H. M. FLETCHER

W. R. FLETCHER · · · R. FLETCHER

RARE BOOKS :: MAPS :: ENGRAVINGS :: PRINTS

27 CECIL COURT
CHARING CROSS ROAD
LONDON W.C.2, ENGLAND
(ONE MINUTE FROM LEICESTER SQUARE)
Telephone : TEMple Bar 2865

Bow Windows Book Shop

128 · HIGH STREET · LEWES · EAST SUSSEX BN7 1XL
TELEPHONE: (0273) 480780 CABLES: BOWBOOKS LEWES

The Old Hall Bookshop

32 Market Place Brackley Northants NN13 5 DP tel Brackley (0280) 704146

TELEPHONE
OXFORD 2342

TELEGRAMS
PARKER BOOKSELLER
OXFORD

PARKER AND SON
LIMITED
BOOKSELLERS SINCE 1798
MANAGING DIRECTOR · W.F. THOMAS
27 · BROAD STREET,
2' · TURL STREET,
OXFORD

JAMES THIN
BOOKSELLER
Partners:
J. AINSLIE THIN
THOMAS THIN
JAMES THIN
ESTABLISHED 1848

54, 55, 56 AND 59
SOUTH BRIDGE
EDINBURGH

Telegrams:
"BOOKMAN" EDINBURGH

Telephone No.:
31068 (2 lines)

Le David Low Booksellers Ltd
Emmington Chinnor
Oxford
KINGSTON BLOUNT SQ.

D.M. BEACH
52 HIGH St
SALISBURY
Wilts · SP1 2PG
Tel: Salisbury 333801.

Beach's

OLD & RARE BOOKS

J. Clarke-Hall Ltd.

Justin Clarke-Hall · · · Adelaide Clarke-Hall

Wine Office Court,
London, E.C.4

RICHARD WAY · SECOND-HAND & ANTIQUARIAN BOOKSELLER
54 Friday Street · Henley on Thames · Oxfordshire · RG9 1AH
Telephone (01491) 576663

Bertram ROTA

Telephone : FOREST HILL 3505.

From

HENRY CORK,

Natural History Bookseller,

73 Queenswood Road, Forest Hill, London, S.E.23.

Also at 365 7 Sydenham Road, S.E.26.

BOTANY	ZOOLOGY	CONCHOLOGY
AGRICULTURE	ENTOMOLOGY	ICHTHYOLOGY
GARDENING	ORNITHOLOGY	NATURE STUDY, Etc.

KENNYS
BOOKSHOP AND ART GALLERY

36, PICCADILLY,
(Opposite St. James's Church.)

London, W. April 6th. 18t.

NRY SOTHERAN & Cº
S & SOTHERAN, 43 CHARING CROSS

OND HAND BOOKSELLERS.
ESTABLISHED 1816

Libraries (at Home or Abroad) Furnished
shortest notice & on the most moderate terms.

E & EXPORT. CITY BRANCH 77 & 78, QUEEN St, CHEAPSIDE.
Cº Post Office Orders payable at PICCADILLY CIRCUS.
Arrangement CREDIT PRICE CASH PRICE

LISTS OF BOOKS
furnished on any subject
LIBRARIES PURCHASED
EXPERT BOOKFINDERS
CATALOGUES ISSUED
VALUERS FOR PROBATE

Galloway & Porter Ltd
UNIVERSITY BOOKSELLERS
30, SIDNEY STREET, CAMBRIDGE, ENGLAND

Telephone CAMBRIDGE 4015
Telegrams BOOKS CAMBRIDGE

Specialists in all branches of
SCIENCE ARTS &
LITERATURE
(New and Second-hand,
Ancient and Modern)

STECHERT-HAFNER INC.
FOUNDED IN NEW YORK 1872

The World's Leading International Booksellers

LONDON OFFICE
STAR YARD, CAREY STREET, LONDON, W.C.2.

HEAD OFFICE
NEW YORK
31 EAST 10TH STREET
NEW YORK 3, N.Y.

CABLE ADDRESS
ALL OFFICES
STECHAFNER

LONDON TELEPHONE
HOL 0526

LONDON MANAGER
G. Edward Harris

PARIS
16, RUE DE CONDE
PARIS VI FRANCE

STUTTGART
HOLDERLINSTRASSE 38
STUTTGART, GERMANY

RF

OUT OF PRINT
& INTO PROFIT

A customer inspecting the stock outside Stanley Smith's Marchmont Bookshop in Bloomsbury, in the late 1960s (photograph: Richard Brown)

OUT OF PRINT & INTO PROFIT

A History of the
Rare and Secondhand Book Trade in
Britain in the Twentieth Century

Edited by
Giles Mandelbrote

THE BRITISH LIBRARY
AND
OAK KNOLL PRESS

First published in 2006
and reprinted in 2007 by
The British Library
96 Euston Road
London NW1 2DB
and
Oak Knoll Press
310 Delaware Street
New Castle
DE 19720

British Library Cataloguing in Publication Data
A cataloguing record for this publication is
available from The British Library

ISBN 0 7123 4920 0 (British Library)
ISBN 1 58456 190 4 (Oak Knoll)

Designed by Bob Elliott
Typeset by Norman Tilley Graphics Ltd, Northampton
Printed in England by Cromwell Press Ltd, Trowbridge

COMMISSIONED BY AND PUBLISHED FOR

THE ANTIQUARIAN
BOOKSELLERS' ASSOCIATION

TO CELEBRATE ITS CENTENARY

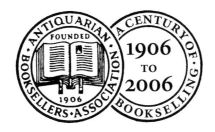

CONTENTS

IV. PERSONALITIES: A TRADE OF INDIVIDUALISTS

APPENDICES

LIST OF ILLUSTRATIONS

Frontispiece: The Marchmont Bookshop, Bloomsbury, in the late 1960s.

PICTURE ACKNOWLEDGEMENTS AND SOURCES

1 *One Hundred Years of Book Auctions 1807-1907* (1908); 2, 23, 49 from Frank Karslake, *Notes from Sotheby's* (1909); 3, 7 Sotheby's; 4, 51 Tony Gibb (Gibb's Bookshop, Manchester); 5 Tony Laywood (A.W. Laywood); 6 photograph by Wilfrid Hodgson/Keith Fletcher; 8, 9 photographs by Javier Molina/Barry Shaw; 10-13, 19, 55, 58 Keith Fletcher (H.M. Fletcher); 14 Marianne Harwood; 15 Museum of London; 16 Magnum Photos, from *Sunday Times Magazine*, 19 May 1991; 17, 18 Javier Molina/Christopher White, from *Saturday Morning, Farringdon Road* [2005]; 20, 21 *Toute L'Edition*, 16 July 1938; frontispiece, 22, 24-28, 30-37 photographs by Richard Brown for *The London Bookshop*, 2 vols. (Private Libraries Association, 1971-7); 29 Maggs Bros. Ltd, from *The House of Maggs* (1939); 38-41 photographs by David Chambers, for *English Country Bookshops* (forthcoming: Private Libraries Association, 2006); 42 The Merton Blackwell Collection, Oxford; 43 Trustees of the National Library of Scotland/Ainslie Thin (James Thin archive: Acc.12384/175); 44-48 H.R. Woudhuysen; 50 Michèle Kohler; 52 David Chambers; 53 *Book Auction Records*, vol. 17 (1920); 54 Maggs Bros. Ltd; 56, 57 Antiquarian Booksellers' Association; 59, 60 Richard Sawyer; 61 Mrs Senga Grant/Ronald Searle; III *Punch* Ltd, from *Punch*, 24 May 1922; IV from *Biblionotes*, the Bibliomites' newsletter (Antiquarian Booksellers' Association, presented by Michael Phelps).

EDITORIAL ACKNOWLEDGEMENTS

I N addition to writing their individual chapters for this volume, the contributors have been immensely helpful in refining and improving it, pointing out omissions and suggesting illustrations. I am grateful to all of them for their interest in the book, and especially to Paul Minet for his reassuring encouragement of the project, to David Chambers for much practical advice about design and illustrations, and to Anthony Rota for reading and commenting on many chapters. Jim McCue brought a keen eye to the book as a second editor; John Collins read most of it and was generous with his own extensive knowledge of the trade's history; Kirstin Kennedy thought up the title. I would also like to thank Keith Fletcher for searching out information and illustrations and Sheila Markham for kindly suggesting relevant material from her own book of interviews with the trade. At the ABA, Jonathan Potter (initially as President and then as Chairman of the Centenary Committee), Paul Minet and Roger Treglown have contributed to every stage of the book's progress, while Andrea Brown, Marianne Harwood and especially John Critchley bore the organizational strain with great tact, efficiency and good humour.

I am also very grateful for advice, help and suggestions from the following: Christopher Edwards, James Fergusson, Colin Franklin, Arthur and Janet Freeman, Roger Gaskell, Paul Grinke, Robert Harding, Ted Hofmann, George Jeffery, John Lawson, Tony Laywood, Richard Linenthal, David McKitterick, Ed Maggs, Peter Miller, Robin Myers, Anthony Neville, Felix de Marez Oyens, Nicholas Poole-Wilson, John Price, Rita Ricketts, John Walwyn-Jones, Veronica Watts, Christopher White and Joan Winterkorn.

Note: The place of publication of books cited in the text and notes is London unless otherwise stated.

LIST OF CONTRIBUTORS

Philippa Bernard, with her late husband Leo, has been the proprietor of Chelsea Rare Books for more than 30 years.-She was General Editor of *Antiquarian Books: A Companion* (1994). Two further books, *The History of Westminster Synagogue* and *Out of the Midst of the Fire*, appeared in 2003 and 2005; she is now working on the authorized biography of the poet Kathleen Raine.

David Chambers is currently researching privately printed books in Britain in the eighteenth and nineteenth centuries, which he has been collecting over the past 35 years. He is joint editor of *The Private Library*.

Retiring from the Royal Navy in 1999 as a Submariner, Engineer and Commodore (in that order), but with no knowledge of antiquarian books, **John Critchley** considers himself extremely fortunate to have landed his current job as Secretary of the Antiquarian Booksellers' Association. He is based in its office in Sackville House, Piccadilly, and hopes to continue in post for a little while yet.

A.S.G. Edwards is Professor of Textual Studies, De Montfort University. A member of the editorial board of *The Book Collector* and co-editor of *English Manuscript Studies 1100-1700*, he is interested in the history of book collecting in England.

Richard Ford is a dealer in manuscripts, printed ephemera and antiquarian books, with a particular interest in the history of bookselling and publishing.

Michael Harris has written about the history of the London book trade and the history of newspapers, mainly in the eighteenth century. He is one of the organizers (with Robin Myers and Giles Mandelbrote) of the conference on book trade history, sponsored first by Birkbeck College and more recently by the ABA, and is co-editor of the annual volumes of essays. He collects old books.

Frank Herrmann FSA worked as a publisher between 1947 and 1976 (Faber's, Methuen, Ward Lock, Sotheby Publications, Hugo's). He was an adviser to Sotheby's Book Department (1977), head of Sotheby's overseas operations (1978-82) and founder-Director of Bloomsbury Book Auctions (1983-2002). He is the author of *The English as Collectors* (1972; revised edition, 1999); *Sotheby's: Portrait of an Auction House* (1980) and *Low Profile: A Life in the World of Books* (2002).

Anthony Hobson is a historian of the book and was Director and Associate of Sotheby's Book Department (1949-77). He has given the Sandars (1975), Rosenbach (1990), and Lyell (1991) Lectures.

Arnold Hunt is a Curator of Manuscripts at the British Library. He has published several articles on book-trade topics, and is writing a life of the nineteenth-century book collector Richard Heber.

Chris Kohler bought eighteenth-century editions of Laurence Sterne whilst a schoolboy and joined Joseph's in the Charing Cross Road after leaving school. He started his own business in 1963 and sold his first collection in 1964.

Michèle Kohler has been a partner in C.C. Kohler since 1974. She particularly enjoys cataloguing Victorian cloth bindings.

Giles Mandelbrote is a Curator, British Collections 1501-1800, at the British Library, where much of his work is concerned with extending and strengthening the national collections by purchases from the antiquarian book trade.

Paul P.B. Minet FSA has been a bookseller since 1955, mainly in the West Country and the Home Counties. He trades under the name Piccadilly Rare Books and also publishes limited edition reprints. A Past President of the ABA, currently Treasurer, he is also one of the six founder-members of the Provincial Booksellers Fairs Association. He founded *Antiquarian Book Monthly Review* in 1974 and has written trade columns in various publications for over 30 years. He is the author of *Late Booking* (1989) and *Bookdealing for Profit* (2000).

Angus O'Neill has been a full-time bookseller since graduating from Cambridge in 1982. He was contributing editor to *Antiquarian Books: A Companion* (1994) and was elected to the Council of the ABA in 2005.

David Pearson is Director, University of London Research Library Services. He has previously pursued a library career in various academic and research libraries. His books include *Provenance Research in Book History* (1994), *Oxford Bookbinding 1500-1640* (2000) and *English Bookbinding Styles 1450-1800* (2005).

Robert S Pirie was born in Chicago, grew up in New York, graduated from Harvard College and Harvard Law School, practised law and subsequently was President of Rothschild, Inc. He compiled the catalogue of the 1972 Grolier Club anniversary exhibition *John Donne 1572-1631*, which included books from his own collection.

A fourth-generation antiquarian bookseller, **Anthony Rota** is a Past President of the ABA and a President of Honour of the International League of Antiquarian Booksellers. His published writings include *Apart from the Text* (an exploration of what a book can teach us about publishing history, even before we begin to read it) and *Books in the Blood* (a volume of memoirs).

Barry Shaw, an enthusiastic book collector and since 2005 an Honorary Member of the ABA, has been in book and magazine publishing since 1953. He was the owner and Editor of *Bookdealer* from 1986 until its closure in July 2006.

Elizabeth Strong purchased McNaughtan's Bookshop from the retiring co-founder, Marjorie McNaughtan, in 1979, expanding into adjacent premises in 1983. Her interests are reflected in the varied stock, which includes children's books, literature, cookery, music, travel, history, arts and architecture. In her spare time she is a landscape artist, exhibiting in Edinburgh and further afield.

Marc Vaulbert de Chantilly has published pamphlets under the imprint The Vanity Press of Bethnal Green.

Anthony James West, after a career as a business executive and international management consultant, has spent a decade and a half studying the First Folio. He has published two volumes in the series *The Shakespeare First Folio: The History of the Book* (Oxford University Press) and is working on the third. He is Honorary Research Fellow, University College London, and Visiting Research Fellow, Institute of English Studies, School of Advanced Study, University of London.

H.R. Woudhuysen is Professor of English and Head of the Department of English at University College London. In addition to publications relating to Sidney, Shakespeare, Johnson and Housman, he has written about sales of books and manuscripts for *The Times Literary Supplement* for more than twenty years.

INTRODUCTION

By contrast with the growing interest in the history of the new book trade, comparatively little has been written about the origins and history of the trade in secondhand and antiquarian books. To take a recent example, the first two volumes to appear of *The Cambridge History of the Book in Britain* (volumes III and IV, covering the period from 1400 to 1695 and running to some 1,600 pages) barely mention this aspect of the trade – with the exception of a chapter on the fate of the monastic libraries. Yet for as long as books and manuscripts have been bought and sold, the trade in new books and the secondhand book trade have worked in tandem, with the latter answering the need for cheaper copies and for copies of works that were no longer available new. Until the last two or three decades of the twentieth century, it was still common for general bookshops to keep new and secondhand copies together on their shelves.

For centuries, buying and selling old books at the upper end of the market has required special knowledge and skills. The more sophisticated collectors of the renaissance hunted for old manuscripts not only to rediscover the ideas and texts of the past, but also because of an interest in their provenance and an aesthetic appreciation of the objects themselves. Towards the end of the seventeenth century – a little later than on the continent – English collectors were becoming interested in the history of printing and the competitive pursuit of rare books had begun. Alongside this came the beginnings of a specialized antiquarian book trade and the rapid expansion of book auctions. As collections of books grew larger, with the accumulated libraries of generations, the book trade struggled with the logistical challenges of buying and selling them. The role played by the trade in helping to create (and disperse) some of the most important libraries of the eighteenth century still awaits the detailed study it deserves.

The golden century of book collecting in England coincided roughly with the lifetimes of two of its heroic figures, Richard Heber (1773-1833) and Sir Thomas Phillipps (1792-1872). The Napoleonic wars and secularization of continental church libraries released waves of books onto the market, at a time when English collectors had the means and self-confidence to buy them. This was the period of the Roxburghe sale (1812), where for the first time a four-figure sum was paid at auction for a printed book, and of the 'bibliomania' chronicled by T.F. Dibdin. It was a formative period also for the antiquarian book trade, as specialist dealers such as Payne & Foss, Rodd and Thorpe issued catalogues which paid increasingly careful attention to rarity, condition and bindings. By the 1840s and 1850s several of the leading firms of the next century were starting up. Of the founder-members of the Antiquarian Booksellers' Association (listed in Appendix 3), eight firms are still in business and remain members to the present day. Almost all of these had put down strong roots before 1870 and were already well established by 11 December 1906, when the Association was founded, at first as the 'Second-Hand Booksellers' Association'.

By 1906 it must have seemed as though the golden age was swiftly turning to iron. The last quarter of the nineteenth century saw a disastrous agricultural depression, with wheat prices undercut by American competition, a series of bad summers and outbreaks of disease among livestock. Land values and rents fell away sharply, and with them went the economic structure which had sustained great estates and country houses. The Settled Land Acts of 1882 and 1884 permitted the sale of 'heirlooms' and libraries were often among the first casualties, less missed than family portraits and silver. A flood of books came through the auction houses, at a time when the trade's traditional customers were short of money. The market was sustained, and dominated, by Bernard Quaritch, buying from Sotheby's on extended credit terms – the firm's debts were not paid off for decades. It was also in this period that the buying power of American collectors came to have a profound impact on the British market, most notably at first Robert Hoe III (1839-1909), to be followed by J. Pierpont Morgan (1837-1913) and others whose relationship with the trade is discussed later in this volume. The export of antiquarian books offered economic salvation for the trade, but American dealers and collectors also became competitors in the auction rooms.

The Antiquarian Booksellers' Association was founded to defend the trade's interests at a time when many of the old certainties seemed to be disappearing. As the ABA celebrates its centenary, the trade in rare books is again changing very rapidly, this time because of new technologies for buying and selling. The twentieth century now appears as a distinct moment in the evolution of the trade; it is this period, ending as the era of internet bookselling begins, which is the subject of *Out of Print & Into Profit*.

This is the first book to attempt to map out the overall shape of the British rare and secondhand book trade in the twentieth century. There are no convenient models to follow, for this or any other period of the trade's history, although the contributors have made considerable use of published memoirs, biographies, interviews and histories of individual firms. Marc Vaulbert de Chantilly has provided a checklist of this material in Appendix 5, but also reminds us forcefully, in his own chapter, that these should be read with a sceptical eye. Book trade archives, surveyed by Richard Ford in Appendix 4, potentially offer the raw material for more specialized studies in the future, though some are currently embargoed for commercial reasons and many are not yet catalogued in any detail. It is hoped that this book will stimulate interest in further research, as well as encouraging booksellers and their institutional customers to preserve their old invoices and runs of annotated catalogues as important historical sources.

The approach adopted here has been a thematic one, beginning with the supply of books from various sources and moving on to look in detail at the range of methods, some old and some new, by which books have been sold at different levels of the trade over the course of the whole century. Widening the historical view, there are chapters on changes in the market and customers' collecting tastes and also on the book trade's relationship to the world around it. This structure offers a contrast to the biographical format of much that has previously been written about the trade, but inevitably it means that there are still many interesting stories to be told about the careers of individual booksellers who are not even mentioned here. In dealing with such a large subject, it has been impossible to be comprehensive: detailed studies of particular periods, places or institutions have sometimes been used to suggest wider issues and themes, for instance in the case of the changing provision of bookshops across Britain over the century or of patterns of buying by institutional libraries.

It is revealing that certain features of the trade have proved stubbornly resistant to being confined within this framework. One notable example is the extent to which books have circulated within the trade. A typical story, told in Anthony Rota's *Books in the Blood*, is of a book taken to a New York book fair by a dealer from England, bought there by another English dealer, and sold in London within a few weeks to a visiting collector from across the Atlantic. Buying (traditionally in this period at a 10% trade discount), selling, sharing and swapping between one bookseller and another has tended to permeate all other activities.

Credit and debt relationships and informal partnerships were one way in which apparently independent booksellers were linked together, depending heavily on trust and reputation, but the trade also had its own social hierarchies. Fred Snelling divided the trade into those who were born into it, those who worked their way up from the bottom and those who moved into it after university. The late twentieth century has seen a movement away from the world of the 'guvs' and apprentices, and the school of hard knocks characteristic of the Depression years, towards a trade largely composed of better-educated (though perhaps less experienced) graduates, with a substantial component of part-time booksellers retired from other occupations. As career paths changed, so too did financial expectations – sometimes dramatically. E.M. Dring has left us with an evocative picture of becalmed booksellers at Quaritch in the 1930s: F.S. Ferguson spending every afternoon in the British Museum, while another colleague read the entire works of Dickens. But to undertake the analysis of changing profit margins, liquidity and returns on investment in the antiquarian book trade over the ups and downs of the twentieth century – crucial though this would be to a full understanding of the trade – would require another and very different book.

The dust has barely settled on the twentieth century and it is too soon for a wholly dispassionate and seamless account of the subject. More than half the contributors to this volume have made their living from the rare and secondhand book trade; some have been closely involved with people and events described here and they write at first hand, from long personal experience of the trade. Other contributors write from the perspective of academics, collectors or librarians, but they have also been committed participants (as customers) in the twentieth-century trade. While they have all been encouraged to reflect on the changing patterns in the trade over the century as a whole, there are many different voices here and a variety of approaches and tone, particularly where the recent past is concerned, which makes the volume more lively and has enabled details to be captured on paper before they are forgotten.

Out of Print & Into Profit was commissioned by the ABA and has been generously supported by the Association as part of its centenary celebrations, but it was decided from the start that it should range over the whole of the secondhand and antiquarian book trade, looking at whichever aspects of its history turned out to be most important or most striking. The role of the book trade organizations, as community and conscience of the trade, is an interesting story, told in Anthony Rota's chapter, but it is, for most of the time, a minor theme in this most individualistic of occupations. Nor is this volume intended as a celebration of the trade, though it certainly celebrates the appeal and excitement of rare and old books. Instead it sets out to offer a more balanced view, without shying away from describing sharp practices and putting on record the trade's transgressions as well as its triumphs. That the trade has been warmly encouraging towards a history in which it does not always appear in the best light is, in itself, an interesting reflection of how times have changed.

GILES MANDELBROTE

I

BUYING

HOW THE TRADE ACQUIRED ITS STOCK

Mr Tregaskis   Mr Quaritch   Mr Leighton   Mr Maggs

Cartoon from *Book Auction Records*, 1908.

The Role of the Auction Houses

FRANK HERRMANN

> Book collecting, I would have you know, is a full-time occupation, and one wouldn't get far if one took time off for frivolities like reading.
>
> A.N.L. Munby

IN a recent poll of members of the Antiquarian Booksellers' Association, they were asked to what extent they obtained their stock from private people, from auction sales, from other dealers and through the internet. Surprisingly, the result showed private buying as slightly in the lead at 32 per cent, auctions at 31.7 per cent and inter-trade buying at 30.9 per cent. The internet figured a shade under 5 per cent. In some cases, buying at auction had increased substantially in recent years: in others it had decreased. The reason for the latter was the high premium which auctioneers now charge purchasers. Against this one has to say that book auctions are generally well supported, not only in London but also in the provinces, though often prices obtained for identical books tend to be rather higher in London.

The auction houses

At the beginning of the twentieth century, there were half a dozen auction houses in London actively concerned with books: Sotheby's, Christie's, Hodgson's, Phillips Son & Neale, Puttick & Simpson and, occasionally, Southgate & Barratt. Sotheby's dominated the field, just as the firm of Quaritch (then run by Bernard Alfred, Bernard's son) still dominated the booksellers. Sotheby's and Hodgson's almost became linked at this time, which would have changed the playing field quite astonishingly.

As it happens, we have a detailed account of how a book sale was conducted at Sotheby's in 1907. It was written by Sir William Osler (1849-1919), a great surgeon, teacher of medicine and collector of medical books, who hailed from Canada. Here he is describing the sale of the library of an American, William C. Van Antwerp, held on 23 March 1907.[1] It started at '1.00 p.m. sharp', as many book sales still do today. Osler even occasionally records remarks made by the 'impressively restrained auctioneer':

One was impressed by the extremely decorous character of the proceedings, without the slightest noise or bluster such as one is accustomed to think of in connexion with sales. The auctioneer, Mr Tom Hodge, presided at a raised desk at the end of an oblong table about which were seated some twenty buyers, the principals or the representatives of the leading English booksellers. Around the room were twenty-five or thirty onlookers, mostly seated, a few standing about. Bids were offered only by the dealers and by a man who held a catalogue marked with the bids sent directly to the firm. The auctioneer, with a soft voice and a good-natured manner, called out the numbers and, as a rule, offered no comments upon the books; in fact, he did not often have to ask for a bid, which was started spontaneously. Occasionally, of course, he could not resist a remark or two. Sometimes he would suggest a bid. It was astonishing with what rapidity the different items were sold. Evidently the dealers knew just what they wanted and what they were willing to pay, and in many cases one could easily see that they had been given a limit by those who had sent the orders.

The first work of special interest sold was the 1817 edition of poems of Keats, a presentation copy, with an inscription by the author. Starting at £20 it rose quickly to £70 and £80 and in less than a minute was knocked down to Quaritch at £90. I say knocked down, but the process was altogether too dignified for such an expression, and no final rap was ever given. The catalogue of the Rowfant Library brought £7. Two books of Richard Pynson's press brought high figures. It was remarkable, also, to see a ragged, rough-looking, unbound, but uncut play of Philip Massinger knocked down to Stevens at £48. Bidding upon the copy of 'Comus', one of the rarest of Milton's works, was started by Quaritch at £50 and ran up pound by pound with the greatest rapidity to £100, and finally to £162. Nothing was heard but the monotonous repetition of the figures by the auctioneer, who simply watched the nodding heads of Mr Quaritch and his rival, Ellis of Bond Street. The 'Paradise Regained', an uncut copy and a great rarity in this state – so much so that the auctioneer remarked, 'Uncut, and need I say more? All you can ask!' – was secured at £94 by Maggs. Three beautiful first editions of some of Pope's works did not bring very high prices, though the 'Windsor Forest', in sheets loosely stitched together, entirely uncut, brought £48. One of the finest sets of the collection was 'Purchas his Pilgrimes, in five Books'. As the auctioneer remarked, 'It is one of the finest copies ever sold and Mr Van Antwerp had had a most detailed and complete collation made.' The volumes were in the original vellum, absolutely perfect. Starting at £50, the fifth bid reached £100, and the set was knocked down to Maggs at £170 against Quaritch – one of the few instances in which Mr Quaritch gave up.

Then ... came the remarkable set of original Shakespeare folios. Just as a foil, it seemed, and to show the contrast between the new and the old, Sidney Lee's facsimile reprint of the first folio, issued by the Clarendon Press in 1902, was put up (£2.12s.). When lot 191 was called out, there was a stir among the auditors, not such as you could hear, but it could be felt, as the famous first folio of 'Mr William Shakespeares Comedies, Histories, and Tragedies' was offered. It was in a superb red morocco binding by Bedford and enclosed in a new crushed red morocco slip case by Bradstreet.

'Language fails me, Sirs,' the auctioneer said, 'I can only ask you to look at the book and give your bids.' Special interest existed as to whether the record price of £3,000, paid by the Bodleian, would be exceeded, but the circumstances were then exceptional, as that copy had originally been in the Bodleian. ... Previously as much as £1,720 had been paid for the first folio, and £3,000 was thought to be a fabulously extravagant price. ... It cheered the book-lover's heart to hear Quaritch lead off with a bid of £1,000, followed immediately by the representative of Stevens with £1,500, and then the figures ran £1,800, £1,900, £2,000, £2,400, £2,800, and at the £3,000 there was a pause. Stevens, thereupon said 'Fifty' and the previous record price was passed, then £3,200. At £3,500 Stevens stopped, and a record – long, let us hope, to remain such – was made when Quaritch secured it at £3,600. Every one in the room applauded his victory.

The second folio brought only £210 (Stevens). The third folio brought £650, and the fourth £75. The quarto copies of the individual plays did not bring such very high prices as were realized the previous year.

Various sets of the four Shakespeare Folios came up with some degree of frequency during the century and, as Anthony James West explains elsewhere in this volume, they represented an important benchmark in book collecting.[2]

The oblong table which Osler comments on was a long, double-sided horseshoe table. Major booksellers who attended sales regularly had their own allotted seats, and woe betide any stranger who strayed into them in error. A porter would circulate inside the horseshoe, holding up the book that was being auctioned, so that buyers could have a last quick look at it before the bidding stopped. The trade attending sales, particularly those at Sotheby's, can almost be divided into a first and a second division. This is clear from a study either of annotated catalogues, in which the price realized and the buyer's name is written in the margins, or of the printed lists of buyers and prices paid which were released a few days after each sale.

Included in the first division up to the middle of the 1920s would be Quaritch, Maggs, Dobell, Leighton, Ellis, Tregaskis, Thorp, Sotheran, Pickering, Spencer and Joseph. The second division, who did not attend sales with the same degree of regularity, included Bain, Bell, Heffer, King, Adamson, Olschki, Allen, Hancock, Sabin, Edwards, David, H. Stevens, McLeish. And then, of course, there were the occasional interlopers from France – particularly when Napoleonic material came up for sale, which it did fairly frequently – and from Germany. But more important, and with devastating effects on prices soon after the First World War, were Dr Rosenbach and G.D. Smith from America, particularly the former, buying not always for the millionaire moguls, such as Pierpont Morgan and Huntington, but also for stock.

Hodgson's saleroom in Chancery Lane had been built specifically for the business in 1863. The firm had its antecedents in Reading, but was later established, by one Robert Saunders, in Soho in 1817. It then moved to 39 Fleet Street where it was joined by Edmund Hodgson who took it over in 1826, and from that time onwards it carried his family name. Later it moved again to 192 Fleet Street and eventually round the corner to 2 Chancery Lane. It was still the same Edmund Hodgson who built the saleroom at 115 Chancery Lane. Later generations of the Hodgson family carried on uninterruptedly until the firm was taken over by Sotheby's in 1967 after holding some 5,500 sales.

Following Sotheby's takeover, books earlier than 1830 were sold in Bond Street, and later books in Chancery Lane. It was the present writer's mournful duty to close the Hodgson business in 1981 and to move its activities to Bond Street. The integrated book department then moved to entirely new premises in Bloomfield Place. But at a stage about halfway through Hodgson's long history, events took place which might have resulted in a very different outcome.

Sotheby's had been run by Edward Grose Hodge and his second son Tom for many years when the father died in May 1907. The elder Hodge had joined Sotheby's in 1847 and had become a partner in 1864. The senior partner beforehand had been John Wilkinson, who had been employed in the late 1820s as an accountant, but became an extraordinarily accomplished auctioneer. After the sudden death of Samuel Leigh Sotheby in 1861, Wilkinson was left in sole charge until he took on Edward Grose Hodge as a partner. The firm then became known as Sotheby, Wilkinson & Hodge, and this continued until 1924.

'Young' Tom had become a partner in 1896 and had run the business single-handed once his father was overtaken by ill health and virtually retired shortly before 1900. But Edward Grose Hodge's death left three sons and two daughters, and Sotheby's was the major item of their inheritance.

Among a deluge of letters of condolence, Tom Hodge began correspondence with a fellow book auctioneer, John Edmund Hodgson. It seems that he was sounding out Hodgson about a merger, or possibly even the sale of Sotheby's to Hodgson's. Although he was only 47, Tom Hodge was not in good health. He drove himself relentlessly, masterminding and taking the rostrum on a vast number of sale days during the year. Thus, in December 1907, he was in the rostrum for seventeen days up to the Christmas break, selling not only books, but also coins and Egyptian antiquities. During the first quarter of 1908, Hodge took 38 sales. It was really not surprising that he was anxious to seek relief from such pressure. He also knew that his siblings wanted part of their inheritance in cash, so he desperately needed a buyer for Sotheby's.

Negotiations between the two men continued sporadically for months on end. Some of the correspondence between them has survived and it is, in part, clear evidence of the relationship between auctioneers and booksellers. Tom Hodge was a dry stick and a great snob. At one time, young Hodgson asked him what he should do about attending a trade dinner of the Second-Hand Booksellers' Association (as the ABA was then called), organized by its secretary, Frank Karslake. Hodge clearly disliked Karslake very much. He thundered in reply:

I too have received an invitation to the dinner but I shall certainly not accept for three reasons. First I consider it entirely a mistake and altogether inadvisable for Auctioneers to be looked upon & ranked as one of the trade; secondly the Association is far too closely identified with its founder [Karslake]; thirdly I am not going anywhere just yet on account of my father's death.

The Association started by the Secretary, is an obvious attempt to reinstate himself in the good opinion of second-hand booksellers but until the Association absolutely eject him I do not see how it can ever get a good reputation & when he is gone the Association falls in pieces. I very much regret that many ever honest men have in any way allowed themselves to be coupled with Mr Karslake.

I do not think you & I need care two pins about it beyond being careful to keep clear of it. We are not of, nor in the trade & booksellers must be made to remember this.

Frank Karslake was the editor of *Book Auction Records*, which he had started in 1903 and which came out in quarterly parts. He had an astounding memory and was something of a self-publicist. It was this quality that evidently did not endear him to Hodge, though it has to be said that when Karslake published his *Notes from Sotheby's* (1909), he did so with Tom Hodge's consent.[3]

In February 1908 events took a new turn. The firm of Knight, Frank & Rutley expressed an interest, but Hodgson rejected a tripartite solution, and there the matter rested for five months, when Hodge brought it up yet again. Sotheby's accountants, Messrs. Cates, Brown & Harding, came up with recent trading figures (and very good they were). They had also calculated what Hodgson and Knight, Frank & Rutley should each pay for one third of the business. After another few weeks, Hodgson's had the opportunity to buy the entire Sotheby business for £6,500 down and a further £3,500 after two years of trading. The stumbling block was that Tom Hodge wanted to retain control until the second tranche was paid for, but the Hodgsons balked at this. Talks petered out and the deal collapsed.

The alternative and successful outcome could not have been more different. The three men who bought Sotheby's were Montague Barlow, Felix Warre and Geoffrey Hobson. At the time of the purchase Barlow was a barrister specializing in ecclesiastical cases. But he had political ambitions, for which he hoped that his career at Sotheby's would eventually provide the financial means: he was a prominent member of London County Council and entered Parliament for the first time in 1910. People remembered him for his efficiency as an administrator, for his integrity and, as we shall hear from Millicent Sowerby, for his progressive ideas relating particularly to conditions of employment. He had a fine sense of fun and his effect on Sotheby's was to give it a completely new character.

The third and youngest member of the new triumvirate was Geoffrey Hobson. Educated at Harrow and University College, Oxford, he was prevented by illness from entering the Foreign Office. Instead, he travelled on the Continent for some years and acquired fluency in French, German and Italian; he could also read and speak Spanish, Portuguese, Dutch and some of the Scandinavian languages, and was an excellent classical scholar. In addition to his linguistic abilities, Hobson was a shrewd businessman and possessed indefatigable industry. In the long term he turned out to be the most brilliant of a formidable trio.

Barlow worked with Tom Hodge on the book side and frequently took sales. Warre became the leading general auctioneer, while Hobson specialized in books and manuscripts and eventually became a renowned bibliographical authority, particularly on early bindings. Felix Warre took charge of the coin and antiquities department, and because he proved to be especially good in the rostrum, he took more sales than any other partner. While he lacked the brilliance of Barlow or Hobson, his charming manners, confidence and integrity endeared him to the trade and collectors alike.

Just as Christie's put out the cataloguing of book sales, so Sotheby's put out the work on coins to Spinks and Baldwin; W.V. Daniell and his assistant, Frederick Nield, tackled autograph letters and Daniell's nephew, with his son (F.B. Daniell & Son) catalogued prints. Later on this work was done by Herbert Breun.

Book sales continued unabated. Hodge had also cultivated major private treaty sales. Barlow turned out to be particularly able in this field and there were astonishing sales to Pierpont Morgan and Henry Huntington. Tom Hodge gradually disappeared from the scene and it was not long before the new partners realized that it would pay them to break into the areas where Christie's had long reigned supreme. Thus it was in the second decade of the twentieth century that Sotheby's, tentatively at first but with increasing confidence, began the sale of paintings, furniture, decorative arts and even jewellery. There was now more space for additional departments and storage of objects because in 1917 the triumvirate had moved the firm from Wellington Street, where it had been since 1818, to the former Doré Gallery at 34 and 35 New Bond Street.

Soon after the move, and in the light of an expanding business, the three partners felt the need for an additional, younger partner. In 1920, with great care, they chose Charles des Graz, who had already gained some experience of the book world in America. During his 33 years at Sotheby's he turned out to be a pivotal figure, concentrating particularly on the book side. He appears in the rostrum in many of the photographs of famous sales of the inter-war period. He took over the chairmanship from Geoffrey Hobson after the latter's death in 1949, shortly after the sale of the great Landau-Finaly library. When des Graz himself died in 1953, Peter Wilson became chairman and Geoffrey Hobson's son, Anthony (A.R.A. Hobson), took over the book department. Anthony Hobson is remembered particularly for his links with sales of material from the Phillipps Collection and his outstanding bibliographical scholarship. After Hobson's resignation, Lord John Kerr (who was to become my partner at Bloomsbury Book Auctions in 1982) headed the book department for seventeen years, a period of many important library sales.

At the beginning of the twentieth century, Christie's, which had been established in 1766, held only occasional sales of interest to the book trade: these mostly consisted of archives, letters and manuscript material, although sometimes a library might be sold as part of the dispersal of a major collection.[4] It was not surprising that Christie's showed relatively little interest in book sales. Such sales required expertise, which the firm did not have in-house. They were also extremely labour-intensive compared to the sale of paintings and jewellery, which generally yielded £5,000-£15,000 or more, whereas book sales at Sotheby's rarely totalled more than £2,000-£4,000.

The few book sales which were held came under the aegis of two long-standing Christie directors, Lance and then Gordon Hannen. The cataloguing work was put out to prominent booksellers. Thus, Maggs did the work from before and until quite a while after the Second World War. Then Dudley Massey of Pickering & Chatto took over. He was paid at a rate of three per cent of the hammer price on books catalogued and sold; one per cent if the book was bought in; the rate (in 1958) for valuations carried out in clients' houses was £5 per day, and on valuations for probate he received two thirds of the total amount of commission payable to Christie's for the work involved. It is quite clear that such payments worked out much more cheaply than employing full-time staff.

The year 1958 was the *annus mirabilis* for Christie's book sales in the middle part of the century. A hundred and seven lots from Chatsworth fetched £109,086 (a staggering £1,000 per lot), and the celebrated Llangattock Book of Hours made £32,000, a world record until broken soon after by H.P. Kraus.

Soon after 1960 a book department came into being. Major William Spowers joined the firm and worked under the direction of Dudley Massey until 1970, when he was put in charge and Massey became a consultant. He was followed by Hans Fellner, and then by Stephen Massey (son of Dudley) who ran the whole show from New York. Book auctions really took off in the mid-1980s after the appointment of Felix B. de Marez Oyens, who had run the old-established New York bookselling firm of Lathrop C. Harper. Christie's also bought up another auction house, Debenham & Coe, which was turned into Christie's South Kensington in 1975 and developed a flourishing secondary book sale business.

Puttick & Simpson had been a serious challenger to Sotheby's in the last quarter of the nineteenth century, but by the beginning of the twentieth century their dominance had faded. Thomas Puttick and William Simpson had themselves taken over the business of Stewart, Wheatley & Adlard in 1841. The firm was based at the Reynolds Galleries, 47 Leicester Square, and for a long period between the wars was owned by W.G. Horseman and R.F. Westthorpe. In 1935 D.R. Rolls became a new partner-director. In general Puttick & Simpson sales consisted of books of relatively low value, which the trade thoroughly enjoyed hoovering up. Occasionally, however, there was outstanding autograph material, which seems to have been catalogued externally. The sales were a good deal shorter than those at Sotheby's. Cataloguing had deteriorated and after the First World War far fewer major properties were sold in their rooms. In 1954 the firm was taken over by Phillips, Son & Neale.

That firm had been founded in 1796 by Harry Phillips, a former head clerk to James Christie. He acquired premises at 73 New Bond Street. The Phillips family continued to control the firm throughout the nineteenth century, with Frederick Neale being taken into partnership in 1881. In 1924, the firm became known as Phillips, Son & Neale, though in 1972 it reverted to the traditional name of 'Phillips'. The original New Bond Street premises were destroyed by fire in 1939 when the firm moved a short distance to Blenstock House, where it is still, now under the name of Bonham's.

Phillips, Son & Neale held regular book auctions but they seldom hit the headlines, and headlines were important – books and, of course, other auction sales, were covered in the major newspapers on an almost daily basis. The Puttick & Simpson takeover seems to have engendered a new sense of purpose under the energetic leadership of Christopher Weston, who became a powerful force on the London auction scene. He enormously broadened the range of Phillips' sales by taking over many independent provincial auction houses, and finished up with regional salerooms in Par (Cornwall), Exeter, Ipswich, Bath, Cardiff, Winchester, Sherborne, Knole, Oxford, Chester, Edinburgh, Glasgow and elsewhere.

In 1998, soon after Weston's retirement, Phillips was taken over by Robert Brooks, who had at one time been employed by Christie's to run their veteran and vintage car department, before forming a very successful auction business dealing in cars under his own name. With backing from a Dutch billionaire, Brooks also bought the old-established firm of Bonham's at the end of 2001; he merged it with the rump of Phillips and called his new combined business Bonham's. Under the aegis of another ex-Sotheby book-man, David Park, Bonham's has become the third most important book auction house by the twenty-first century.

When Brooks took over Phillips, a number of senior staff from the Edinburgh office decided to move to the firm of Lyon & Turnbull, which has since held some very interesting book sales.

From the mid-1960s onwards, however, the Sotheby-Christie duopoly grew to an extent that left all the other auction houses way behind. It had become clear that the two firms were of extreme importance to each other. Between them they gave London its reputation as the centre of the international art market, and that included books. Although the competition between the two firms was in many respects fierce, persistent allegations about fixing of common commission structures culminated in the late 1990s in a conviction under American law and compensation payments to buyers.[5]

There were two separate occasions at times of national emergency when Sotheby's and Christie's entered into serious merger discussions – the first in 1930, after the Wall Street crash and a virtual cessation of trading by dealers with export customers; and again in mid-1940, when economic problems occurred as a consequence of the war. But there was always a lack of unanimity at the last moment. It was agreed that each house would accommodate the other if the need arose. But when Christie's were bombed out of its premises in King Street, it found wartime shelter firstly in Derby House and then in Spencer House.

Peter Wilson at Sotheby's and I.O. Chance at Christie's became chairmen of their respective companies in the same season in 1957. Each man gave his firm a renewed sense of identity, but by the early 1980s Sotheby's turnover had been running at roughly twice Christie's for nearly three decades. Sotheby's opted for innovation and internationalism – they had bought Parke-Bernet in New York back in 1964, a vital factor in the sale of books, and Mak van Waay in Amsterdam in 1974 – while Christie's, more cautiously, decided to continue to concentrate where the cream was thickest. In 1978 Geraldine Norman, then *The Times* sale-room correspondent, wrote:

Sotheby's have turned into the dominant art wholesaling operation worldwide, a type of international operation that had not previously been conceived in this field. Christie's, their closest competitor, are, of course, running a very similar operation but it is because they followed Sotheby's lead.

In Sotheby's case this was globalization, long before the term was widely used. Following Peter Wilson's departure from Sotheby's in 1980, the balance shifted and Christie's soon reached equivalence with its rivals. By 2004 Christie's combined London and New York annual turnover on books was £66 million, representing a sizeable business in its own right, while Sotheby's was only £44 million. The average lot price for books at Christie's in King Street in 2003 has been calculated as £18,500, while at Sotheby's it was £7,400: an amazing transformation in what had been considered a minor branch of the auction world compared to paintings and jewellery.

Few booksellers can afford to buy at such levels. Inevitably a niche appeared at a lower level when the giants decided that selling artefacts at less than £500 or £1,000 did not pay because of their formidable overheads. The first firm to take advantage of these circumstances was Bloomsbury Book Auctions, which began business in Bedford Square in 1983. It was founded by three former Sotheby directors: Frank Herrmann, Lord John Kerr and David Stagg. The firm was given an enthusiastic reception by the book trade and soon had to move further afield to Hardwick Street, near Sadler's Wells Theatre, to accommodate a growing business of some 24 sales a year.

Five years later, Dominic Winter, who had built up a successful book department at Taviners Rooms in Bristol, set up on his own in Swindon. Initially he catered largely for a West Country clientele, but by 2005 his business had become national, if not international, as had Bloomsbury's, and the two firms between them now sell in excess of £10 million worth of books to a market which includes a strong element of private buyers, but also very much appeals to the trade. After 20 years, Bloomsbury sold out to the antiquarian bookseller, Bernard Shapero, and now operates from rather smarter premises at Maddox Street, a stone's throw from Sotheby's in Bond Street.

*

In the old days, if, while viewing a sale, you wanted to find out what a lot was likely to fetch, you asked the porters. As a goodly proportion of their income came from tips, it paid them to be both knowing and knowledgeable. In the 1970s all this changed. Because an increasing proportion of lots were bought by private buyers, the London auctioneers began to print estimates for every sale. Initially they were on separate sheets, but after a while they became integrated into the catalogues. A few members of the trade did not welcome this because they felt it gave private buyers too much information, but estimates have become standard.

After a particularly difficult period in the 1970s, when both Christie's and Sotheby's found it hard to remain profitable, it was generally regarded as counter-productive to raise the commission charged to sellers beyond the average of fourteen per cent then pertaining. In May 1975, the chairman of Christie's informed Sotheby's, as a matter of courtesy, that as of the following day Christie's would be taking the revolutionary step of charging *buyers* a ten per cent premium on their purchases. He was unaware that Sotheby's had been actively considering the same innovation, though it was common practice on the Continent. Sotheby's announced a few days later that they too would charge a buyers' premium.

The trade rose up in arms, with accusations of collusion between the two firms, and this became a legal battleground for many months. Surprisingly, perhaps, Phillips announced a reduction of commission rates to ten per cent and no charging of premium, immediately after its introduction in Bond Street and King Street. Initially this attracted a great deal of business, but three years later Phillips was forced to fall in line and make the additional charge. It had become virtually impossible for an auctioneer to survive without it, and in 2001 the major houses raised the premium to twenty per cent. The wonder is that auction houses in the earlier part of the century could be profitable on a commission of only ten per cent.

There have been changes in bidding procedures too. Commission bids (bids left by buyers not attending sales in person) now represent an increasing proportion of the business. Such bids reach the auctioneers on pre-printed slips before each sale by post and fax, and also by e-mail and phone. More buyers than ever actually bid on the phone to auctioneers' assistants during the sale, so that they are actively participating in the auction. Nowadays banks of telephones festoon the sides of the salerooms.

A custom imported from the USA in the early 1990s – for the sake of anonymity and security – was the use of numbered paddles, with which pre-registered buyers do their bidding. By the end of the decade, few auction houses continued to publish lists of prices *and* buyers' names after each sale. The fear of taxation above all else is the determining factor of this anonymity.

The vast increase in turnover at Sotheby's and Christie's, the need for a bigger capital base and the requirements of accounting regularity forced both houses to become public companies with a multitude of shareowners: Sotheby's in June 1977 and Christie's some years later. The unexpected consequence of this was that an American, Alfred Taubmann, became a majority shareholder in Sotheby's in 1983, after making an offer for the company. Christie's was bought in its entirety in 1990 by a French billionaire, François Pinault. Phillips in the 1990s had been bought by another Frenchman, Pinault's great rival Bernard Arnaud, but his investment proved inordinately expensive and he sold out after only a short time.

Since 2001 a new group of provincial auction houses has emerged, called the Fine Art Auction Group. It is based in Tunbridge Wells and has acquired ten or more formerly independent salerooms, mostly in the south of England. A number of them hold regular book sales. One of the major acquisitions was the well-known firm of Drewett Neate of Donnington, and most of the various acquired firms will in future trade under that name.

It may seem surprising that I have made so little reference to book sales held outside London. Books rarely made up an entire sale: they constituted a special section in a general sale, and provincial cataloguing was relatively rudimentary (very often books were sold by the tea chest). Perhaps this is not surprising when one reads what W. Frederick Nokes wrote in the *Auctioneers' Manual* (ninth edition, 1924), a book which had become the auctioneers' *vade mecum*:

BOOKS: These are perhaps the most unsatisfactory wares that an auctioneer has to handle in an ordinary sale. The owner generally places upon them a price far beyond the market value of such articles, and the cataloguing of many volumes requires considerable skill and not a little patience. After two or three pages of a catalogue thus filled have been dealt with, it frequently happens that the total of the proceeds of the sale has not very appreciably advanced: and the common practice is to sell ordinary books in lots of a dozen or twenty, or in sets according to authorship. Works relating to Local Topography, Chess, Angling, Art and original editions are, however, an exception to the general rule, and should be catalogued separately.[6]

Into the shadows

At this stage, it is unfortunately necessary to step into the shadows and consider one of the murkier aspects of bibliopolic practice. It has to be stated quite categorically that 'rings', and their subsequent knock-outs or settlements, were the absolute norm in the antiquarian and secondhand book trade throughout most of the nineteenth and twentieth centuries, right up to the 1970s. Even today we cannot be certain that the practice is dead. There were some dealers, of course, who did not take part, but for a long period they were the exceptions.

For the uninitiated, a ring is in being when a number of dealers act in combination and agree not to bid on certain lots, thus destroying the element of competition essential for a proper auction. One or more dealers will have been chosen to bid for those lots which have been selected for acquisition by the ring, and all the other members refrain from doing so. At the height of this activity, the trade dominated most auction sales and the chosen booksellers would get what they wanted at the lowest possible price. After the sale proper was over, the ring would adjourn to a nearby pub and stage a second auction among themselves, where the same books would be put up and bid for until they reached a valid price. This constituted the so-called knock-out or settlement. The cash difference between the two sales would then be aggregated and shared out between the participants. In this way, a dealer who did not actually make a bid for a single lot would go home with an appreciable tax-free lump sum. Those who sufferered would be, of course, the original owners of the books and the auctioneers.

In consequence of the ubiquity of the ring for so many years, it is my firm conviction that most book prices quoted in antiquarian bibliographical material and annual auction records up to the 1970s significantly under-represent what the UK trade would have considered a fair price at auction.

Naturally, there were exceptions. The arrival in the 1920s of American dealers, such as G.D. Smith and Dr Rosenbach, literally left the ring standing. The Americans were buying sometimes on commission for wealthy collectors on the other side of the Atlantic and sometimes for stock. Also, of course, occasional very high prices for exceptionally rare books may be regarded as absolute.

A very popular book published back in 1911, *The Bargain Book* by C.E. Jerningham and Lewis Bettany, contains an entire chapter on the ring and warns its readers that: 'the "knock-out" is an iniquitous system. There is no argument which can justify its existence and a respectable dealer who avails himself of the advantages it affords, or in any way countenances it, must bear the odium of taking part in a thoroughly discreditable transaction.'[7]

An early example of these activities occurred in relation to a sale of the books of John Gennadius (1844-1932), a Greek diplomat who lived in London for many years, was an enthusiastic book collector of any early volume relating to his native country and was a particularly good Quaritch client. Quaritch had bought books for Gennadius on commission at many major Sotheby sales in the late 1880s. Without warning, all Greek ministers were recalled to Athens, 'for reasons of economy'. Gennadius was refused a pension and was thus faced 'with the cruel necessity of seeking relief in my beloved books'. A ten-day sale at Sotheby's was planned, starting in March 1895, for which he personally superintended the cataloguing and wrote a preface. But in the event the sale was a disaster: prices realized fell far short of expectations. Gennadius was convinced that the London booksellers, whom he had got to know so well, were operating a ring and preventing the books from achieving their true prices. He began to buy lots in, and for the last five days of the sale he had several agents bidding on his behalf. Later on, he also bought back books from dealers who had purchased them at the sale, for a small mark-up.[8] It was an expensive stratagem to combat the ring's activities, but his story eventually had a happy ending, with the opening in 1926 of the wonderful Gennadius Library in Athens.

The London auction houses usually did their best to protect their clients by the regular use of reserves, as we shall see. Provincial auction houses protected themselves only much later when they felt strong enough to do so; but well into the 1930s, over and over again, their sales were exploited by the ring with devastating consequences.

An extreme case of this has been the subject of a detailed forensic investigation by Arthur and Janet Freeman, a remarkable achievement for its detached and informed scrutiny and covering every aspect of the ring's activities in great depth.[9] The sale studied was that of a wonderfully rich country house library accumulated over many generations by the Foley family of Ruxley Lodge in Surrey. In 1919 the property belonged to the 21-year-old 7th Baron Foley of Kidderminster, who decided to sell the entire property, lock, stock and barrel, including paintings, furniture, decorative arts, the library (which he never seems to have looked at) and the building itself. The sale was handled by a reputable but little-known London and Edinburgh based firm of auctioneers called Castiglione & Scott, who specialized in land sales.

The standard of cataloguing was well below that of the London auction houses. The trade considered it a gift from the gods and no fewer than 81 booksellers agreed to form a ring: 30 'country members' and 51 more established firms, mostly from London, including many of the trade's grandees. The management of so many participants was itself a feat of organization. It was the work of Percy John Dobell of 77 Charing Cross Road, the son of Bertram Dobell.[10]

The Ruxley Lodge sale catalogue was meticulously annotated by the younger Dobell, showing the hammer prices achieved during the sale, together with the buyers concerned, and the subsequent prices for the same books sold to members of the ring, at not one, but four subsequent settlements. The auctioneers obtained

£3,714.12s.6d. for the 637 lots for the owners. After the various settlements, the same books finally reached a total of nearly £20,000 – five times the original sum. Relatively few members of the ring actually went away with books, but each obtained about £120 from the divided spoils, simply by dint of their participation. This was roughly equivalent to an average bookseller assistant's annual salary.

The cheek of the 'ringers' is difficult to believe. Within the sale were good copies of all four of the Shakespeare Folios. The initial auction price of the first, paid by Quaritch, was £100; the Second Folio was also bought by him for £46; the Third, a defective copy, fetched only £28 from James Rimell, and a good copy of the Fourth Folio again went to Quaritch, for £20. It was a well-known and much publicized fact that in the previous year (1918) two copies of the First Folio had changed hands respectively for £1,500 and £2,100, and the Britwell copy, sold only two months after the Ruxley Lodge sale, made £2,300, and we must remember Osler's comments at the Van Antwerp Sale in 1906. In the settlement after the sale, the First Folio finally made £1,550; the Second rose from £46 to £305, and the Fourth from £20 to £160.

In another instance, five bundles of smaller books located in the drawing room were particularly badly catalogued. They consisted of early English plays, poems and pamphlets. One lot of plays contained more than 150 texts. These were very carefully scrutinised and listed by expert dealers among the ring. Quaritch bought the five lots at the sale for £101. After the settlements they moved up to £6,031, and as the Freemans calculate, this was not only sixty times more than the public price, but constituted nearly a third of the entire Ruxley Lodge settlement.

The whole sale was studded with similar examples and, not surprisingly, the press began to take notice and to comment on what had happened. In particular, a well-known crusading weekly called *Truth*, founded by Henry Labouchere and famous for its exposure of fraud, began a series of aggressive articles on the results of the Ruxley Lodge sale, drawing attention to the amazingly poor results of the book auction itself and hinting at the prices obtained at the knock-out. A correspondence resulted in *The Times*, which published a leading article which was highly critical of the practice of ringing. It called the practice 'nefarious', 'noxious', 'an actual evil', and urged legal proceedings against rings as a form of criminal conspiracy.

All the venerable names in the book trade of the period were involved in the Ruxley Lodge ring: Quaritch, Maggs Bros, Tregaskis, Pickering & Chatto, Sawyer, Bumpus, Spencer, Edwards, Thorp, Ellis & Smith, Dulau, Myers, Rimell, B.T. Batsford, and so on. The Freemans have identified which books each dealer bought, analysing their prices through a series of settlements, and what they later fetched on the market.

While it is quite clear that the practice was endemic, it was not strictly illegal at that time. In fact, the practice of ringing was frequently and openly defended on the grounds that booksellers were only using their hard-earned expertise to make the most of an opportunity.

Auctioneers, in particular those outside London, but not exclusively so, certainly realized that the practice was used to the utmost, but generally seem to have felt unable or unwilling to take defensive action by a much more widespread use of reserves because they feared that this might inhibit the trade from attending sales, which would leave vast quantities of unsold goods. This was because private buyers were few and far between; and dealers who would not take part in any settlements were rare and would often suffer malicious or intimidating treatment from the participants in the ring.

Before his retirement, Tom Hodge was once asked what he thought of rings and his often-quoted answer was 'What rings?' But the same could not be said of a new employee who joined Sotheby's just as Hodge was on the brink of retiring. She was Millicent Sowerby, who has left us an enchanting, light-hearted book entitled *Rare People and Rare Books* (1967). Miss Sowerby had started her bookish career with the brilliant Polish emigré bookseller, Wilfrid Michael Voynich, and after the briefest of interludes as librarian at Birkbeck College and later with MI5E in Paris, she joined Sotheby's in July 1916 as their first-ever female cataloguer.

Interestingly enough, one of the themes of her book is the difficulty she experienced as a woman in finding employment, not as a clerk or secretary but as an expert cataloguer. When Montague Barlow shook the trade by employing her in the cataloguing department at Sotheby's (during the First World War, when there was an acute shortage of staff), he insisted that she wore a very plain, dark blue overall and made herself as inconspicuous as possible. He also insisted that she should take her full three-week holiday allowance (at that time virtually unknown) and work no more than the stipulated hours each week. But she was grateful to the Antiquarian Booksellers' Association on two counts. It was their protestations which led to the abolition of Saturday sales, and further pressure from them brought about an improvement of the lamentable heating in Sotheby's saleroom during the winter months.

Miss Sowerby initially had some difficulty in assessing the value of books being sold and in establishing the relevant reserves, 'that most necessary precaution,' she writes, 'for the defeat of the Knock-out'. She goes on to say that 'during all the time I was at Sotheby's the Knock-out was going strong. ... After the sale, these dealers would proceed to the nearest pub, and hold an entirely unlicensed auction on their own of the books they had just bought, and buy them from each other at their proper value, thus doing the owners out of their money and keeping it in their own hands.' She adds that where a dealer had a commission on a lot, 'in which case the higher the bidding the better for him [because he could claim 10 per cent of the final hammer price from the customer], so he would signify this to his group by some gesture known and understood by the initiated, such as putting his pencil into his mouth and tilting it upwards towards the ceiling, or alternatively by letting it droop. In these cases his fellow Knock-outers would bid him up as high as possible so as to put more money into his pocket.'

Another nefarious activity practised at Sotheby's by the trade – and probably not only at Sotheby's – caused problems for the cataloguers. This was the return of books after the sale, as permitted under the auctioneers' terms of business, with the claim that they were not as catalogued, i.e. that there was some minor fault which had not been mentioned in the catalogue description. This would be after the book had been sold at an unusually high price. When, after being returned, it was subsequently re-offered for sale – naturally without a reserve – a dealer could buy it for a fraction of the earlier price and would then be able to sell it on to his own customers at a multiple of the original high price, pointing out that that was what was recorded in *Book Prices Current* or *Book Auction Records*. One particular dealer with a regular habit of returning books is described by Sowerby as having 'the finest set of tools for making wormholes of anyone in the trade!'[11]

The shadows deepen

While rings had often been publicly condemned, they were not yet illegal. The first attempt by Parliament to outlaw the practice was the passing in 1927 of an Act entitled Auctions (Bidding Agreements) Act, framed by Lord Justice Darling in consequence of a particularly exasperating case of malpractice over the sale of a horse. But the Act's major prohibition was against the offering of an inducement to someone else to refrain from bidding, and the book trade had no difficulty in getting around that; in any case, prosecution for such an offence could only be instituted with the consent of the Attorney General. Only one prosecution – and that not in the book trade – is recorded as having taken place. In the event, the book trade did not take a blind bit of notice.

If the law was weak, so too were the rules on the matter governing the members of the Antiquarian Booksellers' Association. Clause 9 of the Association's Code of Good Conduct proscribed participation in the ring on pain of being asked to resign – though only if the miscreant had been found guilty in a court. After a blatant instance of ringing at the sale of the library at Wentworth Castle in 1948, a group of anti-ring members of the ABA devised an ingenious plot to discover the names of the chief culprits. They were successful and provided details to the ABA but, as on many other occasions, the Association ducked behind a wall of silence and hoped that the agitation would die down – as, indeed, it did.[12]

Then, early in 1956, there was a prolonged public outcry over an auction which had been held at Lowther Castle, the family seat in Cumberland of the Earls of Lonsdale. There ringing behaviour had been at its very worst, at the sale of a library built up over several generations and full of highly desirable books. The auction proper of the books fetched £2,200. But there was a ring of 38 participants. The first knock-out in a nearby pub added £11,000 to that sum; a second, from which the smaller – mostly local – dealers had been excluded, raised another £5,000. Knowledge of the event was leaked widely. The cause was taken up by the press, at first by a tiny book-trade weekly called *Desiderata*. An anonymous correspondent who styled himself 'Mr Innocent' wrote four leaders in consecutive issues on what had transpired. He had been introduced into the Lowther Castle ring by a local colleague and promised to pull no punches. 'There is no question of the ring being a jolly brotherhood,' he wrote. 'A den of snarling wild beasts would be more appropriate. ... The prevailing atmosphere is one of mutual mistrust ... their conversation is boastful ... how only they spotted a rarity and bought it for a song.' The consequence was that the trade withdrew advertising from *Desiderata* and cancelled their subscriptions. The paper died very speedily.

The Times soon became involved again. Spurred on by letters from disgusted readers, it headed a Saturday leader 'This Shabby Business'. Why, the leader-writer wanted to know, 'was the Antiquarian Booksellers' Association turning a blind eye to what were undoubtedly illegal practices going on under its nose?'

Two senior ABA members, who had long sought to persuade the Association to strengthen its stance on rings, now became involved. Basil Blackwell (shortly to be knighted in the Birthday Honours of 1956) wrote a blistering letter to *The Times* in support of its leader and announced that he intended to draw up a list of book dealers who would be prepared to sign a formal declaration that they were, and would continue to be, 'innocent of participation in the Book Ring'. He was, of course, head of the famous Oxford bookshop, as well as a former President of the ABA, a very tough businessman indeed, well known and much feared by many of his fellow booksellers for opposition to the ring.[13]

Another former ABA President was the celebrated bookseller Percy Muir, of Elkin Mathews. His particular concern arose from the fact that he had recently become President of the International League of Antiquarian Booksellers (ILAB) and he was exceedingly worried about damage to the ABA's reputation as a member of the international body. He kept a detailed record of the controversy within the ABA itself.[14]

And now a third combatant entered the lists, usually very much behind the scenes: the editor (a great letter-writer) and publisher of *Sheppard's Directory*, an annual which listed all secondhand and antiquarian bookshops in the UK. It had (and still has, though under different ownership) wide circulation among the trade, collectors and book lovers generally. Trefor Rendall Davies, a quiet Welshman with strong Christian beliefs, was horrified that a trade he so much admired should be tainted by so much iniquity. He had already had considerable correspondence with Basil Blackwell on his concerns and offered to circulate to all his readers copies of the suggested formal declaration, promising, furthermore, that any bookseller who signed such a declaration would have his name asterisked in *Sheppard's Directory*. The whole matter was raised in Parliament by Mr R. Chichester Clark and *The Times* again covered the entire debate in detail, causing much alarm to the committee of the ABA.

The Association reacted to this proposal by sending a lengthy exculpatory letter to Rendall Davies and Blackwell, copied to all its members, with strong advice that no one should sign the declaration, and ending with a veiled threat of legal action. The same information was used in an unwise press release put together by the ABA after the Parliamentary debate. This did not have the desired effect: it provoked a scathing *Times* leader headed 'Only a Little Crooked'. The ABA was forced to arrange a special general meeting at which the Association's position on ringing was fully aired. The new President, Peter Murray Hill, announced that the meeting had approved a number of changes: the conduct of auction sales would be investigated and a permanent committee would be established to follow up any findings from the investigation and check any malpractices reported to it in future. Most important of all, the Association's rule was to be changed so that: 'Any member who shall in future contravene the Auction (Bidding Agreements) Act 1927 shall, whether legally convicted or not, be asked to resign from the Association'. All ABA members were to be asked to sign an undertaking that they would observe the new rule.

These decisions were enough to convince Sir Basil that the ABA was now going to take all necessary action, so he withdrew his proposal to publish the list of 66 booksellers who had signed his declaration. Sir Basil told *The Times*, which had covered the results of the meeting very thoroughly, that he was 'highly satisfied' with the ABA decisions. He also wrote to Rendall Davies about the 'triumph of our campaign in the special meeting of the ABA, who have fairly, fully and publicly committed themselves to stamping out the Ring.' Rendall Davies welcomed the ABA proposals but doubted whether they would have any long-term effect on the practice of ringing. It should not be forgotten that there were around 2,000 antiquarian booksellers in the UK, of whom only 300 were members of the ABA, so the Association's declaration could do little more than set a good example to booksellers who were not members.

More than a decade later, in 1969, a second Auctions (Bidding Agreements) Act extended the offences covered in the earlier Act and increased the penalties, and this may have acted as more of a deterrent. Sadly, however, there is still evidence to suggest that any improvement has been limited. At Bloomsbury Book Auctions during the 1980s, I learned from two 'moles' that the ring was active in our room, particularly in the areas of English literature and private press books. I had no proof, but a stiff talk to the suspected participants resulted in much higher prices in the affected areas – at least for a time. It was disturbing.

Trefor Rendall Davies kept up his campaign for years, with the particular and courageous help of *The Bookdealer*. But it was only 30 years later that we found how right he was to have been sceptical. Rendall Davies's article on rings, first drafted in 1956, finally appeared in *The Bookdealer* in September 1989. It brought a response from one of the country's most prominent booksellers, Charles Traylen, who died at the great age of 93 in 2004. He had been a staunch supporter of the ring all his life and indeed a supreme ringmaster/practitioner in the Home Counties. In his letter to *The Bookdealer* he wrote: 'Personally, I can't see how the ring will ever die out. It's too woven into the trade, and those engaged in it simply regard it as the most efficient way of doing business,' declaring quite openly that, to his personal knowledge, 21 out of 36 recent past-presidents of the ABA had been prominent ring members. He based this statement on a scrutiny of his own marked-up catalogues of both London and country sales, going back many years. As late as August 1979 (that is, 25 years after their earlier collaboration), Sir Basil Blackwell wrote to Trefor Rendall Davies: 'as regards the ring generally, I think we are now in a position of those who drove the prostitutes off the streets, though we cannot pretend that we have conquered vice'.

From the early 1990s onwards, *The Bookdealer* also ran a series of interviews with booksellers by Sheila Markham, a selection of which were published in book form in 2004. It was a marvellous conspectus of the book trade. Of course, there were many comments on the ring. Stuart Bennett commented: 'In the mid-80s I began to notice the increasing presence of the provincial auction ring which seemed to be working quite successfully to gain control of both the country and the secondary London sales ... I discovered that many of my colleagues had long since given up on country sales for the same reason that I was beginning to find them so difficult.' Laurence Worms, a strong opponent of the ring, considered by 1995 that there was 'sometimes too much fuss' about the subject. Eric Morten, a convinced supporter, explained how, when young, he was enrolled to handle the calculation of the settlements in the Preston/Liverpool area because he was so quick at mental arithmetic. Robin Waterfield, who died in 2002, made the point that the dispersals of great country house libraries in the late 1940s and early 1950s had been totally dominated by the ring. Peter Murray Hill, he recalled, had a shop in Cecil Court and was a great friend of David Low. 'We went with him to country auctions, although Peter would never go anywhere if there wasn't a ring. It was not uncommon for the auctioneer who had run the original auction to be given a tenner to hold the second sale for the ring.'[15]

Then in 1994 there was a tremendous row when Sheila Markham's interviewee was a recently retired, independently minded Norwegian book dealer, Torgrim Hannås. He hated rings and in his interview commented adversely on the fact that many members of the ABA still took part in them. The ABA President was incensed by his sweeping allegations, which she felt did not acknowledge the work done by the Association since 1956 to stamp out the ring. So the ABA expelled Hannås from membership. The action caused consternation: Brian Lake of Jarndyce, a prominent bookseller known for his dislike of the auction houses, wrote to the President of the ABA over the Hannås case, which he considered most unfair. Chris Kohler, a bookseller who specialized in forming subject-collections for the academic world, sent a letter in the same vein to the President saying:

The ABA needs to confront its past before it can move on to address its future. Courage and humility are needed – pompous righteousness is not the way. I started bookselling in 1961 at Joseph's when that firm was the headquarters of the ring for settling after the London auctions. Remember that in those days auctions were more a wholesale business for the trade than they are now and the involvement of so many dealers must have had a significant effect on prices. The ring was made up of Joseph's, Marks, Thomas Thorp (London), Francis Edwards, Frank Hammond, Charles Traylen and Dawson's. My job was to locate all these good ol' boys through the fog of cigar smoke and give them their tea or coffee, for which I was rewarded with a note dealt off the pile of bank notes on the table. All members of this ring were ABA and five of the seven had been (or were to become) presidents of the ABA.

As any politician knows, an attempt to sack someone for telling the truth –

albeit a partial and exaggerated truth – can backfire. The ABA's treatment of Torgrim Hannås brought out more, and more damaging, information about the ring than even Trefor Rendall Davies could have hoped. Hannås himself died shortly after these events.

So what is the position today? The ABA has certainly tried to put its house in order: its rules governing auctions and rings are as stiff as anyone could wish and, moreover, the Association has made it an offence to fail to cooperate with its Standards Sub-Committee (the permanent committee set up in 1956). It is also evident that ABA members are far more open and condemnatory about ringing. In late 2004, when Maggs published their catalogue 1364 of the Wheldon & Wesley reference library, item 283 consisted of a catalogue of one of the Lowther Castle sales (6-9 May 1947), 'marked up with the sale prices and the knockout prices in ink, in a clear, italic hand'. John Collins, Maggs's omniscient cataloguer, commented: 'It is unusual to have the details presented in such a clear way: such other knockout catalogues as I have seen are usually scuffed and worn with almost illegible computations in pencil.' The annotations showed various purchases that Wheldon & Wesley had made, their relevant auction prices and also their settlement prices. Noting that 'we have to admit that Maggs also joined in', Collins traced some of the ringed purchases to the dizzy heights they reached when they came up in later sales.

Research and reading about the ring makes for an unsavoury diet. It is sad to think that for generations booksellers, some of them venerated in the trade, were really defrauding the people who entrusted their libraries to book auctioneers. And yet it is a subject that seems to arouse more interest than most others among those who care about the book trade. In so far as the practice continues today, it has many obstacles to contend with: more extensive use of reserves; much greater bibliographical expertise among auctioneers outside London; a great number of booksellers who fiercely oppose it; the fact that so much bidding is done on commission, with bids sent by post, fax or e-mail; and telephone bidding while the auction is taking place. Most important, perhaps, is that some of those who did once take part say that the resulting receipts nowadays are inconsiderable and not worth the hassle involved.

The sales

To review the book auctions which took place in Britain in the twentieth century takes us into the realms of the incalculable, the unimaginable and the unmanageable. The highlight sales of famous, specific collections, of which there had usually been perhaps eight or ten per year, may have attracted considerable public attention, but what kept the antiquarian book trade ticking over – and what still keeps it ticking over – are the general, average, humdrum sales where values are not excessive, which include material that can be readily sold on to the average book collector or library, but where the perspicacious and knowledgeable bibliopole can spot items which he hopes that his fellow traders will miss. In recent years, this has helped to breed specialists who deal in niche areas of the market. It is to protect clients against such enlightened marauders that auctioneers have to take particular care. Yet there are few book auctions that do not contain a 'sleeper', a book estimated at, say, £60-£80, which ultimately fetches £900-£1,200 or more because two booksellers compete for what each thought was an unrecognized item. It is this unpredictability that makes the world of book auctions fun, and turns what could be immensely boring into something of a sport.

*

The three magic names in the roster of great sales at Sotheby's during the first quarter of the twentieth century were Huth, Britwell and Morrison. In the case of the first two, truly vast assemblies of books had been built up patiently over several generations from other great libraries dispersed during the nineteenth century.

The Huth sales came along just at the time when Tom Hodge was selling Sotheby's, so that he could rightly state that the new owners would be assured of a steady and continuing stream of material. Henry Huth (1815-78) never bargained and always bought the best. He had entered the family banking business in 1833, but worked so hard that his health failed and he took to travel and learning languages instead. De Ricci, the historian of English book-collecting, looked upon Huth with particular veneration. He wrote: 'He collected fine illuminated manuscripts, incunabula, including Caxtons [of which he had twelve] and *editiones principes* of the classics, early Italian, Spanish and French literature and early books on America in every language. His English books were the best after those at Britwell and were remarkable, as all the other sections of the Huth library, for the choice selection of the editions represented, and the beauty of the copies, chiefly bound by Francis Bedford. The poetry and drama sections were as complete as any man could make them, especially for the earlier periods.'[16]

Huth's son, Alfred Henry (1850-1910), carried on where his father had left off. In addition, he masterminded a five-volume catalogue of the collection which became available in the 1880s and was bibliographically innovative because it included the full title of every book, as well as its full collation. Subsequently, auctioneers began to follow the same methodology.

A first sale of Huth's duplicates took place in March 1906 and twelve sales followed between 1911 and 1922. They netted well over £300,000. Again *The Times* had the last word: 'The Duke of Roxburghe's sale in 1812 created an epoch in the annals of book collecting and book prices, and the Huth Sale, when the last volume is claimed by its new owner, may be fittingly regarded as closing the great sales of the last hundred years.'

Two other facts should be mentioned: Alfred Quaritch gobbled up a high proportion of what was sold for a huge group of vociferous and wealthy collectors – both private and institutional; and it was really the first occasion when the relatively new zest for book collecting in America made itself manifest.

If Huth proved exciting, Britwell was even more so. It was the most gigantic library to pass through Sotheby's in the twentieth century. In many respects it was said to rival the contents of the library of the British Museum (now the British Library). De Ricci lists 21 separate sales between August 1916 and July 1927 (excluding three earlier sales of duplicates, held between 1908 and 1910).

The collection had been formed by a Scottish solicitor and MP, William Henry Miller (1789-1848). He moved to England towards the end of his life and settled at Britwell Court, near Burnham in Buckinghamshire. He seems to have spent most of his time in bookshops and salerooms, buying heavily, for example, when the vast library of Richard Heber (1773-1833) was dispersed by Sotheby's (and other auctioneers) at a very depressed time between 1834 and 1837.

After William Henry Miller's death, his library passed through the hands of various descendents, who each added to it, some quite extensively (the Christie Millers were enormously wealthy hat manufacturers). In 1916, S.R. Christie Miller decided to sell just the Americana, which was bought *in toto* before the sale by G.D. Smith for Henry Huntington for a very large sum. Cheered by the success of this transaction, the owner decided to part with the rest of the library by degrees.

The American railroad king, Henry E. Huntington, played an important part in boosting the competition for rare British antiquarian books, from about 1910 until his death in 1927. He often bought in bulk, whole collections at a time, and he realized that the Britwell sales offered an opportunity which would never recur. He used firstly G.D. Smith and then A.S.W. Rosenbach as his buying agents. The library which Huntington founded in California has continued to make acquisitions and has become one of the great research libraries of the world. Its holdings now run to some six million items.

One of the most outstanding of the long sequence of Britwell sales took place on 16 December 1919. There were only 108 lots but they fetched £110,356, the highest total at that time ever recorded for a single day's sale, and more than four times the previous record total, achieved on a single day at Sotheby's sale of the famous Pembroke library in 1914.

The Britwell sale catalogue must have been a joy to prepare. Over and over again, the cataloguer was able to say: *The only copy known; only one other copy known; of the greatest rarity; probably not more than two copies in existence; believed to be the only copy of this edition in existence.* If there was one thing that tempted Huntington it was a book thought to be unique. He and Smith conferred at length, and Smith went to London with virtually unlimited bids for the sale. The ferocity of the bidding must have given Montague Barlow a jolt too. His carefully calculated reserves were left way behind, being exceeded two, three or four times. George Smith bought 80 lots out of the 108, Quaritch 19 and Maggs two. The trade looked on stunned: the sale constituted a vital lesson in what books were *really* worth. Very soon afterwards G.D. Smith died unexpectedly of a heart attack and Dr Rosenbach took his place.

In the 1919-20 season the firm of Quaritch spent a record £166,172 at Sotheby's. In 1920-21 they spent £66,886 against Rosenbach's £42,089. In 1921-2 Rosenbach shot ahead to £91,300 while Quaritch dropped to £29,232. By 1925 they were virtually neck-and-neck. In 1926-27-28 the London firm remained solidly in the lead and did so right through the slump when the Doctor entered a period of quiescence, though their greatest London competitor, Maggs, who had previously been a very respectable third, overtook them from 1932 onwards and remained consistently ahead for twenty years or more.

The consequences of the incursions of the Americans in the early 1920s were generally beneficial for the whole book trade. E.M. Dring, later managing director of Quaritch, was able to write: 'When I first joined Quaritch's in 1925 the post First War boom was in full flood and any book of any merit fetched a record price whenever a copy was sold, as did some books of little or no merit. With many books, particularly eighteenth-century novels, we were frightened to put a selling price on them knowing full well that the next copy – these books were far from rare – would cost us more than we had got for the one just sold.'[17]

Two more amazing Britwell sales of early English poetry and literature took place in February 1922 (5 days) and March 1923 (also 5 days), when Dr Rosenbach was more firmly in charge. Thus in the case of Richard Edwards, *The Excellent Comedie of the two moste faithfullest freendes, Damon and Pithias*, 1571 (lot 251 in the 1923 sale), Dr R. had noted two earlier prices for the same book – £2 13s. in 1843 and £14 10s. in 1869. The cataloguer opined that 'Only two other copies are known, one of which is imperfect'. Dr R. had to pay £1,250 against stiff opposition.

Lot 42 was Richard Barnfield's *Cynthia, with certaine Sonnets, and the Legend of Cassandra*, 1595, a tiny book (12mo) with a pretty titlepage. Its extreme rarity was fully described and the cataloguer added a long note beginning, 'It is only of late that something like justice has been done to the great poetical qualities of Barnfield; to his melody, picturesqueness and limpid sweetness. That he had some personal relation with Shakespeare seems almost certain.' The book had fetched £10 in the Heber sale, but Rosenbach had to pay £1,550, bidding against Quaritch. There were no fewer than thirteen titles by the sixteenth-century poet, Nicolas Breton (lots 79-91), known principally for his *A Mad World My Masters* (lot 85, £250). Dr R. bought them all.

The impact of the Britwell sales was immense. They fetched a sum well in excess of £600,000 and spawned a raft of handlists and commentaries on both sides of the Atlantic.

*

The Morrison sales were quite different. The collection of historical autographs assembled by Alfred Morrison (1821-97) and his wife Mabel was probably the greatest of its kind in private hands. During his lifetime, Morrison had arranged for the publication of two immensely detailed multi-volume catalogues of the collection. He bought books with enormous enthusiasm. There was always great delay in unpacking his purchases. William Morris was once moved to say that 'Mr Morrison is the only man I know who keeps his books on the floor and his carpets on the wall.'

When finally the Morrison sales came about, the result was disappointing. In 1903, six years after Alfred's death, Junius Morgan, book-collecting nephew of the great financier J.P. Morgan, had heard of the Morrison collection and had asked Tom Hodge whether it could be purchased by private treaty. Mrs Morrison, by that time something of a *grande dame*, refused Morgan's immense offer of £200,000 and asked for £50,000 more. But the negotiations were so long-winded that Junius lost interest and the deal came to nothing.

Eventually there were four sales at Sotheby's in 1917, 1918 and 1919 – not a propitious time for such sales since overseas buyers were virtually excluded. There were some 3,335 lots, taking a total of eighteen days in the saleroom. The purchasers were relatively limited in number but included all the major book trade names: Maggs, Quaritch, Sotheran, Tregaskis, Francis Edwards, Pearson and Dobell. The principal purchaser by far was Charles Maggs, whose firm was to continue selling its Morrison material into the 1960s.

The alphabetical listing of the sale catalogues displayed a delightful jostling of historical characters. Letters by Beethoven were sandwiched between letters from William Beckford (father of the builder of Fonthill and author of *Vathek*), and Bembo (Cardinal Pietro), whose poems have come down to us in the beautiful cursive script of his time; the Buonapartes share a page with the Borgias and James Boswell; on the next page, there are three letters from Buonarotti (Michelangelo) with instructions to pay to Raffaelo de Montelupo the balance for three statues on a papal tomb. There was also a multitude of Byron letters. On the second day's sale, Cranach was followed by Cranmer (Thomas, Archbishop of Canterbury), and then by Oliver Cromwell, and so on. But the result was a mere £53,151, only one quarter of what Mrs Morrison might have obtained if she had been less obstinate years earlier.

*

There was one other sale at Sotheby's that aroused much spirited interest after the First World War, although among a much more limited group of people. Henry Yates Thompson (1838-1928) had become a customer of Bernard Quaritch in 1893 and, in the words of Christopher de Hamel, became 'completely hooked on illuminated manuscripts and began to spend increasingly huge sums on books with high quality illumination, or romantic or aristocratic previous owners'.[18] In May 1897 he made his principal acquisition: 210 illuminated manuscripts from the deservedly celebrated collection of Bertram, 4th Earl of Ashburnham (1797-1878), on which he spent about £30,000, a truly enormous sum at the time.

Yates Thompson now owned more manuscripts than he wanted, and he evolved a strategy to keep only the hundred best, shedding some and buying others continuously to improve the quality of his collection. He disposed of what he did not want to keep in nine separate sales at Sotheby's before 1914. The most notable scholars and experts helped in the cataloguing of what he retained: these included Dr M.R. James, the writer of ghost stories and Provost of Eton, Sir Sydney Cockerell, Sir George Warner (Keeper of Manuscripts at the British Museum), and Sir Edward Maunde Thompson, a great palaeographer and Director of the British Museum. Their work appeared in a long series of catalogues which Yates Thompson published privately over a period of many years. In the last volume of all he included a postscript, which in literary and bibliographical circles – and certainly among the book trade – proved something of a bombshell. The postscript stated that, after long consideration, he had decided to sell the whole of his collection by auction. 'I prefer that the volumes,' he wrote, 'should be in private hands rather than be merged in any public collection.'

When Barlow's attention was drawn to the postscript, he was not slow to respond. He and Yates Thompson met several times to arrange the first sale. Yates Thompson was to undertake the cataloguing himself and Sotheby's would charge only five per cent, half the usual commission. Yates Thompson had hinted in his postscript that if a really tempting offer for the whole collection were to be made, he would at least consider it. Consequently, the planning of the sale was disrupted when C.W. Dyson Perrins, another grandee manuscript collector, offered £100,000 for the entire collection. But nothing came of it. Barlow had also offered to find a buyer in America on his next trip there, but it was felt that Yates Thompson knew all his rivals well and could – if he so wanted – organize a private sale himself.

When Barlow mounted the rostrum on the morning of the first sale in June 1919, the saleroom was crowded to an extent almost unknown, on what the *Morning Post* quaintly described as 'the most important day's sale in the history of the Sotheby firm'. Edmund Dring (then Quaritch's managing director) once again swept the board, buying 21 of a total of 30 lots.[19] He had received commission bids from Chester Beatty, Dyson Perrins, Belle da Costa Greene (J.P. Morgan's librarian), Dr Rosenbach, the British Museum, the Bibliothèque Nationale and others. For Baron Edmond de Rothschild he bought the two most expensive items – a Book of Hours with 108 miniatures, *c.*1334, once owned by Jeanne II, Queen of Navarre. The bidding had started at £2,000 and stopped at an unprecedented £11,800. Baron Rothschild's commission had been £12,000. The under-bidder was Dr Hagberg Wright of the London Library. The other item that Dring bought for the Baron, a Persian manuscript from Samarkand of 1410 with a miniature of a polo match, went for only £5,000 against his top commission of £9,000. Dring bought seven items for the Morgan Library, where Miss Greene thought she had got some great bargains. It is interesting to note the slow pace of the sale. It had taken Barlow an hour and a half to sell 30 lots, though in that time he had established a record figure for a single sale session of £52,360.[20]

In the event, the results of the second sale were even more sensational than the first. Once more Quaritch bought 20 lots for £42,000, out of a total of £78,000. Calouste Gulbenkian's agent, Devgantz,[21] bought four items, and Hugh Blaker, who was acting on behalf of those generous patrons of the arts, the Misses Gwendoline and Margaret Davies of Gregynog in Wales, bought for £860 a fourteenth-century English missal, one of the earliest of its school to have survived, and a fifteenth-century Book of Hours known as the de Grey *Horae*, for £1,270.

A third sale was planned for the following year. It raised only £18,000. To some extent the most avid collectors' appetites had, by then, become sated, and the economic climate in England was bedevilled by a crippling miners' strike and rising unemployment. What irked Yates Thompson enormously was the slow rate at which Barlow was able to pay him, because the purchasers had been so slow to settle their debts. This problem of inertia over payments by the major booksellers and the consequent delay in settling up with proprietors was to bedevil the auction business throughout the 1920s and 1930s. But the sales as a whole had been a great success. Yates Thompson received £150,000 from them, which showed him a good profit over what he had originally spent, and he retained quite a number of valuable books and manuscripts, some of which were eventually bequeathed by his widow to the British Museum.

*

It would be quite wrong to give the impression that sales such as the last four described were the norm. They were the ultimate highlights in an unending drumbeat of weekly mixed sales, each of which often fetched a good deal less in total than some single items in the Yates Thompson sales.

Many of the prices recorded were still in shillings rather than in pounds, and three-figure sums in pounds were the exception. The number of lots in each sale was usually at least 1,200, often more, over three to four days. In the 1930s, certainly at Sotheby's, books were still grouped by size: Octavo et infra, Quarto, Folio, for each separate day. Although the dealers' second division was very much in evidence, the first division was often there in force as well. The wonder is how, with so many sales going on in different auction houses, the trade found time for viewing what was coming up.

If we pick a season of Sotheby's sales at random, in the first half of 1921 there were sixteen sales of books and manuscripts as well, of course, as sales of coins and medals, prints and drawings, paintings, furniture and decorative works of art. Among the sixteen was one Britwell sale and one of the many sales of the enormous library of Sir Thomas Brooke (1830-1908) of Armitage Bridge House, near Huddersfield. This collection had been formed relatively recently, with advice from the bookseller Ellis, one of Quaritch's principal rivals. In 1921 the First World War had been over for eighteen months and the book trade was slowly coming back to life. Families had had time to think over their futures and what they wanted to keep and what could be disposed of. Similar patterns of sales were still true in 1925 and 1928-9. Then the slump hit. Sales to America ceased. Trade fell to a dribble.

Ted Dring wrote in his brief memoir: 'I still shudder at the thought of the

Depression. Business just ceased overnight. ... Looking back on it now one can see that the firm [Quaritch] was like a stranded whale. ... For years we had had things too easy. ... At a stroke it all vanished and no one knew what to do ... and yet it is interesting to note that some of the Charing Cross Road booksellers, the Robinson Brothers, and I think Maggs, all increased their turnover annually during this period.' Earlier auction prices were seriously undermined. Book prices in the trade generally crumbled, and it was not until the mid-1930s that commerce in books began to recover.

By that time, the so-called 'dissolution' of major country houses and their libraries was in full swing. Between 1870 and 1919, 79 mansions were destroyed in the UK. Between 1920 and 1939 the figure was 221. The rise and fall of the aristocracy and landed gentry in Britain and the decline, disposal and demolition of country houses has resulted in an appreciable literature of its own.[22] From our point of view, the most useful such commentary is the one by David Cannadine. Much of his data is taken from the admirable *Estates Gazette*, which kept the score of what was happening in regular detailed analyses of the property market. At first the dispersals mainly affected country houses, but by 1919 the great and expensive London houses were suffering a similar fate, and, of course, they contained some of the most important libraries.

*

If the reader wants an idea of what it felt like to inspect, sort and catalogue the many country house libraries that were coming on the market, he can do no better than to read Tim Munby's experiences as a young man on the staff of the book department at Sotheby's in the 1930s.[23] During the slacker summer months of recess between the sale seasons, Munby's task was to make an extensive tour of the scores of libraries whose owners had sought the firm's advice.[24]

The excitement of those visits lingers still in my memory – the long journeys by train or car, the arrival at the lodge gates, the first sight of some beautiful house and the opening of the library door revealing hundreds of feet of mellow calf, russia and morocco bindings ... steeping oneself in the layers of culture represented by any library which has been maintained for several generations. ... There would certainly have been forebears whose various intellectual tastes and occupations could be discerned – an antiquary, a virtuoso, a traveller, a nabob, a politician, a lawyer or a divine. But there was also a large common factor among these libraries. The phrase, 'a book without which no gentleman's library is complete', contains nowadays an invitation to ridicule, but the conception was a reality. In more leisurely days when visitors came for a month and when the winter mud made the surrounding lanes all but impassable, self-sufficiency in reading matter assumed an importance which it is difficult to envisage.

Munby lists the common denominators among the bookshelves and then recites a long roll call of the houses whose libraries had been dispersed, often because the heirs had been killed in the First World War. Cannadine writes of the 'Cascade of Coroneted Casualties', and that it was only 'in the aftermath of victory that the magnitude of these patrician losses became apparent'. Executors had few other options but to sell, faced with the increases in all forms of taxation, particularly of death duties. Very often the outcome had to be demolition.

*

The continuing sales of books by the major auction houses, from the nadir after the Wall Street Crash and right up to the late 1940s, at what by any standards were low prices, enabled quite a number of booksellers, often with specialist interests, to build up a superb range of stock. In some instances, it seemed to encompass an almost complete bibliography of a particular subject, with multiple copies of titles of major interest. One has only to think of Stanley Crowe in his byzantine, subterranean premises at 5 Bloomsbury Street (actually in Streatham Street round the corner), permanently suffused by a persistent stench of damp, who seemed to have almost any book on British or other topography that one might want – and that, despite having been bombed out during the war in 1941 and two subsequent moves.[25] Or, for private press material, of James Bain of William IV Street (again after several moves). Or Archie McLeish of 22 Little Russell Street. He, and his brother who had died some years earlier, stocked what to my then-untutored eye seemed a remarkably rich collection of sixteenth- and seventeenth-century English literature. Or of a later entrant to the British book trade – he had emigrated from Germany – of Ernest Seligmann of Cecil Court, who had virtually every major work on British art history that anyone could think of.

As a final and later example, there was Ben Weinreb, whose stock of books on architecture was legendary. When at Bloomsbury Book Auctions we wanted to compare a copy of Humphrey Repton's book on Brighton, to check its completeness, he had three to choose from.[26] Weinreb was always most anxious that the prices of books which he stocked should be kept up. He was an inveterate buyer at auction, but like the other three booksellers I mentioned, he also bought heavily from 'runners', who attended the sales and bought what they could with particular clients in mind. This was a not inconsiderable activity on which the salerooms depended for a useful part of their turnover.

A miracle decade

Things started to change in 1957, when all aspects of the antiquarian book trade began to take on a noticeably different character which continued well into the early 1970s. Thus, the decade of the 1960s was particularly significant and it is worth looking at it in detail.

In 1957 Christie's held a sale of books from Chatsworth which raised £110,356, the highest single-session total since Britwell. But it was a one-off. Thereafter Christie's book department continued to slumber for some years. Incidentally, 80 per cent of the Chatsworth books had gone to American dealers.

Sotheby's book sales, on the other hand, took off. In the 1957-8 season the firm sold the ninth section of the André de Coppet autographs (1813-21), which included much relating to Napoleon: 320 lots brought £50,939. A little later the celebrated William White collection of Blake material came up for sale. Fifteen lots fetched £44,310. These were virtually unheard-of figures. Parke-Bernet in New York meanwhile had its worst season for two decades. During 1958-9 Christie's had no sales, but Sotheby's had 28, which achieved a record total of £761,221. That season included the first of three great Dyson Perrins sales: 45 illuminated manuscripts and five incunabula made £326,620 on 9 December 1958. H.P. Kraus of New York made his presence felt for the first time, and the London trade found him a most powerful opponent, who had shouldered the mantle of G.D. Smith and Rosenbach.

In the next season, 1959-60, Christie's staged a charity sale for the London Library. T.S. Eliot had written out a transcript of *The Waste Land* (the original drafts were still missing) and E.M. Forster sold the manuscripts of *A Passage to India* and the related papers. On 19 October 1959, Sotheby's began a huge and many-sessioned sale of the Signet Library in Edinburgh. The first offering consisted of natural history. There were further instalments in November, and March, April and June 1960. The trade loved them. The total reached was £144,101, but the volume of cataloguing had been a nightmare and the size of the lots tended to bewilder buyers.

In the 1960-61 season Christie's held ten book sales, and Sotheby's had 28 in 54 sessions (that is, most were two-day sales). The two portions of the distinguished early English literature collection belonging to Col. C.H. Wilkinson of Worcester College, Oxford, in October 1960 and March 1961 attracted a lot of attention. One of the first sales of a scientific library took place that year. It belonged to Professor Charles Singer. A third portion of the Dyson Perrins material outshone all else. The three parts – 150 manuscripts and five books – brought £888,370 (or $2.5 million). Kraus had again dominated the buying. What was also becoming clear was that the aristocracy was still combing out country house libraries: those involved in sales that year included the Duke of Wellington, the Marquess of Bath (he went on year after year), Lord Tollemache of Helmingham Hall, Lord Elphinstone, the Duke of Leeds and, in contrast, the recently created Lord Bossom (a former Minister of Works). Sotheby's and, a few years later, Christie's benefited from such sales right through the next decade.

The season 1961-2 was less outstanding. Christie's had twelve sales totalling £143,015, a large proportion originating from the well-known Shuckburgh Library. Sotheby's made nearly £100,000 from Lord Bute's library at Dumfries House. But mixed-owner sales were on the increase. The following season at Sotheby's was interesting because institutional libraries began to figure more frequently as sellers, shedding not only duplicates – as had earlier been the case – but substantial parts of their holdings. That year they included the Bristol Baptist College, the Athenaeum of Liverpool, the Royal Scottish Geographical Society and the Linnean Society of London. Booksellers who had for years shunned books with library labels began to accept them, and so, of course, did collectors.

The annual summary of events in *American Book-Prices Current* commented on the 1963-4 season that, 'In London, Sotheby & Company continued in highest gear, grossing £827,713 from its 29 sales (58 sessions). Christie's 11 sales totaled £104,991.' The outstanding single-owner sale at Sotheby's had been that of Dr P.H. Plesch with a first portion of his enormous natural history and science library.

In 1964-5 things heated up again. Christie's suddenly had far more sales and raised £258,358 over the season. But the opposition surged too. The season's total at Sotheby's was £1,250,253. Various commentators used the word 'astonishing'. Book sales were becoming a major factor in the auction houses' turnover. The first of the many marvellous sales of Major Abbey books had taken place in Bond Street. So had the Westbury Collection sale of cookery books and the first part of the 'new series' of the greatest of all libraries, the Phillipps Library.

At this stage three people were working together to achieve the vast expansion of Sotheby's book department. Firstly there was Anthony Hobson who, as we have seen, had become head of the book department in the early 1950s, following in his father's footsteps, and who now concentrated his efforts exclusively towards organizing the Phillipps sales. Lord John Kerr had taken over from him the responsibility of running the book department. His charm and his brilliance as an auctioneer drew in ever more clients. And thirdly there was John Carter in New York, successfully persuading American bibliophiles and libraries to send their collections to London where, he advised them, they would pay less commission and – in all likelihood – achieve better prices than they would in Manhattan.

The changes in the antiquarian book market were discussed in a long analytical piece by the distinguished literary scholar and book collector Professor Gordon N. Ray.[27] Ray had sent a detailed questionnaire to booksellers, librarians and collectors on both sides of the Atlantic and from their answers formed the conclusion that 'it is indeed the institutional libraries, with their paramount concern for the research value of acquisitions, which have chiefly altered the book world'. He also noted that while 'our society is an easy-money society … among cultural artifacts, rare books are only on the outer fringes of affluence'. 'But at the same time, prosperity has also stepped up sharply the activity of collectors. … The current sellers' market has not only made dealers prosperous, it has also played its part in greatly enhancing their status in the rare book world. … No one who remembers what rare bookdealers had to endure in the quarter of a century following 1929 will begrudge them today's prosperity and enhanced status.' In the UK an editorial in *The Book Collector* recognized the perspicacity of Professor Ray's comments and observed that a poll of both British and American dealers showed an average of 60 per cent of their business to be with institutional libraries, and furthermore that the (mostly American) institutional demand was not by any means confined to the upper price ranges, even though that made the news – dealers at all levels were enjoying the boom.

It was Peter Murray Hill's answer to one of Ray's questions that touched on another important new factor. He commented that, while he could buy seminal books in his field with ease in 1945, and with more difficulty in 1955, in 1965 'I find it almost impossible to replace the key books in education, philosophy and literature of the 17th and 18th centuries'. This experience on a large scale very soon led to a major new factor in the book trade: the establishment of the reprint houses, among which, surprisingly, H.P. Kraus was a major player when he joined forces with the newspaper magnate, Lord Thomson, to set up a vast organization to supply what the – mainly educational – world needed.

*

Halfway through the decade, the 1965-6 season turned out to be a most remarkable year. Christie's hit the headlines with their sale of the library of Captain Spencer-Churchill of Northwick Park, as well as his celebrated assembly of paintings and bronzes. Sotheby's was favoured by an exceptional number of institutional libraries which were doing the reverse of acquiring new material. The sales included duplicates from the Folger Shakespeare Library in Washington D.C. and once again the Linnean Society in London, the Ratcliffe College Library in Leicester, the British Medical Association, the Long Island Historical Society, the Garrick Club, the Birmingham and Midland Institute, the London Library, the Royal Academy of Arts and the Royal Institute of Chartered Surveyors. It is worth pointing out that in the late 1990s, serious concerns were expressed about library sales, but in fact such sales had been occurring for generations earlier. They were precipitated not only by a shortage of money (and shelf-space) within the libraries concerned, but also by the deteriorating state of the libraries' contents, and they often helped to pay for thoroughgoing efforts to ensure long-term preservation.

During the 1966-7 season, Christie's growing book department moved into a different gear, with 20 sales held in 24 sessions. They included works from the libraries of the Earl of Shaftesbury and the Duke of Norfolk. Sotheby's sold the fifth portion of the library of C.E. Kenney, one of the greatest aggregations of books on science and surveying: there were eight parts in all eventually. There were further very valuable manuscript sales from the Phillipps collection and another three J.R. Abbey sales. There were four sales of books from the late G.L.T. Brudenell. It was a whirlwind year consisting of 38 sales in 70 sessions. But in the next season, 1967-8, the number went up even further, to 45 sales in 79 sessions. Important sales in Bond Street included two of Major Abbey's sales, more Phillipps sales, no fewer than nine sales which contained books from the library of H.C. Drayton, a property developer (with what has been described as 'good roast beef taste'), and Persian and Middle Eastern material from the Kervorkian Foundation. John Carter and Graham Pollard also sold documentary material which they had used in their exposure of Thomas J. Wise, the infamous bibliophile and forger.

*

To round off the season of 1969-70, Christie's sold books from Warwick Castle and the British Rail Pension Fund, and held some 17 sales in 20 sessions. Sotheby's (not including Hodgson's) staged 43 sales in 76 sessions. There were two Chester Beatty sales of Western manuscripts. In one, a late fifteenth-century Book of Hours made £90,000, and there were many items to match, at continuous price levels which were virtually unknown previously.

Paul Jordan-Smith, writing in the index volume of *American Book-Prices Current* for the years 1965-70 (which, of course, included UK prices), stated boldly that 'every auction house did well during the 1965-70 season', pointing out that the number of priced titles listed in the annual volumes had increased enormously over that period. Above all, the surge at Sotheby's between 1960-61 and 1970-71, from £1,049,1191 to £2,591,397, provided evidence that, in the course of this decade, the market had moved onto a different plateau.

Such trends do not continue indefinitely. The normal economic cycles began to come into play. Many of us would rather forget what happened in 1974 and again in 1981-2. By the later date, Sotheby's had not only swallowed Parke-Bernet in New York fifteen years earlier and built it up enormously, but Christie's also were well established there in their own right. Demand from American institutional libraries went into reverse, but a new market opened up in Japan. British book-sellers hastened to satisfy that demand, though Japanese educational institutions usually worked at one remove through local agents. British auction houses moved rapidly to get a piece of the same action. I listened with astonishment to what our bookseller customers were telling us about the opportunities in Japan. I wrote (in Japanese) to 16 bookshops which dealt in English books, offering an introductory Bloomsbury Book Auctions catalogue subscription at a reduced price. Eight booksellers around Tokyo became subscribers and remained so for years until the Japanese economy went into decline.

Inevitably, the effort of organizing sales on such a scale affected firms in different ways. Christie's built up a young and vigorous team as its book department grew; Phillips became an appreciable player; but Sotheby's powerful machine began to creak. Dealers and clients started to complain that the time taken between bringing in property and its actual sale was growing unacceptably long. By the late 1970s it was no less than fourteen months. I was the lucky one asked to initiate a new approach within the firm and to overhaul procedures.[28] We invented a special form of 'quick sales' with very rapid – if slightly simpler – cataloguing for books up to a value of £300, instituting weekly auctions of this kind and payments to consignees within a week of the sale, which was particularly popular. It cleared the backlog wonderfully. The trade appreciated it and other auctioneers copied it.

*

The pattern of sales in the most recent decade, as we have seen earlier, has changed again. There are new entrants to the auction house field and they have a particularly loyal customer base among the book trade. In all, there are probably no more than 80 or 100 book auctions each year in the UK altogether, but the interest in them has become global. The number of new books put out by publishers has grown enormously. Many volumes tend to go out of print after a relatively short period. There is more interest, therefore, in recent books as auctionable material – particularly where first editions of fiction are concerned. Single-owner sales are now the exception. When they come up, as in the case of Lord Wardington's collection of atlases (at Sotheby's in 2005), or Bernard Breslauer's sale of early catalogues and fine bindings (at Christie's, New York, in the same year), they create exceptional interest.

When a virtually unknown and sensationally rich library of seventeenth- and eighteenth-century scientific books, the Earl of Macclesfield's collection from Shirburn Castle, is discovered and dispersed (in a long series of sales at Sotheby's, starting in 2004), it becomes a milestone. The comment frequently heard among antiquarian booksellers today, that 'there just aren't the books about' is only partially justified. There are still massive quantities about, but the nature of what is being sold has changed. The quality of what was regularly going through the London salerooms at the beginning of the twentieth century is simply inconceivable today.

Private Buying

RICHARD FORD

Booksellers' memoirs have often emphasized the importance of private purchases, usually lamenting their decline. Basil Blackwell commented that by 1922 his antiquarian stock, 'normally refreshed by casual offers of private libraries or smaller lots of books', needed renewal. By implication, fewer private libraries were being offered to him, and he was compelled to consider buying at auction. At much the same time, however, Lionel and Philip Robinson made the purchase of private libraries the cornerstone of their business. Blackwell's theme has been echoed by many booksellers as they look back, usually with the perennial complaint that older books in particular have become increasingly hard to find. Maurice L. Ettinghausen recalled the purchase of incunables and early printed books in the Francis Longe library in 'those blissful days of peace' (before 1914) when 'it was possible to buy in every market'. Robin Waterfield remembered that in the 1930s, 'seventeenth-century books were coming through our hands all the time'. David Low complained about the scarcity of good books in the early 1970s. Jim Thorp described the halcyon days of the 1960s when his firm was buying 'in much larger quantities' than in the 1990s. Meg Kidd recorded Andrew Block (d.1985) feeling that 'the day was fast approaching when he could no longer buy from private collections. Everything was getting into the [auction] rooms.' At the close of the twentieth century, Paul Minet found 'depressing' the standard of books in private houses in his shop's affluent catchment area in Sussex and Kent. While some booksellers find their current buying better than ever (one even claims to be experiencing 'a glut of books') all agree that the quality has diminished.[1]

Booksellers also comment on changes in the perception of the interest and value of books previously little considered. Rusty Mott of Howard S. Mott, Inc. recalled that his parents, in purchasing the residue of the stock of the Museum Book Store during the 1960s, chose not to take the remainder which would now be seen as decent items ('not duds'). Anthony Rota, discussing a buy in Ireland in 1961, pointed out that books rejected by one generation became the collectables of the next.[2]

Current doom-mongers in the trade see a terminal reduction in the scale of their businesses, buying and selling. But while it is characteristic of older booksellers to praise past times and envy their forebears' Caxtons and Shakespeare quartos, each generation has adjusted to changes in the supply of books – so far – and accommodated such innovations in sources of supply and means of selling as bookfairs and the internet. The contemporary rare bookseller cannot now expect to find incunables, seventeenth-century or even nineteenth-century books in private houses. His sights are adjusting to a world in which a private buy may include only a modern first or a children's classic, or in which he is exploring new paths, for example within the fecund field of printed ephemera.

To refresh stock constantly, whether privately or through the trade, is the primary need of the bookseller, and to stop doing so is considered retirement or suicide – except in exceptional circumstances such as war or recession. Many dealers have considered private buying the most interesting, enjoyable and productive means of renewing their stock. Percy Muir, on the subject of buying at auction and in other bookshops in the 1920s, used the phrase 'the hard way', perhaps because it is time-consuming and potentially more competitive than private buying. From the 1950s on, George Sims was in the enviable position of buying so much privately that he did not need to attend auction sales.

For many booksellers private buying also has a dimension of excitement and enjoyment. Block 'loved the chase, the gamble, the bargain', while Harold Reeves evoked the 'romance' which 'in many disguises enters a bookseller's shop'. The bookseller never knows whether a treasure is about to walk through the door, or is to be found on a house call, particularly given (as E.P. Goldschmidt put it) the 'unaccountable manner [books] may stray through the world'. Some booksellers also enjoy the access which house calls give them to different sorts of people. Like John Townsend, they are curious about the character of the collector as revealed through his books: 'Buying a library is rather like buying someone's life.'[3]

At the top of the trade, a bookseller may be experienced and knowledgeable; he may have a reputation for fair dealing; he may be confident; he may be highly moral; he may have good financial resources – but the opposite extremes, and the gradations in between, are also represented. He may be a specialist who is selective or a general bookseller with storage space who swallows large miscellaneous lots. He may have expertise in a wide range of subjects, in a specialist area only, or in scarcely anything at all – for lack of knowledge is not necessarily an impediment to buying. Charles P. Everitt claimed that 'despite everything I believe to the contrary, the best buys I have ever made were the things I knew nothing at all about' and one of Kraus's precepts was not to be put off buying by lack of specialized knowledge, ignorance perhaps leading to highly profitable low offers.[4]

In the past, differences in the status of booksellers have been reflected in the operations of the trade. Richard Sawyer of Chas. J. Sawyer recalled that, 'in the old days' (before book fairs), the provincial bookseller had no market for rare books and sold them on to the London trade. The firms with established reputations had the best customers and could pay top prices, while lesser booksellers had no such access. Booksellers who were out of their depth had the choice of making an offer based on ignorance or referring the item or collection to a more knowledgeable colleague. David Low, for example, was asked for help in a purchase from the Royal Institution by another bookseller and, on another occasion, bought books from an antique dealer who had been 'landed' with them.

Eric Moore recalled that Hatchards would put the best books from a private buy into auction and the rest into its rare book department.[5]

Vendors have also tended to have a wide range of reasons for selling. These have sometimes included a desperate need for money or for human contact. A collector may sell when his tastes have changed or he needs space. An executor is bound to wind up an estate. Unromantically, Giuseppe Orioli mentioned someone who periodically sold a book so that he could dally 'with a public woman'. One central London bookseller described visits to the following: a vet in Wimbledon, a publican in Wigan, and a former customer in the stockbroker belt who had been a sponge merchant and a manufacturer. The collector who periodically sells some of his books – perhaps 'a crafty old man' like Sydney Cockerell – has a fair idea of the current market value. The little old lady may believe that *all* old books are valuable, or may become the prey of the unscrupulous. Or she may turn out to be a suicidal widow, as described in Morley Jamieson's memoir. Some sellers may simply wish to get rid of the books at any price, though this was more common a generation or so ago when books were often seen as encumbrances rather than assets. Others may invite several dealers and auction-houses to fight over their books. Timothy d'Arch Smith mentioned a further type, the charity case, such as the author and eccentric John Gawsworth, from whom the bookseller bought at a loss. The dustman as a source of books has featured occasionally in bookselling anecdotes, an ironical tribute to the lack of awareness of some people caught in charge of books. Booksellers have also rescued material from the dustman: George Sims, for example, caught René Hague in the act of throwing out Eric Gill's ledgers in 1963.[6]

By the end of the twentieth century, many booksellers had observed a great increase in public awareness of the potential value of books. In the past, imagination and avarice may have been stimulated by newspaper stories of great book and manuscript finds, but the general public was unaware of the information obtainable from *Book Auction Records* and the like. Many booksellers felt such reference works were the preserve of the professional and had a vested interest in public ignorance. But since the 1980s, television in particular has not only informed the public but has also encouraged bargain- and treasure-hunting. This may have saved some important books from thoughtless destruction, but it has also often created an unrealistic expectation that anything old must be valuable, while tending to encourage the public to think that auction houses are the natural arena for achieving the best prices for books. Booksellers on a buying call may be asked what an item would fetch at auction. At the same time, as Roy Harley Lewis argued, vendors may think that local booksellers have little more knowledge than they do, by comparison with the corporate expertise of an auction house of any standing – a proposition which booksellers vigorously contest. The fact that many booksellers acquire a proportion of their stock at auction suggests that auction houses do not necessarily get the best prices for a vendor, particularly once commission is taken into account.[7]

Some vendors had always been prepared to do some spadework to get an idea of the potential value of their books, perhaps inviting several booksellers to tender, or getting a view from the auction houses. But the arrival of the internet has given vendors (and the people who price books for burgeoning charity book-shops) a massive reference guide at their fingertips. Booksellers now encounter vendors who have looked up what dealers are asking for other copies of their books, and expect commensurate prices. However, the prices of books on the internet, like those in *Book Auction Records*, require some degree of professional interpretation.

The vendor's view of the bookseller would be interesting, but there is little documentation. Percy Muir wrote of 'those rose-tinted glasses with which the uninitiated view the métier of antiquarian bookseller'. Stephen Mogridge referred to 'the legend of the infallibility of the bookseller', and Paul Minet observed that some people think of booksellers as rogues. Timothy d'Arch Smith described a collector who had become very suspicious of booksellers, 'having dealt with Bert Marley of Dawson's in the sale of the library of C.K. Ogden ... whose executor he had been'. Anthony Rota described a negotiation with the family of John Rodker, whose wife was quoted as saying that, having met numerous dealers in the course of her life, she considered Rota 'more honest than most!'[8]

Since a shop's stock requires constant refreshing most private buying is carried out by the owners of bookshops or retail outlets. Ideally the bookseller would find himself in a similar position to the American acquisitions librarian Lawrence Clark Powell, with his cicerone from Dawson's, in a sizeable house in a central London square, confronted by the Ogden library:

> And so for the next three hours I worked my way onward and upward ... from room to room, through heaps and piles, rows and mounds of books, on stairways and in halls, in bathrooms and closets, big rooms, little rooms, and no rooms – books to the right of me, books to the left of me, above, below, and all around.

The more mundane reality for booksellers involves as wide a range of proper-ties visited as of quantities of books or quality – a storage unit, a palace or a hovel, a monastery or a manse, near or far, sordid or antiseptically neat. Books and other material may also be brought to the shop and bought over the counter. W.T. Spencer told of several such transactions, including visits by Kate Greenaway's aunt, 'Mrs Evans, the wife of a partner in the famous firm of Bradbury and Evans', who 'used to come to me every week or fortnight with a portfolio of her niece's drawings that had been rescued out of the artist's lumber basket'.[9]

The location of a shop has always been a significant factor in private buying, whether over the counter or on house calls. E.P. Goldschmidt recommended a location near the source, rather than the 'estuary' of the books. Many dealers have benefited from being in the right place at the right time. Harry Pratley said that Reuben Hall (Tunbridge Wells, from 1898) 'became THE second-hand bookseller in what was a spa town which was full of retired people absolutely chock-a-block with private libraries'. Blackwell's (Oxford), Broadhurst's (Southport), Maggs Bros (Berkeley Square) and Peter Eaton (Kensington, *c.*1945-80) each had a choice location. At the other end of the spectrum Charles Russell established a bookshop in Battersea High Street in 1980 where he 'had the wrong books in the wrong place. The customers were appallingly low-life and the house calls defied belief'.[10]

There are further practical difficulties beyond the wrong location. Ian R. Grant described the anecdotal circumstances of a traditional bookselling adventure, in this case viewing a country house library. Two or more booksellers have been invited to tender: the house is difficult to find; it is the depths of winter; there are 'vagaries of local pronunciation of place names'; 'the electricity supply is chancy'; and 'heating, if any, is represented by a very inadequate oil stove'. Anthony Rota added one circumstance omitted by Grant: the books are shelved as far from the front door 'as a perverse Fortune could arrange'. A different problem was encountered by John Collins of Maggs at a house call in Lancaster. It was the library of a deceased mathematician and he assured the executors that he could make a selection from several thousand volumes in the course of a morning. When he arrived, it was to discover that every single volume was wrapped up in newspaper and string.[11]

The bookseller has to concern himself not only with the time spent going to, from and at a call-out, but also with what he might otherwise have done instead. For example, it might better reward a bookseller to do some cataloguing rather than respond to an invitation to travel 50 miles to view an inadequately described collection of books. Lack of time or poor choices can lead to missed opportunities, such as George Sims's failure to visit Vita Sackville-West.

Percy Muir perhaps represents the trade in his apparent tolerance of wasted time and effort. He and Greville Worthington once made 'a curious and abortive journey … into a distant part of East Anglia' to view a collection of books and manuscripts. The arrangements for the expedition were 'complicated' and included his requisitioning an expert on illuminated manuscripts, Heinrich Eisemann. All the early books turned out to be defective and the solicitor who represented the estate insisted that the manuscripts (complete, if not 'first-rate') could not be sold separately. Instead of bemoaning at length the time and effort wasted on 'this rather lamentable collection of cripples', Muir simply commented on his colleague's quiet satisfaction when the library was later sold by auction and his estimates for the manuscripts proved to have been slightly higher than the prices realized. Muir seems to have felt that such abortive trips were part and parcel of the trade, a gamble in which losses might be heavy but the potential gains considerable.

At the same time vendors have become more likely than they were a generation ago to invite other dealers to tender or to consult an auctioneer, resulting in a competitive trimming of margins and the greater risk of not buying at all and wasting more time. At the mention of other dealers having seen the books, Clive Linklater decided to 'look at them more closely', but many other booksellers in the 1990s would have walked away. Competition should work to the vendor's advantage, but can be irritating or challenging to the dealer.[12]

The bookseller's financial position inevitably influences, or even controls, his ability to buy. Shortage of capital prevented Orioli from tendering for a Gutenberg Bible from the monastic library at Melk, in Austria. Presumably he did not have the opportunity or credibility to enlist a bank or merchant bank – as the Robinsons enlisted Warburg's for the Phillipps library – or to form a consortium with a bookseller in a better financial position. Shortage of capital might also lead to a low offer, whereas too much cash could lead to a bookseller scorning a collection that in normal circumstances he would snatch at.[13]

Many booksellers baulk at large quantities of books, perhaps lacking the storage space or fighting shy of the physical labour, and prefer to cherry-pick. This often does not suit the vendor, who appreciates dealers like Paul Minet, Richard Booth, and Peter Eaton who would clear everything and had access to substantial storage space (including a country house bought for the purpose in 1969). Anthony Rota and Timothy d'Arch Smith described instances in which they arranged solutions for a vendor: Rota by forming an *ad hoc* partnership with a local 'general bookseller, who still had the equivalent of a "sixpenny box"' and could handle a large quantity of miscellaneous books; d'Arch Smith by using a contact who arranged the disposal of a harmonium, jewellery and other items. Harry Pratley pointed out how important it was to be able to get quantities of books back to the shop, and recalled that just after the First World War, before the car became ubiquitous, one could not hire a van, but hired 'trucks' (barrows) instead. Taxis have been a frequent resource for booksellers and their assistants, and the mass clearers of books think in terms of lorries or pantechnicons.[14]

Pitfalls

Private buying has led booksellers into any number of pitfalls. The vendor's description of the books is likely to be inadequate ('a room full of fine bindings' may turn out to be a shelf of paperbacks.) The prospective vendor may not have the right to sell – in 1993 the bookseller Ron Chapman and the Ballantyne & Date partnership became embroiled with the legal system because of a wife who had no right to sell her divorcing husband's books. Books may prove defective upon later examination. The items offered may have been stolen, as when Ettinghausen at Maggs was offered manuscripts stolen from the Marburg Museum. Or they may have been forged, as when Muir and other booksellers were offered a fake map of the Battle of Bunker Hill. The vendor may make the dealer jump though hoops by putting conditions on the sale: Ottoline Morrell, for instance, required Bertram Rota and Percy Muir not to take any manuscripts or presentation copies. Sometimes there may be an embarrassment of riches: Muir recorded that Morrell's library contained 'a supply of rarities greater than [our] immediate clientèle is likely to absorb'. Occasionally, if clearance of the books is delayed, books on which an offer has been based may go missing or the vendor may change his mind.[15]

The state of the economy in general sometimes made buying risky. In 1915, for example, William Dunlop of Edinburgh declined the offer of a book, giving 'dull times for the book trade' (the war) as the reason not to add to his stock. Booksellers could also be caught out by changes in the market. Percy Muir told of the time when he had to be persuaded by a partner that it was worth buying Mary Webb manuscripts; their profitable sale proved the partner to have been a better judge of their value. George Sims's employer in the late 1940s, Leonard Westwood, bought 'a fine William Blake collection', but was unable to sell it, eventually parting with it 'at hardly any profit'.[16]

Buying technique and psychology

Over the counter purchases have territorial and other implications, and a house call is seldom a matter of walking into a house, casting an eye over a few shelves of books and making an offer. It is a negotiating situation which involves complexities of territory and presentation, the bookseller often being required to exercise skill in assessing the potential of the books and in persuading the vendor to sell.

Booksellers develop individual techniques in buying books. Andrew Block's was 'pantomimic' and employed the poker-face, a ploy that can be traced back at least to Walter Scott's character Jonathan Oldbuck. Oldbuck, a collector with the attitudes and techniques of a dealer, first haggled, giving the impression that he did not really want the item in question, and then, on concluding the purchase, affected 'a cold indifference, while the hand is trembling with pleasure'. The tradition continued with Rosenbach, whose face is said to have 'retained the bland expression of a Chinese mandarin', and Kraus, who said that 'the chief rule in buying is not to show emotion'. Meg Kidd described Block deploying the time-honoured emphasis on the defects and inadequacies of the merchandise, intended to strip the vendor of expectation. Only when the vendor had left did Block reveal his pleasure in the buy – and in getting the better of the vendor.[17]

Morley Jamieson, a Scottish bookseller observing the London trade in the 1950s, described Jack Joseph's bullyboy technique ('the most original shop technique I had as yet seen') in dealing with a student offering 'good class textbooks' to him in his Charing Cross Road shop. He made a derisory offer at which the student was 'aghast; the offer obviously nowhere near his expectations'. Joseph then shouted: 'Well, do you want the f—ing thing or not?' The student promptly accepted the offer, 'no doubt the victim of a very peculiar pressure'. (Such behaviour was not uncharacteristic. E. Joseph Ltd was one of the very rare subjects of a complaint by a member of the public to the ABA – about 'abusive treatment'.)[18]

The techniques of Block and Joseph appear to confirm Paul Minet's suggestion that pre-Second World War booksellers 'had a very different attitude to business forged in the depressed days of the 1930s … leaner days when turnover was much slower and margins had to be larger'. But Richard Booth, in a later generation, had business practices which could have been learned at an old-timer's feet. He expressed copious ideas on technique, from what he described as an 'adage of the trade', that 'you can never refuse a cup of tea', to his belief that 'negotiating deals needs acting ability and I decided that my best persona would be that of a gauche public schoolboy who did not know what he was doing. "Gosh, what do you think they're worth?" was a comment I have made more often than I care to remember.' Booth also put into effect one of the adages of H.P. Kraus, 'experience forbids one to accept the first price asked'. He described a transaction in which he relished beating down the price suggested by the brother of a deceased collector from £500 to £100.[19]

Anthony Rota and Paul Minet were as eloquent as Booth on their buying techniques, but subscribed to a different dispensation. Rota believed in displaying expertise and familiarity with the books on offer, winning the trust of the vendor. Minet believed in openness even to the extent of admitting when out of his depth and recommending a colleague with the requisite specialization. He suggested that an unforeseen consequence of such openness could be further offers of books by word-of-mouth recommendation. Percy Muir's and George Sims's memoirs chronicle the growth of a circle of customers who became friends, sources of stock, and the conduit for further productive relationships. The tone of these relationships is suggested by a letter from Charles Batey of Oxford University Press to Muir in 1969, in which he said that 'I don't like Blackwells and do like (and trust) Percy Muir'.[20]

Another of Booth's adages was that looking at the books was less important than the relationship with the vendor (presumably involving conversation and a cup of tea). The reason for this might be to establish the vendor's expectations, but another function of such a technique is to ascertain whether the vendor has further material beyond what is on offer. Peter Eaton, with his catholic interests, might look up the background of the vendor, using *Who's Who* for clues as to what to expect, and would ask for any letters or other bits and pieces that might be available. His policy resulted in a fine art collection, and a museum of interesting, important and quirky exhibits. Similarly, on one occasion, Charles P. Everitt's line of questioning led to the rescue of important newspapers from a woodshed where they were 'ready to start the next morning's fire'.[21]

Patience and perseverance are also useful weapons in the bookseller's armoury. George Sims called on a productive source three or four times a year, accompanied by his wife, who could act as a diversionary ploy to engage anyone who might interfere with business. David Magee describes one protracted negotiation with the heirs of an old customer. When he made an offer, they could not make up their minds; four years later the books were still in storage in his shop, but he increased his offer and it was finally accepted.[22]

Advertisement and self-advertisement

The imperative for the bookseller wishing to buy privately is to stimulate offers of books. The local bookshop, now something of an anachronism, attracted vendors by its very presence in a neighbourhood. But advertising is the obvious resource, whether through Yellow Pages, the local press, the distribution of handbills in promising areas or other means. Catalogues not only sell books but prompt vendors – many of George Sims's catalogue customers, assiduously cultivated by correspondence, sold their collections back to him. Another form of advertising is the raising of a bookseller's profile in the public eye, at which American booksellers were most proficient, to the detriment of the British trade. Kraus, who inherited Rosenbach's mantle, but with access to television as well as newspapers, quoted a remark made to him by William Randolph Hearst, Jr, that a front-page article about one of his buying coups 'was the best piece of merchandising I ever saw. ... That amount of publicity is worth more than the cost of the book'. Rosenbach himself had developed a superb publicity machine which guaranteed front-page coverage of his exploits. But the articles and books which appeared under his name had the same purpose, to attract important customers and offers of books. The newspaper articles which constitute *Books and Bidders* (1928) were transparent devices for tickling the vanity of the librarians, collectors and the past, current or potential vendors whom he mentions. T.F. Fenwick, Sir Thomas Phillipps's heir, discreetly sold Rosenbach fine items from the Phillipps library and 'possesses an almost unequalled knowledge of old manuscripts'. Lady Swaythling, seduced by her reading of the book, consigned 'her copies of the 1865 *Alice* and the 1872 *Through the Looking-Glass*, both with Tenniel's original drawings, for £6,000' in 1928. The same principle was in operation when the archives of the Earls of Huntingdon were offered to Maggs Bros., following on from an article in *The Times Literary Supplement* about their sale of the Pizarro papers to Henry Huntington in 1925, for which Ettinghausen characteristically took full credit. Ettinghausen was able to sell the Huntingdon papers to Huntington on his second visit to America in 1926.[23]

In a much lower key, British booksellers such as Percy Muir, George Sims, Anthony Rota and Paul Minet published articles or books intended to provide insight and information, while also gaining status and free publicity. Some publications combined information and advertising, such as Henry Sotheran's *Piccadilly Notes* (1933-7), or Peter Eaton's brochure describing his country seat, Lilies, which was in its third edition by 1993. By such means Foyles, who also sponsored literary lectures and advertised extensively, became 'the first choice for anyone wishing to sell books' after the war, but the by-product of this was the envy of individuals in the trade who delighted in referring any time-wasting house calls to them. Some dealers had the knack of stimulating newspaper and television coverage, as Richard Booth did when he crowned himself King of Hay-on Wye in 1977.[24]

Other methods for obtaining stock privately included sending regular circulars to librarians and potential vendors listed in *Who's Who* and other reference books. Richard Booth wrote to big houses in Scotland. A few booksellers have admitted to 'knocking', a term borrowed from the antiques trade. Ken Smith 'bought some of my second-hand stock by knocking on doors in Hampstead Garden Suburb, advertising in local newspapers and talking my way into local jumble sales before they opened to the public'. Even fewer admit to writing to heirs or executors culled from obituary notices.[25]

Purchase of libraries

A private buy might be of one book or of a library. A library could be small and select like the Rowfant collection (sold in 1905) or massive and heterogeneous like C.K. Ogden's (1957). The opportunities to buy large libraries have diminished over the years, but these provided a staple and desirable source of stock until the last decades of the twentieth century, perhaps making the difference between wealth and subsistence for their purchasers. The outstanding private buy of the century was the acquisition of the Phillipps library by the Robinson brothers in 1946. The challenges involved in selling this enormous collection are described by Anthony Hobson later in this volume. The success of the sales greatly augmented the Robinsons' already considerable wealth and status in the trade. Conversely, *shortage* of capital after the Second World War prevented Eric Barton of the Baldur Bookshop from buying 'a distinguished library of French books which might have changed the course of his bookselling career'. Harry Pratley recalled Reuben Hall's windfall purchase of the Baden Powell family library, forced on him for a pittance two or three weeks after he opened his shop in 1898, which gave his business a flying start. Norman Storey described how the purchase of a substantial nautical library led his father to turn one of his Cecil Court shops into a nautical bookshop, specialist knowledge, as it often does, following a buy rather than preceding it. John and Juliet Townsend of Brackley Books 'specialise in the subject collected by the last person from whom we've bought a collection', the case in point being big-game hunting. The specialist knowledge may then fall into desuetude for want of further similar buys.[26]

Any bookseller who has been long enough in the trade can have the consolation of purchasing a valued customer's library from his executors. Long-established booksellers like Maggs Bros. Ltd. (est. 1853) and Bernard Quaritch Ltd. (est. 1847), or even businesses spanning only a couple of generations, have the advantage over later establishments. Michael Hollander observed of Maggs that 'they have customer lists going back to the Duke of Wellington, so someone's always dying with libraries for sale'. Similarly, Hatchards of Piccadilly (est. 1797), with their carriage trade, built up many libraries over the years and remained well placed to buy them on disposal. Not long after moving from Hatchards to another company in 1947, Eric Moore was unimpressed by the library of Sir John Lubbock, since Hatchards had accustomed him to 'having the run of interesting collections'. Lubbock's library, in retrospect, constituted 'a once in a lifetime opportunity'.

Specialists, or general dealers with specialist interests, are also likely to have access to libraries in their field, having formed connections through catalogues, shop, societies, literary circles and so on. Michael Katanka, the specialist in socialist literature (*fl.* 1970), for example, became the obvious purchaser of socialist libraries. A benign cycle by which the customer becomes a vendor, possibly involving a dimension of friendship, has been put in place. This relationship could also lead to word-of-mouth referrals. George Sims, for instance, a specialist in modern firsts, used to buy Golden Cockerel Press books directly from the firm's owner, Christopher Sandford, from 1933 onwards. Sandford introduced him to Mrs Owen Rutter, Robert Gibbings, and other artists who had done work for the press, as well as Eric Gill's family. Bertram and Anthony Rota and Percy Muir established similar networks leading to purchases of private libraries. Bertram Rota 'liked to make friends of his customers' and Barbara Kaye said that 'mostly, libraries came to Elkin Mathews through personal friendship'. The relationship of the collector with the bookseller has often been recognized by executors. J.S. Bain described one occasion when he had the 'privilege' of buying back a collection of Cobden-Sanderson bindings from the estate.[27]

International competition

At the top end of the market, competition for important private libraries in the UK was international, particularly American. The exploits at auction of George D. Smith, Rosenbach, and later Kraus and Lew Feldman, frequently upstaging British competitors, generated wide media attention. Smith also made some remarkable purchases by private treaty through Sotheby's, including the Britwell Court Americana in 1916 and the Bridgewater House Library in 1917. Rosenbach cultivated a network of influential contacts and agents in the UK and Ireland who kept their ears to the ground for potential purchases. The author Shane Leslie was one of these agents and put Rosenbach in touch with Lord Dufferin, the Duke of Marlborough and many others. Rosenbach, most notably or notoriously, bought books from Sir George Holford in 1925 and York Minster in 1930. The Holford books were 'smuggled out of the house, covered with brown paper, in a butcher's cart'. Some of Rosenbach's buying coups in the UK, whether privately or at auction, inevitably aroused nationalistic outrage.[28]

Booksellers as agents

In the first half of the century, Smith (d.1920) and Rosenbach (d.1952) developed the collections of private clients, particularly Henry E. Huntington, on a much larger scale than their British counterparts. After the Second World War, the Harry Ransom Humanities Research Center (HRC), at the University of Texas, often represented by Lew D. Feldman of the House of El Dieff, generated massive publicity by the aggressive buying of archives, again upstaging the British book trade. Timothy d'Arch Smith, for example, described his failure on behalf of The Times Bookshop to secure an important Aleister Crowley archive which 'had already been fed into the Molochian jaws of the Humanities Research Center'. Maurice Ettinghausen compared the activities of the HRC to those of Thomas J. Wise, who had initiated the ploy of contacting heirs and families of literary figures. HRC, as Warren Roberts, its sometime Director, admitted, also directly approached writers to secure their archives, cutting out all middle-men, British or American.[29]

Anthony Rota has described his failure in 1967 to secure the Evelyn Waugh archive for McMaster University, in Canada, against the competition from Lew Feldman, representing HRC. But British booksellers also benefited from HRC patronage, Rota valuing the Vladimir Nabokov archive on HRC's behalf – though later being 'trumped' in its purchase in 1991 by a New York dealer representing the Berg Collection of the New York Public Library.[30]

British dealers also acted as agents for American *booksellers* in the purchase of significant private libraries. The Elkin Mathews correspondence includes a copy of a letter of 1958 from Laurie Deval, the partner of Percy Muir, to Frances Hamill of Hamill & Barker, Chicago, reporting on the high spots of the library of G.L. and Mrs Craik. The following year there was an exchange of letters between Muir and Hamill, in which Muir reported on the purchase of the C.K. Ogden autograph collection. Muir asked for 20 per cent commission on top of the purchase price of £2,000. Hamill & Barker had invited him to take over the negotiations with the Ogden family from the autograph dealer Winifred Myers, a long-standing friend of theirs. Myers's kindness was appreciated by another American bookseller, Howard Mott, to whom she handed over the residue of the stock of the Museum Book Store – presumably to the chagrin of her British colleagues. Myers had not realized that this residue contained important manuscript material, including 'the official 40-foot vellum scroll in manuscript listing the expenses of the British occupation army of New York during the American Revolution executed by the Commissary General'. Hamill & Barker also worked with Leonard Woolf and David Garnett, sometime bookseller, to buy the diaries and letters of Virginia Woolf in 1960 and, incidentally, cultivated their British colleagues with food parcels during the war.[31]

There are also examples of British booksellers representing British vendors in negotiations with American institutions. In 1961-2, for instance, Martin Hamlyn of Peter Murray Hill valued Isaac Foot's massive library (estimated at 70,000 books) for the heirs and arranged its sale *en bloc* to the University of California, having approached Lawrence Clark Powell because of his track record with such collections.[32]

Booksellers and consignment

Elkin Mathews handled a considerable quantity of books and manuscripts on consignment, the property of Richard Curle, Paul Hirsch, Sir Charles Lillicrap, Sir William Rothenstein, A.J.A. Symons, and others. These transactions had advantages for the bookseller. With relatively little risk and without having to find or tie up capital, he was able to derive income and sustain a reputation for handling interesting material. Barbara Kaye likewise commented on the importance of Percy Muir's arrangement with Paul Hirsch, by which Muir catalogued, displayed and sold his books directly 'without capital outlay'. This was during the Second World War when cash was particularly short.

Another reason for a bookseller to encourage or welcome consignment might be his lack of expertise. David Low felt unable to make an informed offer for the H.C. Pollitt collection, but was sufficiently trusted by the heir to negotiate 'an amiable arrangement by which [he] would sell on commission, with no hurry on either side'. When Anthony Rota took a William Faulkner manuscript on consignment from the collector George Lazarus, he suggested too low a figure at which to offer it to the HRC. Lazarus insisted he double the price, and HRC did not hesitate to buy.[33]

The levels of commission which booksellers have felt to be sufficient when working in this way have rarely been put on record. Anthony Rota revealed, however, that he suggested 10 per cent when his fellow bookseller Alan Thomas asked him to evaluate, catalogue and sell Lawrence Durrell's archive in 1969. But Rota described this as a *prix d'amitié*, an insufficient reward for work and expertise. The Elkin Mathews archive provides some evidence of the commission required by that firm or tolerated by the consignor. Sir Charles Lillicrap's books earned the firm 25 per cent of the sale price in 1966, and Sir William Rothenstein's books 15 per cent (33⅓ per cent for the drawings) by agreement with his executors. Martin Hamlyn of Peter Murray Hill received 7.5 per cent of the £50,000 received by the family for the Isaac Foot library in 1962, and found this a more than adequate reward.[34]

Valuation

Booksellers are occasionally called upon to value a library, perhaps for insurance purposes, probate or in mediation between a private vendor and an institution. Bernard Quaritch Ltd. has a well-established tradition in this role: 'The firm has frequently been engaged in the transfers from private to public ownership, acting as agent or arbiter in valuation or purchase', as with the Spencer family archive in 1983 and the Churchill papers in 1995. This has proved good business, especially as the co-operation of charitable grant-awarding funds has become, since the 1980s, a vital component of any major acquisition by a British institution. But valuations are an easily transferable form of intellectual property. Rota described one occasion in about 1970 when he and George Sims were invited to make an offer on the novelist Frank Swinnerton's library and papers, only to discover that his offer had been converted by Swinnerton into a free valuation and used as a guideline for selling direct to the University of Arkansas.

Ad hoc partnerships

Booksellers have also sometimes entered into temporary partnerships to buy particular collections. Percy Muir described one occasion in the 1930s when he and (Cyril) Bertram Rota were invited to Garsington Manor to make a joint offer for some books from the library of Lady Ottoline Morrell: 'there was no difficulty about division of the swag. Cyril and I have done the same sort of thing before and since and ... there has never been a murmur of complaint.' Anthony Rota has explained in more detail how this was achieved: 'it mattered very much who was to start, for what they both wanted most was the very rare pamphlet of verse called *Jonah* by Aldous Huxley. ... A coin was tossed to decide who should have first pick, and the winner went straight to the copy of *Jonah* and plucked it from the shelf in triumph. Then Fortune smiled on the loser, for a second copy, which had been inadvertently concealed inside the first, fell out, and both booksellers went home in a warm glow.' Although a common trade practice, the potential for disagreement in such situations has always been great.[35]

Buying abroad

Most foreign buying trips by booksellers involve visiting bookshops, but some dealers in the British trade have found adventure and fecund private sources abroad. Notable among these were Wilfrid Voynich, Maurice Ettinghausen and E.P. Goldschmidt, whose exploits are described in detail by Arnold Hunt later in this volume. Voynich's reputation as a buyer was so exotic that, in an early example of the hyperbole later associated with Rosenbach and Kraus, the *Chicago Daily Tribune* trumpeted his arrival in October 1915 from 'a remarkable tour of Europe, in which he spent $8,000,000 in purchasing the most valuable articles in the collection of the royal families and monasteries of half a dozen countries', including 'the entire manuscript collection of the Hapsburgs'. Millicent Sowerby, who worked for both Voynich and Rosenbach, characterized the former as a book-hunter who scoured Europe for books and manuscripts, while the latter waited for invitations or bought at auction what others had turned up. These two types of dealer have both been well-represented in the trade.[36]

Percy Muir was another enthusiastic traveller to the Continent and elsewhere, and even made a trail-blazing but frustrating tour of royal and aristocratic libraries in Russia in 1928. He had cut his teeth on a buying trip to Germany with Harold Edwards in 1922. He returned in the 1930s and acted on his intuition that music would be a productive new path for collectors, viewing both private collections and booksellers' stocks. One of his greatest finds, with David Randall, then of Scribner's, was on a buying trip in 1954 to a dilapidated château in France where Randall discovered the manuscript of James II's memoirs and Muir persuaded the owner to part with it to pay for repair of the leaking roof.[37]

Ireland proved productive for several booksellers. In the 1920s Lionel and Philip Robinson found that 'the political situation in Ireland made it a particularly fruitful hunting-ground. Many great houses were likely to become the target of incendiaries, and their owners sought to forestall the holocaust by turning into cash their pictures, plate and libraries.' One of the most interesting of these purchases was the library of the eighteenth-century blue-stocking Mrs Elizabeth Vesey.[38] Anthony Rota and George Sims followed the same path in 1961, taking the precaution to alert Dublin to their arrival with an advertisement in the *Irish Times*. They were kept occupied by the responses to this advertisement and made their most significant find, the magazine containing the first printing of W.B. Yeats's 'Mosada'. Gratifyingly for them, it had been overlooked by Percy Muir a few years earlier.[39]

Libraries and institutions

Other productive sources for booksellers have been the collections of religious foundations and public and institutional libraries, both abroad and at home. Kraus observed that 'Many of the illuminated manuscripts handled by dealers in the early part of the 20th century came from monasteries'. English cathedrals have also proved a happy hunting ground for the enterprising, Rosenbach's 'rape' of York Minster Library being the outstanding example.[40]

Public libraries and institutions have always disposed of books, often with little publicity because of the fear of offending past donors and discouraging potential benefactors. Eric Morten found it easy to list more than 30 northern public and college libraries from which he had bought substantial quantities of books in a career of more than 40 years. His father, who started in business in 1918, had bought surplus books from Manchester University Library. In the 1960s, Richard Booth first came to notice as a wholesale buyer of miners' and country house libraries in Wales, with the aid of a tip-off from an employee of the National Library of Wales and publicity courtesy of the Welsh Tourist Board.[41]

Sales of large quantities of books from English public libraries intensified in the late 1970s. The amalgamation and centralization of libraries encouraged a policy of 'rationalization' by which duplicate copies were sold off, but the quality of the books was poor. Paul Minet, however, described the purchase of a huge quantity of 'surplus library stock' in Ipswich in 1978 which contained much of good quality. Many public libraries (Wigan, Preston, Nottingham, Gloucestershire and Kent County Libraries, for instance) also owned large quantities of valuable antiquarian books, to which the public were allowed little access and which posed significant problems of storage and conservation. The libraries were short of space and money and they had new priorities (for example, the purchase of computers). The tendering system, with all its vulnerabilities, was usually employed to dispose of books. A librarian might have no idea of their value or importance, and the small pool of booksellers operating in this field was sometimes tempted to complicity, leading to bitter allegations by other (excluded) members of the trade.[42]

Finds and coups

Whatever the source of his books, the bookseller relishes the possibility of coming across an item which is special by virtue of its rarity, intrinsic interest and market value. At any time, in the shop, on a call, or assessing the books when he has returned from a call, he may experience one of Jonathan Oldbuck's 'white moments of life, that repay … toil, and pains, and sedulous attention'. In the opinion of many booksellers, such finds are also essential to staying afloat, compensating for loss-making ventures. Charles P. Everitt asserted that the dealer 'remembers and tells about the jackpots [but] averaged out over a business lifetime, the killings melt down to a living wage, sweetened by the adventure of the chase'.[43]

Many 'finds' are made when the bookseller is assessing a collection in the tranquillity of his own stockroom, the circumstances of a purchase often precluding a thorough investigation. 'One of the great joys of second-hand bookselling,' wrote Richard Booth, 'is that one can research values after purchasing. Inscriptions, pamphlets and rare first editions can be bought in total ignorance.' Booksellers have differed in their idea of what constitutes research. In the past, some thought it a matter simply of looking up an item in *Book Auction Records*, but a scarce or unique item had no such pricing pedigree and it became a matter of intuition, experience, knowledge, investigative work and occasionally serendipity. Charles Traylen told the story of his purchase, in the 1940s, of 'the original 1663 charter for Carolina' for £25 and his chance discovery of the deed's significance a year later, when looking at an eighteenth-century travel book in his stock. He sold the charter to the State Archives of North Carolina for £2,500 and, incidentally, claimed to have given his source an extra £500. At roughly the same time Greville Worthington and Percy Muir, helped by the literary scholar R.W. Chapman, a friend of Muir, identified the provenance of some Jane Austen first editions, which led to the 'tremendously exciting and thrilling discovery' of manuscript corrections made by the author or at her instigation, and a comment in the hand of her sister, Cassandra. These failed to sell, however, 'at astronomical prices', from the subsequent catalogue.[44]

Ettinghausen described how he used information from bibliographies to track down copies of rare books in private hands: a long speculative trip to Spain eventually resulted in his locating and buying a sixteenth-century Americanum 'of excessive rarity'. H.P. Kraus provides another example of a bookseller who created his own opportunities by imaginative background reading and research in anticipation of what might become available. 'The coup of my life', trumping all other booksellers, followed a reading of Seymour de Ricci's 'Census of the Mainz presses'. He realized that the Bibliothèque Nationale had two copies of both the 1457 and 1459 Mainz Psalters. After complicated negotiation with an institution which was not thought open to any dealing, Kraus organized an exchange and took possession of the duplicate Psalters in January 1970, becoming the first bookseller ever to have a Gutenberg Bible and the two much rarer Psalters on his shelves.

Edward Goldston's purchase of the Melk Gutenberg Bible for the record price (in 1925) of £9,800 was a considerable coup for him. But when he consigned it to auction in New York after failing to sell it in his shop, Rosenbach gave him a massive profit (hammer price $106,000 – then about £20,000), so gaining his own first major publicity coup.

The word 'coup' also has the connotation that the dealer has out-smarted the vendor – who may well remain in blissful ignorance. This was the case with Rosenbach's purchase of a Bay Psalm Book for £150 in 1933 (in 1946 he was prepared to bid $151,000 for another copy). Voynich's exchange of modern theology ('a cartload of modern trash') for a monastic library of valuable books and manuscripts is an equally resonant coup in this sense.[45]

The ethics of buying

The principle of a fair offer and the attendant consideration for the well-being of the general public were introduced into the Antiquarian Booksellers' Association's Code of Practice only in the 1990s: 'Offers to purchase must be fair, informed and honest.' This was only part of a thoroughgoing revision of the Code of Practice, intended to professionalize the organization. Previously the phrase 'honourable conduct' was the moral catch-all which could be applied to relations with trade and public alike. A reader of the ABA minutes and newsletter could be forgiven for thinking that the general public achieved consideration only if they were book-thieves or bad payers.[46]

Some booksellers have attempted to define a fair price. Anthony Rota believed in offering 'a price at which you would not be ashamed to have your peers know about'. Elsewhere he described a negotiation which 'left both sides well satisfied' and defines 'fair market value' as 'the price which a hypothetical willing seller and willing buyer might agree'. Paul Minet described a call-out to which he was introduced by a dealer of the old school. He estimated the value of the books at £2,500 and would have offered £1,200, nearly 50 per cent, but the other dealer insisted on conducting the negotiations with the 'obviously wealthy' owners and drove a very hard bargain, spinning 'the usual line about hard times, large lots and quick clearing'. To Minet's embarrassment, his associate succeeded in purchasing the books with an offer of £600, less than 25 per cent of their estimated value,. Other booksellers, without committing themselves to paper, will admit to paying anything from one eighth to one half of the anticipated selling price. W.T. Spencer considered he had made a 'fair' offer of £15 for a book which came in over the counter which he expected to sell for £20, perhaps recognizing that the purchase did not involve the overheads of travel and time. Another bookseller's rule of thumb based his offer on the two or three most valuable books, the rest being 'bunce' (windfall). Another tried to divine through conversation what the vendor might *think* was a fair price. All of these might think they are being fair by their own lights.[47]

Charlie Unsworth summed up the moral divide: 'One dealer … gets away with paying very little for his books, while another will always pay an honourable price. One will aim for a moderate mark-up and another will aim for the sky.' Richard Booth admitted that, when he was rampaging through Welsh libraries in the 1960s, he 'simply piled up the books and gave whatever I wanted to pay for them'.[48]

The bookseller's perception of what is 'fair' may be complicated by the problem of offering too much as well as offering too little. W.T. Spencer's story about his purchase of a first edition of the Lambs' *Tales from Shakespeare* had a happy ending. His 'fair' offer led, he claimed, to his being referred to a valuable collection. But he pointed out that 'offering pounds for a book where the owner expects shillings' could be counter-productive if the owner 'is so astonished that his mind goes arguing within itself like this: "If this bookseller offers so much my volume must be worth so much more. I'll try somewhere else."' Charles P. Everitt described a similar dilemma when making an offer to a librarian. If he had offered ten dollars he would have secured the volumes, but he offered five hundred, a market value, leading the librarian to decide to keep them. In a similar vein, supplementing the original agreed payment to a vendor in the light of a larger-than-expected profit can lead as easily to suspicion as to gratitude.[49]

Part of the issue of fair dealing is the question whether a bookseller may elicit a price from a vendor who may know nothing of market value. One advantage to the bookseller of getting the vendor to name a price is that he can assess the vendor's level of expectation. But the implication of the ABA's requirement, advisory not mandatory, of a 'fair, informed and honest offer' is that the bookseller should actually make an offer. There are, however, precedents of eminent, and not so eminent, booksellers leaving the price to the vendor, with no apparent thought of it being unprofessional: Spencer, Rosenbach, Booth and others. Rosenbach, on the occasion when he was offered a Bay Psalm Book, telegraphed the vendor that his company did not make offers – which was untrue – eliciting a price described by Rosenbach's biographer as 'ridiculously little'.[50]

The introduction of the clause into the ABA's Code of Practice may indicate a shift in the trade towards greater professionalism and ethical consideration. The existence of a moral minority (at least) also became apparent in 1996 when Karen Thomson sent out a questionnaire investigating ethical issues. She reported on the results in the *Bookdealer* under the title 'A Question of Ethics'. Only one question (of the ten) had any bearing on buying from the public. 'Would you, having bought a book privately, and made what you regarded at the time as a fair offer, if you then discover it's worth more than you thought, go back to the vendor and offer him more?' One hundred and fifteen booksellers responded, of whom all but eight made it clear that they would offer more.[51]

Some booksellers believe that human nature does not change, but others would claim that the public are likely to get a better deal from booksellers now than they used to, not just because of greater competition and public awareness, but because booksellers are more ethical, perhaps more professional. Morley Jamieson described an era in the London book trade in the 1950s when ruthlessness and profanity were the norm. Perhaps Peter Eaton was remembering this when, in the early 1990s, he said with characteristic bluntness: 'I think earlier booksellers were a load of crooks. But it's greatly improved. There's a more cultured class coming into it.'[52]

Book Trade Weeklies

BARRY SHAW

WHEN the Midlands bookseller Francis Edwin Murray launched *The Clique* in June 1890, bookdealers were provided with a trade weekly, through the 'Books Wanted' columns of which they could, for the first time, readily locate books sought by their customers – a bookfinding medium surely as significant for the trade at that time as was Richard Weatherford's Interloc, the pioneering multi-dealer book database, launched a century later in 1994.

In the 1880s dealers invited offers of books in their specialist fields, along with specific wants, through fortnightly and monthly papers, but for urgent customer orders relied principally on mechanically produced lists mailed to their larger bookselling colleagues around the country. In the early 1930s Andrew Block describes how Murray, recognizing a need, persuaded a number of prominent dealers to become 'members' of *The Clique*, a cachet signified by their names being printed in capitals.[1] The lists of lesser upper-and-lower-case mortals – and the practice was maintained throughout the weekly's 90-year history – were printed after those of members.

Murray was well qualified to assess dealers' book-finding needs, for in the late 1880s he was in a substantial way of business, with shops in Derby (opened in 1884 and from which he ran *The Clique*), Nottingham and two in Leicester, all trading in secondhand and new books under his name. He was also a book publisher, whose list included new editions of some minor literary classics much in vogue at that time, some substantial works on local history, and his own compilation, *A Bibliography of Austin Dobson* (1900). All this changed in 1908 when, leaving his son, Robert Archibald Murray, in charge of the Derby bookshop, he moved to London to develop *The Clique* and the printing side of his business.

*

In December 1906 Frank Murray was elected to serve on the Second-Hand (later the Antiquarian) Booksellers' Association's inaugural Committee and just six months later, responding to an invitation to transfer ownership in his weekly to the Association, he 'absolutely declined to sell The Clique on any terms whatever, but … offered a page each week to the Association, subject to general editorial control'.[2] Nevertheless, he clearly held genuine affection for the Association and in March 1918, when times were hard, offered, as a gift, a debenture of £100 issued by The Clique Ltd and paying five per cent interest, provided only that it was never sold. This was gratefully received and later the gift was repeated.

Although *The Clique* was privately owned, the closeness of its links with the ABA cannot be overstated and, following Frank Murray's retirement in 1919, each new editor or manager, excepting only the last, was immediately co-opted to join the Committee in an ex-officio capacity, when it was expected that his editorial policy would reflect the Association's line.

Clearly this suited both parties. Successive editors sought to use the alliance to stave off potential competition, whilst the Association valued an uncritical trade paper over which its Committee exercised a high degree of control. At times it pushed its luck: 'Mr Last proposed and Mr Fletcher seconded that the Editor of "Clique" be asked to submit names of applicants for membership in that journal, to this Association, for consideration.'[3] On that occasion the Editor concurred. Nevertheless, when a year or two later Robert Murray requested that the Committee urge its members not to advertise in competing papers, its officers declined on the basis that this would not be in dealers' best interests. In a battle of wills that ran for decades, the Editor was, inevitably, always in a minority of one.

On first publication in 1890 the annual subscription to *The Clique* was 2s.6d. and the first issue of six pages included 22 lists, among them those of Blackwell's and Thornton's in Oxford, Maggs of London and James Thin of Edinburgh. By 1919, when its founder retired at 65 and handed over the reins to his eldest son, David Malcolm Murray (whose bookselling background included stints with Joseph Pollard in Truro, the family firm in Derby and Charles Sawyer in London), issues of 80 pages were not uncommon. David Murray continued as Editor until 1932, when he was knocked down by a cab in the Brompton Road (where for long years at no. 180, the paper was both published and printed) and died at the age of 53.

His place was taken by Conrad Davies until 1934, when Robert A. Murray (having abandoned the Derby bookshop) assumed the role of Editor and thereafter represented *The Clique* on the ABA Committee – despite occasional spats with its members over his editorial policy – until ill-health forced his resignation in 1967. The magazine's manager, Lionel Fishman, was then co-opted in his stead, but when in 1976 he sought employment elsewhere no effort was made to continue the long-standing relationship.[4]

*

During its first 40 years the paper knew little competition. But in 1932 my uncle, William Kingston Fudge, decided to start a rival paper, *Book-dealers' Weekly*. His experience was limited. At 28 he had been a publisher for barely three years and had only recently acquired The Pentland Bookshop, which dealt in new and secondhand books from 94 York Road, London SE1. Not surprisingly leading members of the trade, led by the ABA, were unwelcoming of the newcomer. *The Clique* was, after all, 'the official organ of the Association'. There was a quiet first year: the launch issue contained 20 pages with 48 'Books Wanted' lists, including those of Foyles and Elkin Mathews in London, Halewood & Son of Preston and George Gregory of Bath, but nine months later it was averaging just 16 pages. The paper became a popular alternative for non-ABA dealers, however, and received a considerable psychological boost when *Clique*'s advertising manager was persuaded to switch horses.

Fudge's years as a retail bookseller in York Road were made easier, he was fond of recounting, by the craze for Modern Firsts. On publication of almost any new novel by a known author he would salt away six copies, in the knowledge that within a few months they could be sold for several times the unclipped jacket price – welcome business at a time when Britain had not fully emerged from the Depression. But it was indeed too good to be true; overnight the bubble burst and publishers were reluctant to accept returns.

The relative success of *Book-dealers' Weekly* (it was averaging 52 pages by the late 1930s) was sufficient to persuade Fudge to start a second weekly in March 1935. *The Book Trade Journal and Librarians' Guide* was essentially no different from the first except that it was published two days later. The false reasoning behind this decision was that it would be welcomed by dealers whose book-finding service to customers would thus be speeded up. In the event the trade was reluctant to subscribe to yet another weekly and with the issue of 21 April 1939, reduced to just a single page of 'Books Wanted' and 'For Sale' lineage, it was merged into *Book-dealers' Weekly*. *The Clique* also published twice a week for a period until requested to desist by the ABA at the outbreak of war in September that year – imagine the tedium of receiving up to four trade papers each week.

Nevertheless *Book-dealers' Weekly*, which rarely contained any editorial matter, ran profitably in the 1930s under the Fudge imprint. The issue of 11 September 1940, however, contained a statement that it had been sold to its printers, Frederick Samuels Ltd. of Aylesbury, who published it for a few months until paper rationing forced its closure. Thereafter, *The Clique*'s masthead included the note: 'Incorporating *Book Dealers' Weekly* [sic] & *The Book Trade Journal*'.

Paper shortage was the reason Fudge gave for its demise but clearly there was more to it than that. Twenty years ago the Cecil Court bookseller Robert Chris remembered that, with the onset of hostilities in 1939, business dried up to the extent that he was unable to pay the rent. His landlord's response had been that he could remain there rent-free until peace was restored. So if there was little business for dealers, their 'Books Wanted' advertising in trade papers must similarly have been thin. And this is confirmed by reduced issues of *Book-dealers' Weekly* during the final quarter of 1940, under the Samuels' banner, averaging just 24 pages.

With peace in 1945, *The Clique*, free for a while from serious competition, reasserted its dominance and, four years later, from offices now at 170 Finchley Road, London NW3, separated off the 'For Sale' section into a new publication, *The Book Market*. E.M. Dring (1906-90) of Quaritch described *The Clique* as 'compulsory reading for almost every member of the trade, in particular the Charing Cross Road booksellers and the better provincial firms':

readers acquired great knowledge about what books were wanted more than others and I have so often heard it said 'Oh that's a wanted book', meaning you couldn't go wrong in buying it. ... I recall once in the '50s being asked for an STC book of which only one copy was recorded. I told the customer this and said it was not worth advertising for. A month or so later I mentioned this to P[eter] M[urray] Hill who said 'Ha! Ha! I had the same enquiry, put it in *The Clique* and got a copy'.[5]

It was also the principal medium through which staff were found. In 1951 Raymond Kilgarriff moved from Holleyman & Treacher to Quaritch by answering a 'Situations Vacant' ad for 'General Assistant required, experience an advantage. Apply in own handwriting'. Later, when Kilgarriff was established at Howes, he recruited Miles Bartley and Anthony Sillem through the same channel.

*

In fact *The Clique* had always had competition of a sort from *The Publishers' Circular and The Publisher and Bookseller* ('established by the publishers of London in 1837'), a large-format weekly that, as its name suggests, was principally directed at publishers and sellers of new books. Its last few pages contained a 'Books Wanted' section which was well supported by librarians and booksellers (in the 1930s Maggs frequently called for 50 or more titles through its columns) and 'Antiquariana', comprising notes and sometimes articles on the secondhand book trade. These last included, on 2 February 1935, a report on the ABA Annual Dinner at the Holborn Restaurant, and a week later 'The Antiquarian Bookseller To-day and To-morrow!' by the Cockney bookdealer and thrice-published diarist, Fred Bason.

In this *The Publishers' Circular* outdid *The Clique*, where editorial rarely exceeded a single page of trade notes, usually relating to the ABA. Exceptionally, in *The Clique* for 19 June 1954, Robert Murray gave generous coverage to the ABA Annual Dinner and Dance, held at the Mayfair Hotel, under the presidency of Charles Howes, when the after-dinner speaker was the book collector and renowned BBC cricket commentator John Arlott and the principal guest (for the first time a woman), the actress Gladys Young.

However, Robert Murray's real competitor in the immediate post-war period came in January 1948 when a new weekly, *Desiderata*, was launched by the St Leonards-on-Sea bookdealer Eric A. Osborne, from an office at 6 Vigo Street, London W1. In part he hoped to succeed by accepting wants lists from libraries, something *The Clique*, under pressure from successive ABA committees, had always refused to do. *Desiderata* ran for eight years, but when Osborne gave editorial support to Basil Blackwell in his campaign against the auction rings, in which the majority of antiquarian booksellers participated, advertising was withdrawn and in 1956 the paper folded.

Desiderata's ability to survive cannot have been helped by an annual subscription more than twice that of its rival – £3.3s. compared with *The Clique*'s £1.10s. – and the arrival in the mid-1950s of two new weeklies to vie for the trade's lineage advertising. *Books Wanted Weekly* and *Books For Sale Weekly* were published in duplicated form by a dealer in rare books in Tunbridge Wells, T.D. Webster, at a cost of 15s. a year each or £1.2s.6d. for the two. In the event both were short-lived.

*

When in 1953, at the age of 15, I joined Bill Fudge in his publishing business at Sardinia House, Sardinia Street, London WC2, he often spoke of competing again with *The Clique*. Caution restrained him and it was not until 1971, by which time he had sold the company to the arts and soft-porn publisher Charles Skilton (1921-90) and I had become its managing director, that the dream became a reality. For some years prior to this we had been urged to challenge *The Clique*'s monopoly by Mr I. Goldsmith, who had a central London basement bookshop at 76 Chancery Lane and was resentful of *The Clique*, which he identified with the ring. It was not that he was against ringing, but rather that the leader of the knock at Hodgson's Rooms, his auction-house neighbour in Chancery Lane, would not let him in. Ironically Goldsmith died just days before the first issue of *Bookdealer*, in which his 'For Sale' list was printed, appeared on 27 October 1971.

Fudge & Company published *Bookdealer* from 1971 until 1981 under a ten-year licence from Bill Fudge. The first issue had 48 pages with over a hundred advertisers including, in 'Books Wanted', Edith Finer's Frognal Bookshop in north-west London, R.A. Gilbert of Bristol, 'Doggie' Hubbard of Bakewell, B.F. Stevens & Brown of Godalming, George Bayntun of Bath, John Smith & Son of Glasgow and, most usefully, Richard Abel & Co. Inc. of Portland, Oregon, whose many pages of lineage in those early issues helped significantly to get the paper started. 'For Sale' advertisers included

Dr Nothmann's Covent Garden Bookshop, Kenneth Langmaid of Truro, Thelma Harrison of Rotherham and Stevens-Cox of Guernsey.

This launch issue was published at a loss. To get started the annual subscription was a modest £3.40 (or 80p for a thirteen-week initial trial for the doubters) and lineage advertising just 2½p, half the rate charged by *The Clique*.[6] *Bookdealer* subscribers were also provided with free distribution of their weekly book quotations to fellow dealers, a service that proved immensely popular, just as it had been 30 years earlier when Fudge made it part of the subscription package of his *Book-dealers' Weekly*, although in the 1930s he did make a small charge for the report slips.

The trade responded well, so that from issue no. 2 the weekly moved into profit. Clearly the timing was good. In the late 1960s Roy Harley Lewis had begun the first purely book-finding service, Bookfinders, from his home in north London, advertising initially through newspapers and magazines but later relying entirely on referrals. By 1974 a small group of bookdealers, led by Gerry Mosdell, had founded the Provincial Booksellers Fairs Association, and *Antiquarian Book Monthly Review* (now *Rare Book Review*) was beginning to appear on the news-stands. *Bookdealer* grew on the back of the proliferation of book fairs and book-finding, and the consequent awareness among the public at large that just because a book was out of print, it was not necessarily unobtainable.

It was fine of course to have founded the paper on rock-bottom prices and taken many of *The Clique*'s advertisers, but the policy of only increasing advertising and subscription rates in line with inflation did little for the bottom line. What saved the day was massive inflation – it peaked at about 27 per cent – in the late 1970s. Such was the confusion that nobody protested when rates were regularly increased and in a couple of years the profitability of *Bookdealer* was established.

The circulation of the magazine never exceeded 2,300, 90 per cent of which was British trade, with the balance almost equally divided between foreign dealers and UK book collectors who subscribed in order to buy from the 'For Sale' section at what they imagined, often rightly, were trade prices. It is likely that *The Clique* similarly never had much overseas readership. Longer delivery times meant that dealers outside Britain were disadvantaged both in buying and selling, and they responded accordingly. Neither weekly was available on news-stands; they were trade papers and casual sales were discouraged. In this way, if a complaint was made about the conduct of a fellow subscriber and it was found to be justified, the publishers had the power to twist arms.

A year before the ten-year licence expired in October 1981, I quit to start Werner Shaw Ltd., having first set up a deal under which Fudge would sell *Bookdealer* to his old company. Werner Shaw was designed to provide

London office services for foreign publishers and also to take over publication of *The Clique*, by that time published and edited with little enthusiasm by Margaret (Peggy) Pamphilon, Robert Murray's niece, from 75 World's End Road, Handsworth Wood, Birmingham. When my uncle (who had meanwhile fallen out with Charles Skilton over the *Bookdealer* sale) learned that shortly we might be in competition, he offered me publication of his own magazine on terms too attractive to refuse.

Having lost *Bookdealer*, which for some years had been his only profitable business interest, Skilton launched a new weekly on 16 November 1981: *Book World Advertiser,* with Julian Bingley as Editor, was radically different in its style and A4 format. It attempted to combine literary articles, in the style of *ABMR*, with 'Books Wanted' and 'For Sale' trade lineage, but did neither well. Very soon it became a fortnightly, then a monthly, before ceasing publication with the May/June 1984 number (by that time using the shortened title *Book World*), after 27 issues.

Meanwhile The Clique Ltd. had once again merged wants and sale sections in the mother paper. But its decline continued and in 1982 it was sold to Stoate & Bishop of Cheltenham, its printers. They too made no efforts to invigorate the weekly and in 1988, reduced to eight pages and 75 subscribers, it was bought by Michael Cole of York, who discontinued publication but used the name as the publishing imprint for his book trade directories.

*

Fudge remained Editor of *Bookdealer* until his death in 1985 when, under our agreement, I bought the paper for a nominal sum and from offices at 26 Charing Cross Road, overlooking Cecil Court, began to develop its editorial pages. From tentative beginnings these came to include regular articles by Sheila Markham (starting in 1991 with 'Endpaper', especially popular with women readers, to be followed over the next dozen years by more than 90 interviews with leading members of the trade),[7] by Reg Peplow as business correspondent from 1993, and by James Fergusson who has contributed a 'Catalogue Review' since 1994. Between 1995 and 2000, Ian McKay wrote a fortnightly 'Saleroom Selection' and, since 2002, Paul Minet has contributed monthly 'Book Chat'.

At the beginning of June each year a special issue of *Bookdealer* provides the only detailed information available on all the London book and map fairs. Two thousand extra copies of this issue are printed and made available free of charge to visitors at the various fair venues, where their popularity remains undiminished. As a result these bumper issues have been well supported by advertisers – the issue for 19 June 1997 was the largest in the paper's 35-year history, with 404 pages, some 200 of which were filled with display advertisements.

The tradition of book trade weeklies ultimately being published by their printers was followed in 2000 when Werner Shaw Ltd. closed its offices and licensed publication of *Bookdealer* to Alacrity at Banwell Castle in Somerset, although I retained ownership and editorial control.

For 25 years advertising growth in *Bookdealer* was steady. 'Books Wanted' lineage even quickened during the 1989-95 recession as dealers worked ever harder to find books for their customers, peaking in 1996-7 when issues of more than 200 pages (and weekly distribution of up to 10,000 report slips) were unexceptional. Thereafter, as increasingly the trade has sought its books online, issues have diminished to the 40 pages common in 2005.

II

SELLING:
HOW THE TRADE SOLD BOOKS

Gustave David (1860-1936) at his stall in Cambridge Market Place,
drawn by William Nicholson, 1926.

A Century of Innovation
in Selling Books

PAUL MINET

O<small>NE</small> only has to realize that prior to 1920 most booksellers would not have had their own transport to get a flavour of a different age. The major booksellers attended sales around the country, but they arrived by train and had their purchases removed by carrier. I like to think that this was the period that spawned the large metal packing cases that still distinguish a major bookseller from lesser fry. At the auction the big boys would be bothered by a flurry of local booksellers who might have to be outbid or perhaps squared. Most of the major booksellers were London-based and depended for their reputation on catalogues. They *had* to get the better books in order to keep their clientele. There were certain businesses which had been around for 100 years or so – Pickering & Chatto and James Bain spring to mind – but the great growth had been in the second half of the nineteenth century, led by Quaritch, Maggs, Francis Edwards and their ilk. Even outside London, one is struck on looking through an early directory by how many of the larger provincial bookshops originated around the turn of the century, always excepting the vibrant academic book scene long associated with Oxford and Cambridge. The trade magazine, *The Clique*, had also begun over the turn of the century, as did *Book Auction Records* and *Book Prices Current*, the two auction reference books. *Book Auction Records* belonged for many years to Henry Stevens, Son and Stiles, an Anglo-American bookseller, and *Book Prices Current* was issued by Witherby's, the natural history publisher. No less significant, of course, was the foundation of the Antiquarian Booksellers' Association in 1906.

Most large provincial towns had at least one major bookseller, such as Smith's in Reading, Bridger in Penzance, Steedman in Newcastle, Simmons and Waters in Leamington Spa, Henry Young in Liverpool, Thorp in Guildford and many another. They would soak up stock from local private sellers and, in turn, sell to the London booksellers, who would visit their shops fairly regularly.

Underpinning the trade was an efficient railway system and a parcel delivery service which was much envied abroad. Only older booksellers will now remember that until 35 years ago there was a reduced price book service which depended on leaving the ends of the parcel open so that the Post Office could check the presence of a book. The whole pyramid was much more sophisticated than it had been one hundred years earlier, but still in its essentials the same.

The acquisition of motor cars by dealers in the second quarter of the century saw a great expansion of the trade. London booksellers covered many more auctions and bought more regularly from their country sources of supply. Their own businesses were expanding, with more staff to handle books and customers whilst the bosses were out on the road. The 1920s were in many ways one of the high points of the trade: money was plentiful, rare books were collected by wealthy people, wages and rents were still comparatively low and country house libraries were being sold off, as the first wave of down-sizing in living accommodation resulted from the scarcity of servants. As late as 1928 a tyro like Rupert Croft-Cooke could set up and flourish as a bookseller in Rochester High Street with the aid of a good education, a bicycle and £30 capital, although he didn't last beyond 1932. 'I realized soon,' he wrote, 'that the most successful booksellers, in all but the most exalted positions, had little or no knowledge of literary history or of literature, and knew only the bibliographical "points" of books.' An exaggeration, perhaps, but one knows what he meant.

The expansion was brought to an abrupt halt by the Depression. It was in some ways ironic that, at the very time that the price of books at auction was falling and the Depression was forcing people to sell estates and their contents for any money they would fetch, lack of capital meant that times also turned increasingly hard for the top booksellers. I have heard stories from older booksellers of really hard times in the 1930s, with wives having to go out to find other jobs and prices being cut to secure ready money for everyday living. The bubble that had built up around first edition prices, fuelled by a fashion for issuing limited editions, collapsed and many modern books were in 1935 worth a fraction of what they had been worth a few years earlier. Ringing at country house auctions reached its height in this period and this probably reflected real want on the part of at least some of its practitioners.

The Depression saw the end of many older firms, in books as in many other businesses. Those that did survive often carried the scars of their hardships forward into the more prosperous times to come. In these years the London trade was reinforced by a trickle of experienced Continental dealers fleeing the persecution of the Jews in Europe. During the war and for some time afterwards they contributed multilingual expertise to the London trade which expanded its scope greatly, although many had a regrettable habit of moving on to New York after a time. There was also an expansion in the number of 'runners', as smaller dealers in London found it impossible to build stock in straitened circumstances and therefore sold their finds on to more prosperous colleagues. Publishers were in difficulties as well, so that the market became flooded with remaindered books, a field considered an interesting sideline by many secondhand booksellers. This surplus stock was about to find a rather sad outlet.

The Second World War saw many younger members of the trade in the armed forces, with businesses carried on by older members of the established bookselling families, often well past retirement. Some areas of Central London which had been identified with the trade, particularly around St Paul's, suffered badly from the bombing and no one will ever know how many rare book stocks were obliterated. The drives for waste paper also led to a great clear-out of material which might have supplied future stock in trade, particularly ephemera and letters. On the other hand there was a great hunger for reading, in the armed forces and elsewhere, which coincided with fairly strict paper rationing. Suddenly almost anything could be sold. The second half of the 1940s saw a cut in the print runs of new books which was later partly to fuel the modern craze for first editions. I suspect I am not the only bookseller who tends to look carefully at any book published between 1943 and 1950 in the hope that it may be scarce.

The second half of the century divides fairly neatly in two, as far as the book trade is concerned. The immense expansion of libraries, both in Britain and abroad, was allied to a shortage of books in a market to some extent drained by the war. High taxation and further reduction of living accommodation brought more books out, but this time, unlike the 1930s, there were ready customers for them, even if many of these were not private customers but public institutions. The 1950s and 1960s were in many ways a golden period in the book trade. There were still many retail businesses around the country and a small flood of American booksellers made regular trips to exploit stock that was relatively cheap, at least in dollars. What might be styled the terms of trade were now very much in the booksellers' favour. Most of the businesses which had survived the Depression and the war were prosperous and still in their old premises, and the contents of catalogues sold well, especially to libraries. Inflation, at least when it was under control, tended to correct mistakes in purchasing, make leases and properties more valuable and fuel an element of buying books and maps for investment, although it was even then considered invidious to sell on that basis. The country-wide trade was bound together by improved communications and by the advent in 1951 of the reference book *Sheppard's Dealers in Books*, which rapidly became a buyer's bible.

In retrospect it is not difficult to see in this picture the seeds of the quite drastic changes which distinguished the last quarter of the century. As property controls eased, rents and property prices rose sharply. A business which has always been labour intensive was also badly affected by rising wages. In the period from 1970 to 2000 the real value of old and secondhand books fell quite sharply in inflation-adjusted terms.

I do not know of any study which enumerates the decline in retail bookshops, but personal observation tells me that at the beginning of the period there were still retail secondhand booksellers of some standing in most larger towns and cities in Britain: by the end they were becoming a rarity. The decline was much greater in the north than the south. Before the war the Northern branch of the Antiquarian Booksellers' Association had been able to muster social events involving more than twenty businesses. By 1970 they were down to a handful and had no formal branch at all. In 1955 the Manchester area listed eighteen retail bookshops, but by 2000 they were down to five, of which two have since closed. There were exceptions, of course. Horace Commin's in Bournemouth, founded in 1892, was taken over by the talented bookseller Alan Thomas and flourished mightily under him. Another Commin, this time James, had been a fixture in the Cathedral Yard in Exeter for many years: it was still flourishing in 1955 but had long gone by 2000.

Parallel with these physical changes came a change in the books handled. There was a sharp decline in demand for run-of-the-mill seventeenth- and eighteenth-century books, particularly on theology. Academic books were left to the libraries. On the other hand, there arose a great market in colour-plate books and books of topographical engravings, many of which were broken up for framing in the period from 1970 to 1980, until that market became saturated. The late Stanley Crowe's specialization in British topography undoubtedly encouraged collectors into that field, which has not been the same since he died. 'Only professionals have much concern,' wrote John Carter, 'with the why and wherefore of that melancholy class of books which were once fashionable, which are not any longer, but which dealers go on listing and collectors go on buying, or at least eyeing respectfully, because they once were.' It will not have escaped the notice of book collectors that some older booksellers persist in stocking books fashionable when they first came into the trade. This leads to a certain staleness which is sometimes noticeable in shops and book fairs. The really imaginative bookseller creates his own market, as did William Duck in industrial archaeology, Weinreb in architecture and Paul Breman and Eric Korn in whatever they fancy. As the century drew to a close, the two most notable fields in demand were modern first editions and children's books, with which were bracketed 'illustrated' books, meaning finely illustrated modern editions.

For the first three decades after the Second World War there was a good market in social studies and left-wing books, but the cutbacks in university budgets in the 1990s, when amalgamations put some of the new libraries back on the market, led to a collapse in books on social sciences and the changes in Eastern Europe left the dealers in left-wing books high and dry. Theology in general became a pretty dead subject. Firms like Epworth Secondhand Books and Charles Higham, the latter established in 1862, were still flourishing after the war but have become but a memory. They consolidated under the banner of the SPCK, but that chain of shops barely deals in used books now.

There has also been a distinct shrinkage in the services of binders to the trade. Only a few decades ago it was customary to have books rebound or repaired routinely, as well as having a few fine classics bound up for sale as presents. Whilst there are a handful of fine binders still active and one sees traces at book fairs of some not-so-fine ones still operating, the cost of fine binding has become prohibitive to most retail booksellers. This is another example of inflation moving costs in the general economy to a level at which the book trade has been left behind.

During the second half of the century the major auction houses in London moved from being simply one way of disposing of valuable books into being the best known and in some ways most rewarding means of doing so. More realistic estimates and the recruiting of really expert dealers like Hans Fellner as employees of the larger houses must have played their part. In more recent years they have increased their charges to a level which has negated some of those gains, but there is no doubt that the tough attitude carried over by some older booksellers from the hard years of the 1930s led to a public perception that auctions were the best way of proceeding for sellers. I remember years ago being requested as an ABA member to post a notice explaining why sellers got better money from ABA members than from auctioneers, a statement so sweeping that I could never bring myself to display it.

The public's interest in book auctions led to the establishment of specialist houses, Bloomsbury Book Auctions in London (in 1983) and Dominic Winter in Swindon (1988), plus a number of provincial auctioneers who endeavoured to produce special book auctions, not always successfully. As well as competing with booksellers, these auction houses provided the trade with an outlet for surplus stock or, upon occasion, as a means to deal with temporary cash crises. The cash spent in advertising auctions has also been a useful bonus for trade magazines, such as *Bookdealer* and *Antiquarian Book Monthly Review* in its various guises. The proliferation of small specialist dealers which is now a feature of the trade seems to me to have weakened the hold of the old rings, together with a firm policy by the ABA and a changing view within the trade of the moral issues, though there has never been a successful prosecution for ringing an auction of books.

It was inevitable that, in a business where interests were so intertwined, suspicions have been entertained that some major dealers have become too close to the main auctioneers. It is common knowledge that a cash crisis in a major firm can be relieved by a turnout of stock into auction. Smaller dealers have, however, suspected that the credit terms offered to larger firms differed from those offered to them. The late Ben Weinreb, a brilliant bookseller who has left an enduring mark on the architectural book field, achieved terms on occasion which meant he was virtually trading on the auctioneers' capital.

 Another habit which seems confined to the London book trade may be part of a long tradition, but it seems to me to have grown in recent years – the sharing of books. As many dealers have become one-man bands, their capacity to finance major purchases has diminished and one finds increasingly that really expensive books do not necessarily belong solely to the dealer offering them. Several dealers may have an interest in them. This works as long as the syndicate holds together. Some years ago a retail bookseller not a million miles from the British Museum vanished overnight, complete with his stock. Much of it, unfortunately, was not solely his. I am not sure what the outcome was, but it certainly flew a signal for me. Others sell books 'on consignment', effectively either on commission for another bookseller or for a customer. The fewer actual shop windows there are, the more these habits are likely to spread. Owners of sound (rather than rare) books may well find that the auction houses are not interested and that they end up almost in partnership with their local bookseller in achieving a decent price.

As the home market changed, the international market grew. The foundation of the International League of Antiquarian Booksellers, on an initiative which grew out of the ABA after the war, led to increased contacts abroad, doubtless partly fed by air travel. There had, of course, always been a fair amount of contact at the highest levels, with American dealers buying at British auctions before 1914 and famous collectors making an annual pilgrimage across the Atlantic. The weakness of sterling led to an invasion of American dealers in the period to about 1980 and a system of biennial ILAB get-togethers stoked international trade. Curiously enough, there were signs by the end of the century that the free interchange of old books across frontiers was becoming more difficult. Bureaucratic controls on the movement of important materials across frontiers were tightening, as a result of American and European Union regulations and the xenophobic attitude of countries such as Japan.

Domestically, one result of these changes was the rise of the book fair. The Antiquarian Booksellers' Association had been running modest book fairs at the National Book League premises in Albemarle Street since 1958, taking advantage of the shelving skills of Bill Fletcher of Cecil Court in preparing the stands and voluntary co-operation in the planning, since there was in those days only the services of one part-timer in the ABA office. My recollection of those fairs is that the NBL had rather tall French windows on the first floor and that the fairs always seemed to take place on the hottest days of the year.

Membership of the ABA remained something of a dream to many of us in the mid-1960s, but we realized very well that the hub of the demand, as regards both collectors and dealers, was in London. I was based in North Devon in those days and I recollect many talks with Gerald Mosdell about the feasibility of bringing provincial booksellers into London once a month to exhibit and sell our books direct to the London market. The result of this was a short series of fairs in South Kensington which led quite soon afterwards to the foundation in 1974 of the Provincial Booksellers Fairs Association (PBFA), of which I was one of the original members. The PBFA grew apace and within a very few years was running book fairs all over the country from headquarters in freehold premises. Mosdell ran it for a bit, but he was more of an entrepreneur than a manager and he dropped out after a time, running a line of book and antique fairs himself for many years.

The original idea of the PBFA was as a trade fair, to provide provincial book-sellers with access to the London trade. There were already some signs of retrench-ment and visits by London booksellers to distant parts had dropped as costs had risen. As with Mahomet, if they wouldn't come to us, we had to go to them. A few collectors arrived at the fairs from the beginning, in particular A.N.L. Munby, who was most supportive, and we very rapidly dropped a proviso that metro-politan dealers could not participate: Sebastian d'Orsai was one of the very early members, represented by Ian Hodgkins. South Kensington proved slightly sterile territory and various hotels in the Bloomsbury area were tried, sometimes by the original organization and sometimes by rival fairs, which quickly sprang up.

The rise in rents and wages was already leading to a diminution in the number of full-time booksellers and the replacement of the old runners by part-time booksellers, to whom the PBFA fairs were a godsend. The golden period for these fairs was between 1975 and perhaps 1995. At its peak the PBFA had over 800 members and ran fairs all over the country, notably in York, Oxford and Bath. A small army of volunteer booksellers did most of the organizing, belying the usual impression of booksellers as individualists who cannot be made to act co-operatively. By the end of the century the bloom had somewhat gone off the idea and the organization was contracting and also finding it difficult to retain managers for the more far-flung fairs. York remains the largest antiquarian fair mounted in Britain, but there has been a decline in the major monthly PBFA fairs at the Russell Hotel, perhaps due to an element of predictability in stock and prices. There is no doubt, however, that the growth in book fairs filled a gap between the decline of the retail shop and the rise of the internet.

The ABA fair has continued to grow, in central London each June and with the addition (from 1991) of a smaller autumn fair in Chelsea. For many years the PBFA held its most important fairs to coincide with the ABA June fair, and several other independent fairs were held during the same week, notably by Mosdell himself. By the turn of the century the plethora of June fairs was running somewhat out of control, reaching a peak of eight separate fairs in as many days. Visiting booksellers and customers found it virtually impossible to cover everything and unsold stock was moving from one fair to the next, so there has since been something of a reduction. While the high tide lasted, however, there was a liveliness in both ABA and PBFA book fairs which saw the book trade through a distinctly tricky period, attracting new private customers at a time when the habit of collecting was becoming confined to the elderly.

The book fair phenomenon was not, of course, restricted to Britain. It became the custom to bolt international book fairs onto the major ILAB conferences and between times a scattering of British booksellers built up a habit of exhibiting at international fairs, mainly American but on occasions European. In this country, as much as 40 per cent of the British June fairs would consist of foreign dealers, although space considerations kept Chelsea to domestic exhibitors. A large pro-portion of ILAB finances now derives from levies on international fairs held under the auspices of member associations.

By the last quarter of the twentieth century, many specialist dealers were working from home, so book fairs have also proved useful as places to meet existing customers and make contact with new ones, to showcase new stock and to distribute catalogues. The better fairs have sometimes had social events attached, notably the fairs organized by the ABA in Edinburgh and Bath, but rising costs, in particular petrol, have made it essential that booksellers make fairs pay.

The growth of the ABA June fair (charted in the table at the end of this chapter) has not been without its hiccups. When the National Book League moved away from its premises in Albemarle Street, the ABA took a quantum leap by hiring for the 1971 fair a large and splendid ballroom at the Europa Hotel off Berkeley Square. Many older members still look back on that as aesthetically the most pleasant venue. In the 1980s and 1990s, the fair moved to increasingly up-market hotels around Park Lane, which suffered from a total lack of passing trade and a rather marked air of exclusivity. The next move was to Olympia in 1998, a completely different kind of venue, enormous and impersonal architecturally, but with a much friendlier atmosphere than the very select hotels used before. There are still a few members who regret the move out of the West End, but the Olympia fair has been a brilliant success in terms of trade, visitor numbers and perception of the Association as up-to-date. It is expensive to organize, but the autumn fair at Chelsea Town Hall has allowed less financially ambitious members to continue to exhibit in (more or less) central London. The ABA office has been transformed from a single part-timer in pokey surroundings above Cecil Court to a fully professional staff of four, offering a level of support to members undreamt of in the past. Without the fairs it could not have been financed.

One of the more controversial aspects of book fairs has been the practice of allowing exhibitors to trade amongst themselves before the opening of the fair. In fact, for many exhibitors more than half the total business is done before the fair even opens to outside traders and the public. Hardly surprisingly, these customers do not take kindly to this. At one time the ABA made it a rule that no-one could reserve books before the fair opened, but the rule proved unsustainable, although another rule forbidding exhibiting dealers from using non-exhibiting dealer friends as labour in setting up their stands and thereby letting them loose in the fair early has proved more durable. To most exhibitors, however, the book fair is not solely, or perhaps even principally, about selling books, it is as much about buying books in one's own speciality.

The concentration of the trade in London in June has done much to oil the wheels of the book business and cement friendships. In general, exhibiting at fairs has served to introduce booksellers to one another and helped the growing breed of second-career dealers to integrate quickly with their more established brethren. That this intermingling has also tended to iron out prices and eliminate the more esoteric retailers one used to find in isolated places outside London is undeniable, but on the whole the effect must have been beneficial.

Book fairs have not been the only innovation used by booksellers to counteract rising overheads. Richard Booth's experiment with a town of books in Hay-on-Wye started in the 1960s and early 1970s, when he found that space there was cheap and that the redundant fire station, cinema and Norman castle provided room for books on a grand scale. After various ups and downs, it was still flourishing at the end of the century. Whatever one may think of the standards of bookselling which have pertained in Hay, there is little doubt that, in terms of publicity, Booth's little kingdom has been a triumphant success. He is almost certainly more widely known than any other bookseller in Britain, and a tide of books and potential booksellers has passed through Hay in his years there. In more recent years there have been other moves towards spreading the book town concept, but in my view it is too early to say whether any of them can compete with Hay, which still contains some twenty serious bookshops. There are signs that this side may be growing rather than contracting. Hay's relentless publicity through the years, virtually all free, has created an enduring image in the public mind that will probably take decades to dislodge.

Peter Eaton (1914-93), who never mixed with Booth, came from a humble background in Lancashire and never lost his accent or his left-wing politics, although by 1969, when he bought an enormous dilapidated country house called Lilies, near Aylesbury, his style of life had changed beyond recognition. He continued to run a shop in London, moving in 1975 into premises in Holland Park which were specially designed for him by Rick Mather, but his more interesting stock was spread through some 25 rooms full of books at Lilies, which became one of the largest bookshops in England, visited mainly by the trade. He also had a knack of getting on with American dealers and librarians, travelled widely and built up a sound business with American and Japanese libraries.

There have been other shared ventures which do not involve separate bookshops. Charlotte Robinson was pooling booksellers in a London shop over 20 years ago and there have been other experiments in Ludlow, Dorchester and Rochester. The latest (1999), and in many ways the most successful, has been a beautifully fitted building called Biblion in the West End, a successor to a general antiques establishment called the Antique Hypermarket in Kensington High Street. Biblion rents sections of shelving together with staff services to booksellers, and has since started listing its books on the internet and also holding book auctions. It is more professionally run than anything previously attempted in the field and shows every sign of surviving.

At the beginning of the twenty-first century, what was the general position of the trade? The major firms continued to flourish, although there had been casualties on the way – the old and venerable firm of Francis Edwards, for instance, went through a couple of vicissitudes before being taken over and moved to Hay-on-Wye. The loss of its amazing premises in Marylebone High Street, even to such a good new bookseller as William Daunt, was a tragedy for the antiquarian trade. The purpose-built Peter Eaton bookshop in Holland Park is now no longer a bookshop. Hardly any of the major provincial shops still exist and the smaller dealers who have replaced them lack the premises and also the capital to develop into large businesses. Lilies is no more, although Peter Eaton's widow still trades from smaller, if somewhat similar premises. Other select country house operations, such as Foyles' Beeleigh Abbey, a twelfth-century abbey in Essex, and Blackwell's fourteenth-century Fyfield Manor, in Oxford-shire, flourished in the 1980s as fine repositories of stock and a base for catalogue businesses, but neither has lasted. Bayntun's in Bath has passed to a new gener-ation and remains in its splendid premises near the station, but it is very much an exception. Foyles, for most of the century the epitome of both the new and secondhand book trades, is now effectively out of the latter field; the end of this tradition was marked symbolically by the sale, in 2000, of the family's private book collection from Beeleigh Abbey.

I do not wish to embark upon a detailed discussion of the internet, which is essentially a twenty-first century phenomenon. It was fairly well established by the year 2000, but the exponential growth of one site in particular, Abebooks, could not have been foreseen at that stage and this development has undoubtedly had a profound effect upon the business as a whole. Abebooks itself shows some signs of over-exploiting its virtually monopolistic position, but that is for the future. The internet's effect on the retail trade has been, on balance, negative so far. Comparisons of price on a worldwide basis may marginally benefit the customer, but the effect has been to downgrade the expertise and knowledge of the individual bookseller. As Barry Shaw notes elsewhere in this volume, the peak year for *Bookdealer* was 1997, since when the internet has eroded the demand for advertisements. I myself have noticed a falling off in the number of catalogues coming through the post, which must be another side-effect. *Book Auction Records*, for many years one of the most used reference books in the trade, ceased publication at about the same time, although a similar product remains available from America on CD-Rom.

Most dealers now use the internet as an *ad hoc* reference tool, checking all their acquisitions against the various websites to see how prices compare. While understandable, this kind of reference has one notable drawback. *Book Auction Records* recorded prices actually achieved at auction, while the lists of prices published by *The Clique* were based on dealers' catalogues, produced for customers who might be assumed to be relatively knowledgeable. The internet sites offer a great range of prices, many of which have been conjured out of thin air by dealers who may know little about the books concerned: all that the books have in common is that they have so far failed to sell. While a flood of copies of any book may depress prices unreasonably, as dealers seek to undercut each other, the reverse effect may also operate, to an unjustifiable extent, for scarcer books.

The old configuration of the book trade is usually said to be a pyramid, with books moving up from the broad bottom to find their level in more and more rarefied surroundings. That progression is being broken. Customers or libraries in search of a rare book will now turn to the internet before venturing into even a specialist bookshop. It may be that some will learn hard lessons from dealing with sellers who have none of the standards now impressed on their members by the trade associations. The booklover may even be at a loss to know what he wants, without being able to browse and handle particular copies. After all, the internet offers only the title which has been requested. There will doubtless always be expensive shops catering for those with money, but one hopes that the larger retail experience will not become just a memory and that the expert bookseller will not be wholly confined to private premises.

ABA June Book Fairs 1958-2005
(Sales returns per year)

Year	Venue	No. of exhibitors	Take	Average (mean) take per exhibitor	Average take adjusted for RPI (2004)	Average take adjusted for per capita GDP (to 2004)
1958	National Book League	28	No reports			
1959	National Book League	39	£20,000	£513		
1960	National Book League	38	£17,000	£447	£6,700	£17,740
1961	National Book League	39	£34,000	£872		
1962	National Book League	42	£36,750	£875		
1963	National Book League	42	£35,000	£833		
1964	National Book League	41	£41,000	£1,000		
1965	National Book League	42	£45,000	£1,071	£13,500	£31,660
1966	National Book League	44	£54,000	£1,227		
1967	National Book League	42	£50,000	£1,190		
1968	National Book League	42	£67,500	£1,607		
1969	National Book League	42	£100,037	£2,382		
1970	National Book League	45	£66,000	£1,467	£14,775	£30,830
1971	ILAB Congress Fair, Europa Hotel	86	£250,000	£2,907		
1972	Europa Hotel	88	£217,000	£2,466		
1973	Europa Hotel	92	£276,000	£3,000		
1974	Europa Hotel	98	£376,000	£3,837		
1975	Europa Hotel	100	£316,000	£3,160	£17,260	£32,690
1976	Europa Hotel	99	£423,000	£4,273		
1977	Europa Hotel	103	£482,500	£4,685		
1978	Europa Hotel	104	£550,000 (est.)	£5,288		
1979	Europa Hotel	101	£1,208,331	£11,964		
1980	Europa Hotel	101	£663,000	£6,564	£18,330	£31,190
1981	Europa Hotel	103	£620,000	£6,000		
1982	Europa Hotel	101	£558,409	£5,529		
1983	Europa Hotel	104	£731,750	£7,036		
1984	ILAB Congress Fair, Park Lane Hotel	143	£2,062,128	£14,420		
1985	Park Lane Hotel	103	£1,300,000	£12,621	£24,900	£39,130
1986	Park Lane Hotel	107	£1,166,000	£10,900		
1987	Park Lane Hotel	112	£1,892,733	£16,899		
1988	Park Lane Hotel	108	£1,700,000	£15,700		
1989	Park Lane Hotel	113	£2,422,192	£21,435		
1990	Park Lane Hotel	110	£2,336,790	£21,243	£31,525	£42,460
1991	Park Lane Hotel	116	£1,416,540	£12,211		
1992	Park Lane Hotel	109	£1,529,440	£14,031		
1993	Park Lane Hotel	100	£1,413,433	£14,134		
1994	Grosvenor House	86	£1,463,448	£17,017		
1995	Grosvenor House	86	£1,534,400	£18,712	£23,430	£29,360
1996	Grosvenor House	87	£1,526,850	£17,550		
1997	Grosvenor House	92	£1,836,320	£19,960		
1998	Olympia	146	£3,440,486	£23,565		
1999	Olympia	162	£3,101,597	£19,145		
2000	Olympia	145	£3,912,328	£26,982	£29,580	£32,425
2001	Olympia	149	£3,729,938	£25,033		
2002	Olympia	151	£3,097,951	£20,516		
2003	Olympia	157	£2,907,342	£18,518		
2004	Olympia	139	£2,329,352	£16,758		
2005	Olympia	126	£2,115,112	£17,104		

The London Street Trade

MICHAEL HARRIS

I REMEMBER the first time I bought an old book off a street barrow. It was in Dublin just off O'Connell Bridge next to the low wall that ran along the River Liffey, opposite the small cinema where 'The Trapp Family', a non-musical biopic, played for several years. It was a bright weekday morning in early summer in 1959 and the stallholder wheeled his barrow from somewhere on the quays to the pitch, where a crowd of people were milling about in an apparently random way. After a short delay lasting until midday, he whipped off the tarpaulin to reveal a heap of antiquarian books all priced at 6d. In a moment all lack of focus was gone and the crowd threw themselves on the books. By the generous assistance of one of the contenders I acquired volume II of Dodsley's *Environs of London* (1762) with its large, folding street map. This was the beginning of my erratic engagement with the book as an object. It was a good time to buy books in Dublin. Country-house libraries were being emptied out onto the market and the auction rooms along the quays as well as the bookshops were full of modestly priced material. I subsequently filled a hand-cart with books from auction which cost 7s.6d. and were used to insulate my spartan rooms in Trinity College. Others, more experienced and with a sharper eye, used the books to finance their education and living expenses.

Such a glut of cheap antiquarian books was not limited to Ireland. Across the Irish Sea, the first half of the twentieth century saw a massive dispersal of books which appeared on the market finding their own levels of demand and price. The cloud of books released by the French Revolution was still falling in a persistent drizzle and the clouds formed in England, when death duties hit the owners of country houses, created many sharp showers and more persistent downpours. Inevitably the quality of much of this material was mixed, but its quantity was crucial to a complex and dynamic commercial system. The firms of Bernard Quaritch and Thomas Thorp, for example, sailed through most of the twentieth century on the run-off from the general dispersal. At the other end of the spectrum, as defined by socio-economic status and snobbery, the traders working the barrows in the London streets relied on the backwash from the same tides of material. Street selling was an integral part of the book trade and it provided a living, sometimes a very good one, for its practitioners, as well as some rich experiences for their customers. This is over now. It is no longer possible to get a direct experience of what became, in the Victorian period, the street trade in books. In Paris some elements of open-air bookselling persist, but in London the trade has moved on.

It is worth emphasizing how closely the barrow and shop trade were related. The term 'stall' was often applied to the shelves, tables or other displays located on the street outside bookshops, sometimes providing their main source of income. Bertram Dobell was prosecuted for this use of the space outside his shop in the Charing Cross Road in 1902 and even Bernard Quaritch initially had his 1*d*. box, through which notoriously in 1861 he disposed of copies of his first printing of Edward FitzGerald's version of *The Rubáiyát of Omar Khayyám*.[1] The flow of secondhand books linked all members of the trade in a mutually supportive circuit. Barrow booksellers sometimes became shopkeepers, although in the 1890s W. Roberts claimed, in *The Book Hunter in London*, that this was not often the case. 'Occasionally,' he wrote, 'one of these professional book-stallers blossoms into a shopkeeper in some court or alley off Holborn; but more generally they are too far gone in drink and dilapidation to get out of the rut.'[2] But even in the 1890s many street market barrows were run by shopkeepers in a variety of trades, and movement between street and shop seems later to have become more fluid.

The barrow was the cheapest means of independent bookselling. Whatever their shared interests, shopkeepers in general regarded the barrow dealers as unfair competition, who took advantage of the absence of conventional over-heads – rent, rates and, in the case of booksellers, the cost of catalogue production. The feeling of suspicion was mutual. The flexibility and independence of the street trade, which represented its main appeal, meant that although there was a core group of dealers, including long-running family interests such as the Jeffery dynasty in the Farringdon Road, others moved promiscuously between commodi-ties and trades. Books shared many characteristics with any other commodity sold in the street. To the bookseller Peter Eaton, selling books was much the same as selling coal.[3] James Dabbs, who was credited with starting the Farringdon Road book market in the 1870s, began as a hot-chestnut seller, a profitable but seasonal trade.[4] I remember a young Central European named Adrian who in the 1980s regularly turned up at the Farringdon Road barrows with his elderly father and who, after a spell as a shopkeeper in Cecil Court, was last seen selling fruit from a barrow outside Foyles' bookshop. A more disastrous example of mobility from an earlier period involved Charles Carrington the writer and publisher of pornog-raphy. In his early years he was consecutively an errand boy, a van boy and a lavatory attendant before he turned, sometime around 1900, to selling books in Farringdon Market. This may have been a pivotal experience, as his subsequent activities centred on book publishing, mostly in Paris. In the end he came to grief and died 'blind and syphilitic in a lunatic asylum' in 1922.[5] Though extreme, such a passage was familiar enough to the street bookseller. According to Roberts, secondhand bookselling of this kind was frequently taken up to reverse failures in other commercial areas. 'We have known,' he wrote, 'grocers, greengrocers, coal-dealers, pianoforte-makers, printers, bookbinders, cheap-jacks in London, adopt the selling of books as a means of livelihood.' He went on to remark that the result was often further failure.[6]

The book barrows formed a component of the miscellaneous street markets which grew up in central London and the inner suburbs during the Victorian period. Partly because of its size and complexity, London – unlike Paris and most provincial towns and cities – had no central retail market. The authorized markets established in London under statute or letters patent were predominantly whole-saling centres, and as a result the retailing street markets set up without author-ization filled a gap. By 1893, there were 112 locations at which barrow dealers congregated on a regular basis. The starting point for any assessment of these is the reports compiled for the London County Council (LCC) in its first, highly active phase. The main report of 1893 was updated in 1901[7] and supplied inform-ation for the description of street selling in Charles Booth's *Life and Labour of the People in London* (17 vols., 1902-03) and the subsequent *New Survey* (9 vols., 1932), both of which also added new material.

The LCC report of 1893 provided a brief account of each market, its history, number of stalls and a breakdown of the commodities sold at each within the broad categories of perishable and non-perishable goods. The former included fruit and vegetables, the latter clothing, earthenware and books. These sometimes appeared as 'old books'; although George Sims noted penny maps, guides and histories of London as part of the barrow stock, and others mentioned yellow French classics and 'very cheap reprints', most books were evidently secondhand.[8] On some stalls, books were mixed up with other commodities, most often music, pictures and games but also bric-à-brac including old pram wheels. Books were probably also part of the stock lumped under the miscellaneous category, which appeared in most of the entries for individual markets. Though geographically dispersed, this trade took place largely in the poorest districts, where the main roads cut through areas of dense population and squalid housing. In 1893 there were three bookstalls each in the Edgware and Harrow Roads; three and four respectively in South Street, Marylebone and Goodge Street; ten and eight in the High Streets of Shoreditch and Whitechapel, and five in Lambeth Marsh as well as four in Bermondsey, which was described as very poor and thickly populated. In all, in the County of London, books were being sold from 144 barrows at 43 different locations, and there must also have been a number of individual pitches and occasional locations where books cropped up. Cornelius Walford found a long-wanted volume (Weskett on Insurances) in some 'temporary sheds which had been erected over the Metropolitan Railway in Long Lane'.[9]

The largest accumulation of bookstalls was located in the Farringdon Road. It seems to have taken over from the Bishopsgate Street market as the prime site for the sale of old books, and was rivalled only in the High Streets of East End communities, particularly Shoreditch and Whitechapel. At Farringdon Road the usual balance between perishable (21 barrows) and non-perishable (45) was reversed. Of the latter, most (33) were identified with the sale of books. In the 1901 report 19 street markets with more than 100 barrows were identified within the County of London and while some markets were found to be in decline, Farringdon Road was on the up in both the main categories. Here, the perishable barrows had risen to 25 and the non-perishable to 66, an increase which probably reflected an increase in bookselling. Some time between the date of this report and 1914, George Jeffery I moved from the Whitecross Street market, not far from his father's former bookshop, to the Farringdon Road, where he remained until his death in 1927.[10]

The configuration of street markets was continuously modified as the urban environment itself changed. From the mid-nineteenth century the drive to introduce transport links, clear slums and improve sanitation resulted in a programme of redevelopment, especially in the central areas of London. Road building was a major part of this. The construction of the Farringdon Road played its part in the movement for sanitary reform and completed the link between the railway stations on the Euston Road and the City, Blackfriars Bridge and the Embankment.[11] It ran down to the new Holborn Viaduct (completed in 1869), where it joined Farringdon Street and brought a wholesale change to the neighbourhood. The old Fleet Market had already been shifted out of the roadway onto the City side, and it was finally reconstituted as the Farringdon Road market for fruit and vegetables on a large site at the northern corner of Charterhouse Street and Farringdon Road, south of the underground station. The road received its current name in 1863 and the latest rebuilding of the market began in 1890.[12] The construction of a major north-south artery integrated with the railway system brought huge numbers of people into the area and offered a substantial opportunity to street traders. From Charterhouse Street southward, adjacent to the market building, the fruit and vegetable sellers set up their pitches. Northward to the Clerkenwell Road, where it crossed the Metropolitan Railway, stood the barrows of the booksellers, mixed with those of dealers in other commodities. There were barrows on both sides of the road though the majority were lined up along the pavement next to the blank railway wall. One reason for the pervasive sale of books in this unauthorized market was the constant flow of people. At the same time, the presence of street booksellers, already scattered around Holborn and adjacent areas, contributed to the confluence of bookselling in the new Farringdon Road.[13]

In other parts of the central area, the trade was experiencing substantial local upheavals. As the Strand was widened, the Aldwych loop was built over the cluster of mean streets, centring on Holywell Street, known from its concentration of generally seedy shops as 'booksellers' row'.[14] An alternative concentration of commercial activity emerged to the west, as Charing Cross Road was cut through some of the most squalid slums in London. Bernard Quaritch's original premises in Castle Street survived for a while through their proximity to Wyndham's Theatre, but the street itself and the surrounding neighbourhood were entirely reconfigured. Members of the book trade took up premises in the cavernous, modern highway of the Charing Cross Road, creating a new and more respectable 'booksellers' row'. Seven or eight of the shops displayed books on the street and it was here, at number 54, that Dobell was prosecuted for obstruction in the high-profile case brought by the City of Westminster.

The relationship between the street markets and the local authorities which made up the LCC area was mixed. The LCC itself was inclined to accept the social benefits of unauthorised trading; some of the vestries (from 1899 reconstituted as boroughs), particularly Holborn, were not.[15] From the early 1880s the Holborn Board of Works struggled to clear the barrows from the Farringdon Road. The need to keep traffic on the move provided the impulse to action, and the periodic purges were met with sturdy resistance. Meetings, marches, and monster petitions led up to the decision by the Court of Appeal in 1894 that the Farringdon Road costers could carry on their business provided they complied with police regulations.[16] Holborn had failed partly because it was not constituted as a market authority, but partly also because of its geographical limits. The local authority boundary ran down the centre of the Farringdon Road, and the railway side where most of the barrows were located fell within the territory of the more *laissez-faire* borough of Finsbury. The outcome of the court decision was little more than an armed truce. Elsewhere in London the street traders continued to be squeezed. The Aldgate market was closed down as an obstruction to traffic, while across the City of London street trading was slowly strangled. In 1911 licences were issued on a once-and-for-all basis. By 1930, natural wastage had reduced the number of traders from 1,718 to 300. In 1951 there were only two left.[17] It was against this background of continuing struggle that the system of local authority licensing was finally brought in.

It was not until after the First World War, when the return of large numbers of ex-servicemen with gratuities and limited job opportunities created a surge in the volume of street trading, that the licence was added to the LCC General Powers Act.[18] In spite of concerted opposition, from the end of 1927 all street traders were subject to the local authorities and obliged to purchase an annual licence, initially at 5s.[19] There were some benefits. Fixed pitches put an end to the need to turn up in all weathers at about 5am to secure a stand. It curtailed the influence of the police constable who, in some locations, had started the early morning proceedings with a blast on his whistle.[20] It also removed from the costers' overheads the expense of regular backhanders to the police. For the customers, who between the wars were becoming more numerous and more bourgeois, the benefit of some sort of regulation was clear enough.

Yet several boroughs continued to attack the street markets. Holborn council launched a new offensive in 1934 against the Farringdon Road barrows. In the event, the battle-hardened and unionized traders survived.[21] Only 14 of the 111 stalls were located in Holborn and it was probably about this time that all the booksellers gravitated to the railway side.[22] The effect of regulation on the street traders in books was the same as on their fellow costers or 'pitchers': all felt the pinch. After the Second World War, the fashion for traffic-centred planning led to the designation of a network of streets in central London as no-go areas for street traders. In 1947, the itinerant barrow-keepers finally disappeared from the scene. Nonetheless, book barrows remained in Farringdon Road and elsewhere.

The identity of the individuals selling books from barrows is very hard to pin down. Only those active within living memory, or those who moved, like Peter Eaton, from the barrow to the shop trade, have any clear definition. Donald Roome, who had an isolated book-barrow on a pitch outside the Marquis of Granby near Seven Dials (sold on to Bernard Kopps), or James Wolveridge, who ran a row of barrows at the Blind Beggar in the Mile End Road until the 1960s, are among those who flicker across the memory of friends and customers. The two latest booksellers from the Jeffery family, including George Jeffery IV who is still active in the trade, probably have the highest profile through their durable business in the Farringdon Road. Hardly any of the individuals who worked the 144 book barrows identified in the 1893 report are known, even by name. According to Roberts, a namesake of his was the first of the book dealers at this site. Working until his sudden death in 1894 or 1895, he was said by Roberts to be 'fairly' successful and have a 'fairly' good knowledge of cheap books. By the 1890s James Dabbs was running four or five barrows, from which he offered about 2,000 volumes at prices from 2d. upwards.[23] The unattributed illustrations in Roberts's chapter on bookstalls may include one or both of these early dealers. They are representative images of working-class men, indistinguishable from other market people, with captions such as 'A few Types in Farringdon Road'.

In the Booth survey of 1902-03, more than half the families of London costers lived three or more to a room and, collectively, the barrow booksellers do not appear to have risen much above this modest level. As the street markets gradually moved away from the economic life of the poorest neighbourhoods and as the commercial possibilities of trading improved, the (literally) long-standing families became more clearly identified with other commercial sectors. In this respect, the Jefferys, passing the street business on from father to son over several generations, were acknowledged to have become an integral part of the wider London book trade.

It remained a tough business, which required considerable physical resources. In the early 1930s a market dealer in vegetables sometimes sold 10 tons of potatoes in a week.[24] Books could be equally intractable and considerable reserves of strength, possessed in abundance by George Jeffery III, were an essential requirement. Every day the stock had to be wheeled out, the barrows and stalls set up and the books deployed. At the end of each day, the whole apparatus had to be taken down, packed up and wheeled back to a storage place. Early in the century at least, stock and barrows often shared the modest living accommodation of the pitchers. Each of these elements also necessitated some form of financial outlay. The more prosperous of the early street dealers kept a pony or donkey to haul the barrows and, in the case of fruit and vegetable sellers, to collect the stock from the wholesale market. By the 1930s, motorized transport was being used, sometimes shared between several stallholders. George Jeffery III was said to have been one of the first to be licensed to use a van to pull barrows to and from the Farringdon Road. Some street traders employed a 'puller out' at about 5s. a day, while others hired the local children who formed a pool of casual labour in the poorer neighbourhoods.[25] Some traders worked their way into the street market business by this route.

The barrows themselves were usually hired. In the 1950s, it was reckoned that the charge was about 6s. per day and that the purchase price was about £45. A further cost could arise from the hire of an assistant to oversee and sell the stock. This task was often undertaken by members of the stallholder's family or alternatively by some otherwise unemployable member of the local community. George Jeffery III had the help of his mother and various younger relatives to help out over the years. His sister, Joan Richards, was particularly valuable in this role. She appeared in a sketch published in the *Times Literary Supplement* in 1952, standing beside the loaded barrows and viewing the stock in a calm and watchful way.[26] The stock itself naturally represented a very variable outlay. Some market traders relied on weekly loans at exorbitant rates of interest. In the late 1940s, £5 borrowed at the beginning of the week for stock, had to be re-paid by £7 at the end.[27]

Whatever the shopkeepers' opinion, the barrow trade was hedged about with costs and charges, which increased after the licence was introduced and which had to be met out of an unstable income. Trade ebbed and flowed with the seasons and was vulnerable to the vagaries of the weather. Bookselling was particularly likely to be threatened by rain. In October 1881 a hopeful customer found that a book-stall in Bishopsgate Street had not been set up because the prospect of 'uncertain' weather kept customers away. There was also the danger of stock being soaked to the point of destruction when it did actually rain.[28] George Jeffery III was indomitable in this respect. Some of his barrows were covered with a jury-rigged awning, under which his customers huddled on wet days waiting tensely for the start of business. They were seldom disappointed. I remember one winter Saturday in the 1980s when London was engulfed in snow and a huddled group of potential book-buyers were shivering by the the kerb in the Farringdon Road, as much out of habit and unrealistic optimism as expectation. Suddenly, sliding round the corner of the Clerkenwell Road from the direction of the Jeffery book store nearby in Clerkenwell Close, came the familiar dark blue van. Putting out the barrows was impossible, so George dished out the new stock from the sliding door at the side of the van. It was reminiscent of the charitable attempts to feed the urban poor in Victorian London.

As the investigators engaged in compiling the 1893 report found, trustworthy information about income was extremely difficult to obtain. The massive variations – with some street traders making more than their shopkeeping counterparts, while others hovered on the brink of destitution – defied general-ization. Books of account were never available. However, the report did contain a single estimate from a retired coster, who stated that an average income was between 30s. and 60s. a week. What this meant in terms of profit or loss was not explored. Roberts claimed to have carried out his own investigation into bookstall earnings in the mid-1890s. He suggested that profits rarely rose above 30s. or £2 per week and that this fluctuated according to the weather: 'a wet Saturday makes a very material difference to their takings.'[29] During many weeks of the year, the street bookseller might take an average of just 8s. or 10s. In the *New Survey*, two decades later, an attempt was made to arrive at a more detailed set of figures for street traders generally. Two case histories were provided. The first was a fruiterer with an isolated pitch in Central London. Like the book dealers in the Farringdon Road, his main trading period was at lunchtime, contributing to total daily takings of about £3. This produced a profit of about 20 per cent, which over the week came to a surplus of £3 or £4. Out of this came the standard costs of 'garaging' stock, paying an assistant who lived with the family and outlay on rent amounting to 18s. per week. The second case was that of a greengrocer in South London. He had paid £1,000 for his pitch opposite his former shop and, with everything taken into account, reckoned his total profit to be just under £5 per week. Such calculations could probably have been made for most of the street booksellers whose overheads and charges, as well as profit levels, must have been broadly similar. The high-flyers in the London street trade, whether selling books or any other commodity, did very much better, but the detail is missing.

What then, did the book dealers in the Farringdon Road and elsewhere offer for sale and who were the people who clustered around the barrows in the street markets of the late-nineteenth and twentieth centuries? Much of the stock of secondhand books sold from the 144 barrows identified in 1893 was probably poor stuff, relative to what was available at the time. According to J.H. Slater's *Round and About the Bookstalls* (1891), the stock included quantities of sixteenth-century continental books on theology and philosophy, which were virtually worthless (although Dabbs at the Farringdon Road reckoned that theological books were among his best sellers.) Slater claimed that more often than not, 'a protracted search round and about the book-stalls reveals nothing – absolutely nothing – worth carrying away.' He listed ready-reckoners, sermons and 'exhortations', schoolbooks, and 'multitudes of pamphlets on subjects of limited interest and bad and imperfect editions of standard works without end'.[30] This fitted with the experience of the Barber family in the previous decade. When Ernest Baker needed a French dictionary and a copy of *Principia Latina*, which he failed to find in a secondhand bookshop run by an 'old bookworm eaten man', he turned to the barrows in Bishopsgate Street.[31] Here, both he and his father bought dictionaries at different prices. Similarly, in the 1930s, Farringdon Road was described as a good place to find this sort of reference book. The stock to be found outside bookshops and on the barrows was probably broadly similar. According to Slater, every bookstall of the usual sort 'will be found to consist chiefly of technical works, such as scientific books, educational works and the like. The rule here is that none of these are of any value unless quite new (which is seldom the case) or very old.'[32]

The stock of many book barrows in the Victorian period suffered from slow turnover. The leavings of the bookshops transferred to the street sometimes lay around for months, even years, deteriorating in the open air with scant benefit to buyers or sellers. In the 1880s a magazine contributor complained that the reconstruction of large parts of central London had led to fewer barrows and worse books, and this view of a declining street trade is reinforced by comments in the following decade. According to Arthur Morrison, the Whitechapel stall-holders, 'misanthropic men of a gloomy and grim appearance', were 'incessantly brooding over the decline of the book-stall trade of late years, since the second-hand booksellers had increased in numbers and business shrewdness and leave little saleable to the humble stalls'. They had been reduced, he claimed, to labelling Blair's *Sermons* and odd volumes of Bell's *Poets* as 'rare' and 'curious' while offering them for sale at 3*d*.[33]

Bookstall stock continued to be known for its imperfections and limitations but of course there was more to it than this. The existence of a large and persistent group of customers who thought it worthwhile spending 'their leisure moments in searching costermongers' barrows and diving down pestilential courts and alleys in the hope of snapping up some "unconsidered trifle"' suggested the possibility of finds beyond volumes of the *Strand* or copies of Falconer's *Shipwreck*.[34] Slater's short book was intended as a practical guide for such people and it slotted into a series which included *Bicycles and Tricycles of the Year* and *Mushroom Cultivation for Amateurs*. Slater advised customers at the stalls to buy the earliest Aldine editions, any atlas published before 1700 and anything in English published during the fifteenth and sixteenth centuries. He particularly advised looking for association copies, often in broken bindings, and for early materials used in the binding itself. He acknowledged that the reader searching for Shakespeare quartos among the barrow stock was 'hardly likely to be troubled by a superfluity of these'.[35]

Most commentators describe someone who had found such things and they continued to crop up in the heaps of randomly accumulated material, though with striking irregularity. I was a passive but not uninterested observer of one such find at the Farringdon Road. In the early 1990s George Jeffery III sold a box of odd and defective items for £300, which afterwards was found to contain the literary critic and editor Edmond Malone's extensively annotated copy of Hawkins's *Life of Samuel Johnson* (1787). Subsequently the volume moved steadily but obscurely upwards through the trade, ending up at the Beinecke Library at Yale. The final price was said to be in the region of £20,000. The only other great find I witnessed at the Farringdon Road was not a book but a sixteenth-century manuscript copy of a work composed by Thomas More which moved, over several years, from £20 to something over £40,000. This is a well-known story and underlines both the rarity of such heroic mark-ups and also the relative potential of manuscript and print. George Jeffery III was philosophical about such transactions, as had been his distant predecessor Dabbs, who was said to have displayed 'a certain amount of grim humour' as a book sold for 1*s*.6*d*. climbed to £50.[36]

Where did the barrow books come from? The sources of supply in the days of the large dispersals were extremely miscellaneous. At the end of the nineteenth century very large quantities of books were available and the market was becoming saturated. It was getting harder for dealers to dispose of unsold material as waste paper, and one bookseller advertised 'useful old books' at 3s.6d. per hundredweight, with a minimum order of six hundredweight with free delivery.[37] At least until the mid-twentieth century, books were literally lying around in heaps, and access to the materials of the street book trade could be had without much difficulty. As late as the 1960s it was said to be possible to maintain a business at no cost, simply by removing the piles of discards lying outside auction houses. Finding saleable material was another matter, and even in 1895 Roberts was suggesting that the possibility of private deals by stallholders had declined. Whereas once they might have been called in to clear houses and offices, 'the world has grown wiser in respect to books as well as other things, executors, legatees, and so forth have acquired unreasonable views as to the value of old books, and everything in the shape of a volume is sent to the regular book auctioneers'.[38]

Auction houses were and remained the primary source of books for the main London bookstall keepers. In 1895 Roberts identified Hodgson's in Chancery Lane as the principal supplier for this sector of the trade, although individual traders attended Puttick & Simpson's or, occasionally, Sotheby's. As Roberts pointed out, much of the material that arrived at auction had rolled around the shop circuit and then sometimes made repeated appearances at Hodgson's. Here books were sold 'not quite by the cartload, but certainly in lots sufficiently large to fill a moderate sized wheelbarrow'.

The way in which the stallholders formed a regular part of the auction scene in the mid-twentieth century is described in O.F. Snelling's anecdotal account of Hodgson's.[39] Snelling worked there from 1949, becoming a sort of manager. At his retirement in 1981, some years after Sotheby's takeover, he recorded his memories of how the business worked. Early in his career, he remembered 'two of the old "barrow boys"' viewing the cheaper lots – 'those stacks and bundles of anything up to a couple of hundred volumes, mostly pocket editions of no great value'. These were assessed by each of the traders, who then reached their own private settlement in the Front Room and gave their separate commission bids to the porter. It was also, he stated, a common practice for a shelf or two of 'rather worthless books and pamphlets' to be sold off before the auction to any market trader who made the best offer. Snelling did not say much about these booksellers, but he did single out 'George Jeffery *père*' of Farringdon Road along with Pusey, 'an amiable tat-merchant' who had a shop in Monmouth Street near Seven Dials as well as pitches in several street markets. Both were ready to offer a pound or two for a stack of books, although they both rejected a heap of French literature in fancy bindings which was subsequently knocked down for £3 to an aspirant trader. Hodgson's was only one of the potential sources of supply for the street book dealers, who also made use of house and office clearance, probate work and the full spectrum of other ways by which books might get into commercial circulation.

How was the selling itself organized? Mary Benedetta recorded some of her impressions of the Farringdon Road barrows in the early 1930s.[40] Of the three stalls run by George Jeffery II, one was filled with volumes at 6d., including modern fiction and law books. The others carried miscellaneous old volumes at varied prices. Wednesdays were identified as the most active, perhaps as the day the stock was changed, while lunchtime was the busiest time of each day. Her view of the proceedings was benign. Jeffery himself was described as kind and sympathetic, providing information to his customers 'with a wistful little smile'. The customers generally formed a silent fellowship. 'Nobody pushes or jostles, or tries to outdo anyone. They make way for each other politely, while the stallholder trusts them implicitly not to spoil his books.' This is certainly quaint and may not reflect the reality of the book market as it had been before the First World War. It definitely bears no resemblance to the competitive arrangements that were in play towards the end of the century.

From the late 1960s until the end of the book market in 1994, I spent every Saturday morning examining the heaps of books and engaging in some fairly brisk physical struggle, which sharpened up as other sources of reasonably priced books disappeared. For most of this time George Jeffery III (latterly known as 'Old George') was the sole stallholder. He had trained as a printer before the Second World War, fought with the Parachute Regiment at Arnhem and subsequently served in Egypt during the Suez crisis. After he left the army, he worked at the Farringdon Road market until his father died in 1957, when he took over the business.[41] By the late 1960s Saturday had become the day of the regular stock change, though books were sold on the site adjacent to the railway wall every weekday from mid-morning to early afternoon. By this time the site was licensed by the new London Borough of Camden. Two or three trestle-tables and a barrow lined up along the Farringdon Road carried most of the stock.

Both the material and the process were increasingly differentiated. At the northern end of the row Jeffery dumped a quantity of books and miscellaneous materials, which lay partly on the pavement and partly in the gutter. Initially everything in this heap was priced at 6d., although latterly this rose to 25p. Paperbacks, odd volumes, unique pieces of ephemera and bits of paper, often representing the shipwreck of somebody's life, were strewn around and could be rescued from the humiliation of the dust-cart only by purchase. Next in the sequence came a board, supported on trestles, with a general stock of books. These were identified by Jeffery as saleable at between £1 and £5. Most were books from the nineteenth and twentieth centuries, mainly on history and literature, but sometimes including a job lot on German mathematics, or some such subject, left over from a large-scale purchase. Next came the 'auction' board, though any similarity to a normal auction was entirely accidental. In fact, it was a modern version of what was practised in the eighteenth century as a fixed-price sale. Jeffery had written the prices in the books and, holding them up one at a time, he announced the title or price or both; the first customer who agreed to buy the item in hand received the prize. This was where the battle was at its warmest, as books were seized and ownership claimed. The aged or infirm or those of a nervous disposition had no chance unless by favour of the proprietor. Here, books were more expensive, from £5 or £10 upwards. Last in the sequence was a board on which was placed a mixed collection of prints, over-size books and cardboard boxes containing a number of books (on gardening or cookery, for example), which had perhaps already been offered for sale. The van was parked at the end of the row and the whole was surrounded by boxes and piles of books which, for one reason or another, were not accommodated on the boards.

Originally, in the 1960s, all the boards were laid out with books and as the customers arrived they viewed the stock in the sort of leisurely way which Mary Benedetta might have recognized. However, as the pressure from customers grew Jeffery devised a simple mechanism of control which at once heightened interest and contained indiscriminate clashes. The boards with the books on them were covered by tarpaulins, and at the beginning of proceedings, latterly at 9.30am, a sort of commercial striptease began. Starting with the heap in the road, the tarpaulins were sequentially removed by Jeffery or his assistants, each stage being closely followed by the customers. Attempts to identify books by shape, or by surreptitious lifting of the sheet, were vigorously repelled. Jeffery monitored proceedings, drank quantities of tea, took the money and ran a tight ship. Attempts to quibble over prices were met by a stony response and even – if the attempt was pursued – by violent intervention as books were torn in half and thrown over the wall onto the Metropolitan Railway line, 30 or 40 ft. below. George Jeffery III shared many of the personal qualities identified in his father by Mary Benedetta, but the main resource of both was a profound knowledge of books and their value. This underpinned their business and ensured its long survival and high profitability.[42]

So where did all this new stock, some 2,000 or 3,000 books a week, come from? Auctions accounted for a high proportion. Like his father, George Jeffery III was a familiar figure at Hodgson's, Sotheby's and other auctions, latterly standing at the back in his blue working coat, marking up his catalogue. It is impossible to assess the amount of material he accumulated along the way. One of the benefits of such a long-running family business was a network of contacts to keep up the essential flow of materials. At Quaritch in the 1960s there was a regular arrangement with Jeffery to clear out the 'turn out shelves' every month or so; when Quaritch moved from Grafton Street to Golden Square in 1970, it was Jeffery who finally cleared the firm's old premises. Several booksellers, such as John Collins of Maggs, routinely brought Jeffery in on their own house calls, often finding it simplest to sell him the bulk of cheaper books on the spot to ensure that these were removed.[43] Probate work also yielded good results, and the contents of solicitors' offices were a fruitful source of manuscript material, some of it turning up in the Farringdon Road in the original tin boxes.[44]

Material came in from all directions on a large scale, some from the stock of defunct booksellers, some from private houses, cleared with rapid efficiency, some from businesses and institutions of all kinds. When *The Times* moved from its short-term home in the Gray's Inn Road, Jeffery obtained a large part of its archive. I still have some of the monthly volumes of the paper, bound in solid green cloth with the heavy gold titles running down the spine. Jeffery charged £10 for volumes published before 1850 and £5 for anything later. I also have the copy of the *DNB*, the 65-volume edition published in 1900, from the Editor's office, its brown cloth covers stained with smoke and the marks of almost 100 years of use.[45] Public libraries were another fruitful source of supply, as were those of institutions such as clubs and hospitals in which books were likely to accumulate over time. Residues of books from the Brooklyn Public Library and from the library of the garrison at Gibraltar were among the bulk purchases made by Jeffery which filtered through onto the barrows.[46] The Farringdon Road market represented a stage in the general process of dispersal and collection by which the culture of print was continuously renewed.

The final question to be asked about the street trade in books concerns the customers. Whatever changes took place among market clientele in general, the customers at the book barrows seem not to have changed much over the century. The pitches on the fringes of central London, including the Farringdon Road with its mixed economy of stalls, did most of their business at lunchtimes from Monday to Saturday, especially after the steep decline in residential occupancy in and around this area. The many photographs of customers at Farringdon Road and elsewhere show groups clustered round the book barrows, composed largely of men in slightly shabby but respectable clothes. They probably contained a high proportion of clerks and shop assistants on their lunch break, with a leavening of leisured collectors represented in the 1890s by Slater (who lived in Crouch End) and Roberts (who moved from Grosvenor Road to Lansdowne Gardens). Both Slater and Roberts also mentioned an interest in book barrows among the ruling élite, including the Duke of Roxburghe and Lord Macaulay. There were few women, and Mary Benedetta's experience may reflect a sort of smoking-club response to her presence. When Mass Observation carried out a survey of book-shops in 1942, the investigators described a similar customer profile for the books displayed on stalls outside the shops. The table outside John Knox's shop in Highgate Archway attracted some interest from 'C class people. ... These were generally men and the majority were well over 40 years of age.' The investigator counted seven stopping in the morning and 15 in the afternoon. After spending some time in the 'dark and musty shop', he noted tersely 'no one entered'.[47] At the Farringdon Road from the late 1960s, the hard core of between 20 and 30 regulars on Saturday mornings included academics and other professional people, dealers at most levels of the trade, miscellaneous collectors, the destitute and the mentally unhinged. They usually combined several of these categories.

As Slater pointed out, customers were 'not unfrequently strangers to the truth' in their dealings with the stallholders. A clear account of the tense process of book-buying at the barrows was offered by a writer in the mid-nineteenth century. 'How often have I stood haggling on a halfpenny, lest by too ready acquiescence in the dealer's first price he should be led to suspect the value I set upon the article! – how often have I trembled lest some passing stranger should chop in between me and the prize, and regarded each poor student of divinity that stopped to turn over the books at the stall as a rival amateur, or a prowling bookseller in disguise!' As a contributor to *The Times* put it early in the next century: 'These keen, but harmless and even liberal passions of the collector are still to be indulged at the bookstall.'[48] The most hostile comments contained in the accounts of the book barrows in the 1890s were reserved for those customers who fell within the category later defined as the book runner.

The runner earned what could be an even more tentative living than the street bookseller. The barrows were only one source of his omnivorous gathering of books for resale to the booksellers, at what he hoped would be a profit. To Slater runners were 'jackals', while to Roberts and others they were 'book ghouls'.[49] Roberts described how the ghouls haunted the cheap bookstalls 'and buy the better class or more saleable books and hawk them around to the shops, and so make a few shillings on which to support a precarious existence, in which beer and tobacco are the sole delights'. In the late twentieth century the book runners were described collectively as 'melancholy, sinewy men of indeterminate age, tough as rugby players, edgy as bike couriers'.[50] Yet they were an important component of the trade, providing a physical link between barrows, booksellers and auction houses as they moved round their continuous circuit of buying and selling. Snelling described many of the independent, shabbily-dressed exponents of the business of book running. He emphasized their personal temperament as loners and mavericks, while acknowledging that the rising generation of runners were more energetic and upwardly mobile than their predecessors.[51] Dealers and runners mixed in with the amateurs and flâneurs at the bookstalls and brought an ominous note of commercial reality to the proceedings.

By the 1990s the London barrow trade in books had shrunk drastically. Various bookstalls remained within the enclosed markets associated principally with the sale of antiques and bric-à-brac, which had become established as market staples for middling customers between the wars.[52] Books played a declining part in the enclosed spaces, at the Portobello Road in Notting Hill and at Camden Passage in Islington. They were never a focal point within such artificial constructs as the Camden Market established in the 1970s and even when a shop trade continued nearby, as in Bell Street off the Edgware Road, the street trade in books tended to wither away. At the Farringdon Road barrows run by George Jeffery III, commercial activity continued as before. It seemed to its customers that it would never end. In the event, before the millennium arrived, the barrows had gone and the game was up.

There were many causes for this collapse, some inherent in the trade itself. The working conditions of street bookselling, involving heavy and recurrent manual labour in all weathers, were no longer acceptable. George Jeffery III retired in 1993 and died suddenly in December the following year. George Jeffery IV ran the barrows for a while before moving the business to a shop in the Clerkenwell Road, and not long afterwards he took up other forms of bookselling. The emergence of new ways of marketing books in the 1980s contributed to the decline of the street trade and, it is often claimed, to the decline of the shop trade in secondhand books as well. Book fairs initiated by the trade organizations offered a convenient, though much criticised, alternative to street bookselling. The fair was for all practical purposes an occasional covered market, with individual pitches and customers moving around the lanes between them. This arrangement, from the first centred on hotels in Bloomsbury, spread outwards geographically and diversified beyond the book trade.[53] Such commercial organizations as H.D. Promotions attracted shop-based booksellers, as well as individuals only loosely associated with the full-time trade. From the late 1990s, electronic buying and selling through the virtual shops and stalls of the internet has moved the book trade a stage further away from the street and, perhaps, the shop. Meanwhile the volume of old books in circulation was shrinking and the primary street-market principle of 'pile them high and sell them cheap' was becoming less and less viable.

Does it matter that buying and selling books from barrows lined up along the London streets has come to an end? Probably not. Books of all kinds are still available in other ways and barrow dealers *manqués* and their customers are still participating in the mysterious activities of the book trade. Even so, something has been lost. The dynamic and unpretentious character of the street trade, the shared access it offered to the materials of the past (not always expressed through chicanery and physical force) and the continuity it represented have all been relegated to a chapter in the history of bookselling. No online purchase, though, will ever replicate the magpie attractions of the Farringdon Road barrows.

The Bookshops of London

PHILIPPA BERNARD

When the Antiquarian Booksellers' Association asks rather plaintively, as it usually does each year before Christmas, for a London bookshop large enough to host its Christmas party, there are few offers. Nowadays only Maggs, Quaritch, Sotheran, or perhaps Bernard Shapero or Peter Harrington, occupy space enough for 80 or so members of the trade to raise a seasonal glass. It is probably a truism to say that a London bookshop owner now 'works for the landlord'. Overheads have become the most oppressive problem. To give a specific example, a reasonable rent for a shop in a good position outside the West End averaged £300 p.a. at the end of the Second World War; thirty years later it had more than doubled to £700, not unreasonable in the 1970s, but by the end of the century the landlords were seeking a sum of nearly £40,000, virtually impossible for any bookseller except at the very highest level. In this the bookseller is no different from any other city retailer. But unlike large stores and retail chains, antiquarian booksellers cannot take advantage of the opportunities to buy in bulk or sell to a mass market. They are obliged to measure each square foot by the rent they pay for it and small bookshops need to fill every inch of their space with books – on tables, on the stairs, in every corner. Few can afford nowadays the luxury of display windows at street level; indeed, to occupy the ground floor at all is rare, particularly in the West End. The world of the London bookshops so evocatively described by Stanley Brett and shown in the photographs of Richard Brown, published in two volumes in 1971 and 1977, was even then beginning to disappear and has since changed beyond recognition.[1]

By the late twentieth century, the area around Bond Street had become home to at least twelve distinguished bookshops, but the West End had not always been a centre for the upper echelons of the book trade. In 1907, the year after the ABA was founded, the great majority of bookshops were to be found in the West Central area, in Bloomsbury, the Strand, Covent Garden and St Martin's Lane, with only thirteen in Mayfair and Soho. In New Bond Street the firm of Ellis occupied a site that had been a bookshop since 1728, but it was an exception. Ten years later the situation had hardly changed, though there were two bookshops in Bond Street by this time and two in Piccadilly. The City had fourteen shops and there were ten in the area around St James's and Westminster.

After the First World War, some members of the trade considered Mayfair to be the only suitable area for a gentleman bookseller to pursue his profession. When Percy Muir persuaded his partners at Elkin Mathews in the 1930s that the firm could no long afford the luxury of Conduit Street, it did not occur to him to look for premises further away than Grosvenor Street. The estate agent showed him 'locations possibly suited to horse-slaughterers, shipping contractors and motor salesmen … accommodation designed for a fly-by-night mail order business, or an author wedded to garrets'.[2] The firm finally found a handsome Georgian house at a rent of £400 a year and were able to let out the top three floors at a profit. By the 1930s, the number of bookshops in the Mayfair area had grown considerably. This may have been due to the development of the international trade, together with the growth of the nearby auction houses. Albert Myers, for example, moved to New Bond Street in 1919, after 30 years in High Holborn; under his daughter Winnie Myers, the firm remained in Mayfair until the 1970s, specializing in manuscripts and archives. Several other important booksellers, such as Dulau, E.P. Goldschmidt, Maggs, Rota, Sawyer and Kyrle Fletcher, also took up premises in the vicinity of Bond Street in the years between the wars.

The firm of Maggs had started as a bookshop and circulating library in Paddington in the middle of the nineteenth century and had moved to Conduit Street, via shops in Paddington Green and the Strand, in 1918. In 1938, however, Maggs too had to leave Conduit Street, luckily as it turned out, for those premises were bombed during the war. They had the same apprehension about moving away from the immediate vicinity of Bond Street – even Berkeley Square was considered too far. But they settled into an imposing eighteenth-century house at no. 50, where they still remain.[3] The fifth generation of the family in the book trade is represented by Edward Maggs.

The only bookshop now left in Bond Street itself – apart from the London premises of the map dealer Jonathan Potter – is Marlborough Rare Books, formerly linked to the Marlborough Gallery. The business was previously owned by Michael Brand, who handed over to Jonathan Gestetner in 1990. Specializing mainly in art and architecture, the firm keeps a wide range of books on London, a subject surprisingly uncommon in the centre of the capital.

Among those shops whose premises were also in the heart of Mayfair was Bernard Quaritch Ltd. (established 1847), which between 1907 and 1969 occupied 11 Grafton Street. The firm had previously had a splendid double-fronted shop on Piccadilly, which it left when major changes were being made to the area, with the widening of Piccadilly and the demolition of the firm's old warehouse in Castle Street (subsequently rebuilt in what had become Charing Cross Road). Quaritch's most recent move, in 1970 to a former textile warehouse in Golden Square, took it little further from the auction houses and the firm still executes commissions on behalf of many of the world's great collectors and national libraries.[4] For nearly 50 years, from 1922, Quaritch's next-door neighbour at 12-13 Grafton Street was the firm of Charles J. Sawyer. In 1970 Sawyer moved along the street to no. 1, on the corner of Hay Hill, where the firm continued until 1986.

On the other side of Piccadilly, some distance from the Mayfair bookshops, was 16-17 Pall Mall, occupied from 1930 by Lionel and Philip Robinson, of the Newcastle firm of William H. Robinson Ltd. The decision to move to London in the depths of the slump and to take expensive premises in an exclusive location required considerable courage. The Robinsons chose Pall Mall, close to the London clubs, because they realized that it would be an excellent place to make contact with country gentlemen and the owners of great houses, who might sell them books privately. Their promotional leaflet, *A London Bookshop*, probably dating from the mid-1930s, emphasized the proximity of the National Gallery and St James's Palace and shows an elegant book-lined interior, with glass-fronted cabinets, Persian rugs and '4 o'clock tea' laid out on period furniture. Martin Hamlyn has described the atmosphere of the shop where he worked in the 1950s:

The shop, quietly opulent, gleamed with mahogany and morocco. There was not quite the eighteenth century elegance of Maggs, nor the sheer visible size of Quaritch or Edwards. ... But the Robinson atmosphere was extremely dignified and stately. The shop, with a small private room behind it with a divan, easy chairs, occasional tables and (occasional) sherry, was then to the right of the entrance. ... There were then an unpolished floor, tall stools at sloping Dickensian desks at which the brothers preferred to work standing (or hunched; however, flat desks with chairs did finally and briefly appear) ... important clients would be conducted through this working area to the strong-room.[5]

The Robinsons closed their shop in 1956, but much later it became the address of another important firm, Pickering & Chatto. The heirs to the shop of the renowned William Pickering, the publisher, and his bookseller son Basil Montague Pickering, and with links also to the publishers Chatto & Windus, they were originally situated in Chancery Lane. In the early 1980s Sir William Rees-Mogg took over the firm from the distinguished bookseller Dudley Massey, also acquiring Dawsons of Pall Mall, and consolidating the business at Dawsons' premises at 16-17 Pall Mall. More recently Pickering & Chatto, like so many others, have had to give up the shop and have moved 'upstairs', though not too far away.

Further east a new shopping area grew up along the Charing Cross Road. The squalid slums that had occupied the area were torn down in the 1880s.

They were replaced by a hotch-potch of buildings which turned out to be ideal as a bookselling centre. Several bookselling dynasties began there, including one of the most famous bookshops in the world, Marks & Co., established in 1904. Ben Marks and his partner Mark Cohen had begun in the trade by working at Sotheran's, moved to Old Compton Street and then to 106 Charing Cross Road, transferring to no. 84 in 1930. The shop was made famous by Helene Hanff, whose letters to and from the shop manager became so widely known. Another bookselling family firm in the Charing Cross Road was that of one of the founder members of the ABA, Emmanuel Joseph, who arrived there even earlier, in 1902. His sons Jack and Sam continued the business, and were succeeded in the 1970s by a great-grandson, David Brass, who moved out to Vere Street in the early 1980s.

Bertram Rota Ltd. (established 1923) also began in Charing Cross Road, where Rota's grandfather, Bertram Dobell, had had a bookshop for many years. The first bookselling Rota moved several times before settling for nearly 30 years in Vigo Street. The expansion of the business, which had been joined by his son Anthony, led to its migration in 1965 to a modern plate-glass fronted shop in Savile Row, and then in 1977 to a shop in Long Acre, Covent Garden. More recently the firm has traded from office premises above the shop; Julian Rota represents the fifth generation of the family in the book trade.[6]

The largest bookshop in Charing Cross Road, Foyles, no longer sells antiquarian and secondhand books, but this was initially the main business of the brothers William and Gilbert Foyle, who opened a shop there in 1906, after two years nearby in Cecil Court. By 1912 they had moved into a six-storey building on the corner of Manette Street and in the same year they began to trade also in new books. Most bookshops today cannot maintain a large staff. Even some of the largest have only two or three specialists, a couple of all-rounders, and perhaps a packer. But in 1929 Foyles employed 94 assistants, including two full-time buyers for secondhand books. By then the firm was operating on a huge scale, with a stock of more than a million volumes on 22 miles of shelving and a rare book department managed by Gilbert Fabes. During the second half of the twentieth century, under Christina Foyle's management, the shop became as well known for its eccentric and old-fashioned practices as for its large stock; conditions for staff were so poor that there were full-scale strikes in 1965 and 1982.

Cecil Court, which runs between Charing Cross Road and St Martin's Lane, was redeveloped for the Salisbury Estate (hence its name) in 1888-94. The firm of Thomas Thorp (of Guildford) began trading in London in 1903 from a shop in St Martin's Lane on the corner with Cecil Court. Percy Muir has described the shop's 'long side elevation in the Court split into bays, each with a long window. During business hours these were unlocked and slid upwards, making the contents of the shelves accessible to browsers.'⁷ In the 1930s this short pedestrian street became the home of a new generation of bookshops. Harold Storey (and later his son Norman) was one of the first booksellers to set up shop there, at no. 3, in 1934, preceded by Harold Edwards two years earlier. The shops (some specializing in theatrical material) were convenient for theatre-goers and for tourists. After starting in Ramsgate in 1902, the firm of H.M. Fletcher formed a partnership with E. Bolleter in Charing Cross Road, then migrated to Camberwell, Bayswater and Bloomsbury, eventually opening a shop in Cecil Court in 1937 – only to have to close it again for the duration of the war. The shop, at no. 27, reopened in 1947 and continued under Bill Fletcher and his son Keith until 1992, when the business moved first to Docklands and then to Hertfordshire. After changing hands several times, no. 27 became a bookshop again in 2002 under the proprietorship of David Rees and Angus O'Neill. Among other booksellers in Cecil Court were Edith Finer, 'Bell Book & Radmall', Reg and Philip Remington and Watkins & Co. The shops were small and not ostentatious – nor were the rents in those days. But as most shop owners will agree, there are many advantages in being amongst fellow traders. Competition is seldom a problem given the huge range of books on sale, and much business accrues to a shop on the regular route of visitors, especially dealers from out of town.

Another bookselling part of London which benefits from the proximity of other traders is Bloomsbury, long a centre of literary activity. The shops in and around Great Russell Street are within walking distance of each other and are also close to the British Museum – as they were to the British Library until its move to the new St Pancras building in 1997. In the 1930s, Great Russell Street alone was home to Grafton & Co., specializing in bibliography, technical works and railway books, George Harding (economics and history), J. and J. Leighton Ltd. (bindings and incunabula), Luzac & Co. and Arthur Probsthain (both oriental specialists), George Salby (travel and exploration), Henry Stevens, Son & Stiles (America), and James Tregaskis, noted for its scholarly catalogues of rare books and manuscripts. Following in this tradition more recently have been, among others, the architectural bookseller Ben Weinreb (from the 1960s until 1986), Robert Frew Ltd. (from 1986 until 2005, when the firm moved to Mayfair), and (from the 1990s) Jarndyce, specialists in nineteenth-century literature and theatre. The nearby side-streets contained numerous other shops selling large numbers of books, often in very cramped conditions. Among these booksellers were Andrew Block, who moved to Barter Street in 1957, and Louis Bondy, at 16 Little Russell Street from 1947. The most notable dealer in London topography was for many years Stanley Crowe, whose silver-haired gentlemanly presence could usually be found at the bottom of the narrow stair leading down to his basement shop in Bloomsbury Street, where he had moved in 1951.

Much the same could have been said until recently of Chelsea and Kensington. In the 1970s there were twelve secondhand and antiquarian bookshops along the King's Road and many more dealers working from home. Now only one shop remains along the famous highway, at World's End. A few have relocated a short distance away, but the majority have either vanished altogether or their owners, too, operate from home. The Fulham area has fared better. Indeed some dealers from Chelsea have moved half a mile further north, and Fulham Road is now the home of Peter Harrington, Charles Russell and – a long-time resident – John Thornton. Adrian Harrington has moved a little further, to Kensington Church Street.

At one time the seeker after 'yards of leather' in this part of London could be sure to find what he wanted for a few pounds a volume. So easy was it that a shop in Pimlico – The Square Orange – specialized in just that field. The interior decorators of Sloane Square made a beeline for those shelves; as did the private buyers, often American, who wanted to fill an antique bookcase 'as long as the bindings are blue to match the curtains'. Leather-bound sets are still available, but not at the knock-down prices of the post-war decades.

As long ago as 1971, Percy Muir lamented 'the disappearance of the suburban fringe of booksellers', and antiquarian bookshops in the suburbs have become even more reduced since. Hampstead and Greenwich still boast good shops, though few other areas are able to do so. Even the publicity that Notting Hill enjoyed as a result of the film of that name, which was set in a bookshop, could not persuade aspiring booksellers to embark on a venture in that area. The bookstalls in the Portobello Road antique market, however, which developed and flourished in the 1960s and 1970s, still provide an outlet for booksellers such as Paul Hutchinson of Demetzy Books, as well as several map and print dealers. Other booksellers who spent part of their early career on stalls in London antique markets included the Harrington brothers and Bernard Shapero.

Especially disheartening now is the total absence of any antiquarian bookshop in the City, probably the first time that this has occurred since the Middle Ages. Laurence Worms's delightful shop in the Royal Exchange has gone, though the firm is still very active from his home base. The same is true of Clarke-Hall, the specialist in Boswell, Johnson and their circle. How Johnson would have wept.

Every bookseller needs a little time to himself (even if he spends it among his own books), but the attraction of Sunday opening seemed too good to miss, once working restrictions were lifted in the 1970s. This had never been possible in the pre-war days, and indeed until about 1960 every retailer had to close one afternoon a week, usually Saturday in London. As early as 1912 the ABA approached the London County Council to ask for exemption from these regulations. Even today several West End bookshops close for either the whole or half of Saturday, as well as all day on Sunday. The staff of Maggs, Rota, Pickering, and Quaritch enjoy a long weekend. At Heywood Hill and some others, Saturday is half-day closing, but nowadays the shops of Bloomsbury, Kensington and the Charing Cross Road are open for business seven days a week.

1. The supply of books: Hodgson's cataloguers 'unpacking and sorting an extensive library from the country', c.1907.

2. Booksellers cluster around the auctioneer for the Amherst sale at Sotheby's, December 1908.

1. Mr Tom Hodge
2. Lord Ridley
3. Lord Amherst
4. Hon. Sybil Amherst
5. Mr. B. A. Quaritch
6. Mr. Leighton
7. Mr. Tregaskis
8. Mr. B. D. Maggs
9. Mr. B. Dobell
10. Mr Joseph Edwards
11. Mr Hornstein
12. "James" (Head Porter)
13. Mr Snowden
14. Mr. W. Roberts
15. Mr. G. Smith
16. Mr. Bolleter
  (Sotheran & Co)
17. Mr. Robson

3. Charles des Graz presiding over Sotheby's sale of a Gutenberg Bible from the Dyson Perrins collection, March 1947. At the back (far left) is A.N.L. Munby; sitting closest to the auctioneer (from right to left) Winifred Myers, Ernest Maggs and Dudley Massey (Pickering & Chatto).

4. A country house auction in the 1950s: the sale of the Earl of Derby's library at Knowsley Hall, Lancashire. Seated around the table (from right to left) are Charles Traylen (with Bill Fletcher behind him), John Watson (Quaritch), Bernard Simpson (E. Joseph), Walter Harris (Thorp) and Harold Edwards. With back to camera are Frank Hammond (right) and Ted Lowe (Lowe Bros).

578   Smith (Capt. John) General Historie of Verginia, New
      England, and the Summer Islands, and the Names of the
      Adventurers, Planters and Governors from their first beginning,
      1584, to this present 1624, frontispiece containing portrait of
      Queen Elizabeth, James and Prince Charles, the beautiful and
      very rare portrait of the Duchess of Richmond by W. Pass,
      the four folding maps and the rare errata slip, FIRST EDITION,
      *bound in dark red morocco, old style, by Bedford, a fine choice
      copy,* 1624   1

579   Roberts (D.) Holy Land, Egypt and Nubia, plates, *half morocco
      gilt*   3

580   Chaucer (Geoffrey) Poetical Works, edited by R. Bell, *half
      morocco,* 1874, 4; various, 8   12

581   D'Angoulême (Marguerite) L'Heptameron des Nouvelles, *half
      calf*; Poetry, etc., 21   22

582   Prichard (J. C.) Physical History of Mankind, plates (some
      coloured), *cloth,* 1841, 5; various, 10   15

583   Mill (J. S.) System of Logic and Political Economy, in all 4 vol.,
      cloth, 1856-57; various, 6   10

5. The ring at work: detail from a marked-up copy of the catalogue of the contents of Malham
Tarn, Yorkshire, sold by Knight, Frank & Rutley in November 1927, two months before
the Auctions (Bidding Agreements) Act came into force. Lot 578 was the subject of three
successive settlements after the sale, with its price rising from £170 (paid by Quaritch
in the official auction) to £350 (paid by Charles Lowe of Birmingham).

6. The last sale at Hodgson's, 1981: sitting at the table (from right to left) Keith Fletcher,
Pam Douglas (Quaritch) and David Pritchard-Jones. Sitting behind them and to the left:
Eric Barton (Baldur Bookshop, Richmond), John Maggs and Bill Lent (Maggs).

7. A world auction record for a manuscript: the twelfth-century Gospels of Henry the Lion were sold at Sotheby's in December 1983 for £8,140,000. The buyer was Quaritch, acting for the German government. Standing beside the auctioneer Richard Came is Christopher de Hamel.

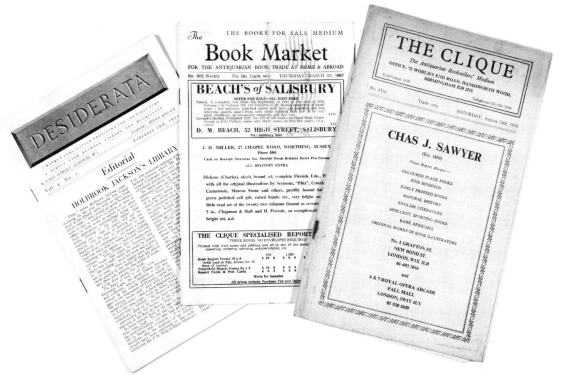

8 & 9. The book trade weeklies were all printed monochrome, with the sole exception of the short-lived *Book World*. (Below) the final issue of *Book World*, for May-June 1984, and the largest issue in the 35-year history of *Bookdealer*, 19 June 1997.

10. Antiquarian book fairs: the under-£5
promotion at the National Book League, June 1969.

11. Martin Hamlyn (Peter Murray Hill) contemplates a purchase from Alan Thomas, June 1970.

12. Europa Hotel, June 1971: Solomon
Pottesman, typically holding a brown paper
parcel, considers whom to visit next.

13. Paul Grinke (left) and Ted Hofmann inspect
the Peter Murray Hill stand, June 1971.

14. The autumn Antiquarian Book Fair in Chelsea Town Hall, November 2001.

15. Lunch-time customers at the Farringdon Road barrows, mid-1930s.

16. George Jeffery (wearing apron) settles up with a customer, while his son (with back to camera) empties out another box of books, 1991.

17 & 18. Calm and frenzy in the Farringdon Road, early 1990s.

19 & 20. Cheap books to attract passers-by along the Charing Cross Road:
(above) the shop of E. Bolleter, c.1914, and (below) E. Joseph, c.1938.

21. The very large premises of Foyles, filling the corner of Charing Cross Road and Manette Street, *c.*1938.

22. Marks & Co., the real 84 Charing Cross Road, shortly before its closure in the mid-1970s.

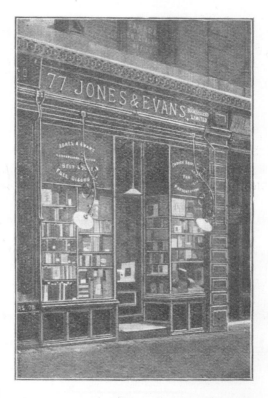
23. A wide range of services for 'the City bibliophile', offered in an advertisement of 1909.

Town and Country Bookshops in Scotland and Northern Ireland

ELIZABETH STRONG

'OLD booksellers bought books because they thought they were lovely books: the profit motive was secondary.' This nostalgic statement and all that it implies sums up both the cause and the effect of the changing face of the antiquarian book trade. In the period covered by this book, there has been a steady decline in the number of antiquarian and secondhand bookshops, as overheads of rates, insurance and salaries have risen disproportionately to turnover. Many towns have been left unserved, throwing into relief the artificial subsidizing of a 'Book Town' in a remote area of south-west Scotland. The inference to be drawn is that grant-giving authorities in a technologically driven age regard book buying as a leisure pursuit rather than a necessity.

Technology is, of course, invaluable for running one's business, be it a large or small antiquarian bookshop, or a specialist business run from private premises. Auction records and other reference material are now consulted on CD and online. The addition of internet sales can help to defray the overheads of keeping an open shop, although in a small shop with few staff the necessary expenditure of time and concentration can conflict with over-the-counter enquiries. Nowadays there are fewer bookshops outside London with a turnover which can sustain a full-time assistant, so that the apprentice of former years is almost extinct. The large general independent bookshops with antiquarian departments are disappearing, and the twenty-first century antiquarian bookshop, with a few notable exceptions, mainly metropolitan, has more the character of a country bookshop, although for obvious reasons boasting a more academic stock in the older university towns and cities. In Scotland and Ireland stock has always been particularly strong in local history and topography, but booksellers countrywide have become more and more specialized. Early in the twentieth century, the majority of booksellers stocked new, secondhand and antiquarian books and publishers' remainders, and many ran a circulating library and perhaps published as well. As the century progressed just one or two of these activities would be singled out and in the latter decades of the twentieth century, especially as more and more academics took early retirement and used a 'lump sum' to set themselves up in business, there was increasing specialization in single subjects. This meant that although the general bookseller in his shop might sell to the specialist, he was in a weaker position when buying – the specialist would most likely be working from home with fewer overheads and could command higher prices, selling directly by catalogue and more recently, of course, on the internet. Conversely, a shop presence does attract stock, albeit much of it unremarkable, but with always the possibility of something exciting tucked away at the bottom of one of those boxes or a house-call from an old and valued customer.

As life has become more pressurized and business more bureaucratic there is, sadly, less time to spend in conversation with customers, and often the customer is also driven by lack of time and, in the city centre, by traffic restrictions. Troughs of cheaper (and expendable) books may still be seen outside some shops, but planning regulations forbid this in some areas, and tempting piles of books on floors and staircases and in corridors would be likely to invite criticism from any visiting fire inspector. A back room may increasingly be used to hide clutter rather than choice stock – nowadays one is only too glad to have the choice stock to display, although one is likely to have it locked behind glass. Security of personnel and stock has become more of an issue, and health and safety arrangements are now strictly regulated. As behaviour has become less formal over the last hundred years, restrictive regulations and the formality of business practice has increased.

One of seven Scottish founder-members of the Antiquarian Booksellers' Association was William Brown, whose firm moved from Princes Street to Castle Street in 1906. Sadly Brown (who had founded his firm in the mid-1870s) died in December 1906, in the very month the Association was founded. However, the firm continued and in 1908 James R. Abbey (1898-1983) joined as a young apprentice. Apart from a break for service in the First World War, when he apparently lied about his age in order to volunteer, Mr Abbey was employed in the firm for over 70 years, latterly as Manager of the antiquarian section of the Edinburgh Bookshop. (The amalgamation of Robert Grant and William Brown to form the Edinburgh Bookshop in George Street took place in the mid-1950s.) We are fortunate that one of Mr Abbey's customers, Professor Roland Paxton, had the presence of mind to record a conversation they had had in 1981, about a year before the bookseller's retirement. Abbey remembered starting work with the firm in 1908, as one of five staff including a cashier:

It was very nice working there, we had a view looking across to St Cuthbert's Church. The pay was half-a-crown a week and the hours 9 a.m. to 6 p.m. We went in half an hour before to get things cleared up. Much of the work was cataloguing – we didn't depend on passing trade. Old William Brown had a saying that as far as Edinburgh book buyers were concerned 'interest expired at the sum of five shillings'. Most business was then from abroad by catalogue of which four were issued each year. … We didn't have an open fireplace for warming the shop but an anthracite stove. It was very warm. I used to copy letters in an old-fashioned letter press with a turning handle. The letters were damped into the book. If you damped it too much the copy became blurred. It used to be the bane of my life. The letters were copied each day after the customers had gone.

From the time he joined the firm Mr Abbey helped with the time-consuming task of cataloguing:

the use of previous catalogues helped, as a number of the books had already been described and the entry was cut out for the catalogue currently being prepared. Another task was the collation of all books priced at ten shillings or more. On completion of checking you put 'cp' and your initials at the back of the book, which meant that it had been collated perfect. ... The firm was always keen on getting books in good condition so that people, particularly from abroad, could buy with confidence and thus a good reputation was built up. ... Before the Great War many books were relatively more highly priced than now, especially genealogical books, family histories, Scott, Galt and people like that. There was not a lot of interest in atlases, travel, medical or agricultural books. A dear book then was probably two guineas. Prices remained very stable over many years.

William Brown had been on the committee of the Edinburgh Bibliographical Society in 1891 and Mr Abbey in his turn became a loyal member of the Society. Mr Abbey only allowed customers to buy the books he thought were 'for' them. He would keep things aside for particular people – to ensure their continued interest – in his inner sanctum and it was only at the end of his career that customers were allowed to browse there. Professor Paxton was able to buy from Mr Abbey *The Complete Surveyor* 'and other lovely books' but was obviously tantalized by the hidden treasure.

A visitors' book was kept from 1953 and notable customers were invited to record their visits. Colleagues Winnie Myers and Jack Steedman were recorded alongside Joyce Grenfell, Edward Heath and Will Y. Darling, the proprietor of Darling's the ladies' outfitters on Princes Street, author of the prophetic *Private Papers of a Bankrupt Bookseller* (Edinburgh, 1931) and eventual saviour of Robert Grant, the Princes Street bookseller. 'Will Y', who became Lord Provost of Edinburgh and also served as a Member of Parliament, loved the bookshops, which he celebrated in his *King's Cross to Waverley*, published under the pseudonym of 'Timolean'.[1] He not only preserved the firm of Robert Grant, but also bought the business of F. Bauermeister, Foreign Bookseller, during the Second World War, when the proprietor became senile and the sons who were old enough were serving with the forces. The firm had been started by Bauermeister in Glasgow in the early 1890s and later moved to Edinburgh. A daughter managed the shop until the end of the war and when the family could afford it they were able to buy the business back in about 1960. The Bauermeisters dealt solely in new books and periodicals, apart from the completion of some back numbers of periodicals for the university trade and their involvement in the photo-mechanical reprint industry and the reprinting of antiquarian books. One of the founder's grandsons, William F. Bauermeister, has been Secretary of the Edinburgh Booksellers' Society for the last fifteen years. Earlier in the century, the firm had taken over that of Otto Schulze and although there is no record of its having continued the Schulze business of fine binding and publishing, after the Bauermeisters' firm was wound up in 2004 two extensive albums of illustrations of bindings which had originated with the Schulze firm were sold to the National Library of Scotland.

For those who have lived through the second half of the twentieth century it is hard to believe how static prices and wages were in the nineteenth and early twentieth centuries. Seventy-two years before Mr Abbey's apprenticeship began, James Thin was apprenticed in 1836 to James McIntosh in Edinburgh at a salary of 2s.6d. a week, from which he had to provide his own pen and pencil.[2] There may have been some disparities between firms, however, and it is evident from the records of John Grant of George IV Bridge that in 1900 the lowest paid of their seventeen staff received four shillings a week.[3]

The firms of James Thin and John Grant became two of the most powerful players in the Scottish book trade. They acquired property which enabled them to expand their businesses on South Bridge and George IV Bridge and jointly bought the publishing firm of Oliver and Boyd which remained in the families until, to avoid the effects of death duties, it was sold to the *Financial Times* in 1962.[4] Both of these firms, and some others in Edinburgh and, of course, John Smith and Son in Glasgow, employed young men who would then go into business on their own account, either in those cities or further afield. In April 1948, Henry M. Meikle, a director of W.R. Holmes (Books) Ltd. of 488 Sauchiehall Street, Glasgow, wrote in acknowledgement of the gift of the commemorative volume, *James Thin, 1848-1948*:

when I joined the firm in 1898 the 'Old Man' as we called him had more or less retired but was still coming about the shop. I think he must have thought I was the only one who could do his messages, because all the time that I was in the Bridges (some 4¼ years) it was always for me he called when there was any little errand to be run although there were many other junior apprentices on the premises at the time. I can still hear his deep gruff voice calling down to the back shop and asking me to get him a glass of milk and two wine biscuits.[5]

In January 1901 Robert Steedman was presented with a portable wooden writing desk by the staff at Douglas and Foulis of Castle Street in Edinburgh on leaving the firm and moving to Newcastle, where in 1907 he founded the firm bearing his name and now owned and managed by his grandson, David Steedman. Robert Steedman had served his apprenticeship with the Edinburgh firm, which was noted for serving the dual function of bookshop and circulating library and was one of the last survivors of the type when it closed in the early 1970s. In 1977 Mr Abbey was still writing letters on paper headed 'The Edinburgh Bookshop' and with the description 'Antiquarian, Fine Art and General Booksellers, Librarians, Stationers and Art Dealers'. There had been many circulating libraries in the city in the earlier years of the century, and in the Edinburgh and Leith Post Office Directories of the time publishers, stationers, booksellers (both new and secondhand) and circulating libraries are all listed under the one heading. We know that some businesses covered several categories, one of these being Williamson's on Leith Walk, founded by R.M. Williamson, author of the most entertaining *Bits from an Old Bookshop*.[6]

Another of the seven Scottish founder-members of the ABA was W. Dunlop of George IV Bridge – he had served his apprenticeship with John Grant and remained on George IV Bridge until the 1950s. In the late Ian Grant's files there is a list of booksellers' employees who branched out into business on their own account. Those from John Grant were Robert Aitken, Alan Anderson (the first secretary of the Scottish branch of the ABA, but later to abandon bookselling in favour of fine printing, producing highly collectable work with the Tragara Press), William Dunlop, Kulgin Duval and Alan Rankin. Another of Grant's assistants who remained a notable figure in the Edinburgh trade was Edward McLachlan. In 1964 Kulgin Duval, with his partner Colin Hamilton, produced a most attractive and still useful catalogue, *Eighteenth Century Scottish Books*, designed by Ruari McLean. At the time of Grant's centenary in 1974, Duval wrote:

My training with John Grant was not only my first, but my only connection with a bookshop, and I was fortunate to be in one so ideally designed for book lovers, with endless shelves packed with books for exploration and delight. Amongst many members of staff whom I remember with affection, I would like to mention two; Mrs Wright who was the cleaner and caretaker who lived above the shop, and who was a sort of mother earth figure; and Mr Wilson, who held complete control of the underworld where the packing was done and where other members of staff entered at their peril!

The present author remembers being impressed with the neatness and organization of the shop when, as an undergraduate in the mid-1960s, she found the requested secondhand copy of Brahms' *German Requiem* precisely filed in one of many boxes.

The Book Hunter's Stall, which was run from John Grant's original shop along the railings towards the statue of Greyfriars Bobby, was a much-loved part of Edinburgh's scenery until Gordon Grant closed Greyfriars Remainders in 1985. The Stall is illustrated in W.B. Hole's etched portrait of John Hill Burton in the 1882 edition of Burton's *The Book Hunter*.[7] Fresh stock was added every day and Edward Nairn, who was employed by James Thin from 1948 to 1954, remembers hastening up Chambers Street during his lunch-hour in order to scan the stall before Mr Riddell arrived. Mr Riddell, a local bank manager and a customer well remembered in Edinburgh and Glasgow, would call at Thin's every lunchtime before proceeding to the Book Hunter's Stall. His collecting interests expanded from books to nineteenth-century Scottish photographs, and after his death in 1985 this collection was presented to the nation.[8] He particularly enjoyed illustration of the turn of the century, but had been collecting since his childhood days in Glasgow when he was able to spend his Saturdays scanning the Glasgow barrows, so he found it hard to adjust to latterday pricing and would often claim to have bought books which we prized highly 'for 6d. from the Barrows' – or for the same amount from Mr Willis, the MP who had a shop at 9 North St Andrew Street in Edinburgh from the early 1930s until the late 1950s. (Mr Willis himself was still trawling the Edinburgh shops in the 1970s.)

The original John Grant, who opened the small shop on George IV Bridge in

1874, became a very successful dealer in remainders, which must have both necessitated and enabled his expansion across George IV Bridge in the late nineteenth century. In the firm's stocktaking ledger of 1900, shop-fittings are listed in detail, conjuring up a picture of a prosperous business of which the secondhand department was just a part, though no doubt an important part.[9] Lord Rosebery was one of the firm's most distinguished customers, to quote notes in the late Ian Grant's files:

No self respecting bookseller-cum-publisher of this period could be without his political allegiance and J.G. pinned his allegiance to the Liberal cause. Gladstone was an early political hero and by the same token Rosebery thought of J.G. as more than a bookseller. Gladstone acquired books from many sources and his links with Scottish booksellers were widespread. ... Within the emerging 1900s J.G. was to develop a closer link with liberal politics. This with Lord Rosebery and the surviving correspondence gives some indication of the contacts between collector and bookseller, coloured to some extent by political affinity.

In 1910 John Grant's remainders were valued at over four times as much as the secondhand stock, but by 1920 more than half the stock value was secondhand and by 1930 there was almost four times the value of secondhand stock as of remainders. By 1940 the value of the remainder stock had remained much the same, but the secondhand stock had dropped in value from £5,565.16s.2d. to £3,817.5s.11d., presumably reflecting difficult times. The firm was also, of course, publishing new books: a selection of John Grant imprints was offered in the *Centenary Catalogue* of 1974 (designed by Alan Anderson at the Tragara Press), including the Winchester Edition of Jane Austen (12 vols., 1911-12), John Grant's *Piobaireachd; its Origin and Construction* (édition de luxe, one of 130 copies, 1915) and McKenney and Hall's *History of the Indian Tribes of North America* (3 volumes, 1933-4). A Gaelic speaker, the founder of the firm published many Gaelic titles.

By 1912 of the twenty staff on John Grant's books, six were women. Robert Grant received £6 per week and John Grant (Ian Grant's father) £3 per week, while apprentices still received 4s. per week. In 1914 one of the staff joined the Red Cross and, as with those called up for military service, the firm topped up his wages so that he took home the same amount as he had earned during peacetime. According to the records, those who returned received a small rise in salary, though apparently it rankled that it was not what it might have been had they not 'lost' the years of bookselling experience.[10] Bookselling seemed to have continued seamlessly while those men were away. Grant's estimate book gives details of customers' accounts, showing that many well-known figures were buying strongly over the period between 1914 and 1925.[11] Professor Patrick Geddes (who listed himself also as a bookseller in the Post Office Directory) had a secondary 'Town Planning' account; we see Sir Rowand Anderson, Hippolyte Blanc, Professor Grierson, and William Roughead.

Dr Charles Sarolea, first head of the French Department at Edinburgh

University and for over 40 years the Belgian Consul in Edinburgh, had a running account which sometimes took two years to be paid. He lived at 21 Royal Terrace in Edinburgh – a four-storey Georgian house – and eventually had to buy the house next door to accommodate his expanding collection. Despite the fact that he appears to have sold some of his books and manuscripts in 1929 and 1946, his was reputedly one of the largest private libraries in Europe. In the year 1930 he estimated that it was more than 200,000 volumes strong.[12] Following Sarolea's death, Thin's bought a share of the library during Edward Nairn's time as an assistant at the shop. Nairn describes how Sarolea's housekeeper threatened to leave because of the collection. Books were three-deep on the shelves, piled up against the windows, and the rooms had become a series of corridors, with ornaments and antiques scattered amongst the mishmash. On the housekeeper's day off, Sarolea would take a taxi to tour the bookshops and pick up all his week's purchases. When the collection came to be sold, the National Library of Scotland had the first pick, Blackwell's came second, and Thin's took the remainder. Chutes came down from the windows of the two houses into pantechnicons and it took a team of boys three days to unload Thin's share into the shop. In due course catalogues of the library were produced and orders were received from Blackwell's, who presumably needed to fill gaps as viewing the collection thoroughly had been well nigh impossible.

Nairn remembers Thin's shop as having had books everywhere – under the building there were cellars- and cellars-full. A run of the *Edinburgh Review* from its commencement and in original boards was priced at £25. Above his desk were shelved quantities of sixteenth-century editions of the Greek and Latin classics and in the lower shelves folio editions of the classics by many of the great printers, priced at around two guineas each.

Another Edinburgh bookseller's memories of the firm of James Thin date back to the 1940s. David Hyslop, who now operates as Yeoman Books from his home in Haddington, East Lothian, had the task as a schoolboy apprentice in the 1940s of delivering books to Thin's, which had been purchased from his father's shop nearby. In the light of this it is interesting that in the later part of the twentieth century the firm of Thin's were not renowned for allowing local booksellers to buy from their antiquarian stock, keeping 'catalogue stock' strictly segregated, and sending catalogues abroad initially in order to keep up their international reputation. In the 1940s, Hyslop says, the main part of the shop was filled with secondhand books, with the new books tucked upstairs. 'Old' Ainslie, the proprietor at the time, would oversee the front shop and the late Jimmy Thin, in the firm's 150th anniversary history, described Ainslie sitting

at his table at the back, from which he could clearly see everyone coming through the door. He liked to think that he knew all his customers personally. He didn't, of course, but he did not do too badly. 'Who's that fellow who has just bought Osbert Lancaster's *Drayneflete Revealed*?' 'I don't know,' I replied 'he just paid for it and went out.' 'That's no good,' he said. 'Who is he? Where does he live? What does he do for a living? What are his interests? Bookselling is all about books and people – nothing else matters.'

David Hyslop's contrasting duties as a ten-year-old during the Second World War included tearing the covers off unwanted books to prepare them for collection by the salvage lorries. He would sometimes be in the shop until 2 a.m. and then sent home alone – on one occasion being 'lifted' by the police (by the ear, apparently) and returned to the shop for identification. My own earliest memories of Thin's are from the mid-1950s as, towards the end of the summer holidays, my mother and I queued along with many other mothers and children on rows of chairs in the education department. Obliging staff would fill the requirements on our book lists, if possible with secondhand material but failing that with new books. All my purchases would then be covered with brown paper wrappers to protect them during my period of ownership.

Jimmy Thin went on to remark that over the years it grew more difficult to keep the personal contact with customers 'partly because of the natural increase of both books and people, and partly because – although there remained a hard core of customers who liked to be welcomed personally, and asked about their golf and their summer holidays – I really believe that the increasing pace of life militated against this, and many of our customers preferred to remain anonymous'. Olive Geddes, in an article published in the National Library of Scotland's *Folio* magazine, quotes Arthur Birnie's diary for 24 August 1935: Mr Birnie was looking in Thin's window 'when a member of the family who is always to be seen in the front shop came out and told me my book was selling very well. ... Was very glad to hear the news and grateful to Mr Thin for his kindness in telling me.'[13] Looking back to the earlier part of the century, there is a touching passage in an anonymous 'Informal History' of Robert Grant & Son in the late James Abbey's papers:

It was during the Great War that Grants built up a multitude of friendships among men and women whom the exigencies of the service brought North. The bookshop became a port of call for men of the Battle Cruiser squadrons stationed in the Forth. With half-a-day's leave there was little to be done, but at Grants one might be sure of meeting a friend as well as picking up a book to pass the dull hours on board. ... Nearly every officer of the Battle Cruisers dropped in at one time and when at Jutland three of these great ships went down in as many minutes there were sore hearts in the bookshop.

Soon after the end of the Second World War, a mature apprentice took up employment with William Dunlop on George IV Bridge. This was Alex Frizzell, who was demobilized after war service with the RAF and joined Dunlop for about five years before opening his own shop in Bruntsfield Place. Starting a business with little in the way of material resources was a considerable challenge in the early 1950s, and initially life was so hard that the Frizzells, Alex and Marion, slept in the back room of the shop on a table which had been cut down for the purpose. (This is reminiscent of the young William Chambers who had appropriated 'a small back room as a dwelling, so as to be near [his] work' in Leith Walk more than a century before.) Alex Frizzell had been brought up in the country and the couple always felt the pull of the countryside, balanced by a love of company. For this reason they left Edinburgh for Berwickshire, then returned to keep a shop in Thistle Street, before eventually settling at Castlelaw, the house in a valley near West Linton in Peeblesshire from where numerous catalogues were issued until the late 1980s. Always the kindest and most hospitable of booksellers, the Frizzells' parties remain legendary. The house was lined with books and the designated bookroom also contained the printing press on which Frizzell produced his Castlelaw Press imprints. Weekly visits to Edinburgh would bring the couple to McNaughtan's Bookshop, where Frizzell used to buy generously in all sorts of areas. Again there would be great chat and one would be injected with fresh confidence and enthusiasm – one of Alex Frizzell's gifts being his ability to encourage younger colleagues in a sensitive and unassuming way.

Another of the Scottish trade's great conversationalists was Alasdair Steven, bookseller, writer and broadcaster, who started his business in the early 1950s selling around the Highlands from his bicycle – perhaps the last of the 'chapman' booksellers. In 1964 he began to produce lists from his house in Perthshire and this continued until the late 1990s. Alf Jamieson served as an assistant at Thin's before becoming manager of Brunton's, the shop founded by Alexander Brunton, which in about 1950 moved from Hanover Street to George Street, where its basement premises were piled up with enviable material, interesting and in good condition. In the 1970s the business moved to Dundas Street and eventually ended up in Bruntsfield, closing in the early 1980s when Jamieson retired. Alf Jamieson always seemed the down-to-earth lowland Scot, but, as Morley Jamieson, produced the most sensitive and romantic poetry and short stories. He also issued a literary periodical, *Brunton's Miscellany*.

There were other post-war booksellers who started their businesses in what might seem unlikely ways – David MacNaughton and William Blair both drove taxis, but this, of course, afforded them ample opportunity to visit the bookshops and build up a stock between fares. MacNaughton, after some years at the Book Cellar in Dundas Street, where he commenced trading in 1965, has been a somewhat peripatetic bookseller, but always tremendously industrious, and a great support to the Scottish branch of the ABA in the early days of the book fairs. He now works from Dalmellington, the town which Richard Booth had hoped would rival Wigtown, the Scottish Book Town supported by Scottish Enterprise, the Scottish Arts Council, and the European Union among others. Bill and Isobel Blair had a wonderfully stocked shop, the Grange Bookshop, until Mr Blair died in 1984. Their shop was well placed on the edge of the Grange district of Edinburgh, home to many Edinburgh University staff, and this must have contributed to the success of their business. It was always very neatly kept, with Mrs Blair serving at the front of the shop, clad in an overall, and meticulously brushing any dust which had escaped her housekeeping from the top edge of each book before it was wrapped for the customer. Domhnall MacCormaig, brought up a Gaelic speaker, trades from his private address in Edinburgh in all aspects of Celtic culture. He was employed by the GPO while building up his collection and took the bookselling plunge in the mid-1970s, thriving on the independence allowed to the dealer from home, travelling about 45,000 miles each year in search of stock, combing auction sales, booksellers' stock and catalogues and buying private collections. Perhaps the highlight of his career was the discovery in a shop in Leamington Spa of an album of photographs taken in 1911 on Heisker Island, off North Uist, and featuring his own mother-in-law as a child with her mother and grandparents.

My own shop, McNaughtan's Bookshop, was founded in 1957 by Major John McNaughtan and his wife, Marjorie, whose early training with the Yorkshire Penny Bank informed her bookselling career. The couple had both collected enthusiastically since their youth and, while serving as a barrister in the army, Major McNaughtan would travel the country appearing at courts martial and purchasing law books from provincial bookshops, which he was able to sell in London for profit. In the meantime Mrs McNaughtan was collecting in the fields of literature and art, so that by the time 'the Major' had retired from the army they had built up enough stock to launch their business. According to early accounts, they purchased the shop which was the original McNaughtan's for just under £600. They fitted it out, with the help of their young son's joinery skills, with shelving from Dunlop's shop, which had closed on George IV Bridge after more than 50 years in business, and with bookcases purchased at auction which were fitted together like patchwork and gave the shop its character. Similar resourcefulness was in evidence during the miners' strike and 'three-day week' in 1974. There was no question of a three-day week, but a car battery was used to install temporary lighting and, with the addition of calor gas lamps and paraffin heaters, business continued without interruption.

The McNaughtans patronized the auction rooms in Glasgow and Edinburgh, sifting shelf lots for the more desirable items and discarding the 1920s and 1930s novels, many in dustwrappers but most of which held little interest for the collector in those days. With annual turnover starting at around £2,000 per annum and rising to just over £5,225 for the year ending 31 March 1965, the first seven years were lean. However, the McNaughtans' eye for interesting material ensured a constant turnover of stock, meriting the close attention of customers in Edinburgh and from further afield. The carriage and postage bill in 1960-61 was £183.2s.6d., compared with purchases for the same year of £1,121.15s.4d. and wages of £180. Mrs McNaughtan formed a particularly warm relationship with the late Professor and Mrs Eudo Mason. Professor Mason had a fine collection of children's books and it was in helping him to extend and enhance this collection that Mrs McNaughtan gained her special enthusiasm for the subject. She was to play an important part in ensuring that the Mason Collection went to the National Library of Scotland following the tragic deaths of Professor Mason and his wife.

Mrs McNaughtan was a formidable presence in the auction room. Her catalogue would be marked on the left-hand side with the price she was prepared to pay (not discreetly in code, as was the case with most of her colleagues, but in actual money) and on the right with the price realized. When she was particularly enthusiastic no price was entered on the left, simply the word 'BUY!' She had no patience at all with the games sometimes played in auction rooms, nor had she any patience with time-wasting tactics, to the extent that if the bidding was slow to start, the auctioneer would often look in her direction to get things moving.

After the death of her husband in 1972, Marjorie McNaughtan continued to manage the business as a sole trader until she sold it on her retirement in 1979, with characteristic judgement arranging terms which would allow a young book-seller to make a living while also allowing herself to retire relatively comfortably. She was an exacting employer, but took pleasure in passing on her enthusiasm and was brave in the delegation of responsibility, allowing staff to buy and price books from an early stage, but always expecting a price to be justified. During the period when Mrs McNaughtan was in sole charge of the shop, inflation was at its height and it was her regular practice to go through the more expensive stock in the locked cabinets increasing the prices, as otherwise it would have been difficult to replace. At the same time, her profit margin could initially be quite small, as she preferred to turn over large quantities of stock quickly. In those days, when there was a real hunger for books of all sorts and at all levels, the practice worked. By the time she sold the business, her annual turnover must have been about 50 times what it had been in the early days about twenty years before. Unfortunately, 25 years later, turnover remains much as it was in 1979.

It was to the McNaughtans' shop that 'Wattie' (Walter Blaylock) gravitated in old age. A former travelling man with a pronounced Hawick accent, which he would adjust to suit the ear of the listener, Wattie had in his later years earned a living transporting booksellers' purchases in a pram from the Lane sales to their premises. It was typical of the McNaughtans that they continued to pay Wattie a weekly retainer when that source of income dried up and physical infirmity limited his activities to gossip and coffee-drinking. They were also pleased to encourage young booksellers such as Gus McLean and Jennie Renton, both of whom are still in the trade, Gus McLean selling books in his basement stall at the University of Edinburgh and Jennie Renton with her partner at Main Point Books in Edinburgh. Jennie Renton founded the *Scottish Book Collector* and has now moved on to found the online literary magazine, *textualities*, and to edit the National Library of Scotland's *Folio* magazine. The McNaughtans were proud to be members of the ABA and were founder-members of the Scottish branch of the Association in 1972. The firm was represented at the first Scottish Antiquarian Book Fair in 1973, as it has been at all the Association's subsequent Scottish fairs. Mrs McNaughtan took an increasing interest in branch affairs, serving her turn as Chairman in due course. She also began to support the Association's annual Antiquarian Book Fair in London as an exhibitor in 1977, having visited it for many years previously, and again the firm continues to play its part as an exhibitor south of the border.[14]

In 1967 St Andrews had no secondhand bookshop and another intelligent and energetic woman took note. Gillian and Ralph Stone were living in St Andrews with their family of five children. While her husband was at work in Dundee, Gillian Stone began to attend auction sales to furnish the large family house they had bought. The bookcases she bought at auction came complete with books, so she decided to open a secondhand bookshop. Forming a partnership with Pat Hunter and Margaret Squires, she traded in the market for eight months, before opening in 1968 the Quarto Bookshop, which was still owned and managed by Margaret Squires until its closure in 2006. In 1971 Ralph Stone's work took the family to Devon, where Mrs Stone continued bookselling independently, to be joined in due course by her husband and it was then that they decided to call the business 'Titles'. The couple began to take part in fairs organized by the Provincial Booksellers Fairs Association and in 1979 Ralph became Chairman of the PBFA, and was instrumental in the formation of its constitution. Moving first to a bookshop in the Cotswolds, at Shipton-under-Wychwood, in 1981 they also took the lease of a bookshop in Oxford. They ran the two shops concurrently for two years before concentrating on Oxford, where they remained for seventeen years. Having joined the ABA in the late 1970s, the Stones have always supported the Scottish book fairs and maintained their connection with Scotland. Since closing the Oxford shop, they work from home in Jedburgh, trading mainly on the internet and at book fairs.

Women have played a not inconsiderable part in the Scottish trade throughout the century. Although I have not found any evidence that she was an antiquarian bookseller, the first bookseller to mention a specialist subject in the *Edinburgh and Leith Post Office Directory* during the twentieth century was Catherine L. Taylor of 7 Dock Place, Leith. She advertised in the 1907-08 *Directory* that she specialized in nautical books. Her listing continued to appear until 1915-16, when the business was listed under the name of William Salmon, and then in 1917-18 the owner was listed as Maude Gottwall. However, the business then disappears. In the 1900-01 *Directory*, out of 141 'Booksellers and Stationers' there were three women booksellers and two circulating librarians. These, of course, were women who owned their businesses and the record does not take account of the female staff members in the larger shops. In 1920 100 booksellers were listed, of whom five were women; in 1930 two out of 55 were women. By this date fourteen secondhand booksellers were listed separately. The apparent decline in numbers was partly due to the fact that peripheral areas were given a separate listing.

Thanks once again to Ian Grant's files, we have a customer's (typewritten and unsigned) record of his collecting in Edinburgh which started over Christmas in 1933. He describes purchasing from the Grants' stall beside Greyfriars Bobby and from the shop, and I quote:

Edinburgh in those days was with reason reputed to be the best hunting ground in the Kingdom, if not in the whole world. The whole city seemed full of secondhand bookshops and stalls. There was Mrs Haxton in Chambers Street. She was the widow of an erstwhile taxi-driver with a literary bent; she used to sit crouched over the hob in her back room with her cat. For cat lovers her prices were reduced and included a cup of tea; she also owned a dark cellar where, in the gloom, there was a first (or was it a second?) edition of Erasmus' *Adagia* in mint condition, as well as a large folder full of coloured Cruikshanks, Gillrays and Rowlandsons to be bought for 1*d.* each. Dear Mrs Haxton died during the war. ... Finally, of course, there was Grants. In those early days it seemed frighteningly expensive, a place where books were marked 5/6d., 9/6d. and even 18/6d. As time went on, however, Grants became more and more the centre of attraction for visits to Scotland. One was allowed by Ian Grant to go downstairs. Downstairs meant access to two corridors, each some forty yards long and with rooms and alcoves, most of which had fat piles of old stock. There was an enormous cellar, too, across a yard and behind an oak door opened by a giant key, where shelf upon shelf of dusty books were waiting to gladden the heart. It was a very sad day for the writer when he arrived at George IV Bridge to discover, unbeknown to him, the premises had become a bank.

The firm of John Grant left the George IV Bridge premises in 1973, just before its centenary, and then after a period in Dundas Street in Edinburgh, took a small stock to their shop on Gullane High Street, convenient for golf. Sadly Ian Grant died in 1990 and his widow, Senga, decided to retire from the trade after a short time specializing in golf books. (She shared this speciality with another Scottish bookseller, Rhod McEwan of Ballater, who does much of his business at golf trade exhibitions all over the world.) The Grants remain the only couple who have both achieved the distinction of serving as President of the ABA. Ian Grant was instrumental in the formation of the Scottish branch of the Association and in the inception of the Scottish Antiquarian Book Fair, which in its first year attracted 31 exhibitors from Scotland, England and Italy (Olschki) and was reported in very favourable terms by *The Book Collector*. The success of the Fair during the 1970s and 1980s owed an enormous amount to the couple's energy, enthusiasm and organizational abilities and perhaps, above all, to the hospitality for which the branch became renowned. This reputation and Edinburgh's many attractions led to the city's being chosen as the venue for the millennial Congress of the International League of Antiquarian Booksellers. In 1977 the Scottish branch organized *Landmarks in Science*, an exhibition of about 100 books mounted at Edinburgh University on the occasion of the 15th Annual Congress of the History of Science. In the early 1990s the branch mounted an exhibition at the Edinburgh Book Festival in order to raise the Association's profile, with the support of Anthony Rota and John Saumarez Smith who faced the Festival audience and fielded questions.

Three antiquarian booksellers were also among the first members of the Edinburgh Bibliographical Society, which was founded in 1890. George Pyper Johnston was the first Secretary and Treasurer of the Society, William Brown a committee member, and James Thin an ordinary member. Both William Brown and George Johnston produced papers, Johnston writing a short history of the Society, which appeared in 1934. Johnston's catalogue 101 was reviewed in *Book Auction Records*: 'A beautifully-printed catalogue, which is explained by the fact that Mr Johnson [sic] is secretary of the Edinburgh Bibliographical Society.' Of the booksellers advertising in the *Edinburgh and Leith Post Office Directory* early in the century, Johnston stands out as insistent on his status as a purely antiquarian bookseller. In the 1900-01 volume he listed the services available: 'Catalogues of libraries compiled, Libraries valued for all purposes ..., Bindings of Old books in appropriate and Characteristic styles carefully and artistically executed, Libraries of old and Rare Books Bought.' He then stated that 'Executors and others having old Family Libraries to dispose of are invited to communicate with the advertiser, who, having an extensive connection of buyers of curious, old and rare books, can offer high prices.' Of course, as Secretary and Treasurer of the Edinburgh Bibliographical Society, he was well placed to build up this connection. Lord Rosebery was a member of the Society and among the library catalogues Johnston compiled was a *Catalogue of Pamphlets in the Library of Barnbougle Castle* ([Edinburgh], 1903), as well as a *Catalogue of the early and rare books of Scottish interest in the Library at Barnbougle Castle* (Edinburgh, 1923).

Antiquarian booksellers have also been prominent within the membership of the Edinburgh Booksellers' Society, both Ian Grant and James (Jimmy) Thin having served their turn as Preses. The Society was founded in 1792, and the author, its first lady member, was proud to reply to the toast of the Society at its bi-centenary dinner. It is an interesting reflection on the trade that of the 24 members of this society, which requires that its members be 'principals' within their firms, only one of these could at present be described as a full-time antiquarian bookseller. The majority of those who are still in employment are publishers or printers, or combine printing and stationery. When the Society was founded, the members would have undertaken all of these activities, including, of course, the selling of new books.

The best-known shop in Glasgow and until recently, when it closed its retail premises, the longest-established in Scotland, was John Smith & Son (Glasgow) Ltd. The firm's reputation was greatly enhanced with the issue of its catalogue no. 8, *Bibliotheca Scotica* (1926). Orders and notes of appreciation from an international clientele have been preserved in the National Library of Scotland.[15] Many colleagues and librarians wrote to say that they would be glad to keep the catalogue for reference purposes – some copies were issued interleaved to allow space for notes and additions. The author A. Boyd Scott wrote that 'even in the eyes of the casual and the unenlightened it must complete the establishment of the House of John Smith and Son among the greatest of the great Booksellers', and communications were received from H.V. Morton, J.B. Priestley, and John Buchan. Among the colleagues who sent congratulations was a K. Mackenzie, proprietor of The Book Shop, Baghdad (Bookseller, Publisher and Stationer). The artist E.A. Hornel, who already had almost 10,000 items in his collection of Dumfries and Galloway material, ordered ten Burns items and suggested that he would be back in touch when he had had time to look at the rest of the catalogue. Favourable reviews appeared in the press – including the *Sunday Times* and various other non-specialist periodicals.

The antiquarian department of John Smith provided a training ground for two prominent booksellers who subsequently set up in their own right. George Newlands was there in the 1970s and now specializes in maritime books at Helensburgh. Cooper Hay started with John Smith & Son in the early 1970s; after a spell selling secondhand and antiquarian books on his own account, he returned to Smith's antiquarian department. In 1985 he set up independently in Bath Street, conveniently placed for Christie's and Phillips' auction rooms. His shop gives the lie to the general rule that nowadays north of the border the choicest stocks are to be found in private premises.

In H.D. Hopkins, Glasgow produced one of the founder-members of the ABA and the Associations's first Scottish President. Hugh Hopkins was President in 1931 and is remembered by Kulgin Duval as having the most lovely shop in Scotland, selling to many libraries, and having access to large private libraries in the west of Scotland. He was well-known for his opulent style – driving a big car, dressed in his bowler hat, and decanting sherry or brandy in his shop. Among the most prestigious items he handled were Shakespeare quartos and the manuscript of Allan Ramsay's *The Gentle Shepherd*. Kulgin Duval remarks that it was the Hopkins style of business which first attracted him into the antiquarian book trade.

From an Aberdeen bookseller, James G. Bisset, came one of the fulsome tributes to John Smith & Son on the production of *Bibliotheca Scotica*. Although Aberdeen's book trade had expanded greatly in the second half of the nineteenth century,[16] only four businesses were listed in the ABA's 1932 *Directory of Antiquarian Booksellers in the British Isles* (which included non-members of the Association): Bisset, Low's Bookstalls, Milne, and Wyllie. Wyllie's most interesting publications were family and local history and topography, but some vanity publications and many sermons and tracts were produced: in 1904 Dr Stewart's *Should the Wine of the Sacrament be Intoxicating?* reached a third edition, while 1936 saw the publication of Donald J. Macleod's *Drips from my Old Umbrella*.[17]

There is a long historical connection between the book trade in Scotland and that in Northern Ireland. Jack Gamble, of Emerald Isle Books, wrote in August 2005 that 'the wealth of Scottish books in Ireland' had only dried up some twenty years earlier. However, he has continued to buy Scottish Gaelic and family history whenever possible because of his interest in the Scots-Irish identity. Gamble has had access to large quantities of 'Covenanter' books in Ireland, as so many Ulster ministers had been educated in Scotland, but he has also been in the habit of visiting Scotland to buy books. He has long been one of the most respected Irish booksellers and his importance is reflected in the substantial catalogues produced by Emerald Isle Books in the latter decades of the twentieth century. Gamble also possesses catalogues of Scottish books produced in the Antrim Road in the 1930s by dentists who bought and sold antiquarian books as a hobby, purchasing much of their stock in country house sales in the lowlands of Scotland.

In the *Directory of Antiquarian Booksellers* for 1932, seventeen Scottish members of the ABA are recorded. They spread from Aberdeen, Coldstream, Dundee (Frank Russell, where in the 1930s schoolchildren queued down Barrack Street for their secondhand school books at the beginning of the academic year), to Dunfermline, Edinburgh and Glasgow. In Northern Ireland there were three ABA members: The Cathedral Book Store (H. Greer) at 18 Gresham Street in Belfast, H. Greer at Smithfield, and Mayne at 3 Donegal Square West. (There was one ABA member, Fenning, in the Republic of Ireland, based in Dublin.) In 1928 the Cathedral Book Store advertised in *Irish Book Lover*, claiming to have the largest stock of books in Ireland. In 1929 it offered 3,000 items in its catalogue no. 8; again in 1934, catalogue nos. 11 and 13 were advertised, each containing 3,000 items. In 1910, W.H. Taggart & Co. of 9 Battenburg Street, Belfast, offered a catalogue of over 400 items relating to Ireland; by 1913 they had moved to the Antrim Road. Apart from the Cathedral Book Store, there were a further three Greer bookshops listed in the ABA's guide but not flagged as ABA members, and a further four bookshops in Smithfield and Donegall Place. Mullans, the large general bookshop in Donegall Place, had an antiquarian department up to the time of its closure following the arrival of Dillons. In the 1938 *List of Members* published by the ABA only one member survived in Belfast: the Cathedral Book Stores at 18 Gresham Street. In the 1958 ILAB *Directory*, we find only the same firm listed in Belfast as 'Greer, Hugh, Cathedral Book Store, 18 Gresham Street', specializing in 'General Literature (antiquarian books) Irish Literature, Theology, Topography (Ireland)'. The Greers had been the most celebrated Belfast booksellers since the 1840s: Henry Greer had supplied books to the Linen Hall Library from 1852 until 1874, when he was made an honorary member.

From at least the 1940s Smithfield covered market was the centre of the secondhand book trade in Belfast, but when the market was bombed in the 1970s, many of the secondhand book businesses were destroyed. Jack Gamble also suffered a bombing in the 1970s when the main warehouse at the back of his house on the Antrim Road was attacked. Some of the books survived, but such was the trauma that he has found it hard to look at them since. Richard Booth, in *My Kingdom of Books*, recorded visiting Ireland in the 1970s. He quotes a Belfast bookseller describing the streets after bombing as being 'full of seventeenth-century pages' but says that 'even in Londonderry, and at times of extreme violence, we still managed to fill a container with books. By the mid-70s, the small house-dealer with a lot of bargains was a very rare bird. A new type of dealer was emerging who would scour book fairs throughout Ireland. As the books became more difficult to find we stopped going.'

As elsewhere, more and more Irish booksellers began to work from home, and it was no surprise that most specialized in Irish books. Gordon Wheeler (formerly of Queen's University Library, Belfast) notes among the principal dealers P. & B. Rowan (Peter Rowan) of Belfast, who started trading in 1973. With specialities in the history of ideas and Ireland, he has issued 66 catalogues, which have been singled out as the most substantial and well-researched catalogues ever issued in Ireland. Prospect House Books (Colette McAlister) of Donaghadee traded from a bookshop in Belfast from 1982 until 1992, but has since been dealing from home via the internet and by appointment. Her specialities are Ireland, natural history, philosophy and travel. Arthur Davidson of Ballynahinch, a regular buying visitor to Scotland, has produced more than 30 catalogues on Ireland over the last twenty years and has published facsimiles of local history rarities. Other contemporary antiquarian booksellers with substantial miscellaneous stocks are Foyle Books of Londonderry, Greens Books of Newtonards and Craobh Rua Rare Books of Armagh. Until recently Lucy Faulkner, the widow of Lord Faulkner, the last Northern Irish Prime Minister, combined two of Ireland's greatest enthusiasms, the book and the horse, dealing at first by catalogue and then on the internet in equestrian books from her peaceful house on the outskirts of Downpatrick. Like many colleagues before, she would make buying trips to Scotland in the 1980s and 1990s. The choice of Wigtown as Scottish Book Town may have seemed eccentric and off the beaten track to many, but situated in beautiful countryside and close to the route to the Stranraer-Larne ferry from northern England and eastern Scotland, it is well placed to catch such trade as may be passing along that road to and from Northern Ireland.

The spread of secondhand and antiquarian bookshops in Scotland and Ireland earlier in the century has already been noted. At the time of writing, country shops are still in evidence, one of the more recently established being the attractive and carefully stocked shop at Comrie in Perthshire. Jim Macmaster, the founder, a delightfully eccentric and enthusiastic bookseller, caused astonishment a year or two ago when he was discovered by potential customers plucking a brace of pheasants beside the open fire in the bookshop, bottle of whisky to hand. John Marrin works from what was formerly the gamekeeper's cottage on the Ford and Etal estate, just over the border in Northumberland, with an opportunity to fish on the estate water. In Peeblesshire Spike Hughes works from home on the outskirts of Innerleithen, thus enabling him to combine a successful business, much of it on the internet, with his love of country pursuits. In Edinburgh too, some of the most talented booksellers have retreated from shop premises to work from home: Edward Nairn and Ian Watson from their top-floor flat crammed with nineteenth- and twentieth-century material in the finest condition; Alan Grant selling mainly eighteenth-century books; and Peter Bell cataloguing at home in the mornings and crossing central Edinburgh to sell from his shop in the afternoons.

Determination is required to keep shop premises going in the twenty-first century. So much that in the past was left to common sense is now regulated. In Edinburgh the Second-hand Dealer's Licence has been a requirement for all those keeping secondhand and antiquarian bookshops, and incidentally for exhibitors at book fairs, since the introduction of the Civic Government (Scotland) Act 1982. Despite approaches made to the City of Edinburgh Council and to Lothian and Borders Police, it has proved impossible to alter the stringent conditions which include an undertaking not to deal with anyone under the age of sixteen. This has always seemed inappropriate to the antiquarian book trade. One of the McNaughtans' original customers was the six-year-old Eric Robertson – now a musician in Toronto – who would rummage in the sixpenny boxes outside the shop and was soon discovered to be so seriously interested that he was welcomed into the shop and became a lifelong customer.

Overheads are, of course, another deterrent to keeping an open shop. Business rates can take approximately 5 per cent of annual turnover. It is a continuing cause for comment among booksellers that the plethora of specialist charity bookshops now operating – six in Edinburgh – can disregard many of these overheads. As long ago as 1971, Ronald Mavor, retiring Director of the Scottish Arts Council, expressed no surprise when asked if he envisaged subsidized bookshops. He was mainly concerned with the deterioration in new bookshops: 'now there's hardly anything but books for tourists about Scotland, records and fountain pens. The business of running a bookshop has become much less an artistic and cultural one.'[18] At that time there were still fine antiquarian bookshops in Scotland, with the solidity that came from decades of building up stock and property. In the intervening 35 years, the bookselling landscape has altered almost beyond recognition, with smaller businesses coming and going. R. & J. Balding, for instance, a firm which was run successfully from a flat in Edinburgh in the 1970s, expanded into an entire New Town house at a time when trade was about to slump following the expansion of the previous few years. The firm also bought heavily from Sotheby's Signet Library sale, where all multiple lots were sold not subject to return. Without long-accumulated stock and goodwill to offset these problems, the business failed.

In the early twenty-first century, as shop trade tends to become quieter, sales can be boosted by printed catalogues, an internet presence, and by exhibiting at book fairs. The ABA and the PBFA have cooperated in the staging of a book fair in central Edinburgh, planned to be an annual event. Better communication between Edinburgh and the Continent since devolution is an advantage which one hopes can be made to work for the trade, particularly on these occasions. However, the small shopkeeper needs to conserve resources to finance the private purchases which may still result from having a presence on the high street. Despite all this, in Edward Fenwick's 2005/6 *Secondhand & Antiquarian Bookshops in Scotland*, 21 new entries are cited as evidence that 'some people are still brave enough to want [to] realise their romantic vision and open a bookshop'. Fenwick lists 132 shops from Aberdeen to Wigtown, as far north as Kirkwall and as far west as Iona. For some the day-to-day contact with the public and the sense of being a valued amenity is rewarding, but in an economically stringent atmosphere and at a time of sweeping cultural change, confidence needs to be boosted continually by customers who make purchases. The well-meant 'What a lovely shop! I could spend all day in here' is not quite enough.

West Country Bookshops in the 1960s: A Memoir

PAUL MINET

THE writing of this book in the early years of the new century is in some ways convenient to those of us who traded through the second half of the old one. The changes that have taken place in the trade in the past five or ten years have in some respects been greater than those in the previous three centuries. Trying to recapture what it was like trading in the provinces in the 1960s and 1970s is an exercise not just in memory but almost in belief.

I remember a day in the early 1960s when my wife and I were driving back from a house near Newton Abbot, where we had been successful in buying a roomful of books for around £250, a fair sum at that time. The condition was that we must clear the lot within 48 hours because the house was being sold. My only recollection now of the actual books is that they included three or four long shelves of A. & C. Black colour books in the larger format which even then were desirable. Our bid was successful solely because we offered to clear them all within the time limit, which trumped a slightly higher offer from the Neptune Bookshop in Paignton.

I think it was on the second of three trips in our small car that I misjudged the petrol. We were clearly going to run out before we got back to our home in Hartland in North Devon. It was quite late and there was only one filling station between us and Hartland, a filling station where we didn't know the owner. Credit cards and even bank guarantee cards did not exist (or, if they did, they hadn't penetrated to a customer like me). I had only a business cheque, which would not be acceptable. We turned out our pockets and the car's pockets and came up with three shillings and ninepence, enough for one gallon of petrol, with threepence to spare. We made it home, rustled up a little money from the local pub and made the third and final trip that night, dropping the house key back through the door and drinking soup from a thermos flask on Dartmoor at 3 a.m. I can still conjure that sparkling night as if it were yesterday

We were always on the edge, as indeed were most of the booksellers we knew. One whole winter we survived by driving up to Ilfracombe where there was an old bookseller named Smith who had a cinema full of marvellous books which one could buy for £1.10s. each provided one took more than a hundred. I always went after lunch on a Thursday, so that my cheque would not come in until the Tuesday, when I had sold enough of the books to cover it. The Friday would be taken up with the market in Tavistock, where we traded for several years on a range of tables under glass skylights in the great market hall. Takings might top £100 on a good day, with occasional much better days if the haul of the previous week had yielded some real goodies. If it were a poor day, I might have to leap in the car and take a few boxes to Bristol, where Tony Heath was always good for a cheque, or even as far afield as Hay-on-Wye, where Richard Booth was in the first flush of his desperate expansion in what was becoming a town of books, although we would not have used that particular phrase then.

I would take in the odd auction, although my already fixed aversion to joining a ring usually ensured that I was frozen out of the buying. There were, however, occasional auctions in country houses or in Exeter where the presence of a particular character named Heap would disrupt the best-laid plots of the ringers. Heap was an ex-classics master who had moved into a select small shop in Wells in 1950 and applied a fine taste and fearless bidding to auctions across the West Country. He would never join the ring and his buying ability, unlike mine, disrupted their arrangements. Like everyone else, I never really got to know him, but I was grateful to him nonetheless. I was, on the other hand, very friendly with Mr Burbridge of the Neptune Bookshop in Paignton, who took my unwillingness to join the ring in good part even if he quite failed to understand it. He had a large shop with some tens of thousands of books, although the cream of it was always concentrated into a room at the front of the first floor, or else immediately behind his desk at the front in a range of locked bookcases. He shared the desk with a stamp dealer who looked after the shop whilst he was out book-hunting. I don't think he ever had an assistant although I think his wife occasionally helped out.

There were other large shops in the West Country. One massive place in Exeter was called the Iron Bridge Bookshop in the trade, although its real name was the Caledonian Bookshop; then there was the famous J.A.D. Bridger in Penzance, established in the 1890s but soon to be bought out; and Mr Smith in Ilfracombe – these were our lode stars, but there were other, smaller shops either in the same towns or nearby, so that it was possible to go through six or eight shops in the course of one trip, ending with a worthwhile haul.

Plymouth was rather barren until a university teacher, Tony Clement, set up in the Barbican with a stock bought largely from me. He had a strange idiosyncrasy in that he would never send anything anywhere. This was unfortunate because almost all of us depended for such jam as we managed to get on our bread on visiting American booksellers, for this was the period of the free-spending US dealers and librarians who, as we vaguely knew, were the staple customers of those London booksellers who also made their way down to us. I remember in particular David Low, Peter Eaton and George Walford making lucrative raids upon my stock in Hartland, as well as smaller booksellers such as Bill Duck, just starting out in the technology field that he made his own over the next 40 years, and a curious atheist named Walker who traded as the Nelson Bookshop in Brighton, specializing in theology but with a good nose for anything that would sell better up-country than in the fastnesses of the West Country. Tony Clement insisted on two things: that you paid for and removed the books yourself and that he had a decent lunch hour, spent largely exercising his wife's dog. It cost him a lot of money in the long run. My wife and I, on the other hand, would stay up with a visiting bookseller into the small hours, feeding and putting him up if necessary (a travelling bookseller was then always 'him').

I have touched on another of the great changes in that paragraph. We had only our experience of other shops and our own knowledge to price books. The ABA had been running a book fair in London for a few years, but we were barely aware of that and few of us were members. There were no other fairs at which to compare prices with one's peers. Our main avenue of communication with the rest of the trade was a weekly magazine called *The Clique* which had been printing wants lists every week since the 1890s, but one had to guess the prices to be quoted and learn from who took what. There was a reference book called *Book Auction Records*, always known as BAR, but we couldn't really afford that and in any case the books treated in it barely came our way. It was in fact taken for granted that our prices had to be quite sharply lower than London prices in order to tempt the big boys down to visit us. That was the way the pyramid worked.

This was a period when rents were beginning to rise and old-established shops were going. I remember an old couple in Castle Cary who had traded in a small shop for decades on a strictly local basis, buying in a small area and selling there also. I never heard of any bookseller other than myself visiting them. There was another Victorian shop tacked onto the back of a tobacconist's shop in Okehampton, in the middle of Devon, with room after room of books which had clearly been there for most of the century. The property changed hands in the end and we cleared out thousands of theological commentaries, old novels and nineteenth-century biographies which I would like to find again today.

Our trade reference book, then as now, was Sheppard's *Dealers in Books*, although the edition in the mid-1960s ran to a bare 200 pages. West Country bookshops were dominated by Bayntun's in Bath, George's in Bristol and Commin's in Bournemouth, although there were other smaller shops in all three towns, some of them ABA members. George's was an outpost of Blackwell's in Oxford and cornered a lot of the buying in the region: indeed, I am sure that that was why it was there. In Bournemouth, as well as Commin's splendid retail shop, there was also Alan G. Thomas, who later rose to great prominence in the trade, and a bookshop called Modern Books, otherwise Turll's, which listed itself as being founded in 1921. In Dorset and Somerset there was the legendary Stevens-Cox in Beaminster, established in 1930 and prolific producer of lists, who shortly afterwards moved to the Channel Islands. Dorchester boasted H.V. Day, which had made the prices in Dorset books since 1937 but went out of business at about this time. I did a lot of dealing with a charming man named Ernest Hardy who also traded in Dorchester before he semi-retired to a neigh-bouring village, selling me all his surplus stock. There was a general bookshop on The Cobb at Lyme Regis which I believe is still there, but not much else. Further west, in Devon, there was Burbridge in Paignton and an ABA shop called the Priory Book Store, which had traded since 1940 but which I could never catch open. Near Crediton, trading from private premises, was a very knowledgeable bookseller named Morton-Smith who specialized in books far above my head. In Dartmouth was Eric Hooper, who had been in the trade since demob in 1946. I dealt with him first in a rambling farmhouse near Bere Alston not far from Plymouth, but he was tempted away to become a junior partner to Christopher Robin Milne for a few years in Dartmouth. To the north was Gerry Mosdell in Barnstaple, Smith in Ilfracombe and myself in Hartland, although in some ways the most pleasant shop to visit was one trading in Westward Ho! as Robert Harper and Daughter, the remaining outpost of a major business which had had shops in the middle of both Bideford and Barnstaple before the war. It was run by the remaining daughter, Joan Harper, and a very elderly assistant, selling books from a packed terrace house at very cheap prices and both fuelled by the most remarkable consumption of cigarettes.

Further down still and only visited occasionally because of the distances involved were a number of Cornish shops. Jill Holiday in Padstow created a major market in Cornish books, which largely collapsed when she stopped trading, and there was a shop in Truro specializing in and reprinting books on Cornish mining. Aside from them, and Bridger's in Penzance, Cornwall hosted a few small shops and quite a number of antique shops with book sections, notably in Looe, but nothing very serious. It was a period when local topography was a bigger seller than it has been since. As I subsequently discovered, the subject was largely fuelled by a delightful gentleman in Bloomsbury named Stanley Crowe, who specialized in it for twenty years or so. Gentleman is an accurate description of him, since he was always impeccably dressed and he hid his extraordinary expertise behind a suave and almost jovial manner. When he died and his basement shop was sold up, the craze for local topography almost stopped in its tracks. For a time, two of the staples of my business were topography and steel plate books, which were being progressively broken up to feed the antique trade's appetite for framed prints. I could live for a week on one decent 1840s plate book picked up in seaside junk shops.

Gradually the scene changed. Petrol was no longer 3s.6d. a gallon, shops were worth more empty than full of books, the auctioneers in London were doing a magnificent job publicizing their services and creaming off the good libraries. The gaps between shops were becoming noticeably greater so that one couldn't take in so many in one trip.

I wasn't the only one locally in North Devon who was noticing the changes. Gerry Mosdell, at the Porcupine Bookshop in a rather pokey alley in Barnstaple, was also thinking that things would have to change. I would drop in there regularly en route to points east to exchange gossip and the odd book. We would discuss whether it might be possible to take car loads of books to London and display them to London dealers, thereby short-circuiting the necessity of their coming down to see us, which happened, in our view, too rarely. This germ of an idea did not come to fruition until personal circumstances had led to my departure from the West Country, but it did mean that I was eventually one of the initial six dealers who exhibited at the first London book fair run by what developed into the Provincial Booksellers' Fairs Association.

My visits to Hay became more frequent as I got to know Richard Booth better, until I was acting as a kind of unofficial agent for him in my area, buying loads of books and running them up to him. Since he was always spending ahead of himself, I would sometimes take my payment in books and run them to London, often selling them to Peter Eaton or to others more specialist than him. In effect, I was doing on an individual basis what the book fairs later institutionalized. One could, at least after a time, buy locally, but one could not sell enough without either a specialist catalogue business or turning oneself into a kind of glorified 'runner' for the London shops, where the business was.

The PBFA fairs came into existence to solve the problem. Almost all of the successful provincial bookshops I know today are very long-established and none of them are in the West Country. There were retail shops in places like Guildford, not too far from London, but even they have now closed. Before I went to the West Country, around 1958, I had a retail bookshop in a very good position in Reading, which I combined with a coffee bar, but even the fact that we were almost opposite a large bookshop called William Smith and in a university town could not save me there. I thought that my rivals opposite, who had been there 100 years and issued large catalogues, were a fixture but even they went when some new owners discovered that the new books they sold were much more lucrative than the secondhand. The owner when I first knew Smith's was a delightful ex-Indian army officer named, I think, Redway who was permanently cold. The William Smith shop had been there since 1832.

In the 40 years since I first knew them, I have seen a multitude of bookshops open in Torquay, Exeter, Barnstaple, Ilfracombe, Launceston, Penzance and other desirable West Country towns, but few have lasted. Some were run by locals, but the majority represented a double escape, from urban life and from working for someone else. I was one of the escapees. It is interesting that the 1964 edition of Sheppard's directory does not feature Totnes in the town index at all, whereas a decade later there were half a dozen small bookshops there. When bookshops did last, it was usually because there was some other kind of income coming in, a flat let or a partner working at something else, or perhaps because the owner was already enjoying a retirement income from another occupation. During the main inflationary period in the 1970s and 1980s, it was the value of the property that came to everyone's rescue. One sold on the lease or the freehold, paid the debts and started up somewhere else. It was only narrowly specialist dealers who built up an expertise and an in-depth stock in some subject who could prosper, usually in a private house. It has only been with the coming of the internet, which is outside my field here, that the mountain has at last come to these remoter Mahomets.

In those days before the PBFA revitalized much of the provincial trade, there was not much consciousness of trade associations beyond the reach of London. We knew that there were ABA members in London, but there were very few beyond Bristol, where George's was to be found and occasionally encountered at a country house auction. We trusted the bigger firms implicitly: medium-old books were sent to Maggs, old books to Quaritch and bindings and binding copies to Bayntun's in Bath, although even then our major contact with them was through quoting books via *The Clique*. Booksellers from all over the country advertised books wanted every week, reputedly to the tune of 20,000 titles a week. The magazine was slightly past its best days by then, with even the title raising a slightly sceptical laugh. I don't recall that I knew that its editor sat on the ABA committee and I certainly would not have known that the ABA held a debenture on its shares. George Walford, who specialized in steel plate books at this time, began advertising in its pages for named books at named prices until the London trade protested that this was letting the cat out of the bag for small provincial booksellers like me: at least, that is what they meant, even if they didn't quite put it that way. Walford was very much the successful eccentric, with his shop in Islington's Upper Street never changing its window and the trade confined to the front office. He used at one time to run a kind of large camper vehicle, in which he would sit and collate his purchases before paying for them. He was always very courteous to me, although he had a bit of a prickly reputation. After he died, I wrote a longish piece on him with the help of his family and found that he was a much more varied and interesting man than I had thought. He didn't quite measure up to David Low, who sent me a cheque once after a visit to Hartland, with a note saying that the books had been too cheap.

In the provinces we operated far more remotely from the rest of the trade than dealers do today. Now there is the internet, but even before that there were great numbers of book fairs where dealers from many areas could compare notes and observe each other's prices. It is quite difficult to recall just how cut off we were before the advent of those fairs. I was unusual in travelling around quite a bit, but most of the booksellers whose shops I frequented were genuinely pleased to get news from elsewhere. While I acquired a significant proportion of my stock from trade buying, I still bought far more privately than I do now, as did most of the other small booksellers in the West Country. One followed up 'call-outs' religiously and I seemed to spend a great deal of time crawling around attics on my hands and knees. Nowadays I am regrettably aware of how much a morning or half a morning investigating one dubious lot can cost me, but in those days that was just what one did. If one turned up one's nose at a private call or a tip-off about some junk shop in a side street, where else were one's books to come from? Then, after buying the lot, one had to make the prices and find a market, in my case usually in Tavistock on a Friday. One applied experience to the pricing, often experience learned the hard way by once selling a book too cheaply. The few regular collectors I had at my stall in Tavistock taught me quite as much as I taught them. One customer in particular, Charles Beckerleg, who ran a local electrical shop, had a major collection of Devon books. He could always be consulted about anything I bought in return for first choice on the local books. Even the regular dealers were more forthcoming, at least in my experience, than they are today, when everyone is pitched against the prices of (unsold) books listed on the internet. The local junk shops in various small towns were far more ignorant than they are today, when those that survive seem to have traded up to antique shop status. I do not wish to paint a picture of some ultra-rosy past, but rather the reverse. We were to some extent trading in the dark, although we were aware that the major London dealers at that period were making serious money from American dealers and librarians. We just couldn't think of any way to tap into it without working through the London shops.

The larger shops had, in most cases, been going since the 1930s, when I presume there had been a shake-out connected with the Depression, I have since heard stories of the difficulties of even such people as the Fletchers of Cecil Court at that period and, if it was bad there, one hates to think what it must have been like in the West Country. Of the shops I have mentioned here, only Bridger, Bayntun, Commin in Exeter and George's date back beyond the 1930s and of those only Bayntun is still going now. I have noticed, however, that the Sheppard's directory I have been delving into includes a listing for a business called Simmons and Waters in private premises in Bridgewater which is listed as having been established in Leamington Spa in 1844. They were ABA members in 1964 but I know nothing else about them.

After I moved back to London around 1968 and before I became established in North Buckinghamshire with a proper business, with employees, catalogues, reprints and overdrafts, I ran an office in London for a bit and continued my running from there. Runners have almost died out now, subsumed into book fairs and now the internet, but they had an honourable history of many years. 'Running' pure and simple consisted of ascertaining what several bookshops wanted to buy, rushing off to find the books somewhere else and coming back to sell them, usually for cash. It was called running because the people who did it usually worked on a minute amount of capital and had no vehicle, so they had to move their purchases on fast, perhaps within the day. I remember my mother, who ran a small bookshop in Reading in the late 1950s and who was something of a soft touch for some of them, dealing with several old boys whose charm was matched only by their extreme penury. I later discovered that one in particular, Stretton by name, used to buy books from Tony Doncaster in Colchester and peddle them down to my mother by bus within a few hours. He was a large, soft-spoken man who always dressed in a white flannel suit and a panama hat and had to be revived after his trips with copious amounts of tea. Tony, who later became a friend of mine, had a soft spot for him and used sometimes to give him credit, to his ultimate cost. When he died of a heart attack in a boarding house in Oxford, Stretton still owed my mother for a roll of road maps taken on approval years before.

Catalogues

H.R. WOUDHUYSEN

I

THE scene is Hammersmith in the early years of the last century: the school is a lightly disguised version of St Paul's and Mr Olim is similarly recognizable as an impersonation of the Revd H.D. Elam:

Minutes later than all the other masters, Olim came along the silent corridor … He was browsing, through his steel spectacles, over a second-hand book catalogue, as he came slowly, heavily, towards us. Probably, for such was his habit, he had been studying the catalogue most of the way from Shepherd's Bush to the school. Each time his eyes met a title he'd like for his own he raised his eyebrows in a wonder or his shoulders in a despair.[1]

Ernest Raymond's affectionate portrait of the schoolmaster's rapt attention, his astonishment and despair at the prices he read as he walked, captures something of the fascination, the pleasures and the pains which booksellers' catalogues bring. 'I shall never forget the arrival by post of the first slim Bellew catalogue,' Michael Sadleir wrote, describing the catalogues of late eighteenth- and early nineteenth-century novels discovered at Mount Bellew in the West of Ireland by M.J. MacManus in 1933:

After tearing through the catalogue's eight pages, I felt so breathless that I had to sit a few moments before I was capable of going through the whole thing item by item. I made pencil-crosses; I drafted a long telegram. Then I commended my cause to Providence and went through the catalogue all over again.[2]

In a similar but less excited vein A.N.L. Munby's description of the subject has probably not been bettered:

Current book-sellers' catalogues present a grave problem. Space forbids that they should all be retained, yet it is a sad wrench to part with them. No ephemeral literature approaches them in fascination. To receive one at breakfast, to skim through it with one's porridge, possibly leaving the table to dictate a telegram if circumstances demand it, to note complacently how the books one bought for modest sums in the past have risen in price – these are among the highest pleasures of life. Only when a mountainous accumulation of catalogues demands drastic action can I bring myself to throw a proportion of them away. Then – perhaps once in three years – there is a gigantic sorting; some are earmarked for permanent retention as works of reference; the rest are reluctantly destroyed after certain material such as plates of bindings and manuscripts has been cut out and transferred to a growing series of folio scrap-books – 'cutting up books to make other books', as an unsympathetic friend once described it.[3]

The excitement of receiving new catalogues is perhaps matched only by the peculiar heartache of reading or rereading old ones, which has all the pain and some of the pleasure of revisiting old love letters – pleasure and regret about what we did and did not do. As the Robinsons put it at the end of a long introduction to their splendid catalogue 77 in 1948, when post-war conditions seriously upset trade and the economy:

we suggest that it will not be a hundred years – perhaps not even a decade – before collectors will re-scan … even such a comparatively modest catalogue as the present, and will look back with nostalgia to the opportunities of the present moment, some, at least, of which can never recur.

Sunt lachrymae rerum; or, as Peter Opie put it, 'When I die my heart will be found pressed between the pages of a book catalogue.'[4]

From the bookseller's point of view the subject is more complicated, but may still involve a delicate negotiation between pride and humiliation – the hundredth catalogue, with rare and expensive books which are all sold, or the books woefully underdescribed, wrongly identified and got rid of too cheaply, or priced too high and not sold at all. There are troubles with printers, the post, assistants, packers, and most of all with customers. As with most publications, anything that can go wrong with a catalogue has a tendency to do so: getting the books together and selling them is almost the easy part. Catalogues interfere with the real business of bookselling – the buying and study of books, the keeping of a shop, talking to customers and colleagues, avoiding customers and colleagues, making money, or having lunch – and they may play an essential or an inessential part in the bookseller's life.

An account of how the trade sold its books during the last century might well set Mr Elam, Sadleir and Munby against E. P. Goldschmidt's famous remark that his ideal customer lived a long way away, occasionally ordering a book by catalogue on a postcard and A. Edward Newton's huffy printed circular of 1930 that 'Owing to the discourtesy with which I have been treated by a prominent London book-seller [Quaritch], I … request that you send me no further catalogues'.[5] Its narrative would trace a relatively simple trajectory, taking in the decline of the bookshop as premises and assistants became increasingly expensive, the decline of the catalogue as production costs rose, and finally the decline of the bookfair as the internet conquered all before it. It would touch on the beginnings of the collecting of modern literary authors in the 1870s and 1880s, when American money also started to enter the market. The age of Wise, the boom of the 1920s, the obsession with 'points', and the development of higher bibliographical standards would all be discussed. New paths in what was considered saleable – early and detective fiction, music, books on medicine, science, politics, economics, sociology, law, education, architecture, cookery, fashion, children's books, ephemera, maps and cartography, photography, books on the history of the book trade – could all be traced. The slump of the 1930s and the effect of the two World Wars could help explain the changes in the market in the 1950s and

1960s, especially the growing importance of selling by catalogue to America and in particular to university libraries. Along with this would go the gradual decline in the large general catalogue and the increasing specialization by subject or by period of what dealers offered for sale. Finally, the rampant inflation of the 1970s and the appearance of new money in the 1980s and after, the sudden emergence and disappearance of Japanese buyers, would do much to account for the constant obsession with modern firsts and the developing market for cult works of the period. Such a narrative would provide a rich store of anecdote and illustration, but there may be a little more of a specific kind to say.

Catalogues play an important part in the trade, but they have a number of different uses. Most simply they are a convenient way of selling stock to customers: old or new stock to old or new customers. They allow dealers to reach customers who cannot visit their shops, in the hope that they will buy books that will not move from their shelves. Catalogues add value to books: by describing their appearance, history, and contents, by placing them in context with books of a similar or related kind, their status is enhanced, new subjects for collection are suggested and a spirit of competition between collectors is promoted.

What is a catalogue?

Printed catalogues containing second-hand books, imported from the Continent, for sale in England have survived from the 1630s; by the beginning of the next century they were quite common and from about 1730 they started to list books with their prices.[6] The nineteenth century saw the general pattern of selling books by catalogue well established. Substantial catalogues by such dealers as Thomas Rodd, Thomas Kerslake, Payne and Foss, and Thomas Thorpe showed how central this form of bookselling was to the higher end of the trade. Long runs of these sorts of catalogue, issued four or five times a year, might be collected, uniformly bound and used as valuable reference works by collectors and scholars, as well as by dealers. The lower part of the trade also made extensive use of cheaply produced catalogues, which might be issued stitched or stabbed or even simply folded: these were put out regularly, on a monthly basis. The production of these two different types of catalogues, and many that came in between them, continued into the next century.

A catalogue may arrange books in any order – by author, date, place of printing or publication, subject, and so on – and may contain any number of them: the grandest catalogue may describe one book, while the less pretentious may list many hundreds or even thousands. To a certain extent content determines form: cheap books rarely get long descriptions. Dealers also have to bear in mind the time and patience that reading catalogues demands from customers. There is no 'standard' size or length for catalogues, but many dealers have found lists of 32 pages with around seven items on each page a convenient format. A general catalogue, of the kind Quaritch produced in the nineteenth century, may in effect be a stock list of everything on the shelves – but material for a catalogue on a specific topic may be assembled over a long period. The catalogue may be produced by any process, in an edition of one copy or for widespread distribution – between 1935 and 1937 A.N.L. Munby wrote out lists of eighteenth-century books which he offered for sale to his friend Harold Forster alone.[7] It may be targeted at many collectors or at just one or two, but even so, that one or two will have more confidence in the level of prices being demanded if the catalogue has been published. Items offered for sale may be described at great length or very briefly; illustrated or not; numbered or not; their previous owners may be mentioned or, especially in the case of their last owners, not; they may be priced or (more rarely) not. The catalogue may be compiled by the bookseller named on its cover or titlepage or by someone quite different; it may be issued by one bookseller or by two or three acting together; it may contain the stock of just one seller or items contributed by other dealers or collectors. The catalogue may consist of one or of many different parts, issued at the same or at different times. The books in the catalogue may genuinely be for sale, or may already have been sold (and marked or not marked as such in the catalogue). The dealer may intend to sell items individually or in small groups, or he may hope to sell the entire catalogue to one buyer. The books in the catalogue may represent the sort of stock which the dealer might like to think he should have for sale but has not, or they may represent an elaborate joke on the dealer's behalf. Second-hand books may be combined with new books and remainders or not: items may all be of about the same price or the cheap and the costly may be mixed promiscuously to form what Peter Opie called 'mishy-mashy catalogues'.[8] Booksellers may do all their trading by catalogues; alternatively, catalogues may play a comparatively unimportant part in their business.

The advent of email has meant that catalogues do not necessarily have to take a tangible form – Adam Mills, for example, emailed catalogues to customers as attachments. Internet search engines for books, such as abebooks, have allowed customers to browse a bookseller's stock, which can be arranged into different subjects, each one of which is called a 'catalogue'. Equally, booksellers may use their websites to publish their catalogues, alerting customers to new material by email. The internet has allowed booksellers to describe more items at greater length (often with digital images of the item in question) but lower cost than in a paper catalogue and to reach an international audience. The purchaser can look at an almost infinite number of descriptions and compare prices at a glance – something which has had the effect of driving prices of some sorts of books, particularly academic ones, down. However, there is little pleasure to be had from reading descriptions on the internet; in addition to this there is an occasional anxiety about the security of paying for material, and a more frequent concern with the accuracy of descriptions of books, especially their condition. Selling books at an electronic distance to an unknown clientele requires quite different abilities from those involved in compiling a pleasing catalogue for an established list of collectors.

Where are catalogues?

The ethereal nature of electronic catalogues makes them particularly elusive for collectors and scholars who want to trace specific items or look at more general trends: there one day, they are gone the next. The situation for paper and ink catalogues is in many ways not very much better.

Generally speaking, institutions such as libraries, especially ones far from major dealers, tend to buy from catalogues or from dealers' quotations, while individual collectors tend to like browsing shelves. When booksellers' catalogues arrive in libraries they are often used by staff; for that reason they are not always preserved and, if they are kept, tend themselves to be poorly catalogued or not catalogued at all. Any attempt to recover the total output of catalogues by British antiquarian and second-hand booksellers in the twentieth century is problematic and almost certainly impossible. Libraries would be the obvious places to start. The main collections in the British Library, at Cambridge (especially in the Munby collection), Oxford, and elsewhere are well described by David Pearson, the pioneer in this field.[9] The holdings of British catalogues in libraries in the United States remain a more or less unexplored subject, but there are substantial numbers in such obvious places as the Grolier Club, New York, the Folger Shakespeare Library, Washington, DC, and so on.[10] A substantial number of the catalogues owned by the Dutch booksellers' association and deposited in Amsterdam University Library were issued by British booksellers. These have been described in some detail; an earlier catalogue describes a smaller selection of non-Dutch items with, for example, an almost complete list of the catalogues of G.H. Last of Bromley (1916-30).[11] British booksellers' catalogues in the Belgian Royal Library have been catalogued by Jeanne Blogie.[12] Some investigation of what is available can be undertaken through internet search engines such as COPAC or individual library catalogues, but these need to be used with care since they rarely distinguish between series of catalogues and individual items or between booksellers' and auctioneers' catalogues.

Catalogues themselves are by no means easy to catalogue. There is often a maddening confusion about different parts of catalogues and their relation to the bookseller's numerical sequence (if that exists). The difficulty can be further complicated by the habit of issuing lists, bulletins, and supplementary catalogues, as well as of starting (and not always keeping to) new and subsidiary series of catalogues and of renaming series. Especially in hard times booksellers sometimes change their names and identities, so that it is not always easy to be certain how a run of catalogues issued in one name relates to another in a similar or different name. Furthermore, many booksellers prefer not to date their catalogues accurately or at all – the absence of dates may be unintentional or deliberate so that customers will have no sense of when the catalogue was really published, only of when they received it or picked it up at a shop or fair. Reading a catalogue from G.V.M. Heap in a state of high excitement and anxiety Peter Opie recorded that 'The list had come by second-class mail, the postmark was indecipherable, I had no way of knowing how long it had been in the post.'[13] There are ways of dating undated catalogues: by the most recently published book in the catalogue or advertisements for them; by changes in address and the forms telephone numbers and addresses (post codes) take; by the presence or absence of telegraphic or email addresses, of references to VAT; by prices before and after the introduction of decimal currency and by exchange rates, especially of the dollar. (See Appendix 2, 'A Note on the Dating of Catalogues'.)

The other obvious way to explore the subject is by investigating not what survives but what catalogues were issued. Again, David Pearson points out the best sources for this: the catalogues mentioned in journals and noticed by *Notes and Queries* between 1903 and 1946; the seventeen issues of the *Book-Collectors' Quarterly* (1930-35), containing a section called 'The Booksellers' Register'; the 'News and Comment' essays in the *Book Collector* (from 1966), and the catalogues noticed in *Antiquarian Book Review* (formerly *Antiquarian Book Monthly Review*) since 1975.[14] To these sources might be added the occasional advertisements in journals such as *The Times Literary Supplement* and trade publications such as *Book Prices Current* and *Book Auction Records*. These would also help to establish a list of British booksellers at work between 1906 and 2006, but they would still not supply a complete account of them. There are useful directories and guides to book dealers published by the ABA, PBFA, by Sheppard Press from the 1950s, The Clique from at least the 1960s, by Gerald Coe in 1967, the Coles in the 1980s, and so on, but these can only be partial accounts of the trade as a whole and information about which firms issued catalogues is not always forthcoming.

In a trade in which anyone can set up as a bookseller for a few years or even months and issue just one catalogue, it is not surprising that it is unknown how many booksellers there are or have been at any one time or how many issued catalogues. In 1855 *Notes and Queries* recorded the existence of 104 second-hand booksellers in the United Kingdom, of which 37 issued catalogues; in 1870 John Power printed a list of just over 500 dealers in old books, of which about 170 issued catalogues – around two-thirds of the last group in London.[15] The directory issued by the International Association of Antiquarian Booksellers for 1921 also lists just under 500 booksellers in Britain, with just over 150 in London. The third edition of a similar directory, published by the ABA for 1932, lists around 640 booksellers, with just over 200 of them in London. Unfortunately, neither of these directories says which firms issued catalogues.

Several lists of the more prominent book dealers exist.[16] A further source for the history of the trade can be found in catalogues relating to bibliography and book collecting, which describe either the history of the business and its catalogues or the catalogues of another dealer.[17] The following sketch of the subject can do no more than scratch the surface and is largely based on material in the author's own haphazard collection.

II

It was the proud boast of the firm of E. Joseph that since 1936 it had issued no catalogues for 40 years.[18] In the general scheme of bookselling issuing catalogues may be a sign of desperation or of worldly success. There is always something to be learned by looking at catalogues; reading them can in itself change what is sold, collected, or studied and how selling, collecting, and academic research are carried out. In rare cases catalogues can even provoke writers to fits of imaginative creation. Lionel Johnson wrote a poem, 'Ballade of the Caxton Head', to celebrate the publication of James Tregaskis's 900th catalogue; the manuscript of it was reproduced photographically c.1930, presumably by the firm.[19] An unidentified bookseller's catalogue served as the inspiration for the play *Meeting Point* by June Braybrooke (1920-94), who wrote under the pseudonym 'Isobel English'.[20] However, catalogues do not emerge in a vacuum, and the following section will describe the progress of catalogues through some of their different stages.[21]

Sources

Booksellers have tended to be cautious about identifying the immediate sources of the books in their catalogues. If they are issuing what is in effect a stock list, this information would be difficult to compile and not very interesting to the potential purchaser. In more specialized catalogues the information may be suppressed so that buyers cannot easily trace an individual book or a group of books from a collection from one dealer's catalogue to another or back to the auction house to see what sort of profit the dealer is making. In any case interest in a book's provenance – beyond medieval manuscripts, incunabula, and association copies – is a relatively recent phenomenon in the trade and among collectors.

Nevertheless there are some exceptions to this reluctance to name sources. This was the case with the catalogues of the libraries of scholars and writers issued by firms in university towns such as Blackwell's and Heffer's. For example, Blackwell's catalogue 187 (1922) advertised itself as made up of the bulk of the library of Sir Walter Raleigh, with a photograph of the professor of English Literature on the upper cover; Heffer's catalogue 7 (1971) offered the library of E.M. Forster. However, as scholars have become less able to build up notable libraries and as booksellers have become more wary of identifying their immediate sources of supply, the sale of large, named collections has declined. Although Blackwell's sold John Masefield's library in three catalogues (858 (1968), 867 (1969), 896 (1970)) and Dennis Wheatley's in one (A1136 (1979)), reprinting most of his notes and annotations, among the last named academic libraries they sold by this means were those of Percy Simpson and H.W. Garrod in catalogue 749 (1962). In the famous case of the sales of part of A.E. Housman's library by Blackwell's (included in catalogues 395 (1936), 403 (1937)) the firm named him as owner at the start of the catalogue, but followed his wishes by erasing his marks of ownership, including annotations.[22]

Some more general dealers have been willing to state where they bought what they offered for sale – a practice related to the development of single-author collections. There was nothing especially new about these when they were devoted to contemporary writers, the process beginning with the sale of the author's manuscripts, correspondence, and library. Bertram Dobell's catalogue *Browning Memorials* [1913] is an early example of a catalogue devoted to a single author. What he offered for sale was 'purchased at the recent dispersal of the Browning Collections' at Sotheby's in May 1913 and he gave a long account of his finds among the lots he bought.[23] Catalogue 4 (1920) of Everard Meynell's The Serendipity Shop contained the library, manuscripts and correspondence of Coventry Patmore.[24] A measure of the precocious ambition and financial problems of 'John Gawsworth' (Terence Ian Fitton Armstrong) can be seen in Bertram Rota's catalogue 25 (1933), which contained the twenty-one year old's 'Personal Library', along with a sketch of him by Tristram Rainey. Francis Edwards (624 (1938)) was able to offer books and manuscripts from the library of J.M. Barrie. From a later period, Gilbert Foyle issued three catalogues between 1949 and 1951 containing the remains of Henry James's library after the bombing of Lamb House in Rye.[25] Similar sorts of catalogues have contained David Garnett's library (Michael Hosking at the Golden Hind Bookshop, catalogue 22 (1983), with an introduction by Nicolas Barker), and several from Bertram Rota, such as the special catalogue of the Herbert M. Schimmel collection of Noël Coward (1997) and the more frequent catalogues of books belonging to V.S. Pritchett (292 (2000)), John Ryder (295 (2001)), and Simon Nowell-Smith (300 (2002)). The firm has been especially associated with the sale of what can amount to a contemporary literary archive.[26] Its other side was the ready-made collection of a single-author's works, a practice Elkin Mathews developed in its catalogues, which offered the opportunity to create research collections of great authors from the past. Less scholarly accumulations might relate to more recent authors: probably the outstanding example of this was Winston Churchill. As early as 1950 Charles J. Sawyer in catalogue 203 had a complete set of Churchill's major writings and some pamphlets in 42 volumes in original bindings for sale at £195.

In other, more general, cases the source of the material on sale would be mentioned as part of its attractiveness, especially if, having been bought at auction, it was already in the public domain. Sotheran's Piccadilly Series 67 [c.1920] had books on the fine arts from the libraries of Sir Edward J. Poynter and William Michael Rossetti. Books from the library of Edmond Bonnet featured in Quaritch 382 (1924), from the genealogist George W. Marshall in 656 (1948), and from the cactus expert R. King Byrd in 663 (1949). W.H. Robinson 12 (1925) contained books for the most part from the library of Newburgh Priory, Yorkshire, and later catalogues, such as 19 (1928), with books from the Huth, Hoe and Britwell libraries, also advertised their sources. Charles J. Sawyer 91 (1928) had over twenty books from the library of David Garrick, 'purchased at the recent sale of effects of the late Major Henry Edward Trevor', the actor's great-great-nephew and, rather unexpectedly, their catalogue 120 (1934) had a 'Supplement of Books from Lord Northcliffe's Library'. In the next year Pickering and Chatto offered books from the library of Edward Gibbon (catalogue 289) and Bernard Halliday 191 (1935) had over a dozen from Arnold Bennett's. The firm offered early seventeenth-century books from the Duke of Newcastle's library at Clumber in 226 (1938) and their catalogue 237 (1939) contained Shakespeariana owned by J.O. Halliwell-Phillipps. Maggs seem to have been much more relaxed about mentioning sources in their series of *Mercurius Britannicus* catalogues, begun in 1933, than in their main series. The previous owners of quite a few scientific libraries were named when their collections were sold: for example, Dulau disposed of part of the library of the botanist G.C. Druce in 1942 and Quaritch had a series of similar collections of books in the 1930s and 1940s. After the war Charles W. Traylen offered the Wentworth Woodhouse library in two portions (catalogues 14, 21) in 1949 and 1951. Ernst Weil catalogue 23 [1956], *Astronomy, Navigation, Astronomical Instruments*, was concerned with sixteenth- and seventeenth-century books from the Nordkirchen Library, and in 1983 George's catalogue 666 described Chatsworth books. In all of these instances a general statement of who had previously owned the books offered for sale helped give them a fine pedigree and some sort of guarantee of condition and genuineness: thus Dulau's catalogue 144 (1926) proudly announced on its titlepage that it included duplicates from the library of John Drinkwater and beautifully bound French books owned by the former Brazilian Ambassador to Washington, the late Domicio da Gama.

In the past few years there has been something of a revival of interest in offering catalogues devoted to an individual's books. G. Heywood Hill have made a speciality of this with catalogues of books from particular libraries (with appropriate introductions and codewords for orders), including John Fuggles (Spring 2003: 'Trust'), Enoch Powell (introduction by Simon Heffer: 'Intellect'), A.L. Rowse (parts 1, 2 and 2½: 'Tamar', 'Thames', and 'Animation'; part 2 with an introduction by Richard Ollard), Jack Simmons (introduction by J. Mordaunt Crook: 'Britannia'), Sir Stephen Tumim ('Garrick') and John Cornforth ('Country Life'). More unusually, the various collections made by Hugh Trevor-Roper (Lord Dacre) were divided between several dealers: Heywood Hill had general books (2004, with an introduction by Jeremy Catto: 'Mercurius'), E.M. Lawson 312 (2004) had antiquarian books, while Toby English catalogue 29 had 'The Working Library' followed by catalogue 30 (2005) 'The Third Reich, Intelligence and Espionage'. Other dealers, including Waterfields with the libraries of Vivienne (later Vivien) Greene, Owen Barfield, and Christopher Hill, or Bennett and Kerr with many academic collections, have continued to offer this sort of catalogue.

A relatively common practice has been for one bookseller to place books in another's catalogues. This recycling can be sensible when the other bookseller's stock provided a more suitable context for the books, encouraging their sale. Less respectably, putting the same book in several different dealers' catalogues at the same price helped to suggest a 'usual' or fair price for it: by this means a market could be created and even inflated. Equally, collectors who had a good relationship with a dealer might put material they wished to sell in catalogues.

Cataloguing

Although word-processing packages and computer programmes for cataloguing books have made an enormous difference to the production of catalogues, the actual process of writing entries still requires a great deal of time, knowledge, and experience. In the past dealers might keep a set of stock cards for books whose descriptions could be easily recycled (some of Bernard Quaritch's cards, which include clippings from other booksellers' catalogues, are now in the British Library); many dealers now simply download descriptions of books from the internet and alter them as they see fit. For printed catalogues a large number of decisions have to be taken about form, content, and arrangement, all of which depend on the part catalogues play in a dealer's business.

As the last century progressed, fewer dealers, even large ones like Maggs, Pickering and Chatto, Quaritch or Sotheran's, issued general catalogues in which old and relatively new books, cheap and expensive ones, were promiscuously mixed up. The subjects in which booksellers specialized are fairly well known: Myers for autographs, Dobell and later Peter Murray Hill for Restoration and eighteenth-century literature, Rota for modern firsts, Maggs for autographs, travel, and bindings, Weinreb for architectural books, Zwemmer for art books, Weil for medical literature, Dawson for science, Rosenthal for music, and so on. While the larger firms could afford to issue a range of catalogues, each devoted to a particular subject, smaller and successful ones, such as Goldschmidt or Alan Thomas, were free to include anything they liked.

Pioneering catalogues

Some catalogues can be considered pioneering or important because of the splendour of their contents. It was the boast of Sotheran's 1907 catalogue, *Bibliotheca Pretiosa*, offering just under 600 items in a particularly 'choice state', that their total value was about £40,000: the contents largely came from the library of John Gott (1830-1906), and with their sale Sotheran's claimed an 'era will have come to an end'.[27] The larger firms, such as Maggs and Robinson, sometimes dressed their best catalogues in very fine clothes, but there are other ways – for example through outstanding scholarship – in which a catalogue may come to be seen as particularly distinguished. Writing about Quaritch, Nicolas Barker, a connoisseur of the genre, singled out two especially important pre-war catalogues: one, devoted to the Powis and Holford collections of Aldine books (1929) and 436 (1930) the two-part catalogue of English literature before 1700, produced under F.S. Ferguson's supervision.[28] In addition to over 2,000 items the latter contained a particularly fierce note about not using *The Short-Title Catalogue*, to which Ferguson devoted so much of his working time, as a census of extant copies. Among other more recent outstanding Quaritch catalogues, no. 926 (1973) devoted to books and pamphlets from the library of Maurice Buxton Forman had an introduction by Graham Pollard and heavily implicated Harry Buxton Forman in Wise's forgeries. In a different field in 1932 the specialist dealer in oriental books, Arthur Probsthain could say without false (or any) modesty that:

it has been a great satisfaction to have had some of my catalogues favourably reviewed in the best newspaper in England. I have been advised that my catalogue on Pali and Buddhism, for instance, is the best guide to the subject, and my catalogue on China and Chinese literature, consisting of 4,624 items, is supposed to be to-day a vade-mecum to this literature. These catalogues with all the research which they involved have been entirely compiled by myself.[29]

Among other scholarly catalogues which still serve as valuable reference works are ones which are particularly well illustrated, such as Maggs's long series of bindings catalogues (324 (1914), 407 (1921), 489 (1927), 665 (1938), 845 (1957), 893 (1964), 966 (1975), 1014 (1981), 1075 (1987), 1212 (1996)) or Patrick King's catalogues (for example, 8 (1979), 9 (1980)) or Edward Bayntun-Coward's for George Bayntun (for example, 13 (2005)) on the same subject.

Scholarly descriptions of items for sale might be supplemented by booksellers' using their catalogues as independent vehicles for their own researches. An unsigned 'Note on Advertisements', arguing that early, dated adverts do not necessarily indicate priority of issue ('advertisements by themselves signify nothing at all unless accompanied by other "points"'), appears in the preface to *Rare Books in English Literature of the Last Sixty Years* from the First Edition Bookshop, April 1932: it may have been written by A.J.A. Symons. In Dulau's catalogue 144 (1926) there is a brief account of the life and work of the emerging Irish writer Liam O'Flaherty (1896-1984), including an autobiographical note by the author, with a bibliography of first editions. John Carter contributed an introduction 'With Special Reference to Binding Variants' to Elkin Mathews catalogue 48 (September 1932) with two-and-a-half further pages of addenda to his recently published book on the subject (to be continued). Going beyond even the single-author catalogue, Ken Spelman's catalogue 53 (2005) was entirely devoted to editions of Sterne's *A Sentimental Journey*: the catalogue was the work of the Sterne scholar Geoffrey Day and carried a brief introduction by him.

Some booksellers also used their catalogues to publish new and scholarly material which was not directly offered for sale: for example, Frank Benger's catalogue 4 (the first he issued after the Second World War) contains 'A Calendar of References to Sir Thomas Benger', Master of the Revels 1560-72. Bound in at the end of Frank Marcham's account of *William Shakespeare and his Daughter Susannah* (1931) is *A Small Selection of Rare Books and Manuscripts*, listing 53 items from his stock: here it is not entirely clear whether the scholarly account is supplemented by the catalogue or vice-versa. The same overlap occurs with James Stevens-Cox's *The Literary Repository*, which he ran from 1954 to 1975, as 'a quarterly devoted to the printing of unpublished manuscripts and original articles of archaeological, historical, literary, sociological and theological interest', as well as including a catalogue of 'rare and scholarly books' for sale.[30]

In addition to lavish and scholarly catalogues the most obvious way in which dealers could contribute to the development of the trade in books was by opening up new areas for collectors. By Percy Muir's own account the three catalogues issued by Elkin Mathews on the edge of the chasm of the Depression changed the way people thought about collecting English literature. The catalogues (5, 28, 32) were devoted to Samuel Johnson (1925), Byron (January 1930 'the first thing of its kind on anything like the scale in the history of bookselling'), and the early nineteenth century (October 1930). According to Muir, quoting Wilmarth S. Lewis:

It was one thing ... to issue a catalogue of eighteenth-century literature with 'books priced from ten shillings to two guineas which had never appeared in any West End catalogue before'; and quite another to catalogue 'Childe Harold' at £950, the Bristol 'Lyrical Ballads' at £1,100, and 'Guy Mannering' at £385.

None of these last sold at these prices.[31]

Muir was perhaps playing up the novelty of the subject-matter to offset the monstrous prices: Maggs 382 (1919) was devoted to the eighteenth century, and this was the field in which Dobell dealt – Dobell's five-part catalogue of eighteenth-century verse (99, 102, 122, 128, 133) extended to 3,216 items.

Just as some dealers sought to promote the relatively neglected eighteenth-century field for collectors, others saw the importance of, for example, authors' original manuscripts. This is the explicit aim of J. Pearson and Co.'s catalogue of *Rare and Valuable Autograph Letters, Historical Documents and Authors' Original Manuscripts*. On the wrappers of the catalogue there are quotations relating to the subject from *The Connoisseur* (October 1907) and *The Observer* (October 1909), the latter stating that since 'The typewriter has superseded the pen', 'the personal interest' attached to an original manuscript will disappear and typewritten copies 'would not have any special attraction, unless' bearing the author's autograph corrections.

One convenient way of charting the development of new subjects for collectors is through the complete lists of catalogues (issued during similar periods) that have been published for Maggs and Blackwell's – two very different booksellers. Blackwell's stock until the 1960s was on the whole academic and the business naturally included catalogues or sections of catalogues devoted to science, political science, 'Orientalia', and more occasionally the fine and applied arts. The first major English author mentioned by name as forming a distinct collection in a catalogue is, intriguingly enough, Alexander Pope in 260 (1929), followed the next year in 262 by Byron. Catalogues solely devoted to bibliography and palaeography (568) were first issued in 1951, to criminology (621) in 1955, to colour-plate and illustrated books (731) in 1961 and to antiquarian music (734) in the same year. The 1969 catalogue devoted to transport and technology (865) was particularly striking both for its design and contents. After Pope and Byron, arguably no single-author catalogue was issued again, although there was a catalogue in 1973 (988) devoted to the Powys family; catalogues containing material relating to T.E. Lawrence in 1975 (1018), Norman Douglas (A1064) and Robert Graves (A1073) in the next year, and then to both Henry James and D.H.

Lawrence (A1101) in 1978, mixed together items by those authors with other rare modern books. It also has to be borne in mind that books in Blackwell's catalogues were generally described in two or three lines so that a catalogue of as many as 1,500 items might fill only 30 or 40 pages.

The catalogues Maggs issued between 1918 and 1968 present rather a different picture. However, the firm did not issue its first single-author catalogues until 1936. In that year they had one in their main series devoted to Milton (620), largely from Hugh C.H. Candy's library, and special catalogues of Arnold Bennett's manuscripts, autograph manuscript material relating to T.E. Lawrence, and in 1937 to Elizabeth Barrett Browning. In the following year there were two catalogues (663, 664) devoted to Kipling and Hardy, but then a long interval until Johnson (809) in 1952, Voltaire (910) in 1967, and the next year Rousseau (914) – both these last were compiled by Clare Lightfoot. Before this in 1956 the firm had issued an unusual catalogue (837), consisting entirely of books from the library of Edward Herbert, Lord Herbert of Cherbury. In 1923 on the tercentenary of the First Folio the firm issued a Shakespeare catalogue (434) which it claimed was 'the most extensive that has yet been attempted by a Bookseller', describing 1,042 items; a similar catalogue (493) four years later ran to 1,383 items. The main series of catalogues of English literature before 1800 began in 1922 with two volumes (422-3) containing over 2,300 items. Between 1946 and 1958 the firm could still produce two sets of catalogues, each of seven parts, covering books before 1800, the first (750, 754, 770, 781, 786, 793, 800) with over 3,000 items, the next (817, 826, 834, 841, 848, 851, 858) with over 3,500. A third series in seven parts (865, 874, 882, 887, 895, 901, 906) contained 3,800 items and took eight years to complete.

Maggs issued some less conventional catalogues and sought to develop new subjects for collectors. In more or less chronological order these might include: *Bibliotheca Aëronautica*, 387 (1920), 'Probably the first Aeronautical Catalogue issued by an antiquarian bookseller'; association and presentation copies, 406 (1921); medicine and alchemy, 410 (1921), and Judaica and Hebraica, 419 (1922). Catalogue 437 (1923) included Indian and Persian miniatures, while 440 in the same year had a supplement of books on printing, bibliographies, and so on; the firm's first full bibliography catalogue did not appear until 468 (1925). Catalogue 451 (1924) described authors' original manuscripts and in the same year 453 was a catalogue of incunabula of which, according to Goff's *Census*, there was no copy in the United States. The firm issued a second catalogue of this kind, 704, *A Catalogue of Fifty Incunabula not in America* (1941), according to Goff's second *Census*: both were presumably aimed at the American market. Before that in 1930 Maggs continued the incunabular theme with catalogue 533, *Bibliotheca Incunabulorum*; this consisted of 113 items (a second part covering the rest of Europe was never issued), and was preceded by a map of fifteenth-century continental printing with towns represented in the catalogue marked in red. An appended slip stated that 'An additional copy of the Frontispiece Map, without any red printing, will be supplied to clients desirous of marking in red the towns represented in their own Collections of Incunabula.' The catalogue also contained a brief section of 'Suggestions for Incunabula Collecting' for 'the collector whose taste is for the earliest printed books', but who evidently did not know what to collect.

The firm's first music catalogue, 512 (1928), included books from the library of Dr Werner Wolffheim sold in Berlin in the same year, while 520 (1929) was concerned with medicine, alchemy, astrology, and the natural sciences (1253 items). In 1931 catalogue 564, represented a new departure for the firm, with books on architecture, costume, furniture, gardens, and ornament: it would have been still relatively unusual in the trade at that time. Even more original – however clichéd it may now appear – was 574 (1932) *A Catalogue of Strange Books and Curious Titles*, which was headed (opposite Tenniel's illustration of Alice with her elongated neck) '*"Curiouser and Curiouser!" – cried Alice*'. Food and drink, 645 (1937), including books from the library of the Parisian restaurateur Robert Viel, may seem hackneyed to modern dealers and collectors, but is one of the first British catalogues concerned with the subject: it is still cited in standard bibliographies. (Birrell & Garnett's catalogue 37 also devoted to cookery books (from the collections of J.E. Hodgkin and A.W. Oxford) had appeared in about 1931.) Harder-edged subjects from the late 1930s to which Maggs devoted catalogues of their own included economics 658 (1938), slavery 677 (1939), and law 680 (1939). The firm gave over a whole catalogue, 689 (1940), to '*Thrillers' of the Victorian Age, Comprising 'Penny Dreadfuls' Loved by Schoolboys and Similar Literature for their Elders*, and followed it in the same year with one devoted to cartography (693). Finally, from a modern perspective it is interesting to notice, *Women in Literature: A Catalogue of Books by or about Women*, 829 (1955), which, despite its winsomely off-putting title, '*Shall We Join the Ladies*', was an imaginative development for such a smart West End dealer.

Names and titles

Maggs's periodic fondness for playful and allusive titles reflected a desire to escape the purely functional forms of most dealers' catalogue titles. The firm regularly employed series of catalogues, such as Autograph Letters & Historical Documents, a European Bulletin, and Voyages & Travels, which began with 638 (1937) and eventually reached fifty parts. One of their most celebrated series, begun in 1933, was called *Mercurius Britannicus, or Mercuries Swift Messenger*. Other firms also issued subsidiary series under similar short titles: catalogues designated periodicals enjoyed a lower rate of postage than catalogues deemed to be advertising. Sotheran's monthly *Price Current of Literature* was begun in 1845 and continued until 1958; a further series of *Piccadilly Notes* started in 1933. Pickering and Chatto's *The Book-Lover's Leaflet* dated from 1886. Colbeck Radford & Co., in which P.J. and A.E. Dobell were partners during the 1930s, issued catalogues of autograph letters and manuscripts under the title *The Ingatherer*.[32] Arnold Muirhead's minor series of catalogues, issued from 83 Limes Avenue in north London, was called *The Lime Tree Miscellany*. More recently

Jarndyce issued a series of catalogues (for example, 67 (1989-90), 136 (2000), 156 (2003-4)) under the title, taken from Quaritch's earlier lists, 'The Museum'. 'Second-string' catalogues might take a separate physical form: until about 1994 Claude Cox used to add a loosely inserted Supplement, printed on thinner paper, of cheaper items. In the nineteenth century some booksellers modestly described their catalogues as 'rough lists', as if they would be later worked up into full-dress descriptions. From the 1890s until at least c.1912 Pickering and Chatto bound up their catalogues in hard covers and, by adding a new titlepage, formed substantial and well-illustrated volumes: the firm still modestly referred to the contents as 'This rough list'. Titles might also range from the pompous to the mildly pretentious: Charles J. Sawyer's catalogue 125 (1935) was called *An Imposing Collection of Books Issued During the Last Four Hundred Years*, while Birrell & Garnett's catalogue 30 [c.1930] had the title largely in roman capitals ranged top left on an otherwise blank cover: 'LIBRI SCIENTIFICI | PROSTANT VENALES | Apud BIRRELL & GARNETT'.

Similarly, cables and telegraphic addresses (as well as code words for orders from a particular catalogue) varied between the obvious, the imaginative and the facetious. Voynich employed the address 'Sessa', perhaps after the Venetian family of printers, 'Vespucci' served for Charles J. Sawyer, Pickering and Chatto appropriated 'Lycidas' and Otto Haas used 'Solmifa'. Plain 'Bibliograph' was used by Martin Breslauer, 'Bibliopole' by Tobias Rodgers, and 'Finality' by Francis Edwards, while Louis Bondy advertised his own speciality with 'Miniliber' and George McLeish alluded to his name and address with 'Skotusbuk, Hammer [later, 'Estrand'] London'. In Newcastle W.H. Robinson were simply 'Books, Newcastle-on-Tyne'; when they moved to Pall Mall in London they became, rather more pretentiously, 'Fineboke, Piccy, London'. Winifred Myers claimed to be 'Unique' while H.W. Edwards of Newbury gloried in 'Dryasdust'. The choice of code-words for ordering books from catalogues also gave similar scope for invention and to cite only one example, Roy Davids used 'Gobbet'.

Arrangement

Catalogue entries can be arranged in any number of ways – alphabetically, by date, by subject, by printer or place of publication (the Bradshaw-Proctor method), and so on. Each arrangement has its advantages and disadvantages. An unbroken alphabetical sequence does not stimulate readers to look beyond their immediate interests; arranging entries by subject-matter is potentially confusing and risks what Quaritch (1034 (1983)) once called 'taxonomical distinctions' of which the reader may not approve. 'We beg pardon,' says the preface to Marlborough Rare Books 71 (1972), *A Touchstone for the Arts*,

for the somewhat haphazard arrangement, which despite the problems of overlapping subjects, is mainly due to the incompetence of the compiler, who, nevertheless, hopes that it may compel the reader to wade right through, instead of dipping in here and there. (There is an index.)

Indexes certainly help to find books, especially when a catalogue has been issued in several parts, although most indexes are of authors or titles only and rarely mention, among others, binders, previous owners, and printers. One ingenious way of distinguishing between parts of a catalogue was used by Simon Gough in at least two stock lists (2 (1982) and 4 (1984)), with sections printed on different coloured papers. Traditionally, booksellers liked to arrange their catalogues by century, but the growing scarcity of earlier books meant that few dealers could show a respectable display of items before 1700 or even 1800: in 1974 Peter Opie recorded receiving 'a catalogue from George's divided – most unusually these days – into sixteenth century books, seventeenth century books, and eighteenth century books'.[33]

Descriptions

In their catalogue descriptions dealers have a chance to show their bibliographical knowledge, their discriminating taste, or a mixture of these. A good description (and mailing list) can find a buyer for a hard-to-sell book. This is what the Parisian dealer André Poursin characterized as 'selling catalogue slips rather than books'.[34] There is, no doubt, an art to writing catalogue entries which involves explaining why a book is being offered at a particular price. Issues of historical or personal importance, rarity, and condition all come into this, along with a question-able host of bibliographical references and booksellers' abbreviations and conventions.

There was perhaps no subject which exercised dealers and collectors more between the wars than condition. At first sight it might seem to apply mainly to modern first editions but, with tastes changing away from wholesale rebinding, it also affected older books. 'All Books are in the original publisher's binding', Ingpen and Stonehill announced in their *First Editions of Modern Authors*, NS 17 (1930), 'most are in finest possible state'. 'We wish to draw the attention of our readers to the fact that we specialise in Books in the finest possible condition', the First Edition Bookshop maintained in *A Catalogue of Rare Books of English Literature in the Last Fifty Years* (June 1931). In the same year, showing the immediate effects of the Depression, Bertram Rota's catalogue 19 offered on its titlepage 'an Extensive Collection of Modern First Editions Offered at Remark-ably Low Prices', varying the description with the running-title at the head of each page 'First Editions in Original Bindings'. The concern with condition was reflected in the nice discriminations which dealers made (and still make) between what they mean by 'fine' or 'very good' and how these terms are generally understood. John Carter's *ABC for Book Collectors*, first published in 1952, had a great influence for the good in helping to promote some sort of general agreement about their meanings. Yet the concern with condition was not limited to modern books. It is still surprising to read in W.H. Robinson's catalogue 12 (1925) that 'Every Collector realises that an old book should be in an old binding, preferably that in which the volume was originally issued', but this was written when the appetite for eighteenth- and early- nineteenth-century books in their original boards was at its height. Nevertheless, as an axiom marking the end of an age of surrender to morocco, it is worth noting.

In describing books dealers could draw on a whole range of abbreviations and codes which applied to condition ('vg in dw') or referred readers to standard reference works ('Proctor', '*GKW*', 'ESTC', and so on). In both cases, there may have been an element of deliberate mystification about these rather indigestible mouthfuls, a desire to make the reader feel part of a coterie and in the know, or simply a desire for scholarly accuracy. The ever-increasing number of reference works allowed dealers to demonstrate they had done their homework and, perhaps, to show off their own reference libraries. A more charitable explanation would be that shorthand saved space in catalogues. The general rule for most dealers must presumably have been that the cheaper the book the less time and space should be given to its cataloguing. 'With a superb disregard of commercial value,' Sarah de Laredo at Maggs 'would do as long a note, amounting often to an essay, for a book worth two or three guineas as for one valued at several hundred'.[35] This may have resulted in excellent reading, been satisfying for the dealer in leaving a more permanent record of his work, and helped collectors to decide which catalogues to keep and which to discard, but publishing catalogues for instruction and entertainment was beyond the means of most dealers. There was also a danger in over-describing a book and leaving the potential purchaser with nothing to find out about it for himself. Conversely, the pleasures and risks of buying underdescribed books are well evoked by Peter Opie in relation to G.V.M. Heap's stencilled lists, as being 'like taking tickets in a lottery'.[36]

Developments in enumerative and descriptive bibliography during the last century were of extraordinary value to booksellers, who themselves contributed a great deal to the subject. It could be argued that the concern which flourished between the wars with 'points' sometimes (or often) signified that dealers lacked an entirely firm grasp of how books were produced and what the real implications of those minute features might be. In some newer fields of collecting, such as colour plate books, reference to standard catalogues might serve to validate the whole enterprise (if it was good enough for Major Abbey ...), show that a work was complete, that it had an unusual feature, such as an uncalled-for plate, or that it had escaped previous bibliographers. Especially with the development of online catalogues it became possible for dealers to give a fairly convincing account of a book's rarity: the familiar 'No copy has appeared at auction during the last twenty years' was replaced by details of how many copies are recorded in North America and in Great Britain. Catalogues, such as *STC*, Wing, *GKW*, which included lists of known copies, allowed dealers to press claims for the rarity of a particular book (often on very shaky grounds, as Ferguson pointed out in his Quaritch catalogue) or to indicate the pressing need, usually for an American library or collector, to buy the book. Citations from old editions of reference works might simply reflect what books of this kind were in a dealer's own collection, but they might also result from a wish to put a volume in the best possible commercial light.

The use dealers made of reference works was by no means uniform. To give only one example: although dated on its titlepage 1926, the *Short-Title Catalogue of English Books 1475-1640* was published early in 1927, which was also when R.S. Crane and F.B. Kaye's *Census of British Newspapers and Periodicals 1620-1800* was issued; by the end of the year, in their December catalogue 17, Birrell & Garnett noted in a preface their use of both works, adding references to them for particular items. By contrast Maggs seems only to have started paying proper attention to *STC* in catalogue 691 in 1940.

Personal notes

Although many dealers' catalogues maintained a studied impersonality – the mask at Quaritch, for example, rarely slipped in the last century and dreary manilla covers were abandoned for something less austere only in the early 1970s – others were generous with making their own presence felt. Complaints about the cost of issuing catalogues often revealed a fiery personality. 'The printing and posting of my Rough Lists is a considerable expense to me', Bernard Quaritch's catalogues announced on their front covers during his lifetime and shortly after, 'I therefore appeal to the recipients to favour me occasionally with an order, otherwise the sending of these Catalogues must be suspended.' John Metcalfe-Morton of Ye olde Booke Shoppe in Brighton (motto: 'Be Square without being Angular' – Lao-Tzu) had a box with this plaintive message printed at the top of the titlepage:

WILL YOU DO THIS, PLEASE?
When you have ordered all the books you want this time, if you have a friend who is also interested, he will thank you to pass this list along to him – and so will Yours Truly. As costs of production are so heavy, if this is the first catalogue of mine that you have received will you kindly say if you wish to have further issues as published, in order that I may register your address.[37]

Both of these are positively mild compared to the much fiercer message in bold capitals from Arthur Rogers of Newcastle-on-Tyne in about 1951:

This catalogue is not only expensive to print, but has only been produced as a result of very many hours of hard work – sometimes pleasant work – sometimes forced drudgery – on my part. Please do not waste it.

Of course, what lay behind these pleas was the expense of sending catalogues to customers who may have read and enjoyed them, but never ordered anything. As the Covent Garden Bookshop put it in catalogue 56 [1974]:

We will therefore assume that customers who receive two subsequent Catalogues without placing an order do not wish to remain on our mailing list unless they specifically notify us. This of course does not apply to Institutions and Libraries.

In capital letters Bernard Halliday's catalogue 92 (1927) betrayed an anxiety that its recipients would not even bother to read it: 'Attention is drawn to the exceedingly varied and interesting nature of the contents of this catalogue, which will well repay perusal.'

Dealers often used catalogues to indulge their journalistic abilities and, it was hoped in the process, entertain their readers. Claude Cox's catalogues are still notable for their discursive paragraphs on the inside of the upper cover and in the 1970s and 1980s Sanders of Oxford had a series of 'Fables for Bibliophiles', followed by 'True Tales for Bibliophiles', on their wrappers. The practice of including these sorts of pieces can be dated to before the Second World War: Sotheran's *Piccadilly Notes* contained a series of 'Adventures in Bookselling', edited by J.H. Stonehouse. More unusually, in their catalogues during the 1980s Any Amount of Books set competitions and literary quizzes with book prizes, a practice continued by Peter Stockham.

Other substantial prose matter might take the form of an introduction or preface to the catalogue, extolling its merits, by an invited contributor. Edmund Blunden, John Carter, Winston Churchill, Holbrook Jackson, Michael Sadleir, and H.M. Tomlinson wrote prefaces for Elkin Mathews catalogues.[38] The witty doctor and natural historian Philip Gosse (1879-1959) contributed a preface to Maggs catalogue 630 (1936), *A Gallery of Rogues*. Bertram Rota also made something of a practice of inviting suitable experts to write prefaces to catalogues: Sir John Betjeman for Rota at the bookshop of Frank Hollings for a catalogue (NS 3 (1970)) of nineteenth-century verse, Edward Lucie-Smith for two catalogues of modern poetry (143 (1966), 155 (1968)), the Pre-Raphaelite expert William Fredeman for 180 (1973) Rossetti family books, and the historian Keith Simpson for 245 (1988), the Great War. In the same way Paul Grinke's first solo catalogue (1984), devoted to Suffolk, was introduced by J.M. Blatchly. On other occasions a prominent collector might introduce a special catalogue; for example, A. Edward Newton wrote a 'Prolegomenon' to the thousandth Caxton Head catalogue in 1931 and Lord Wardington performed this task for Charles W. Traylen's hundredth catalogue in 1985. Not all such associations with writers of whatever eminence were successful. Maggs's catalogue 860 (1959), *Plays of the Palmy Days*, reproduced a postcard from George Bernard Shaw refusing permission for the firm to issue a catalogue of plays (775, published as 'The Play's the Thing') in 1948 under the title *Plays Pleasant and Unpleasant*. In the catalogue preface Maggs lament, 'We wish now that we had pursued the matter further, and possibly elicited further letters of a like nature.'

More personal elements could be briefer than a preface. For example, Traylen's catalogue 9 [*c*.1947] was dedicated to Charles P. Porter 'who at Cambridge, in 1923, fostered my career as a Bookseller' and Thomas Thorp of London's catalogue 434 (1981) announced the birth of a child. Yet the main place for personal remarks was in the catalogue descriptions themselves. One example must stand for thousands: after a description of Richard Oke's *Frolic Wind* (1929), first edition signed by the author for two guineas, G.F. Sims, catalogue 59 (October 1964) noted 'About fifteen years ago we foolishly said that this book was "neglected", posing as critics instead of booksellers. Now we merely state that it is a nice copy in a faded d.w.' Dr Andrew Jones's catalogues, mainly devoted to history, frequently contain thoughtful and acerbic comments on books and individuals, as well as the occasional invented title. In extreme cases the whole or much of a catalogue might be given over to the dealer's idiosyncratic views. This was the case with the celebrated 1932 catalogue from the Ulysses Bookshop issued by Jacob Schwartz in which some books were priced at the level – pennies and halfpennies – he thought they actually deserved in relation to literary merit.[39]

Some booksellers clearly enjoyed ruling their own literary empires. C.S. Millard printed customers' comments about previous catalogues: 'Prices more reasonable than usual. – Wimbledon' or 'Your preposterous prices. – New York'.[40] Alan Thomas had fairly robust political views, for example complaining in 1980 about the imposition of VAT at 15 per cent on unbound documents: 'This does seem a perversion of the intention of Parliament ... It cannot have been in the minds of those who framed the act that scholarship should be taxed' (catalogue 41 (1980)). A more plangent note was sounded in Marlborough Rare Books catalogue 71 (1972), *A Touchstone for the Arts, being a Catalogue of Manuals, Treatises, Drawing Books, Pattern Books, Price Books and Trade Catalogues Relating to the Fine and Applied Arts*: 'If this catalogue should lead to the publication of just one bibliography, it will have been to some purpose.' George Sims used to preface his catalogues with a few literary quotations, usually of a fairly morbid kind; Roy Davids's prefatory quotations were of a more familiar kind, but might include specimens of his own poetry. More conventionally, the back wrappers of a catalogue supplied a useful place where dealers could advertise for books they wanted, as Bernard Halliday (188 (1935)) and Charles J. Sawyer (188 (1948)) both did.

Events

Even before the Depression, economic events regularly affected dealers and figured explicitly in their catalogues. As early as 1909 in 'Forewords' to a *Catalogue of Old English Literature* Francis Edwards sought to explain why some old books were so expensive and to reassure purchasers that they would hold their value: 'the millions of our race and speech in America and elsewhere are realizing that these works are quite as much their heritage as ours, and are claiming their share of it'. Less happily, paper rationing during the First World War meant that only catalogues requested by customers could be sent out: James Wilson of Birmingham informed customers of this change, issuing reply cards for requesting future issues.[41]

After the Wall Street Crash, in May 1931 Myers & Co. published a *Special Clearance catalogue of Old & Modern Books ... with a few Autograph Letters offered at Extremely Low Prices* (279). In October of that year the First Edition Bookshop added a note to *Rare Books in English Literature of the Last Sixty Years*: 'To bring ourselves into line with the present financial slump and purchasing depression in all countries, our stock has been heavily marked down ... Now is the time for collectors to fill their shelves with definitely cheap purchases.' At about the same time Maggs added a slip to catalogue 561 (1931), evidently aimed at American customers, pointing out the advantageous rate of exchange for sterling since the suspension of the gold standard in September 1931. In the spring of the next year I. Kyrle Fletcher bravely asserted that 'Our view of current events is coloured by our faith in books' (catalogue 27).

The effect of the Second World War on the trade was both economic and personal. In 1940 Maggs (692) inserted a slip printed in red explaining that from June 1940 payment in sterling for goods exported to the USA could not be accepted; four catalogues later in the same year, under the heading 'CARRYING ON' was the news that the street windows of the building had been blown in, but that stock and staff were undamaged: 'We are carrying on business as usual.' On the lower cover of W.H. Robinson catalogue 72 (1940) there is an 'Excerpt from a leading article in the London "Evening Standard" at the beginning of the intensive aerial attacks on the city' ('We can do it, too. The eyes of the world are upon us.'). The same catalogue also carried the note 'We beg to assure our American customers that *there is no difficulty whatever in sending books to America.*' After the war new possibilities opened up and Charles J. Sawyer in catalogue 194 (1949) were unashamed of their pitch:

The de-requisitioning, by the Government, of many large country houses may present some perplexity to owners in view of the social changes and domestic difficulties of the past few years.

Many libraries in these houses were sealed during this period and Messrs. Sawyer are prepared to give maximum prices for complete libraries or any small collections of books of interest, and their experts are at the service of all who seek advice in this matter.

In the post-war years the exchange rate proved a great anxiety even after it was fixed at an 'official' rate in 1940. In 1928 W.H. Robinson (20) had quoted $4.87 to the pound; by 1940 in Maggs (692) this had slipped to $4; by around 1950 it was $2.80 (E. Weil (15)). Dealers had to be brave or optimistic to supply agreed conversion rates and the inevitable happened:

Owing to the Exchange Regulations in force since 8th June, 1940, we are obliged to request payment in dollars for all books exported to U.S.A. In order to make things as simple as possible for our American customers and to do our best towards assisting this country's exports, we have printed the prices in this catalogue in dollars ... excuse us for presenting [British customers] with prices marked in American currency. (Goldschmidt cat 107 [1953])

In addition to dollar prices, dual pricing was current in post-war Quaritch catalogues (with a brief interlude in 1949-53, when a red heading was added to the upper covers of their catalogues instructing purchasers to calculate remittances at $2.80 to the pound). As time wore on and the British economy weakened the practice of dual-pricing had to be used, as in Hugh K. Elliott catalogue 21 (1965), and became a regular feature. Even this could not accommodate the problem: 'In the present situation,' Colin and Charlotte Franklin mournfully noted on an errata slip pasted in to their second catalogue (1971), 'dollar prices printed here are not valid.' By 1977 Quaritch (963) chose to price only in dollars, but they returned to sterling prices at the start of the 1990s.

More local problems, especially with the post, were common both in Great Britain and overseas: 'My last catalogue coincided with the American dock strike,' Alan G. Thomas noted in catalogue 13 (1963), 'and some copies went astray. If you did *not* receive Catalogue 12, yellow cover, I should be pleased to send it now; many items are still available.'

Format, design and production

Economic factors also necessarily influenced the physical form catalogues took. Until relatively recently most booksellers seemed generally to choose a particular shape and size for their 'normal' catalogues and stick to it, although different series might well have different formats. Equally, some dealers liked to make the covers of each catalogue quite different, while others – Alan Thomas from at least 1968 was a notable example – kept to the same basic design, only changing the wrappers' colour. Diana Parikian adopted the same practice, but using a fine eighteenth-century engraving of a library interior, during the 1970s. Sizes might vary from the really quite small, although 'unusually attractive', catalogues issued by H.W. Edwards (4 × 5½ inches),[42] through the smaller volumes of Simon Gough's *Food for Thought* series, to the Myers and Rota forma – Rota's 'charming little catalogues are eagerly read, especially by the author of this book':[43] the firm changed the format to a larger size only in 1985. An A4-envelope size is currently favoured by Alex and Emily Fotheringham and John Hart, and a set of unfolded, stapled A4 sheets by Ximenes. The catalogues issued by Robin Waterfield during the 1980s (with a drawing on the covers of the Park End shop by William Bird) and by John Wilson shared the same tall, thin (approximately 4 × 11 inches) format. The most common dimensions are 5½ × 8½ inches, with larger sizes for special catalogues, such as Thomas Thorp's catalogue 380 (1927), several magnificent Maggs catalogues (500 (1928), 555 (1931), 812 (1953)), illustrated in red and black, and Robinson's 77 (1948) and 83 (1953).

Until the 1960s or 1970s many less elaborate catalogues were arranged in double columns with more important and expensive titles set across the whole page: Alan Thomas kept to this layout when he traded as Horace G. Commin and under his own name until at least 1963. It was 'bad policy' according to Michael Sadleir, because the displayed item was distracting.[44] Dealers often sought to produce typographically distinguished catalogues, but on the whole catalogues mirrored the age in which they were produced. For example, J. & J. Leighton's 1899 *Catalogue of Books in Fine Bindings* was very much in the private press style, printed on good paper, with generous use of printers' flowers to mark notes on items and to divide sections, while Pickering and Chatto catalogues of perhaps a decade later were printed in grey ink on paper which is rapidly decaying. Reginald Atkinson's catalogue 81 (1929) had a cover in an interesting shade of orange, with arts and crafts woodcuts and a decorative initial letter A, while Heffer 300 [c.1927] had a green-patterned cover design slightly reminiscent of Bloomsbury.

The most common trope for catalogue covers was to adapt some item for sale: an early example of this was in Maggs's catalogue 246 (1909) of *Old Time Literature*, where the firm's title is printed in red in a suitable fount within a woodcut titlepage border from an early sixteenth-century Italian book. This could be taken further: the upper cover of Birrell & Garnett 29 *Novels and Romances* [c.1930] was done up to imitate the sort of book being sold; Arnold Muirhead did the same thing as *A Catalogue of Old Books* (1951-4), Peter Murray Hill 114 (1970) as *A Collection of Poems on Several Occasions*, and Claude Cox 140 (2000) as *Poems on Several Occasions*, with a suitably adjusted title and imprint. Peter Murray Hill, John Price, and Maggs have adapted eighteenth-century engravings and woodcuts for the covers of their catalogues, adding captions to them of one kind or another. More unusually it is possible to detect asymmetric typography on the titlepage of Bertram Dobell's catalogue 155 (1907) of *English Dramatic Writers*. Simon Finch's catalogue 40 *Unchained* (1999) was arranged in 'a number of sections, temporarily held together by a removable wrapper' in a box; the sections were 'intended to be read in a random order' or rearranged 'into any other random order before reading'. The conceit was clearly influenced by B.S. Johnson's novel *The Unfortunates* (1969).

Although most catalogues were probably designed in consultation between dealer and printer some exhibited a suitable degree of typographic self-consciousness. Six inter-war Elkin Mathews catalogues were designed by William Maxwell of R. & R. Clark 'each in a different type, and each with a short proem on the type that was used'.[45] Some dealers commissioned the great typographers of the last century to design their catalogues. Stanley Morison was responsible for Maggs 456 (1924), which at one time the firm considered probably their best, although they were alarmed by his omission of the full stop at the end of paragraphs. Morison was also involved in the production of Birrell & Garnett's catalogue of type specimens, printed at Cambridge University Press under his supervision.[46] Goldschmidt 106 [c.1953] had a simple and elegant calligraphic cover designed by Jan Tschichold, and John Ryder frequently worked on catalogues for Bertram Rota Ltd.[47] Catalogues could also be used as showcases for printers and new types: Breslauer's catalogue 60 (1946) stated that it was set in Monotype, Plantin Series with cover, titlepage and headings in 'Bologna', 'a new type designed by Stephenson & Blake Ltd., The Caslon Type Foundry', with reproductions by Emery Walker Ltd. (who also made blocks for Maggs catalogues); unusually, the edges of the leaves of the catalogue were stained a bluey-green colour. R. &. J. Balding's catalogue (33) of books relating to Hume and the Scottish Enlightenment (1976) was designed and set in Bembo at the Tragara Press and printed at the Summerhall Press, Edinburgh.[48] Bernard Crossland designed the Blackwell's transport and technology catalogue (865 (1969)) which was printed by Burgess and Son of Abingdon. Montague Shaw designed J.F.T. Rodgers & Co.'s first catalogue [1971] dressing it in attractive coloured card wrappers, and John Lewis was responsible for Ben Weinreb's catalogue 39 (1978).

Dealers might also commission special art-work for their catalogues. Pickering and Chatto's large format catalogue of 1902, filling some 434 pages with over 6,000 items with many plates (some in colour) and facsimiles, had fine wrappers on green paper with a bold design, possibly by Archibald MacGregor, of a rich man being served in a medieval bookshop. Maggs's fourth series of English Literature 1500-1800 (929, 951, 978, 987, and 994) issued in the 1970s had a calligraphic cover design by Pamela A. Neads. Catalogues issued by R.A. Brimmell and Percy Muir as Elkin Mathews were ornamented by reproductions of attractive wood engravings; G.F. Sims catalogue 75 (1970) had a cover design '(from a brass plate engraved for our door) by Will Carter'. More unusually, Rota 244 (1987), describing Lloyd Emerson Siberell's Powys family collection, included a loose facsimile of his bookplate.

On the whole, however, in comparison with some North American and French examples, most British booksellers' catalogues have been fairly modest in design and production: with the exception of a handful of dealers such as Simon Finch, Bernard J. Shapero and Roy Davids, the swagger catalogues Maggs produced between the wars have had few imitators.

Typewriting

Until computer technology allowed dealers to produce their own camera-ready copy most catalogues were set in type by printers. The chief exceptions to this were catalogues reproduced from typewriting or from stencils. Writing in 1950 Michael Sadleir urged booksellers who produced catalogues in this way to use one side of the paper only:

I am not complaining of the duplicated catalogue *per se*. Indeed, with printing costs and printing delays as they are at present, carefully laid-out and not over-crowded roneo'd lists are a natural and useful part-solution of a bookseller's catalogue-problem.[49]

That problem was a long-lasting one and affected even some of the larger and more successful firms. Blackwell's catalogue 616 in 1955, for example, was reproduced from typewritten copy, and there is a marked decline in the production values of Peter Murray Hill's handsome catalogues in the beginning of the 1970s to the crude typewritten catalogue 127 (1974), later going to electric typewriter by 167 (1983-4). Subsidiary catalogues might well be produced in this way: for example, Marlborough Rare Books in the early 1960s reproduced their 'lists' from typewriting, using stiff coloured covers – by 1966 they were using an electric typewriter. All of Keith Hogg's catalogues from at least the mid-1960s were produced from typewritten copy on yellow-tinted paper covered by different coloured wrappers bearing a striking calligraphic cover. Even at the higher and more scholarly end of the trade Hofmann and Freeman's catalogues during the 1960s, 1970s and 1980s were consistently reproduced from typewriting. Among the last survivors of this practice were the crudely duplicated, typewritten catalogues in foolscap format produced by W. Forster who specialized in bibliography and books about books.[50]

Printers

The enormous changes in technology and the mixed commercial fortunes of both the book and printing trades are reflected by the printers that dealers used for producing their catalogues. With some dealers, such as Tregaskis, it is hard to discover who printed the catalogues; other firms, notably Heffer's, produced them in-house from their own printing works. Among the more distinguished and general presses which have produced catalogues for dealers are the Alden Press (for Bertram Rota), the Chiswick Press (for J. Pearson), T. and A. Constable, Edinburgh (for Sotheran's in the 1940s), Hazell, Watson & Viney Ltd (for W.H. Robinson in 1938), Latimer Trend & Co (for J.F.T. Rodgers & Co. in 1971), W. & J. Mackay, Chatham (for Thomas Crowe in 1969 and Rota in 1970), Maclehose, Glasgow (for Francis Edwards in the 1920s), Smith Settle, Otley (for Quaritch in the late 1980s-90s), Waterlow & Sons (for Quaritch's larger catalogues in the earlier 1920s). Some dealers stayed with the same printers for many years. Maggs, for example used the Courier Press, Leamington Spa, for over seventy years:[51] the same firm, with its distinctive letter-spaced typography, was responsible for catalogues by Goldschmidt and Pickering and Chatto in the 1920s and 1930s. Francis Edwards stayed from 1919 to 1973 with Robert Stockwell, although there were a few interruptions when the firm went to George Flower. Other dealers might regularly use different printers. John Grant's catalogues in the 1930s were produced by three different printers (Turnbull & Spears, Oliver and Boyd, and the Darien Press) in five years, yet at first glance they all look indistinguishable. Over a longer period a dealer might change his printer many times: Charles J. Sawyer was using the Bath firm Harding and Curtis in 1922; by 1926 the firm had moved to George Flower; a couple of years later it employed Turnbull & Spears, Edinburgh; in the 1930s and 1940s it used both the Hawthorne Press and H. Sharp & Sons, Bath, until it settled from the 1960s to 1970s on the Blackett Press. A similar tale could be told about Bertram Rota's printers.

Much of this switching around was probably due to demand and capacity and, of course, wartime rationing of paper. Catalogues provided many small printers with the regular jobbing work they needed to survive. In addition to the numbers of printers throughout the country engaged in this work, the field was dominated by two or three firms. The leaders were Robert Stockwell in London and Frank Juckes in Birmingham: most of the major and many minor dealers used one or other or both. Stockwell was working for Bertram Dobell before the First World War and for Weinreb in the late 1970s. Juckes was printing for James Wilson during and probably before the First World War, for Blackwell's and George Y. McLeish in the early 1920s and for Rota in the late 1970s.[52] The nearest competitors to these firms were Harpur and Sons, Derby, whose clients included Thomas Thorp (Guildford) in 1921, and Harding and Curtis, Bath, who worked for Sawyer, Dulau, W.H. Robinson, Birrell & Garnett, in the 1920s, The First Edition Bookshop in the 1930s, for Quaritch from 1933 to the mid-1950s, Henry Stevens, Son & Stiles, for Breslauer, P.H. Muir (for Elkin Mathews Ltd.), and Rota in the 1950s. Around this time Harding and Curtis produced a catalogue of 'A Selection of Styles suitable for Booksellers' Catalogues' illustrating 28 different styles and arrangements, in different founts and sizes, ranging from the simple ('8 pt. Garamond, with Cap. Sideheads') to the complex ('8 pt. Bodoni with Heavy Cap. Sideheads and Small Cap. Titles, double column'), with examples of a wide variety of priced books.

More recently E. & E. Plumridge, Linton, Cambs, printed for J. Clarke-Hall, G. David, Peter Eaton, Claude Cox, Paul Grinke, Thomas Thorp (London and St Albans), and Charles W. Traylen. W.E. Baxter, Lewes, worked for the smarter end of the trade, such as Dawsons, Quaritch, Traylen, and Marlborough Rare Books. It is unlikely that any firm will again develop such a monopoly of the trade, although Quacks Catalogue Printers, York, who worked, for example, for both Gekoski and Rota in the 1980s, were evidently important. It seems more probable that printing centres will share work between a number of firms. This was evidently the case with Oxford from the 1970s which in addition to the Alden Press and firms such as Halls the Printers (who worked for Sanders), was home to Commersgate (Quaritch), Parchment (Goldschmidt), the Bocardo Press (Sanders), and Joshua Horgan (Ulysses, Howes Bookshop, Rota, and Alex and Emily Fotheringham).

The copy dealers supplied for printers was presumably most often typewritten and later in electronic form. However, Frank Maggs, who was responsible for the fifty catalogues of Voyages & Travels from 638 (1937) could not type and seems to have submitted handwritten copy.

Photographs

Photographs of dealers and their premises are particularly valuable for historians of the trade. The habit of including photographs in catalogues is quite old: Ellis and Elvey's 438-page *General Catalogue of Rare Books and MSS* (1894) had a photograph on the titlepage of the interior of their premises at 29 New Bond Street, with a cluttered desk, glass-fronted, wall- and revolving-bookcases and a Turkish carpet. More pretentiously Charles J. Sawyer catalogue 86 (1926) had J.B. Manson's portrait of Sawyer in his Grafton Street shop; this was exhibited at the Royal Academy in that year. The upper cover of Birrell & Garnett's catalogue 17 (1927) shows the interior of their shop in Gerrard Street. In the same year Maggs issued eleven views of their premises in London and Paris and in 1939 a similar number of the Berkeley Square shop. Maggs centenary catalogue 812 (1953) had photographs of the Berkeley Square premises as well as a brief history of the firm. Some of the books and illuminated manuscripts offered in Francis Edwards catalogue 619 (1938) were shown *in situ*. Part of the interior of 16, Pall Mall was shown in W.H. Robinson catalogue 73 (1941). In the 1950s C.A. Stonehill catalogue 152 had a frontispiece of 'The Reference Library, Great Bookham', showing glass-fronted bookcases, easy chairs and a sofa, a briefcase on its side on the floor, and the cataloguer at work behind a desk. The interior of Arnold Muirhead's fine house in St Albans with one plate of the seventeenth-century books and some reference works and another of the eighteenth-century books was displayed in *The Lime Tree Miscellany* 10 (1955). Bernard Halliday 280 (1961) had a photograph of the two brothers who then ran the business in their shop. Charles W. Traylen catalogue 58 (1963) had photographs of the exterior of Castle House in Quarry Street, Guildford while catalogue 123 (celebrating 76 years in the trade) had a fine colour photograph on its cover of 'Charles and Caroline' in formal dress, he seated, she standing by a large globe.

Who actually did the cataloguing?

It was relatively rare for there to be any indication of who was responsible for producing a catalogue, and most dealers would probably expect to do their own cataloguing. A certain amount of recycling of descriptions took place within but also between firms. Cataloguing also served as a good training-ground for learning the trade. In larger firms, especially when the material was of a specialized nature, one or two individuals might be permanently employed to produce catalogues, or external help might be bought in. In about 1908 Wilfrid M. Voynich thanked the two professional librarians R. Rye and R.A. Peddie (who later worked for Grafton & Co.[53]) for their help in compiling his catalogue 24 of early printed books not in the British Museum. Other important scholars (present or future) were employed as cataloguers: for example, E. Gordon Duff catalogued books for Pearson and Co.[54] and A.N.L. Munby catalogued for Quaritch in the mid-1930s. Robert Dougan worked as a cataloguer for Goldschmidt and his set of catalogues 1-100 is in Cambridge University Library;[55] in the late 1970s and early 1980s Robin Halwas was credited with cataloguing for the same firm for which Ernst Weil also worked. A string of cataloguers worked for Quaritch in addition to F.S. Ferguson: Nicholas Poole-Wilson, Ted Hofmann, Arthur Freeman, Paul Grinke, Roger Gaskell and Derek McDonald. Eric Osborne catalogued books for Dawsons and R.V. Tooley, Jean Archibald and David Park for Francis Edwards.

In my copy of six catalogues of autograph letters and manuscripts issued by Dobell in 1922-3 the bound collection has been inscribed by P.J. Dobell 'To Myles Radford whose collaboration has so materially helped in the production of these Catalogues': Radford was presumably later part of the firm Colbeck Radford & Co. Similarly, Michael O'Neill Walshe catalogued for Hodges Figgis in Dublin, before founding Falkner Greirson[56] and Peter Selley compiled Rick Gekoski's catalogue 12 (1989). Those responsible for a grander catalogue might be named in it: for example, W.H. Robinson 81 (1950) listed Ralph Lewis, Elizabeth Cook, and Frederick Wolff as the authors.[57] But credit might also be given for more modest volumes: Priscilla Wrightson was named on the titlepage of Ben Weinreb's catalogue 39 (1978) of architectural books and Martin Dyke was credited with George's 674 (1984) of bibliography. For larger firms dynasties of cataloguers can be identified. At Maggs Maurice Ettinghausen started with catalogue 380 (1919); Alice Martin spent 40 years producing autograph catalogues between 1922 and 1961 and was succeeded by Hinda Rose from the 1970s and John Wilson; Sarah de Laredo was responsible for their Spanish catalogues for many years; later, John Collins produced catalogues of bibliography and still produces ones devoted to natural history. At Blackwell's Eddie Milne, Philip Brown, John Manners, Barry McKay, John King, and Edward East all had a hand in the writing of catalogues (see also catalogue 1000 (1974)).

Mistakes

Those who did the cataloguing were presumably responsible for the mistakes from which almost no catalogue is ever wholly free. As the *Book Collector*'s occasional Christmas *sottisier* shows, cruel fun can be had at the expense of the ignorance, laziness, or carelessness of dealers who commit their descriptions to print. It is easy for catalogues to be wrongly numbered (Frank Hammond 112 [1950s]), for the numbering of pages and plates to go wrong (Maggs 871 (1960)), for items to be wrongly priced or not priced at all (R. & J. Balding, *Hume and the Scottish Enlightenment* (1976)) and for incorrect details to be compounded by hopelessly inflated prices: in Gekoski 12 (1989) item 10 Lawrence Durrell's *Panic Spring* should have been £875 not £8750 and the limited edition of Pound's *Hugh Selwyn Mauberley* should have been attributed to the Ovid Press not the Egoist Press. Booksellers have consistently sought refuge in errata slips.

Costs, terms, etc.

One final element to appear in the catalogue was a description of the dealer's commercial terms. However, this is a surprisingly problematic area, since setting down precisely what terms might be expected by private, institutional, and trade customers seems to have been largely a post-1945 phenomenon: the majority of catalogues before the end of the war were silent on the subject.

Advance copies of catalogues might be reserved for private customers or for institutional libraries, with copies for the trade not sent for a fortnight or four weeks after issue – or vice-versa. For example, an 'Advance Copy for Overseas' was prepared of Elkin Mathews's catalogue 48 (September 1932). Libraries and the trade might be offered the usual 10 per cent discount, but sometimes only after a month. Practice varied extensively and it is hard to get a sense of what conditions actually applied. 'No books sent on approval during the first fortnight after the issue of this catalogue,' Alan G. Thomas laid down in his first catalogue (1957), while George's in 1966 extended the embargo to a month. In 1927 Ingpen & Stonehill offered '5 per cent discount for cash with order', while Quaritch reportedly sent out catalogues to the trade and to customers who haggled over prices only after a month.[58] Arrangements could be fairly arbitrary: 'Will customers please note,' Thomas Thorp of Guildford stated (645 (1964)), 'that for this Catalogue overseas buyers will receive priority.' They might seek to accommodate libraries – 'We can offer extended credit to Libraries, Institutes and similar bodies to suit their various requirements and budgetary arrangements', Covent Garden Bookshop 48 [1972] – while in the same catalogue refusing a trade discount for three weeks after date of postage. Similarly, 'Libraries may arrange for deferred billing to meet their budgeting requirements,' as Gekoski (1987) put it rather delicately.

One particular douceur for purchasers was curious and unusual. Sotheran's Piccadilly Series 17, advertised that the blocks from which the illustrations in the catalogue were made would be presented to the purchasers of the originals; Charles J. Sawyer 65 (1922) offered the same practice and again in 200 (1950) ('The catalogue has no pretensions to "high spots"'). The hardback W.H. Robinson catalogue 83 (1953), with about 135 plates in colour or gravure, was issued with a prospectus explaining that it would be issued free to regular customers, but that for others a charge ('less than the cost of production') of two guineas would be raised which would be refundable against orders. The balance in the terms and conditions between the cost of the catalogue and getting future orders was always a delicate one: as J. & J. Leighton put it in their catalogue NS 6, 'The smallest order secures delivery of future Catalogues'.

In the nineteenth and early twentieth centuries a usual way of paying for a catalogue was by sending stamps: John Wilson in 1870 would send a catalogue free for a stamp and Ellis & Elvey (94 (1900)) said that catalogues would be sent post free on receipt of six stamps, the same number Henry Sugg asked in exchange for his last six catalogues post free. It is not clear whether the stamps were just a convenient way of sending small amounts of money or whether they were specifically designed to cover postage. Some dealers never charged for their catalogues, others asked for a token amount, while grander catalogues were relatively costly. Of course, some of these charges were purely nominal and would be waived for good customers.

At the beginning of the last century Sotheran's charged 3s. subscription for a year's catalogues, while some issued by Grafton and by Davis and Orioli in the 1940-50s were only 2d. each. One of Otto Haas's wartime catalogues 18 (c.1943-4) carried a cover note stating that 'By recent Government restrictions my Catalogues can no longer be forwarded free of charge to my customers in the United Kingdom' and asked UK customers to pay a subscription fee of 1s. for six catalogues. Alan Thomas as Horace G. Commin charged 3d. in 1948, but seems to have issued them free from about 1954. Thomas Thorp of Guildford was still charging 3d. for each catalogue in the 1960s. Zwemmer's catalogue 29 (1948) cost 1s., the same price as most of Quaritch's in the 1920s and 1930s, but their bigger and better ones might be 5s. or 7s.6d; after 1945 their regular catalogues generally came down in price to 6d. until 1950 when they went to a shilling and shortly after (686 (1951)) to two shillings, where they remained until around 1957 – they then seem generally to have been issued free. Early in the century Voynich's catalogues cost 1s. and Leighton's three parts of *Early Printed Books Arranged by Presses* were the same price for each part or 2s. with facsimile reproductions. Charles J. Sawyer charged 5s. for catalogue 65 (1922) and although some of Robinson's were free, others varied between 3s. and 6s. or were more expensive. Maggs's catalogues could be similarly expensive, with the folio 555 of 1931 priced at a guinea.

There were no hard and fast rules about catalogue prices: most Birrell & Garnett catalogues were free, but the one offering writing books was to cost 3s.6d. (it was never published). In more recent times it became less common for dealers to charge for catalogues, although in 1988 Nial Devitt charged 50p and a decade earlier Ben Weinreb £2 for one of his catalogues. More crucial for a time, at least before electronic communications became so universal, were different rates for air-mail catalogues: in 1971 Joan Barton and Barbara Watson wanted only 50p for three issues and during the 1980s Robert Clark asked for £5 for six issues.

It is relatively surprising how rarely dealers mentioned their professional affiliations, which would offer some guarantee of their trustworthiness. Francis Edwards is unusually early in signalling membership of the ABA in 1938; Alan Thomas as Horace G. Commin did the same a decade later.

Despatch

Dealers with shops usually display their catalogues fairly prominently, but they must still send them out to collectors and institutions, either in bulk or piecemeal. Large mailing lists entail a great deal of work, addressing and filling envelopes, sticking stamps to them or having them franked before taking them to the post office. Some printers, like Plumridge and Joshua Horgan, offer this sort of service, but the families of dealers must often be roped in to do it. Customers with names in the second half of the alphabet might well receive their copies several days after those in the first half. In times when the arrival of posted material in different places could be reliably calculated dealers might stagger the despatch of catalogues in an effort to ensure that they were all received at more or less the same time.

Most were presumably sent in envelopes, but the evidence of franking on the lower cover of some catalogues shows that some dealers – for example, Horace G. Commin (Alan Thomas) from at least 132 (1948) to 147 (1956), on his own 2 (1957) and Bernard Halliday 188 (1935), and Thomas Thorp 638 (1963) – sent them out with a paper wrapper of some kind around them. The cost of postage for these franked catalogues was 2¼d. A less satisfactory expedient was tried by Bell, Book and Radmall with catalogue 1 [1975]; its covers slightly overlapped the text, which was sealed on three sides with tape and an address label was pasted on the lower cover which was franked at 5p. Peter Jolliffe's early catalogues and Robert Temple's were sent out in a similar fashion without envelopes.

Orders

In addition to instructions relating to telegrams and cables, letters, and telephone calls ('Please do not 'phone before 9am or after 6pm'), some dealers helpfully printed order forms or post cards with their catalogues so that customers could buy books with minimum effort. In the 1920s Foyle's did this, with an order form bearing the firm instruction 'Please write distinctly'. In an earlier catalogue (number 9 for 1919) a printed postcard could be filled in and sent with orders for new or second-hand books on approval or quoted at the lowest price, along with requests for catalogues. Different changes could be rung on this arrangement: Charles J. Sawyer 218 (1953) included a prepaid post card, which read (the ellipses represent the number and any name which the sender chose to insert): 'Kindly send me on approval from your Catalogue … If I decide **not** to keep these I will return them to you within two days of receipt. I think … would like to receive your Catalogue'.

Economics

The most mysterious part of any consideration of the role catalogues have played in the trade during the last century is how they worked financially. Of course, this varied from time to time and dealer to dealer. The issuing of a large number of catalogues might simply indicate that this was how the dealer did most of his business – alternatively it might signal a dealer in real difficulties, desperate to shift stock. 'On average,' Nial and Margaret Devitt told Sheila Markham in 1993, 'we expect to do 40 per cent of our catalogue business with the trade, 40 per cent with private customers and 20 per cent with institutions.'[59] Precise figures are hard to come by and can vary wildly: in the 1930s Quaritch apparently reckoned on doing three-quarters of its business with the trade and the remainder through catalogues.[60]

Dealers who run their own businesses without staff can only produce catalogues when they have sufficient time to write them: slack times in trade, during the summer or over Easter or Christmas, were suitable for this. Equally, dealers became more and more prone to issue catalogues to coincide with bookfairs and other bookish events: Maggs 838 (1956), their first of this kind, was 'Issued on the occasion of the 10th Annual Conference of the International League of Antiquarian Booksellers' and 861 (1959) was 'Issued on the occasion of the visit of the Grolier Club of New York to England'.

The frequency of catalogues varied a great deal. Despite the call-up of many staff, Francis Edwards was able to get out between 30 and 35 catalogues during the First World War: when it ended the catalogues became monthly until the Second War during which about 50 were issued.[61] In the 1930s Bernard Halliday also issued monthly catalogues, but by 1955 this had diminished to three a year. On the other hand, large firms like Maggs issued a monthly series of autograph letters and manuscripts, and Quaritch in the 1930s issued fourteen catalogues a year. Falling numbers of catalogues might signify declining postal trade or generally adverse economic conditions. W.H. Robinson issued eight catalogues in 1933, four in 1936 and only three in 1937. Thomas Thorp of Guildford managed only three catalogues in 1964, but seven in 1965, six in 1966 and five in 1968.[62] Bertram Rota was still publishing six catalogues a year in 1970.

The financial success of a dealer's catalogues was determined not just by how many he issued each year, but by how many copies he sent out through his mailing list. Dealers are naturally reluctant to reveal much about these, but occasional information about their size is revealing. In the early part of the century J. Pearson

& Co.'s catalogues were generally printed in runs of between 750 and 1,250 copies; but some, for example, the folio or quarto *Autographs of the Rulers of France* [1905] and catalogues of Bossuet, Corneille, Fénelon, Le Sage, Racine, and Regnard were issued between 1905 and 1907 in editions of 50 or 54 copies and the contents were intended to be sold as discreet collections – J. Pierpont Morgan bought up several of them (see Maggs, 1118 (1991)). The first of Maggs's series devoted to bookbinding in Great Britain (893 (1964)) was limited to 1,400 copies, of which twelve had a coloured frontispiece, while nearly quarter of a century later their catalogue celebrating 50 years at Berkeley Square (1088 (1988)) consisted of 1,250 ordinary and 50 hard-bound copies. John Wilson told Sheila Markham in 1992 that he had a mailing list of 3,000 customers.

The actual economics of catalogue production itself are strangely elusive, although it is clear that plenty of rules of thumb exist. Graham Weiner told Sheila Markham in 1999:

When I came to do my first catalogue, Paul [Minet] advised me that the cost of producing and mailing it should not be more than a quarter of the value of the books. It was a useful calculation although I find that it no longer holds today, as I sell a much smaller percentage of each catalogue than in the past. He also posted my first two catalogues to his mailing list and, although they were not specifically science customers, it produced orders.

The figures here might seem quite disproportionate to modern eyes, more used to production costs of a very few percentage points of the total value of the books being sold. They are presumably based on the assumption of at least 50 per cent profit margin and 50 per cent sales: this would leave no surplus at all, of course, and disaster would ensue if fewer books were sold. A different set of figures was reported by Sheila Markham for Simon Finch's eighth catalogue in 1992: this had a sale value of almost a million pounds and reportedly cost over £30,000 to produce.[63] Writing in 1974 Gordon N. Ray described the inflation which caused books in catalogues to become more expensive: 'A large English firm breaks even only if it shows more than a £4 profit on a book, a smaller firm only if it shows more than a £2 profit.'[64] Given the constant inflation and occasional deflation of the past thirty or forty years, the economics of producing catalogues must probably remain largely a matter of luck.

One way of offsetting the cost of catalogues was by charging customers for them; another way was by taking advertising. Apart from advertisements for new books which the dealer might be able to supply, this was always relatively unusual. Foyle's was one of the few firms which was willing and able to take such advertisements: in their first catalogue for 1922, which had the motto 'Cultivation of the mind is as necessary as food to the body' at the head of the titlepage and the less lofty advice 'Please keep for reference, it will save you money' at its foot, there was advertising for books and journals, as well as for educational courses – the Premier School of Journalism, the School of Simplified Study ('Languages & Sciences Made Easy'), and the Cambridge Correspondence College. Catalogues also have a more general advertising role: dealers can use them to list books (or odd volumes) which they wish to buy and they give a clear indication of the sorts of books in which a dealer is interested.

Purchasers

Vanity aside, the main purpose in issuing catalogues is to sell books. If successful, this usually takes place with something of a rush soon after the catalogue reaches customers and then by dribs and drabs. There are, however, occasions, when a single purchaser buys the entire contents of a catalogue. It is worth distinguishing here between catalogues which were designed to sell a collection as a whole and ones which were not: some of the limited edition Maggs catalogues belonged to the first kind. For example, Henry E. Huntington bought the whole of Maggs 387 (1920) which was devoted to aeronautical books; he also bought subsequent collections *From Panama to Peru* (1925) and the Huntingdon Papers (1926), along with most copies of the catalogues. The South American catalogue was limited to 100 copies, suggesting that it was intended for sale as a whole. The 35 medical works bound for Nicolaus Pol, court physician to Maximilian I, and described in a special catalogue, were sold *en bloc* by Maggs in 1929 to the Cleveland Medical Library. The Lilly Library, Indiana, bought the Pforzheimer Collection of George Gissing, which left Quaritch's 1992 unnumbered and unpriced catalogue by Arthur Freeman of the collection as a record of the sale. Such sales might be very pleasing to dealers but frustrating to customers who could not buy copies of books they wanted. Booksellers were, however, left with largely obsolete copies of the catalogue. Lawrence Clark Powell bought the entire contents of the Beauchamp Bookshop's catalogue of children's books (catalogue 19 [c.1955]) along with many of the copies of the catalogue that had not yet been sent out;[65] making a virtue of necessity in catalogue 21 (1955) the bookshop noted it still had a few copies of the earlier catalogue for sale at 1s. each.

Practice among dealers varied about whether to include sold items in catalogues and whether to mark them as 'Sold' or not – some might think the question almost an ethical issue. Many catalogues contained a sprinkling of sold books, but these may reflect different circumstances. Goldschmidt's catalogue 100 (1954) was a personal selection of favourite items which he had sold privately over the years but now wished to record in a more permanent form.[66] Colin Franklin's early 1970s catalogue 3 of books printed on vellum was never issued because the collection was sold *en bloc* when the catalogue was in proof.

Old catalogues

There can be few things more pleasing to a dealer, besides selling all the books in his catalogues, than to see the catalogues themselves become sought-after items, of interest not just to the trade and collectors but more generally to scholars. Yet even the most dedicated collector must from time to time submit to Munby's 'gigantic sorting'. The literary scholar R.W. Chapman annotated his copy of Breslauer catalogue 60 (1946), which had a section '"The Tenth Muse": A Collection Illustrative of Forgery and Alleged Forgery in History, Science and

Literature', with the words 'FORGERIES' and 'Keep'. Just after the First World War J. & J. Leighton, NS part 1, offered a range of back catalogues for between 1s. and 3s.6d. each, but also an entire *General Illustrated Catalogue* in nine parts (1,738 pages, 6,209 items, with upwards of 1,350 reproductions in facsimile), bound in half-morocco for 30s. Goldschmidt in about 1930 (20) was offering catalogues 1-17 for 2s. each, although numbers 5 and 10 were unavailable. A history of the appearance of booksellers' recent catalogues in the catalogues of other dealers would be an interesting one: Colin Richardson catalogue 38 (1946), for example, had over a hundred such items, with a good run of Maggs catalogues from 1908. Marked-up sets of a dealer's own catalogues can contain very valuable information about particular copies of books, their provenance, purchasers, and profit.

The difficulty of finding catalogues and the anticipated pleasures they may bring are hinted at in a final reversal of expectations. In catalogue 5 issued during the 1970s J.F.T. Rodgers & Co. offered 50p 'for any copies in good condition' of their first catalogue [1971]. A decade later H.W. Edwards wrote to James Stevens-Cox in November 1980: 'Sorry that I cannot help you over my old catalogues. I think I have some, but cannot find them – lost among 2 or 3 cwt. of odds and ends!' adding as a postscript 'I haven't 119 myself!'

III

By their very nature booksellers' catalogues are ephemeral items – however useful or interesting they may become in time, the moment of a catalogue's greatest interest is an alarmingly brief one for both the dealer who compiled it and the customer who reads it. 'The Scufflers', as Iain Sinclair calls those who haunt jumble sales and street markets,

have their pretensions: have seen books change hands for money, have hoarded catalogues, from which they never order (not realising that the catalogued books are the ones that the big boys can't sell, sour stock).[67]

Yet, despite their ephemeral quality, catalogues are essential to the history of the trade, the history of collecting and to other larger histories. Catalogues have certain sorts of stories to tell; the stories may be of an obvious kind – this copy of this book was once offered for sale at this price – but they may also conceal deeper and quite hidden tales of friendships and feuds, brilliant coups, and terrible disasters. The lists issued by Peter and Helen Kroger as part of their cover for their involvement in what became known as the Portland Spy Ring may be an extreme example of the use to which catalogues can be put, but they are also part of the hidden story of how the trade sold books – as such they deserve to be collected, catalogued, and studied.

The Phillipps Sales

ANTHONY HOBSON

THE Robinson brothers' purchase of the Phillipps collection was the greatest bookselling coup of all time, exceeding in scope, size and value even those of the eighteenth century, such as Thomas Osborne's acquisition of the Harleian printed books or James Edwards's of the Pinelli library, let alone Dubrowsky's purchase of the early manuscripts from Saint Germain-des-Prés.

Thirlestaine Hall, Cheltenham, formerly the residence of Sir Thomas Phillipps, had been requisitioned at the outbreak of war in 1939 by the Ministry of Aircraft Production. The entire Phillipps collection of books and manuscripts, still present in vast numbers in spite of the 22 sales since the Baronet's death, had had to be hurriedly removed in Sir Thomas's box-shelves and stored in the cellars. There was no catalogue, and both Harvard and the British Museum declined to purchase on the grounds of lack of information. Subject to the Phillipps trustees' condition that they retain a token 29 manuscripts, the Robinson's offer of £100,000 was accepted and judicial consent to the sale was given in February 1946.

One hundred thousand pounds was a large sum in 1946. Through the good offices of one of their clients, Sir Louis Sterling, the Robinsons were able to obtain a loan of £80,000 from a merchant bank, but on harsh conditions. They were required to pledge their homes as well as their business and stock, and to pay the bank half of any profits from sales.

Philip Robinson published a description of moving the collection to London.[1] The principal manuscripts, the most valuable printed books and the Catlin Gallery – the collection of paintings of North American Indians by George Catlin – were first removed to a rented house in Gordon Square. Day after day convoys of lorries carrying the box-shelves followed. Manuscripts were taken to Gordon Square until every room had been filled. Meanwhile the printed books went to a neighbouring church crypt, until that substantial space, 36,000 cubic feet, was packed from floor to ceiling, with not even a gangway left open, and with a residue stacked outside. Philip Robinson had supervised the packing at Cheltenham, while his brother Lionel oversaw the reception of the books in London.

Within a year sales privately and by auction had realized more than enough money to repay the bank loan. Nine sales were allocated to Sotheby's, three of lesser value to Hodgson's and an Americanum of the utmost rarity, *The Journal of Major George Washington* (Williamsburg,

1754), was given a catalogue to itself at the Parke-Bernet Galleries, New York, and sold for $25,000 in 1955. Meanwhile eight catalogues were issued and substantial sales were made privately to Sir James Caird (naval papers for the National Maritime Museum), D.M. Colman (late illuminated manuscripts), Dr Martin Bodmer (early manuscripts), Sir David (later Viscount) Eccles (the Ker Porter papers), Sir Chester Beatty (a famous Armenian manuscript), and J.W. Hely-Hutchinson (manuscripts and fine bindings, bequeathed by him to Eton College).

In June 1947 the brothers had bought back, at considerable expense, the bankers' interest in future profits. By 1956 their success had the bizarre result of forcing their business into liquidation, since owing to the fiscal arrangements of the Attlee Government, not repealed by their Conservative successors, almost 90 per cent of any future profits would have been forfeit in tax. The elegant premises on Pall Mall, where a decanter of sherry was kept in readiness to welcome visitors, were sold and the substantial residue of the Phillipps manuscripts was transferred to a trust for the benefit of the brothers' families.

The Robinsons had been advised to allow seven years to pass after the creation of the trust before holding any sales. The Revenue might otherwise claim that they were still trading and tax the proceeds. These years were not wasted. The manuscripts were sorted by country of origin and some of the more important charters were mounted in fitted cases. The Robinsons had invited A.N.L. Munby, Librarian of King's College, Cambridge, to write Sir Thomas Phillipps's life and had placed the Baronet's personal papers at his disposal. This was an inspired choice. The five volumes of *Phillipps Studies*, published between 1951 and 1960, and later abridged in a single volume *Portrait of an Obsession* (1967), were written with impeccable scholarship but at the same time with such felicity, humour and lightness of touch as to make the omnivorous collector a subject for collecting in his own right.

*

In 1964 I was approached by the Robinsons. They were kind enough to say that they had formed a favourable impression of my discretion and abilities, and wished to advise the trustees to consign the remaining manuscripts to Sotheby's for sale under my direction. I had then been in charge of Sotheby's Book Department for thirteen years. I realized that I could not combine the day-to-day work of the Department, together with the other administrative responsibilities that fell to me as a senior director, with the attention that the Phillipps collection would require. I arranged to give up the Department, and a younger brother of the Marquess of Lothian, Lord John Kerr, who had been running a bookshop in Oxford, was brought in to take it over.

Visits to inspect the manuscripts followed. The house in Gordon Square and the church crypt had long since been given up and the bulk, though still considerable, had been drastically reduced. Three hundred and ninety-four medieval manuscripts were shelved in a strong room in the City. A typewritten list was provided and was annotated by me during many sessions. Though some, I commented, were 'very fine', many, of interest primarily for the text, were very different from the Books of Hours, Italian Renaissance copies of classical authors and other illuminated volumes that the English trade was familiar with. Special marketing would be needed.

The post-medieval manuscripts were stored in a nondescript Victorian terraced house in a side street in Barnet. Steps had been taken to preserve its anonymity. The curtains were kept drawn and I was warned not to park my car outside. Behind its unassuming façade the rooms were unexpectedly spacious. On my first visit I was dumbfounded by the quantity of neatly arranged volumes in contemporary vellum or Middle-Hill boards. The Italian manuscripts, the most numerous category, occupied a large ground-floor room shelved on each side almost to the ceiling and with two lines of double-fronted shelves down the centre. Other rooms held the English, Spanish, French and Oriental sections; Greek manuscripts were in a tall bookcase behind a grille door; charters occupied a room on the top floor. I was to spend many days in this house over the next seventeen years.

I divided the sales into two groups: Phillipps New Series to include the post-medieval manuscripts and Phillipps New Series Medieval for the medieval ones. The first New Series sale took place on 28 and 29 June 1965. It consisted of English material, chosen by the Robinsons, and the papers of Madame de Grafigny, containing many references to Voltaire. The Grafigny papers were divided between the Bibliothèque Nationale and H.P. Kraus. English booksellers – Dobell, Quaritch, Traylen, Maggs, Sawyer, Myers, Alan Thomas – were prominent among the other buyers, but the chief lot fell to the University of Texas bidding through their usual agent, L.D. Feldman of the House of El Dieff, New York. This was a commonplace book in which P.J. Croft, by a brilliant piece of literary detection, had recognized the hand of Robert Herrick.[2] It sold for £34,000. The sale realized £84,000, a very encouraging start to the series.

Sotheby's Book Department had been joined in time for the sales by a newcomer of great scholarly distinction. Andreas Mayor had been a Queen's Medallist at Cambridge and an expert in the Department of Manuscripts in the British Museum. He catalogued the whole of the first medieval sale which took place on 30 November 1965. Later sales were divided between us.[3] The Robinsons had certain favourites among their manuscripts. As the late Frederick B. Adams remarked, they were like owners of a racing stable eager to see how their horses would run. One of these pets was the only Icelandic medieval manuscript in private ownership, the fourteenth-century 'Codex Scardensis', *Lives of the Apostles*. It was offered in the first sale and fetched the high price of £36,000 bought by T. & L. Hannas. There was good support for the other lots and a total of £187,150. Purchasers were divided almost equally between England – Maggs, Quaritch, Dawson, Traylen, Eisemann, Otto Haas, Hammond, Breslauer, Abramsky, and Major Abbey bidding in the room – and elsewhere – H.P. Kraus, Georges Heilbrun, Bernard Rosenthal, Florimond Tulkens and the Bibliothèque Nationale.

Another volume of which the brothers were justly proud caused a considerable stir when offered in the second non-medieval sale in June 1966. This was the long-lost manuscript of Books 1-9 of Caxton's translation of Ovid's *Metamorphoses*, complementing the second part, preserved since the early eighteenth century in the Pepys Library of Magdalene College, Cambridge. It had been discovered, disbound and disordered, in a heap of old papers. There was no indication where Phillipps had found it. This too was bought, for £90,000, for the University of Texas, but the export was stopped, and the manuscript rejoined the second part through a generous advance made by an American citizen, Eugene B. Power of Ann Arbor.

The first medieval sale had included a more than average proportion of the most attractive manuscripts in the strongroom and had been judged a success. The second one the following year fell perhaps below the average. The result was a sad contrast. Though Dr Martin Bodmer secured three lots and buyers included the Bibliothèque Municipale of Nancy, five lots were bought in and the total sold was less than £50,000. I had had high hopes of an early fifteenth-century Missal written in Glagolitic letter and with illuminated initials. It was probably the only pre-1500 Glagolitic manuscript that was likely ever again to be available to collectors. It had last appeared in the rooms in 1830, when Sir Frederick Madden had tried to obtain it for the British Museum, but had been outbid by Phillipps. No one in England could read the script and I took it to Vienna to be described by the great Croat scholar, Professor Josef Hamm. Madden's successors in Bloomsbury viewed its reappearance with total indifference, and it was Bernard Breslauer, displaying his characteristic flair and imagination, who was the only bidder at £4,000. It is now one of the more singular and remarkable possessions of the Pierpont Morgan Library.

This unfortunate sale showed that fatigue had already set in at the prospect of an almost endless series of offerings of unfamiliar and somewhat indigestible material. Something had to be done. From the third medieval sale (1967) onwards, I took the manuscripts of most sales to New York for an advance exhibition at Sotheby's Parke Bernet Galleries. The first effects at any rate were excellent. The Italian Government, bidding initially through the Libreria Leo S. Olschki, later through the Italian Institute, began to acquire lots for the national libraries. They were agonisingly slow payers, every payment having to be referred to the Court of Cassation, but the competition was most helpful. Bernard Breslauer's indignation at their intervention was expressed in letters to *The Times*, but did not deter continued Italian acquisitions. For the tenth medieval sale (1975) the remaining manuscripts of German origin were exhibited at Sotheby's office in Munich. This attracted many visitors, but there were no German buyers. Breslauer bought the eleventh-century Greek Josephus, one of the earliest witnesses to the text (£27,000), and the British Rail Pension Fund invested in the German fourteenth-century Bestiary (£60,000) and the fifteenth-century Freudenberg Breviary (£36,000).

In early 1969 the Robinsons announced, with happy smiles, that instead of the usual early summer post-medieval sale there would be an auction of Americana at Sotheby's Parke Bernet in New York, allegedly as an act of politeness to their friend Mary Vandergrift, Vice President of Parke-Bernet, though I suspected the real reason was to finance a jaunt to America at the trustees' expense. The Americana they sent over, both printed and manuscript, had until then been withheld. (There were rooms at Barnet I was not encouraged to enter.) Much of it, especially the manuscripts in Spanish, tested the Parke-Bernet cataloguers to breaking point. When proofs of the catalogue were sent over, the brothers were appalled. I was begged to intervene and spent a week of intense editorial work on Madison Avenue, later returning to take the sale. The results were generally satisfactory, though one of the brothers' 'pets', a document of 1610 transferring an interest in a ship called 'The Mayflower', aroused little interest and was knocked down for $5,000. Its subsequent owners, Hofmann & Freeman, proved conclusively that the ship in question was indeed the one that carried the Pilgrim Fathers, and priced it accordingly.

Greek manuscripts were catalogued by Andreas Mayor up to and including the sale of July 1975. After his tragically early death the responsibility became mine, greatly helped by Mr Nigel Wilson, Fellow of Lincoln College, Oxford. Four were of special interest: one of three known manuscripts of *I Erofigli*, the Cretan play by George Chortatzes (£680, Quaritch for the University of Birmingham); *The War of Cyprus*, an unknown epic poem (£1,900, the Greek Academy); the commonplace book of John Mavrocordato, a significant document of the seventeenth-century Hellenic renaissance (£3,400, bought by a Greek businessman for presentation to Archbishop Makarios, President of Cyprus, and lucky to survive the revolution that occurred on the island shortly afterwards); and the personal papers of Cyril Lucaris, the 'Calvinist' Patriarch of Constantinople (£5,200, Leiden University Library). Forgeries had already become popular in the saleroom and those by Constantine Simonides of early Greek manuscripts were no exception. Kraus, Quaritch, Myers, Breslauer, Pickering & Chatto, and Hofmann & Freeman were among the buyers, and the Greek Academy paid £1,900 for the Homer alleged to have been copied in the first century BC.

Cataloguing the Spanish section was an education in Spanish literature. I should have been unable to do it without the generous help of Professor Edward Wilson of Cambridge University. There were three sales. The first was a relative failure. Spain showed no interest although I took the proofs to show the National Library in Madrid. The extensive papers of Juan de Iriarte, first librarian of the Royal Public Library, were bought in, as were poetical manuscripts of Quevedo, Antonio de Solis and Lope de Vega. The first named was sold afterwards to D. Bartolomé March, the others to Cambridge University Library. Only the poems of the Marqués de Santillana were well received (£7,000 Traylen, for Yale University Library). The second sale, thanks to the valiant support of J.L. Gili of The Dolphin Book Company, was a considerable improvement; the third one was a runaway success. Spanish Americana that Parke-Bernet had been unable to catalogue had been returned to London. We invited the ambassadors of Spain and of eleven Latin American countries, as well as the High Commissioner for Trinidad and Tobago, to a private view. This led to lively bidding, but the Spanish embassy swept the board, buying 74 lots or 45 per cent of the total. Letters of Philip II and Philip III unsold in the first sale six years earlier now went to Madrid for almost three times as much.

Two more Glagolitic manuscripts came to light, both post-medieval, but the crown of the Slavonica was a collection of the poems, twelve of them previously unknown, of Marko Marulić, the leading poet of the Croatian renaissance, together with the second earliest pastoral in the Croat language, by Petar Hektorović. Against spirited bidding by Breslauer it fell at £7,000 to the Croatian National Library, Zagreb.

The medieval series was interrupted by two oriental sales. The second contained manuscripts in 29 languages and the catalogue required the collaboration of seventeen experts. Brill of Leiden, Maggs and Alan Thomas were prominent among the buyers. The earliest manuscript of the Malay epic, *The Ballad of the Macassar War* (£2,200) now belongs to Singapore University.

A specialized Italian Renaissance sale was held in 1968. The great Professor Giuseppe Billanovich wrote to me, 'Quite frankly I never saw in my life a catalogue of manuscripts on sale so filled of humanistic treasures … it was a thrilling adventure to go with astonishing eyes [*sic*] through all the items'. Competition was keen. Nevertheless by 1972 interest was again flagging. To revive it I suggested a dinner to celebrate the centenary of Sir Thomas's death. The Robinsons, always most generous with hospitality, seized on the idea. The evening before a post-medieval sale, 138 guests were entertained at Stationers' Hall. They heard speeches by Viscount Eccles, M. Marcel Thomas of the Bibliothèque Nationale, Herman W. Liebert of Yale and Dr A.N.L. Munby. The effect on the next day's sale was electric, but it did not last. In 1975 I tried a selection of Italian seventeenth-century manuscripts on the room with disastrous results. If it had not been for Alan Thomas many lots would have received no bidding at all. Alan, whose faith in Phillipps never wavered, bought more than two thirds, 94 lots, some for as little as £5. Fortunately in the meantime the Robinsons had enlivened the process by introducing sales of printed books, many of which, it must be admitted, came, not from Phillipps, but from their successful forays into stately homes. STC books were sold to start with, then Wing, finally a first selection of Continental imprints.

Nevertheless, after twelve years of sales, the large Italian room at Barnet seemed no emptier than at the beginning. The rows of shelves tightly packed with volumes of vellum-bound seventeenth-century manuscripts still seeemed endless. I shuddered at the thought of presiding over more sales like the last one, with no buyer except the courageous Alan Thomas. In 1977 I resigned from Sotheby's. The trustees decided that the time had come to look for a purchaser of the remainder *en bloc*. There was only one firm with both the capital and the will to take on so large a quantity of difficult material: H.P. Kraus, of New York.

The deal was soon completed, for an undisclosed sum. The charters filling the attic room at Barnet would never have received an export licence and were excluded. Sotheby's refused to deal with the bulk and I spent several weeks over the next four years identifying placenames and personalities and sorting out ten large county groups. What remained, by now reduced to a manageable size, provided a successful sale at Sotheby's, totalling £82,148, in April 1981. Gloucestershire was the largest of the county groups I had assembled, though of low individual value, Norfolk the most valuable. Kent was acquired by a private buyer, the others by their respective County Records Offices.

On 7 May 1982 I was able to report to the trustees that except for a Swedish-English dictionary, on offer to Alan Thomas (and acquired by him), the mission they had entrusted to me in 1965, of carrying out the dispersal of the Phillipps Collection had been completed. A celebratory luncheon was held on 11 August and a toast drunk to the immortal memory of the bibliomaniacal Baronet. The total achieved, omitting the bulk sale to Kraus but including the charters and a few small private sales, was £3,522,806. Subject to deduction of commission and capital gains tax, it represented pure profit. The Robinson brothers and the trustees expressed their satisfaction with the result. With hindsight, however, it can be seen that the sheer quantity of material had tended to depress prices. Present-day figures, even allowing for inflation, might be very different. Jacques de Longuyon's *Les voeux du paon*, for example, sold in 1965 for £5,800, was resold at Sotheby's in 1997 for £166,500, and a sixteenth-century Greek manuscript of Porphyry's commentary on Ptolemy's harmony, sold for £380 in 1975, fetched £14,950 22 years later. Nevertheless, once the collection had been conveyed to trustees, its sheer bulk and heterogeneous content made a sale through a large auction house the only possible choice.

Making Collections

CHRIS KOHLER

COLLECTIONS of books and manuscripts have been passing from private to institutional ownership for hundreds of years. These collections, or sometimes blocks of coherent material from larger collections, were usually assembled by private collectors – sometimes over several generations – and the materials would pass into institutional ownership by gift or sale. The bookseller's role, if any, was that of agent and booksellers have continued to be active in this role until the present day.

Although a few earlier instances can be found, bookselling in Britain in the twentieth century saw a largely new development – booksellers themselves assembling collections. My general criteria for such collections are that they are put together and funded by the bookseller, in a series of purchases over a period of time, with a view to offering the collection *en bloc* on the market seeking an institutional buyer. 'Typical Kohler criteria,' said one bookseller, and they may wobble a bit as I go through the century. I exclude archives because they are rarely assembled piece by piece and almost always sold on commission. Collection booksellers, my own firm included, have been secretive about their activities and I am grateful that so many have shared much of their history with me.

The first half of the twentieth century (by Michèle Kohler)

The earliest examples of dealer-assembled collections that I have been able to find were offered for sale by J. Pearson & Co.[1] The firm was founded by John Pearson in the 1860s. Pearson retired in about 1890 and the firm was continued by F.A. Wheeler and C.E. Shepheard (who may have been a sleeping partner). The last letter from Wheeler in the Morgan Library archives is dated October 1933. W.C. Hazlitt describes Pearson as 'almost the introducer of those stupendous prices for really first-rate books or rarities in book form'.[2]

Wheeler was just as secretive as Pearson and, as yet, little is known about the firm. Wheeler sold collections to Pierpont Morgan from the late nineteenth century onwards. On 9 November 1906, he offered Morgan four collections of first editions – by Fénelon, Le Sage, Regnard and Bossuet – sending him short preliminary lists and a seven-page handwritten letter, identifying high spots and explaining significances. 'Perhaps, however, *the* feature of this unrivalled collection is the number of volumes of Bossuet's own writings which belonged

either to Bossuet himself or to his followers and intimate friends – for example ...'
Four days later he wrote again: 'I forgot to say that should you purchase these sets
I propose compiling catalogues. ... Of course, as on previous occassions [*sic*],
I shall be pleased to compile the catalogues *con amore*.' Morgan sent a cable on
4 December indicating that the price of £3,400 for the four collections was 'too
high', but an arrangement was reached – £2,640 – and the collections are in the
Pierpont Morgan Library. On 2 April 1907 Wheeler sent a letter to Morgan about
'my scheme to place in your library unrivalled ... sets of the first editions of the
seven greatest French authors of the 17th Century. ... You will see, therefore, that
we *commence* with the author of 'Le Cid' and *end* with that of 'Gil Blas' – and I
hope you will agree with me that my carefully considered scheme is worthy of
your endorsement. ... I told you (when you were here) I have taken the greatest
possible pains to prevent the inclusion of *any duplicates* whatever.'[3] Wheeler's
collections sales pitch has not been bettered in a century: he shows how the
collections fit into existing holdings, guarantees to eliminate duplicates, highlights
the exceptional qualities of the material – and makes the sale.

In 1917 Quaritch offered for sale the Spedding Library of Baconiana.[4] Quaritch
added a few volumes 'to strengthen the collection', which is described in the sale
catalogue as one that 'should be an invaluable acquisition to a public library or to
a collector of Baconiana'. The collection was sold *en bloc* to a private collector.
Twelve years later Quaritch issued 500 copies of a catalogue devoted to its
collection of Aldine Press publications. This was based on Quaritch's purchase of
the Holford collection, to which further material had been added. The total cost
of the books to Quaritch was £4,019.18s.2d. The contents of the catalogue were
offered for sale for £10,000, but the timing was not auspicious and the books were
eventually priced and sold individually.[5]

Maggs approached 'collection selling' in a different way. Several catalogues
devoted to modern technological subjects were produced, in which the books
were priced individually, but with the expectation that the contents would be
bought *en bloc*. Subjects offered in this way included aviation, photography and
ballooning. During the inter-war period, some 30 special catalogues describing
particular collections of books and manuscripts were also issued out of series
from the firm's normal sequence of catalogues and in limited numbers. Several of
these collections were acquired for the Huntington Library in California, as
described by Henry Woudhuysen in a preceding chapter; other examples included
'a Unique Collection of Early Editions of Ronsard' (1927), consisting of 95 items
described by Seymour de Ricci, 'Six Block-Books' (1931), purchased by R.E. Hart
of Blackburn and bequeathed to Cambridge University Library, and a collection
of 21,000 books about books (*c.*1937), offered on behalf of a client.[6]

Harold Reeves, working in his shop in Shaftesbury Avenue, came from a long
line of antiquarian music sellers. He enjoyed putting together single-composer or
single-genre lots which he knew would interest his institutional library customers.
His most notable collection was also his least successful – a collection of original
editions of Sir Henry Rowley Bishop's operas. James B. Coover has analysed

Harold Reeves's catalogue entries: 'The description made them sound magnificent: 43 works bound in 15 red morocco volumes, dated 1808 to 1827. They were offered first in Catalogue 66, 1926, again as lot 15032 in Catalogue 111, 1934 (though now there were 46, not 43 volumes), [and] yet again in 122 in 1937, each time with lengthy annotations full of praise.'[7] When I asked his nephew, William Arnold Reeves, the last of the line of booksellers stretching back to the early nineteenth century, about his uncle's Bishop collection, he laughed and said that it didn't sell because Bishop's operas weren't any good.[8]

In 1937 Leon Kashnor of the Museum Book Store in London sold a large collection of books, pamphlets and periodicals dealing with British social, economic and political history to the International Institute of Social History in Amsterdam.[9] The Institute's website describes Kashnor as 'among the first booksellers to gather a large collection around some movement or person, before selling it as a whole'.

The final major player in the collection business in the first half of the twentieth century was Henry Sotheran Ltd. A six-page brochure, probably printed in 1929, described – without indicating the asking price, later said to have been £30,000 – the remaining 858 volumes from Isaac Newton's library that had descended to Mr and Mrs Wykeham-Musgrave of Barnsley Park in Gloucestershire.[10] The collection remained unsold until purchased by the Pilgrim Trust in 1943 for £5,000 and given to the library of Trinity College, Cambridge. This collection fulfils some of my criteria – sold *en bloc* by a bookseller, ultimately to an institutional library – but it seems that it was offered by Sotheran on behalf of the Musgrave family and neither put together nor owned by the bookseller. The other collection handled by Sotheran was 'A Remarkably fine Collection of Old English Plays' consisting of 124 quarto plays (1604-64), bound in twelve volumes, priced at £3,250 and offered for sale 'to a private collector or a great Public institution' in a flyer that also re-offered the Newton Library for £5,000.[11] The plays collection was offered for sale on behalf of the American bookseller Gabriel Wells and was finally sold by Wells's New York firm after his death in 1949.[12]

From 1945 to the late 1970s

After the war, increasing prosperity and the growing university population across the world began to stimulate a market for collections that grew slowly through the 1950s, 1960s and 1970s. Japan entered the market in the late 1970s, leading to explosive growth and the heady years of the 1980s and first half of the 1990s.

Dawsons, Quaritch and Heffer's announced collections (often author collections) in their general catalogues from the early 1950s. Rapidly expanding American university libraries liked to buy collections. Raymond Kilgarriff managed the antiquarian department at Heffer's and sold D.H. Lawrence, Aldous Huxley and H.G. Wells collections (from Lord Horder's library) in this way: 'All this was in the 1950s and collections trades were still novel.'[13] Dawsons' catalogues carried announcements of collections from the mid-1950s through the

1970s, but the only definite sale was an 'Anaesthesia' collection sold for £1,000 to Kansas Medical Library in 1955.[14]

In 1953 the National Library of Australia bought Leon Kashnor's private collection covering political economy from 1640 to 1870.[15] In 1955 Peter Eaton sold his 'Robert Owen and Co-operation' collection, for about £1,250, to Goroshiro Toike who gave it to his alma mater, Hitotsubashi University in Japan.[16] The same year saw Peter Murray Hill sell his private collection of Edmund Curll to the University of Kansas.[17]

Martin Hamlyn remembers Keith Stock visiting Peter Murray Hill's shop in the 1950s to buy eighteenth-century British plays. Stock traded as John Rothwell and dealt in old plays and theatre books. In 1956 an academic from Rice Institute (now Rice University), Professor Carroll, happened to be in London and saw a Rothwell catalogue advertising a collection of 2,100 eighteenth-century plays. Carroll consulted and Rice bought the collection, which has since grown to more than 5,000 plays. The price in dollars was the equivalent of about £5,350.[18]

Dawsons were becoming important booksellers by the mid-1950s, both for rare books and runs of periodicals. The driving force was Herbert Marley, who was 'hard, but a very good boss to work for', according to Nigel Phillips.[19] Marley was selling collections to the University of California at Los Angeles from the mid-1950s.[20] Lawrence Clark Powell, UCLA's Librarian, recounts in *Books in My Baggage* how in 1957: 'I labored to carry out my resolution to acquire the Ogden library for the University of California, sole agent for which was the firm of William Dawson & Sons Ltd., managed by Herbert Marley.'[21] The collection cost UCLA $100,000.

Harold Edwards bought heavily at the Harmsworth sale in 1957. After his death Arnold Muirhead wrote:

I well remember that when Sotheby's sold the large Harmsworth collection of 17th-century theology and after Peter Murray Hill and I (and probably many others) had spent a lot of time viewing and estimating, when the sale took place Harold practically swept the board, paying what many thought ridiculous prices. But how right he was – within months he had catalogued the collection and Larry Powell had come down and bought it for the University of California Library – and paid the cost of the catalogue into the bargain.[22]

Martin Hamlyn of Peter Murray Hill told me about his involvement with the sale of the Isaac Foot collection to the University of California. Foot had met Lawrence Clark Powell while travelling on the Santa Fe Chief in 1945. After Foot's death in 1960, a note had been found among his papers suggesting that an approach be made to Powell. Hamlyn contacted UCLA and two librarians from Santa Barbara viewed the collection and sent a favourable report. Powell's response was brief and telegraphic: 'Keep Hands on Foot'. A sketch of Foot's 24 book-filled rooms and assorted corridors, corrected in detail by Hamlyn, made it possible for the various campuses of the university to allocate sections of the collection before it arrived in California. The purchase price was £55,000.[23]

I left Joseph's just before my twenty-first birthday in 1963 and sold my first collection – a G.K. Chesterton collection of 32 items for £17.10s. – in 1964. In the same year Noel Bolingbroke-Kent, then aged 24, sold a collection of 80 nineteenth-century Irish pamphlets to the Free Library of Philadelphia for £40. He went on to sell eight other collections in the 1960s, all to North American libraries. I sold ten collections in the 1960s for a total of £13,337, mainly to the same market. In 1967 I bought a collection of early Socialist pamphlets and tracts at Hodgson's and offered them *en bloc* for £700. The new University of York bought them, and 16 other libraries, including even Fort Wayne Public Library in Indiana, were sent 'regret sold' notices. That changed my life. We went on selling both individual books and collections for some years, but in 1974 decided to concentrate all our energies and time on collections and we have done so ever since.

Other booksellers forming collections at this time included Richard Hatchwell and John Lawson. Richard Hatchwell set up shop in Malmesbury in 1952 and by the mid-1960s had built up an extensive collection of first and important editions of the works of Thomas Hobbes – a Malmesbury man. David Esplin of the University of Toronto library saw the collection in 1967 and bought it.[24] John Lawson sold a St Helena collection to the National Library of Australia in 1963 and an important 4,500 item Mauritius collection to the same customer in 1968: it remains their principal resource on that country. Why would the National Library of Australia buy these collections? Because St Helena was the first and Mauritius the last watering station for the convict ships leaving England for Australia in the 1790s.[25]

Our collections business increased dramatically during the 1970s, when we sold 129 collections for £446,709. Most went to Britain, North America and Australia, with a few to Germany. A small number of other booksellers were selling collections. We visited libraries, gently built collections and enjoyed life. But the market was about to change.

The demand from Japan

Hamish Riley-Smith recently observed that 'I suspect we have – by good fortune – lived through a remarkable but short period of extraordinary prosperity in bookselling which will almost certainly not return in our lifetimes'.[26] One of the main reasons for this was the number of sales to Japan in the 1980s and 1990s.

Booksellers started to sell collections to Japan in the late 1970s. Sales are usually made by sending catalogues to Japanese booksellers, who then sell to libraries. Occasionally sales are made direct to Japanese libraries. We sold our first collections in 1977 ('Eighteenth-Century French Plays' to Yushodo and 'Nineteenth-Century British Biographies' to Maruzen). Noel Bolingbroke-Kent and Hamish Riley-Smith first sold there in 1979, followed by Rudi Thoemmes around 1982. Others followed their lead.

By the later 1970s America and Europe were pressing Japan to reduce its enormous trade surplus.[27] Buying books was one way to do this. New colleges and universities meant a demand for instant libraries. The government's response was increased funding and 'special budgets' to help private institutions buy scientific equipment and books. By the mid 1990s the Japanese economic bubble had burst and a large part of the market disappeared. There have latterly been reports of new life in the market, but it is very sketchy.

Japanese booksellers sell collections through their many salesmen. The largest companies, such as Maruzen and Kinokuniya, have about 200 salesmen; smaller companies such as Far Eastern Booksellers have fewer. The salesmen were already in place to sell new books, textbooks and serials, and would take the catalogues (with Japanese language preliminaries) to the relevant academics, check library duplication, and so on. Kikuo Sakamoto, who joined Maruzen in 1953 and retired in 1995, notes that 'many university libraries purchased competitively collections and rare books of Japanese and foreign countries as treasures and also pride of their library' and that 'our business was very active and aggressive'.[28] Kinokuniya report buying collections from some twenty British booksellers, Maruzen and Far Eastern Booksellers each say about fifteen. They say that Britain was always the main supplier, followed by Germany, but far fewer booksellers offer them collections now.[29]

Assembling and selling collections[30]

The demand from Japan is mainly for collections on Western civilization in all its aspects. British booksellers built collections in subjects that interested them or which they thought would sell. Japanese booksellers sometimes suggested subjects. Subject specialists had most of the material in stock, whereas 'collection' specialists would either buy a block of material and add to it or assemble from scratch. The trade, home and abroad, is overwhelmingly the biggest source of supply, followed by auction and private buys. Allowing for duplication is increasingly an issue. We now check institutional catalogues online to ensure that books in our collections are 'unknown' to our customers.

Some booksellers have spent up to twenty years assembling collections. It can also be done in a day. An urgent request from a Japanese bookseller to a supplier whose stock is computerized and searchable by subject can result in an offer being made immediately. In 1996 we were asked for 300 books on youth education 'quickly'. Driving to Hay-on-Wye to trawl the shops (Booth best as always) and then, twenty books short, a train and rucksack to London enabled us to send the catalogue less than a week after the commission. Good profit was earned, based on mutual trust built up over many years.

Most 'standard' collections – a few hundred books selling for a few thousand pounds – take a few months to assemble. Most collections of rare books take up to five years. There is a distinction between 'assembling' and 'selling' collections. Some booksellers like to sell their collections themselves, some like to sub-contract the selling and some prefer mainly to sell other booksellers' collections. Roles may change as circumstances dictate. Collections are usually sold by means of a detailed catalogue and the scholarship and standards are the same as when selling individual books – varying in proportion to value. The only difference is that the catalogues of many outstanding collections are completely unknown – often only the bookseller and the purchaser will have copies. Selling by overseas visits is hard work, but customers like to be met and collections are sold during such trips – in the months following – or the mutual goodwill will pay dividends later. A few booksellers still do it.

Profit margins are good, with a selling price of two to three-and-a-half times cost – sometimes more for standard collections. But collection bookselling can be capital intensive. We have had up to 60 collections 'being assembled' at one time (1986) and in 1996 we had £365,000 tied up in collections, though most booksellers would report a much smaller capital investment.

Booksellers know that nothing beats buying books. Those who have sold them will tell you that using their talents to assemble and sell collections and make good profits from so doing is as good as it gets. But it is a gamble. The gamble is that the booksellers' money and skills will result in a collection whose value as a whole is greater than the sum of the parts. It may take a long time to come off, or it may not come off at all. Simon Finch bought Chris Johnson's 'Provincial Poetry 1789-1839' collection but was unable to sell it on; the break-up value, sold at auction, was less than the whole. Whole or parts of failed collections can be returned to stock, consigned to auction or sold within the trade. We pioneered another strategy by taking our 'never-to-be-repeated' Catholic Truth Society collection to the dump. Yes, a purchase order followed shortly. 'Regret no longer available,' we said.

We have received good feedback on the hundreds of collections that have sold direct to libraries in Britain, Europe, North America and Australia over the past 40 years and I believe this to be true for other booksellers. In the Japanese market some report good and a few bad feedback. A senior British bookseller said that the collections trade was 'a trade that had some abuse'. At the height of the boom some standard collections were padded out with poor-quality books. One bookseller told me that, early on, he inadvertently included imperfect books in a collection, was told about it and it never happened again. Reputation is all and many of the big players have successfully repeated several times 'their' particular subject or author collections – both 'standard' and 'rare' books.

In 1982 Hamish Riley-Smith and John Boyle had a brilliant idea. I asked them to tell their tale in their own words:

In the autumn of 1982, after assembling and selling an Adam Smith collection, we decided to put together a collection of Adam Smith's source books. Our plan was to assemble the exact editions possessed or referred to by Adam Smith – that is to say the authorities he was known to have consulted – in writing *The Wealth of Nations* (1976). Our shopping list was based on the authorities, both direct and conjectural, identified by Cannan's 'index of authorities' in 1904 and Skinner and Todd in the Glasgow edition of 1976. It was possible to identify the exact edition used by Adam Smith from the research into his library by Bonar at the end of the nineteenth century and Mizuta and Yanaihara in the twentieth century, and in many cases the exact location of the copy he used.

Having established a detailed list of titles and exact editions, the search began. The collection was to be put together on a 50/50 basis, sharing all costs of purchase equally and therefore any subsequent profit.

The first book, the first edition of Dupré de St Maur's *Essai sur les Monnoies* (Paris, 1746) was bought on 23 December 1982. The last two books to be purchased were William Blackstone's *Commentaries* (first edition; Oxford, 1765-9) and James Steuart's *Political Oeconomy* (first edition; 1767) and the collection closed on 11 May 1985.

The collection contained 120 'authorities': 81 books in English, 23 in French and 16 in Latin and Greek. Some had been bought at auction, not only from the grandees of Mayfair but also from more modest establishments such as a country house sale near Wetherby held by Tennants, where Hamish Riley-Smith secured four items in one swoop. But the antiquarian booksellers were to provide the majority of the books that were acquired, from book fairs, from catalogues and from their shops. In America books were found from Jake Zeitlin, and Pergamon New York; in Paris from Professor G. Sabbagh, Magis, Polak, Raymond Katz, Viardot, Clavreuil, Scheler; in Holland from Max Israel, Nijhoff, Beijers of Utrecht; and at home from McDowell & Stern, Franklin Brooke-Hitching, Peter Murray Hill, Reg Remington, Martin Orskey, Maggs, Tony Laywood, Roger McCrow, Waterfield's, John Lawson, Simon Gough, Robert Steedman, Spike Hughes, Rowan of Belfast, Nigel Phillips, Grant of Edinburgh, Edith Finer of Frognal, Quaritch, and Sanders of Oxford. Several arduous journeys to Paris were undertaken (if there wasn't a 'source book' in sight then there might be 'quelque chose en Arabe' or dentistry, both which could easily be marketed east of Calais). A detailed catalogue was produced by Hamish Riley-Smith, with an introduction by Professor Andrew Skinner, one of the General Editors of the Glasgow Edition of *The Wealth of Nations*.

Some of the books were expensive, but had to be found to give the collection any sort of integrity. They included François Quesnay's *Physiocratie* (Leiden, 1768-7), found in Max Israel's shop in Amsterdam in June 1983, and Richard Cantillon's *Essai sur la Nature du Commerce* ([Paris], 1755), found at Scheler's in Paris. There was one book which at the outset we thought we would never find. It was a French book which Adam Smith had used as a source for the development of his theories on taxation, Jean Louis Moreau de Beaumont's five-volume *Mémoires concernant les Impositions et Droits en Europe* (Paris, 1768-9). Adam Smith's own copy was given to him by Turgot. He lent it to Sir John Sinclair in 1778 and wrote, 'If any accident should happen to my book, the loss is perfectly irreparable.' A copy was found in February 1983 at Nijhoff in the Hague. They had bought it at the Signet Library sale in Edinburgh in 1979. Remarkably we found another copy at Magis in September of the same year and sold it separately. Neither of us have seen another copy since.

Some of the books were not necessarily expensive, but were elusive because we were looking for the exact edition used by Adam Smith. Among these were William Hay's *Remarks on the Laws Relating to the Poor* (1735), Cicero's *Opera* (11 parts in 16 volumes; Amsterdam, 1724), Jenyns's *Thoughts on the Causes and Consequences of the Present High Price of Provisions* (second edition; 1767), David Hume's *Political Discourses* (first edition; Edinburgh, 1752), and *A Summary, Historical and Political, of the First Planting, Progressive Improvements, and Present State of the British Settlements in North-America* (second edition; 1755) by William Douglass, whom Adam Smith described as 'the honest and downright Doctor Douglas'.

As complete as could reasonably be expected, the collection was offered in May 1985 on an exclusive basis to one of Japan's oldest and largest booksellers. The price was quite high, as were our hopes, but within six weeks that most damning telex a bookseller could receive from Tokyo was transmitted. A 'P.F.F.' they were known as, and for those lucky enough never to have received one it means 'Please Feel Free' to offer elsewhere. So the collection did the rounds of the other big booksellers in Japan but no one expressed any real interest. A good two years later, in June 1987, the original Japanese bookseller was in London and we tentatively enquired about possible progress. 'Very sorry, unsaleable.' A few days later the same gentleman rang us at midnight (his time) and asked if it was still available. On receiving the affirmative answer he said, 'we now place firm order'. Two days later we were again contacted by him. 'Please to supply immediately second copy of collection for another customer.'

Who were the important players in the collection business?

Leading players were Noel Bolingbroke-Kent, John Boyle, Jim Burmester, David Chilton, Kulgin Duval and Colin Hamilton, Chris Johnson, Conor Kenny, Chris and Michèle Kohler, Maggs, Quaritch, Hamish Riley-Smith, Jeffrey Stern, Rudi Thoemmes and Paul Wilson.

Noel Bolingbroke-Kent, in Norfolk, has sold more than a thousand collections since 1964, more than any other bookseller in the world. He is a good buyer and a persistent seller of books in many countries. He says that the best collection he ever built was of books and manuscripts by and about Comte Claude-Henri de Saint-Simon (1760-1825). 'Kinokuniya suggested the idea to me. My friend Comte Fernand de Saint-Simon and I found the basis of the collection in a back room of a Paris bookseller. I then spent three years buying from booksellers in Britain and Europe – about 50 different transactions. Dr Robert Wokler wrote the introduction to the catalogue and the collection was so good that Kinokuniya bought it for their stock.'

John Boyle started at Dawsons in 1961 and remembers building up there 'off my own bat' a John Locke collection. He first visited Japan (for Dawsons) in 1967, selling mainly runs of periodicals and a few rare books. He started on his own in 1976. His visits to Japan continue to this day. He has been involved with many significant rare book collections in the fields of philosophy, economics, literature and dentistry – often working in partnership and friendship with others.

West Country bookseller Jim Burmester's favourite collection is his accumulation of 'Publishing abroad, as illustrated by printing in English on the continent in the eighteenth and nineteenth centuries' which now numbers close to a thousand books acquired over the course of twenty years. He finds endless fascination in discovering the texts that were chosen for Continental distribution, and their relative popularity. The collection has not been offered for sale yet. Most of the collections he has sold have been to North America and they included three series – a sort of Victorian 'three-decker' – on 'Victorian Fiction by Women', 'Victorian Travellers in Europe' and 'Victorian Travellers in North America'.

David Chilton in York and Paul Wilson in Shrewsbury are two independent booksellers who both separately and jointly have assembled some of the more significant area studies collections in their specialist fields of Africa and the Middle

East. A collection on West Africa, developed from an initial core purchase of an academic's working library, was sold to a Japanese university in the late 1980s. That encouraged the building over the following several years of a much larger collection on the same theme, which comprised some 4,700 titles. This collection was sold to a newly established national library in the Arabian Gulf in 2000. David Chilton spent more than a decade putting together a major collection on the history and geography of the Arabian Gulf region. The project began in the late 1980s. Maggs became a minority shareholder in the collection in 1993 and were instrumental in its sale in 2001. The collection of more than 5,300 items, almost all in European languages and including books from the sixteenth century to the twentieth, is now in the Gulf.

Kulgin Duval and Colin Hamilton sell their books from Perthshire. They have built a number of collections on subjects that interested them, from the Enlightenment to social studies and economics. In 1972 they had the innovative idea of commissioning 39 bindings from leading artists and craftsmen in Great Britain. They sold the collection to the Lilly Library in 1975 who say 'the results were spectacular. The range of techniques and aesthetic effects defy categorization, but the spectrum serves as a basis for the study of the best in contemporary fine binding.'[31]

In 1969 Chris Johnson attended a course on bibliography given by David Foxon at Oxford for students for the B.Litt. One day Foxon brought in some volumes of early nineteenth-century verse, explaining how such material was now inviting the attention of collectors and librarians. Johnson started bookselling in Manchester in the early 1970s and spent eighteen years fanatically searching for minor verse printed in the provinces between 1789 and 1839. He sold the resulting collection of a thousand titles to Simon Finch. The published catalogue, *Provincial Poetry 1789-1839*, is frequently cited.[32] The collection was later dispersed at auction. Now in London, Johnson drew upon the best materials which came on the market, developed an interest in British social history and has assembled collections on 'Poverty and Poor Laws' for nearly twenty years.

In 1940 Conor Kenny's parents rented two rooms in High Street, Galway and started a bookshop in the front room. Kenny still trades from Galway. He sold collections to North America in the 1980s, but did not sell collections to Japan until 1995 – a move prompted by British dealers buying books for collections cheaply from him for re-sale to Japan. He has now sold over 650 collections. His success in a declining market is due to flexibility, ability to respond to requests for collections instantaneously because of his catalogued stock of several hundred thousand books, and offering credit to the Japanese trade. He told Sheila Markham in 2002 'we all have to adapt to changing markets. ... We have always gone to faraway places in search of new buyers. When we meet librarians, we don't bring books – we bring ourselves.'[33]

The Dorking booksellers Chris and Michèle Kohler have sold just over 700 collections to fourteen different countries since 1964, for a total turnover of £4,287,278. They sold some 9,000 titles of British poetry between 1789 and 1918 to the University of California at Davis, more than 1,500 titles of 'British Poetry of the Romantic Period 1789 to 1839' were purchased by Stanford, and a gathering of 1,601 Victorian three-deckers went to the University of Sydney. A collection of editions of Sir Walter Scott's writings published outside Britain, in English and in translation, is now in the National Library of Scotland. In 1985 they bought 74 books on evolution from the Guildhall Bookshop in Kingston; in the spring of 2006 the Kohler Darwin collection was acquired by the Natural History Museum in South Kensington.

Maggs built few collections themselves – 'not our style of trading' – but sold quite a number in these years, often modern English literature and travel, always on behalf of a third party. Robert Harding, writing in the introduction to Maggs catalogue 1350, *STC & Wing. Books printed in England 1500-1700 from the library of James Stevens-Cox (1910-1997)* (2003), explains that Stevens-Cox was not only an antiquarian bookseller:

On leaving school JSC was apprenticed to his parents, receiving a thorough grounding in ladies' hairdressing and wigmaking. ... Some dozen years ago Maggs Bros had the distinction of selling the Stevens-Cox hairdressing collection which as well as books included a vast array of hardware, including bigoudis, curling tongs and hairpieces (sadly no merkins, although he was fully trained in their manufacture and delighted in retailing their history). ... The collection was sold to a Japanese 'Museum of Femininity' sponsored by a manufacturer of ladies' underwear, causing disruption at the Tokyo docks as customs agents tried to work out what these machines were.

Based on the idea that a good story is the best source of a good opera, Quaritch sought out the literary sources, from the world-famous to the trivial, for their 'Literature of Opera' collection. They enjoyed assembling it and the fact that no other bookseller had attempted such a thing. Quaritch have assembled other imaginative, ground-breaking collections, including 'From Wunderkammer to Museum' (in 1984, with Diana Parikian); 'The Philosophy of Language 1668-1926'; 'Gelegenheitsdichtung: A Collection of German Celebratory Verse 1550-1750' and 'Bernard de Mandeville and the Fable of the Bees'.

Hamish Riley-Smith is a Norfolk bookseller. In his interview with Sheila Markham he described himself as 'a simpleton; I go for brand names'.[34] Other booksellers see him as a brilliant bookseller who assembles important collections: on David Ricardo, 'Thomas Mun and Mercantilism in the 17th Century', Sir William Petty, 'Book-keeping and Accountancy before 1800' and Isaac Newton, among many others.

The York bookseller Jeffrey Stern believes that British booksellers have assembled many definitive collections of Western books, of enduring importance to the progress of scholarship in the countries that purchased them. He, like others, has enjoyed the challenge of using his academic and bookselling skills to create collections that have not only extended the bibliography but have also, potentially, laid the foundations for new research. Stern has built 144 collections during the past twenty years, on social history, education, economics, technology, literature and art. Of particular note were his collections on Lewis Carroll, Pestalozzi, Maria Montessori, the history of education, Wordsworth and Robert Owen. 'It's fantastic what you can discover, piecing together the bibliographical past,' he says.

Rudi Thoemmes started bookselling whilst reading philosophy at the University of Bristol and he still works from Bristol. During the early 1980s no one else was specializing in philosophy and he moved into the gap. He told Sheila Markham: 'I was also lucky to be starting when it was still possible to sell large collections, especially to Japan. In my second year of bookselling I began concentrating on that aspect and, by the mid-80s, it was almost too easy to make a lot of money.'[35] Thoemmes has sold collections on philosophy, economics and accountancy, as well as author collections on Kant, Locke, Hume, Berkeley, Descartes, Mill, Adam Smith, Hegel, Schopenhauer and, like a number of other booksellers, several professors' libraries.

What does it all add up to?

In terms of both the number and the value of collections sold, Japan (mostly from the 1980s to mid-1990s) has been by far the largest market. In second place is North America (mostly late 1970s to early 2000s) and third are Great Britain and Ireland (mostly mid-1970s to early 1980s, and again in the 2000s). Germany (mostly mid-1970s to 1980s) and Australia (mostly 1970s to mid-1980s) have been good markets in the past for some booksellers. Others are now selling to Taiwan and China. I know that collections have also been sold to libraries in the Arabian Gulf, Belgium, Hong Kong, Israel, Italy, Malaysia, the Netherlands, Nigeria, Norway, Saudi Arabia, Singapore, South Africa, South Korea and Sweden. In terms of turnover, 98 per cent of Kohler sales were to four markets: 37 per cent to Japan, 30 per cent to Great Britain and Ireland, 24 per cent to North America and 7 per cent to Australia, but these will not be representative of the whole collections business.

Booksellers wanting to continue to sell collections have learned that to survive they must adapt. The Far East will remain a market. Intelligently designed, specialized research collections will continue to be sold successfully to libraries in North America and Britain. In this country, support from the Heritage Lottery Fund and the National Heritage Memorial Fund has been, and will continue to be, significant in enabling institutional libraries to acquire collections.

In just 50 years, between 1955 and 2005, some 75 British booksellers have sold between 3,250 and 3,500 collections. My best estimate of total sales is £35-40 million. Most collections were sold for less than £4,000. Few collections were sold for more than £500,000. What it all adds up to is not only that British booksellers have pioneered a new way of selling books, but also that two generations of booksellers have assembled world-class collections. As Jeffrey Stern says, 'Making collections is a glorious thing.'[36]

The British Trade and Institutional Libraries

MICHÈLE KOHLER

BRITISH booksellers, great and small, have been selling old books and manuscripts to institutional libraries worldwide for hundreds of years. The relationship between the trade and its institutional customers is a relatively unexplored subject, however, and it is only possible here to give a brief overview of that relationship during the twentieth century and to point the way to further research. It is interesting to see the trade through the eyes of a significant customer: Cornell University has been selected as a case study, to demonstrate how much material remains to be discovered in institutional archives.

At the beginning of the twentieth century, the antiquarian bookseller and library supplier Edward G. Allen & Sons Ltd. was dealing with the Library of Congress, Yale, Harvard and Cornell.[1] B.F. Stevens & Brown was selling to American public libraries, universities and government departments.[2] James Bain supplied books to the Library of the Parliament of Queensland in Brisbane, the Shanghai Library and the Royal University Library in Uppsala.[3] He also notes that after the First World War he sold books to the Rockefeller Institute for Medical Research in New York City.[4] Following the Second World War, books were seen as dollar-earning exports; firms like James Wilson's bookshop in Birmingham were selling to the Library of Congress and the Newberry Library in Chicago.[5] The increase in student numbers and government funding made the institutional library sector even more powerful purchasers in the second half of the century.

Most dealings with institutional libraries are by catalogue and booksellers must develop mailing lists. Among the traditional tools for doing this are Bowker library directories, the *Commonwealth Universities Yearbook* and other specialist library directories. Booksellers can purchase mailing lists and may be given them by elderly colleagues. Many of the same libraries will be on many booksellers' lists. Pickering & Chatto has a notebook listing its customers that was begun early in the century and added to as recently as 1960. The list is a roll-call of major research institutions. The absence of zip codes and modern names for some of the libraries gives it a wonderful period flavour.[6] Although booksellers' specific mailing lists cannot be easily reconstructed, it is possible to work out which booksellers dealt with various institutions. Princeton University Library, for example, is one of several libraries to list as a special collection its antiquarian booksellers' catalogues.[7]

Beyond catalogues, how do booksellers establish links with their institutional customers? The simplest way is to get involved with local institutions. Iain Campbell is best known as a dealer in printed ephemera who has devoted many hours to the various libraries of Merseyside. His list of institutional customers includes record offices, museums, art galleries and commercial and industrial archives.[8]

Most institutional customers, however, are not local. Prior to the Second World War foreign travel was costly as well as time-consuming. Relatively few booksellers visited their overseas customers, although Quaritch, Maggs and Lionel Robinson were among those who did. Once hostilities ceased this began to change. The great ocean liners once again plied the Atlantic, making business travel easier. A few booksellers, such as Percy Muir, were able to cover the costs of visiting the United States by lecture fees.[9]

By the 1960s booksellers were able to take advantage of quicker and more convenient air travel between Britain and the United States. While his father was still making annual trips to the United States, Anthony Rota's only visit was to the University of South Carolina. But from 1967 and for the next 21 years, Anthony visited his library customers on a very regular basis. He participated in the Rare Book School at Columbia University and gave a course of lectures at the University of Tulsa. His warm relationships with numerous librarians and institutions are evident from the testimonials published to celebrate his 75th birthday.[10] At about the same time John Lawson visited America with John Maggs, was smitten and thereafter made frequent visits to library customers. He became a regular supplier of books to the John Carter Brown library at Brown University, Rhode Island. In 1967 he flew to Winnipeg in Canada and then travelled by train to the University of Calgary and to the University of Alberta at Edmonton. He also went with John Maggs to Australia, where he met librarians in Sydney and Canberra.[11]

Today booksellers can meet librarians at book fairs, but before these fairs became commonplace booksellers had to organize their own exhibitions. Earlier in the century Maggs regularly booked exhibition space in America and put on displays for its American customers.[12] In 1968, Chris Kohler held book exhibitions in Chicago, Washington and New York 'to meet our most important group of customers – the North American Librarians. ... So here we are with our books. Come and visit our exhibitions.'[13] The entrepreneurial spirit is maintained nowadays by booksellers such as Christopher Edwards and Roger Gaskell, who are constantly looking for new and interesting ways to offer their books to customers.[14]

The best and most rewarding relationships with institutional libraries have always required the ability to be a good listener and to pay close attention to detail. The bookseller must deal with the library on at least two levels – books and personalities. Familiarity with the library's holdings is of prime importance. In the past this might have been achieved through a marked-up bibliography[15] or by repeated visits to the library to consult its catalogue. More recently it has become possible for the bookseller to do this from home, by using the internet. Finding the right person used to be hit and miss – the most rewarding contact may not be the first person suggested or the one with the obvious job title. The librarian must then be nurtured. And just when the bookseller is enjoying a rewarding relationship, the librarian moves to another position or another institution. Perhaps that new institution will want the bookseller's books, perhaps not. The replacement may be an old contact from somewhere else, or someone with his or her own favourite suppliers.

Some booksellers have built up close relationships with institutional libraries: well-known ones are between Quaritch and the British Library and between Rota and the Harry Ransom Humanities Research Center. Paul Wilson, John Titford and John Coombes are representative of a great many other names quietly building amicable relationships with institutions: Paul Wilson of Oriental and African Books of Shrewsbury has had a close involvement with the development of the Abdul Karim Mirghani Cultural Centre in Sudan,[16] while John Titford of Derbyshire, a genealogist and part-time bookseller, has specialized in supplying the Library of Congress with genealogical works. John Coombes of Dorking has specialized in British local history and topography and for many years also dealt in Ordnance Survey maps. He devoted much time and attention to customers such as Cambridge University Library, the State Library of Victoria and the National Library of Australia, using marked-up lists of Ordnance Survey maps to help them build their holdings.[17]

One sign of the close relations between booksellers, their customers, and the books and manuscripts they sell is the public recognition that a library sometimes gives its supplier. Thus the webpage of the Spencer Library at the University of Kansas mentions that the core of their Curll collection came from Peter Murray Hill, and that other important items in their holdings were supplied by Maggs, E.P. Goldschmidt and Wheldon & Wesley.[18] The Lilly Library at Indiana University acknowledges, for example, that the Hannah Whitall Smith papers and the Browning papers were purchased from Colin and Charlotte Franklin.[19] In 'One Curator's Apology', the preface to the exhibition catalogue celebrating his career, Roger Stoddard of the Houghton Library, Harvard University, observes:

The true curators of 'special' collections and historical libraries are antiquarian bookdealers. The books on exhibition and in the notes – together with other purchases among the sixty-five thousand books acquired since 1965 – came to Harvard by collaboration between a librarian and hundreds of antiquarian bookdealers from around the world. If only they could all be cited here, every one of them named. Here at least are a few to whom I feel special debts for what they taught me, what they showed me, what they sold to me. …

He mentions Arthur Freeman, Theodore Hofmann, Stephen Weissman, Diana Parikian, James Burmester, P.N. Poole-Wilson, Alex Fotheringham, Bryan Maggs, Robert Harding and Detlev Auvermann.[20] To give another example, Ian Rogerson in his exhibition catalogue of the Shakespeare Head Press (1988) notes that 'the collection in Manchester Polytechnic Library has been built over a fifteen year period. Among those booksellers who have directed material towards this library, Blackwell's Rare Books, Claude Cox, Barry McKay, Eric Morten, Shaw's Bookshop and John Bevan have been most helpful.'[21]

What of the other services that booksellers offer their institutional customers? Quaritch began to act as an agent at auction for libraries, including those of the British Museum and the Natural History Museum, as long ago as the end of the nineteenth century; by the middle of the twentieth, it had a virtual monopoly on English institutional bids. Booksellers have also been regularly called on by institutional libraries for insurance valuations and to assist with grant applications. Libraries occasionally give booksellers special one-off commissions. When the University of Tulsa wanted to build up women's studies holdings for a visiting academic, they contacted Charles Cox to fill the order.[22] In 1997 C.C. Kohler was asked by the Hoover Institution at Stanford University to offer material dealing with British General Elections. They already collected manifestos and candidates' biographies. 'But the ephemera is more difficult. ... Stickers, banners, silly stuff, anything colourful I could use for a mini exhibit for students is also very welcome.'[23]

Trade, as we know, is a two-way street, and just as British booksellers enjoy meeting their customers in their libraries, so librarians enjoy meeting their suppliers and viewing their stock. Lawrence Clark Powell of the University of California at Los Angeles documented his visits to Britain, most notably in *A Passion for Books* and *Books in My Baggage*.[24] He writes about travelling to the West Country and meeting James Commin of Exeter, visiting Harry Pratley in Tunbridge Wells, Beach's in Salisbury, Thomas Crowe in Norwich and Percy Muir in Essex; he describes combing the basements of Maggs for hidden treasure; he reports his visits to Harold Edwards's Newbury bookshop and also the Aladdin's cave of a garden shed in the bookseller's Ashmore Green garden.

An important frequent visitor in the middle of the century was Eleanor Pitcher, who selected books for the Folger Shakespeare Library. In 1949 she had moved from the Huntington Library to Washington DC, to become assistant to the Director of the Folger and head of the accessions department. Her boss Louis B. Wright described her skills:

Miss Pitcher has a quality envied by all librarians and bookmen. She can remember titles for years and keeps books in her head on the prices of thousands of items. Spotting a book on a shelf in Edinburgh, let us say, she will remember whether the Folger needs that title and will know probably as well or better than the dealer what it is worth. One of her great assets is that through twenty years of contacts with scholars she also knows what kind of rare books the research worker in history and literature most likely will need.[25]

She regularly spent six months of the year in London, using it as a base for visiting bookshops throughout England, Scotland, France and the Netherlands. Martin Hamlyn remembers her, with bags full of reference material, sitting 'in the chill grime of the crypt, wrapped in blankets and with a coffee flask and an electric fire', sorting out Wing pamphlets from the Phillipps collection, at that time stored by the Robinson brothers beneath a church in Gordon Square.[26] Wright too visited British booksellers, enjoying himself at Blackwell's, 'a sort of club where we met several scholars and bibliophiles whom we had been hoping all summer to see'. He singled out for special praise George Harding's bookshop in Great Russell Street, where George Wheeler had the reputation of understanding better than any other bookseller the needs of customers undertaking historical research.[27]

One visitor who was always welcome – and always welcomed visiting booksellers in return – was Marella Walker of Emory University in Atlanta. Up through the early 1980s she would arrive at Gatwick and begin her rounds, visiting Kohler, Quaritch, Jarndyce, Maggs and Blackwells.[28] Ginger Cain, the University Archivist at Emory, first worked for Marella as an undergraduate. 'She was amazing, quite shrewd, tyrannical to the staff at times (she reduced each of us to tears at least once), and hilariously funny.'[29] In 1954 Marella became the Head of Acquisitions in the Woodruff Library at Emory, where she was described by Ted Johnson, the Director, as 'a woman astute in business practices and possessing a fantastic memory'. She had the 'ability to recall with great accuracy those titles from any century that Emory had or still was seeking'.[30] After a trip to England with Marella, Johnson observed that 'relations with particular dealers were strengthened and new ones developed which have resulted in purchases throughout the year'.[31] Brian Lake of Jarndyce notes that 'the most important thing about Marella was that she was not only an enthusiast, but methodical about pursuing her enthusiasm on behalf of her library. Helen Smith painstakingly marked our copy of Wolff with her nineteenth-century fiction "wants", together with the books already in Emory, which greatly assisted us in adding to their holdings. I can't think of many, if any, librarians today who pursue their quarry in such a determined and organised way.'[32]

Other initiatives to improve relations between libraries and the trade included James Babb's programme for bringing booksellers to Yale University. Bryan Maggs was offered one of these internships at the Beinecke Library just after his father's death in July 1960, though he was unable to take it up, while Keith Fletcher took up a similar opportunity soon afterwards.[33] Between 1943 and 1981 the National Library of Australia had a liaison officer in London, whose duties included meeting antiquarian booksellers and discussing possible purchases – a process that included cocktail parties at Australia House.[34]

This gives a sampling of the relationship between British booksellers and institutional libraries which can be garnered from interviews and memoirs. But it does not give a continuous quotidian picture. To single out one bookselling firm to the exclusion of all others has not been an option – but a preliminary study of a particular institution may serve as a marker for future research. Cornell University, an Ivy League institution founded by Ezra Cornell and Andrew Dickson White in 1865, seemed a good choice. Cornell's great good luck was that its first president, Andrew Dickson White, and first librarian, Willard Fiske, were bibliophiles and got its library off to a flying start.

By the beginning of the twentieth century Cornell's library of 250,000 volumes ranked fifth among American university libraries after Harvard, Yale, Columbia and Chicago. By June 1965 the number of volumes had grown to 2,700,000 and at the end of the century it was approaching 7,000,000, making the university's library the tenth largest in the United States.[35] In other words a major player by anyone's definition. A more detailed history would show various ups and downs in status, in spending, in satisfaction; however, this is not a history of Cornell but rather a tale of its relationships with British booksellers.

Cornell is unique among non-British universities in that two of its alumni are outstanding active members of the British trade, having spent their entire bookselling careers in England: Joan Winterkorn and Ted Hofmann of Quaritch. Joan Winterkorn was not the first Cornell librarian to work in the London book trade – Felix Reichmann spent time with E.P. Goldschmidt before the Second World War and Donald Eddy produced the highly regarded Samuel Johnson catalogue for Maggs Brothers in 1983.

At the beginning of the twentieth century most of Cornell's British book buying was from E.G. Allen & Sons in London. Cornell purchased both new and out-of-print books from Allen, as well as serials and journal subscriptions. During the First World War these were supplemented by the occasional order from J. Wheldon, Dulau & Co., B.F. Stevens & Brown, and Spink & Son. After the war there were also orders from Galloway & Porter, Quaritch and James Thin.[36] As the 1920s progressed further booksellers were involved, including J.G. Commin, George Harding, P.J. & A.E. Dobell, Thomas Thorp, Maggs, Grafton & Co., Probsthain, Kegan Paul, Luzac, G.H. Last, John Grant and Heffers.[37] In the 1930s and 1940s the list of suppliers reads like a volume of Sheppard's directory of the book trade.[38]

Our understanding of Cornell's relationships with the British book trade owes much to the meticulous record-keeping of Felix Reichmann, who was hired in 1947 as Acquisitions Librarian and served as the Assistant Director of Technical Services from 1948 to 1964 and then as Assistant Director for Collection Development from 1964 to 1970 – in the years when these positions were power centres in libraries. In January 1956 he visited Europe, mainly to buy books for the South-East Asian collections, and sent the following report back to Ithaca:

London. I visited the following bookstores: Francis Edwards, E.P. Goldschmidt, Wm. Dawson & Sons, Myers & Co., Pickering and Chatto, W.H. Robinson, Maggs Bros. Bernard Quaritch, Henry Sotheran, George Salby, Charles J. Sawyer, Arthur Probsthain, Kegan Paul, Trench & Trubner, Luzac & Co., W. Foyle, Edward G. Allen & Son. In these stores holdings with regard to Southeast Asia were inspected, the dealers prepared lists which were sent to Cornell, the Acquisition Department checked these lists against our catalog, and we bought everything which we did not have. I also looked over their holdings with regard to India, and missing titles were ordered. I searched in the stores for other titles which we wanted, and was able to select several interesting ones. Among the books acquired were two early editions of Chaucer, Varclius, Anatomia, several interesting Wordsworth items, etc.

The holdings of the English book markets with regard to Southeast Asia material were extremely meagre. Dealers unanimously reported that very little is being offered and that purchases made by Oriental libraries and American institutions deplete their stock immediately.

My most important objective was to impress on selected members of the London book trade the interest and needs of the University library. I hope I have been successful in this respect. Offers are still coming in currently and certain very important items could be bought because of recent offers.[39]

Academics were also encouraged to scout bookshops and Reichmann followed up a visit to Blackwell's by the leading Cornell Wordsworth scholar and curator of the Cornell Wordsworth Collection with an order: 'Professor Healey of our University saw in your shop a set of Wordsworth … bound in decorated cloth. This set is stored on the highest shelf above the books on English language and philology and not with the other Wordsworth material.'[40]

Reichmann's correspondence shows high expectations and a keen under-standing of the trade, reflecting many years' experience, including his time as a cataloguer with E.P. Goldschmidt. While much of it deals with accepting or rejecting offers, ordering from catalogues and returning duplicates, other letters tell us more about the relations between the trade and one of its customers. Reichmann was not above criticising members of the trade – in this case Luzac – when they did not meet his high standards:

This will acknowledge with thanks your letter of June 12. We have checked your many lists carefully; however, as in many cases you have not given us enough information – for instance, you have fairly everywhere left out the first names – I am sure we may be ordering some unwanted duplicates. A small amount we shall accept, and add as second copies, but we could not do this indefinitely. Will you from now on send us complete entries – author, family name and Christian name, publisher and date. The date especially is important.[41]

Offers from British booksellers were reviewed by librarians and the following comments were attached to an offer from another London bookseller: 'This collection, though parts of it are of interest, does not as a collection, fit the pattern of our holdings and interests, and we could not easily justify the purchases at this time. [And by the way it is dreadfully over-priced, aimed at the American market for manuscripts]'.[42]

Although other booksellers, including the Soviet spy Peter J. Kroger,[43] were occasionally used by Cornell as agents at auction, most such work in the period was carried out by Maggs. The relationship was one of trust and good advice. Sotheby's offered a Wordsworth manuscript in a sale on 23 July 1962 (lot 295) and Reichmann suggested a bid limit of £200. 'If in your opinion this would not be adequate, will you please write immediately to Professor George Healey … I am going to be out of town for the next two weeks, and as we are anxious to buy this manuscript, please contact Professor Healey immediately.' Maggs obtained the item for Cornell for £60.[44]

In the 1960s Cornell dealt with Blackwell's, C.K. Broadhurst, Thomas Crowe, Dawsons of Pall Mall, Peter Eaton, Harold Edwards, Hugh K. Elliot, Ifan Kyrle

Fletcher, E.P. Goldschmidt, R.D. Gurney, Frank Hammond, Hannas, Hollett, Howes, Kohler, Harold Landry, Maggs, Quaritch, F.S. Read, A. Rosenthal, E. Seligmann, Geoffrey Aspin, Tony Appleton, K.D. Duval, The Bookshop in Wells, Guernsey Books, H.T. Jantzen, Merrion Book Company, Eric & Joan Stevens, Alan G. Thomas, Traylen and Walford.[45] The list is a snapshot of the trade at the time: small and large businesses, metropolitan and provincial, mail order and shop premises, old and young. Felix Reichmann retired in 1970 and died in 1987.

When archives are as wide-ranging as Reichmann's correspondence, they may reveal many minor players in the institutional library's dealings; the memories of more recent librarians are more focused. Donald Eddy, whose special interest was the eighteenth century, remembers most vividly dealing with Maggs, Arnold Muirhead and Peter Murray Hill. David Corson stressed the role of Roger Gaskell in the world of antiquarian scientific books. Katherine Reagan's list of current contacts in the trade includes Dylan's Bookshop, Amanda Hall, James Burmester, Christopher Edwards, Timothy d'Arch Smith (supplier of a masturbation collection) and, of course, Quaritch. She emphasized that Cornell alumna Joan Winterkorn continues to take an interest in the library.[46]

Cornell is just one of the thousands of institutional libraries worldwide to which the British rare and secondhand book trade sells. Its archives provide an example of the range of material that is available for research into the numerous contacts between booksellers and librarians that make up the relationship between the trade and institutional libraries. The history of this relationship is a broad subject, encompassing the history of taste, of education, of collecting, of international finance, advertising, tourism and travel – readers can probably add to this list. It is hoped that this brief chapter has told some good stories and highlighted some pathways for future research.

24. Cecil Court, looking east, in the mid-1970s.

25. The view from the inside: H.M. Fletcher's shop (27 Cecil Court), *c.*1970.

26. E.M. Dring of Quaritch, in the midst of packing for the move from Grafton Street to Golden Square, 1970.

27 & 28. Bernard Quaritch
Ltd, 11 Grafton Street,
*c.*1970: (above) elaborate
display cases; (left) the safe.

29. The eighteenth-century grandeur of Maggs Brothers Ltd, 50 Berkeley Square, as pictured in a promotional brochure of 1939.

30. The top-lit gallery at Francis Edwards Ltd, 83 Marylebone High Street, c.1975.

31. Concrete and plate glass at Bertram Rota Ltd, 4-6 Savile Row, c.1970.

32. Bundles of prints in the basement of Suckling & Co., 13 Cecil Court, c.1970.

33. Printed ephemera: the Bloomsbury bookseller Andrew Block cataloguing his stock, *c.*1970.

34. The inner sanctum: Louis Bondy's shop in Little Russell Street, in the late 1960s.

35, 36 & 37. Three London booksellers in the late 1960s: (top left) Stanley Smith (49 Marchmont Street); (bottom left) George Suckling (13 Cecil Court); (above) Harold Mortlake (24 Cecil Court).

38 & 39. English country bookshops, *c.*2003: (left) Claude Cox, College Gateway Bookshop, Ipswich, a fifteenth-century merchant's house; (below) George Bayntun, Bath, a nineteenth-century postal sorting office.

40. Howes Bookshop, Hastings, a Victorian parish school.

41. Bow Windows Book Shop, Lewes, in the medieval High Street
(the 'bow windows' remain in the former premises further up the hill).

42. Blackwell's bookshop, Broad Street, Oxford, 1938.

43. James Thin in the office of his South Bridge bookshop, Edinburgh, *c.*1904.

Dealers and the Specialist Collector

DAVID CHAMBERS

BOOK collecting can often be simply a matter of buying whatever is easily found in catalogues or at book fairs, with no greater purpose than to have entertaining books on the shelves. Such a collection, though, may well develop into something of more independent consequence, a collection constructed with a purpose, with a meaning that will give its final catalogue a place on the reference shelves of other collectors and dealers. The nature of this intent is not the question, but rather that there was a well-defined object in the first place. The purpose may, of course, have been the result of serious consideration by the collector, or may have been engineered by some dealer luring him along a particular path. But there has plainly to be a purpose to the collection if it is ever to be of any consequence.

The influence of the dealer is obvious, even if made less personal nowadays through the use of the internet. In some cases a single dealer may have been employed to search for and buy the books, but more often it is the collector who leads the chase, cultivating a number of dealers, but issuing wants lists to as many others as he dares. One might pursue the history of specialist collecting through some closely analysed account of those searching for papyri in Egypt, manuscripts in Rome, or printed books over the last 500 years. There are reminiscences of such relationships in all the 'books about books' that provide entertainment during occasional lapses from one's own quest for the impossible.

T.J. Wise (1859-1937) might serve as opening player from the past century, declaring himself to be a collector rather than dealer, yet creating – by forgery – the first editions which he persuaded fellow collectors to buy from him. Apart from the sale of recently printed 'first editions', Wise used his eminence in the world of books to persuade a wealthy stockbroker, John Henry Wrenn from Chicago, to build a collection of seventeenth-century plays – a project worthy enough in itself, were it not that Wise had torn some of the titlepages from copies in the British Museum. He was elected President of the Bibliographical Society on the strength of his bibliographies of nineteenth-century authors, though he included forgeries within his detailed lists.[1] Wise was not greatly liked by booksellers and was eventually caught out because the trade became suspicious. The story is too well known to consider in any detail, but Wise's relationships with other collectors and with the trade, for all his dishonesty, manifested in an extreme form the elements of a fertile imagination, obsessive acquisitiveness, dogged determination and persuasive advocacy, all of which are a necessary part of creating and fulfilling the object of a specialist collection of books.

Two or three decades later, in the five years just before the Second World War, Percy Muir was asked by Ian Fleming (1908-64) to search for what the two men called 'milestones of progress'. The idea was Fleming's, who had just made £250 in a stockbroking deal, but it was Muir who sought out and bought the books. What they were looking for were scientific books and those concerned with philosophy, inventions and even sports and pastimes. Such subjects were not in great demand, and were consequently available for relatively modest prices, so that when Muir helped organize the great Printing and the Mind of Man exhibition in 1967, more of Fleming's books were included than from any other private collection.[2]

George Lazarus (1905-97) had a similar arrangement with Bertram Rota, who alone was charged with forming his collection. Lazarus was an active member of the Stock Exchange and had little time available for searching shops or catalogues on his own account. The object of pursuit, following an early enthusiasm for Galsworthy, was the work of contemporary authors for whom he felt similar excitement – and he could have made no better choice than Bertram Rota for the task. Rota described the guiding principles behind Lazarus's collection:

Determine the field and stay within it. Choose and use one reliable expert. Buy courageously when good opportunities occur, but not beyond reasonable judgement. Gather every separately-published work by each chosen author. Buy the first edition, wherever printed, and the earliest issue, whatever its form. Insist upon fine condition. Try to enrich each author collection with original manuscripts, letters and interesting association copies.

Following these sound if ruthless conditions, the collection of some 30 novelists that Rota put together was extraordinarily rich, in particular the collection of D.H. Lawrence, for which others had to be sacrificed as it grew in size – the sales then handled by Rota's son, Anthony. In the end the Lawrences were bequeathed to Nottingham University.[3]

The use of a single dealer, whether at the dealer's instigation or that of the collector, has often enough resulted in the finest of collections, but far more often the collector has controlled the whole affair, following his own paths, though often influenced initially by the books that were available from his regular dealers. The well-tried method was to search through catalogues and send out wants lists, at the same time establishing close relationships with particular dealers.

Writing in *The Book Collector* in 1954, Albert Ehrman (1890-1969) commented: 'This is an age of specialists in all walks of life, and not least among book collectors.' By his own account, however, it was a chance purchase in Eastbourne, while he was recovering from influenza, of a Venetian incunable in a contemporary binding, that provided the inspiration for not merely one, but two specialist collections, about the invention and spread of printing and about the history of different styles of binding. In both cases, Ehrman proceeded to buy up several small collections which had already been formed by specialist collectors or booksellers:

Many are the disappointments in collecting: one's telegram was just too late, or one was careless in reading the catalogue and missed the book entirely; on the other hand, the greatest opportunity any collector can have is to be offered the first choice of an entire Library or specialized collection.

The first such opportunity which Ehrman describes was his purchase in 1933 of the 'personal collection' (or so he was led to believe) of early panel-stamped bindings belonging to E.P. Goldschmidt: 'At first, he was unwilling to sell anything before his American customers had seen the collection, but after a battle-royal, lasting several hours, I emerged with … the nucleus of our Stamped Binding Collection.' Ehrman was also a customer of Birrell & Garnett, buying a number of early type specimens from the specialist catalogue of this material issued by the firm in 1928. In the early 1930s, he seems to have pre-empted plans for a Birrell & Garnett 'Catalogue of Catalogues' by buying up many of the early book trade catalogues which had been brought together by Graham Pollard with this purpose in mind. The 'Catalogue of Catalogues' never appeared, but 30 years later Ehrman presented to the Roxburghe Club an important book by Pollard on the subject, with a detailed listing of Ehrman's own collection of this material. Other purchases *en bloc* included a small group of incunabula from C.S. Ascherson's collection, bought from Quaritch in 1945, and another group from Lord Bute's library, from Francis Edwards in 1949.[4]

'If not the most learned,' according to Anthony Hobson, 'certainly the largest English book collector of his time,' was J.R. Abbey (1894-1969). Abbey was fortunate in being able to begin collecting seriously in the buyer's market of the 1930s, concentrating at first on private press books, which led him to appreciate and then to commission and collect modern fine bindings. As his interests extended to include antiquarian bindings, he relied heavily on the advice of G.D. Hobson and A.N.L. Munby. Meanwhile, from 1935, he was also forming a separate collection of English colour-plate books of the eighteenth and nineteenth centuries, for which he sought guidance from a different part of the trade, enlisting as his agent the bookseller George Stephenson of James Rimell & Son Ltd., who was followed by George Bates of Hove. This collection alone amounted to nearly 3,000 volumes.[5]

Sir Geoffrey Keynes (1887-1982), by contrast, was a collector whose own knowledge in his chosen fields so outstripped the trade that he could buy against it at auction, knowing, as it did not, the rarity of the books for which he was bidding. At the same time his friendships within the trade meant that he was offered known rarities, and at prices he could afford. In 1914 Percy Dobell sold him a copy of Winckelmann's *Reflections on the Painting and Sculpture of the Greeks* (1765), signed by Blake (though Dobell thought not) for 3s.6d. Lionel Robinson had offered to allow Keynes to buy at cost price the next Blake item which he coveted, and was held to his promise in 1938 over another book, by Swedenborg, with Blake's annotations. But Keynes continued to pursue his quarry by every means possible. His greatest coup came in 1942 when he was able to buy privately a collection of paintings and prints by Blake, from a book auctioneer who had been offered £350 by a furniture dealer and was happy to take £500 instead.

Keynes formed numerous author-collections in the course of a long life; the bibliographies which he published drew wider attention to what he had been collecting, and prices rose accordingly. Writing in his autobiography in 1981, Keynes observed:

> The interest of my own collections depends rather on a principle ... of choosing to study in depth the works of an author whom I found interesting though unfashionable. ... my method avoided competition and high prices – until I had compiled my bibliography. ... by that time I had acquired good copies of all the books and could view with complacency the change in market values. The principle is no longer applicable since the supply of the right kind of books has dried up and all books have become expensive.[6]

Yet fortunately there *are* still books that can be collected at affordable prices, before the rest of the world understands, even if they are not so exceptional in their beauty as Blake's miraculous images.

Simon Nowell-Smith (1909-96) was another collector whose acquisitions do not seem to have been especially influenced by particular dealers. In 1961, in two letters to Percy Muir, he gave an extended, critical commentary on the dealers in London and the country, ending his first letter:

> Hell! When did you last report a book to me? I don't ask much: the Bristol Lyrical Ballads, Fugitive Pieces, Pauline, The Battle of Marathon ...

Muir must have responded with the suggestion that a wants list might help, to which the response was as complex as would be that from any eclectic collector:

> My proper answer to you should be to send you a specific wants list: but that is no answer to my complaint about booksellers leaving London. And my difficulty with a wants list is that I don't know myself what I want until I see it. I collect the early and/or rare books (but not factitious rarities) of English poets from about 1780 to about 1900, and some later. My special enthusiasms at the moment are Landor, Rogers, Southey, Wordsworth, Coleridge, Byron: and though I have (for example) nine of the first dozen titles in Wise's Landor Library, my wants list would include the whole dozen in case better or more interesting copies than mine turned up. So in effect I should have to send you Vol. III of CBEL and ask you to report all poetry in it, even if you knew that I had copies already!

In one of his wants lists, Nowell-Smith later wrote a note in red ink:

> Desiderata – Not necessarily books I should go out of my way to buy, but such as I might be happy to happen upon. S.N.S. '87

Nowell-Smith's canter through the dealers still about in 1961 makes entertaining reading, and, so long after the event, may be quoted here – as Adam might have said, when turned out of paradise, the world is never so good as it once was:

> When a fit of extravagance comes over me – and there is no knowing when it will come or how soon it will go – I greatly regret the disappearance from London of almost all booksellers of intelligence and understanding. Dudley [Massey] remains: but if I ask him

for a particular book, and he admits to having had it since King Street days, I wonder whose stupidity it is – his or mine or a bit of both – that has resulted in his not having offered it to me before. Maggs is (for 1790-1850) hopeless: there is no one there who knows anything. Quaritch is agreeably old-fashioned. Sawyer? well, I ask you! Francis Edwards has a vast stock, not for me, and only buys my sort of book on commission for Americans. Dawsons have the stock I knew so well at Raphael King's. I adore both Winnie Myers & Nellie Clark, but the one has no books and the other cares only for prints. The Robinsons were pricey when on the ground floor, and I have no courage to take the elevator. Like John Betjeman, though for other reasons, I should be content to see the Charing Cross Road pulled down.

And outside London? It is true that I have never known much about the old-established provincial-town booksellers: but if Oxford – Cambridge – is any guide, the trade is dead. The one-or-two-man London-expatriated firm is little better: the bookseller either cares more for his garden than for his books (Edwards, Low, the man who runs Days, whose name I always forget); or he is too smart for me (Sims); or – and this I can admire while I deprecate it – he is more a collector than a seller (Colbeck).

And if any of these dear friends have any books, they sell them to Bill Jackson or Gordon Ray, who triumphantly tell me of their successes.[7]

This was all, of course, something of a posture, for Nowell-Smith had, in fact, a deep respect for the dealers from whom he bought so many remarkable books, and his friendships within the trade helped immeasurably in his many successes – evidenced by both the Bodleian exhibition catalogue (*Wordsworth to Robert Graves and Beyond*, 1982) and Rota's sale catalogue of his collection.[8]

Sir Paul Getty (1932-2003) was able to approach matters in a different way, heavily influenced by dealers in the first place, becoming eventually the more knowledgeable himself, but still relying on their skills to create one of the finest private collections in the country. Starting to collect whilst in America, it was not until he settled into Rossetti's house in Chelsea that his collection began to absorb so much of his time. Colin Franklin, among others, fostered an interest in private press books. When he bought a Kelmscott Chaucer on vellum, the die was cast: he went on to buy all the Kelmscott Press books, and much else besides, all on vellum. He was similarly drawn to illustrated books, particularly aquatints. His collection of early manuscripts followed the same pattern, as the impressive catalogue of the exhibition of his books at the Pierpont Morgan Library amply showed.[9]

Driven by a love of fine workmanship and of well-made books, Getty's collection of bindings was built up by Bryan Maggs, who took over as librarian when Sir Paul and his wife, Victoria, moved to Wormsley in Buckinghamshire. Maggs's advice, and the advice of the firm in general, was of great value, though Sir Paul's knowledge of historical bindings could sometimes rival even that of his mentor. In the earlier years Sir Paul had insufficient funds to buy all that was offered, but after the death of his father he was able to buy more or less without restraint. So he was able to fill the shelves of his newly built library, and the rolling cases below, with a collection that had been inspired by his dealer friends, but was then driven by his own enthusiasms.

My own relationship with the trade extends over the past 60 or so years, from the days when there were several bookshops to be found in any major town to the situation now, when one is glad to be able to find but one. So the progress of my own mania may illustrate the way in which friends in the trade have pandered to it.

My first needs were simple enough: to have all the English classics in the cheapest possible style, Nelson Classics, Everyman, World's Classics preferred. Seymour Smith's *An English Library* (1943) listed all that I thought I needed, so I copied the titles into a quarto hardbound notebook, with columns for when the item was bought, and when read. Before I left school, I made only monthly visits to Charing Cross Road, and Foyles in particular, where everything displayed on the outside stalls could be had for 6*d*. Then I went to work in the city, and fell at once under the influence of Hugh Jones and Cyril Nash – 'Jonash' they called themselves – who had just opened a shop in Cullum Street. Every tea-time, and once a week at lunch-time (with weekly visits to the four other city dealers), I spent my time browsing their tiny shop, and buying on occasion. They led me towards books illustrated with wood-engravings, and the less expensive private presses. What they made of my tastes at that stage I cannot tell, but their influence was considerable – though fortunately I never fell for the first editions of Bernard Shaw they offered, at two guineas apiece. When I had started my own press they would sometimes offer nineteenth-century printing manuals; from them, too, came the first of my Lee Priory books, *Nymphidia*, in a very worn binding, at 25*s*., the beginning, it turned out, of a major part of my collection.

Thus far my relationship with the trade was really as a beginner, learning what I liked and what did not appeal. Catalogues from some of the dealers in this field widened my range: George Sims, who was only a year or two my senior, provided many fine books, as did Elkin Mathews, and Bertram Rota. I bought a lot of the Eragny Press from Jonash, and started a long series of wants lists, searching for twentieth-century fine printing.

Alan Thomas bought well at the Phillipps sale in 1971, and offered a lot of minor ephemera as well as some of the Middle Hill Press books – and I was away on another trail. Shortly before, I had bought a Holtzapffel Parlour Printing Press, had edited with James Mosley the third edition (1846) of its manual, and had started to search for books printed on similar machines. My enthusiasms were now for privately printed books of the eighteenth and nineteenth centuries, and new lists had to be compiled and circulated among the dealers I knew might help.

Soon the dealer-collector relationship was reversed, for it was comparatively easy to become better informed about what I wanted than most of the dealers who had my lists, though, of course, it was vital that I still had their support. My dear friend Bob Forster was wont to ask why I was so foolish as to tell his colleagues in the trade what it was that I wanted. Prices would be raised against me, he said, if I told everyone what I was after. But how else to find them, was my response, unless one had a runner searching all the shops in this country and, indeed, elsewhere. One or two dealers have multiplied prices as I watched the vital book move from one to another at fairs, or even while I chased from dealer to dealer after missing something in a catalogue. One dealer, forever damned – not a member of the ABA, of course – sold to another dealer one Sunday morning what he had promised to sell to me the previous Wednesday. Such trials (but how will *he* burn) have often been made up for by tips from bookseller friends, who have simply told me that they have noticed something that I might want in someone else's catalogue. Indeed, despite Bob Forster's cautious advice, if one tells dealers what one is after, declining only the most outrageous quotations, then everything that is to be had may – eventually – come to hand.

The internet has turned the tables still further to the collector's advantage. He can search the trade world-wide, coding his search words to locate what is needed, leaving wants lists on some sites, and enjoying more general searches on Addall. True, the net allows dealers to compare their books with other copies that are already available, and to raise their prices if need be – but it also compels them to reduce the price if their book is not so rare as they had thought. The same applies to the collector, who is free to choose the best of many copies and, where the book is truly rare, his greater knowledge in a specialist field will still give him the advantage. Where he is searching for some genuinely obscure work, then there is no artificiality in the price, and rarities can sometimes be found like herring with golden rings in their bellies – or Aldines from a charity shop.

In a century the world has indeed changed: paperbacks fill the shelves of secondhand bookshops and many antiquarian dealers are selling from home, using the internet to advertise their wares. Collectors, though, have hardly altered, only distinguished one from the other by the size of their purses – the absorbing mania ruling all. Good relations with the trade remain of the utmost importance – with prompt payment of bills an underlying essential.

Reminiscences of a Book Buyer

ROBERT S PIRIE

My earliest visits to London bookshops were in 1951, during my family's first post-war visit to Europe.* Most of our time was spent at the usual tourist sites and visiting friends, but I also remember getting violently ill after a spin in the barrel at the Festival of Britain. However, I did spend a good deal of time at Foyles – a paradise for someone whose prior knowledge of bookshops was limited to the excellent but small Housatonic Bookstore in Salisbury, Connecticut, run by Maurice Firuski – and upstairs at Hatchard's where there were some old books, and I bought a nineteenth-century edition of Thomson's *The Seasons* in a polished calf binding – I wonder where it is now.

Serious book hunting came five years later when I arrived in Germany as a very young 2nd Lieutenant. Letters went off to Quaritch, Maggs, Francis Edwards, Thorp, Traylen, Pickering & Chatto, McLeish *et al.* asking for their catalogues and, in due course, a great many arrived including a substantial package from Maggs, but none from Quaritch. The Maggs catalogues, which I naively assumed were current, listed a number of works by John Donne so I ordered the lot. Many of them turned out to be still available – an indication of the state of the book market since the Depression. I managed to wangle a free flight to London as a top-secret courier in April, my first leave, found a room through the USO, and started on my visits. At Francis Edwards I was taken up to Mr Harris's office where the early books were, introduced myself and after a half hour or so asked the price of the Harlech copy of Heywood's *A Mayden-Head Well Lost*. Just then the tea lady arrived with a tray set for two. 'How pleasant,' I thought, but Mr Harris's partner arrived. I was told the price, agreed, and then was asked to leave so they could enjoy their tea. It was several years before a third cup appeared on that tray, but I bought some splendid books and always enjoyed the visit.

At Maggs, Kenneth and Clifford were most friendly and let me loose in the bookcases on the first floor. I remember buying the Hoe copies of Beaumont and Fletcher's *Monsieur Thomas* and *The Elder Brother*, and going from there to tea with John Carter, whom I had met through his wife, Ernestine, the fashion editor of *The Times* and a friend of my family. We

* I have limited this, with few exceptions, to my dealings with British booksellers and have therefore left out many wonderful memories of friends in the United States.

went to a spot near Sotheby's, where tea was produced IN TEA BAGS! 'American influence,' grumbled Carter, 'Let me see what you have bought.' He opened each book, buried his nose in the gutter, inhaled deeply and pronounced 'washed'! So much for them, but they are still happily on my shelves. In those days, Maggs produced a regular bulletin, *Mercurius Britannicus*, and while we were on manoeuvres in northern Germany, a copy arrived describing a first edition of Donne's *Devotions*. I quickly found my driver, hopped in our jeep, headed for the nearest Deutche Post some 20 kilometres away, darted in, put through a call to Kenneth Maggs and heard him say 'I wasn't going to sell it until I heard from you.'

I vaguely remember visiting McLeish – a small dark shop on a side street – but don't remember buying anything. A visit to Pickering & Chatto at first produced nothing, but then, out of his pocket, Dudley Massey produced a 1598 edition of Adams's writing tables in a contemporary doeskin wallet binding. When it was shown to Bill Jackson, the Librarian of the Houghton Library at Harvard who was then revising the *Short-Title Catalogue ... 1475-1640*, he remarked that it fell into one of his favourite STC categories – books of which he had found ten or more editions *not* in STC. A few years later I bought a lovely copy of Waller's *Poems* (1664) and asked that it be sent to the States. Months went by; I inquired, and Dudley wrote back that it seemed to be lost. Several years later he found it – on his desk!

I did walk by Quaritch's premises at 11 Grafton Street several times, but was too intimidated to enter, until finally in June I got up my nerve, walked in, was greeted by a ruddy-faced Mr Newton and sent upstairs to see Mr Dring and Mr Howard, who worked in a dark and dusty back room. (Years later, as we were leaving London, my wife and I sent Ted Dring a proper swivel chair to replace his straight-back one, which was covered in an old skirt belonging to his wife Pat. His first reaction was shock, but I think he learned to like it.) We talked briefly and then I was let loose in the front room. Quaritch records show that on 19 June 1956 a Lieutenant Pirie bought a Donne *Pseudo-Martyr* in contemporary calf for £65. Dring asked if I got their catalogues. I indicated that though I had written requesting them none had arrived. 'Ah, yes,' he said, 'I remember, we thought the military address somewhat unstable.' He later became a close friend and, with the possible exception of Seven Gables, more books on my shelf have come from Quaritch than any other source. I did once meet Mr Ferguson, but just to be introduced as he was darting out to his usual haunt – the British Museum.

In 1959, on our honeymoon, my wife and I came to London for three weeks and much of our time was spent in bookshops. I remember being shown at Quaritch the remains of a set of Pavier Shakespeare quartos in contemporary vellum; three were left I believe, for £2,000. Too much for us, but bought by Lou Silver and now, I believe, in the Newberry Library. Also, at Christie's, a splendid 1559 *Mirror for Magistrates*. Many years later I bought it in the Bradley Martin sale, through Quaritch as usual. My wife found a Cuvier on the second floor at Quaritch and this started a collection of books about antelopes which led us to Wheldon & Wesley, from whose catalogues a fair number of books came our way. Bradley Martin once showed me a newly arrived W & W ornithological catalogue in which he had checked off his holdings. Of the hundreds of books listed he had all but about ten. Dawson's of Pall Mall, where Miss Violet Diver reigned supreme, was also a good source of natural history books and of some wonderful watercolours of the wildlife of Ceylon, which currently fill a wall of my dining room. But my 1667 *Paradise Lost*, in contemporary calf and with the title-leaf slit for cancellation, also came from there.

The walk from the Harvard law school to our apartment led past the Houghton Library, and I would regularly stop in to see Bill Jackson. Frequently on Saturday mornings we would meet and go to the Club of Odd Volumes for lunch. One evening the phone rang. It was Bill saying to get over to Houghton quickly as he had the galleys of a Peter Murray Hill catalogue with books we both would want. They had just bought a portion of the angling library of a Mr J.C. Lynn. We poured over them and made a list of our choices which Bill said he would cable overnight, but he was worried that Jim Babb at Yale would have the proofs as well and might beat us to it, so I volunteered to track down the Managing Director, a Mr M. Hamlyn. About 7pm, back at the apartment, I called directory inquiries in London, miraculously got an answer and asked for the phone numbers of all the M. Hamlyns in the London directory although I had no reason to believe this mysterious figure even lived in London. I got three numbers and dialled the first. It was now after midnight in London and a very sleepy voice answered the phone. 'Are you the M. Hamlyn of Peter Murray Hill?' 'Yes.' 'Good, I have an order from Bill Jackson and myself.' We got the books and Martin became a friend – a tribute to his patience – although he once caught me sneaking an early look at the Book Fair and heaved me out.

In 1962, having finished law school, we went to England and with Bill Jackson drove down to Guildford to visit Charles Traylen, who had recently purchased the bulk of the Fairfax of Cameron library, an acquisition Bill had learned about from Arthur Freeman. Bill bought six or seven minor rarities to tie down for the STC, and I bought 43. Mr Traylen wasn't there and the books weren't priced so the invoices arrived much later. Bill was somewhat put out to learn his was bigger than mine. Mr Traylen apparently assumed that if Bill wanted them they must be valuable. I recently found, in a copy of Harris's *Voyages*, a printed form which reads as follows: 'The maps in this volume are most attractive when coloured. This colouring by hand can be expertly executed at 15/- each map (Postage 9d). Extract your plain map, send it on a cardboard roll and it will be returned to you beautifully coloured. Charles W. Traylen, 87 North Street, Guildford.' This now hangs framed, but uncoloured, in the library bathroom. Bill was giving a talk to the Oxford Bibliophiles so we went down to hear him. Afterwards he had arranged for us to visit John Sparrow, the book-collecting Warden of All Souls College. I later learned that the Warden's response to Bill's request that he entertain us was 'Bill, if there is anything I don't want to do, it is to meet a nice young American couple!' We went, had tea, gazed on the rows of seventeenth-century vellum with awe, admired his presentation copy of *Pseudo-Martyr* and started a friendship which lasted till he died. (I have a lovely memory of my daughter, Amanda, aged five, sitting on his lap in the library eating a peanut butter and jelly sandwich.) Finally, he had to excuse himself to coach Lord Halifax for his Latin speech at the Encaenia, but there was time to spare before our train, so he arranged a visit to Colonel Wilkinson at Worcester College, another great if somewhat eccentric collector. After a while we were invited into Wilkinson's bedroom where he dived under the bed, producing one great rarity after another.

It was on this trip that we first met Lionel and Philip Robinson at the shop on Pall Mall. I remember longingly handling Sir Walter Raleigh's notebook, including a catalogue of the books he had with him in the Tower, which they had recently acquired from Walter Oakeshott. As we left Lionel invited us to tea with his daughter Pat and her husband, which resulted in an invitation to the Eton and Harrow cricket match, where we discovered the joys of curry puffs and champagne and that boxes at sporting events in England came with attached dining rooms. The brothers joined us for a lunch at the Mirabelle and as we were leaving there was some mumbling between them, and then Lionel said that if we could spare the time Philip would take us to the crypt of the church where the Phillipps books were stored. It was some years before we realized that this offer was, apparently, unique. Needless to say we had the time, hopped in a cab and, in due course, arrived. Philip banged on the door, the verger appeared and we descended. A room was unlocked which Philip said contained the English books. I remember a whole case labelled 'Not in STC', and when I later told Bill Jackson of this he went into a frenzy and ultimately got a list. Foolishly assuming that repeat visits were on the menu, I limited my purchases but did manage to get four very rare books, including the Farmer copy of the second edition of Donne's *Anniversarie* in contemporary vellum and one of two known copies of both parts of William Corkine's *Book of Ayres*. A year or so later when I suggested a repeat visit the answer was a polite 'no', but Lionel came for tea and fished out of his raincoat pocket an unrecorded book from Donne's library which he thought I should have.

Over time our farm became a regular stop for visiting members of the trade, if possible on a weekend so lunch at the Odd Volumes could be included. Anthony Hobson looked at the little writing tables from Pickering and, to my amazement, was able to identify the barely visible blind-stamped arms as those of the city of Antwerp. I also showed him a letter from Philip and Mary to Cosimo de' Medici and mentioned that the diary of one of the letter's bearers, Thomas Thirlby, Bishop of Ely, had been reprinted in the nineteenth century but the volume was missing from the Widener Library. 'Don't worry,' he said, 'you can buy the original in the next Phillipps sale.' The letter and the diary are now in closer proximity than they have been for 400 years.

John Lawson and John Maggs were regular guests and were staying when the terrible news of Bill Jackson's death came. Bill set a standard for scholarship, librarianship and friendship which few have equalled. It was through him that I first met David Foxon, Frank Francis, Anthony Hobson, Geoffrey Keynes, Tim Munby, Howard Nixon and John Sparrow amongst others. He once suggested that I might succeed him as the Houghton Librarian because, he said, I was the only person he had ever met as greedy as he was. To him this was the ultimate compliment; I wasn't so sure. John Lawson's catalogues have always been a treat, and we have met regularly at sales and on his trips to America. Just recently he published a catalogue of seventeenth-century books with a picture of himself leaning on the road sign for the town of Wing in Buckinghamshire – a pun on Donald Wing's *Short-Title Catalogue … 1641-1700*. I called to order a book, and to chat. We agreed that few besides the two of us would remember a similar photograph of Peter Murray Hill at the same spot, in one of his catalogues some 50 years ago.

Geoffrey Keynes and I corresponded a good deal and, finally, a visit to Lammas House was arranged. We were introduced to his wife Margaret and went to the library. It was a collection far beyond what I had imagined and several hours passed quickly there and in the dining room where, amongst other things, some amazing Audubon and Bewick watercolours were stored. We adjourned to the sitting room where Margaret had produced tea. Geoffrey went to a small bookcase to the left of the fireplace which he said contained 'Margaret's books' and extracted a rather marginal copy of Donne's *Six Sermons*, then still a common book. This, he said, had been his engagement present to Margaret. To my horror, I heard myself asking if, when he gave it to her, he already had a better copy himself. He turned quite red and then, fortunately, burst out laughing. Many years later, when I borrowed for an exhibition one of his copies of a book dedicated to Donne, he gave it to me, so I guess I was forgiven.

It was John Sparrow who introduced us to Dick Lyon where, generally, something agreeable was to be found, but the pricing discussions were occasionally a bit arduous. I remember a subscriber's copy of Robert Adam's *Ruins of the Palace of the Emperor Diocletian* in contemporary boards and, not long before Dick died, a lovely copy of John Evelyn's diary (1818) in contemporary pigskin, with the rare third volume in boards uncut. But I also remember John Gould's *Birds of Great Britain* in contemporary green morocco at £300 which I turned down. John Sparrow also suggested once that as we were driving up to Wales to see Lord Kenyon and had an introduction from Bill Jackson to the Probys at Elton Hall, we might visit a certain bookshop in Birmingham. We parked our car outside and went into a smallish shop where four or five other customers were present. In due course the proprietor appeared and, when told we were interested in early English books, asked in a rather hostile tone if we would pay £1,000 for a book. When told that it was possible, he disappeared and came out with a rebacked copy of the 1603 translation of Montaigne's *Essayes*. When I enquired as gently as I could if by any chance he thought the final quire, which was ¼ inch shorter on all three sides, might have come from another copy, he exploded and ran around the room locking all the cases, while screaming 'Get out, get out, we won't have the likes of you in here.' Mortified, we fled, followed by the curious looks of the other customers. That night, when told the story, Lord Kenyon murmured 'I wonder what you did to annoy John that he sent you there?' The Kenyons had become friends several years earlier, but we did not meet through the book world. In the fall of 1961 I had arranged to visit them at Gredington in connection with the purchase of several Welsh ponies, and had asked Dring if he could organize a car to take me there. I arrived in London only to be greeted by a very suspicious Ted Dring who wanted to know what this Welsh pony business was all about. It turned out, to my amazement, that Lord Kenyon was a well-known book collector and a member of the Roxburghe Club, and Ted suspected that I was up to some nefarious activities. I don't know who was more surprised – Ted to discover that I really was buying Welsh ponies or Kenyon to discover that I was a book collector. I do remember from that visit a rather well-lubricated look at his library and then, at two in the morning, Kenyon insisting that we had to look at ponies so, flashlight in hand, off we went to the stable. Other than being asked to admire the ears of one animal I am somewhat vague about that excursion, and my recollections of the next day's auction are not very coherent either, but a fair number of ponies ended up at the farm.

Toby Rodgers became a friend while at Quaritch's. One night, after he had set up in business with Paul Grinke, I came home and found the galleys for their first catalogue. In it was the only copy of Robert Heath's *Clarastella* (1650) that has been on the market in my lifetime. I got up at 4.30, called him and got it. Mike Papantonio who called him at 9.30 was not best pleased to find it was already sold. Years later Toby catalogued a volume of lithographs of the French attack on Garibaldi's headquarters in Rome, now part of the American Academy campus. I called to order it. 'Oh dear,' he said. 'I already have three orders for it. Well, two unhappy customers or three, what's the difference, if it hasn't been sent it's yours.' And it hadn't been.

Davis & Orioli always had interesting catalogues and I remember particularly buying a copy of the beautiful engraved *Laws of Denmark*. Each page has spectacular borders, and we reproduced the one with a lobster and used it on the menu for a Club of Odd Volumes outing to the farm. Some books came from Steve Weissman in New York, particularly a copy in contemporary morocco of the very rare 1634 Donne *Devotions*. Since he moved to England in the late 1990s much more has come this way, including lots of Gibbon and some very fine early books from the library of Jim Edwards which he sold. I don't remember buying much from Ben Weinreb, but I do remember with regret not buying a book from Donne's library which he had. I thought four was enough, but the truth is, in book collecting, too much is a bare sufficiency.

As the old guard retired new members of the trade have come along, dedicated with equal zeal to keeping me in poverty. Nicholas Poole-Wilson, who knows my likes and dislikes better than I do, Bryan Maggs and Robert Harding, Christopher Edwards, Steve Massey, Felix Oyens, Ted Hofmann, Arthur Freeman, Meg Ford, Christopher de Hamel and Jim Cummins have all become friends and made their contribution to my basic collection of seventeenth-century English literature and also the manuscripts and letters to accompany it. Lately, in addition to Chatterton, Gibbon and Lamb, I have started to buy books that would have been in an eighteenth-century country house library – but they must be bound in morocco and, to make it more difficult, preferably not red, though that requirement is not rigorously adhered to. I only hope that a new group of collectors will develop to maintain the symbiotic relationship. Having recently been described in Christie's catalogue of Mary Hyde's early books as the last surviving customer of the Rosenbach Company, I recognize that the baton has passed but, thanks to wonderful friendships and countless acts of generosity, I have acquired over the last 50 years some respectable books and hope to continue. I was once asked to define a book collector and replied that you weren't a collector unless you were in debt to the trade, probably not a definition members of the ABA would like spread around.

III

CREATING FASHIONS AND
CHANGING TASTE

AUTOLYCUS, U.S.A.

Uncle Sam. "NOW, THAT'S REAL DISAPPOINTING. I'D SET MY HEART ON THAT SKELETON."

Shade of Shakspeare. "BUT ALL THE SAME I SHOULD FEEL MORE COMFORTABLE IF IT WAS INSURED."

Cartoon from *Punch*, 24 May 1922, referring to the Burdett-Coutts sale at which Rosenbach carried off the Daniel copy of the Shakespeare First Folio, destined for the American collector Henry Folger.

Patterns of Collecting and Trading
in Antiquarian Books

DAVID PEARSON

Introduction

THE aim of this chapter is to look at changing trends in the sale and collecting of antiquarian books during the twentieth century, and the forces that have influenced them. It focuses specifically on old books – early printed books and manuscripts – rather than modern literature and first editions, which are considered in a following chapter.

The immediate reaction of most people with some knowledge or experience of the book market is that the century was one which saw great changes. 'Things, it is generally agreed, are not what they were,' as Nicolas Barker wrote when analysing 'The book trade in 1984 – and after?' in *The Book Collector*.[1] The truism that book collecting is not what it used to be has a long history; in the 1720s, Humfrey Wanley was already lamenting that the supply of good-quality old books was in decline. The perception that fashions in book collecting have undergone much change also has a documentary pedigree: a piece in *The Times* in 1906 on 'Some recent phases of book-collecting' stated that 'Upside-down would seem to be the neatest phrase to apply to fashions of book-collecting today as compared with those of 20 years ago. Fashions … begin no one knows quite where and change for no obvious cause'.[2] 'Book-collecting is very much influenced by fashion, which has its effect on the esteem enjoyed by the pursuit as a whole,' wrote G.L. Brook in 1980.[3]

On the other hand, looking at the books and sales which made the headlines at each end of the century, the observer might be struck as much by similarities as by differences. Reporting on Sotheby's sale of Lord Amherst's collection in 1909, *The Times* picked out a number of highlights which made high prices, including two copies of Shakespeare's First Folio, handsome copies of incunables, a fifteenth-century manuscript of Richard Rolle, and the first book printed in Dumfries in a fine contemporary Edinburgh binding.[4] These are all books which would have been as desirable in the marketplace at the end of the century as they were at the beginning, and the kinds of books which have always made column inches in the newspapers when they pass through the auction houses. Shakespeare folios still make good news stories, as do major collections that come up for sale. The topsy-turvydom of the marketplace is primarily noticeable in the area of recent or contemporary literary authors, and first editions, where swings in popularity are more evident. *The Times* piece of 1906 mentioned above was concerned with Rudyard Kipling, Robert Louis Stevenson and Kelmscott Press books, rather than incunabula or illuminated manuscripts.

The story is therefore more complex than might at first appear, and is not so much about a linear process of change as about a matrix of influences, including cultural and academic values, developments in historical bibliography and the availability of material. These factors were all identified by A.J. West in his analysis of twentieth-century trading in Shakespeare's First Folio, a subject to which he returns later in this volume:

> To summarize for the century: the forces already affecting sales and prices of the First Folio ... were joined by at least four new influences that derived from four separate but interrelated events. These were Lee's search for copies and the publication of his *Census*, the volume's central role in modern bibliography, the extensive purchases by Henry Folger, and the reduced number of copies, especially after the twenties, available for purchase.[5]

Availability of books in the marketplace always influenced what people bought, and the fact that many antiquarian books moved from private ownership into institutional libraries during the century meant that the volume of this material in circulation became much less as time progressed. We should however be wary of assuming too readily that the glory days all belonged to the earlier part of the century and that great private collections can no longer be formed; John Paul Getty (1932-2003) assembled a large collection of fine bindings and manuscripts of outstanding quality which would bear comparison with some of the great collections auctioned before the Second World War.[6] Old-established family libraries can also still enrich the marketplace with unexpected treasures; the Earl of Macclesfield's library from Shirburn Castle, which Sotheby's began to auction in 2004, brought a sizeable quantity of rare and valuable books into the saleroom from a collection which had been largely undisturbed since the eighteenth century. 'The market in medieval manuscripts has seemed well fuelled,' wrote *The Book Collector* as recently as 1990, 'suddenly, but no doubt temporarily, there are plenty.'[7]

Two catalogues compared

The various influencing factors can be seen at work more broadly if we compare catalogues of antiquarian books published at either end of the century. Pickering and Chatto's *Illustrated Catalogue of Old and Rare Books*, issued in 1902, is a typical example of the kind of catalogue issued by any of the upmarket London firms of the day, just as Maggs catalogue 1293 (2000), *Books and Readers in Early Modern Britain (1510-1815)*, is representative of the same kind of offering from the last years of the century. But while both contain miscellaneous antiquarian books covering many subject fields, the catalogue titles themselves reveal significant differences: the earlier is presented straightforwardly as a list of books for sale; the later has a more sophisticated title which deliberately aligns itself with contemporary trends in book history. *Books and Readers in Early Modern Britain* could be the title of a scholarly monograph rather than a catalogue of books for sale.

The Pickering catalogue contains 6,014 items, presented in 434 pages. The Maggs catalogue contains just 99, spread through 187 pages. These two significant differences, both again broadly representative of their time, point to some important underlying factors. The quantity of antiquarian books available for purchase, and circulating between booksellers and collectors, was much greater at the beginning of the century, and generally declined as time progressed and more material became locked up in libraries. Although high-quality and expensive books still change hands today – it is still possible to buy a First Folio or a Grolier binding, as long as you can afford it – no one can produce the kinds of blockbuster catalogue issued earlier in the twentieth century, containing thousands of early printed books. Most of the books in Pickering's catalogue were English, and well over half were printed before 1700.

Where Pickering has quantity of books, however, Maggs has quality of description. The figures show that Pickering averages 14 items to a page, whereas Maggs devotes an average of just under two pages to every book. Where Pickering has a few lines of description with brief notes on condition, rarity and (occasionally) provenance, Maggs gives each book a brief scholarly essay, with a detailed and comprehensive account of its significance, provenance, binding, and bibliographical citations. The first edition of John Donne's *Poems* (1633) merits twelve half-lines in the Pickering catalogue (no. 1808, £13.13s.), despite being associated with Henry King, Donne's executor; a different copy of the same book in the Maggs catalogue (no. 34, £35,000) has almost three pages devoted to it, with illustrations of both binding and titlepage. A hundred years after the Pickering catalogue was issued, there were fewer antiquarian books in the marketplace, but a great deal more literary and bibliographical scholarship available.

Price comparisons over time are always difficult, but it is clear that Donne's *Poems* was being more highly valued in 2000 than in 1902; standard price inflation tables come up with various translations of thirteen guineas into pounds and pence at the end of the century, using either the retail price index, average earnings, or gross domestic product, but they vary from £875 to £6,830, a long way short of £35,000. It is perhaps more illuminating to compare prices within the Pickering catalogue, to see what relative values were being applied to various books.

The great majority were priced somewhere between two shillings and ten pounds, so the thirteen-guinea Donne was certainly at the upper end of the market. We might however be surprised, today, to compare its price with that asked for John Suckling's *Fragmenta Aurea* of 1646 (£22.10s., 'the book is becoming rare, and steadily increasing in value'), or the 1630 *Workes* of John Taylor the Water Poet (£25, half the price asked for a copy of the 1632 Shakespeare Second Folio). In 1902, these were both better-known and more celebrated seventeenth-century writers than Donne; the Pickering catalogue was published before the first serious scholarly edition of Donne's works appeared in 1912, before the first edition (1914) of Geoffrey Keynes's bibliography of Donne, and before twentieth-century literary scholars had got to work on establishing Donne's place in the canon as we think of it today. The fact that a copy of the 1633 *Poems* had gone up to £52.10s. in a Quaritch catalogue of 1922, after these key publications had appeared, reflects this evolution of values.[8] It had then overtaken the 1646 Suckling, still robustly priced at £48, and the Water Poet, whose *Workes* could then be bought for £10. In 2000, when the William Foyle collection was sold at Christie's, all three of these books came under the hammer; the 1633 Donne made £11,000, while Suckling and Taylor, both bundled up as part lots with other books, made £1,400 and £950 respectively.[9]

Further analysis of the Pickering catalogue reveals other examples of relative valuations which would today have changed in line with literary and historical reassessment. In 1902 a first edition of George Herbert's *Remains* (1652) could be had for five guineas, less than half the twelve guineas of William Wycherley's *Miscellany Poems* of 1702. It is unlikely that we would today value a first edition of Aphra Behn's *Pindarick* on Charles II's death (1685), or an apparently rare STC pamphlet 'unknown to Lowndes' (Thomas Bell, *The Tryall of the New Religion*, 1608) at the same five-shilling standard price that was applied to numerous seventeenth-century tracts or eighteenth-century plays. The single most expensive printed item in the catalogue was a complete set of first editions of the novels of Captain Marryat, 'a beautiful set of these charming sea tales, uniformly and choicely bound in blue morocco extra', £185 for 80 volumes. Although the 1911 *Encyclopaedia Britannica* devotes a column and a half to Marryat and speaks of his 'admirable gift of lucid, direct narrative, and an unfailing fund of incident' his star waned during the early decades of the twentieth century and by 1927 Sawyer and Darton could dismiss Marryat in their *Signpost for Collectors* with a single mention ('more popularity than financial value').[10] De Ricci's *Book Collector's Guide* (1921) does not mention Marryat at all. It seems unlikely that anyone today would pay nearly four times the price of a Shakespeare Second Folio (the Foyle copy in 2000 made £64,250) for this set of Marryat. All the books in the Pickering catalogue would be saleable and collectable today, but relative valuations would have changed in line with broader cultural assessments.

Subjects, and specialism

Within its alphabetical author sequence the 1902 Pickering catalogue includes a number of subject categories, many of which would be familiar today as areas of collecting interest. These include America, Angling, Architecture, Chap Books, Children's Books, Cookery, Freemasonry, Gardening, Medical Works, Military Works, and Sporting Books. The categories are broadly in line with a list of 56 areas of collecting interest identified in *The Book-Hunter at Home* (1922), which embraces all of these as well as Bibles, Bibliography, Dictionaries, Early-printed books, Economics, Legal, Natural History, and School Books.[11] The similarities with the chapter headings in a more modern guide to book collecting, *Miller's Collecting Books* (1995) are more striking than the differences: Early Printed Books, English Literature, Modern First Editions, Fine Printing, Bindings, Illustrated Books, Children's Books, Natural History, Travel & Topography, Americana, Science & Medicine, Sporting Books, Architecture & Design, Aeronautical & Maritime, Performing Arts, Cookery.[12]

The key point here is that a broad range of collecting interests, subject-wise, is not a characteristic of any one part of the twentieth century, but is observable throughout. Some of the published guides to book collecting of the earlier part of the century can give an impression that English literature was really the only concern of the time; in his *Book Collector's Guide* (1921), Seymour de Ricci said that 'as the backbone of my work, I have sought to list … the first editions of the chief works and in many cases of all the works of the greater British and American authors from Chaucer to Swinburne'.[13] De Ricci's view was that 'nothing is scarcer, nothing is more desirable for a collector than … the earliest plays in English literature'. The near-absence of such subjects as classics, natural history, medicine and science from de Ricci is noticeable; such authors as Darwin, Hooke or Vesalius are not mentioned. Sawyer and Darton's 1927 *English Books 1475-1900: A Signpost for Collectors* focused likewise on literary authors. However, the breadth of approach of other guides and catalogues, combined with observation of some of the collections being formed at this time, shows that interests actually ranged much wider. Silvanus Thompson (1851-1916) left a library of nearly 13,000 volumes on electricity; Sir William Osler (1849-1919) accumulated a celebrated collection of 7,600 early medical books; Frederick Ashley-Cooper (1877-1932) collected 4,000 books on cricket. Throughout the first half of the twentieth century, the firm of Maggs was issuing catalogues not only of English literature, but also of Americana, voyages and travels, early science and medicine, and music.[14] New specialisms emerged as the century progressed, in line with developing trends in popular or academic interest, or in response to new phenomena; in 1920, Maggs issued a catalogue of *Books and Engravings Illustrating the Evolution of the Airship and the Aeroplane*.[15] An exhibition held at J. & E. Bumpus Ltd., in November 1934, intended to demonstrate 'New Paths in Book-Collecting', proposed among other subjects 'The Development of the Theory of Evolution' and 'The Evolution of "Trade" and Publishers' Binding, 1600-1900'.[16] Booksellers certainly influenced the development of such themes, by identifying niches or opportunities and opening up new collecting enthusiasms. Ben Weinreb (1912-99), whose business in architectural books grew to 'outdo every bookseller in the world in the field', not only expanded and shaped interest in antiquarian architectural books, but also became a prominent and highly respected figure in architectural history.[17]

The theme of specialism, of focusing on a particular interest, is one which runs through the literature of book collecting in the twentieth century. 'The specialists now rule the book market,' said the introduction to the 1899 edition of *Book-*

Prices Current.[18] 'Every collector should become a specialist,'advised *The Book-Hunter at Home* in 1922, 'it will give him a definite ambition, something to look for.'[19] 'It is sensible for collectors to specialize, to choose an area of interest that they can make their own,' wrote F.B. Adams in 1977.[20] This is partly a matter of observation, but also one of advice and encouragement to budding collectors. It was certainly felt, in the first half of the century, that omnivorous library-building on a grand scale was now beyond the means of individuals. As Wilfred Partington put it in 1927, 'the days of the giant book-collectors are passed. Gone our Cottons, Harleys, Bodleys, Ashmoles, Hebers, Huths and Christie-Millers. Book-collecting has become more democratized. There are many more collectors today, with a tendency to smaller and more specialized collecting.'[21] There is nevertheless an upbeat note in this, sounded by the words 'many more collectors' and 'democratized'; the key point, made many times in collectors' handbooks, is that specialisation in a particular and ideally uncharted area allows people of relatively modest means to accumulate significant collections.

To quote *The Bookman's Journal*, just after it was launched in 1919, 'the collecting of old books is wrongly supposed to be a rich man's hobby. Competition to secure rare early printed books has, it is true, sent the prices of these soaring ... There are, however, thousands of forgotten books not considered sufficiently scarce for the wealthy collector.'[22] Exactly the same theme is found in a report in *The Times* in 1960, entitled 'Book collecting on a small budget', on the opening of the third Antiquarian Book Fair ('One of the objects [was] ... to persuade the more timid book lovers that it was possible to indulge in book collecting without being a millionaire').[23]

In 1919, the advice was to look in bookshop cellars for 'once popular old books' that could be had relatively cheaply ('less than ten shillings'), starting with works by seventeenth-century English authors such as George Sandys and Gervase Markham.[24] Half a century later, Tim Munby's advice was to look to the nineteenth century: 'It is often said today that good books are so rare and expensive that very few undergraduates can afford to collect at all. I myself do not believe this. I believe that the great increase in the study of the Victorian period, combined with the emergence of the social sciences, has opened up whole fields of significant subject-collecting.'[25] Here, again, we see changes driven by a combination of availability and academic values, but a certain constancy in the underlying themes about the desirability and interest of acquiring old books.

The influence and impact of bibliographical scholarship

'All book collectors ... find that they cannot progress very far without reference to what has been written on their subjects.'[26] Thomas Tanselle's remark summarizes the close relationship which has long existed between academic bibliography and the trade in antiquarian books. Both dealers and collectors wish to find out what is known about the book in front of them, where it stands in the canon of cultural values, and particularly how rare it is. 'Scarcity is still the force that drives most collectors,' wrote Christopher Edwards in 1995, and rarity or uniqueness is a great selling point for a book, irrespective of its content.[27] An apparently unremarkable or even dull book becomes much more desirable if it can be stated with confidence that it is the only known copy, or is one of a few surviving exemplars. The 1581 edition of *A book of Christian questions and answers*, £4.4s. in 1902 in the Pickering & Chatto catalogue mentioned earlier, was of interest because 'this early edition of the little book is unknown to Lowndes and other bibliographers'. The 1539 edition of *The boke for a iustice of peace* commanded the hefty price of £50 in Quaritch's 1922 *English History and Literature* catalogue partly because it was 'extremely rare; the only other copy known is in the British Museum'. Booksellers' catalogues throughout the century have been liberally sprinkled with phrases describing the rarity of their offerings: 'unknown to X'; 'no copy in the British Library'; 'only two copies recorded in the UK'. In order to make these assertions with some degree of authority, there needs to be a framework of published bibliographies and catalogues to which both booksellers and customers can refer.[28]

The twentieth century was one during which descriptive and enumerative bibliography made great advances, with the antiquarian book trade contributing towards, benefiting from and helping to disseminate those developments in knowledge. At the beginning of the century, the panoply of available reference tools was neither extensive nor, in the main, recent, although work was in hand to bring improvements. J.H. Slater's manual on *How to Collect Books* (1905) stated that 'for English printers before 1600, Herbert's edition of Ames' *Typographical Antiquities* is generally consulted, and for those of the eighteenth century Nichols's *Literary Anecdotes* … mention must, of course, be made of Lowndes' *Bibliographer's Manual*, useful in every way'. These books were originally published in 1785, 1778 and 1834 respectively. Slater did add that 'collectors of English printed books have been considerably helped of late by the various publications of the Bibliographical Society, but a great deal yet remains to be done'.[29]

The Bibliographical Society had been founded in 1892, both a symptom and a driving force of a movement towards a more rigorous approach to mapping the printed heritage, which began in the late nineteenth century and blossomed in the twentieth. Robert Proctor, who 'found the history of early printing guesswork and left it a science', set the study and cataloguing of incunabula on a new path with his *Index to the Early Printed Books in the British Museum* in 1898; the first volume of the detailed catalogues of British Museum incunables, commonly known as *BMC*, appeared in 1908, and the German-led initiative to produce an international census of incunabula, the *Gesamtkatalog der Wiegendrucke*, issued its first volume in 1925. The first edition of the *Census of Fifteenth-Century Books owned in America* appeared in 1919. Studies and listings of early English printing and printers appeared, led by scholars like Duff, McKerrow, Madan and Plomer, and in 1926 the Bibliographical Society brought knowledge of English books up to the Civil War period onto a new plane with the publication of Pollard and

Redgrave's *Short-Title Catalogue of Books printed in England, Scotland and Ireland ... 1475-1640 (STC)*.[30]

Although the first edition of *STC* was far from complete – its subsequent revision and enlargement took many decades and was ultimately published in three volumes, between 1976 and 1991 – it set a new standard for usefulness and a comprehensive approach, valuable for scholars, collectors and booksellers alike. With *STC* in hand, it became less necessary to trawl through separate library and private collection catalogues to verify the rarity of a book, or to place a particular edition within its sequence. Its extensive canvass of the holdings of many libraries, much enhanced in the second edition, created a new level of authority; 'unknown to *STC*' is a far more potent phrase than 'unknown to Lowndes'. We can now consult *STC* and realize that the 1581 *Book of Christian questions and answers* offered by Pickering in 1902 was not in fact unique (five copies are known), while Quaritch's 1539 *Boke for a iustice of peace* was one of six surviving copies, not two. The enduring authority of *STC*, and the power of those listings in establishing locations and rarity, was demonstrated by Maggs catalogue 1350 (2003), *STC & Wing: books printed in England 1500-1700 from the library of James Stevens-Cox (1910-1997)*, in which a preliminary section consisting of those copies which were actually cited in *STC* was reserved 'for sale *en bloc* to a recognised institutional library only'.

The format established by *STC* was followed by Donald Wing to bring the census up to 1700 (published 1945-51, second revised edition 1972-94), and the creation of the *Eighteenth-Century Short Title Catalogue* at the British Library in 1976 (first published on microfiche in 1983 and in a fuller version in 1990, but more importantly available in a constantly updated electronic form) formed a backbone for English enumerative bibliography for the entire handpress period, supporting more detailed work. Bibliographies of particular genres, such as Greg's *Bibliography of the English Printed Drama to the Restoration* (1939-59) or Foxon's *English Verse 1701-1750* (1975) could flesh out descriptive or collational details, and give additional information on the whereabouts of copies.

Exhibition catalogues can also sometimes be influential in creating listings of books which are noteworthy and therefore desirable to own – the Grolier Club's 1902 exhibition of *One Hundred Books Famous in English Literature* was an early example, leading to people assessing their collections in terms of the number of books from 'the Grolier Hundred' which they contained. The best-known example of such a catalogue is probably *Printing and the Mind of Man*, originally mounted as an exhibition at Earls Court in 1963, followed up by a full-dress catalogue published in 1967.[31] 'PMM', as it came to be cited in booksellers' catalogues, selected more than 400 books identified as having had a transforming impact on the development of Western civilisation over the past 500 years; its simple but multidisciplinary approach ensured that it has had a lasting authority and influence.

The creation of bibliographical listings of individual authors or topics was an idea which took off seriously in the late nineteenth century, focusing particularly on recent or contemporary literary authors (and essentially therefore the subject of a later chapter). T.J. Wise is commonly recognized as one of the driving forces here, although listings of numerous nineteenth-century authors, compiled by various hands, appeared during the last two decades of the century. Works such as Thomas Westwood's *Bibliotheca Piscatoria: a catalogue of books on angling* (1861, expanded 1883) or Henry Bolton's *Select Bibliography of Chemistry, 1492-1892* (1893) had also appeared before the century was out. The twentieth century saw continuing generation of such works, as well as refinement of technique to make for greater accuracy and consistency of bibliographical method. Already by 1922, *The Book-Hunter at Home* could state that 'there are bibliographies for almost every class of books, and a great number dealing with the works of individual authors'. A good overview of developments in this kind of 'enumerative and descriptive bibliography' in the middle and later twentieth century can be found in Trevor Howard-Hill's essay of that title in *The Book Encompassed*.[32] All of these developments created new opportunities for 'the interplay of bibliography and profit', in Stephen Weissman's phrase, 'which is the constant feature of a bookseller's existence'.[33]

For the antiquarian book trade, the key point was the creation of an ever more detailed framework of knowledge within which to fit the books they were offering for sale, and to validate the importance, scarcity or interest of their wares. Philip Gaskell's published bibliographies of John Baskerville (1959) and the Foulis Press (1964) undoubtedly helped to promote interest in buying books from those presses, for their place of printing rather than their texts, and booksellers have cited Gaskell numbers to encourage that ever since. Returning to Donne's 1633 *Poems*, the brief description in the 1902 Pickering catalogue includes no references to bibliographical or other secondary works about Donne. Quaritch, in 1922, could make use of Keynes's bibliography of Donne (1914) to note that their copy had 'the first issue of the leaf Nn1 in which there is no headline on the recto', although there is no reference to Keynes or to any other bibliographical sources. (Keynes numbers were, however, already being cited by Leighton as early as 1921.)[34] By 1950, when the Robinson brothers offered a copy of the 1633 *Poems* in their catalogue 81 (£200), it could be described as 'STC 7045. Pforzheimer 296. Keynes 98. Jaggard, *Bib. of Shakespeare* 81. With Nn1 in the first state, without headline on recto'. Similar examples could be multiplied endlessly to show how booksellers have made use of emerging bibliographical knowledge to improve the sophistication of their catalogue entries, increasingly considered incomplete if they omit mention of the relevant standard reference works. This line of development has not always been welcomed – John Carter, in a radio talk on book collecting broadcast in 1950, grumbled that 'It is difficult ... to read more than a page or two of a bookseller's catalogue to-day without stumbling on phrases like ... "Q6 is a cancel as usual", "secondary binding", "not in STC"'.[35] Stephen Weissman drew a distinction between the needs of institutional and private customers in this respect.[36] On the other hand, it stands to reason that 'cataloguers, whether booksellers or auctioneers, dearly (and understandably) love to add lustre to their productions by citing unimpeachable sources', as Grant Uden put it in 1982.[37]

The book trade has not only exploited these advances in bibliographical knowledge, but has also made significant contributions towards them. The relationship is a symbiotic one; the published fruits of bibliographical scholarship generate interest in acquiring the books concerned, and help to create new collecting trends. Bibliographers are often collectors themselves, and published bibliographies of particular authors or subjects are not uncommonly based to some extent on the compilers' own holdings: T.J. Wise and Geoffrey Keynes are well-known examples. Those collections may in turn rely to no small extent on many years of fruitful dialogue between the collectors and the booksellers who supply them. It is clearly in the interests of the trade to foster such things (and also of collectors, as the overall result for them is a marked increase in the value of their books). Antiquarian booksellers, like rare book librarians, have the privilege of handling and directly experiencing early books in great quantities, allowing them to build up the kind of knowledge upon which bibliographical scholarship often depends, and the discipline has often been taken forward by people whose careers were primarily or partly based in the book trade or auction house, as Tony Edwards explores in his chapter elsewhere in this volume.

Booksellers' catalogues can become works of bibliographical reference in their own right, and subsequently cited, when they contain descriptions of scarce books, or ones with unique qualities. This is particularly the case with bookbindings, where the professional literature is liberally sprinkled with references to bindings which have been reproduced in auctioneers' and dealers' catalogues, and whose subsequent whereabouts may not be known. The influence of booksellers' catalogues both on the development of bibliography and on the encouragement of collecting trends can be seen in the catalogues issued by Percy Dobell around the 1920s and 1930s, focusing on English literature of the Restoration period and early eighteenth century. As he said in the preface to his 1918 catalogue of *The Literature of the Restoration*, '[no] work exists from which a general view of the activities of the poets and playwrights of the last forty years of the seventeenth century can be obtained'; this was poorly charted bibliographical terrain. During the following decades Dobell issued a series of extensive and well-ordered catalogues which were presented both as lists of books for sale, and as contributions to bibliography; his catalogue 105, *Works by Dr. Jonathan Swift*, says in its modest preface that 'I can only claim to have made a very small contribution to the subject – nevertheless it will be seen that I have added slightly to the labours of former workers in this field'. His efforts also contributed to the fact that 'there has been a recent revival of popular interest in the Restoration period [where] the literature is undergoing assiduous research', as *The Bookman's Journal* noted in December 1925. Dobell's *Catalogue of XVIIIth Century Verse and ... of books by and relating to Dr. Jonathan Swift* (1933) is presented with a titlepage that suggests a scholarly bibliography will follow, rather than a list of books for sale. Dobell did indeed publish purely bibliographical works, based on the stock he built up, with no prices attached, such as *John Dryden: Bibliographical Memoranda* (1922). 'Mr Dobell's monograph on Dryden, while it may yet be extended, must be the foundation of all knowledge of the first production of that great poet's works,' wrote Sawyer and Darton in their 1927 *Signpost for Collectors*.[38]

Interest in condition, binding and provenance

Criteria for appreciating the condition and binding of early books have changed considerably during the course of the twentieth century, although the principle of the desirability of original condition can to some extent be seen throughout. The worst excesses of zeal for replacing old bindings with new morocco extra belong to the nineteenth century rather than the twentieth, and the reaction against this thinking is commonly said to have been pioneered by T.J. Wise and his associates, from the 1880s onwards. They were concerned primarily with contemporary or near-contemporary literature, and although 'Wise thought no more than a chronic rebinder like Huth of putting his seventeenth- and eighteenth-century books into morocco and gilt edges' (as John Carter put it), by 1905 Slater's guide on *How to Collect Books* was positive about respecting the value of early bindings: 'An old binding, whether of leather, boards, paper, or cloth, should, whenever possible, be restored rather than removed altogether.' Collectors were advised to be 'very careful about the binding of any book offered ... [which] should, if possible, be in its original state'.[39] A. Edward Newton actively counselled against putting old books in smart new leather bindings: 'I want the book as originally published, in boards uncut, in old sheep, or in cloth, and as clean and fair as may be.'[40] His argument was not just an aesthetic one, as he recognized the loss involved in rebinding: 'invariably in binding a book, in trimming, be it ever so little, and gilding its edges, one lops off no small part of its value'.

Good contemporary condition, without later intervention, was regularly noted as a virtue in the 1902 Pickering catalogue; the 1624 folio edition of Robert Burton's *Anatomy of Melancholy* (£8.8s.), a 'fine sound copy in the old calf' was 'now becoming a very rare book in good state'. A copy of Samuel Johnson's *Irene* (1749) could be had in (later) half calf gilt for £2.10s., but another copy, 'totally uncut, as issued' (albeit also in 'a neat half binding') was £7.17s.6d. Internal interference with books, through washing, making up or the addition of facsimile leaves, has always been a less transparent process than rebinding and although it certainly went on in the twentieth century, its heyday, like morocco extra, fell more in the century before. No collectors' guide from 1900 onwards would disagree with the advice in *The Elements of Book-Collecting* (1927) to 'warn the collector to be on his guard against made-up copies'.[41] Pickering offered a Shakespeare Fourth Folio (1685) in the 1902 catalogue at the robust price of £85 on the grounds that it was not only fine, sound and clean, but also that it was 'perfect throughout, every leaf being genuine'; another copy, also sound, but with the portrait in 'excellent facsimile' was only £31.10s. The principle of integrity of condition without subsequent sophistication was well established by the beginning of the century.

Writing mid-century and looking back, John Carter could say that 'it has been fashionable for the past fifty years to place a strong emphasis on 'original' condition: to prefer even a battered copy in this hallowed state to another in the handsomest of subsequent (or even contemporary) coverings. This respect for the integrity of the outside was a healthy reaction from the indiscriminate, and sometimes tasteless, rebinding of our forefathers'.[42] Carter was nevertheless of the opinion that '"fine" would be equally applicable to a copy of the Jenson *Pliny* (Venice, 1472) in contemporary stamped vellum, [or] to another in the sober but handsome morocco which Lewis or Hering would have put on it for Lord Vernon', a judgement we might question today. We would also increasingly blanch at Carter's observation, written in 1948, that 'it has been discovered by the discriminating ... who revere original or contemporary condition but recognise that they cannot always get it, that a careful binder, carefully instructed, can produce a quite acceptable modern version of the plain calf or vellum of 1650'.[43] Bernard Middleton's *Recollections* testify to the regular practice of making 'antique-style bindings' – he writes about the second half of the twentieth century, but the practice goes back well into the nineteenth – and although this still goes on today, and 'calf antique-style' is still quite often seen in booksellers' catalogues, this kind of approach has become less widely accepted.[44]

The consolidation of achievements in enumerative bibliography towards the end of the twentieth century led bibliographers to broaden their approach, to look beyond what was printed to explore more how books were read and used, how they were distributed and sold, and how their contents influenced contemporary thought. The move from historical bibliography to the history of the book brought an increasing concern for attention to be paid to the copy-specific aspects of early books, to consider their bindings to be potentially interesting even if not aesthetically 'fine', and to consider their ownership evidence to be important beyond the confines of interest in association copies and books from the libraries of famous people. The entry on 'provenance' in the *ABC for Book Collectors* expanded from three paragraphs to six between its first edition in 1952, and its eighth in 2004.[45] This was accompanied by a growing professional recognition of the importance of preserving the nation's documentary heritage, stimulated by an influential national survey published in 1984 which highlighted the need for action and new attitudes.[46] The closing years of the twentieth century saw an increasing professionalization of book conservation, and a growing emphasis on preserving the original, whatever its condition, rather than repairing and restoring.

In 1919 *The Bookman's Journal* encouragingly reported that 'old volumes, some in vellum, some in calf, with bindings made to defy centuries ... are no longer burned as rubbish or sold for a song'.[47] Only 30 years earlier William Blades had published his *Enemies of Books* with numerous horror stories of rare early

English books used as tobacconists' wrappings or lavatory paper, and while the *Journal* may have been right in thinking that books printed by Wynkyn de Worde were less likely to meet that fate in 1919, the advances were only relative, as the level of respect for old books which is generally taken for granted in the early twenty-first century developed only gradually during the twentieth. Parish libraries were being discarded because the books were 'dirty and unread' as late as the 1950s.[48] Eighteenth-century printed theology is now less likely to be pulped (though it may still be difficult to sell) primarily because we have developed a respect for all kinds of historic documentation, and it is less likely to be rebound, because we have developed an appreciation of the potential of books of all kinds as historical evidence, beyond their textual content.

Later twentieth-century catalogues therefore tend towards an increasing description of ownership and binding details, as a selling point of the books, however humble or ordinary these may be. While Maggs catalogues of the earlier part of the century might include sections on 'association copies', in 1997 they issued a catalogue entitled *Provenance*, in which a miscellaneous collection of antiquarian material was presented in terms of the previous ownership of the books. Sotheby's and Christie's catalogues from the 1980s onwards not uncommonly include provenance indexes, such as would only exceptionally be found earlier. In 1995 Yale University Library acquired a collection of 242 books assembled by the bookseller Bernard Rosenthal, mostly European imprints before 1600, whose interest lay not in their textual content but in the fact that they were all heavily annotated by early owners, who were neither celebrated nor even necessarily identifiable scholars.[49] Responsible booksellers today share the concerns of book historians to respect the integrity of books that pass through their hands, and avoid the destruction of evidence, however mundane it may seem. In 2005 Quaritch offered for sale a copy of the first edition of Johnson's *Vanity of Human Wishes*, 1749 (£5,000), 'in a tract volume of verse of the 1740s, rebound in early nineteenth-century polished half calf, spine directly labelled "Poetical Miscellany"'.[50] The other contents of the volume are only cursorily described; the point is that previous generations would have broken the volume up, to rebind the valuable item and sell it separately.

There are various reasons for buying, and owning, antiquarian books. Books were generally made first and foremost to be read and that has, obviously, always been a motivating factor for acquiring old books as well as new ones; to read their texts, or to use them in some way as reference sources for leisure, education or research. People may also buy old books because they find them aesthetically satisfying, or because they offer a tangible link with the past; they may be motivated to collect them through a desire to preserve, to assemble something comprehensive and unique, or through a sheer hard-to-rationalize delight in ownership. The growing availability of early texts in modern editions, or in some other surrogate form such as microfilm or online, has inevitably meant that buying antiquarian books for reading has become less important as time has progressed, and those other collecting purposes have become more prominent. As the potential of digital technology marches forwards and more and more early books are available, textually, in an electronic form which can be easily accessed and printed out from a computer, that trend looks set to accelerate; books will become more interesting for their artefactual qualities than their textual ones. Antiquarian books, which are perhaps more readily appreciated in this way (being more likely to be written in, to be bound by hand, and to have other unique qualities), probably have a less doubtful future than modern ones. Their status as desirable objects that people will continue to buy and sell looks fairly secure.

The Market Fortunes of the First Folio

ANTHONY JAMES WEST

AT the beginning of the twentieth century the Shakespeare First Folio had already been a collector's icon for a long time, arguably since the Duke of Roxburghe's widely reported purchase in 1790.[1] Since the 1860s, its rate of sale had increased continuously. In the last three decades of the century, its price averaged well over £300. In 1899, Sidney Lee wrote that 'a fine copy of the First Folio is worth at least £1,000', commenting later (1924) that the record price of £1,700 in 1899 'was regarded as a fantastic extravagance'.[2]

The standing of the First Folio was greatly enhanced at the dawn of the new century by the publication in 1902 of two folio volumes: Sidney Lee's *Facsimile* edition and his *Census* of (156) extant copies. These publications had remarkable consequences. Lee's Introduction to the *Facsimile* marked, even provoked, a shift in bibliographical history – from the nineteenth-century traditions of scholarship to the New Bibliography of the twentieth century. W.W. Greg roundly criticized it in *The Library* in 1903 and A.W. Pollard's trail-blazing *Shakespeare's Folios and Quartos* (1909) was written in reply to it. At the same time, Lee's *Census* changed the perception of the Folio in the antiquarian book trade and among collectors. From the moment of its publication, dealers could refer to each copy by a number and quote condition and provenance information from Lee's short descriptions. Copies were universally identified by their Lee number or dubbed 'Not in Lee'.

A sampling of events will illustrate the Folio's fortunes and the trade's dealings. Between the 1890s and 1928 the American collector Henry Folger (1857-1930) bought no fewer than 82 First Folios, a third of the copies now located.[3] He purchased discreetly, through book dealers and other agents, notably through Quaritch, Gabriel Wells, and A.S.W. Rosenbach. In 1903, through A.B. Railton of Sotheran, Folger paid an astronomical sum (uncharacteristically for him) for the Sibthorp copy. In 1905, he tried through Sotheran to pre-empt the Bodleian's reacquisition of the deposit copy it had sold in the seventeenth century. In 1915, he asked A.H. Mayhew of Charing Cross Road to write to 35 owners listed in Lee's *Census* to test their interest in selling and to value their copies. Owners resisted, some disdainfully.

Not many books have been featured in cartoons. In 1922, when Rosenbach bought (for Folger) the two First Folios in Sotheby's much-publicized Burdett-Coutts sale, setting a new price record of £8,600 for one of them, *Punch* published a cartoon showing Uncle Sam carrying off a First Folio (see

p. 199). Others, including Lee, had already commented unfavourably on the exodus of the national heritage across the Atlantic. The following year was the anniversary of the Folio's publication: the very fact of recognizing the tercentenary of a book says something about the regard in which it was held by 1923. The tercentenary events propelled its status ever higher: there were several exhibitions; a celebratory volume was edited by Israel Gollancz; Maggs Bros. issued a special catalogue 'in Commemoration of the Tercentenary of the First Folio'; and The Old Vic celebrated the culmination of a ten-year cycle of performances of all 36 plays in the Folio.

The leading First Folio bookseller, by far, during the century was Bernard Quaritch.[4] This dominance continued a position well established in the nineteenth century. Quaritch handled at least 32 Folios in the first three decades and four more later (1972-90); Maggs handled at least eleven, mostly in the 1920s and 1930s. Around the turn of the century Tregaskis sold four. Sotheran and Pickering handled at least seven and six, respectively, in the first decade. Other leading booksellers, such as Frank T. Sabin, the Robinson brothers and Francis Edwards, each sold three or more. The dominant American dealers, by comparison, were Gabriel Wells (who sold at least 24), A.S.W. Rosenbach (17), George D. Smith (12) and John Fleming (12). Sotheby's dominated the auction market.

Before addressing sales and prices, one special aspect of the history of the First Folio needs to be mentioned – namely the extraordinary degree and the extreme variety of treatment the copies have been accorded. Leaving aside the care and misuse of owners in the course of nearly four centuries, copies of the Folio have been subjected to: the making-up of copies and treatment by binders and re-binders (since the seventeenth or eighteenth centuries); repairers – skilled and unskilled, often misguided by our standards (since the eighteenth century); and expert, skilful, well-equipped and sensitive conservators (increasingly during the twentieth century). Perhaps no other book has received so much, and such varied, attention.[5]

As for the volume of trading, on the basis especially of auction records, the number of copies sold peaked in the first three decades of the twentieth century, with between 45 and 50 sales per decade. These figures exclude many sales by dealers and many of the Folios purchased by Henry Folger during his most active years in the market. Then, as supply dwindled, the numbers sold declined to the upper teens in the 1930s and 1940s, and ranged between seven and twelve copies in each of the century's last five decades. (Six copies have been auctioned, 2001-2005.) This decline is symptomatic of a general reduction in the supply of antiquarian books during the course of the century, but it also reflects the institutional confinement of copies of the Folio in particular.

Any study of prices, especially one based largely on auction results, must take account of the effect on prices of 'the ring'. The way the ring operated is discussed in more detail in Frank Herrmann's chapter in this volume, but four things can be said with some assurance: hammer prices were likely to be extremely low compared to open market prices; vendors did not receive their just return; auction houses did not earn their due commissions; and dealers profited nefariously. The effect on market prices is less clear. When the dealer bought a book at the post-sale settlement, he would presumably prefer, in most circumstances, to sell it at the top retail price the market would bear; if so, market price would be unaffected. With well-known, high-priced, collectors' books, such as the First Folio, there was a greater risk of public exposure and of competition at the sale from private buyers and foreign dealers; to the extent that ring-members had to respond by excluding particular lots from the ringing operation, the auction price itself would not be affected. In such cases, the ring was irrelevant. Certainly, it is difficult to find evidence of the ringing of First Folios. One case in point, however, is revealing. At the Ruxley Lodge sale, in October 1919, Quaritch took the First Folio for a derisory £100; in the post-sale settlement, Charles J. Sawyer, Ltd., had to pay £1,550.[6] The factor of 15.5 is a measure of how much Gerald Henry Foley, the vendor, was deprived. But £1,550, for 'a decent copy in modern morocco,' is already (before Sawyer added a mark-up) above the average price for First Folios in the 1910s. Thus the effect of the ring was to distribute gain improperly, not demonstrably to affect the final open market price. Since over 100 First Folios went to America during the century, it was American demand that largely determined prices.

The average prices per decade which follow, based more on auction than dealer sales, are mostly from sales in London and New York – by far the most important markets.[7] They rose in the first four decades from £1,200, to £1,400, £3,500, and £3,800. They declined to £3,000 in the 1940s and to £1,800 in the 1950s. With inflation beginning to rise at an unprecedented rate, there were then two significant jumps, to an average of £9,400 in the 1960s and to £16,800 in the 1970s. In the 1980s, there was a mighty leap: to £313,000. The market dwindled in the 1990s to an average of about £150,000. (These last two averages are shaky, being based on only five and four prices respectively.) The two highest auction prices in the century were $580,000 (£411,000) in 1985 for a copy now in Japan and $1,064,000 (£691,000) in 1989 for a copy now in Ohio.[8] Five new price records were set, between 1960 and 1989.

When one turns to comparing Folio prices with prices of other books, the issue of 'like' is ever-present, especially when little is known about the condition of the books being compared.[9] Three very similar books, except for date of publication, are the Shakespeare Second (1632), Third (1663/4), and Fourth (1685) Folios. Prices of the First Folio began to rise away from those of the other seventeenth-century editions in the eighteenth century; by the twentieth century they were consistently in a different price category altogether. For example, in the last two decades when the First Folio averaged around £313,000 and £150,000 respectively, the Second did not exceed £36,000, the Third £62,000, and the Fourth £21,000. These figures omit three extraordinary exceptions in the William Foyle sale, at Christie's on 12 July 2000. The poor copy of the First Folio was bought in.[10] By contrast, the Second reached a record of £55,000, the Third a remarkable record of £420,000, and the Fourth a record of £38,000. High as these prices were, they do not challenge the general conclusion that the First Folio was in a different price category. This was proved at the Berland sale, at Christie's New York in 2001, when a copy of the First Folio sold for a record $5,600,000 (£3,864,000), the Second for $250,000, the Third for $500,000, and the Fourth for $240,000.[11]

For the purpose of choosing 'like' books, I have tried using the criteria of (i) well-known writer, (ii) nearly contemporary and (iii) folio format. This led me to editions of Ben Jonson's *Works* (1616 and 1616-41), and to Walter Raleigh's *History of the World* (1614 and 1634). The content and appeal of the Jonson make it a better comparison than the Raleigh. There were enough sales of these works in the last two decades of the twentieth century to provide a reasonable sample of prices. The average price of all nine First Folios auctioned in these decades was £240,000, with six of them in the hundreds of thousands of pounds. By comparison, Jonson (1616) exceeded £1,000 four times, with a top price of £1,831; and Jonson (1616-41) exceeded £2,000 four times, with a top price of £3,614. Raleigh (1614) exceeded £1,000 three times with a top price of £2,139 (excluding a copy with Raleigh's autograph); and Raleigh (1634) exceeded £550 on one occasion with a price of £900. Clearly the Folio is again in a different price realm.

By contrast, there is one book in a different league in the other direction. It is not directly comparable for several reasons: it was published over 170 years earlier; it has the distinction and prestige of being the first book printed with movable type; furthermore, it is rare. But like the First Folio, the Gutenberg Bible has been the dream, if not the realistic goal, of countless serious book collectors. No Gutenberg Bible sold for less than £2,000 in the twentieth century. In 1911, a copy sold for nearly four times the price of a First Folio in the same sale (Hoe). In the 1920s, when the Folio was averaging £3,500, a Gutenberg Bible (on vellum to sure) sold for the equivalent of £61,000. In 1978, when the highest price of a Folio was the equivalent of nearly £77,000, three Gutenberg Bibles averaged around £1.3 million.

One of the notable outcomes of the First Folio's passage through the book trade in the twentieth century has been a marked change in its pattern of distribution. Geographically, 55 per cent of the Folios are now concentrated in four places: Washington, DC; the London area including Eton and Windsor; Tokyo; and New York City. By 1899, Bernard Quaritch was already intimately familiar with the dramatic exodus of copies across the Atlantic: 'Perfect copies are usually sold by us dealers to American collectors.'[12] In 1902, Lee recorded 39 copies (25 per cent) in the USA; by 2000, there were 145 (64 per cent). In 1902, in the UK, there were 100 copies (63 per cent); by 2000, 44 copies remained (19 per cent). At the end of the century the First Folio had become a global book, with 27 copies spread around the world beyond the USA and UK, fifteen of them in Japan.

There was also a striking, huge shift during the century from private to institutional ownership. As early as 1889, the editor of Book Prices Current, explaining the scarcity of First Folios, noted 'every available copy [is] being secured at any price for Libraries'.[13] In 1902, about 112 copies (71 per cent) were in private hands; by 2000 there were merely some fifteen (7 per cent).

We have seen that the Folio's value in the market rose from an average of £1,200 in the first decade to a peak in the 1980s of over £300,000. In 1900, the Folio had no claim to be a rare book; by 2000, since institutional copies tend not to move, it had become rare.

Patterns of Collecting and Trading in 'Modern' Literature

ANGUS O'NEILL

Introduction

THE canon of antiquarian English literature was largely established by 1900, and while there are innumerable instances of writers gently rising and falling in esteem, even the occasional rediscovery, there has been no wholesale reassessment on the scale of that in, for instance, art history or musicology. Modern literature, by its very nature, is another matter. The pattern of buying, selling and collecting the literature of one's own time has changed almost out of recognition since 1900, and the following pages will attempt to examine some of the developments – from the perspective of a dealer in rare books, rather than a literary scholar.

The very word 'modern' itself presents a problem. Does it mean 'recent', or 'contemporary', or 'in the style of the Modern Movement'? Even in 2006, some dealers in 'modern firsts' stock authors as remote as Henry James, who died in 1916. Others seem to think Martin Amis belongs with the incunabula. 'Modern' is used loosely here, to identify works from around 1880 to 2005 which appear to be of lasting significance – of some kind. The 'modern' books of the 1920s may appear hopelessly old-fashioned now, if they are not forgotten entirely; but some of the most avidly collected books of the 1990s are already gathering dust, and the neglected experimentalist of 1913 may be reassessed at any moment, so (in the manner of George Sims, as quoted by Henry Woudhuysen elsewhere in this volume) I have decided to abjure value judgments and try to be inclusive.

Most 'modern' books had not even been written in 1900. A few writers from the first stirrings of modernism – Kipling, Wilde, Shaw – are worth examining because they have been consistently collected throughout the century, leaving a trail of evidence in booksellers' catalogues and auction records. And certain modern books were always 'rare' simply because they needed to be produced under expensive circumstances, whether for political reasons (*Seven Pillars of Wisdom*) or cultural ones (*Ulysses*, *Lady Chatterley's Lover*). But these are the exceptions. In general, it was most unusual for any but the most valuable of recent first editions to be lotted separately in the auction rooms, and disappointingly few catalogues have survived from the smaller booksellers who were instrumental in forming taste. Collectors have tended to hang on to lists issued by the doyens of the trade in preference to those of the minor players, and one has to look long and hard through a pre-1925 Maggs or Quaritch catalogue to find anything recognizable as a 'modern' book.

Much of what has been published on this subject seems to have been written from a perspective of nostalgia, and is hardly evidential. There is a more precise measure we can use, which distils lifetimes of experience in assessing supply and demand, and relating those criteria to the economy as a whole. It is vulgar, but it is factual and computable. In short, the hardest evidence of changing taste is changing prices.

Rather than using the retail price index, a crude and often inappropriate measure, I have chosen to base my calculations of relative value on 'per capita GDP'. The reasons for this are set out in Appendix 1. As with any such index, it is far from perfect, especially when applied to the earliest periods discussed, but I believe it is more suitable and more useful than RPI in the context of rare artefacts.

The influences: bibliographies

The impact of academic study and scholarly bibliography on the collecting of antiquarian books has been very considerable. This is not yet true of 'modern' books. Most of the early work in the field was done by the dealers, some of it with flair and accuracy (P.H. Muir), some less so (Gilbert H. Fabes, William A. Foyle); the academics followed later. As a result, the concepts of analytical bibliography, book history and so on are only now beginning to have a significant impact on most day-to-day collecting and dealing in modern books, and (see below) are not always welcomed when they intrude. Although the twentieth century has seen a steady improvement in the standard of author bibliographies, and the principles of sound and consistent description have been applied to modern as well as older books with increasing regularity, there are still exceptions, such as 'bibliographies' which are merely checklists of criticism, and otherwise excellent and scholarly works which simply ignore dustwrappers: this omission may appeal to traditionalists, but it is no help to the collectors or dealers of the twenty-first century. If there is a trend in all this, perhaps it is as follows: the subjects of the most thorough bibliographies are the authors who are taught as 'serious' literature in universities (Eliot, Larkin, Pound); those who are outside the modernist canon are less well served. (It is perhaps worth noting that the absence of a Waugh bibliography is largely due to the persistent rumour that comprehensive notes for the definitive one already exist – compiled by a bookseller.) A generation or two ago, enthusiasts may have been drawn to modern books because they seemed easy to deal with, but anyone who thinks that they are all bibliographically straightforward should look at, for instance, Michael Juliar's *Vladimir Nabokov: A Descriptive Bibliography* (New York & London, 1986, and xeroxed supplements) to see how complicated modern firsts can get. And most of the impetus for this insistence on bibliographical accuracy came from academics, admittedly with the aid and encouragement of collectors and book-sellers. 'Not in Gallup', for instance, really means something: if Donald Gallup missed an Eliot or Pound item, that item was genuinely uncommon (unless it was one of Frederic Prokosch's forgeries, which now have their own market.)

These bibliographers did not, for the most part, live in splendid isolation with their collections (although some, like Geoffrey Keynes, were firmly in that tradition). Much more often they were attached to universities, and the role of institutional collecting (usually North American) in expanding the trade in modern literature was immensely important. This began in earnest after the Second World War, when libraries such as Yale (with the help of Donald Gallup) and, perhaps most notably, the Humanities Research Center at the University of Texas had unprecedented budgets and exercised enormous influence. Dealers such as Lew D. Feldman ('The House of El Dieff' – if the name seems obscure, read it aloud; it has three syllables) in the USA, and Bertram Rota in the UK, helped feed this appetite. In more recent years the University of Tulsa, again with the help of Anthony Rota and his co-director George Lawson, has built a collection of international importance. By the end of the twentieth century, however, things had changed considerably. Only the grandest firms dealt with institutional collections on the scale that was widespread in, say, 1980. A few libraries still had the budgets, and needed archives now that they had most of the books: the rest, alas, appeared to be a spent force. (The present writer is aware of only half a dozen American librarians who have visited his shop, in four years. Three bought books. Two paid for them.) Among all but the most prominent dealers in modern literature, library purchases account for perhaps only a tenth of their 1980 figures, and by most accounts their share was even greater ten or twenty years before that. Now the trade is driven by collectors.

Thematic bibliographies have not, in general, had so much impact on the collection of literary first editions, but *Printing and the Mind of Man* (1967) has been a pointer towards thematic collections of previously unconsidered subjects and authors. No one would dispute the place of the Gutenberg Bible as Item One: but the later entries, key books on Futurism, the Boy Scout Movement, and X-ray crystallography amongst many other topics, were something new. And one of the principal private collections which was used in compiling the catalogue (and on which the 1963 IPEX exhibition had been based) was formed by a writer whose own works of light fiction will feature in this study of first edition price move-ments: John Carter's near-contemporary at Eton, Ian Fleming (1908-64).[1]

Another important guide in this field, an influence on at least one generation of collectors, was Cyril Connolly's *The Modern Movement: One Hundred Key Books from England, France and America 1880-1950* (1965), which, while necessarily limited by its period, includes (as one might expect from the compiler of *The Unquiet Grave*) a highly intelligent and informed selection of worthwhile books, many not at all well known. Everyone has read Henry James and James Joyce: not everyone is familiar with Edmond Dujarin and Ivy Compton-Burnett. But they ought to be.

Sources of information to help dealers and collectors assess rarity (always a selling point) have changed considerably over the last hundred years, and these have been influential. In 1900, much 'evidence' about scarcity was merely lore, the comments in Lowndes or its equivalent just expressions of opinion; this began to change, for earlier books, with Wing and STC. But there will never be a twentieth-century equivalent: there is simply too much published material, and not enough of it is of interest. Online sources (OCLC, RLIN and so on) can give a reliable indication of the scarcity of individual books, but these do not quite replace the National Union Catalog, 754 large volumes (plus 458 supplements) weighing, perhaps, two tons. This work, an almost Borgesian attempt at enumerating the locations of every printed book in the libraries of the USA, will never again be realized in printed form, which is regrettable. Though online information can be accurate and efficient, it is too easily tampered with, and the risk of history being rewritten is real: a few years ago, records at a leading English museum were altered to provide spurious provenance for some fake modern paintings, and books cannot be far behind.[2]

Having said this, most modern books do seem to pose fewer bibliographical problems than earlier ones. In the machine age, changes in a book's text during the production process are less likely to be authorial: consequently these books have often escaped the minute attention of bibliographers. And we can all name dozens of twentieth-century books whose 'points' are complicated by any standards. But very few need to be collated page by page. Most modern books have no variants at all: if such a book is not a reprint, it is a first edition, 'period'. As such, it is perfectly feasible for a leading dealer to issue a catalogue without the refrain of 'Ramsbottom A40' and so on, if there is no possibility of confusion between the item on offer and another book. (Moreover, when these references do appear, they are all too often just copied from other catalogues. Some dealers, especially on the internet, seem to think their purpose is purely decorative, and do not appreciate that they may not apply to every copy of the book!)

The influences: guides, good and less good

Collectors' guides are a more established influence on the market in rare modern books, but they have not always served their subject well. The price guide, until synthesized into something useful by Allen and Patricia Ahearn, has gone through some strange phases.[3] Joseph Connolly's variously titled guides were successful enough to go into three editions (1977, 1984 and 1987): yet even the last of these contained howlers enough to provoke magisterial criticism in the trade press. The Ahearns wrote with some accuracy in their 1998 edition 'It is our feeling that in 1987 there were probably not more than twenty twentieth-century literary first editions selling for more than $750'; but Beckett's *Murphy* (1938), valued by Joseph Connolly in 1987 at 'up to £500' in a wrapper (itself a marked increase on his 1977 valuation of £40!) was certainly one of them. Even without a dustwrapper the book, one of the notorious rarities of the century, was worth something close to that. Other price guides, mostly based on minimal research and unleavened with Connolly's wit (he went on to become a successful novelist), have come and gone like marsh gas, and to similar effect. The most recent, Catherine Porter's *Collecting Modern Books* (2003), has a sensible introduction by Peter Selley and some excellent colour illustrations. The main text is not to be relied upon.

Most general guides to book-collecting have been unhelpful about twentieth-century literature. One exception, which was for a while influential and still contains much interesting material, was Percy Muir's *Book-Collecting as a Hobby, in a Series of Letters to Everyman* (London & Chesham: 1944). The book's format might be thought off-putting (it certainly seemed so to this writer, 30 years ago), but, despite a lamentable tendency to 'talk down', inevitably compounded by the use of the second person, the advice given (on, for example, how to treat booksellers) is very clearly based on personal experience. Muir is sound on hagglers: 'if there is an alternative customer for a book, do you think the bargainer gets the first offer of it?' Some of what he writes would have appeared dated even at the time ('the jacket is still a thing apart from the book itself ... [Never] pay a higher price for a book because it has something unusual about the dust-jacket or the inserted advertisements') but he does point his readers towards relatively new areas of collecting such as detective fiction.[4] (Muir was a director for many years of Elkin Mathews, and their catalogue 43 of 1932 already illustrates some of his preoccupations: of A.E. Housman's *Last Poems* (1922), the cataloguer writes, 'Like most copies of the First Edition, this has faulty punctuation on p.52 which is said to denote the first issue. It probably does nothing of the kind'; 'exceedingly fine' copies of Conan Doyle's *Adventures* and *Memoirs of Sherlock Holmes* (1892 & 1894) were offered here at £35 the two, exactly ten times the price of a 'repaired ... but good' first-issue *Dr. Jekyll*.)[5] Percy Muir counsels at length against pursuing the fashionable subjects of the moment. But then he can never have expected to appear, very thinly disguised, in a novel which is now a necessary component of a Booker Prize collection: Sybille Bedford's *Jigsaw* (1989, shortlisted for that year's award.)

John Carter has been so influential that he risks more frequent mention in this volume than any other writer. Alas, his calm authority and unimpeachable taste have yet to be matched by his successors. The works of Anthony Rota, notably *Apart from the Text*, are full of good advice and sound observations, but no individual book covers the ground as Carter's *ABC* did. However, one of the distinguishing features of early twenty-first century collecting is that the customer is sometimes the last person to realize that he may not know best. Most people who spend large sums on books are not idiots – the money has to come from somewhere, after all – but too often they are scared of missing the new Damien Hirst or J.K. Rowling, and in their haste they may rely on information readily supplied by fools or knaves.

Other influences, including the baneful and the banal

The cinema, 'investment' and the internet have emerged as three of the most powerful motive forces on the market at the beginning of the twenty-first century.

The first of these, cinema (and indeed television, with radio represented to a much lesser degree), is especially influential. Literary people bewail the fact that there are, seemingly, no longer any books that 'everyone has read' (except, apparently, for Harry Potter); but there are certainly films that everyone, or nearly everyone in affluent Western society, has seen. This has led many to concentrate on collecting novels which inspired celebrated films (and of course other manifestations of performing art). It sometimes seems as though the 'author collector' is dead and buried, with the rare pamphlets on the writer's pet subjects, the variant states, the suppressed polemics all brushed aside in the stampede for the dust-wrappered highlights. In 1973, a proof copy of T.S. Eliot's *Collected Poems 1909-1962* (1963) fetched £18 at auction, a little more than late, dull Eliot proofs usually made, but not much; in the same year *Old Possum's Book of Practical Cats* (1939) made a modest £26. In 2006 these prices would equate to about £250 and £350; but, thanks to the decline in 'completism' (the assembly of a writer's entire output, including when practicable all the forms in which at least the principal titles were issued)[6] the proof would now struggle to reach £100, even if it were separately lotted at all, while *Possum* would be over £1,000 – largely because of the musical *Cats*. In the early 1970s the auction price for Evelyn Waugh's *Basil Seal Rides Again* (1963), an artificial rarity if ever there was one, climbed from about £20 to about £40, a steady £350 at the 2006 equivalent: Maggs have one on offer as I write, priced at ... £350. But during the same period *A Handful of Dust* (1934), perhaps Waugh's finest novel, fetched £22-£24, and £36 for an inscribed copy. It would look like a very good swap for *Basil Seal* today.

'Investment' is a problem. There will always be proponents of 'alternative investment vehicles', or whatever this year's phrase may be, and few of them are distinguished by bibliographical acumen. Many, indeed, are simply sharks. Financial gain, as a motive for owning books, has only ever attracted a certain type of buyer, usually one who makes the grave mistake of supposing that, because antiquarian books are so obviously complicated, modern ones are not. These buyers are happy dealing with each other, or with unscrupulous dealers, over the internet, but all too often their compounded errors do not stand up to the harsh light of day. Anyone with a shop will have their own stories of appallingly misdescribed books offered at outrageous prices by the gullible – and, indeed, by the gulled.

The internet's profound impact on the book trade is discussed by Paul Minet elsewhere in this volume. As a source of instant information it is a wonderful thing: the only snag is that nearly all of it is wrong. The credulous should recall the words of Robert Wilensky: 'We've all heard that a million monkeys banging on a million typewriters will eventually reproduce the entire works of Shakespeare. Now, thanks to the Internet, we know this is not true.'[7] Another influence that should not be ignored is the literary prize. Booker Prize winners have been enthusiastically collected since the 1980s, and the interest has widened to include all six titles shortlisted each year: some of these (the prize began in 1969) have become surprisingly elusive. Possibly the 'longlist', introduced in 2001 and bringing the annual tally close to twenty, will now begin to attract collectors. Other prizes are slowly gaining attention as well, though it is not clear whether the discontinuation of the Whitbread, recently announced, will stifle this trend or stimulate it. In any case, these awards, unsatisfactory though they may be *sub specie aeternitatis*, do highlight some excellent writing, offer a valuable insight into the reading tastes of a generation, and generate useful publicity for the book trade as a whole.

The origins of the modern first edition trade

There are some grounds for believing that the trade in first editions of contemporary books – in effect, first impressions of newly published titles – owes its inception to the firm of Pickering and Chatto. Its catalogues from the 1890s include, for instance, many of the works of Robert Louis Stevenson, for most of his career a Chatto & Windus author (the firms were as closely linked as their names suggest): the marked copy of a Pickering catalogue from 1892, for example, lists RLS's *Across the Plains*, published in that year, as 'First Edition. New. 6s.'.[8] The manuscript note on the interleaved blank opposite, 'I copy / i/-' (four shillings, in Pickering's price code of the time) suggests that this was not an isolated listing. Later in the same year, the firm offered 'A Complete Set of his Works, 25 Vols, All First Editions, And Uncut Copies, in the Original Bindings, As Issued, £36': most of these were Chatto and Windus titles.[9] (The set was sold to 'Bangs', possibly the American writer John Kendrick Bangs, and carried a cost of 'pr/-/-', or seventeen pounds.) The strong trade in Stevensoniana continued until well into the new century: catalogue 166 (*c*.1915) included *Dr Jekyll and Mr Hyde* ('original paper boards') at a guinea ('£325' – perhaps a tenth of the 2006 price), while the 1910 limited edition of *Virginibus Puerisque*, with illustrations by Norman Wilkinson, was soon on offer at an ambitious three guineas (nearly '£1,000'!), with the assurance that it 'will speedily become a much sought after item'. (Fine copies are clusive, but passable ones can be bought in 2006 for little more than £100. A copy sold at auction in 1915 for £1.4s.)

Oddly, there are few if any entries for another Chatto and Windus author, Mark Twain: perhaps Mr Bangs was buying them up before they reached the catalogue; perhaps Pickering and Chatto had simply not laid down copies of his books as assiduously as they might have done. Or perhaps more customers then 'followed the flag' and collected only American editions of American writers, even when (as often with Twain) the English ones preceded them. Maybe, however, the market for Twain was still undeveloped: I can find no trace of single titles (as distinct from library sets) appearing at auction before 1913.

Not all the newer books came from the publishers, of course. The purchase of William Morris's vast library in 1897 had been another source of relatively recent material; a catalogue of about 1900 included such resonant items as Walt Whitman's *Poems* (1868), the provenance 'from the library of William Morris' proudly stated, at a modest 10s. ('£200'). But it seems likely that much of the market in 'modern first editions' was fuelled by the synergy between 'P&C' and 'C&W'.[10]

The competition: a Maggs catalogue from 1916

Not many modern books appear in Messrs Maggs' catalogue 350 of 1916 ('First Editions ... of the XIXth and XXth Centuries'). Perhaps the Berkeley Square location encouraged a more conservative clientele, the 'carriage trade' indeed; perhaps (as so often) the stock simply reflected the taste of the bookseller responsible for stocking the department. But with the exception of Joseph Conrad (half a dozen titles), George Bernard Shaw (five items) and Oscar Wilde (two pages, including the 1894 *Salome*, one of 100, at £8.15s. or about '£2,300'), most of the taste shown here is firmly rooted well before 1890. One or two titles catch the eye: the first American edition of Herman Melville's first book, *Typee* (New York, 1846), in original wrappers, now seems cheap at 18 shillings ('£240'), for instance; but artificial rarities and forgotten humorists are there in far greater number.

One familiar name does feature, however. While Pickering and Chatto's marked catalogues contain many familiar buyers' names, one who appears in their archives neither as a buyer nor as a supplier is the infamous Thomas J. Wise. Perhaps they saw through him?[11] The 1916 Maggs catalogue, however, contains a number of unascribed Wise forgeries, including the first of all his efforts, Shelley's *Poems and Sonnets*, edited by 'Charles Alfred Seymour' ('Philadelphia', 1887). The cataloguer quotes the pseudonymous Seymour's introduction: 'It is, I suppose, hardly necessary to add that not one of these thirty copies will at any time, or in any manner, be offered for sale.' An extraordinary claim indeed! And here it is, priced at 25 shillings, or around '£330' adjusted to 2006.

Modern first editions: a refreshing development

Under the heading 'modern' the *OED* gives, as printed authority for the use of the word in the phrase 'modern first editions', a catalogue issued by the bookseller Bertram Rota. This is no accident: the firm, which exists to this day, was founded in 1923 and rapidly established itself as the leader in a new field. On reading Rota's early catalogues one is struck by the freshness of layout, the economy of description, the absence of pomposity, and above all by the taste and dis- crimination of his selection of stock: this was clearly a man who knew his books. The very first of these ('1923 / A Catalogue of / Modern Books / mainly / First Editions ... C. Bertram Rota / 108 Charing Cross Road') is interesting. Carefully cross-referenced, all the staples of the trade of his time are there, of course –

Galsworthy, Masefield, Shaw, Hugh Walpole[12] – but so are Ezra Pound (*Cathay*, 1915, that fragile and charming book, three shillings or, at 2006 prices, '£30') and Virginia Woolf (*Monday or Tuesday*, 1921, five shillings, or '£50'). Catalogue 4, of 1924, was to offer a fine copy of T.S. Eliot's *The Waste Land* (1923) at 7s.6d.! ('£75'). Three shillings seems to have been the lowest price: the highest was twelve guineas (c.'£2,500') for Samuel Butler's *Erewhon* (1872),[13] or fifteen pounds ('£3,000') with the second and 1901 editions thrown in. Perhaps more tempting to a buyer in 2006 would be Synge's *The Playboy of the Western World* (1907), 'very rare', ten pounds ('£2,000') – with a 'long and interesting autograph letter' inserted.[14] Visual material is present as well: Boulestin and Laboureur's charming *The New Keepsake* (1921), with original engravings by Laboureur and Marie Laurencin, and a Paul Nash woodcut, is on offer at 12s.6d. ('£125' – yes, please!), and there is a three-guinea ('£630') Beaumont Press book on Karsavina which would have appealed to Rota's West End clientele. He clearly knew how to find his books: the complete set of that attractive periodical *Coterie* (1919-21) is here priced at two guineas ('£420'), but was intermittently available as a remainder until around 1985, when this writer sold several sets for £175 each; I imagine Rota did a good trade with it, too. Rota always mentions the presence of dust-wrappers. He was probably the first successful dealer to realize their importance, modest though the price increment was in those days; for example, he had two copies of Lawrence's *Aaron's Rod* (1922), one fine in dust-wrapper at 10s.6d. ('£105'), another, 'cover slightly soiled', at 7s.6d. ('£75').[15] Again, in 1931, the firm's catalogue 20 offered two copies of Woolf's *To the Lighthouse* (1927), one 'fine in dust-wrapper' at £2 ('£400'), the other 'end-papers defaced, otherwise a fine copy' at 14s. ('£140'). One other noteworthy feature is that, even then, the firm was using research to explode the myths of the trade, as a footnote to Masefield's *Ballads and Poems* (1910) illustrates: 'The publishers state that there is no justification for the statement that the issue of this book on watermarked paper is earlier than that on plain paper. Both forms were issued simultaneously.' So much for the point-maniacs.

In 1927 Rota's catalogue 10 was issued from a new address, 76a Davies Street, with a Mayfair telephone number instead of a Regent one; the wrappers are thicker, blue and mention 'association copies' for the first time. The star item, after a set of Galsworthy (the Manaton edition, 21 vols., 1923) at £20 ('£4,000'), was a Robert Nichols manuscript at £15 ('£3,000'), with a number of newish press books between £5 and £10 ('£1,000-2,000'); the signed limited *Winnie-the-Pooh* (1926), 'as new in dust-wrapper' cost five guineas ('£1,100'), the trade issue, in the same condition, a modest nine shillings ('£90'). (The limited *Pooh* was competitively priced: Maggs paid £5 for a copy at auction in the same year.) One of Eric Kennington's drawings for *Seven Pillars of Wisdom* at twelve guineas ('£2,520') would have been a better buy than the Nichols manuscript; so would a large-paper *Salome* (with an impression of the suppressed plate inserted) at the same price. This last was cheap at the time, if the First Edition Bookshop's price in the following year (see below) is to be believed. This catalogue, especially when compared to others of its time, is remarkable for the scrupulous attention to bibliographical accuracy: Rota even points out textual changes between editions, something few of his contemporaries did with much more valuable books. The association copies show real imagination and flair: D'Annunzio's *The Child of Pleasure* (1898), with the ownership signature 'Jas. A. Joyce, Mullingar, July 5, 1900' would have been a good find at 30 shillings ('£300'). But one of the most refreshing characteristics of Rota's catalogues is the way in which he spends seven lines explaining the printing history of some Lovat Fraser items worth a little under five shillings apiece, yet dismisses the £20 Galsworthy set with five lines in total: rightly, since nothing need be said about it other than that it is in fine condition and cheaper than when it came out.

A case study: Kenneth Grahame's *The Wind in the Willows*

This was never a common book. Copies in the dustwrapper now appear only rarely, and fine copies even without it are scarce and expensive; a handsome one was on offer in 2005 at £12,500. In 2000, a copy in a 'defective' wrapper, with over half the spine missing, fetched £14,000 at auction; two years earlier, an evidently better one ('frayed') made £39,000 (plus buyers' premium in both instances). A really crisp one would fetch – who knows – £100,000? It is not impossible. (ABE currently lists a copy of the Barnes and Noble edition of 1995, 'lavendar [*sic*] boards ... lovely dust jacket ... as new' at £93,787.26, but this may be an error.)

The first, presumably wrapperless, copy we can trace at auction fetched £7 in 1930, equivalent to around £1,300 in 2006. (The next was in 1936: again £7, this time to Quaritch.) And yet, in June 1931, the First Edition Bookshop Ltd. felt it had to apologize, in an unnumbered catalogue 'Rare Books in English Literature of the last Fifty Years', for asking £20 for a copy in a dustwrapper: 'in such state ... a consummation we had hardly ever hoped to meet with'. That would be a little under '£4,000' by our measure. It wasn't even the most expensive item in the catalogue; Wilde's *Salome* of 1894, one of 100 on japanese vellum, was £32.10s. ('£6,500'), and the signed large-paper *Importance of Being Earnest* of 1899 was a round £40 ('£8,000'). These would have performed soundly enough over three-quarters of a century; but £30 ('£6,000'!) for H.M. Tomlinson's *The Sea and the Jungle* of 1912 ('almost mint but for slight bruising of one corner and there is a name on the end-paper', and no mention of a dustwrapper) seems extraordinary to us. Hugh Walpole's copy is currently on offer at $500, with Lew D. Feldman's 'original 1950 slip', showing a price of £100, laid in; £30 in 1931 equates to around £85 in 1950, so it held up well enough for two decades, and Feldman was nobody's fool, but how it has fallen since! Robert Bridges's *The Testament of Beauty* (1929: one of 50 signed) fared if anything worse, from £32 in 1931 to £150 on the internet in 2005, and I dare say even that is negotiable.[16]

Of course the First Edition Bookshop copy of *The Wind in the Willows* may have changed hands several times in the next fortnight to the mirth of the whole trade; often the best bargains are the books whose owners feel they have priced them to the full. (Bertram Rota's catalogue 16 had offered an 'unusually nice bright copy' at six guineas in the preceding year). But the canny time-traveller to 1931 would have found other bargains, from *The Thirty-Nine Steps* (1915, 'a fine copy', £1/7/6 or about '£275'), or *A Passage to India* in the dustwrapper (£1.10s., or '£300'), to *A Room of One's Own* (1929, 'as issued in dust wrapper') at a tempting £1.5s. ('£250'). More tempting, certainly, than *The Voyage Out* of 1914, 'covers slightly soiled and slight stain and erasure on front endpaper … otherwise a very good copy' at £4; '£800' sounds about right, if you wanted to sell it (the internet gives prices for non-association copies in original cloth from £500 to £2,000, but there are a dozen of them out there.) A literate descendant of one of the firm's customers might weep to find some of the invoices neatly folded inside their inheritance: Sheila Kaye-Smith's novels at prices up to £11, a signed limited Masefield for four guineas, a George Moore ditto for two (in 2002 we sold all ours from outside, at £4 each, after they failed in the shop at £10). None of the books actually appears to be worth less, unadjusted for inflation, than it was then, but these and the Hugh Walpoles (at prices up to £12.10s.) must run very close. And yet some of the staples of our trade are not so very different; *The Yellow Book* at six guineas would have to be a very superior copy to fetch £1,250 in 2006, but the signed limited D.H. Lawrences at 30 shillings and two guineas ('£300'/'£420') seem spot on.

Post-war trends: an examination of two general catalogues, from The Times Bookshop and George Sims, both *c.*1964

The undated catalogue 12 (New Series) from The Times Bookshop inches, tentatively, towards the modern. 1964, or perhaps a year or two later, is a likely date for it: the catalogue includes a book published in 1964, and all-figure telephone numbers would probably have replaced 'WELbeck 3781' by 1966. The cover is boldly entitled 'Rare books' in American Uncial, and it reproduces a sketch from Chagall's *Dessins pour la Bible*, to this day part of the stock-in-trade of the accessible avant-garde, and on sale within at £70 ('£2,150', or about two-thirds the going rate in 2006);[17] the contents, however, are mostly traditional. The catalogue is set (not unreasonably) in Times New Roman, and the descriptions are brief but efficient; the contents are divided into centuries, and show a taste for the bizarre (alchemy, sorcery, erotica) which, however, does not exclude the familiar, perhaps even the trite. It is an uneven catalogue, and unlike some other Times Bookshop catalogues of the time, notably the thematic ones produced by Timothy d'Arch Smith, it conveys no strong impression of individual taste; or perhaps, to be more precise, it conveys the impression of several competing tastes, some more informed than others. There are highlights, such as the manuscript of Lawrence Durrell's *Cities, Plains and People*, written in Alexandria in 1943, on offer at a cool £1,000 ('£30,000'),[18] but their impact is lessened by a large number of worthy but dull titles such as James Pope-Hennessy's *Queen Mary* (1959, one of 50 signed, £5 5s., or around '£160'). Even the altogether more covetable signed, limited Yeats *Poems* (1949) seems fully priced at £100 (£3,000): the three copies sold at auction around this time fetched the remarkably consistent figures of £58, £60 and £60.[19] That common book by Conrad, *The Rescue* (1920), surely needed a wrapper to merit the description 'A superb copy' and the price of £4 ('£125'), and a plethora of proofs from contemporary private presses – the most artificial of artificial rarities – suggests a slight lack of discrimination; the most amusing items (historically rather than textually, one suspects) are some manuscripts by F.R. Leavis, 'written on the versos of students' examination papers' at £20 (over '£600') a throw.

Lack of personal taste is not a criticism which could be made of G.F. Sims's catalogue 59, dated October 1964. Eric Gill is on the cover; but the text (printed by the same printer as the Times catalogue, Robert Stockwell of London S.E.1) is more imaginatively and effectively set in double-column Bodoni. There are flashes of the driest wit, and elsewhere Sims berates himself for missing a chance to buy, of all things, D.H. Lawrence's gravestone – 'foolishly we refused to purchase this'); there are, too, any number of genuine scarcities, often perhaps under- rather than over-catalogued. More might have been made, I suspect, of a proof copy of Robert Graves's *Lawrence and the Arabs* (1927), described laconically as bearing the legend 'Advance copy only – not for sale'. Given the closeness of the relationship between author and subject (Graves wrote to many of Lawrence's friends at the latter's own suggestion), and the rapid developments in T.E. Lawrence's personal life at the time, textual comparison might have been extremely rewarding. (Evidently someone at the time thought so too, as the book is frustratingly marked 'Sold'.) The face value of the catalogue must have been only a fraction of the Times's (the most expensive item, at £42 (c.'£1,300'), is the scarce first of Norman Douglas's *Some Limericks* (1928), followed by the rare first issue of D.H. Lawrence's *The Lost Girl* (1920) at £35, or c.'£1,100'): but there is nothing in it that we would scorn 40 years later.

A Seventies curiosity

The Covent Garden Bookshop is still remembered with mixed feelings. Through apparently limitless credit facilities, it built up a substantial and wide-ranging stock, and pioneered a highly speculative trend in collecting modern first editions which is still with us in 2005. By the time it issued its two-part catalogue 55 (undated, but references to the 'three-day working week' fix it at the last few days of 1973 or early in 1974), it was in expansionist mood. The owners had started a sister business, Covendell Books – nothing to do with covens or dells, alas, merely based in Covent Garden's Endell Street – where 'in order to maintain the high standard that our customers expect, we have secured the services of Mr. Eric Osborne, the well known bibliographer who will represent us at all major sales and will be available to advise collectors or librarians on the sale or purchase of Antiquarian books'. This excerpt perhaps conveys the almost Fawlty-esque flavour of a firm which, according to one London dealer, insisted that its purchases be delivered by taxicab. The catalogue ran to 3,872 items, most of which – even those 'specially selected for their particular interest by Mr. Osborne' – are of staggering dullness; high spots are almost completely absent (although it seems likely that many of these had, simply, already sold) and the typesetting, done on an IBM machine of which the Nothmanns were proud, is full of errors. There is no attempt at discrimination, just alphabetical order at its crudest: Ted Hughes rubs shoulders with W.H. Hudson; Kate Greenaway nestles uncomfortably (and in-accurately) between Thomas Gray and Henry Green. The firm's own publications (plus a few more they were evidently trying to shift) are printed in bold; sometimes the fussiness of the prices is a result of conversion from guineas (£4.20, £21), but elsewhere it is just wayward (£15.03). The predominant impression it leaves is one of bafflement, the question 'Who could possibly want that?' unanswered. A proof copy of the first edition of Joyce Cary's *An American Visitor*, for instance, might not be that easy to sell, but a proof of the 1952 collected edition? For £6.30? Or, at 2006's rate, £63?

In issue 8 of *Antiquarian Book Monthly Review* (September 1974) the editor reported that 'Reactions to our article on the Covent Garden Bookshop affair in ABMR Seven have been mainly favourable'. This article, unsigned but by Paul Minet, describes at some length the collapse of the Nothmann empire. Evidently the Covent Garden Bookshop and its associated businesses (including an extraordinary venture known as the 'First Night Bookshop' in Henrietta Street, which stayed open until after midnight) had been launched on a wave of cash from the Overseas Development Bank, a subsidiary of Bernie Cornfeld's collapsed Investors Overseas Services. Cornfeld himself was one of the most successful crooks of all time (his 'losses' amounted to about half a billion dollars, in 1970, and he spent less than a year in a Swiss jail.) When the ODB foreclosed on Nothmann's six-figure overdraft, there was little sympathy. Much of the stock was dispersed and the Nothmanns went to the USA to pursue another career. The Covent Garden Bookshop itself was bought out, but maintains a shadowy presence even in 2006: despite the firm's various changes in name, ownership and address, the original telephone number, with only the prefix changed, is still in use by a leading specialist in modern first editions.

1980s to the Present

This is so close to the present day that discretion and commercial survival become the enemies of the good story and the telling example. Perhaps it will suffice to remark that most of the impetus in the market has come from the USA, which was always important, but by now may be considered defining: Robert Dagg, Mark Hime, Glenn Horovitz, Peter Howard, James Jaffe, Maurice Neville, Peter Stern and John Wronowski are amongst the dealers whose knowledge, flair and in some cases sheer nerve have helped make the early twenty-first century's market what it is. The trend has been towards perfect copies of 'big books'. Dustwrappers are crucial, even when they bear no text at all (Rick Gekoski discusses this with reference to Hemingway's *Three Stories and Ten Poems* (Paris, 1923) in his amusing *Tolkien's Gown* (2004): a few months after a 'pretty' but wrapperless copy had sold at auction for £22,000, a copy with the plain glassene still present fetched £70,000).[20] To paraphrase the catch-phrase of the estate agents, it's 'condition, condition, condition' that matters. Where the canny dealer or collector once hoarded the rarities – the squibs, the anonymous pamphlets, the unfindable ephemera – now it is 'high spots', preferably ones that have been successfully filmed. And the trade is increasingly one in *objets* rather than books: Mark Hime's (Biblioctopus) catalogue 20 offers Michael Jordan's own 1992 Nike Air Jordans (that's a type of basketball shoe, if you've been away) for $7,500, in between Washington Irving and Sinclair Lewis. The salesmanship in this catalogue is impressive; it's hard to imagine a Rota catalogue, for instance, insisting that 'your hallucination of another copy, this nice at this price, has been left by the 1st edition fairy under your pillow at book collector fantasy camp'. But, lapel-grabbing prose aside, the scholarship is there too (it isn't always, even at this price level), and that's what matters.

Another case study: the Fleming phenomenon

If anyone ever doubted the almost magical power of cinema, the Bond movies would prove them wrong. Ian Fleming's oddly dated bodice-rippers about the Old Fettesian were transformed by clever casting and superb special effects into wonderfully atmospheric depictions of the international intrigues of the 1960s. In the novels, characterisation is minimal and the plots absurd (no wonder *The Spy Who Came In from the Cold* caused such a shock when it appeared in 1963), but the films went from strength to strength, and their viewers eventually took the collecting market with them. It took a while: *Casino Royale*, the first, appeared in 1953; the first film (*Dr. No*) appeared in 1962; Fleming died unexpectedly young in 1964; but the novels seem not to have been lotted separately at auction until John Hayward's inscribed copies came up at Sotheby's in 1966, some ten years after that firm inaugurated its specialist sales of 'modern firsts'. Then, the prices were solid but not enormously high (£22 to £60: buyers included Berès, Blackwell, El Dieff, Frank Hollings, Rota, Sawyer and G.F. Sims). More appeared in 1971: inscribed copies ranged from £10 to £32 (for *Casino*, of course), to many of the same buyers. In the same sale El Dieff paid £40 for an admittedly rough *Ulysses* (Paris, 1922): in the same year you could have had Greene's *Stamboul Train* (1932) for £12, or *To the Lighthouse* in dustwrapper for £50. Not a fortune for the Flemings, in other words, but older heads were probably shaking nonetheless. The signed, limited *On Her Majesty's Secret Service* (1963), now fetching £5,000 or so, went for £14 and £22 in the same year. (cf *Basil Seal*, above). Very roughly, these figures represent between two and six hundred pounds in the money of 2006, proving among other things that time travel does not exist.

The prices waxed: in 1978 the bookseller Iain Campbell produced a witty catalogue to celebrate *Casino Royale*'s quarter-century, and in 1979 Richard Booth paid £420 at Hodgson's rooms for a copy of that title, a fourfold advance in real terms on the 1971 price. The book stayed around £350 to £500 for a while: Bertram Rota offered a fine copy (and, as ever, Rota's 'fine' really did mean fine) inscribed to one of Fleming's secretaries at £2,500 in 1983. (The same copy fetched £9,500, plus premium, at Sotheby's in 1997). Within a couple of years, the (uninscribed) book was fetching a thousand pounds. (Quaritch, of all firms, paid £2,000 for an inscribed copy in 1985, thereby illustrating this writer's conviction that the buyer's identity is always at least as interesting as the price – *autres temps*, alas). The title broke the five-figure barrier in 2001; as I write, ten or so copies in 'collector's condition' are on the market, for between ten and twenty-five thousand pounds. Of course, if the demand were really buoyant, some of those would be *off* the market, but the price now seems established, at least for the moment.

'You cannot be seriosu!': analytical bibliography versus 'point-mania'

In 1928 a celebrated misprint occurred on page 66 of the first English edition of Hemingway's *A Farewell to Arms* (1928). The error was noticed, and corrected, half-way through the print run, and considered too slight to justify replacement of the faulty sheets: so some copies of the book give the word as 'seriosu', and others 'serious'. By the time the sheets had been to the binders, and the finished book had been wrapped, and the wrapped copies had been distributed, it is obvious that no priority of issue could ever have existed, and clearly the error is of no possible meaning as far as the history of Hemingway's text is concerned: yet some misguided collectors still insist on the misprinted state.[21] Collectors should use their own discrimination and intelligence, and seek out the first states of books when their variations are of textual or historical significance, and, conversely, they should have the wit to ignore them when they aren't.

The dustwrapper debate, and an easy solution to the problem

This is a controversial subject, and ultimately a matter of discrimination. There has been much debate recently about the ethics of swapping dustwrappers between books. Like everything else in the world of books, there are no simple rules. The bibliographical purist would say, immediately, 'Don't.' This is praise-worthy, but not quite the full story.

Most bibliophiles, if they buy a new novel from their local bookshop, will cheerfully 'marry' an unbumped book to an unblemished wrapper; a glance at half a dozen books in a new bookshop will show that only one or two at most are in fine condition, even at that early stage in their existence, and no great harm seems to be done by this activity. But, as Nicolas Barker sensibly and succinctly remarks in his recent editorial in *The Book Collector*, 'The practice in new bookshops of replacing shop-soiled jackets with new ones is irrelevant. This is a pre-natal event in a gestation that ends when the book is first sold, the point of bibliographical birth.'[22] And if one accepts this eminently reasonable definition, this pre-first-sale swapping seems to pose no problems at all.

A little further down the line, a bookseller might possess two manifestly identical books, one with an ownership inscription but a perfect wrapper, the other with a tatty wrapper but no inscription. ... Most booksellers will swap them. The temptation is considerable. But there may well be some minute difference between the wrappers, which the bookseller has not noticed (or, worse, decides to overlook), and the waters of bibliography are muddied for short-term gain. (It's worth remembering, also, that much of the value of valuable books lies in their scarcity, and if fine copies of them become commoner, it doesn't take a genius to work out what will happen.) And if either copy is marketed as possessing any sort of association, of course, this practice instantly becomes wholly unacceptable, because then it is no longer 'the dustwrapper the author touched'.[23]

Finally, there are instances which are, to me, well outside the limits. Let us consider three. One is a poor, stained copy of the first edition, with a dustwrapper whose very presence belies the state of the book beneath: but everyone knows the second impression wrappers were identical, and perhaps the culprit still has a pristine, wrapperless reprint lurking at the back of his premises. Second, a decent copy of a book in a decent wrapper, with an old (but substantial) price pencilled in it. Superficially sound – but recent research has identified that this wrapper can only have come from the third impression. Curiously, the original vendor doesn't want to buy it back. Third, a 'presentation copy' which has acquired a nice clean wrapper since its (well-documented) sale, by catalogue, from a library which was noteworthy for its poor condition. The first of these is, we are often told, acceptable to some people, if correctly described – but it seldom is, and I would neither want such a book on my shelves nor encourage a customer to buy it. The second corresponds precisely to the superficially venial example of the swapped wrapper, the only difference being that the perpetrator has been caught out: another good reason, if one were needed, to avoid this practice. The third is a suggestion that something is that which it is not, since the supplied wrapper was not part of the original copy when it acquired its valuable association: it renders meaningless the book as historical object, and should not be tolerated.

The 'easy solution' referred to in the heading is, of course, 'Don't swap dustwrappers.' After all the special pleading has been heard, this is the only way to preserve the integrity of the book as an object, the historical record and (incidentally but importantly) the reputation of the trade.

Marryat vs. O'Brian: a sort of tailpiece?

David Pearson refers to a set of Captain Marryat's first editions in the 1902 Pickering catalogue, offered at the apparently vast price of £185: equivalent, under the indexation of per capita GDP, to nearly £72,000. This is indeed a huge sum of money, even for 80 volumes of leather-bound first editions. But a set of Patrick O'Brian's 20 Jack Aubrey novels, as close a contemporary parallel to Marryat as we could hope to find, and 'finely bound in recent full navy blue morocco … gilt' was in 2005 on offer (Peter Harrington) for £8,500: at 2005's value, not much below half the price per volume of the scarcer Marryat, which was, as will be remembered, 'uniformly and choicely bound in blue morocco extra'. Perhaps things have not changed so very much after all.

A Short Look at *ABMR*

PAUL MINET

FOR a trade dependent on the written word, there has been a surprising dearth of successful periodicals devoted to themes of common interest to book collectors and dealers alike. The oldest example I have amongst my own books is *The Philobiblion: A Monthly Bibliographical Journal*, published in New York in the 1860s. That indefatigable Victorian publisher Elliot Stock produced a magazine in the 1880s and 1890s entitled *The Bookworm*, which was sub-titled 'An Illustrated Treasury of Old-Time Literature' but which did, in fact, impinge on the rare book trade to some extent. I also have a great run of *The Book Monthly*, from 1903 until its demise in 1915, which is mainly to do with new books but also strays into the field of old books. Copies of that attractive magazine *The Bookman*, from the inter-war period, are still collected, though chiefly for the quality of the illustrations; in any case it was mainly concerned with new books.

When I first thought about starting a magazine catering for collectors and dealers, I had for years been a subscriber to *The Clique*, the book trade advertising journal. I was an occasional reader of both *The Book Collector* and *The Library*, but I considered them to be on a different, perhaps more exalted, plane from what I wanted, which was something both useful and entertaining, a mixture of news, background information and practical tips. Charles Skilton ran a magazine called *Book World Advertiser* for a time and there was an *American Book Collector* which came slightly closer to what I had in mind, but it did not last. More recently there has been an American magazine called *Book Source Monthly*, a fairly modest production based on advertised information, and there have been other American ventures such as *Firsts: The Book Collector's Magazine*, but it seems always to have been a fairly transitory field.

During a turbulent part of my bookselling career in the 1960s, I had had to devote my main efforts to working in a publishing business and, although back in full-time bookselling before long, I had been left with a certain amount of publishing ambition allied to a less certain level of printing expertise, which I fancied might qualify me to fill a perceived gap in the market. I had discussed my ideas with Gerry Mosdell at the same time that we had talked about founding a provincial book fair organization. By 1974 I was ready to launch a small quarto monthly magazine, initially aimed mainly at the trade since that was my only mailing list. Despite being known initially as 'Minet's trade mag' in certain quarters, it was from the start designed for collectors and the public as well as the trade. Indeed, a considerable spur to its foundation was a series of lunches I had with A.N.L. Munby, the well-known librarian and collector, who was enormously helpful. I called it the *Antiquarian Book Monthly Review* and, although it has since changed its name a couple of times, I will refer to it here by its most familiar acronym, *ABMR*.

A couple of years earlier I had started a small printing company called Comersgate Ltd., which took advantage of the rapidly changing printing technology. My partner in that venture was a renegade American named Stef Mulkey; from the start I put the editorial content of the magazine together, with the help of my assistant Elke Sadeghi, while Comersgate did the technical side. We sent out about 1,000 copies of the first issue, for February 1974, most of which fell on stony ground, but there was enough positive response to continue. Various trade friends rallied round with advertisements and we managed to build the circulation to almost 2,000 within the first two years. That may sound a small number, but in the field of small magazines with little capital it takes a deal of achieving. We tried many expedients in the early days: auction reviews, catalogue inserts, articles by many experts in niche collecting fields and, not least but quite unsuccessfully, efforts to sell copies retail through bookshops.

There was little doubt that at first *ABMR* was very much an insiders' magazine, commenting on the book trade in a way which had not, to my knowledge, been done before. There were certain high points. The collapse of Dr Nothmann's Covent Garden Bookshop was handled in depth and on one occasion we created a furore by hiring a City analyst to examine the top four firms in the trade in strictly financial terms, using their listed accounts from Companies House.[1] Whether for that reason or not, *ABMR* never received much advertising from the top of the trade in its first 20 years, although this has been reversed in recent years under different ownership. Those who did advertise, many of whom were personal friends, were some of the up-and-coming second-string members of the trade like Weatherhead's of Aylesbury, Peter Eaton, Bob Gilbert of Bristol, Ian Hodgkins, R. & J. Balding of Edinburgh, and Titles, then of Torquay and later of Oxford. It was still a period of quite marked expansion in the rare book trade and, in retrospect, not a bad time to launch a magazine.

To say *ABMR* ever made much of a profit would be to exaggerate, but it had its moments. I owned it for most of the 1970s and then sold it to Comersgate, which had moved to Oxford and flourished as a book-catalogue printer. I had relinquished my holding in the firm, so that for much of the 1980s the ownership of the magazine rested with Stef Mulkey, who ran it through a series of underpaid but devoted editors on a string tight enough to keep its finances under some control. At its peak it achieved a circulation of 4,000, but I suspect that a figure of around half of that would be more accurate as an average. Certainly in the 1980s it became a respected medium, carrying a variety of interesting articles and book reviews and reporting on activities in the trade in depth, something which it has lost in subsequent years. It also had its eccentricities. Joanna Dodsworth, a respected bibliophile who edited it between 1976 and 1979, managed to reveal in print, in response to a letter from an impecunious collector, that she herself earned £64 per week. Perhaps not entirely coincidentally, she moved to pastures greener about two months later. The next two editors, Julian Bingley (1979-82) and Jennifer Hainsworth (1982-5) lasted a little longer and they were succeeded by John Kinnane, who provided much-needed continuity until 1994.

Stef eventually moved abroad and, faced with the prospect that the magazine would close, I bought it back from him and installed it in offices in Oxford, where it ticked along for a few years with the aid of an occasional subvention from me. Eventually, in 1992, I sold out to Dawson's, the large magazine and book distributor based in Folkestone, and they in their turn sold what became known as *Antiquarian Book Monthly* to Countrywide Editions, a small printing firm which had for some time handled its production and distribution. At the end of 2001 the magazine changed hands again and, rather more decisively, passed into the hands of Bernard Shapero, a prominent member of the ABA and owner of Bloomsbury Book Auctions. Under his ownership it has changed its name twice, first to *Antiquarian Book Review* and then to *Rare Book Review*; the most recent development is that it is now published every two months. The change of ownership produced a very much more up-market layout and its new owner has managed to introduce more advertising from the upper end of the trade. After 31 years it is now justly regarded as the leading magazine for antiquarian and rare book collectors.

With the distinguished exception of *The Book Collector*, which achieved its fiftieth anniversary in 2002, *ABMR* has become the oldest periodical in its field.[2] Monthly magazines are a different kind of beast to quarterly journals, not least in their resemblance to a treadmill – the months succeed each other with breathtaking speed. The foundation of the magazine coincided, as I have indicated, with the formation of the PBFA and that organization has been a continuing support, in the form of both advertising and information, down the years. The first twenty years were also the golden years of book fairs and the magazine has excelled in comment on the June book fair season, as well as in its reviews of auction sales and of new catalogues. It may be that, in a small way, *ABMR*, along with the book fairs, the expansion of the ABA's services and the rise of the PBFA, has contributed to making the trade less fragmented in the last third of the century. Whatever the reason, there is little doubt in my mind that the rare and secondhand book trade as it ended the twentieth century was a much more knowledgeable and integrated trade than it had been 30 years earlier.

A striking aspect of the magazine has been the remarkable diversity of contributions from both dealers and collectors. The articles were generally slanted towards the period from 1800 to the present, a field which was less well represented in the more erudite journals. To take just one year, 1985, as an example, we find Roger Dobson on Arthur Machen, Ruari McLean on 'The Life and Death of *Picture Post*', Fred Snelling on Dornford Yates and Edgar Wallace, Arthur Chick on Pickering bindings, Elizabeth Gant on *Orlando*, and Ken Swift on collecting Penguins. The advertisements for the same year form a commentary on the book trade, running from the major auctioneers (who were never as snooty as the top end of the trade) to small advertisements for dealers who have often later become names to be reckoned with. *ABMR* itself was collected to the extent that in the late 1970s we had to reprint Issue 1 to replace those discarded from the original mailing, the only time I can recall such a thing in relation to any of the magazines with which I have been connected.

There have been other ventures into the field since *ABMR* was founded. The maverick Driffield, whose guides to British bookshops had had a considerable success in the early 1980s, launched a scurrilous but always amusing *Driff's Fortnightly* in 1986, which lasted almost a year. The last issue described itself as now being 'owned by a Workers Collective. Mr. Driffield and his debts have departed', but unfortunately that was the end of it.[3] In 1989-90 a firm in Colchester had a quite determined shot at the same thing entitled *Books, Maps and Prints*, but it folded after ten issues. I wrote a column in it under the pseudonym 'Janus'. Perhaps the most lasting and successful of the others has been a small monthly magazine called *The Book and Magazine Collector,* which caters for collectors of modern books and magazines on an unabashedly commercial basis, although its author summaries have continued to be useful down the years.

Upon reflection, I think that the failure of magazines aimed at book collectors to achieve any real breakthrough rests with the nature of book collecting. Each collector is interested in one particular sector, his own, and it is impossible to provide enough specialist information on every speciality to retain a proper market. I like to think that *ABMR* has come nearer to achieving that impossibility than any other attempt, but it may be that such success as it has enjoyed has owed as much to the trade chat as to anything else, for, as with Ratty and his boat talk in *The Wind in the Willows*, book trade chat flows on forever.

IV

PERSONALITIES:
A TRADE OF INDIVIDUALISTS

Device of the 'Bibliomites', the Society of Antiquarian
Booksellers' Employees, founded in 1950.

Foreign Dealers in the English Trade

ARNOLD HUNT

AᴺᵀɪQᴜᴀʀɪᴀɴ bookselling has often gone hand-in-hand with antiquarian habits of mind. The popular image of the antiquarian book trade – 'crusty old men selling dusty old books in musty old shops', as I once heard it described – may be only a myth; but for much of the twentieth century, the trade remained stubbornly attached to business practices that would not have seemed out of place in the age of Dibdin. At Ellis's shop in New Bond Street in the 1920s, all transactions over the counter were solemnly recorded in copper-plate in a vast ledger; and Percy Muir recalled that the firm had only just taken the bold step of introducing blotting-paper, as a reluctant concession to 'the devastating inroads of modernism'.[1] Ellis's – 'the oldest bookshop in London', as they proudly described themselves – may have been exceptional in making such a fetish of tradition, but even a more progressive firm like Pickering & Chatto apparently saw no need to invest in a typewriter, and continued to issue handwritten invoices until the 1950s.[2]

In general, the trade was extremely slow to exploit new opportunities or new ways of selling books. Muir has described how, working at Dulau's in the 1920s, he gradually became convinced that the history of science represented a promising new field for collectors, but was unable to persuade other members of the firm to share his enthusiasm. As one of the leading specialists in natural history, Dulau's were ideally placed to develop a sideline in scientific first editions; but the head of the natural history department, John Knowles, 'resented and resisted the intrusion of a new school of thought that threatened to give his department a new orientation by creating a value for what he regarded as antiquated and superseded texts simply because they were first editions'. Knowles knew his business: he was, in Muir's words, 'an expert shopkeeper who knew exactly what was required and exactly how much to charge for it'. But he was totally impervious to new ideas, and preferred to deal in 'the kinds of books whose prices were fixed by current practice' rather than trying to create a market for books that were undeservedly neglected.[3]

This general conservatism was the result of several factors. First, there was the fact that the trade, as a whole, was chronically under-capitalized. Most firms had their assets largely tied up in their stock, and simply could not afford to take the risk of branching out into new areas. Secondly, there was the steady demand for antiquarian books to furnish upper-class libraries. At least until the 1930s, it was possible to make a good living supplying well-bound copies of standard editions to the West End carriage trade, without needing to explore new markets. Thirdly, and most significantly, there was the existence of the ring. As Arthur and Janet Freeman have shown, the ring in the early twentieth century was essentially a mechanism whereby the larger firms, especially Quaritch, shared some of their profits with the rest of the trade in return for first pick of all the best items on the market.[4] The ring is often portrayed as a criminal conspiracy designed to defraud vendors and auctioneers, but this, though important, was only incidental to its main function, as one of the ways in which the trade organized and regulated itself. The case against the ring is not merely that it was unfair or unethical (though it was both of those things), but that it discouraged competition and innovation in the trade.

In these circumstances, dealers in search of new ideas, or new ways of looking at old books, often had to look outside the London trade. Once again, Percy Muir provides a good example. Having failed to persuade his colleagues at Dulau's to take an interest in the history of science, he had to go further afield for support and encouragement: 'to Friedlander and Niederlechner in Berlin, Taueber in Munich, Thiébaud in Paris, and in London to Ernst Weil, then in partnership with E.P. Goldschmidt'.[5] It is an instructive anecdote. There has been a tendency to write the history of the English antiquarian book trade in Anglocentric terms, with the emphasis on the great Anglo-American libraries – Huth, Britwell, Folger, Huntington – most famous for their collections of early English printed books. By contrast, the European dimension of the trade has received relatively little attention. Yet the London book trade, over the centuries, has been profoundly influenced by a succession of talented European immigrants – from Wynkyn de Worde to Quaritch and beyond – and the twentieth-century antiquarian trade was no exception.

This chapter deals with three foreign booksellers – a Pole, a Frenchman and a Dutchman – who each brought fresh ideas and wider horizons to the English trade and, in doing so, helped to shake it out of its complacency. It is not intended to be a comprehensive account of foreign booksellers in England; in particular, it deals only briefly with the Jewish refugees from Nazism – 'that distinguished list of gifts from the Third Reich to the book trade of London and New York' – who deserve separate and fuller treatment elsewhere.[6] Nevertheless, I hope it may illustrate some general themes. My main thesis – that foreign dealers gave the English trade a much-needed shot in the arm – will already be clear. But my three case-studies, taken together, also tell a story about the changing pattern of supply and demand in the twentieth-century trade. Between them, they cover a period of about half a century, from about 1900 to about 1950, when – thanks to the rich supply of antiquarian books available on the Continent, and a handful of London-based dealers uniquely placed to take advantage of it – the London trade briefly became the crucial point of contact between European sellers and American buyers.

The revolutionary: Wilfrid Voynich

Wilfrid Michael Habdank Woynicz (1864-1930), better known by the anglicized version of his name, Wilfrid Michael Voynich, is one of the most remarkable characters ever to have passed through the antiquarian booktrade. He was born in Lithuania, in what was then part of the Russian Empire, and studied chemistry at the University of Moscow, where he was drawn into the Polish nationalist movement. In 1885 he was recruited by the Polish revolutionary group *Proletarjat* to assist in organising the escape of two of its members from the Warsaw Citadel. Unfortunately there was a police spy in the group, and the plot was betrayed: the two prisoners were summarily executed, and Voynich was imprisoned for two years without trial before being transported to Siberia. Somehow he managed to escape, and after five months on the run, finally managed to get clear of Russian territory and made his way to Hamburg, where he bartered his last remaining possessions, including his waistcoat and glasses, in exchange for a berth on a merchant vessel bound for England. In 1890 he arrived in London, penniless, not speaking a word of English, and clutching a small scrap of paper on which was written the name and address of the leading Polish revolutionary exile in London, Sergei Kravchinsky (Stepniak).[7]

In London, Voynich quickly became part of the circle of Russian political exiles and English fellow-travellers – including his future wife, the novelist Ethel Boole – clustered around the charismatic figure of Stepniak.[8] In 1891 he was one of the five founder members of the Russian Free Press Fund, set up to translate and publish revolutionary propaganda for clandestine distribution in Russia. This was his introduction to the business of publishing and bookselling, and brought him into correspondence with booksellers all over Europe, an experience which would serve him well in his subsequent career as an antiquarian dealer. It seems he managed the financial affairs of the Fund very efficiently, bringing its income up to about £400 a year, but resented the fact that he had little influence over its editorial policy. In 1894 he resigned from the Fund in order to set up a rival organisation called the Booksellers' Union, designed to carry on the work of the Fund on a larger scale by publishing books in a variety of other languages – 'Polish, Armenian and Jewish' (presumably Yiddish) – as well as Russian. It was not a success. Voynich was unable to raise enough money to get the enterprise started, and having issued a prospectus vigorously denouncing the Russian Free Press Fund for its 'narrowly nationalist and narrow party views', the Booksellers' Union immediately sank into oblivion.[9]

It was Richard Garnett, Keeper of Printed Books at the British Museum, who first proposed to Voynich that he should try his hand at antiquarian bookselling. Talking to Garnett's son Robert many years later, Voynich recalled the decisive conversation that had launched him into the rare-book business. 'I was very miserable, not knowing what to do, and very poor, when it occurred to me to ask your father (to whom I had chatted about books on many occasions in the reading room of the British Museum) if he could possibly help me.' Garnett replied without hesitation. 'Nothing is easier. You have only to travel and pick up incunabula and rare books, and sell them in London, There is success in front of you.'[10] It was a surprising suggestion, but a fortuitous one. Voynich was not obviously suited to the antiquarian book trade – by his own admission, he did not even know the titles of the standard reference books – but he seized on the idea at once and pursued it with characteristic energy.

He issued his first catalogue in July 1898, in partnership with Charles Edgell, a young Cambridge graduate who presumably helped him with the cataloguing and may have put up some of the capital to get the business going.[11] It is an impressive catalogue by any standards; but as the work of someone just starting out in the trade, with little previous experience, it seems positively miraculous. The focus is on fifteenth- and sixteenth-century Continental books, with a particular bias towards religious heterodoxy and freethought, reflected in books such as Charron's *De la Sagesse* (1662), La Peyrère's *Prae-Adamitae* (1655) and the Socinian Bible of 1563 (described as 'excessively rare' and priced at £45). Titles are transcribed in full, with line-breaks marked – a most unusual level of bibliographical detail in a catalogue of this date. Even more remarkably, the incunables are arranged in 'Proctor order', according to their place of printing, following the system devised by Robert Proctor for his *Index to the Early Printed Books in the British Museum* published in the same year, 1898. The first bookseller to cite 'Proctor numbers' in his catalogues was apparently Joseph Baer of Frankfurt, but Voynich was the first English bookseller to follow suit.[12]

In 1900 Voynich opened his first shop, at 1 Soho Square. The Quaritch sales ledgers show him buying various modern books – including Hain's *Repertorium* (the standard bibliography of incunabula) and Deschamps' *Dictionnaire* (the standard guide to places of printing) – presumably to equip his reference library.[13] His second catalogue, issued later that year, is in many respects an even more impressive production than his first, and introduces a number of features that would become standard in his later catalogues, such as a section devoted to the works of British authors printed abroad, and a final section of 'Unknown, Lost or Undescribed Books'. The star item is a copy of the 1493 Malermi Bible (an Italian translation of the Vulgate, famous for its woodcut illustrations) which Voynich sold (for £300) to Quaritch before the catalogue appeared. There were also some important early Polish books, including a copy of the first Polish Bible (Cracow, 1561) with a long catalogue description in which Voynich gave fleeting expression to his political views, lamenting the fact that many of the relevant records in Polish archives had been destroyed 'by the brutal vandalism of illiterate Cossacks'.[14]

How did Voynich do it? Above all, where did he get the money to build up such a magnificent stock? Millicent Sowerby, who worked as his assistant from 1912 to 1914, and left an affectionate portrait of him in her autobiography *Rare People and Rare Books* (1967), related a tradition that he had set himself up in the rare-book business on the strength of a half-crown borrowed from Stepniak – but 'how exactly the money was invested I was never informed'.[15] Giuseppe Orioli, who left a much less flattering portrait of Voynich in his *Adventures of a Bookseller* (1938), recorded the advice that Voynich had given him on starting out in business: 'always keep the price as high as possible, if you ever have a book to sell' – good advice, certainly, but one cannot help feeling that there must have been more to Voynich's success than that. If Orioli is to be believed, then Voynich's methods of acquiring stock were not entirely above board. 'What I have discovered in Italy is altogether unbelievable!' he records Voynich telling him (though in a tone that sounds, suspiciously, more Oriolian than Voynichian). 'I once went to a convent and the monks showed me their library. It was a mine of early printed books and codexes and illuminated manuscripts. I nearly fainted – I assure you I nearly fainted on the spot. But I managed to keep my head all the same, and told the monks they could have a most interesting and valuable collection of modern theological works to replace that dusty rubbish. I succeeded in persuading the Father Superior, and in a month that whole library was in my hands, and I sent them a cartload of modern trash in exchange.'[16]

In fact, Voynich's success seems to have been based on a combination of factors. He was one of the first English booksellers to make regular buying trips to the Continent, and had the good fortune to be doing so at a time when the supply of early printed books was astonishingly rich. He took advantage of the new tools of bibliographical scholarship – Holtrop, Pellechet, Proctor, et al – to identify rare and unrecorded editions which other booksellers would not have recognized. He built up a very large mailing-list of customers – and claimed to have distributed as many as 4,000 copies of his early catalogues, though they are surprisingly rare today – but also benefited from his close connection with the British Museum, which at this time was actively seeking to fill in the gaps in its holdings of fifteenth-century printed books.[17] And the fact that he was an outsider, with no previous experience of the antiquarian book trade, may actually have been a positive advantage, as it meant that he was not handicapped by any preconceived notions about market value. Almost single-handedly, he seems to have brought about a revolution in the price of early printed books, with books that had previously been priced in shillings now being priced in pounds. The rest of the trade was slow to catch up, though in his ninth catalogue, in November 1902, Voynich observed that the price of early books had 'greatly increased of late years'.[18]

One of Voynich's greatest achievements was his Eighth List, issued in June 1902, which consisted of a collection of 'unknown and lost books', that is, books not recorded in any bibliography or located in any library. (The preface to the catalogue adds, slightly gratuitously: 'we have, of course, not searched works of recognized unreliability, such as sale catalogues and booksellers' lists.') One of the most striking features of this catalogue is its emphasis on printing history: it included a book printed in Venice in 1518 with contemporary proof-corrections (how many other booksellers at this date, one wonders, would have drawn special attention to this?), two editions of a Milanese incunable, one a piracy of the other ('of peculiar interest, on account of the light which it throws upon a curious side issue of the history of early printing'), and a large number of books from small provincial presses (Aix, Assisi, Loreto, Montpelier, Tivoli) – this last a special interest of Voynich's which, according to his assistant Herbert Garland, he never quite succeeded in persuading any of his customers to share. The British Museum was interested in buying the collection, but turned it down as too expensive: it appears from the BM archives that they valued it at £800, which – even adding a generous 50 per cent to reflect the fact that all the books were unknown – still fell far short of Voynich's asking-price of £1,575.[19] Undeterred, Voynich wrote, on his own initiative, to some of his wealthier customers, asking them to put up the money to present the collection to the Museum as a gift. The books duly came to the Museum, and are still shelved as a discrete collection in the British Library – making Voynich one of only two booksellers to have a BL shelfmark named after them.[20]

The one book with which Voynich's name will always be associated, however, is the famous 'Voynich Manuscript', which he bought in 1912 from the library of the Jesuit College at the Villa Mondragone in Frascati, near Rome. This manuscript, which Voynich dated to 'the latter part of the thirteenth century' (though others have put it later), is illustrated with bizarre and fantastical alchemical drawings, accompanied by a text written in a mysterious cipher or invented language which has, so far, resisted all attempts at decipherment. Many interpretations of the Voynich Manuscript have been put forward over the years, with varying degrees of plausibility. It is the work of the medieval philosopher Roger Bacon, recording his invention of the telescope and the microscope.[21] It is a sixteenth-century fabrication, concocted by John Dee and Edward Kelley in order to deceive the Emperor Rudolf II.[22] It is a liturgical manual compiled by a Catharist suicide cult, drawing on secret wisdom handed down from ancient Egypt by the priests of Isis.[23] Last but not least: it is a modern forgery by none other than Voynich himself, using the knowledge of ciphers and chemical inks which he had picked up during his undercover work with the Polish revolutionaries, and written on a stock of old paper which he had conveniently acquired in the course of his work as a bookseller.[24]

The theory of Voynich as forger has proved surprisingly popular, despite the fact that the Voynich Manuscript has a well documented provenance going back to the seventeenth-century Jesuit polymath Athanasius Kircher. The result is that a romantic legend has been woven around Voynich's personality, with one recent book describing him as 'a lovable rogue, living a flawed but admired life which sometimes took him to the edge of the law'. Even the layout of his bookshop – 'two large rooms and a back room with high bookcases' – is given a conspiratorial spin, with the claim that it was deliberately designed to give customers the illusion of going on a 'cloak-and-dagger adventure'.[25] All this is highly fanciful. When Voynich applied for British citizenship in 1904, his application sailed through without any difficulty, backed by two members of the British Museum staff, Garnett and Fortescue, who would have been in a position to know if there was anything shady about his business dealings.[26] With regard to the Voynich Manuscript, the most that can be said is that Voynich took pains to conceal its immediate provenance, claiming to have acquired it from 'an ancient castle in

Southern Europe'. When H.P. Kraus, who acquired the manuscript after Voynich's death, visited the Vatican Library in 1963, he was surprised to find that the Vatican officials thought the manuscript was still in the Mondragone collection and were unaware that it had ever been sold.[27]

All the same, there is an air of mystery about Voynich that cannot quite be dispelled – partly because of his involvement with the *demi-monde* of anarchists, spies and secret agents. At this period there were said to be more Russian spies in London than anywhere else in Europe, and Voynich, as a prominent member of Stepniak's circle, would certainly have been under surveillance. On one occasion, while travelling in Switzerland, he fell into conversation with a stranger on a train, and showed him the forged passport he had used to escape from Russia, which he still carried as a souvenir. The stranger examined it with care and returned it courteously. 'I am interested in such things,' he explained to Voynich, 'because I am the head of the Russian police.'[28] No one, however, even in the overheated world of Voynich studies, has seriously suggested that Voynich himself was involved in espionage. Jessie Conrad claimed that he was the model for Vladimir, the Russian spymaster in Joseph Conrad's novel *The Secret Agent* (1907), but this implausible claim was firmly rejected by Ethel Voynich and has been generally disregarded by Conrad scholars.[29] It might have made more sense for Jessie Conrad to have identified him as the model for Verloc, the eponymous 'secret agent', who also kept a bookshop in Soho; but Verloc's seedy shop, selling cheap pornography and rubber goods, bears no obvious resemblance to Voynich's more salubrious establishment.

The financial basis of Voynich's business remains mysterious, but it is possible to glean a few clues from contemporary book-trade archives. It is clear that Voynich was a slow payer who relied heavily on credit arrangements with other booksellers. In 1910 he owed Quaritch more than £1,300, and in 1913 more than £500, some of which was still unpaid more than two years later.[30] The records of the firm of J. & J. Leighton also throw an interesting sidelight on his business. They show that he was buying large numbers of fifteenth- and sixteenth-century books – most of them fairly inexpensive, costing no more than a few pounds each – and offsetting them against a roughly equal number of books sold to Leighton's. In effect, this was a stock-sharing arrangement which enabled Voynich to keep his stock turning over at little or no cost. It may, in fact, have been a three-way arrangement between Voynich, Leighton's, and Leo Olschki of Florence, as the Quaritch sales ledgers record a comparable number of sixteenth-century books sold to Olschki but delivered to the other two firms.[31] A surviving letter from Voynich to Leighton's shows the extent to which he treated the latter's stock as his own. 'I have a customer for three of your books. ... Your price is £51 13s. I can offer you £46 otherwise I cannot sell, the prices are too high. Please let me know at once as I must wire.'[32]

The Quaritch archives also give us a glimpse of Voynich through the eyes of other members of the trade. In 1909, E.H. Dring reported to his chief Bernard Alfred Quaritch, in New York, that Voynich had just placed a large order with the firm. Quaritch responded: 'Voynich seems successful, I presume it is mostly with the Trade. However I am glad to get rid of second rate stock. Our policy is to realize and get rid of dead stock even at very little profit, a good bank balance puts it into our power to take advantage of good opportunities.'[33] From Quaritch's point of view, it seems, Voynich was a fairly small operator, who dealt mostly with the trade rather than with private customers, and performed a useful service in taking over other firms' unsold stock. However, this letter was written just as Voynich's business was starting to expand. In 1909 he moved from Soho Square to a more upmarket address in Shaftesbury Avenue, and his purchases from Quaritch may have been intended to fill the shelves of his new shop. At the same time, he began to shift the focus of his business away from the cheap fifteenth- and sixteenth-century books that had previously formed the majority of his stock-in-trade, towards more expensive items targeted at a wealthier clientele. In the words of his assistant Herbert Garland: 'Illuminated manuscripts became a prominent feature, and two erroneous theories, previously held, that Voynich did not sell English books and that his prices were prohibitive, began to have more substance.'[34]

Voynich's correspondence with J.P. Morgan's librarian Belle da Costa Greene provides an interesting insight into his business at this period. His first letter to her is uncharacteristically hesitant: 'I have thought for some time that there were books in my collection suitable for your library and I have had introductions to you from the late Prince Essling and Mr Hoskiers, but I was unable to decide to use them.' As Voynich must have known, it was no use trying to tempt Morgan's librarian with second-rate stock; only the very best would do. 'I usually try to procure the best available manuscripts in Europe,' he went on, 'and this spring I showed to Mr Berenson in Florence some very fine things. The best of these, however, have been sold to (1) booksellers in Florence (2) to Mr Walters [presumably Henry Walters, founder of the Walters Art Gallery in Baltimore]. I still have about twenty of these manuscripts ... but they are what I term trade manuscripts at prices varying from £400 to £800 and I doubt if you would care to see them.'[35] Sure enough, it took some time before Voynich succeeded in making a sale to this most demanding of private buyers, but in December 1912 he succeeded in selling her a copy of the *editio princeps* of Augustine's *De Civitate Dei* (1467), which, at £1,200, was quite possibly the most expensive single book or manuscript he had handled up to that date.

With the outbreak of the First World War, Voynich's buying trips to the Continent came to an abrupt end. Once again we can catch a glimpse of him through the eyes of a colleague in the trade, F.S. Ferguson of Quaritch, whose trip to New York in the spring of 1915 happened to coincide with Voynich's first visit to America. By this stage Voynich had progressed from a mere scavenger of other people's stock to a potentially troublesome competitor, and his presence in New York plainly caused Ferguson some disquiet. 'Voynich is said to have done very badly in America,' he reported to Dring. 'His prices have made him a laughing stock. I think he has now returned but if not I am certainly not going to look him up as I do not want him to worry me.' Several days later he visited Belle Greene at the Morgan Library to find that Voynich had been there before him, trying to sell a fourteenth-century manuscript of the *Vitae Patrum* with illuminations optimistically attributed to Giotto. 'Miss Greene was much amused at Voynich,' he told Dring. 'He asked £30,000 for his 'Giotto' MS, which of course she thinks is preposterous, though she acknowledges the MS is a very fine one.' Several days later there was more news to report. 'I hear Voynich has moved from the Savoy, a very swell hotel on Fifth Avenue, to the MacAlpin on Broadway, an ordinary businessman's hotel. He is said to have done very badly.'[36]

Voynich may not, in fact, have done quite so badly as Ferguson supposed. A year later he succeeded in selling the *Vitae Patrum* manuscript to Morgan, though at a stiff reduction, $75,000 (= £15,750), half his original asking-price of $150,000. He must have been reasonably satisfied with his success in America, for in 1916 he settled permanently in New York and gradually transferred his stock across the Atlantic, while retaining a small office in London. His later career in America lies beyond the scope of this article, though his business records, now in the Grolier Club, provide abundant material for study. He appears to have had some difficulty getting started in America, as he wrote in 1921 that 'private collectors are shy of me and my name'; but he was later credited with a pioneering role in encouraging American university libraries to collect medieval manuscripts, and his sales to the Morgan Library alone amounted to about $25,000 over the course of the 1920s.[37] 'His influence upon the promotion of medieval studies has been great,' wrote one American historian after his death in 1930 – a remarkable tribute from a scholar to a bookseller.[38] In many ways H.P. Kraus was his natural successor, although the two never met. Kraus had great admiration for Voynich, describing him as 'a towering figure in the rare book trade', and although Kraus's achievements were on an altogether grander scale, it is perhaps no exaggeration to say that Voynich blazed the trail which Kraus was to follow.

The courtier: Maurice Ettinghausen

An obituary of Maurice Leon Ettinghausen (1883-1974) described him as 'probably the oldest active antiquarian bookseller on the international scene'.[39] By that time he had been active in the trade for more than 70 years – the last surviving link with the era of Pierpont Morgan and Henry Yates Thompson. Yet he has been curiously neglected in histories of the trade, partly because he never went into business under his own name, preferring to act as the *éminence grise* behind other firms, and partly because his autobiography, *Rare Books and Royal Collectors* (1966), is so discreetly uninformative. In the preface to that volume, Ettinghausen writes tantalisingly that there are many stories he could have told 'to the discredit of eminent persons ... but I have neither the time nor the inclination to dwell on unpleasantness'.[40] Most notably, the firm of Maggs Bros, for whom Ettinghausen worked for over twenty years, is never once mentioned by name in his autobiography, but only referred to in passing as 'the London firm with which I was then connected' – and thereby hangs a tale.

Ettinghausen was born in Paris in 1883. His mother was a member of the Oppenheimer family, one of the leading Jewish families in Frankfurt; his father was a businessman and entrepreneur who moved to England in 1888, bringing his wife and children with him. Maurice was sent to St Paul's School and then, in 1901, went to work as an assistant to the Oriental bookseller C.G. Luzac at 46 Great Russell Street, opposite the British Museum. The following year he went up to Queen's College, Oxford, to study Oriental languages, and then went on to the École des Hautes Études, in Paris, where he took a doctorate in Sanskrit. His intention was to return to Luzac's as a junior partner, but in 1903 Luzac died suddenly, and Ettinghausen's father, feeling that his son needed more experience of the general antiquarian book trade, found a job for him in the firm of Ludwig Rosenthal in Munich. It was the best apprenticeship he could possibly have had. Rosenthal's stock was enormous – Ettinghausen estimated that their warehouse in Munich contained more than a million volumes – and the firm did business all over Europe on a scale unmatched by any English dealer with the possible exception of Quaritch. The job brought Ettinghausen into contact with some of the greatest private collectors of the day, including C.W. Dyson Perrins, Baron Edmond de Rothschild and J. Pierpont Morgan, and also gave him an excellent training in the persuasive skills required to sell expensive books to rich men.[41]

Ettinghausen was still in Munich when war broke out in 1914, and spent the next four years in the internment camp for British civilians at Ruhleben. Characteristically, he turned even this experience to bibliographical advantage, forming a complete collection of the newspapers, magazines and ephemera printed at the camp, which he sold to the Harvard Law Library after the war. About one aspect of life at Ruhleben, however, his autobiography is silent. For the first two years of the war, the Jewish prisoners at Ruhleben were segregated in a makeshift ghetto known as Barrack 6, which became the target for a good deal of anti-Semitic hostility from the other prisoners. One occupant of Barrack 6 wrote that it became 'a sort of by-word in the camp, invariably uttered in a tone of contempt', and recalled the hurt astonishment of some of the Jewish inmates on finding their fellow prisoners acting as persecutors. Ettinghausen says nothing of this in his autobiography, which describes his time as a prisoner of war in the blandest possible terms ('among the five thousand inhabitants of Ruhleben Camp I met old friends from St Paul's School and made new ones'), but the experience undoubtedly reinforced his sense of Jewish identity, which became increasingly pronounced in later years, and left him with a strong fellow-feeling for other Jews suffering persecution.[42]

At the end of the war, Ettinghausen was taken on by the firm of Maggs Bros and, in his own words, 'plunged at once into the London world of antiquarian books'. Maggs was a solidly respectable and slightly old-fashioned firm, specializing in the safe and well-established fields of English literature and travel, but its principal director, Ernest Maggs, was keen to see the firm expand, and

Ettinghausen was hired specifically to build up the Continental side of the business. No one else in the firm knew much about Continental books, so Ettinghausen was given an empty desk and a fountain pen and left to his own devices, which suited him very well. On his first week in the job he acquired a new customer – Eugène Scheider, 'one of the most important manufacturers of artillery in Europe' – who subsequently ordered books worth £1,000, 'two and a half times my annual salary', Ettinghausen proudly records, from which we may deduce that his starting salary was £400, a fraction of what it would later become.[43] Ettinghausen's preference for buying and selling privately, rather than exposing himself to the glare of publicity in the auction-room, accorded perfectly with Ernest Maggs's aspiration that the firm should offer its clients the level of personal, confidential service that they would expect to receive from their banker or their solicitor.

The most important customer that Ettinghausen introduced to Maggs, however, was the exiled King Manuel II of Portugal, whose brief reign had been ended by the republican revolution of 1910. They had first met in the autumn of 1913, when the 24-year-old Manuel was on honeymoon in Munich, attending a festival season of Wagner operas, and Ettinghausen, thinking that the newly married king might be 'rather bored' – with his wife, or with Wagner? Ettinghausen does not say – wrote to him with the offer of some early Portuguese books. This direct approach paid off, as Manuel promptly called in at Rosenthal's shop to inspect the stock, and had a long conversation with Ettinghausen. They met again after the war, when Manuel, now living in Twickenham, announced that he wished to form a collection of Portuguese books, including every book printed in Portugal before 1600, and commissioned Maggs as his sole agents.[44] It was an extraordinary opportunity, which effectively gave Ettinghausen the entrée to every important aristocratic library in Spain and Portugal, just as many of those libraries were coming onto the market. As an added bonus, it gave Maggs the patronage of the British royal family, after King Manuel, at his weekly luncheon at Buckingham Palace, persuaded King George V to appoint the firm as his booksellers.

Manuel was perhaps not the easiest of customers. When the three volumes of his great catalogue, *Early Portuguese Books 1489-1600 in the Library of His Majesty the King of Portugal* (1929-35), were being printed at Cambridge University Press, he insisted on supervising the production himself, and plagued the University Printer, Walter Lewis, with a stream of peremptory instructions. Lewis gave as good as he got. On one occasion Manuel was late for an appointment at the Press, and arrived to be greeted by Lewis with the words: 'I thought punctuality was the politeness of princes' – much to the horror of Ernest Maggs, hovering nervously in the background.[45] But Ettinghausen, always the perfect courtier, knew exactly how to handle his man. On another occasion it was his turn to be late for an appointment, and he arrived at Twickenham to find the King pacing up and down, obviously furious at having been kept waiting. With a flourish, Ettinghausen produced from his briefcase a sixteenth-century world map, and spread it out on the floor. 'Your Majesty, I am placing the world at your feet.'[46] Who could resist a sales pitch like that? The association with Manuel lasted for thirteen years, until the King's death in 1932, and laid the foundations for Maggs's post-war prosperity. By the end of the twenties they were the only firm who offered any serious challenge to Quaritch's position at the head of the London antiquarian book trade.

Nothing reveals the scale of Ettinghausen's ambitions for Maggs more clearly than the plan he hatched in 1931 for handling the sale of books from Russia. In its desperate need for hard currency, the Russian government had been pouring huge quantities of goods into Austria and Germany for sale at auction, often at knock-down prices; and Ettinghausen was quick to grasp the commercial possibilities that this presented. His proposal, in brief, was that the Russians should appoint the firms of Maggs and Sotheby's sole agents for the sale of all books, antiques and works of art. The sales would be conducted through a private company in London, formed specially for the purpose, under 'a name … that will offer no indication of the business that it is to carry on'. In order to sweeten the deal, Maggs and Sotheby's were even prepared to waive their usual percentage commission. Instead, Ettinghausen proposed an alternative arrangement, whereby the Russians would set a reserve price on all items consigned for sale, and any profit over and above this reserve price would then be divided equally between the three parties.[47] How well this would have worked in practice is debatable, since it depended on the Russians setting the reserve prices well below the actual market value. Had it succeeded, however, it would have propelled Maggs right to the top of the antiquarian book trade; and the prospects looked sufficiently promising for Ettinghausen, Ernest Maggs and Geoffrey Hobson of Sotheby's to make a special visit to Moscow in 1931 in an attempt to sell the deal to the Russians.

Ettinghausen prepared for the trip in his usual meticulous way, by taking lessons in Russian conversation and learning a selection of useful phrases such as 'Please give me a cup of tea', 'May I have some plain-boiled potatoes?' and 'Have you any illuminated manuscripts?' Unfortunately, these preparations were largely wasted. Their visit took place on the eve of the Great Famine of 1932-3; there was no tea and no potatoes, and Ettinghausen later claimed to have spent the entire two weeks of the trip living on a supply of tinned sardines which he had prudently taken with him in his suitcase.[48] Nothing ever came of the proposal for a grand alliance, but the journey proved profitable in other ways. In Leningrad they called on the official responsible for the export of art and antiques, who exclaimed in astonishment: 'How was it that you timed your visit to Russia in such an extra-ordinary way that you arrived here on the very day that we received a Gutenberg Bible for disposal?' It was the copy from the former Imperial Public Library, and at that time the only copy in Russia. Ettinghausen had no difficulty in selling it by cable to Martin Bodmer, for what he coyly describes in his memoirs as a 'reasonable price' – unspecified, but yielding a profit of £2,600 which Maggs split 50/50 with Sotheby's.[49]

But the most remarkable result of the Russian trip was yet to come. While visiting the old Imperial Library, Ettinghausen had been shown the famous Codex Sinaiticus, one of the three great fourth-century codices of the Greek Bible, tucked away in a leather box on a lectern 'in a dark corner of the room'. Later, in Moscow, he facetiously remarked to the Vice-Commissar for Foreign Trade that if ever he was short of money, he could tie up the Codex in a brown paper parcel and send it to London with an invoice. There the matter rested; but two years later Ettinghausen was approached by the Russian cultural attaché in Paris with the information that the Codex was indeed for sale at a price of £200,000. There followed a classic Establishment fix. Ettinghausen told Stanley Morison that he had an option on the Codex, and Morison passed the word on to Sir Frederick Kenyon, the recently retired Director of the British Museum, who went to see Ettinghausen and came away promising to 'see some friends and find out what could be done'. These friends turned out to be the Prime Minister and the Archbishop of Canterbury. After some high-level diplomatic haggling the Codex was secured for the nation for £100,000, and Ernest Maggs and Ettinghausen bore it in triumph from the Russian Trade Delegation to the British Museum, accompanied by two plain-clothes detectives and a newsreel photographer – the first time that filming had been permitted within the hallowed precincts of the Museum.[50]

It later transpired that the Russians had originally offered the Codex to Dr Rosenbach.[51] Money was scarce in 1933 and even Rosenbach could not afford to make such a large purchase for stock, but he had been looking for a likely customer and apparently came very close to finding one. A letter preserved in the Quaritch archives alleges that 'Texas University very nearly got the Codex. ... Ettinghausen only just beat them in time while Miss Ratchford was interesting one of the local millionaires in it.'[52] The Americans did not accept defeat easily: as late as 1936 the British Museum received a letter from the Librarian of the University of Texas, on behalf of an American syndicate, offering to buy the Codex for £200,000 so that it could be placed in the Library of Congress.[53] But if this takes some of the romance out of the story, it hardly detracts from the glory of the transaction, which remains one of the greatest coups in the history of the antiquarian book trade. The Codex Sinaiticus is the oldest surviving manuscript of the entire Bible, and the most valuable witness to the textual transmission of the Greek New Testament. No more important book or manuscript has been offered for sale in modern times: and the fact that it had been snatched out of the jaws of Dr Rosenbach must surely have given Ettinghausen great private satisfaction, even if he chose not to trumpet this aspect of the deal in public.

John Carter has left us a vivid description of Maggs's premises in Conduit Street at about this time. 'The atmosphere downstairs was dignified and businesslike,' he writes, 'but on the first floor all was exuberance and gaiety; for this was the domain of Dr Maurice Ettinghausen and his delicious Portuguese secretary. Here, surrounded by his beloved Romantique bindings and the literature of France, was a dedicated enthusiast before whose whirlwind enthusiasms you either capitulated or, if your own customers were as unsophisticated as most of mine were in those days, beat a reluctant retreat.'[54] The description is not quite as complimentary as it may seem, for the implication, delicately conveyed, is that Ettinghausen's 'foreign department' was effectively a separate entity, independent of the rest of the firm. This may not have seemed so important in the roaring twenties, when, with the firm at the height of its prosperity, there was enough money to equip the Conduit Street premises with an 'Americana Room' and an 'Incunabula Room' specially designed by the architect John A. Campbell, an old acquaintance of Ettinghausen's from Ruhleben days. But in the thirties, with the economy in recession and the book trade feeling the pinch, mutterings of discontent began to be heard in the firm about Ettinghausen's style of doing business.

Much of this discontent was focused on Maggs's office in Paris. This is a fascinating story which deserves an entire article to itself, but can only be summarized here. Ettinghausen had established the Paris office in 1925 and installed Arthur Rau as manager, but Rau resigned in 1931 after a blazing row in which each side accused the other of bad faith, the London partners complaining that Rau was buying and selling on his own account, and Rau, for his part, complaining that Ettinghausen treated him as a mere 'commissionaire' (that is, a salesman) and allowed him no independence.[55] After Rau's departure, Ettinghausen took over as manager of the Paris office and began to spend most of his time there, producing a number of outstanding catalogues, notably the great Baudelaire-Verlaine-Rimbaud catalogue of 1937, based on the collection of Edward Titus, husband of the cosmetics queen Helena Rubinstein and publisher of *Lady Chatterley's Lover*. The Paris office was something of an innovation in the antiquarian book trade. Maggs was not the first London firm to open an office in Paris – Voynich had done so, briefly, in 1912 – but this was the first time that a London firm had played such an active role in the Paris trade, buying and selling in direct competition with French dealers. It was particularly successful in attracting the custom of wealthy American collectors like Charles W. Clark, as they passed through Paris each year en route to the South of France, and thus has a small but not insignificant place in the history of American francophilia.

But by the late 1930s the Paris office was rapidly turning into a liability. In 1937 it made a net profit of about F 200,000 (just over £1,600), quite a respectable sum, but more than swallowed up by Ettinghausen's salary alone.[56] The following year an ominous discussion took place among the London partners when the Paris balance-sheet was presented. 'Although Paris showed a fair margin of profit this year, it was realized that after the deduction of the Dr's salary, this profit was in reality small. Agreed to stress to Paris the need for real economy & ask them to refrain from purchasing unless items easily saleable or real bargains. It was felt that unless Paris showed a good profit, it was really not worthwhile. The high salaries paid would have to come up for revision.' In June 1939 it was agreed to reduce Ettinghausen's salary from £2,250 to £1,500, with the promise of a small percentage bonus if profits improved.[57]

There was a further source of friction between the Paris and London ends of the firm, although the full story did not emerge until much later. In December 1935 the London partners noted that 'Dr Ettinghausen was in the habit of receiving exiled Germans and approaching the Foreign Office on their behalf' and agreed that 'on no account should the firm's notepaper be used for this purpose'.[58] Ernest Maggs assured the other partners that 'the only Germans so helped were either book or print sellers', but this proved to be far from the case, as he subsequently learned from Hélène Kormann, the firm's acting manager in Paris during the war. Early in 1944, according to Mlle Kormann's account, the Gestapo searched the Paris office and 'discovered here carbon-copies of the Dr's private correspondence with Jewish people who had emigrated in Holland, Switzerland, America and even to South of America ... of course I knew all about those letters, but I pretended to be surprised and I assured them that you knew nothing, otherwise you would have strongly objected that such a correspondence should be written on your own heading paper'.[59] Maggs, to its credit, was extremely generous in supporting the German and Austrian booksellers who sought refuge in England, but Ettinghausen's activities were clearly on a much larger scale, and undertaken without the knowledge or consent of the firm (though it is possible that Ernest Maggs knew more than he let on).[60]

Ettinghausen plainly had no illusions about Hitler, but even so, the outbreak of war caught him unprepared. In May 1940 he was in Paris when he was informed by a friend that, contrary to the optimistic reports in the French press, the German army was rapidly approaching the capital. On 30 May – just two weeks before the fall of Paris – he drove south to Biarritz, taking with him a selection of the stock. Even then he did not suspect that the whole of France would soon be under German control. Bizarrely, his first action on arriving in Biarritz was to look for a local printer 'who could be trusted to make a fine job of a catalogue of the important books which I had brought with me'.[61] This was soon overtaken by events. On 17 June Ettinghausen fled to Bordeaux, leaving the stock – valued at nearly two million francs – with the Biarritz bookseller Henri Matarasso for safe-keeping. At Bordeaux he was lucky enough to get a place on the last boat leaving for England, and embarked the following day on an old P. & O. liner crammed with 1900 passengers (and lifeboats for only 400) – his last view of France being the surreal sight of dozens of Daimlers and Rolls-Royces left abandoned on the quayside.[62] It is hard to see what else he could have done. As he wrote laconically in his memoirs, he had no wish to fall into German hands 'to meet with the inevitable fate that they meted out to their unfortunate victims'. But he had kept no inventory of the books he had taken to Biarritz, and arrived in England with nothing more than a suitcase full of French banknotes (rendered almost worthless by currency regulations) and one book valued at £180.

In July 1940 the London partners met to decide what to do next. 'Now that Maggs Bros Paris had temporarily ceased to function, the matter of the further employment of Dr Ettinghausen in London was fully discussed. His value to the business in the past was fully realized, but it was [regretfully] decided' – the word 'regretfully' is crossed out – 'that owing to the financial situation of the business it was not possible to continue his employment in London. Besides the financial consideration it was felt that there was no opening for him in the London House.'[63] It was a brutal way to terminate a profitable business relationship of more than twenty years. From his eyrie in Old Bond Street, E.P. Goldschmidt – who seems to have had little liking for Ettinghausen as a person, but considerable respect for his abilities as a bookseller – provided a forthright commentary on the whole affair in a letter to W.A. Jackson, the eminent bibliographer and rare book librarian of Harvard University. 'That the younger generation of M's had been striving for years to get rid of the great Dr E. was a notorious fact. But apparently it was ultimately achieved under circumstances of astonishing meanness.'[64] Ettinghausen promptly sued the firm for £1,500 in unpaid salary and £3,000 compensation.

Before the case came to court, however, Ettinghausen dropped two bombshells. The first was a letter signed by Ernest Maggs in which Ettinghausen was described as 'Managing Director' of the Paris office. This had apparently been written merely to assist Ettinghausen in obtaining a *permis de séjour* from the French authorities; but it completely undermined the firm's argument that Ettinghausen was merely an employee who could be dismissed at will. The second bombshell was Ettinghausen's revelation that he had in his possession a private letter of 1929, in which Ernest Maggs was highly critical of the younger partners, Frank and Kenneth Maggs. It is not clear what use Ettinghausen was proposing to make of this in court, but it would certainly have caused the family severe embarrassment if it had been made public and it led to a furious argument between the directors, in which Frank and Kenneth expressed themselves 'very strongly about the injustice of such a letter'.[65] It was the final straw. The firm dropped the case and settled out of court, paying Ettinghausen compensation of £1,200 plus costs.

Ettinghausen spent the rest of his career as an associate of Albi Rosenthal in Oxford. Albi's brother Bernard recalls that the partnership was not an entirely easy one. 'Their characters were totally different – Albi was by nature very generous, loved a bit of ambiguity, had a wonderful light-hearted sense of humour, and had no patience with religion, any kind of religion. Ettinghausen had none of these traits, his ideas were set in concrete, and he was totally matter-of-fact.'[66] As a result they gradually drifted apart, with Rosenthal specializing in music, his first love, and leaving Ettinghausen to specialize in early printed books, especially Hebraica and Judaica. He grew increasingly conservative in religion as he grew older. On one occasion, the Israeli Prime Minister David Ben Gurion, an avid and knowledgeable collector of Greek classical texts, was on an official visit to England and called in at the firm's Oxford premises to look at the stock. It was a Friday afternoon, and Ben Gurion, who had to attend an official function that evening, promised Ettinghausen that he would return the following morning to complete his purchases. Ettinghausen was unmoved. 'I am sorry, Your Excellency, but we are closed on the Sabbath.'[67]

Ettinghausen was by this time a legendary figure, whose awesome reputation attracted a regular stream of foreign dealers on their summer buying-trips to

England – though a visit to A. Rosenthal Ltd could often be something of an ordeal. Leona Rostenberg and Madeleine Stern found him an intimidating figure, whose 'huge dark beard and sonorous voice … reminded us of some gigantic movie villain'.[68] Anton Gerits, some years later, had a happier experience: he had been warned that Ettinghausen was not an easy man to deal with, but to his surprise, the 'elderly gentleman with the impressive beard' received him courteously, and after selling him a few books, entertained him to lunch and took him on a tour of the Oxford colleges. 'I left Oxford with an admiration of English gardening and a warm feeling for the dreaded man.'[69] Nicholas Poole-Wilson recalls another side of Ettinghausen's character. While bidding for Quaritch at a Sotheby's sale, he had been pleasantly surprised to acquire a rare item of Spanish Americana at an unexpectedly low price. The following lunchtime the telephone rang, and as his boss E.M. Dring was out of the office, Poole-Wilson took the call. It was Ettinghausen, who asked in a quavering voice whether 'as a special favour to an old man', the book could be quoted to him at a small advance on cost. Poole-Wilson named a figure, which Ettinghausen instantly accepted. On returning from lunch, Dring was incredulous: 'You didn't fall for that old trick, did you?'[70]

The dispute with Maggs was not forgotten – nor, apparently, forgiven. When Ettinghausen came to correct the proofs of his autobiography, *Rare Books and Royal Collectors*, he grew so irritated by the constant repetition of the firm's name that he ruthlessly excised it from the published text.[71] Maggs, for their part, were more magnanimous; and Clifford Maggs's review of the autobiography, which describes Ettinghausen as 'one of the outstanding figures of the antiquarian book trade' and pays tribute to his 'long and fruitful connection' with the firm, must have been intended as a peace-offering.[72] A few relics of the man referred to, not unaffectionately, as the 'dickery Doc' can still be seen at 50 Berkeley Square today. Downstairs in the basement is a shelf of Spanish-language pamphlets which may well have been in stock ever since Ettinghausen's time; upstairs is some of the panelling from the Incunabula Room, salvaged when the firm moved from Conduit Street in 1938; while in the firm's reference library is the most evocative relic of all – an English-Russian pocket dictionary preserved from that momentous trip to Russia in 1931.

The scholar: E.P. Goldschmidt

Ernst Philip Goldschmidt (1887-1954) was, by common consent, the greatest scholar-bookseller of the twentieth century. In the words of his friend John Carter: 'There have been scholars before now who have dabbled in bookselling. There have been – and are – booksellers who are also scholars. But I do not recall, in the long and honourable history of the book trade, any man since Giovanni Aurispa (one of Goldschmidt's favourite characters in his favourite period, the Renaissance) who, being by nature, aptitude and avocation a scholar, embraced the antiquarian trade as his means of livelihood and used it as a platform from which to deploy his scholarship.'[73] Yet it is not solely as a scholar that Goldschmidt deserves attention here. He also reflected very deeply and seriously on the mechanics of buying and selling, the rationale of collecting, and the 'metaphysics of value' (his own phrase) – all of which made him an exceptionally astute commentator on the workings of the book trade. Nor did he allow the disinterested pursuit of scholarship to divert him from the more worldly aspects of the profession. To quote Carter again: 'there has been no shrewder dealer in the business in our time'.

The first thing that needs to be said about Goldschmidt is that he was accustomed to great wealth – a fact which determined his attitude to money for the whole of his life. He was the son of a Dutch banker, a descendant of Lazarus Goldschmidt, founder of the Banque de Pays-Bas, and related to many of the great Jewish banking families of Europe. The family firm of Bischoffsheim & Goldschmidt was one of the leading financial houses in the City of London (and the model for the fictional firm of 'Brehgert & Goldsheimer' in Anthony Trollope's novel *The Way We Live Now*). He grew up in Vienna – where, in the words of his future bookselling partner Ernst Weil, he was 'brought up like a young prince' – and went up to Cambridge in 1905, where he was reputed to be the richest undergraduate in the university.[74] He seemed destined for a career in *haute finance*, and a job had already been found for him with the investment bankers Kuhn, Loeb & Co. in New York. Goldschmidt, however, had other plans. On leaving Cambridge in 1910 he went to work with Dr Konrad Haebler on the *Gesamtkatalog der Wiegendrucke* (GKW), the giant union-catalogue of fifteenth-century printed books. His work for the Wiegendruck-Kommission, which he partly financed out of his own pocket, took him to many of the most important private libraries in Europe, first in Italy and later in Austria-Hungary. This paid unexpected dividends in later years, when several of the Austrian monasteries he had visited, including Admont and Melk, fell on hard times and invited him back to purchase some of the books from their libraries.[75]

Goldschmidt's background in the world of high finance and entrepreneurship makes his move into antiquarian bookselling seem almost inevitable. In 1913, after the death of Bernard Alfred Quaritch, he made an unsuccessful offer to buy the firm of Quaritch; and in 1917 he took over the firm of Gilhofer & Ranschburg in his home town of Vienna. The story goes that he went past the shop one day and saw several items on his wants-list on display in the window. On complaining that these items had not been quoted to him, he was told that if he was dissatisfied with the way the firm was being run, he was welcome to come in and run it himself – which he duly did.[76] In later years he was inclined to make light of the purchase of Gilhofer & Ranschburg – 'it was available', he told his assistant Jacques Vellekoop, 'and I had the money' – but in fact it proved to be an excellent investment, though for reasons that he may not have foreseen. His personal fortune was badly affected by hyper-inflation after the war, and from being a rich man's hobby, Gilhofer & Ranschburg was suddenly transformed into his main source of livelihood.

By the early 1920s, however, Goldschmidt was growing restless, and in 1923 he sold his shareholding in Gilhofer & Ranschburg and moved to London to set up as an independent dealer, taking with him his own personal collection and a proportion of the stock. There, he established himself at 45 Old Bond Street, where he remained for the rest of his life.[77] Bond Street in those days was home to a number of small businesses, a far cry from the luxury shops that dominate it today. Goldschmidt's premises – which doubled as his private flat, with a showroom on the first floor, a bedroom on the second floor, and his reference library on the third and fourth floors – were located directly above a tobacconist's shop, and sandwiched beween two 'complexion specialists', Madame Verdi on one side and the unfortunately-named Madame Swastica on the other. But it was right at the heart of the London antiquarian book trade. Sotheby's were in New Bond Street, as they still are today, and around them were clustered most of the leading West End dealers, including Quaritch in Grafton Street, Maggs in Conduit Street, Ellis in New Bond Street and Dobell in Bruton Street.

Goldschmidt's daily routine hardly varied. He was not an early riser, and often found it a struggle to get up in time for Sotheby's sales at 11 a.m.[78] On days when there were no auction sales, he would rise at about 11.30, open the post and play with the cat before going out for lunch at Brown's Hotel, where, if he was in an especially bad mood, the waiters would place a screen around him so that he could eat his meal in peace. Then, in the afternoon, he would make a tour of the bookshops and auction-rooms, returning home in the early evening to finish the *Times* crossword before dinner. After dinner, there was time for some more games with the cat, or perhaps a chat with a friend who might have dropped in to see him, knowing his nocturnal habits. Only then, late in the evening, would he finally settle down at his desk, working into the early hours of the morning to produce a neat pile of catalogue-slips before slipping out for a glass of milk at the all-night Lyons Corner House in Piccadilly.[79] Many of his letters to W.A. Jackson look as though they were the product of these late-night sessions, with the letters developing into miniature essays – composed directly on the typewriter, with marvellous fluency – as Goldschmidt gradually warmed to his theme, fortified by black coffee and cigarettes. He was a heavy smoker (forty a day), and his cigarettes were made specially for him, with his own highly distinctive blend of Turkish tobacco. On one occasion Albi Rosenthal and several other booksellers were debating the provenance of a book coming up for sale at Sotheby's. Rosenthal solved the problem by opening the volume and inhaling deeply. 'E.P. Goldschmidt,' he pronounced.[80]

What, then, of Goldschmidt the bookseller? His catalogues quickly became famous for their erudition – the first three were praised by the *Times Literary Supplement* as being 'well up to the high standards set some years ago by Mr W.M. Voynich' – and are still valuable today as works of reference.[81] But as Weil commented, Goldschmidt's style of bookselling was, at heart, a very personal one: 'His aim in buying was to find something for a collector he liked, or a library, or some extraordinary book or manuscript which appealed to him.'[82] His earliest catalogues are dominated by incunabula and early bookbindings, but after the publication of his magnum opus, *Gothic and Renaissance Bookbindings* (1928), his interest in bindings gradually waned, and he came to specialize more in sixteenth-century humanism and in what would now be called the history of ideas. Weil joined the firm in 1933 to develop a parallel specialism in the history of science and medicine, in which he proved so successful that he eventually set up on his own and, in financial terms, did far better than Goldschmidt himself.

Although Goldschmidt had lost most of his money after the war, he remained a comparatively wealthy man. Weil described him as having 'a complete disregard for money' and claimed that he always spent right up to the limit of his credit, but it is unlikely that he was ever seriously short of money. Jacques Vellekoop recalls that he always maintained a balance of £1,000 in his private bank account, as an emergency reserve.[83] This gave him a degree of financial independence denied to most booksellers, and meant that he could afford to buy the books that interested him and keep them in stock for years, even decades, waiting for the right buyer to come along. In this context Weil relates a revealing little anecdote. One day in June 1940 – just as the Germans were advancing on Paris – Goldschmidt returned to Old Bond Street in high good humour, clutching a seventeenth-century heraldic manuscript illustrated with the coats-of-arms of the medieval noble families of Serbia, Croatia and Dalmatia. He was delighted with the purchase, describing it to Weil as 'ein kleines Freuderl', a small delight. Weeks of painstaking research followed, as Goldschmidt immersed himself in the medieval history of the Balkans and the genealogy of the Frangipani family of Naples, first owners of the manuscript. At last it was sold: for £20.[84]

To those who might have objected that this was a hopelessly uncommercial approach to bookselling, Goldschmidt had an answer ready to hand. One of his favourite themes was that book prices were purely arbitrary, bearing little or no relation to the intrinsic importance of the books themselves. To anyone tempted to regard antiquarian books as a long-term investment, his advice was simple: 'Keep away from every book that is sought after now! There is no telling what will be "valuable" forty years from now; the possibilities are too varied and too manifold to be predictable. But there is just one thing you can know with positive certainty: whatever is the height of fashion in 1860 is sure to be practically valueless in 1900. If you will spend one day only in studying the history of book-prices you can make certain of that.'[85] The wise collector would thus be a contrarian, pursuing his own interests and developing his own field of collecting with sublime disregard for contemporary fashion – though still with no certainty that he would ever see a return on his investment. And the wise bookseller, knowing that value was in the eye of the beholder, would seek to create value by being a skilful and persuasive advocate for his stock. 'He starts with a virginal book and in describing it, he must plead for it: he must exercise his ingenuity to bring out any point hitherto not noted, to advance any claim that can reasonably be maintained. ... He must be sceptical and critical of all accepted tradition, and he may be quite justifiably bold and even fanciful in his conjectures, provided he can support them with a reasonable measure of evidence.'[86]

How does this look with hindsight? Goldschmidt was scornful of the fashion for modern first editions, which he regarded as nothing more than a passing fad. Every generation of book collectors, he remarked in 1947, had its 'articulate enthusiasts', like Wise, Gosse or Sadleir, who set the fashion for others. 'Their enthusiasm is genuine, and it is infectious. But infectious only by contact, not at long range. Twenty years after their day, their "points" of interest, their criteria of value, will certainly be of no account.' Their emphasis on 'chronological priority' was 'a very modern and a very parochial limitation, and, I should expect, a very passing one. The earlier book-collectors were as much interested in the best edition and in the finest edition as in the first.'[87] In fact, as we can now see, Goldschmidt seriously underestimated the staying-power of first-edition collecting. Sadleir's criteria of value – particularly his insistence on original condition – have proved to be remarkably long-lived; and a collector who had set out in 1947 to form a library of nineteenth-century first editions, following Sadleir's example, would have had no reason to complain of a bad investment twenty, forty or even sixty years later. As for Goldschmidt's argument that the bookseller must be 'bold and even fanciful in his conjectures', John Carter reasonably pointed out that this was all very well where Goldschmidt himself was concerned, but that not all booksellers were as scholarly and responsible as he was.[88]

Goldschmidt's own criteria of value, on the other hand, have stood the test of time far better than he might have expected. His enthusiasm for text manuscripts, for example, has proved to be extremely far-sighted, and it is no longer possible to say, as he did in 1952, that 'a manuscript lacking all pictorial decoration, whatever its content or its historical interest, is a thing of little commercial value', or that 'from the business point of view the handling of old manuscripts without pictures in them is unattractive and unprofitable'.[89] His taste for antiquarian bibliography and book sale catalogues has also been borne out, in market terms, by the sale of his own reference library in 1993 and more recently, the sale of the Bernard Breslauer collection.[90] Seldom can Goldschmidt's vision of the bookseller as a persuasive advocate for a neglected field of collecting have been more spectacularly vindicated. It is interesting, too, to observe that Goldschmidt's views on first-edition collecting underwent a significant change in later years. Having previously dismissed the cult of the first edition for its irrational insistence on chronological priority, by 1952 he was prepared to give it his guarded approval, as reflecting a 'way of looking upon a book as valuable as a historical document, as a concrete stepping-stone in the march of knowledge and of ideas'.[91] This emphasis on the role of the material text in intellectual history – á la *Printing and the Mind of Man* – is arguably the single most important development in modern book collecting; and Goldschmidt was one of the first to articulate it.

After the war, Goldschmidt increasingly sank into depression, convinced that the great days of bookselling were over. Writing to him in 1945, Jackson tried to console him with the reflection that he would soon be able to begin buying on the Continent once again. 'Your "pipe-dream" of a tour on the Continent in the near future appears to me more like a nightmare,' Goldschmidt snapped in response.

'What, for goodness sake, should anyone want to go to the Continent for now? To watch people perishing in misery and filth? You say something about finding out "where the books are". The books, if they have not been burned or otherwise destroyed, are where they always were; but the time when they can be bought is still far, far away. Why should anybody want to sell books now?'[92] In his view, there was no point in selling books because there was nothing to buy with the money – no food, no fuel, no means of transport – and because any dealers with a decent stock, like the Robinson brothers, would do much better to hold onto their assets and wait for them to appreciate in value. By 1947, Goldschmidt was writing that 'I see no livelihood for me in the booktrade, and I am urgently anxious to get out of it'.[93] In the last years of his life, he deliberately ran down his stock and, in Robin Halwas's phrase, elected to commit 'commercial suicide' by ceasing to buy books.

When John Carter was invited to take over the business after Goldschmidt's death, he wrote a blunt assessment of its prospects in which he concluded that Goldschmidt the firm could hardly be continued without Goldschmidt the man. 'Did not the business ultimately depend on EPhG's own learning and sagacity, on his personal reputation with his customers for scholarship and imagination? That is irreplaceable … I should have thought that it was the specialisation (plus the authority, plus the personality of the man) which had made the business a modest success.'[94] As it turned out, Carter had underestimated Goldschmidt's chosen successor, Jacques Vellekoop, who carried on the business with great success for another forty years (and gave several younger booksellers, including Paul Breman, Robin Halwas and Lord John Kerr, their start in the trade). But in one sense he was right, in that Goldschmidt's style of bookselling was very much a product of the inter-war years and could not easily have adapted to post-war conditions. Goldschmidt once told Weil that his ambition was to die like Quaritch, with no cash, a sound overdraft and a magnificent stock.[95] That style of doing business was hardly possible any more.

Conclusion

The story of our three booksellers – Voynich, Ettinghausen and Goldschmidt – is, in effect, the story of one distinctive period in the history of the trade. This period may be said to have begun in the 1890s, when Voynich began travelling on the Continent and importing early printed books to England. It reached its height in the 1920s and 1930s, when Ettinghausen held a commanding position in the trade – controlling, through Maggs's Paris office, a steady flow of books from Europe to America. It was coming to an end by 1949, when Goldschmidt returned from a buying-trip to France, Italy and Austria feeling 'very depressed about the prospects of ever getting any books again in the same way and to the same extent as I used to do'.[96] Why was it so short-lived?

One reason was the geographical shift in the trade brought about by the emigration of many Continental booksellers to America. Increasingly, American librarians and collectors found that they no longer needed to rely on booksellers in England or the Continent. 'The books they wanted,' as Bernard Rosenthal observes, 'were no longer out of reach somewhere in Europe, or confined to the shelves of a few rather intimidating establishments; and the expert dealers one previously visited in Munich, Frankfurt, Vienna or Berlin were now in mid-Manhattan or Los Angeles.'[97] Of course, American buying-trips to Europe did not cease overnight; and some libraries, like Harvard, maintained fruitful relationships with European dealers for many years to come. But London dealers were no longer at the centre of the international book trade in the way that they had been before the war.

Another reason was, quite simply, that the books were no longer there. 'The supplies of books worth buying are everywhere diminishing at a rapid pace,' Goldschmidt lamented in 1949. 'This last week was the first week in my memory that at this time of the year there was no booksale at all in London, neither at Sotheby's nor at Hodgson's nor elsewhere ... Both Hoepli and Olschki are closing their branches in Rome, because they cannot keep them supplied with books. I know of no bookseller anywhere outside Switzerland (where the currency is good) who has a stock at all comparable to his pre-war holdings.'[98] It is, of course, a common illusion among dealers and collectors that there is nothing worth buying any more; but in this case there was a good deal of truth in Goldschmidt's prediction that while the most expensive books would continue to pass from one private collection to another, the supply of less valuable items, 'emerging without noise in small sales and small bookshops', would not be replenished. Many of these books had now passed into permanent institutional collections from which they would not re-emerge – a situation for which, as Goldschmidt wryly admitted, 'I am as much to blame as anybody'.[99]

If Goldschmidt feared that this would lead to the total extinction of the antiquarian book trade, he was mistaken. The drying-up of old sources of supply caused dealers to pay new attention to books they might previously have disregarded, and to enlarge their ideas of what might be worth buying or collecting – all of which has been wholly beneficial. But although the trade at the beginning of the twenty-first century is in some ways more international than ever before, in other ways its horizons have narrowed. In general, British dealers today are more likely to be found selling books in San Francisco or Tokyo than buying books in Rome or Madrid, and the entry that catches one's eye in their catalogues is more likely to be a neglected piece of eighteenth-century English provincial poetry or a minor nineteenth-century novel than an unrecorded example of seventeenth-century neo-Latin verse or a sixteenth-century edition of a classical text. Europe may be closer than ever, but the cosmopolitan European culture inhabited by Voynich, Ettinghausen and Goldschmidt now seems, paradoxically, further away. If so, then their example may still have something to teach us.

The Antiquarian Book Trade
and the World of Scholarship

A.S.G. EDWARDS

THE connections between the commercial and the scholarly worlds of books have always been close and pervasive. They are partly demonstrated in the various institutional collaborations that link these worlds. The Council of the Bibliographical Society has very often included dealers among its members.[1] Members of the book trade have, like other scholars, made important contributions to scholarly bibliophily in the publications of the Roxburghe Club and to the activities of the International Association of Bibliophiles. They have been invited to give bibliographical lectures, such as the prestigious series of Lyell Lectures at Oxford and Sandars Lectures at Cambridge. These connections are the most general manifestation of the role of the antiquarian book dealer in the wider world of scholarship.[2]

I am concerned here mainly with publications, with specific contributions to particular fields of scholarship. Yet what is published as scholarship is only a fraction of the book-dealer's scholarly activity. For most of this activity appears in that ephemeral printed form, the catalogue. Many people retain files of the catalogues of particular dealers or subjects because they form important contributions in their own right to the scholarship of certain fields or periods. Some booksellers have, through their catalogues, effectively invented new scholarly or bibliographical fields. Some have poured their erudition into their cataloguing and published little else. The extraordinary knowledge of Restoration and eighteenth-century literature possessed by Percy J. Dobell (1871-1956) is most evident in his catalogues on these subjects.[3] The sale catalogues of incunabula and other early printed books compiled by Felix de Marez Oyens have become essential reference tools in their field. Peter Murray Hill's premature death meant that he published only the smallest fraction of his knowledge of eighteenth-century literature,[4] while Bertram Rota's expertise in modern literature found only occasional expression in print.[5] The importance of catalogues is discussed elsewhere in this volume, but it is appropriate to begin here with some acknowledgement of the crucial, unobtrusive, achievements of many book dealers, both in their descriptions of books and in the materials brought together in their catalogues. These achievements range from identifying rare or unique editions or uncovering provenances, to placing books in their proper historical or cultural contexts, and, at times, assembling collections that can create new fields of intellectual enquiry. Such services to the world of scholarship are rarely explicitly acknowledged. For many dealers, their catalogues are the only enduring record of their knowledge and vision.

For some dealers, scholarship has been an extension of the particular expertise developed through handling and researching their stock, their bibliographical research prepared and published as circumstance permitted. But not all dealers have shaped their intellectual pursuits around their professional activities. Some have found scholarly distinction in an unrelated field. John Edmund Hodgson (1875-1952) wrote his standard *History of Aeronautics in Great Britain to the Latter Half of the Nineteenth Century* (Oxford, 1924), while a partner in the family firm of auctioneers. Cyril Beaumont (1891-1976) was a bookseller and publisher for more than fifty years, but his chief claim on posterity's attention is as a dance historian, critic and bibliographer of his subject, with such works as the *Complete Book of Ballet* (1937; revised 1951 with supplement) and *A Bibliography of Dance* (1929). Frederick Henry Evans (1853-1943), who owned a business in Cheapside, wrote about photographic technique and was a famous photographer.[6] Ifan Kyrle Fletcher (1905-69) made important contributions to the study of ceremonial and dance,[7] in addition to his bibliographical researches.[8] Andreas Mayor (1918-75), in his later years a manuscript cataloguer at Sotheby's, was known to a wider public as a translator of Proust.[9] And George Holleyman (1910-2004), of the firm Holleyman and Treacher in Sussex was a distinguished prehistoric archaeologist.[10]

Others have for a time juggled the conflicting attractions of scholarship and the book trade before retreating to academe. An early precedent was set by R.B. Haselden (b. 1881), who moved from Sotheby's in the 1920s to the firm of Gabriel Wells in New York, before becoming keeper of manuscripts at the Huntington Library in California, where he published his still-useful *Scientific Aids to the Study of Manuscripts* (1935). The Book Department of Sotheby's has continued to provide an academic training ground, chiefly for scholars who have later been translated to Cambridge. A.N.L. Munby provides the model. He joined the book trade in 1935, after coming down from King's College, Cambridge, and worked briefly for Quaritch before joining Sotheby's in 1936. After the war he returned to the firm before becoming librarian at King's in 1947. During his period in the trade he laid the foundations for his later studies of the collecting and circulation of manuscripts among collectors: *The Cult of the Autograph Letter* (1962), *Connoisseurs and Medieval Manuscripts* (Oxford, 1972) and, most famously, the series of five volumes of *Phillipps Studies* (Cambridge, 1951-60) which chronicle the growth and dispersal of the collections of Sir Thomas Phillipps.[11]

Munby was succeeded at King's in 1975 by Peter Croft (1929-84), who had joined Sotheby's manuscript department in 1953, after abandoning a research degree at Oxford. The principal published fruit of his years at Sotheby's was his remarkable two-volume *Autograph Poetry in the English Language* (1973). This was far more than a judiciously chosen series of plates with meticulous transcriptions; the accompanying commentaries on each manuscript demonstrate a grasp of bibliographical, textual and palaeographical detail that makes the documents live for the user. During his all too brief time in Cambridge, Croft was able to complete his edition of *The Poems of Robert Sidney* (Oxford, 1984), but long-projected undertakings were left incomplete at his untimely death.[12]

Christopher de Hamel (b. 1950) was another Sotheby's recruit who has become librarian of a Cambridge college. But before his appointment to Corpus Christi College as Donnelley Librarian he had already established himself as one of the leading experts on medieval western manuscripts. His researches have often drawn on his experience of more than 25 years of cataloguing medieval manuscripts and are reflected in a range of important books and other writings, including *A History of Illuminated Manuscripts* (1986; 2nd edn., 1997), *Syon Abbey* (Roxburghe Club, 1991), *Scribes and Illuminators* (1992), and *The Book: A History of the Bible* (2001). Few scholars have embodied so brilliantly the fruitful connection that can exist between the academic and the commercial worlds of books.

Peter Beal (b. 1944), a Fellow of the British Academy, has recently retired from Sotheby's to take up a research position at the Institute of English Studies, University of London. Probably his greatest scholarly monument to date is his *Index of Literary Manuscripts 1450-1700* (1980), a meticulously detailed bibliography of the manuscript sources for literary writers of the English Renaissance.[13] This work has been supplemented by his Lyell lectures, *In Praise of Scribes* (Oxford, 1998), by numerous articles on Renaissance manuscripts and texts and by his co-editorship of the important series, published by the British Library, *English Manuscript Studies 1100-1700*.

Anthony Hobson (b. 1921), son of Geoffrey, of whom more below, followed his father to Sotheby's, where he was director for nearly 30 years before devoting himself to his scholarly interests. As with his father, bookbinding history has been a central scholarly concern, albeit one that has led him in a different direction and which is part of a range of academic and literary interests.[14] His study of continental bindings found its first major expression in his *French and Italian Collectors and their Bindings, Illustrated from Examples in the Library of J. R. Abbey* (Roxburghe Club, 1953) and achieves its fullest development in a trilogy of books examining Italian Renaissance bookbinding: *Apollo and Pegasus* (Amsterdam, 1975), a re-examination of a group of Roman sixteenth-century bindings on which these figures appear in a plaquette; *Humanists and Bookbinders* (Cambridge, 1989), on the development of gold-tooled and other decorated bindings;[15] and *Renaissance Book Collecting: Jean Grolier and Diego Hurtado de Mendoza, Their Books and Bindings* (Cambridge, 1999). He is the only person associated with the book trade to have been elected both a Fellow of the British Academy and a member of the Roxburghe Club, to have delivered both the Sandars and Lyell lectures, and to have received the Gold Medal of the Bibliographical Society.

Norma Hull Lewis (1902-97) graduated from Somerville College, Oxford, and in 1933 married the auctioneer John Edmund Hodgson (q.v.). She became a cataloguer of books and manuscripts for Hodgson's and this enabled her to develop her bibliographical interests. The discovery of a manuscript notebook belonging to a seventeenth-century London bookseller, Thomas Bennet, resulted in her first major publication, in collaboration with Cyprian Blagden, the historian of the Stationers' Company.[16] Following her husband's death, she became librarian of Somerville in 1955. As Norma Russell (she remarried in 1956) she produced, among much else, *A Bibliography of William Cowper* (1963). Her edition of the complete poems of Crabbe (Oxford, 1988, with Arthur Pollard), appeared under her third married name, Dalrymple-Champneys, and was awarded the British Academy's Rose Mary Crawshay Prize in 1990.[17]

The career of Graham Pollard (1903-76) also took many turns.[18] The son of a distinguished academic, he went to Shrewsbury School and then to Oxford, where he took a third in history. On coming down in 1923 he bought a share in the firm of Birrell and Garnett. His time in the trade led to some publications of fundamental importance. His first major catalogue, published in 1928, of typefounding specimens and related works, is itself a collector's item and has been reprinted in a limited edition.[19] In 1934, he achieved a wider and rather different standing when he collaborated with John Carter in exposing the forgeries of T.J. Wise in *An Enquiry into the Nature of Certain Nineteenth Century Pamphlets*. Birrell and Garnett was dissolved in 1938, after which Pollard left the book trade. During the war he entered the Civil Service, where he remained until early retirement.

Pollard continued to research and write, however, often on subjects which he had begun to investigate during his time in the trade. His later publications have two main thrusts. One is book trade history, adumbrated in his early paper on 'The Company of Stationers before 1557',[20] elaborated in his various contributions to the *Cambridge Bibliography of English Literature* (Cambridge, 1940) on 'Book Production and Distribution',[21] and receiving fullest expression in his 1959 Sandars lectures on 'The English Market for Printed Books'[22] and in his Roxburghe Club volume with Albert Ehrman, *The Distribution of Books by Catalogue from the Invention of Printing to A.D. 1800* (1965).[23] His second main interest was early English bookbinding history, to which he contributed a number of fundamental studies in the last twenty years of his life.[24] But the range of his knowledge is not fully reflected in his publications. His 1961 Lyell lectures on 'The Medieval Book Trade in Oxford' were never printed, for example. As one obituarist concluded: 'He was indeed a scholar who put into print but a small fraction of his learning.'[25]

There has been, on occasions, a reverse movement, away from other worlds to the trade. Jocelyn Baines became managing director of Quaritch after he had completed his important biography of Joseph Conrad (though he had started life as an antiquarian bookseller). Paul Quarrie moved to Sotheby's book department after twenty years as Librarian of Eton College Library. Not all these moves into the trade were happy. For Christopher Millard (1872-1927), bookselling was the final stage in the tragic trajectory of a career in which he was tortured in equal measure by his homosexuality (for which he was imprisoned on several occasions) and his devotion to Oscar Wilde. He became a bookseller only for the last eight years of his life, after he had completed his great *Bibliography of Oscar Wilde*, written under the pseudonym Stuart Mason, which was published in 1914 in two volumes.[26] Its scope and method anticipated later developments in descriptive bibliography in its detailed enumeration both of editions of Wilde's works and of his contributions to periodicals; it also presciently included numerous reproductions of titlepages.[27] But Millard became the victim of his own commitment to scholarly accuracy: in 1926, the year before his death, he lost a civil suit for libel brought against him for challenging the authenticity of a play ascribed to Wilde by the implausible Mrs Chan Toon.[28] Some aspects of his solitary life and bibliographical intensity can be glimpsed in his letters to the young Anthony Powell.[29]

Millard is untypical of the trade in very obvious ways. One could perhaps compare him with his near-contemporary Bertram Dobell (1842-1914), who, though mostly self-educated, opened his first bookshop in the early 1870s, and went on to produce nearly 240 catalogues, often of considerable erudition, notably on the subject of privately printed books (1891). Dobell wrote studies of his friend James Thomson ('B.V.') (1910) and of Charles Lamb (1903), scholarly articles and several volumes of verse. He was responsible for editions of various authors, but his most important literary achievement was the rediscovery of the seventeenth-century poet Thomas Traherne, whose manuscripts, found on two London book barrows, he identified and published as *Poetical Works* (1903) and *Centuries of Meditations* (1908).[30] His son Percy J. Dobell and his nephew, Bertram Rota, followed him into the trade.

Not all the figures from this period were specialists. Indeed, one of the most remarkable demonstrates a capacity to combine a trade career with other interests, which seem in retrospect bewilderingly diverse. R.A. Peddie (1869-1951) produced books on incunabula and the history of printing, as well as the history of trade unionism, engineering and metallurgy, and railway history, in addition to a monumental – and highly idiosyncratic – subject index to books published before 1881. Few can have matched the range of his interests and the unobtrusive energy with which he pursued them.[31]

Dobell and Peddie are models for the scholarly embodiment of the book trade in the following generations, of men (they were mainly men) who were often not university educated, but who thrived because of the range and depth of their scholarly curiosity and the resolution that enabled them to bring the fruits of their knowledge to published form.

This embodiment received possibly its fullest expression in the figure of Percy Muir (1894-1979). He left school in his teens to work in a paint factory. Like Millard he saw service in the First World War. Afterwards he worked the music halls before a chance meeting with Harold Edwards led him into the world of rare books. He set up on his own in 1924; two years later he joined Leslie Chaundy at Dulau. It was several years later that he found his proper home at the firm of Elkin Mathews with which he was to be associated for the rest of his life.[32]

Muir was also a bibliographer, as Millard was, rather than a man of letters, like

Dobell. His books include *Points 1874-1930* (1931), *Points Second Series 1866-1934* (1934), *English Children's Books 1600 to 1900* (1954), and *Victorian Illustrated Books* (1971). But a fuller sense of the range of his bibliographical interests is provided by his numerous editions, edited collections, articles and reviews in bibliographical journals, particularly *The Book Collector*, on whose editorial board he served from its inception.[33] He also produced several books on book collecting, including *Book-Collecting as a Hobby* (1944), and *Book-Collecting: More Letters to Everyman* (1949).

Muir's entry into the rare book world was closely followed by that of another figure from a very different background, with whom he was to become closely associated. John Waynflete Carter (1905-75) was one of the most remarkable scholar-booksellers of the twentieth century. Educated at Eton and King's College, Cambridge (where he took a double first in Classics), Carter's background and early achievements held the promise of some glittering career appropriate to the well-connected and academically brilliant. But on graduation in 1927 he became the English representative of the American publisher and bookseller, Charles Scribner's. The late 1920s were an unpropitious time to begin a career, not least as an antiquarian book dealer. But for the next quarter of a century Carter stayed with this firm, with one foot in England, the other in North America. He subsequently joined Sotheby's, with whom he remained until his death.

Carter's determination and intellect found fulfilling expression in the world of rare books. Over a period of nearly 50 years he produced an extraordinary number of articles and books to do with bibliography in a variety of aspects: *Binding Variants in English Publishing 1820-1900* (1932), *Publisher's Cloth: An Outline History of Publisher's Binding in England 1820-1900* (1935) (this allegedly 'written in forty-eight hours in a New York hotel bedroom'), *More Binding Variants* (1938), bibliographies of Stanley Morison (1950) and A.E. Housman (1952; with John Sparrow), as well as several collections of his own essays, most notably *Books and Book Collectors* (1956). But while these books testify to his range of interests they give only a partial picture of his influence within and beyond the book trade. Possibly his most widely used book was his *ABC for Book Collectors*, the first edition of which appeared in 1952 and the seventh in 2004. Probably the most significant of them, though, was *Taste and Technique in Book Collecting*, his 1947 Sandars lectures.[34] The first part ('Evolution') surveys the development of book collecting and the various factors that shaped it from the nineteenth century to the immediate post-war period. Time has done little to lessen the force of most of its points. The same cannot be said for the second part ('Method') which is now rather dated. But its authority and urbanity, allied to its sustained elegance of expression, make it a book still to be studied with profit.

Hundreds of articles, reviews and contributions to books came from Carter's pen on topics from Thomas Browne to the invention of stereotype. He was also, like Muir, a member of the editorial board of *The Book Collector* from its beginnings (and, like him, a regular contributor) and for many years bibliographical advisor to the *Times Literary Supplement*.[35] His importance within the world of books cannot be adequately summarized.

In spite of their differences in background, Muir and Carter were close friends (Muir dedicated his autobiography to him), and they were associated in other enterprises, particularly the revised and enlarged version of *Printing and the Mind of Man*, the catalogue which they co-edited in 1967.[36] This had first been published in 1963 to mark the International Printing and Allied Trades Exhibition. In its enlarged form it is defined by its sub-title: *A Descriptive Catalogue Illustrating the Impact of Print on the Evolution of Western Civilization During Five Centuries*. It comprises separate descriptions of 424 key works in the history of Western culture, from the Gutenberg Bible to Winston Churchill's speech to the House of Commons on 20 August 1940, and including books on science, religion, economics, philosophy, law, medicine, literature, art and architecture. The scope of the undertaking required a range of historical and bibliographical knowledge that drew heavily on the rare book trade. In addition to Carter and Muir, H.A. Feisenberger and S.H. Steinberg were among the contributors to the catalogue (together with Nicolas Barker and Howard Nixon). It remains one of the most imaginative and stylish testimonies to the scholarly resources of the trade. Muir termed it his favourite book among his many writings.

Equally important in scholarly terms was Carter's association with Graham Pollard, with whom he wrote the most famous account of bibliographical detective work, *An Enquiry into the Nature of Certain Nineteenth Century Pamphlets* (1934). This exposure of the forgeries of T.J. Wise swiftly gained the status of a bibliographical classic and spawned a cottage industry of writings on Wise and his activities that continued over the next 50 years, until the publication of a second edition of *An Enquiry* by Nicolas Barker and John Collins in 1983.[37]

Carter, Pollard and Muir were perhaps the most productive scholarly book dealers of their generation. The friendship they all shared seems to have provided a stimulus to their researches. They were, from its beginnings, part of the circle that became known as the Biblios, an informal sodality that did much to shape bibliographical study in England for more than 40 years.[38] But in the 1930s such study already had a vital place in the trade. For example, Pollard's partner at Birrell and Garnett was Jane Norton (1893-1962), the editor and bibliographer of Gibbon.[39] And when Muir joined Elkin Mathews he found himself part of a firm in which bibliographical expertise abounded. The chief shareholder was Greville Worthington, author of *A Bibliography of the Waverley Novels* (*Bibliographia*, no. 4, 1931).[40] One partner, A.W. Evans, was the author of *Warburton and Warburtoniana* (1932); another, Robert Gathorne-Hardy (1903-73), wrote about seventeenth- and eighteenth-century bibliography before fully developing his interest in flowers and gardens.[41]

While firms like Birrell and Garnett and Elkin Mathews reflected the bibliographical energy in the book trade during the inter-war years, other journeyman-dealers produced works of widely varying significance. These ranged from individual bibliographies of very limited value, such as Frederick T. Bason's bibliography of Somerset Maugham,[42] to the much more prolific Andrew Block (1892-1985),[43] historian of the London book trade and author of a guide to book collecting, and of bibliographies of Barrie and of the English novel,[44] and to Gilbert Fabes (b. 1894) of Foyle's, who produced numerous bibliographies of modern writers in the late 1920s and 1930s.[45]

Three figures, however, dominated their chosen fields of scholarship during the years between the World Wars. Geoffrey Hobson (1882-1949) had joined Sotheby's in 1908 as a partner and remained with it for the rest of his life. He played a crucial role in establishing the firm's dominant position in the rare book trade. He was also a scholar of exacting standards and one of the most important historians of European bookbinding.[46] He began his study of the subject before the First World War and in the 1920s started to publish a range of significant studies. His method is set out in the first, *Maioli, Canevari and Others* (1926), an arresting series of reattributions. By rigorous analysis he demonstrated that a group of books hitherto associated with Demetrio Canevari, physician to Urban VII, were made for Pier Luigi Farnese, and that another group of bindings, linked to one Maioli, were made for Thomas Mahieu.

The book set a standard of scholarship and analysis that was maintained in Hobson's subsequent writings. In 1927 he was the first member of the book trade to deliver the Sandars lectures, published as *English Binding before 1500* (Cambridge, 1929). In this and such other studies as *Bindings in Cambridge Libraries* (Cambridge, 1929), *Les Reliures à la Fanfare* (1935), *English Bindings 1490-1940 in the Library of J. R. Abbey* (1940) and *Blind-Stamped Panels in the English Book-Trade c. 1485-1555* (1944) and in various essays,[47] he brought to the history of bookbinding, particularly in England, an unprecedented authority and perceptiveness. Much of his writing in this field remains fundamental.[48]

Ernst Philip Goldschmidt (1887-1954) has been described as 'the most learned book seller, I suppose, that any of us have ever known ... his favourite customer, he used to say, was one who lived at least a thousand miles away and from time to time sent an airmail postcard ordering one very expensive book'.[49] The characterization captures something of the personality of an exotic in the world of English book-dealing. The youngest son of a Dutch-Jewish banker, Goldschmidt went up to Trinity College, Cambridge in 1905, at a time when it was rich in book collectors.[50] He was quickly drawn into the study of early books and became a dealer, moving from Vienna to London in 1923.[51]

Goldschmidt's scholarship achieved its most monumental expression in *Gothic and Renaissance Bookbindings* (2 vols., 1928), a work published early in his career. Based on his own collection, it presents a survey of European bindings, organized chronologically by place and type. It was immediately recognized as 'another milestone in getting the history of bookbinding on the right lines'.[52] Goldschmidt was himself always inclined to downplay the importance of bookbinding history: 'The study of old bookbindings is a sideline of the main course of bibliographical research,' he was later to assert;[53] but his work, like Hobson's, established the scholarly importance of the subject in England. Nor was the range of his interests limited to binding history. Among his other important publications was *Medieval Texts and their First Appearance in Print* (1943). In 1953-4 he was elected Sandars Reader in Bibliography but was too ill to deliver his lectures, which were published posthumously as *The First Cambridge Press in its European Setting* (Cambridge, 1955).

The third crucial figure was of a very different social and scholarly caste. F.S. Ferguson (1878-1967) joined Quaritch in 1897. Largely self-educated, he became Managing Director of the firm in 1929 and retired from it after the Second World War.[54] He published relatively little under his own name: the most substantial work was *Title-Page Borders in England and Scotland, 1485-1640* (1932), with R.B. McKerrow; there are also a few articles in bibliographical journals.[55] But his publications do not properly reflect his contribution to enumerative bibliography, which he seems increasingly to have preferred to the more commercial activities of the book trade.[56] In the original *Short-Title Catalogue of Books Printed in England ... 1476-1640* (1926) his important role is emphasized in the preface (p. ix). But his involvement with *STC* was to be lifelong. He became one of the compilers of the second edition (1976-91), which began to appear only after his death. The preface pays tribute to his 'meticulous collations and his collection of woodcut ornaments and initials, which he began to amass early in the century' (p. xviii). Ferguson's devotion to the service of bibliography was acknowledged, in 1951, with the Gold Medal of the Bibliographical Society and later, in 1955, with honorary degrees from both Oxford (MA) and Edinburgh (LLD).

The forcible emigration of German-Jewish booksellers brought to England both new talent and knowledge which was to enrich bibliographical scholarship in the post-war years. One such was Bernard Breslauer (1918-2004), son of the distinguished European dealer Martin Breslauer. After the family's escape from the Nazis in the 1930s and his father's death in the Blitz, Breslauer patiently developed both his business and his scholarly interests.[57] In his later years he moved to the United States and it was there that he produced some of his more substantial writings: his assessment of *The Uses of Bookbinding Literature* (New York, 1986), his reconstruction of the library of Count Henrich IV zu Castell (Austin, TX, 1987) and his introduction to the facsimile of Federico Frezzi, *Il Quadriregio* (Roxburghe Club, 1998), as well as his important Grolier Club exhibition catalogue (with Roland Folter) of *Bibliography: its history and development* (New York, 1984).[58]

Among other notable exiles was Albi Rosenthal (1914-2004), who was driven from Germany in 1933. After an early flirtation with art history (his earliest article was in the *Burlington Magazine*), he became a book dealer in 1936. His scholarly career reflected his professional one as a (possibly *the*) specialist in music. In collaboration with Alan Tyson he wrote *Mozart: A Thematic Catalogue* (Ithaca, NY, 1990) and *Mozart and the Keyboard Culture of his Time* (Ithaca, NY, 1991). A number of his shorter writings are collected in *Obiter Scripta* (2000).[59]

Ernst Weil (1891-1965) found the scholarly focus to his career long before he left Germany. He had joined the Munich firm of Hans Taeuber in 1924 after completing his doctorate. During the 1920s he produced a flow of scholarly monographs and editions on early scientific subjects. In 1933 he joined E.P. Goldschmidt's firm in London before setting up independently. He was also the bibliographer of Albert Einstein and the author of numerous articles and reviews on aspects of scientific bibliography.[60]

H.A. Feisenberger (1909-99) was another emigré who entered the trade, working first with Davis and Orioli (1934-40), then with Dawson's (1952-60) and finally, for the longest period of his career, in Sotheby's book department (1960-75). Feisenberger, a stranger to the rare book world on his arrival in London, quickly established himself as a distinguished scientific bibliographer. His publications were relatively few: they include his edition, with introduction, of the sale catalogues of leading scientists of the seventeenth and eighteenth centuries,[61] his study of the libraries of Newton, Hooke and Boyle,[62] and his catalogue entries for scientific books for the *Printing and the Mind of Man* exhibition.

The importance of these incomers cannot be overemphasized. Their energy and scholarship helped reinvigorate the trade after the war. But the post-war years also saw an influx of younger dealers eager to contribute to the disciplines of their trade. They received some support from the creation of *The Book Collector*, which came to provide a crucial link between the commercial and scholarly worlds of the book. Several of the new generation of dealers appeared in its pages, often as initial steps towards larger scholarly enterprises. Among these was Timothy d'Arch Smith (b. 1936) who has written widely on later nineteenth- and twentieth-century English literature, including a study of the Uranian poets, bibliographies of Montague Summers and of the Fortune Press, as well as a deliciously scandalous series of reminiscences of the Rare Book Department of the Times Bookshop (2003).[63] George Sims (1923-99) was a novelist and poet as well as the author of a number of valuable studies, particularly of writers of the 1890s. Some of these are collected in *The Rare Book Game* (Philadelphia, 1985), *More of the Rare Book Game* (Philadelphia, 1988) and *A Life in Catalogues and other essays* (Philadelphia, 1994).[64] Cecil Woolf has produced bibliographies of Norman Douglas and Frederic Rolfe, baron Corvo[65] for the Soho Bibliographies series as well as bibliographical articles on figures such as Sir William Watson, William Lisle Bowles, George Darley and Hawker of Morwenstow. The personality of Alan Thomas (1911-92) is reflected in his splendidly idiosyncratic catalogues; it can also be seen in a substantial survey of books and collectors[66] and in his writings as the faithful bibliographer and editor of Lawrence Durrell.[67] Arnold Muirhead made contributions to the bibliographies of William Cobbett and Jeremy Bentham.[68]

On occasion, firms that emerged after the war have created new subjects for collectors and for research. Ben Weinreb (1912-99) opened the first bookshop devoted to architectural history in London in 1961. Although he published relatively little apart from his *London Encyclopedia* (1983, with Christopher Hibbert), his contribution to scholarship is reflected in the Ben Weinreb Collection of Architectural Drawings, now lodged in the Humanities Research

Centre, University of Texas at Austin.[69] Paul Breman (b. 1931), his erstwhile partner, has written extensively on the architectural studies of *Vitruvius Britannicus* (New York, 1972), *Writings on Architecture, Civil and Military, c. 1460-1640* ('t Goy-Houten, 2001; with John Bury) and *Books on Military Architecture Printed in Venice* ('t Goy-Houten, 2002). Tony Campbell, who worked under R.V. Tooley at Francis Edwards and then at Weinreb and Douwma, became an expert on early printed maps and the history of cartography, moving in the 1980s to the British Library. On a smaller scale, the preoccupations of Louis Bondy (b. 1910) as a dealer led to his publication on *Miniature Books* (1981).

Colin Franklin's interest in forming collections has helped to provide the impetus for his studies of fine press books, including catalogues of *The Ashendene Press* (Dallas, TX, 1986), *Poets of the Daniel Press* (Cambridge, 1988) and (with J.R. Turner), *The Private Presses* (Aldershot, 1991). David Rees has compiled checklists of a number of contemporary novelists.[70] Brian Lake has written a standard guide to collecting newspapers (1984). And Chris R. Johnson's survey of provincial printing of Romantic poetry opens new possibilities for collecting in this period.[71]

This generation also includes a number of important scholar-dealers who have entered the trade from academic life. Rick Gekoski (b. 1944) is the bibliographer of William Golding (with P.A. Grogan).[72] He spent his early career as an academic (Oxford and Warwick universities) before turning to book dealing, as did Arthur Freeman (Harvard and Boston universities). Freeman's range of interests resists summary categorization. He has written extensively on Elizabethan and seventeenth-century bibliography and with his wife Janet has produced a classic analysis of the operation of 'the ring', *Anatomy of an Auction* (1990) and a massive bio-bibliography of the nineteenth-century scholar and forger, John Payne Collier.[73] Paul Goldman, who became a bookseller after a career in the Prints & Drawings department of the British Museum, has published studies of Victorian book illustration (1996) and of John Everett Millais.[74]

The book trade continues to make contributions to the wider bibliographical world. One testimony to this is the extremely useful *Antiquarian Books: A Companion* (1994), edited by members of the trade and containing contributions from many more.[75] At Christie's, such figures as Margaret Lane Ford and Kay Sutton, at Quaritch, Richard Linenthal, Ted Hofmann and Nicholas Poole-Wilson, at Maggs, Robert Harding and John Collins, the co-author of the second edition of Carter and Pollard's famous *Enquiry* and the biographer of Wise and Harry Buxton Forman,[76] at Sam Fogg, Alixe Bovey – to name but a few – are representative of those currently at work who demonstrate the continued vital links between the trade and scholarship.

Bernard Rosenthal, the American dealer and younger brother of Albi Rosenthal, is reported as telling a story about Leonardo Olschki, the son of the famous Italian dealer, Leo Olschki. After receiving his doctorate, Leonardo was asked if he now planned to follow his father and enter the rare book trade. He replied: 'I don't think I am smart enough for that, and I have decided to devote my life to scholarship.'[77] It would be hard for anyone with an understanding of the rare book world to convict him of irony. Knowledge alone is not sufficient, in selling rare books. To deal in them with authority requires equal measures of imagination and sensitivity, an understanding of the needs of individual collectors and institutions, and the motives that inform their collecting, as well as an ability to respond to the distinctive physical qualities of a text or a particular copy of it. The greatest dealers have been able to combine exact knowledge with a wider sense of historical, bibliographical and cultural context to produce scholarship that few professional academics can emulate.

I conclude with an unusual example of the ways in which book dealing and the scholarly world are intermeshed. In 1967 Norman Colbeck (1903-88), sold the entire stock of his Bournemouth firm to the University of British Columbia library in Vancouver. He also agreed to go with it and to be paid to catalogue the stock for publication.[78] The result, *A Bookman's Catalogue: The Norman Colbeck Collection of Nineteenth Century and Edwardian Poetry and Belles Lettres*, was finally published by the University of British Columbia Press in 1987. Has any other dealer ever made not just his books, but also himself, part of his own deal?

Part I.   Price 6d.

An Illustrated Catalogue of

Old and Rare Books.

Pickering & Chatto,
66, Haymarket, S.W.

44. Pickering & Chatto catalogue, 1902.

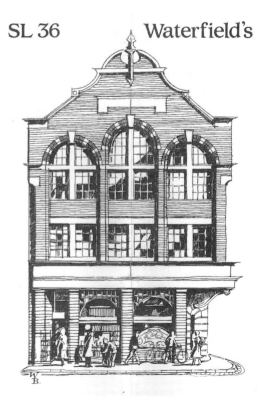

45, 46, 47 & 48. Catalogues (clockwise):
Blackwell, 1922; Breslauer, 1946, annotated by
the scholar and collector R.W. Chapman;
Waterfield's, 1980, showing the Oxford shop;
Maggs, 1971, of 'books from famous libraries'.

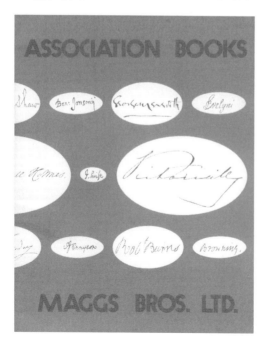

49 & 50. Selling to libraries: (above, left) an advertisement of 1909; (above) Chris Kohler and Lyn Elliott loading a collection, Dorking, 1976.

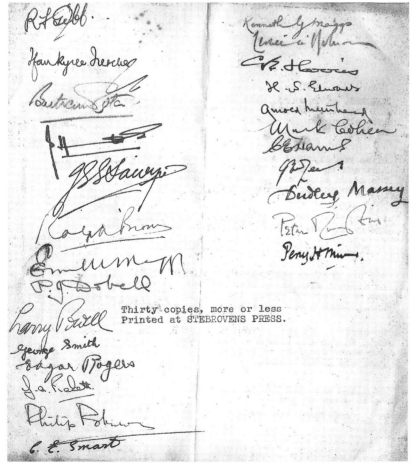

Thirty copies, more or less
Printed at STEBROVENS PRESS.

51. Keepsake from a lunch at The Ivy, 4 June 1951, signed by the American librarian Lawrence Clark Powell and his many friends in the antiquarian book trade.

52. Lionel (left) and Philip Robinson outside their Barnet storehouse, an unlikely home for the Phillipps post-medieval manuscripts, c.1980.

53. Frank Karslake (1851-1920), founder of the Antiquarian Booksellers' Association.

54. Ernest Maggs displaying the Codex Sinaiticus after its acquisition from the Soviet government by Maggs, on behalf of the British Museum, 1933.

THE MORAL BOOKSELLERS
PALACE of VARITIES.
MAMMOTH
PROGRAMME of STAR TURNS.
THE KARSLAKE TROUPE
IN THEIR GREAT SENSATION.
"WHITEWASHED! or
THE (FORE) EDGE of THE PRECIPICE!"
RE-ENGAGEMENT of
BENNET JUNIOR
in his SCREAMING ABSURDITY
"WHAT I KNOW ABOUT FIRST EDITIONS."
LAST APPEARANCE of THAT CHARTERED
LIBERTINE EDGAR ROGERS
WITH HIS PATHETIC BALLAD
"THEY GAVE ME THE BIRD FROM MY BIRTH."
MAGGS BROTHERS
The GREAT MORAL ILLUSIONISTS.
LOTTIE COLLINS IN
HIS KNOCK(AB)OUT ACT.
JOSEPHs (WITHOUT HIS BRETHREN)
WITH HIS SOUL-STIRRING MELODY –
"HARK HOW THE CHOSEN SQUEAL!"
CHAS MEUEL & Cº IN
"A ROYAL (SCOTCH-HOOSE) DIVORCE"
THE CHAS. J. SAWYER – LTD, COMBINATION
IN THEIR LATEST AMERICAN SUCCESS
"RUNNING WITH THE HARE AND
HOLDING WITH THE HOUNDS"
SIC ITUR AD ASTRA.

55. Satirical cartoon from the 1920s, in which Robert Fletcher (of H.M. Fletcher) introduces his fellow antiquarian booksellers as a succession of variety acts. Along with more familiar book-trade names appear Edgar Rogers (of Myers & Co.) and George Good, nicknamed 'Lottie Collins' after a music-hall singer, who worked for Quaritch. 'Kyd' (Joseph Clayton Clark) was employed by the book trade for many years as an illustrator and fore-edge painter.

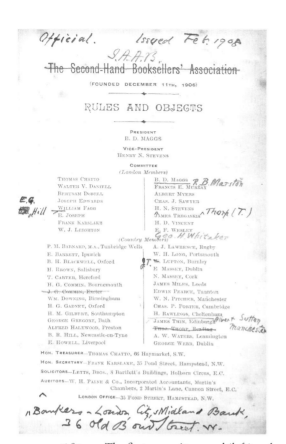

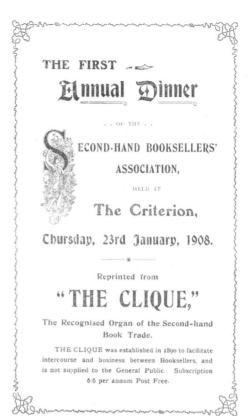

56 & 57. The first committee card (left) and report on the first annual dinner, 1908, of the Second-Hand Booksellers' Association, which became the International Association of Antiquarian Booksellers later that year.

58. President and Past-Presidents of the Antiquarian Booksellers' Association, 1962: (left to right, standing) Bob Williams (Quaritch), Dudley Massey (Pickering & Chatto), Thomas Thorp, Alan Thomas, Harry Pratley, W.R. Fletcher, Mark Cohen (Marks & Co.) and Jack Joseph; (seated) C.E. Harris (Francis Edwards), Winifred Myers and Bert Marley (Dawsons of Pall Mall).

59 & 60. International Conference of Antiquarian Booksellers, London 1949. (Above, left to right) Robert A. Murray (of *The Clique*), Ernest Maggs, Mark Cohen and F.S. Ferguson (Quaritch). (Below, left to right) the Parisian bookseller Pierre Berès, Mme Berès and Ian Grant (John Grant, Edinburgh).

Anatomy of an Antiquarian Bookseller [175×60cm]

t.e.g

Small dent in fore-edge
Lacks headband
Hinges weak
One corner slightly 'bumped'
Dogeared
Slightly worn at head
Spotted
Dentelles nicely tooled
Edges untrimmed
One section loose
Rebacked
New as issued
Lovingly thumbed by former owner
Contents very good
Trifle soiled
Back defective
Spare label tipped in
Slightly split
Some creasing
Spine cracked
fore-edge shaken
Corners rubbed
Leather label
Name on fly
Stitching loose
Original cloth slightly discoloured
Some inkstains
Blank at end
Some foxing
Rear hinges cracked
Tear neatly repaired
signature detached
Joints badly worn
Mottled calf

lower margins frayed
Worn at foot
Running title

61. Ronald Searle's cover illustration for John Grant's Centenary Catalogue, 1974.

Booksellers' Memoirs:
The Truth about the Trade?

MARC VAULBERT DE CHANTILLY

WHILE the British Twentieth-Century Antiquarian Booktrade Memoir is never likely to dance trippingly off the tongue and into the heart of the wider reading public, it does appeal to more than the odd academic. If the scholar wants facts, the journalist wants copy, the fellow bookseller and customer want gossip and the casual reader just wants to be entertained. 'The comedy and pathos of bookselling,' writes Tommy Spencer, 'are homespun threads intermingled in what to some of us is as fascinating as an oriental carpet.'[1]

It is disheartening therefore to find that, viewed from any angle, the standard of such memoirs is not exactly high. 'Things,' as one of the better writers in the field, Fred Snelling, puts it, are 'pretty lean'. Nor should we be surprised. There is no reason why someone who sells books should be able to write them, any more than a picture-dealer needs to know how to paint.

In 1982 Snelling could find only three books on the subject worth mentioning: Spencer's *Forty Years in My Bookshop* (1923), Muir's *Minding My Own Business* (1956), and Low's *'with all faults'* (1973). There was no lack of stories worth telling, the problem was getting the booksellers to put them down on paper. 'They talk it,' Snelling complained, 'but they will never write it. The major part gets forgotten, and lost forever.'[2]

That booksellers like to 'talk it' there can be no doubt: theirs is a business that lends itself to gossip. The 'lore and history' of the trade, Peter Murray Hill observed in the 1950s, 'live mostly in stories told over strong tea in dim back-rooms or over strong ale in country pubs'.[3]

For Hill, the reason why so few stories find their way into print is quite straightforward: booksellers 'are for the most part shy men'. Touching as this vision of faltering diffidence may be, Snelling is probably closer to the mark when he observes, with the libel laws in mind, that 'the best stories are those you daren't relate'.[4]

It need not be fear of anything as grave as legal action which deters publication. 'The integrity of a seller of books,' Fred Bason points out, 'is a very precious thing.'[5] Engaged as they are in a business – as Paul Minet puts it – 'much given to cliques and back-biting',[6] booksellers are jealous of their reputations, and only a fool would risk the antagonism of colleagues for the sake of an anecdote.

A paucity of material forces us to interpret the word 'memoirs' loosely, and to look for any account which emphasizes the human element of the booktrade, which awakens in us a feeling of what it was really like to be a secondhand or antiquarian bookseller in the twentieth century. Viewed in these terms the range of the subject is apt to prove quite bewildering. What is the link between, say, the eight men conducting the fourth settlement at the Ruxley Lodge 'knock-out' of 1919, and an individual setting up a 'commercially-run, technology-based booksearch business' 80 years later? Or, for that matter, between a leading West-End dealer who travels to Austria in the 1930s to buy a Gutenberg bible; a young lad having to sell twelve books on his father's stall in Manchester in the 1940s to pay for his 'butties and tea'; and a woman in the 1970s opening a shop in Elstree with stock so 'pathetic' that she manages just six customers in the first month?[7]

If we cast our net wide enough we may find enlightenment in the most surprising places. A visit to the *Fortean Times* website provides some unexpected comments by the writer Iain Sinclair about guns and drugs during his time in the trade.[8] A book of verse by a Newdigate-Prize-winning poet contains an affectionate memoir of the author by his employer, a Hammersmith bookseller.[9] A list of bookshops in *Time Out's Book of London* (1972)[10] evokes the 'drab, dusty and useless' Charing Cross Road of the 1970s, with Foyles at its centre – a 'dirty and impersonal warehouse masquerading as a bookshop'. Mention of the army of 'young underpaid foreigners' forming the shop's staff brings to mind the story of the Foyles customer 'who asked for *Ulysses* and was told that he had gone to lunch'.[11]

The *Time Out* list also throws up a rare reference to a notable London bookseller:

Henry Pordes is the remainders' King. His blurb says he is interested in 'almost everything'; for him, unusually modest.

A snap judgement, certainly, but also the type of punchy, irreverent, immediate comment – made 'from personal knowledge' – that carries more of a feeling of authenticity about it than any number of quotations from the various 'histories' of the big firms, 'turgid, and constipatedly compiled', as Snelling puts it, 'by "official" and designated biographer-historians'.[12]

We need to be wary of the sort of company histories Snelling has in mind. They have, we must not forget, a palpable design upon us. Their primary purpose is to inspire confidence in whichever long-established, well-run, trustworthy and supremely successful business happens to form their subject.

If one thing is guaranteed to get the reader's back up it is the frequent attempts by such histories to gloss over the everyday realities of business with an appeal to loftier sentiments. The following, from Gilbert Fabes's celebration of the twenty-fifth anniversary of Foyles in 1929, is egregious:

The bookseller places the works of the great thinkers into the hands of the readers, thereby providing the essential link in the chain by which genius may be appreciated, and happiness broadcast, as the result of his work.

Let us therefore accept the genius as a dreamer and the bookseller as a labourer, and we have the most ideal combination to combat the unhappiness of the world, but even so we cannot eliminate the possibility of the bookseller being also a genius.[13]

Faced with this sort of *guff* – and there is no better word for it – our suspicions are naturally aroused that the writer is not dealing fairly with us. And when we are told, later on, that W.A. Foyle (trade nickname: 'With All Faults') is referred to by his staff 'very often, affectionately but secretly, as "Papa"',[14] we are unlikely to feel much inclination to read on.

As head of the rare book department at Foyles, at least Fabes had the excuse of being an employee, but even academics are not immune. In his book on Blackwell's, Sir Arthur Norrington – president of an Oxford college no less – extols 'the Founder' in quasi-religious terms:

His staff learned from him the true Blackwellian attitude to the customer. They learned, also, every detail of their daily work, and they honoured him as a complete bookman and a just and generous employer. He had trained them, like children, in the way that they should go, and he remembered them in his will.[15]

Such encomiums – duplicated in Rita Ricketts's gushing and untidy *Adventurers All* (2002) – are, for our purposes, practically useless. One would far rather read that T.E. Lawrence employed the firm of Bain to clean the camel droppings from the vellum covers of his Kelmscott Press books, or that the founder of Bumpus 'used to deal with book thieves in the good old English fashion of marching them into the inner office, and giving them a sound trouncing at fisticuffs', or even that Aleister Crowley made the entire stock of the Cecil Court bookseller John Watkins disappear into the ether.[16]

It comes as no surprise to find Sir Basil Blackwell – regarded by his rivals as something of a prig – writing in a similarly exalted vein. His entry on J.G. Wilson in the *Oxford Dictionary of National Biography* (2004) strikes an incongruous note. Wilson, we are told in language better suited to a mission statement than a work of reference, regarded bookselling 'not so much as a matter of retail trade as a service in which bookseller and customer met and shared the experience of contact with the precious manifestations of the spirit of man'. And then Wilson banked the cheque.

Company histories make for dull reading but they do have their uses. As vague and badly-written as Fabes's book on Foyles is, it does show how William and Gilbert Foyle used modern advertising methods to exploit the new market for educational books among the aspiring lower middle classes to which themselves belonged. One publicity scam involved the brothers sending the notoriously anti-British mayor of Chicago, 'Big Bill' Thompson, a cable reading 'Can offer high prices for all English Books from the Chicago Public Libraries. Will you negotiate?'[17] The answer, as anticipated, was 'no'. A few years later Adolf Hitler received a similar telegram, offering to save from the pyre all 'German banned books'.[18]

Fabes was presumably speaking for his employers when he dismissed the disapproval felt by many at the use of such techniques: 'Other trades scheme and stunt in all manner of ways, and it is known by the simple phrase of "pushing your wares," but seemingly literature must not be pushed!'[19]

Invaluable as this information about 'the world's greatest bookshop' is, we have begun to stray from the field of book-trade memoir into the neighbouring territory of book-trade history. There is in Fabes's little book perhaps only one passage which carries authenticity: a description of Gilbert Foyle, toiling away in a dust coat at the height of his twenties success, being asked to 'catch hold' by a messenger who had mistaken him for 'one of the lads'.[20]

Fabes had left Foyles by the time the second edition of his book appeared in 1938. The latter part of his career was spent at Rye, whence, shortly after the war, he issued catalogues containing books from Henry James's bomb-damaged Lamb House. After his retirement David Low visited him at Winchelsea, and the two sat together in the railway carriage Fabes had converted into a bookroom. What account, Low wondered, would the first historian of Foyles have given of the firm in the years following his departure?[21]

It would not be hard to improve on the version of events given by Christina Foyle in her father William Foyle's entry in the *Oxford DNB*,[22] a piece which raises once again the wider question of the reliability of sources.

For whatever reason, Christina Foyle seems to have gone to some trouble to write her uncle Gilbert out of the story of W. & G. Foyle Ltd. Nowhere is he mentioned in the description of the firm's origins she gave to the *Oldie* magazine in 1994. Instead we are told that William Foyle 'abandoned the law' in 1904 (in fact he was sacked for incompetence from his job as a clerk) and set up as a bookseller in Cecil Court, where he was soon 'joined by his wife, who shared his passion for books and for dealing, and went on selling him second-hand books after their marriage'. In 1907, the article informs us, husband and wife 'merged forces, moving into their well-known site in Charing Cross Road'.[23]

In the *DNB* Christina Foyle gives a different, but no more accurate, account. 'In 1903,' we read, 'at the age of eighteen, he opened, with his brother Gilbert, a bookshop in Islington, north London.' That, as far as the *DNB* entry on William Foyle is concerned, is the sum total of the involvement of Gilbert Samuel Foyle in the affairs of the company he co-founded and co-owned. Neither his full name nor his dates are given.

If Christina Foyle is to be believed, her uncle played no part in his brother's other activities. She claims, for example, that the formation of the First Edition Club, and the ownership of the seven-ton ketch the *Griffin*, concerned A.J.A. Symons and her father alone. That Gilbert Foyle was party to both ventures is made clear in Julian Symons's biography of his brother, which gives a good description of the 'caution and expansiveness, combined with an unvarying industry' with which William and Gilbert Foyle built up their business. It also contains an amusing account of how William was once knocked almost senseless into the *Griffin*'s hold after being stranded in the North Sea for two days with nothing to eat but potato crisps.[24]

Christina Foyle's own *DNB* entry – by the aptly-named Jason Tomes – is in marked contrast to her father's. It describes the 'famous inefficiencies that eroded Foyles' reputation' under her reign, not least the 'complex sales system reminiscent of communist eastern Europe'. During this period the ability to read Roman numerals was apparently all that was required of the manager of the firm's antiquarian department.[25]

Tomes can be supplemented by Timothy d'Arch Smith's recollections of his time with the company in the 1950s, including the following description of William Foyle in old age:

Long white locks and dilapidated clothing suggested a foreign maestro of the piano exiled without warning to the purlieus of Soho, only a whining accent pitched rather high evincing London, utilitarian, origins.[26]

This is however to stray from the point. If we cannot depend on the *Oxford DNB* to provide a reliable account of a bookseller as celebrated as William Foyle, what source can we trust? A couple of examples may perhaps shed light on the question: first W.T. Spencer and then the celebrated firm of Marks & Co.

Walter Thomas ('Tommy') Spencer of 27 New Oxford Street died, after more than half a century in business, in 1936. His autobiography, *Forty Years in My Bookshop*, appeared thirteen years earlier, and was reprinted twice in two years. For David Low, who admired the book and urged its republication, it is

the story of two great episodes in book collecting – that of the nineteenth-century literary authors in the original parts of their works as published monthly, and of the colour plate book, with the sketches of the collectors who sat in the little Spencer parlour at the back of the shop – the Lords Rosebery and Derby, the wealthy, the English and American, the librarians from all over the world.[27]

Spencer's editor Thomas Moult appears to have been responsible for the book's florid prose, which one reviewer found gave off 'something of the mental aroma of a rare bookshop'.[28] The text – in contrast with such punchy chapter headings as 'My "Millionaire" Bookie and How I Began', 'the Book-Collector who grew too Fat to Collect' and 'The Dickensians who were Afraid of their Wives' – is more Edwardian than Georgian in its unhurried, stilted style.

Low, who visited Spencer's shop in the 1920s, describes it as an 'impressive and frightening' place, its windows 'piled with Dickens, Thackeray, Trollope, and Lever in the original monthly parts, each tied in pink tape'. Inside,

Under the hissing of the gas, a staff of young women were sorting and pulling out these hundreds of folders. It looked chaotic, but there was complete central control of every folder, with these young women able to produce 'Americana', 'Australiana', 'Sporting', 'Literary', or whatever the collectors coming from all over the world, might ask to see.[29]

For many years the owner of this thriving enterprise was, as Moult puts it, 'the chief living authority on Dickens from the collector's standpoint'.[30] 'Dickensiana', Spencer states simply, is 'where my heart is'.[31]

A major source of material was Dickens's sister-in-law Georgina Hogarth, whose acquaintance Spencer made around 1907. She lived beyond her means in Brompton – an excessive liking for cut flowers is mentioned – and was in the habit of sending her maid with Dickensiana to New Oxford Street several times a week. It is from Miss Hogarth that Spencer obtained the manuscript of Dickens's *Cricket on the Hearth* (now in the Pierpont Morgan), an item which, incidentally, she had no right to sell.

Forty Years in My Bookshop is significant, not least because its author's career bridges two centuries. 'I have observed many migrations in my time,' Spencer observes. 'Mr. Quaritch from Piccadilly, Mr. Walford from the Strand, Mr. Rimell from Oxford Street, Mr. Sabin from Garrick Street, Mr. Robson from Coventry Street; and in naming these gentlemen I have recalled only a minority of their number.'[32]

The changes wrought by time make for some interesting contrasts. By the 1920s Spencer was having to deal with a correspondence that included '(such is the influence of a speeded-up civilisation on bookmen) feverish telegrams of enquiry about particular volumes or prints, and perhaps a Marconigram or so'.[33] Before the turn of the century matters had proceeded at a more leisurely pace. Spencer had time for regular Saturday-afternoon strolls with Queen Victoria's dentist, the eccentric Dr Edwin Truman, while Truman's four-wheeled carriage waited outside his shop.[34]

Booksellers love to name-drop, but few could match the array of celebrated customers Spencer is able to muster: Sir Henry Irving, Aubrey Beardsley, Walter Pater, Richard Jefferies, George Gissing, Hugh Walpole and Israel Zangwill. Thomas Hardy features in the story of a dispute over a 'presentation library' assembled for an American customer around 1902 'on behalf of a good cause'. Spencer buys from the 'pathetic, faded' Lady Wilde. ('I said: "What will you take for these, your ladyship?" She answered with splendid indifference, "Whatever you offer, Mr. Spencer, whatever you offer."') Lord Curzon invites him to Carlton House Terrace to view his 'numerous treasures'. Robert Louis Stevenson even writes him a poem:

> I thank you, Spencer, courteous chap,
> For many a volume quaint and neat,
> Which would not have been mine perhaps,
> Had I not known New Oxford Street.[35]

Spencer's memoirs are not a mere roll call of the rich and famous. There is the Pimlico greengrocer who employed a variety of ingenious ruses to smuggle his purchases into his potato store without his wife noticing; and the American bookseller who 'fitted a gag over his nose and mouth every time he entered my shop, to keep the dust out of his lungs'.[36]

What, then, are we to make of *Forty Years in My Bookshop*? For David Low it tells 'the full, rich, Walter Spencer story',[37] but Snelling is not so sure. 'Much of what he knew,' he writes, 'has certainly gone into limbo. Most definitely, some of the best tales I ever heard about Spencer's dealings never got into his book.'[38] As early as 1918 the American collector A. Edward Newton had hinted at an irregularity about those dealings. 'How he does it,' Newton wrote in his *Amenities of Book-Collecting*, 'where he gets them, is his business.'[39]

We can thank John Collins and Timothy d'Arch Smith for clarifying the nature of that business. In *The Two Forgers* (1992) Collins reveals Spencer's ownership of 'a shady country house in the Isle of Wight where indentured young ladies were said to improve plate books with modern colour and engage in other doubtful bibliographical sophistications'.[40] Collins leaves us in no doubt as to these sophistications. 'There was little Spencer did not turn his hand to: bogus provenance (Dr Johnson's teapot; Dickens's chair); books imperfect or made up with facsimiles; modern colouring; facsimile wrappers for his favourite Dickens in parts; and so on.'

D'Arch Smith, who describes his dealings with Spencer's after the firm's relocation to Upper Berkeley Street,[41] has cast a bibliographer's eye over the 'otiose stab-holes' often found in the Dickens part-issues which were its speciality. 'Spencer's back-room workshop', he concludes, was a 'rehabilitation wing for bibliographical cripples', in which ideal copies were 'cobbled together' from defective ones.

D'Arch Smith also suggests that Spencer may have made Georgina Hogarth sign the 'small stack of authentication labels unattached to any memorabilia' now at Dickens House. These, he points out, might just as well have been 'slapped on to a junkshop inkwell or a rickety dining chair'. Similar exercises in creative provenance won Spencer a cameo as 'X' (who 'induced bibliomania by hypnotism and spells')[42] in Wilmarth Lewis's *Collector's Progress* (1951).

Spencer is at pains to emphasize 'the dignity that is undoubtedly a predominant quality in the bookman's enthralling pursuit'.[43] (D'Arch Smith is more honest, and more accurate, when he speaks of the 'unalleviated dullness' of most collectors.[44]) He ends with a tribute to the owner of 'the first private library of its kind in England', 'that most dignified and honoured of book-collectors, Mr. Thomas James Wise'. 'To me,' he writes, 'he has always been a true friend.'[45] In fact the two men loathed one another, Wise characterising Spencer as 'one of those persons who never speak the Truth save by way of accident, or under great provocation'. He had good reason to hold this view: around 1904 Spencer managed to out-Wise him with a forgery of one of his forgeries. Spencer would also seem to be the bookseller whose fake manuscripts Wise boasted about destroying.[46] *Arcades ambo.*

The second of our examples will always be associated with Helene Hanff, whose *84, Charing Cross Road* is the one book about the booktrade everybody knows. Published in America in 1970 and in England the following year, there is clearly something about it that the public likes. There have been theatre and television adaptations and even, in 1984, a Hollywood movie starring Anne Bancroft and Anthony Hopkins. The film's tagline does not inspire confidence in its subtitle of 'A true story': 'She's in love with a place she's never seen. A way of life she's never known. And a man she's never met.'

Whether the film is true to the book is not what interests us: the question is whether the book is true to the firm of Marks & Co. At first glance it is hard to see how it could not be, as it appears to consist of an unmediated transcription of a twenty-year correspondence – some 80 letters between 1949 and 1969. The story is a simple one: brash New Yorker wins over staff of staid London bookshop. Hanff sends food parcels with her orders and together with her books receives a recipe for Yorkshire pudding and an Irish linen tablecloth embroidered with the names of the firm's six employees. Time passes and family and friends get in on the act; but, despite much goodwill on all sides, Hanff never quite manages to make it across the Atlantic before the death in 1969 of her main correspondent, the 'blessed man who sold me all my books',[47] Frank Doel.

While many readers will agree with the writer who described *84, Charing Cross Road* as 'tender and funny and incandescent and beautiful',[48] it is hard to find anyone in the trade with a good word to say about it. Snelling admits it has been 'sneered at' (although 'gimmicky' he finds it 'absolutely absorbing').[49] John Saumarez Smith of Heywood Hill is less complimentary; in his view the book 'has a lot to answer for'. The notorious Driffield, adopting his customary extreme position, describes it as a 'classic example of American naivety, gaucheness, infantile exuberance, loggorhea [sic] and total inability to perceive anybody else's point of view'.[50] More valuable is the opinion of the Cecil Court veteran Bill Fletcher:

Helene Hanff glamorized everything. That's her prerogative. But I know Charing Cross Road and Marks & Co. intimately, and the book just doesn't ring true. (That's all I'm saying in print!)[51]

This intriguing comment poses a problem with which we are fast becoming familiar: how to arrive at that truth the unprintable nature of which Fletcher can only hint at?

The best place to start is Andrew Block's *Short History of the Principal London Antiquarian Booksellers and Book-Auctioneers* (1933). Of the 58 firms listed there, Marks & Co. was one of six that wrote their own entries.[52] From it we learn that 'B. Marks and M. Cohen (trading as Marks & Co.)' both entered the trade in 1904. They spent twelve years together at Sotheran's, and became 'inseparable friends'. From Sotheran's they progressed via a small warehouse in Old Compton Street to first-floor offices at 108 Charing Cross Road, before taking over the neighbouring business of the Dickens specialist George W. Davis. In 1930, on the expiration of the lease, the business moved to its celebrated premises.

The size of the operation is unexpected: ground floor, basement and four upper floors. David Magee recalled the enormous tabby that sat in the unchanging window display.[53] Raymond Kilgarriff was struck by the number of employees:

I was always surprised at the size of the Marks staff, although wages then were nearly negligible. Prior to the outbreak of war there must have been a half dozen male 'assistants' as they were called, in addition to the principals and female office staff. They seem to have worked very long hours. Always to 6 or 7 p.m. and before Christmas and at other busy times the shop would remain open until 10 p.m.[54]

David Low, who dealt with the firm for 40 years, could not be more complimentary. Marks & Co. was not only 'the most complete bookshop in the road', but also 'the fairest, no-nonsense bookshop I ever knew'. He provides a partial floor plan: ground floor, 'with cloth for the browsers' (and Ben Marks at the far end reading *The Times* – 'I never saw him doing anything else'); basement with library bindings; first editions and handsomely bound sets on the first floor; 'Freemasonry and less obvious Rariora' on the second; topography and unpriced items on the third.[55]

Snelling found the shop's stock dull and tatty: his interest lay in the personnel. Mark Cohen was 'a swarthy, bald-headed and bespectacled gentleman of Jewish extraction', with 'a perennial pipe in his mouth and a fund of reminiscence and bibliographical erudition forever on his lips'. The firm's packer – known only as 'Pat' – 'was "butch" in the extreme in his appearance, but as fluffy and feminine in his actions as any girl'. He cleared auctions in a 'powder blue suit of tight and advanced cut'. Doel – 'a very quiet and unassuming chap', came across as 'a rather dull and dry old stick'. The 'whole of the antiquarian book trade turned out' for his funeral in 1969.[56]

Anthony Rota recalls Cohen and his Charing Cross Road neighbour Jack Joseph at the major London auctions of the 1950s, sitting 'staunchly side by side through the whole of every sale, snapping up any unconsidered trifles that the other players let fall'.[57] Between them the pair would buy every copy of *Encyclopaedia Britannica*. 'There was,' according to the Cecil Court bookseller Norman Storey, 'a saying in the trade that a set of books was either a Joseph or a Marks set. A Joseph set had to be immaculate, but a Marks set could have a bit of damage.'[58]

Rota – who finds it curious that a 'great man' like Cohen should have wasted his time saving the string from incoming parcels – remembers with gratitude the 'gentle' Doel's willingness to place his 'amazing memory' and 'incredibly wide knowledge of books and booksellers' at the disposal of his friends in the trade, 'absolutely free of charge'.[59]

Doel was a leading member of the 'Bibliomites' (the Society of Antiquarian Booksellers' Employees) – a benevolent society for 'booksellers' assistants' set up in 1950 along the lines of a 'First Assistants Association' of the 1920s – and he regularly acted as umpire at their annual cricket match against the 'guv'nors'. In 1958, having served as treasurer, he was elected president, his vice-president being another Marks employee: George Plummer, the head of the firm's 'Occult and Masonic Department'.

Plummer – who does not feature in Hanff's book – was a respected figure, giving talks on bibliography at Bibliomite meetings. His obituary in the March 1960 issue of the Society's bulletin *Biblionotes* is interesting for its use of the word 'collector' in a sense now obsolete: that of an employee responsible for the collection of purchases.

Like most assistants of his generation, George came up the hard way, shop-boy, errand-boy, collector, etc. for a meagre few shillings a week, but keeping eyes and ears well open; he gradually acquired knowledge, and became one of the best assistants in the trade.[60]

Fresh information about Marks & Co. is to be found on an enthusiastic website set up in 2003 by Steve Maggs.[61] This is a useful if uncritical contribution, with some good photographs, and interviewees including Doel's elder daughter Sheila Wheeler, and one would like to see it preserved in a more permanent form. From Maggs we learn that Hanff used pseudonyms for several Marks employees: 'Daphne Carr' for Cecily Farr; 'Megan Wells' for Doreen Wellsbury; and 'Bill Humphries' for Pat the packer, whose surname turns out to have been Hynes.

When Hanff finally reached England in 1971 Doel's widow held a party, at which Hanff was informed by 'the rare-book dealers' that 'after the war there were too many books and not enough bookshop space, so all the dealers in London BURIED hundreds of old books in the open bomb craters of London streets'.[62]

On the same trip Hanff made the acquaintance of Marks's son Leo, whom she describes as 'a TV and film writer'.[63] While Leo Marks certainly was those things (he wrote the script of Michael Powell's *Peeping Tom*) his main achievement was as chief cryptographer with the Special Operations Executive. It is his book *Between Silk and Cyanide: The Story of SOE's Code War* (1998) which decodes Fletcher's hint and explodes what he calls 'the gentle little myth by Helene Hanff'.[64]

Born into a milieu of successful Jewish booksellers – his grandfather was Jack Joseph's father Emanuel, and his cousins the Myers family of Bond Street – Leo Marks was trained up to the trade. One piece of advice he received was that a good bookseller strums, rather than turns, the pages of a book.[65] Another lesson was the 'one trick' for which his father was 'infamous':

Whenever he was ready to bid for a library he'd conceal two pieces of paper with a different offer written on each. He'd then invite the vendor to write down what he thought his library was worth while he pretended to do the same. As soon as he saw the vendor's estimate, he'd produce whichever piece of paper was closest to it, and the deal was done.[66]

Many firms used substitution codes to note down at the back of their more valuable books the cost, and it was this practice which helped awaken Leo Marks's interest in cryptography. After breaking the Marks & Co. code at the age of eight, he turned his attention to those of his relatives, whose profit margins, he discovered, were even greater than his father's.

Marks gives a vivid description of 84 Charing Cross Road, from the unmanned basement concealed by a door covered in book spines, to the 'war room' on the fourth floor, where the firm engaged in distinctly Spencer-like activities:

Everything in it was locked away in bookcases whose doors it was impossible to see through. Behind the dark glass were thousands of coloured plates, title-pages and frontis-pieces – spare parts which could be transplanted into any book which needed them.[67]

According to his son, Ben Marks and his partner 'made one perfect bookseller': Marks providing 'the acumen' and Cohen – ABA president in 1943 – 'the knowledge'. The pair worked together for twenty years without a written agreement.[68]

Marks & Co.'s customers included Charlie Chaplin, Bernard Shaw, Field Marshal Alanbrooke (who addressed his letters to 'Dear Ben'), Michael Foot and an unnamed member of the royal family, who 'liked his pornography bound in vellum'. Freud visited the shop while writing *Moses and Monotheism*. Too ill to climb the stairs to Plummer's department, he sat in a chair pulled out for him by J.B. Priestley, while Doel carried down books for him to see.[69]

The financier Clarence Hatry purchased most of his huge library from the firm. Following Hatry's exposure as a fraudster in the 1920s, Marks – a fellow freemason – bought the books back at a considerable loss, and pulled strings to have him made prison librarian. Hatry would go on to acquire the 'Royal Family's favourite bookshop', Hatchard's of Piccadilly. It is unclear whether he was still in control of the company in 1955, the year it took over the book-wholesaler Simpkin Marshall, following the latter firm's collapse under an even greater crook, Robert Maxwell. (The 'bouncing Czech' must surely be one of the more surprising members of the trade. Paul Minet recalls 'I. R. Maxwell and Co.' dealing in secondhand books from Fitzroy Square.)[70]

Leo Marks, we are told, 'kept secrets as well as any man'.[71] There is one secret in particular which we are fortunate he has chosen to divulge. The story – which can be dated to between 1948 and 1955 – concerns the surgeon Evan Bedford, who bequeathed his cardiological library to the Royal College of Physicians. Unable to attend an auction at Hodgson's, Bedford asked Doel to bid up to £300 on his behalf for an edition of Harvey's *De motu cordis*. Finding that the book had sold to another dealer for £200 he rang Doel at home, demanding an explanation. What Bedford could not know was that Marks & Co. were 'kings of the book ring', one of five firms who regularly engaged in the illegal activity of auction rigging. When a distracted Doel let slip that the book had sold at the knock-out for £650 a furious Bedford had the matter raised in parliament. We will let Marks finish the story.

The then editor of *The Times Literary Supplement*, himself a collector of rare books, was anxious to avoid a scandal and invited the five leading firms of antiquarian booksellers to sign an undertaking that they would take whatever steps they thought necessary to put an immediate stop to the book ring – if such a thing existed. The Big Five arrived at the editor's office a quarter of an hour earlier than expected and, whilst waiting to sign the undertaking, held a knock-out in the ante-room. It was far better security for them than a Lyons tea shop and the tea was free.

I asked the normally discreet Frank why he'd told a client about the book ring.

'Well, you see,' he said, 'when the phone rang the wife and me were having a jolly good fuck in front of the fire.' He hesitated. 'And I don't think too well on my back.'[72]

It is good to see Doel receiving some satisfaction in the position of underbidder.

The names of the 'Big Five' are easily discovered. In 1951 Doel told Hanff he had been 'chasing round the country in and out of various stately homes of

England trying to buy a few books to fill up our sadly depleted stock'.[73] Four decades later the Guildford bookseller Charles Traylen (dubbed by *The Times* 'the last of a breed of grandees of the trade')[74] reminisced to Sheila Markham about those trips, ruffling a few ABA feathers in the process:

When I was at Thorp's and later on my own, I used to go to several auctions a week, racing all over the country with a group of buddies – Bernard Simpson from Joseph's, Frank Doel of 84, Charing Cross Road, Johnnie Watson from Quaritch [who began his career with Marks & Co.], Charlie Harris from Francis Edwards, and my great friend, Frank Hammond. I drove the car, and they all crammed in with all the books. We thought nothing of doing a morning sale in East Anglia and then tearing over to Hereford in the afternoon.

We always viewed the books together and told each other about any discrepancies. When it came to bidding, we had a little arrangement.[75]

Traylen's handwritten calculations survive,[76] showing that as late as 1963 the same firms – without Quaritch but with the addition of Thorp and Dawson – continued in their 'little arrangement' of auction ringing.

It is a relief to turn from the seamier side of the trade to happier examples. There is no reason to doubt Richard Goffin's description of Harry Pratley of Hall's Bookshop as 'an extremely loveable man' from whom 'benevolence radiated',[77] or to question Bertram Rota's account, given two years before his death, of his own 'happy life amongst books, rich in interest and in daily discoveries, made entrancing by friendships amongst colleagues at home and abroad'.[78]

Two notices in *The Times* bear witness to the respect in which Rota was held. The military historian Basil Liddell Hart describes him as a 'deeply wise man' with a 'sense of integrity', while the critic Edward Lucie-Smith recalls his 'gentleness and humour', adding that 'those who have laughed with him will not quickly forget his gift for the appropriate anecdote'.[79]

As for Pratley – whom Rota's son Anthony remembers as 'a saintly man, loved by all who came to know him'[80] – his kindly nature comes across in a slight production worked up from tape-recorded reminiscences made shortly before his death in 1987.

Born in 1905, Pratley was apprenticed as a fourteen year-old orphan to a Tunbridge Wells bookseller named Reuben Hall, a 'dour Nonconformist' who, despite keeping no accounts, had prospered in business over two decades.

Looking back Pratley considered himself unique in the trade in having been legally indentured for four years ('A very grand document it was too'). The wages, as he recalled, 'were absolutely pitiful':

I was to be offered seven shillings a week for the first year [1919], ten shillings for the second year, fifteen shillings for the third year and one pound for the fourth year. But it was that or nothing.[81]

(To put this in context, in 1920 Charles Traylen was earning seven and six a week working in Cambridge for Galloway and Porter, while in 1932 the oriental bookseller Arthur Probsthain could point out that – unlike 'the young generation'

– he had served a formal apprenticeship: 'three years' work without pay' in Germany at the end of the nineteenth century.)[82]

To transport his books Hall employed a licensed station porter, in crimson hat with brass lettering, who pushed his costermonger's cart with its waterproof sheet to and from villages as far as six miles away. Before the internal combustion engine such carts were in general use for transporting books. Around 1906 one of the 'hardest and heaviest tasks' Walter Harris had to perform for his employer the London bookseller James Westall was the clearing of purchases from the salerooms: they

had to be trundled back in an old Coster barrow, hired at fourpence an hour from a firm in Drury Lane. These barrows, even when loaded, were very easily handled on the level, but negotiating one up the inclines of Drury Lane, Chancery Lane, or Charing Cross Road, needed the strength of a horse.[83]

Pratley grew too frail to continue and his account ends abruptly. A similarly cheerful and fragmentary memoir of the provincial trade is given by George A. Wheeler, whose 'random recollections' describe his employment by George Gregory of Bath six decades earlier, loading books into sacks in a rat-infested cellar for sale at the rate of 12s.6d. per hundredweight. A three-volume manuscript catalogue of the Cotton library was once found among the rubbish.

Returning from the provinces we find the origins of Bertram Rota Ltd equally humble. Rota's grandfather Bertram Dobell was born in 1842. The son of a journeyman tailor, he began life as a grocer's errand boy. Around the age of 30 he broke free from 'a thankless and sordid trade'[84] and set up as a newsagent in Kentish Town. Fifteen years later he opened the first of two bookshops in the newly-built Charing Cross Road. It was here, in 1901, that he played the lead in what he calls 'the battle of the bookstalls'.

In the 1870s and 1880s the Charing Cross Road had been carved through what Dobell describes as 'a congeries of mean and squalid streets'.[85] It was, as a local councillor conceded in 1902, 'one of the ugliest thoroughfares in London';[86] 'a fine example', in Dobell's view, 'of the way how not to do it'. The turn of the century saw an influx of booksellers, including several displaced when the old 'Booksellers' Row' – Holywell Street – was demolished to make way for the Aldwych. The bookshops were generally considered the new street's sole attraction, but in the opinion of Westminster City Council their outside stalls – seven or eight in number – caused an obstruction.

In response to council pressure Dobell reduced the size of his stalls so that they projected only a few inches over the building line. When this proved insufficient he dug in his heels on principle. 'The matter in itself,' he explains, 'was of little importance to me, since my bookstall trade is only a small part of my business.' The Council now decided to make an example of him and brought the case to court. The resulting fine of one shilling was hardly a triumph for the authorities, and here they let the matter rest. Dobell gives a brief account of the affair, with extracts from the newspapers, in a supplement to his hundredth catalogue.

The story is used by David Low as the starting point of his *'with all faults'*.

Dobell's friendship with the chemist Samuel Bradbury – himself the author of a slight piece entitled *Bertram Dobell: Bookseller and Man of Letters* (1909) – is the subject of a recent article. As much for his scholarship as his bookselling, Dobell is also accorded an entry – by his great-grandson Anthony Rota – in the *Oxford DNB*.

On Dobell's death in 1914 his business passed to his sons Percy and Arthur. Percy Dobell's diary forms the basis of Arthur and Janet Freeman's meticulous reconstruction of a ringed country-house sale, *Anatomy of an Auction: Rare Books at Ruxley Lodge 1919* (1990). From the Freemans we learn that Percy Dobell was one of the eight dealers left in the fourth and final settlement of a ring whose 80 and more members (around 50 'town' and 30 'country') saw to it that the treasures of Lord Foley's library – including the four Shakespeare folios – were auctioned at a fraction of their value.

The year before the Ruxley Lodge sale the Dobell brothers took their nephew Cyril Bertram Rota into the business. 'Give us your boy,' they told his mother, 'and we will teach him all we know.'[87]

It was while trying to execute his uncles' bids at his first auction that Rota was introduced to the ring:

When the first Lot marked came up, he took a deep breath, looked up at the auctioneer and opened his mouth to call out. Suddenly he felt an excruciating pain in his foot. He looked down and found that one of the Joseph family was standing on his toe. 'You do your bidding in the public house afterwards, young man, and if you're lucky you'll get a poached egg on toast for your tea.'[88]

In 1923, after a four-year apprenticeship, the nineteen-year-old Bertram Rota set up on his own, viewing auctions in his lunch hour and earning extra money by playing drums in a dance band after work.

The business took time to recover from the loss of stock through enemy action during the Second World War, but by the time Anthony Rota joined in 1952, it was employing five people in John Lane's Bodley House in Vigo Street.

The younger Rota is sensitive to accusations of preferential treatment. He was only allowed to catalogue his first collection after stints dusting the stock and drafting correspondence, his training also involving standing in the rain in Sackville Street until he had correctly identified the bindings in Sotheran's window.

Rota's was one of the main British firms to benefit from the 'learning explosion' of the 1950s and early 1960s. Links with several North American institutions were strengthened by annual trips across the Atlantic. 'Many good books seemed to be coming onto the market,' Anthony Rota recalls, 'and the appetite for them among university libraries seemed insatiable.'[89]

On his father's death in 1966 Anthony Rota inherited a staff of fifteen and spacious premises in Savile Row. He tells his story in *Books in the Blood* (2002).

A past-president of both the ABA and ILAB, Rota has more than a touch of the head prefect about him. By his own account he likes the sound of his own voice, enjoys committee work, and can never resist telling 'the other side' they have 'got everything wrong'; but on reading his autobiography three qualities shine through: his sense of duty, his loyalty to his friends and to his father's memory, and his relish for the trade in which he has been employed for half a century. 'Oh I am sure I could have made more money in other fields,' he exclaims, 'but what other jobs could have brought me such unalloyed pleasure – pleasure in the materials I deal in and in the people I work with?'[90]

'Such,' Rota writes in his diary, 'is my life: aching back and dirty shirt cuffs – and I love it.' No other memoir gives such a clear impression of the physical side of the trade. Working with rare books is, he declares, 'no job for weaklings'. Assistants 'must be able to bench-press at least 200 lbs'. He yearns for the days when, on the arrival of a container-load of books, 'word seemed to spread round the firm like wildfire and all the cataloguers, together with the man who kept the accounts, would strip off their jackets, roll up their shirtsleeves and set to'.[91]

One passage neatly exemplifies Rota's nostalgia for the more rigidly hierarchical past. He describes a typical 1950s Sotheby's or Hodgson's sale, with the auctioneer's rostrum 'at the head of a pound, or inverted horseshoe', bounded by the tables at which the dealers were seated 'in strict accordance with custom and protocol'. 'Indeed,' he writes, 'places could be said to pass from father to son, rather like the privileges that went with a porter's badge at Billingsgate fish market.'[92]

Rota devotes a chapter to changes in packing materials, from the 1950s – when the firm 'kept supplies of three kinds of string' – to the 'advent of bubble wrap'. As for the parcels themselves, 'there are few sights finer', he declares, 'than large quantities of them being loaded into the Post Office van in response to orders brought in by the publication of a new catalogue'.[93]

Some dealers, he finds, are not so well-organized. On buying out rival modern-first specialists Frank Hollings, Rota asks the proprietor A.T. Miller to explain the system by which the firm's stock is arranged. 'The system,' Miller replies, 'is that if I buy a short fat book I look for a short fat hole on the shelf.'[94]

From first to last Rota comes across as high-minded to the point of quixotism. 'Ethics and etiquette' are, he declares, 'two subjects close to my heart'. A staunch opponent of the ring, it was his habit during his ABA presidency to warn off those he 'suspected of illegal bidding' at private meetings – a practice which must have met with much the same response as greeted the Bishop's sermon in Browning's 'Holy-Cross Day'.[95]

Friendship can on occasion conflict with Rota's quest for 'the highest ethical standards'. In the dispute between the Parisian bookseller Fernand de Nobele and one of his own assistants, most readers will feel that Rota should have sided with the assistant.[96] And then there is Jake Schwartz, New York dentist turned London bookseller, who, 'in the days when auctioneers at Sotheby's wore black jackets and sponge-bag trousers, and when jackets and ties were *de rigueur* for bidders', arrived at an auction 'in a sports shirt, aquamarine towelling shorts and open-toed sandals worn sockless'.[97] From the stories Rota tells it seems doubtful that he and his father would have been as forgiving if Schwartz had been a less engaging character.

Rota's association with fellow modern-first dealer George Sims was a more straightforward affair. Around 1960,[98] and trailed by an advertisement in the *Irish Times*, the pair went on a buying trip to Dublin. Their greatest success was at the house of the widow of the writer James Starkey ('Seumas O'Sullivan'), where – despite a previous visit from Percy Muir, who had sent home his purchases by goods wagon – they made a number of discoveries.

Sims's story can be pieced together from the four volumes of his essays ending with *A Life in Catalogues* (1994). Lacking what he calls 'sociability', he dealt from his Berkshire home, issuing a hundred and seven catalogues between 1948 and 1987.

Sims was a young soldier around the end of the Second World War when he came across two books that were to influence his future career: A.J.A. Symons's *Quest for Corvo* and the second series of Percy Muir's *Points*. 'Messrs. Muir & Symons', he recalls,

fostered in me the illusion that antiquarian bookselling largely consisted of literary detection, the tracking down of unsuspected sources for rare books, salvaging manuscripts from attics and 'rat-haunted cellars', but with some leisurely periods of more scholarly investigations.[99]

On discharge Sims took a job with a Harrow bookseller called Len Westwood, but soon realized he was not cut out for shop work: 'my ambition was to model a business on that of Elkin Mathews and issue catalogues from a country retreat'.[100] The next eighteen months were spent learning as much as possible from Westwood, whose 'sober, scrupulously correct appearance … masked an anarchic comic spirit',[101] and from the dealers who visited his shop. These included Bill Fletcher, and the runner Harry Mushlin, who acted as a 'Dutch Uncle' and became a close friend.

Sims issued his first catalogue from a room in his parents' house. It was followed by a series of excellent private buys. As he recalled, 'One contact seemed to lead effortlessly to another so that I rarely had to attend auction sales or search through another dealer's stock.'[102]

Sims's success did not go unobserved. In 1951 he was informed that a bookseller in London's Gloucester Road wanted to see him.

Entering Ivor Poole's office I found that Philip Pearce of the Beauchamp Bookshop was already there, just nodding in my direction but saying nothing. Poole wasted no time – he told me that the modern rare book & first edition market was very small and already had enough dealers in it: he mentioned Bertram Rota, the Beauchamp Bookshop, Frank Hollings, Heywood Hill and Elkin Mathews Ltd. He made it clear that there was no room in it for me. I found it hard to credit that he was actually asking me to leave the book business; I had worked hard for four years to build my business, and I had a wife and two small children to support. I thought of succinctly refusing with one of my father's favourite swear words but decided against it, shrugged silently and left the Poole premises.[103]

Clearly not a suitable candidate for a porter's badge.

Sims found a warmer welcome elsewhere. One dealer about whom he reminisces – as does the Thackeray scholar Gordon N. Ray[104] – is Norman Colbeck, whose large stock ('rivalling that of major bookshops') filled two houses in Bournemouth. Colbeck was for many years one of the more active figures at country-house sales. He once found himself the sole bookseller at an auction in a cottage on the Isle of Wight, 'where there were only some ten bundles of books on a bedroom floor, but where not one title-page was dated later than 1625'.[105] Colbeck retired from the trade in 1967 and followed his private collection of 50,000 books to the University of British Columbia.

In the 1920s, while managing the Rare Book Room at Foyles, Colbeck dealt with the author and *bon vivant* A.J.A. Symons – an associate, as we have seen, of the Foyle brothers. Like Wise before him, Symons dabbled in bookselling, to the extent that it may for some years have provided his principal source of income. He summed up his business philosophy in verse:

> When Mr. Symons buys a book
> He buys it cheap, or not at all.
> He sells it, and the price is tall.[106]

(As fond of 'a big mark-up' – and just as brazen – was Antony Rota's friend Boris Harding-Edgar: 'Book collecting is a disease and I am the doctor. It is a very expensive cure'.)[107]

Symons's *Quest for Corvo* (1934) begins in the back garden of 'The Bungalow at 8 Abercorn Place', St John's Wood, London – home to a figure eccentric even by bookselling standards, Christopher Sclater Millard, the subject of a lacklustre biography by Montgomery Hyde.

A Roman Catholic homosexual socialist and Jacobite, whose will directed that 'The Red Flag' be sung over his grave, Millard turned to bookselling in 1919, following his release from Wormwood Scrubs Prison at the end of a second sentence for gross indecency, the two incidents involving a total of three boys, two youths, two army officers and a priest.

In the eight years before Millard's death in 1927, 'The Bungalow' saw the production of sixteen catalogues, strong in Wildeana – Millard was Wilde's bibliographer under the name Stuart Mason – and peppered with entertaining and informative comments. It was from Millard that Symons obtained Baron Corvo's notorious 'Venice letters', and the purchase exemplifies his 'buy small, sell tall' philosophy. Having acquired the correspondence at a drastic reduction, Symons sold it at a ten-times mark-up to the honours-broker and putative murderer Maundy Gregory.

Although he now considers *The Quest for Corvo*'s subject 'irretrievably second-rate' and 'probably insane', in his youth Timothy d'Arch Smith was inspired, like Sims before him, by the book's 'hypnotic features'.[108] As camp as a row of tent pegs, and written in a style so convoluted that it makes Henry James look like the Revd Wilbert Audry, d'Arch Smith's own memoir *The Times Deceas'd* – a gossipy account of his period as manager of the rare book department of the *Times* Bookshop during the 1960s – has upset those of its readers who would rather not be told that the founder of the booktrade journal the *Clique*, Francis Edwin Murray, was a purveyor of pederastic literature, and that the married curator of the Berg Collection, John Gordan, visited gay bars while on London buying trips. D'Arch Smith's book is nevertheless an entertaining description of its author's efforts to smuggle a little decadence and 'New Bibliography' into an ailing British institution. The following depiction of some 1950s Charing Cross Road and Cecil Court booksellers – 'graceless of manner and unsightly of aspect' – is a fair example of his style.

Cohen of Marks looked like an ill-conditioned mole planning subterranean damage on a wide scale. Jack Joseph cast himself in a mould of unamiable buffoonery after the image of Mr Punch whom he much resembled, Punch knocking on a fair bit more than in puppet representation, that in itself never especially youthful. His brother Sam possessed the temperament and physique of a nightclub bouncer. Harold Storey's vegetative moustache endowed its owner with the air of a suicidally inclined grocer contemplating a trading period of deep financial recession.[109]

Millard frequented the Plough pub in Little Russell Street, a favourite with the Bloomsbury set and near to the London premises of Davis & Orioli, a firm with which he did occasional business. Sharing his sexual – if not his literary – proclivities, Giuseppe ('Pino') Orioli is the author of a necessarily coy memoir entitled *Adventures of a Bookseller* (1938). This was presumably aimed at a similar market to *The Early Life and Vicissitudes of Jack Smithers* (1939), a work dismissed by its publisher Martin Secker 'in an apt, succinct phrase', in which the passages dealing with the author's father the 'decadent' publisher and bookseller Leonard Smithers are, Sims observes, 'based on very vague memories'.[110]

Richard Aldington's claim, in his disappointing *Pinorman* (1954),[111] that Orioli's autobiography was ghosted by his companion Norman Douglas, is supported by a comparison of the book's description of 'the first autochthonous Anglo-Saxon I had had occasion to study at close quarters' with an undoubted example of Orioli's prose, a diary entry describing how, after an act of bestiality, Douglas 'farted so lowdely that it frighten the dog'.[112]

The son of a pork-butcher, Orioli was born in Italy in 1884. In 1907 he travelled to London, where he found employment as an umbrella-mender, a street-singer and the back end of a pantomime cow. At the front was an Italian named Gilodi, who during the day ran a bookshop without shelves in Wardour Street, its 'rubbishy books piled up in mountainous masses against the walls'. Gilodi's 'singular speciality' was odd volumes and incomplete sets, acquired for a pittance from the stalls in Farringdon Road, and quoted to advertisers in *The Clique* and *Publishers' Circular*.[113] Seeing in him a future bookseller, Gilodi introduced Orioli to the celebrated Voynich.

Wilfrid Michael Voynich is dealt with elsewhere in this volume. Two of his cataloguers have left admiring accounts: Walter Garland, whose piece in *Library World* is more matter-of-fact (it is preceded by an equally businesslike account of the firm of J. & J. Leighton by its managing director H.W. Davies), and Emily Millicent Sowerby, whose *Rare People and Rare Books* (1967) is a faux-naïf tongue-in-cheek attempt to defend Voynich's assertion that the rare book trade is no place for a woman. Sowerby has a fine ear for dialogue, and conveys Voynich's distinctive style with such phrases as 'Oh, did she went?', 'By mistake they sent me skunk' and 'As for you, Mees Sowerby, you are *eempossible*'.[114]

Sowerby's subsequent employment as a Sotheby's cataloguer was, as Frank Herrmann puts it, a 'wartime expedient'.[115] She was made to wear 'a most unbecoming dark blue overall', and to promise never to 'catch a man's eye' deliberately. Her tasks included the examination of returned items, some of them rendered 'temporarily imperfect' for cheaper repurchase. She soon learnt which dealers were involved: one removed plates with a piece of wet string (a method still in use in the 1970s),[116] and another 'was considered to have the finest set of tools for making wormholes of anyone in the trade'.[117]

During her eighteen months with Voynich between 1912 and 1914 Sowerby developed an affection for him bordering on hero-worship, and she was displeased to read that Orioli did not share her recollection of his 'great Norwegian god-like appearance'.[118]

At the time of his meeting with the man he remembers as a 'bent kind of creature' Orioli's chief employment was as a teacher of Italian.[119] His pupils included Dr Crippen and an undergraduate named Irving Davis, who agreed to open a bookshop with him once he had taken his degree. Orioli paid frequent visits to Davis at Cambridge, where he learned a good deal by observing the French bookseller Gustave David, who merits his own digression.

David settled in Cambridge in the 1890s, and ran a bookstall there from 1898 until his death in 1936. The greater part of his stock came from London, where he attended the Thursday sales at Hodgson's and Sotheby's. Shrewd rather than knowledgeable, he dispensed bargains to generations of academic customers including J.M. Keynes, Lord Rothschild and that modern-day Heber, C.K. Ogden, who formed a syndicate to buy the books stored by the bookseller in two cottages. David was honoured with a 'gala luncheon' at Trinity College, and a posthumous book of 'appreciations' by Quiller-Couch and others.

In 1910, after a brief partnership with an Italian ex-anarchist named Barberi, owner of the Polyglot Library in the Charing Cross Road, Orioli opened a bookshop in Florence with Davis. In 1913 the pair argued over the same 'creature' and returned to London, where they set up in Museum Street.

The firm had begun to make a name for itself when war was declared. 'Little by little our clients dropped off,' Orioli recalls, 'partly in order to economize their means and partly because they were drafted into the army. Books were becoming luxuries.' Orioli was called up, Davis set to work in the same War Office department as Millard, and the shop was left in the hands of R.A. Peddie, who had previously catalogued for Voynich. After the war trade revived, but in 1920 – at the 'highest point of prosperity' – Orioli grew tired of the partnership and returned to Italy, setting up on his own in Florence.[120]

Irving Davis continued to trade under the name Davis & Orioli until his death in 1967. One can only regret that this fascinating figure – quite capable of absent-mindedly throwing the morning's correspondence, cheques and all, into the waste-paper basket – did not live to complete the autobiographical fragments which accompany his *Catalan Cookery Book* (1999). The editor of that volume Patience Gray remembers Davis as a gourmet and a friend in *Honey from a Weed* (1986).

H.A. Feisenberger numbered Davis among 'a remarkable circle of London dealers, many of Continental origin, led by the greatest scholar of them all, E.P. Goldschmidt, whose knowledge was based on an unequalled experience of the splendid books they had seen over more than 50 years all over Europe during a period when the supply of fine books seemed almost unlimited, a time which has now passed for ever'.[121] A 'strange, original figure', Goldschmidt was, in Percy Muir's view, 'something new in the English antiquarian trade' – a bookselling scholar.[122]

A regular at the Saturday 'bibliographers' teas' held by Goldschmidt and other bookmen at a restaurant in New Oxford Street was Andrew Block – to *The Times* 'the doyen of London booksellers';[123] and to Driffield, 'the apotheosis of all a bookseller should be, all that people imagine and all that a customer could want'. (Elsewhere Driffield remarks: 'I've always had a soft spot for Mr. Block ever since he told me that not everybody in the ABA was a bastard, but all the bastards he met were in the ABA.')[124]

Andrew Block was a bookseller for three-quarters of the twentieth century, a record only surpassed – although Joseph Allen, Maurice Ettinghausen and Albi Rosenthal come close – by Charles Traylen's 80 years in the trade. For the last three decades his assistant was Meg Kidd, whose *Four Book Walls* (1997) gives an intimate portrayal of her exasperating employer and friend: loud, enthusiastic and opinionated; as theatrical as the books in which he dealt. Essays by Block's customers Edward Craig and David Robinson accompany Kidd's account, and the book's illustrations include some taken from the first of two volumes of photographs of nineteen London bookshops by Richard Brown, a work which also contains a 'broad conspectus' of the 1920s London trade by Percy Muir, and articles by Stanley Brett which call to mind Block's groundbreaking *Short History* four decades before.

The striking feature of Block's Barter Street shop was, as *The Times* explained,

the mountainous, slithering heap of disintegrating brown paper folders which house, Block claimed, a million items of ephemera – playbills, programmes, billheads, prints, postcards, newspaper cuttings, a treasury of reference and nostalgia.[125]

It was Block's boast that any item could be plucked from the seeming chaos within two minutes.

The Walworth 'book barrow bloke' Fred Bason is another London character. While not quite the 'modern Samuel Pepys' he believed himself to be, Bason wrote with humour and spirit, and the selections from his diary published with introductions by Nicolas Bentley, L.A.G. Strong, Michael Sadleir and Noel Coward met with deserved success. There is, as Sadleir points out, an 'underlying pathos' about this working-class South Londoner who, for two of his five decades in the trade, dragged his barrow from Walworth to Bermondsey Market, where he stood in all weathers selling books from the gutter.

Bason's career began in 1923 when, aged fifteen, he did so well touting jumble-sale purchases along the Charing Cross Road that he threw in a job as a carpenter's mate. A lifelong collector of autographs – he amassed at least 12,000 – Bason cultivated celebrities, and after seven years as a runner the sale to Jake Schwartz of a collection of books inscribed by Somerset Maugham allowed him to open a small shop in Camberwell. With the depression he lost heavily on de luxe signed editions of Francis Brett Young and Martin Armstrong. In 1939 he shut up shop, but the start of the war gave trade a 'needed flip up', and he invested in 'books that, because of the blitz, folks were selling for a song'. In 1941 his own home was bombed, and a year later he suffered a nervous breakdown. Thereafter his writing brought him some fame but not, it would seem, much money.[126]

The war dealt the London trade its share of punishment. In 1940 a bomb killed Leslie Chaundy of Dulau's and blew his stock all over Dover Street.[127] The following year Thomas Thorp's Jermyn Street premises were hit, and every book destroyed.[128] By 1943 Batsford's – whose antiquarian department specialized in architecture and the fine arts – had lost, from the bombing of its warehouses, 'no fewer than 250,000 precious volumes', many of them 'quite irreplaceable'.[129] When Arnold Haskell's house was hit, Maggs were asked to recover the books. On querying the absence of a bill, Haskell was told 'It is no part of our business to profit from the misfortunes of others'.[130]

Something of the wartime mood is conveyed in the letters – collected in *A Bookseller's War* (1997) – which Heywood Hill received from his wife Anne in the six months following his call-up at the end of 1942. Assisting Anne Hill during her time in charge of G. Heywood Hill Ltd, and a later partner in the business, was Nancy Mitford, whose own correspondence with Heywood Hill between 1952 and 1973 has been published in *The Bookshop at 10 Curzon Street* (2004). All three correspondents write without pretension, and their sensitive, intelligent letters have an emotional range unusual in the field. The story of Hill's feud with his junior partner Handasyde Buchanan unfolds throughout the second volume with painful fascination.

Heywood Hill is an odd omission from David Low's *'with all faults'*, a good-natured book stuffed with plums, from the excellent introduction by Low's friend Graham Greene, to the account of the proprietor of Rosen's bookstall in Rupert Street, Soho –

The most ill-suited bookseller of all time, he had not only never read a book, but most of the time, hated them. When business was bad, he used to walk around the basement where the books were stored overnight, kicking the poor bundles, and muttering 'Bleedin' things!'[131]

Low's career began at Hodgson's in Chancery Lane, but he was long gone by the time Fred Snelling joined the firm in 1949. Snelling's *Rare Books and Rarer People* (1982) paints garish pictures of some of the characters he encountered in the course of three decades as a sales clerk, including his friend the Ruislip bookseller/spy 'Peter Kroger' (Morris Cohen), who hid microdots on the pages of books he sent abroad. With a million-seller (*Double O Seven*, 1964) under his belt, Snelling knows how to spin a yarn, but he is as brash as Low is subtle, and his book is the closest thing to a potboiler the genre has to offer.

In terms of brashness, Rick Gekoski is every bit Snelling's equal. The blurb of his *Tolkien's Gown* (2004) describes him as 'the Bill Bryson of the book world', but his talent for self-publicity is more likely to call to mind P.T. Barnum. Discussion of the publication history of 'twenty significant modern books' by such 'Great Authors' as Beatrix Potter and J.K. Rowling provides him with the opportunity to advertise his acquaintance with 'Graham', 'Ted' and 'Julian', while a discreditable anecdote told along the way settles the score with 'Bill' – William Golding, who satirized Gekoski as 'Rick L. Turner' in *The Paper Men*.

Gekoski's glib account of his transformation from academic to bookseller grates, and his attempt to imbue the world of modern first editions with scholarly significance only leaves one with a sense of the futility of the whole enterprise. Graham Greene's inscribed copy of *Lolita* is sold the day after purchase to the wife of Elton John's lyricist. Tolkien's college gown (one of several) is bought for an American academic to parade around in. The owner of the 'finest James Joyce collection of his generation' turns out to be a 30-stone New Yorker who pays for his purchases by raiding the Teamsters' Union pension fund.

The Hastings bookseller Clive Linklater sees more Reader's Digest condensed novels than Joyce firsts. His *Reflections from a Bookshop Window* (1994) is an unpretentious attempt at writing a funny book. Ostensibly consisting of a year's diary entries detailing the author's efforts to advance by geometrical progression from the sale of a £5 book to one worth £10,240, it takes a rueful look at the trade from the point of view of a struggling provincial dealer.

At the other end of the market, Oliver Davis has worked in the Charing Cross Road for twenty years, and it shows. He has clearly developed the battle fatigue that affects every veteran on that retail front line. His *Second-Hand Books: A First-Hand View* (2001) is a study rather than a memoir, but it does refer to such characters as the indefatigable 'Tram-ticket Man' and the 'notorious bookseller' (John Adrian) whose Cecil Court shop was stocked with books arbitrarily priced in multiples of twelve pounds. (A close associate of Driffield, Adrian regularly flooded the West End with yellow fliers, and later supplemented his income by running a fruit stall outside Foyles.) Davis's scornful account of the process by which, every three months, Quintos of Charing Cross Road 'reciprocates' its stock with a sister bookshop outside London should be contrasted with Pharos director Greg Coombes's defence of the practice to Sheila Markham.[132]

Davis can be urbane, but for all his playful wit and allusive punning he is at his best when he breaks into obscenities and describes 'How to Put a Customer Down' and the '20-Odd Ways/20 Odd Ways ... to Annoy a Bookseller'. The latter piece may owe something to 'How to enrage your bookseller: no. 258 of an occasional series' in *Remainders* (1989), a collection of Eric Korn's articles in the *Times Literary Supplement*. Korn's erudition and love of wordplay are as obtrusive as Davis's, but his approach is less crude. He has long been a fixture of the book fair circuit, but *Remainders* only rarely touches on the trade.

It is curious – and we have Walter Harris of Messrs Thomas Thorp to thank for the information – that 90 years before Davis, and a few yards from his place of work, an individual had surveyed the trade with similar disenchantment. From Harris's reminiscences of the days before the Great War in *Biblionotes* we learn that Lionel Britton's extraordinary novel *Hunger and Love* (1931) draws on his experiences as an assistant to A.H. Mayhew at 56 Charing Cross Road.[133]

Although unreliable, Harris's memoir cries out for publication, with its tales of the runners Mad Jack, Born Drunk, Turkey Bird and the Slab, and its references to forgotten figures like Teddy 'the Baron' Bolleter and 'Whitechapel George' – owner of Gladdings purpose-built bookshop ('one of the finest in London') in Whitechapel Road.

One of Harris's booksellers was 'allergic to rain':

Having no staff he used to employ an old down and out, (a match-seller as a matter of fact) to run messages and deliver parcels for him, whose stand was at the Gent's Toilet in Cambridge Circus, consequently this particular place was usually referred to by the boys as Uncle Solly's Office.[134]

From Jack Joseph's account of his father Emanuel, also contributed to *Biblionotes*, it seems that 'Uncle Solly' was Emanuel's brother S.H. Joseph, 'a very brilliant, but most erratic and unreliable man'.[135]

Emanuel Joseph's career began at the Holywell Street shop of his uncle S.H. Lazarus, who also employed Albert Myers and Charles James Sawyer. When Lazarus died in 1888 his widow Esther Lazarus sacked the three men, and while waiting for a lease to come up in 'the Row' Joseph 'took a barrow and filled it with books and stood for four years at the top of Aldgate'.[136]

Nicolas Barker writes well about the trade, and his obituaries in particular are always worth reading, but he errs in describing Joseph's as a firm in 'a quiet tradition of shopkeeping and service'.[137] In fact the family's rudeness was a byword. Two examples of Emanuel Joseph's milder banter are given by his son. Tastes change, and what Jack Joseph calls 'the most humorous incident ever to take place in this or any other Bookseller's shop', though 'pretty well-known right through the Trade in all parts of the English-speaking world' in 1954, is now forgotten. It concerns a clergyman who complained that a religious book he had purchased from Joseph smelt, because while on the bookseller's outside stalls 'every dog in London had transacted his business on it':

> 'Well,' said my Father, 'I cannot see that you have a grievance of any kind because I sold you Theology - - - I have made certain that it is DOGMATIC THEOLOGY.'[138]

Joseph's reply to the medical student who asked if he had 'Redhare on the stomach' has fared rather better: 'I'll take me ruddy breeches down and let you have a look!'[139]

The Charing Cross Road was a hard school, and Joseph's more than any other firm exemplifies the contrast with the 'soft' West End dealers. 'Now, you boys, don't take advantage. You're dealing with a gentleman!' Emanuel Joseph told his sons regarding a 1920s business arrangement with the Revd A.W. Evans, senior director of the Mayfair booksellers Elkin Mathews.[140] The story of the 'rise and decline' of that most fashionable of firms is told by another of its directors, Percy Muir, in his well-crafted and thoughtful *Minding My Own Business*. Muir's earlier experiences as a partner at Dulau's are the subject of 22 chapters of 'Further reminiscences', published in *The Book Collector* between 1956 and 1964.

The innovative and influential Muir is a surprising omission from the *Oxford DNB*. Those interested in the latter part of his career should turn to his wife Barbara Kaye's *The Company We Kept* (1986), which describes the wartime relocation of Elkin Mathews Ltd to two wooden sheds near the couple's house in the Essex village of Takeley, and her *Second Impression* (1995), which chronicles Muir's ILAB activities and struggle against the ring. *Second Impression* is tough going, but it does describe a 'stampede' at Beeleigh Abbey by an ILAB delegation 'eager to get at the Foyle hospitality'; and it reproduces a letter warning Muir that 'the Emperor of C. X. Rd.' – clearly Jack Joseph – is conducting a 'vendetta' against him. The hardheaded Joseph is unlikely to have shared Muir's faith in ILAB's future as a 'great power for good'.[141]

Muir's friend, associate and fellow 'Biblio Boy' John Carter – rare book specialist in Scribner's London office and latterly Sotheby's American agent – is the subject of a biography by Donald C. Dickinson, an academic who has done useful work on American dealers and collectors. Carter is an elegant and incisive writer, and his work with Graham Pollard has opened up a field of research not limited to the activities of Wise and his stooge Herbert Gorfin.

As the 1920s boom ended Muir was taken to task by his neighbour Dr Maurice Ettinghausen for admitting in print that book prices were falling.[142] 'A man of mystery', Ettinghausen had joined Maggs in 1919. As head of the firm's continental department he was, his colleague Clifford Maggs recalls,[143] 'something of a phenomenon'. Such was his success that he was able to convince his employers to fit up their Conduit Street shop with 'an Incunabula Room in the monastic style and an Americana Room in the Spanish Renaissance style'. Ettinghausen's 1931 visit to Russia – discussed elsewhere in this volume – can only have been inspired by a similar buying trip by Percy Muir and his employer the Dulau director Leslie

Chaundy three years before, a 'madcap venture' which ended in almost complete failure.[144]

Ettinghausen managed the Paris branch of Maggs, and his association with the firm ended unhappily in the chaos preceding the German occupation. As a consequence his *Rare Books and Royal Collectors* (1966) is rather like *Hamlet* without Denmark. The author describes a number of interesting circumstances – from the ransoming of a trunk of books stolen from Southampton docks during the General Strike, to the efforts of the Nazi propagandist Otto Vollbehr to corner the market in incunables – but he cannot bring himself to mention Maggs by name, referring to it instead by such circumlocutions as 'the firm with which I was then connected'.

Ettinghausen's punitive reticence only serves to reinforce his employers' reputation for discretion. In fact none of the great London firms provides much in the way of memoir. Edward Maggs is an entertaining columnist and has printed a couple of unassuming talks. As for Sotheran's – a company which has, Snelling suggests, 'produced more first-rate bookmen than any other shop in London'[145] – there are J.H. Stonehouse's 'Adventures in Bookselling' articles (1933-7) in *Piccadilly Notes* and not much else. The 1997 *Book Collector* special number celebrating the 150th anniversary of Quaritch yields little beyond Ted Dring's 'Fifty years at Quaritch', with its description of the firm's main 'outside man' John Watson's skill in 'the hard graft of bookselling', such as the seeking out of 'the local Woolworths or some store' from which to buy up 'used cartons and string'.[146]

Once, when the Hay-on-Wye bookseller Richard Booth was competing against Quaritch for the Countess of Huntingdon's library at Trefecca, his carpenter Frank English – responsible for 25 miles of Hay bookshelves – came up with a novel plan to discredit the opposition.

After a few pints en route he proposed to knock at the door and, smelling strongly of beer, say, 'I'm from Quaritch, lady. Can I have a piss?'[147]

Richard Booth – styled 'King of Hay-on-Wye' and 'Emperor of all the World's Second-hand Book Towns' by himself, but 'King Richard Rubbercheque' in Hay graffiti – is an avowed 'eccentric bookdealer with questionable financial and sexual habits'. He is also a mass of contradictions. In *My Kingdom of Books* (1999) he describes his role in the depredation of the same Welsh workingmen's libraries whose closure he now considers a 'tragedy', and the supply of collections to the same university libraries which he now feels have 'a deadening effect on the culture of the book'. His own cultural achievements include the pulping of 300,000 books in 1967.[148]

Booth claims to have imported more than a hundred twenty-foot containers of books from America during the 1980s. The only comparable logistical exercise is the transportation of the great Phillipps collection from Cheltenham to London, following its purchase by the Robinson brothers in 1946. Philip Robinson's account of the move, first published in *The Book Collector*, has been reprinted in *The Pleasures of Bibliophily* (2003), a collection which also features Alan

Thomas's vivid portrait of Solomon 'Inky' Pottesman, an obsessive collector of incunabula in the mould of Dibdin's friend Dr Isaac Gosset. The fifth volume (1960) of A.N.L. Munby's *Phillipps Studies*, *The Dispersal of the Phillipps Library*, gives an account of the Robinsons, and Martin Hamlyn's *The Robinson Legend* is an elegiac tribute to his former employers.

Booth features in one of the better chapters of Paul Minet's *Late Booking* (1989). Minet can write (witness his *Bookdealer* obituary of Henry Pordes,[149] 'amalgam of aggressive foul-mouthed dealmaker and cultivated, intelligent charmer'), but his self-published autobiography founders for lack of an editor. He describes his career between 1958 and 1983 as 'a literary St. Vitus's Dance, an uncomfortable and pecuniarily unrewarding affair', during which a 'burgeoning private income' allowed him to 'pump money' into a succession of concerns, from a bookshop/coffee bar in Reading to the Sackville Street emporium 'World of Books'. His aim throughout was to recapture 'something of the feel of the browsing bookshops of my youth', and his explanation for his 'rather persistent failure' is that 'the kind of business I am trying to build is no longer feasible'. He has nevertheless been at the forefront of a number of developments, including the rise of the book fair and the remainders boom of the late seventies. The *Antiquarian Book Monthly Review*, which he founded in 1974, gives an insight into the trade during a turbulent period.[150]

Another 'snapshot of bookdealing during a time of unprecedented change'[151] is provided by Sheila Markham's *A Book of Booksellers* (2004), a selection of around half of the interviews she has conducted for *Bookdealer* since 1991. Of the 52 subjects, ranging from Bill Fletcher to Bernard Shapero, eight are women, with a sprinkling of foreign dealers.

Markham's articles are arranged chronologically, and to begin with differ little in form from those published by 'Bibliophile' in *The Publisher and Bookseller* a hundred years before. A piece on Sally Edgecombe of Clarke Hall sees a change in approach, with Markham adopting what she calls 'a monologue style in which the interviews are reported entirely in the subject's own words'.[152] In the deceptively simple articles that follow, skilful construction allows the character of the interviewee to come through strongly.

Although interesting and informative, *A Book of Booksellers* needs to be treated with caution. In her willingness to show the trade in its best light, Markham gives her subjects an easy ride. One interviewee at least claims to have made substantial changes before publication.[153]

Markham is careful not to rock the boat. Despite her claim that the full texts of those interviews which are not in the book are on her website,[154] the 1994 article which resulted in Torgrim Hannås's expulsion from the ABA[155] is absent from both. It is curious that Bill Fletcher's comment 'That's all I'm saying in print!' should only feature in the *Bookdealer* version.

It comes as no surprise that our final subject should object to Markham's 'Hello style interviews'.[156] Driffield – or Driff, Drif, drif field, etc. (real name unknown) – burst in on the booktrade like a hooligan launching himself into a crowd of rival supporters. A bicycling vegetarian transvestite in kilt or plus fours, a Stentor boasting of views 'to the extreme right of Adolph [sic] Hitler', this self-styled 'skinhead gorilla' traversed the country from Penzance to Stromness – a crazed leech gatherer in search of books on suicide, midgets, masturbation correction devices, scatologic rites, cranial deformation and the literature of adult bed-wetting.[157] His celebrated *Guide*, six editions of which appeared between 1984 and 1995, is a bibliopolic Leland's *Itinerary*, the strange fruit of a visitation that took in more than a thousand shops.

Driffield's bugbears include book fairs, trade associations, charity shops, and redundancy and retirement booksellers, and he records his judgments in a little language replete with acronyms. A bookseller might be a BSN INBie (*bibliographically subnormal* member of the *important neckwear brigade*), a CLOT (*candidate for librarian on the Titanic*) who AWYW, WYLAH and FARTS (*asks what you want, watches you like a hawk* and *follows around recommending the stock*).

It was inevitable that Driffield's trenchant observations should cause offence in a business blessed with more than its fair share of po-faced sole traders. Charles Traylen (a fine one to talk) dismissed him as 'a thorough disgrace to an honourable trade',[158] and the Richmond bookseller Eric Barton was not alone in deciding that he was not worth suing.[159]

Emboldened by his *succès de scandale*, 'Britain's favourite book-hunter', as *The Times* dubbed him,[160] started a fortnightly magazine called *driffs* in 1986. It folded after 22 issues, but its best feature, the gossip column by 'Charles of the Writz', was revived in *d notice*, a photocopied typescript distributed to the favoured few in two series between 1989 and 1994.

Driffield next turned his attention to the case brought in 1992 by David Brass of Joseph's against his American partners, who included a former associate of the junk-bond dealer Michael Milken. Ignored by an embarrassed trade press, it was a story that needed telling, but although he sat through the 26-day hearing Driffield was not up to the job: his *Not 84 Charing Cross Road* (1994) is badly written and riddled with errors from the first sentence. The 126 copies sent out for review failed to produce a single response.[161] In 1995 Driffield disappeared, resurfacing nine years later in circumstances touched on in a recent piece by the present writer.[162]

In *Liquid City* (1999) Iain Sinclair contrasts Driffield with the legendary runner Martin Stone, a figure whose iconic status is confirmed by a handsome eulogy by former ABAA president Peter Howard and John Baxter's enjoyable *A Pound of Paper* (2002). Driffield and Stone are transmuted into Dryfeld and Nicholas Lane in Sinclair's first novel *White Chappell: Scarlet Tracings* (1987).

Anthony Rota concludes a surprisingly sympathetic portrait of Driffield with the claim that his writings have 'died the death'.[163] On the contrary, the passage of time only serves to place his strengths in sharper relief. His account of his inadvertent creation of a market for the novels of John Lodwick, and his obituary of the runner A.W. Howlett show what he can do.[164] He asks awkward questions, and at his best – in *d notice* and the early editions of the *Guide* – his vicious wit and Yahoo energy counterbalance Markham's stage-managed prose. The truth about the trade lies somewhere in between.

Defending and Regulating the Trade: A Hundred Years of the Antiquarian Booksellers' Association

ANTHONY ROTA

BOOKSELLERS, especially those concerned with secondhand and rare books, are notorious individualists. It is difficult to get any two of them to walk forward at the same time, and to many of us who have tried to arrange such a simple co-operative manoeuvre, it seems almost unbelievable that the secondhand and antiquarian booksellers of the United Kingdom should have banded together voluntarily, albeit for the common good, as long ago as 1906.

The man responsible for the launching of a trade association to foster the interests of dealers in secondhand and rare books was Frank Karslake (1851-1920). A successful businessman, he is said to have made most of his money from land deals in North America, where he owned at least three ranches. Around the turn of the century he returned to his native England and once more took up the trade which he had earlier found so satisfying. Back in London, in 1902 he became founding editor of *Book Auction Records*. His work in building up the subscription list for this invaluable reference book brought him into contact with secondhand booksellers throughout Great Britain, as well as a number overseas. He realized that as things stood, booksellers had little chance of getting to know one another or of having their interests mutually protected, and he decided that both problems could be answered by the formation of a trade association. In 1902 he floated this suggestion in the pages of *Sale Records*, which he published from his imposing house in Pond Street, Hampstead: 'Why should there not be a Second-hand Booksellers' Association for the United Kingdom, similar to the existing New Booksellers' Association? Its object would be the safeguarding of the interests of the trade on vital issues. Union is strength.' A year later he complained through the same medium of the 'great apathy' that existed, but he persevered.

On Friday 11 December 1906, in answer to a printed invitation sent out by Karslake, a host of booksellers met at the Criterion restaurant in Piccadilly Circus to hear more about his proposal. By now Karslake was able to point to a list of 112 provisional members. It was agreed that these should be regarded as original members.[1] The prime object of the new body would be 'the safeguarding of the interests of the trade on vital issues'. Those present went on to decide on its name. 'The Antiquarian Booksellers' Association' was proposed by Thomas Chatto and seconded by James Tregaskis, but this was defeated by 28 votes to six. The humbler 'Second-hand Booksellers' Association' won the day, though not without a lengthy and inconclusive debate about the definition of the term. (How long was it, one wonders, before the old chestnut about the difference between a second-hand bookseller and an antiquarian bookseller arose? By the millennium it was still in circulation, the answer to 'What is the difference …?' having increased to 'About £10,000 a year'.

The meeting went on to appoint officers and a Committee. It was decided that there should be 35 Committee members, sixteen from London and nineteen from the country (a large Committee by today's standards). There is little doubt that Karslake could have had any position or office that he wished, despite his alleged unpopularity with some of the more important members of the trade, but he chose to be Secretary of the new Association, working hard at secretarial duties.

The honour of being the first President of the Association was offered to B.D. Maggs, who declined, and it went instead to Henry N. Stevens, with Ben Maggs succeeding him the following year. As early as May 1908 the grander name finally triumphed and 'The International Association of Antiquarian Booksellers' was formally born. The prefix 'International' was added because at that time this was the only trade association for secondhand and antiquarian booksellers and it was hoped that the best dealers from overseas would also join. At the 1928 AGM, the name was changed again, to Antiquarian Booksellers' Association (International), which stated the Association's purpose more clearly.

The Association has gone through many changes over these hundred years; in 2005 there were 264 members. Candidates seeking election to the ABA must be able to show that they have traded satisfactorily for a minimum of five years; each must have four sponsors, all of whom must be members of the Association. The sponsors are asked searching questions about their candidate's experience and expertise, stock, reference library, and much else. If successful, the candidate must also swear to abide by a strict code of practice.

Early concerns

An early task for the new Association was to set up a Benevolent Fund to help members in financial need, and to promote 'entertainments', the profits from which would swell the Fund. Whist drives, concerts and annual dinners were organized to this end. If the Fund alone was not enough to meet the need, or if too strict a rule stood in the way, members of the Committee would literally pass the hat round, a practice that continued for many years.

The Committee minutes record a speedy change of mind about the proposed annual subscription, which was increased from one shilling to five. Then, in January 1907, it was agreed that the Association should help members collect bad debts, charging for the work on a commission basis. In this connection it was resolved that the names of what the minutes call 'doubtful persons' be advertised in the trade paper, *The Clique*. Cautious souls suggested that there should be at least two apparently valid debts against a person's name before he or she was put in the 'doubtful' category.

In 1907 ABA members found it 'a nuisance' that auctions were sometimes held on a Saturday, and a delegation went to Sotheby's and asked them to restrict their sales to weekdays. Sotheby's agreed, provided that it did not cause a big sale to run over into a second week. The Committee's next initiative was to attempt to buy *The Clique* from its founder publishers, the Murray family, but Mr Frank Murray, the editor of this useful trade journal, refused to consider any offer. He did however suggest to the ABA that it should take advertisement pages free of charge to address its members or indeed a wider constituency. The ABA accepted, and *The Clique* became the official organ of the Association.

January 1908 saw the first ABA annual dinner. It was held in the Criterion restaurant and tickets cost six shillings each. The object had been to raise money for the Benevolent Fund, but the dinner made a loss and there had to be a whip-round among the Committee members to make that loss good. A smoking concert at Anderton's Hotel raised nine pounds for the Benevolent Fund, although a second concert made a loss. Guests invited to the annual dinner in January 1910 included Victor Gollancz, Israel Zangwill, Buxton Forman and G.K. Chesterton.

In 1912, when the ABA was barely six years old, it sponsored a remarkable exhibition at Stationers' Hall in London, on the theme of 'the history and progress of printing and bookselling in England from 1477 to 1800', with a catalogue extending to 218 pages and listing 1229 exhibits.[2] Most of the big names in the trade were represented among the exhibitors. The catalogue begins with fifteen Caxtons and continues with books printed by Wynkyn de Worde, Richard Pynson and William Middleton. The first editions of Hobbes's *Leviathan* is there, and so is Sir Thomas Browne's *Religio Medici*. Indeed, the catalogue is virtually a roll-call of the great names in English printing.

Wars

Any historical overview of what happened to institutions during the last hundred years must take account of the influence of the two world wars. I do not know of any concerted attempt to discover what ABA members did during those wars, but this would be an interesting exercise.

In October 1914, just two months into the Great War, it was resolved at a 'private meeting' of members that it was undesirable that book auctions be held for the remainder of the year. It was subsequently agreed with Hodgson's that there should be only a few such sales. (Perhaps the Committee held the popular belief that 'the boys will be home for Christmas', or at least that the market would have settled down by then.) A contribution was made to the Belgian Book Trade Relief Fund. Soon afterwards a grant of £5 was paid to a member who was found to be 'in distressed circumstances in consequence of the war'. This is an early example of the generosity with which the ABA has helped its members throughout its existence. Benevolent grants were made throughout the Great War, the largest amounting to some £800.

On 6 September 1939 the ABA Committee held a meeting postponed from the outbreak of war on 3 September. This emergency meeting acted to suspend some activities and cancel others. *The Times* National Book Fair came into this second category. War risks insurance had to be arranged. *The Clique* would only be published once a week. Bookshops' opening hours would be earlier so that staff, 'could get home before dark'. Prompt payment of bills was encouraged. It was thought that key members of staff could be regarded as having a reserved occupation, as they undoubtedly did, in supporting an export trade. Details of the Board of Trade insurance scheme were reported to members, although, at ten per cent of full value, the Committee thought the premiums far too high for the book trade.

In 1940 the ABA applied for the release from detention of three dealers who were foreign members. Mr Eisemann, who later managed Maggs Bros.' showroom in Paris, was released almost at once and showed his gratitude by contributing to the Benevolent Fund and the Spitfire Fund. It was agreed that the former should be used to make grants to booksellers who lost their stock, and perhaps their premises, in air raids. An auction sale at Hodgson's also raised £600 for the Air Raid Distress Fund.

In 1943 it was reported that the National Book Recovery and Salvage Drive had been a great success, resulting in the collection of fifty million books. What treasures were lost when those books were recycled, one wonders?

In 1944 a 'doodlebug' or a V2 rocket fell on the premises of Dulau and Company in the West End. As the proprietor F.W. Chaundy remarked, he had lost everything, including the life of his son, Leslie. We also know that G. Seaford of Portsmouth and I.G. Hewkin of Manchester lost their bookselling businesses, and booksellers' lives were lost during these air raids. One London bookseller, Peter Eaton, made saving lives his daily routine. A conscientious objector, he was part of the rescue team based at Paddington. After the strong men of the Heavy Rescue Squad had dragged girders and huge blocks of masonry to one side, it was the task of Peter Eaton and his slighter colleagues to crawl into the wreckage and rescue any wounded or trapped survivors.

Norman Storey, who joined his father Harold in business after the war, served as a rear gunner in the Royal Air Force, first on Lancaster bombers and later on Flying Fortresses (sent up to draw enemy fighters away from the real targets). He was offered a commission but preferred to remain a Warrant Officer. Also serving on Lancasters, but just a little later, was Bill Fletcher (H.M. Fletcher). He was a Flight Engineer. When George Holleyman joined the RAF at the beginning of the war he packed up his entire stock and stored it in lock-up garages. It is said that the increase in its value by the time he was demobilized was the foundation of his success.

Constitutional change

In the late 1950s and early 1960s a small but not insignificant group of dealers, was unhappy about the ABA Committee's action, or lack of action, in two areas. The so-called 'Ginger Group', also known as 'the Young Turks', thought the Committee much too slow and cautious when it came to support for and promotion of book fairs. The Committee, the book trade's 'establishment', was made up of men (and one woman) of conservative mind. Perhaps they were anxious that the independent fair held in Sotheby's book sales room, hired in a period during which no auctions were to be held, had succeeded only because it was a novelty. How dreadful it would be if the ABA sponsored the fair and it was a financial disaster. In June 1958, however, the first annual Antiquarian Book Fair was held under the auspices of the ABA at the National Book League.

The second bone of contention was more serious by far: the issue of the 'ring' (sometimes called the 'settlement' or, less formally, the 'knock-out'). Who were 'the Young Turks' who eventually managed to achieve constitutional and professional reforms in the 1960s? Seen as an impatient few, they kept no membership list, but their identities were an open book. Those who made the running included Laurie Deval (Elkin Mathews), Rodney Drake (James Bain), Boris Harding-Edgar (Charles Rare Books), Max Brimmell (R.A. Brimmell), and the present writer. Our position was that the Committee appeared to be ignoring the unpleasant publicity about the ring and seemed to be hoping it would just go away.

The ring

It can well be understood why the older members of the trade, those with the longest memories, so liked the ring and were sorry to give it up. They regarded as 'greedy' those owners who would not sell their books to a dealer but required perhaps as many as twenty or thirty booksellers to attend an auction, where they felt they were making such owners a free gift of their hard-won expertise. The sums involved could be quite large, too. Master booksellers could sometimes take home from the 'knock-out' as much as they paid their first assistant for a year. It must be remembered that until 1927 this was not against the law. Nor did things necessarily stop after one private auction. There might be 'town versus country', then 'West End versus Charing Cross Road', and so on.[3]

We are principally concerned here with book auctions, but the legislation to outlaw the ring is believed to have been brought on by the effrontery of a group of dealers in oriental carpets, who are understood to have held a settlement on the steps leading down from Sotheby's galleries. In addition some scrap metal dealers were indiscreet in their bidding for a surplus battleship. Be that as it may, the passing of the Auctions (Bidding Agreements) Act of 1927 made it an offence to receive a 'consideration' not to bid. Yet for at least 30 or 40 years thereafter, a number of decent and otherwise honourable booksellers continued to participate in what were now illegal rings. They argued that if two booksellers who were friends, and who had different fields of specialization, found themselves the only dealers at a given sale, it would be natural not to bid against one another but to leave books in the other's specialization alone. They could see no harm in that – and nor, perhaps, can we – but when there were, let us say, a score or more of dealers at a sale, and the benefits of a low cost at the public auction had to be shared out, things were very different. There have been very few prosecutions under the Act, partly because evidence was hard to come by, but in 1948 a letter to the ABA from Mr John Sparrow seemed likely to change all that. This astute lawyer was an important and influential collector. He had placed a commission bid at an auction sale through an ABA member, but had failed to buy the lot because his agent had lost it during the second or private auction which had followed the public auction and which by this date was illegal. The editor of *The Times* was disposed to publish details of the affair in his newspaper and was dissuaded from doing so only when virtually every member of the Association signed a pledge not to participate in future settlements.

It was Laurie Deval who warned, in 1956, that unless the ABA showed it was serious in its attempts to crush the ring, his firm (Elkin Mathews) and other like-minded firms would resign and form a new association, a 'Guild of Antiquarian Booksellers' (whose badge would be triangular rather than circular). Happily things did not come to that pass. At an Extraordinary General Meeting in September 1956, the Association's rules were amended to require members, on pain of expulsion, to comply with the 1927 Act. Today the ABA Code of Good Practice, which all members are sworn to uphold, has this to say about auctions:

The Association opposes all forms of malpractice at auction. No member shall engage in any activity, or be party to any covert or undisclosed agreements, whether with buyers, sellers, or auctioneers, that artificially distort the price paid in open sale. No member shall for any consideration agree with other persons not to bid at auction, or take part in a private re-auction of lots bought at public auction. Furthermore every member shall pledge full support to the Committee of the Association in its opposition to the activity of any ring with the trade in antiquarian books.

While it is the 'settlement' or 'knock-out' that is being addressed here, this is only one of the misdeeds that may occur at auction. For example, it is alleged that at some auctions where the house and contents were sold *in situ*, where large lots were the order of the day and the cataloguing was not as detailed as it might have been, corrupt porters could be bribed to move, say, one volume of a three-volume set from one lot to another. Again, one has heard it said that auctioneers have been known to run a bidder up in price when he or she actually faced no legitimate competition at all. The most outrageous of all the stories of bad behaviour at auction sales is of an auctioneer who, in exchange for a ten-pound note left under the blotter, allowed the members of the ring to hold the second or illegal sale in his office.

Representing the trade's interests

Over the years the ABA has defended its members' interests in a wide range of contexts and against different adversaries: three examples are described here.

In 1944 the government introduced Bulk Export Licences. These were intended to simplify the arrangements for sending printed books abroad – provided that they were not priced at more than £50. But manuscripts over 100 years old could not be exported without a specific licence, however low their value. The Association sent a delegation to the Board of Trade and a compromise was reached. Holders of Bulk Licences (later Open Individual Export Licences) were allowed some useful, time-saving concessions. Manuscripts valued at not more than the OIEL limits had only to be declared on a quarterly basis. The British Library could not insist on having microfilms of these. For their part, the Bulk Licence holders had to give an undertaking that they would apply for a specific licence if they thought an item was potentially of national interest.

The ABA has two seats on the Documents Working Party, a small but hard-working body in which academics, librarians and curators meet dealers and auctioneers to thrash out improvements to the operation of the export controls. The chair is taken by a member of the Reviewing Committee on the Export of Works of Art, which advises whichever Minister currently has the power to issue, delay or refuse export licences. Responsibility for the export of manuscripts has passed between no small number of ministries and departments over the years. Despite considerable efforts, the ABA representatives (on behalf of *all* exporters and would-be exporters) have been unable to achieve the abolition of the age and value criteria for the export control of manuscripts. Indeed, the age criterion for individual items has become more restrictive and has gradually reduced from 100 years to 50 years; there has been more success with the value limit for OIELs, which has been adjusted upwards. Perhaps the best result of the deliberations of the Working Party has been a marked improvement in relations between what used to be seen as the two sides. Keeping a reasonably free market while preserving the national interest in historical material is not easy. It is a question of the owner's property rights on the one hand and the expectations of future generations on the other.

In 1974 *The Clique*, the 'official organ' of the ABA, had a falling-out with the committee. Some 95 per cent of *The Clique*'s contents consisted of lists of books wanted by trade subscribers. Advertisements from private buyers, which is to say from collectors, were not accepted. Bearing this restrictive practice in mind, readers were surprised to find in one particular issue a list, from a subscribing bookseller, which had against each title the price the dealer was prepared to pay for it. The 'old school' of booksellers on the ABA committee were horrified. This specialized list offered high prices for books that many a dealer would hope to be able to buy for less. Moreover by giving these prices the advertiser was revealing enough about the values of the books concerned for tyro booksellers to be able to trade successfully in this field to the detriment of the booksellers already established in it. The ABA committee sought to have *The Clique* give an undertaking not to accept any more priced wants lists. Lionel Fishman, *The Clique*'s manager, who now attended ABA committee meetings as *The Clique*'s representative, refused to give such an undertaking and there appeared to be an impasse. The ABA's officers thereupon arranged to meet the journal's Board of Directors. Exactly what was said at that meeting is not known, but the fact that *The Clique*'s policy was changed specifically to exclude prices from advertisements for books wanted gives an idea of the line that must have been taken. This, I repeat, was in 1974: I cannot think that this restrictive attitude would prevail today.

The year 1975 was a bad one for the fine art trade. While the dealers tightened their belts and waited for times to improve, the auctioneers sought a more radical solution. They hit on the notion of getting additional funds from a new source: instead of merely charging the vendor a percentage commission on the sale price achieved, they would introduce a percentage buyers' premium as well. Thus the auction house would take two slices of the same pie. Sotheby's and Christie's announced this radical change of policy virtually simultaneously and in remarkably similar terms. To the dealers this looked like collusion, and a breach of fair trading legislation.

All of the fine art trades were hurt by the new policy. Their associations conferred together and appointed a delegation to ask the auctioneers if they would make any concessions towards the trades' position. The answer they were given was a definitive 'No'.

Soon the day of the first London sale of books to be sold subject to the premium came around. On the stroke of eleven o'clock Lord John Kerr, then the Director in charge of Sotheby's book department, mounted the rostrum and looked around the crowded room. He bade us good morning and began the day's litany. 'Lot one. I must say fifty pounds to start it ...' Before he could go further Howard Swann, head of Wheldon & Wesley, specialists in natural history, who was then President of the ABA, rose to his feet. Apologizing for interrupting the proceedings, he asked whether the buyers' premium would extend to purchases in this sale. Lord John said that it would. Charles Swann replied that in that case he and his colleagues would not be bidding. The ABA members withdrew quietly – and gave a press conference on the pavement in Bond Street. Lord John and Charles Swann had both behaved with dignity and impeccable manners. The dealers achieved very good publicity for their cause. A few days later the ABA received a letter from the Office of Fair Trading, warning us not to repeat an exercise in which we urged members to refrain from bidding on specific lots or at specific sales. We felt rather hard done by.

The trade alliance had begun a legal battle and had high hopes of winning, but Sotheby's said they would fight all the way to the House of Lords – which meant the dealers could be looking at a bill for £250,000. The ABA had only to raise a small part of that, but it was still a lot for mere booksellers to find. We needed the participation of six book dealers who (a) were members of the ABA, (b) could afford their possible share of the lawyers' bill and (c) had 'clean hands' where auction rings were concerned. Finding all three qualifications in one dealer was not easy: to do so six times over was a hard task indeed. Then there was the added problem of ensuring that the litigants would not be too vulnerable should the auctioneers cut off their credit.

After many months of argument and name-calling a compromise was reached: the buyer's premium remained, but another talking-shop was set up. It consisted of the chairmen of Christie's, Sotheby's and Phillips, together with the Presidents of the Society of London Art Dealers, the British Antique Dealers' Association and the Antiquarian Booksellers' Association. These worthies were to meet under the chairmanship of a lawyer well versed in the fine art trade: first, the solicitor, balletomane and painter, Anthony Lousada, and later His Honour Sir Stephen Tumim, formerly a consultant to Christie's and latterly Her Majesty's Inspector of Prisons. He was also a bibliophile and a connoisseur of paintings. This new group worked under the title 'The British Art Market Federation'. Meeting quarterly or whenever there was a matter that needed speedy attention, its formal business usually followed a lunch given by one of the constituents. This hospitality fostered the building of friendships between the various parties, frequently resolving quarrels which might otherwise have escalated to public rows as fierce as the argument over the buyer's premium itself.

Thefts

The essays in the present volume have much to say about books entering and leaving British bookshops. It ought perhaps to be remembered that not all such comings and goings were legitimate: in short, there is the problem of the book thief. The relatively high prices at which rare books change hands today have led to particularly serious levels of theft.

Over the years, booksellers had become conscious of book thieves' habit of wearing loose clothing, handily equipped with poachers' pockets. In the 1970s and 1980s one well-known collector used to visit the West End bookshops in his lunch hour. He would chat to the assistants and would make the occasional small purchase whilst talking of much grander things. After this customer had gone back to his office, the bookseller often found that a rare pamphlet had gone missing. It had been removed under the cover of a neatly folded copy of *The Times* which the thief had been carrying under his arm. Such amateur book thieves are nuisance enough, but skilled professionals are even more of a problem. The advent of fast and relatively inexpensive air travel meant that books could be stolen from, say, a country bookshop in England on a Monday and offered for sale in New York or California on the following Tuesday or Wednesday. Any counter-measures required prompt discovery when books had gone missing and swift communication with any dealers who might innocently purchase the stolen goods. The book trade took an enormous leap forward when it set up a telephone chain, a swift method of passing information across the country that has led to a number of arrests and the recovery of many rare books. The electronic age takes us further forward as first the thief and then the legitimate dealer edges ahead. This is a race, with a handicap, that bears close watching.

Educating the public and training booksellers

One of the best pieces of public relations work the ABA ever did was in 1944, when it commissioned Percy Muir to write *Book-Collecting as a Hobby in a Series of Letters to Everyman*. This simple little book contained 100 pages of sound advice for beginners and was priced at only 3s.6d. I suspect the ABA subsidized it. The first edition bore the little-known imprint of 'Gramol Publications Ltd' of London and Chesham, which rather suggests that in the days when paper was rationed Messrs Gramol had an allocation to use up. In his prefatory letter, Muir gives Mark Cohen (Marks & Co.) credit for suggesting that Muir should write it. Now, some 60 years later, there are other elementary works on book-collecting, some arguably better than Muir while others are not so good. What is clear is that Muir's book was the primer from which several generations of collectors learned the delights of book collecting.

The success of this little book seems to have encouraged the ABA Committee to publish, or at least to sponsor, more books about books. In 1952 Cassell & Co brought out *Talks on Book-Collecting*, edited by Muir and 'delivered under the authority of the Antiquarian Booksellers' Association'. The talks had been given by Muir himself, Simon Nowell-Smith, John Carter, E.P. Goldschmidt, Ernest Weil and others, at the headquarters of the National Book League during the winter of 1948-49. Also in 1952 there appeared the *ABA Annual*. This published the text of the first Annual Lecture, given by Michael Sadleir, together with contributions by Lawrence Clark Powell, Dudley Massey, Peter Murray Hill, Percy J. Dobell and others. The second annual publication came out in 1953 under the title *Books and the Man*. The contents included A.N.L. Munby's lecture on Sir Thomas Phillipps, and work by W.A. Jackson, A.T. Miller, Alan Thomas and Ian Grant. Unfortunately it did not sell as well as had been expected and the series of lectures came to an abrupt halt. In October 1958 the BBC broadcast a talk by my father Bertram Rota on collecting modern first editions, and later one on H.G. Wells.

In 1961 H.W. Pratley (of Hall's Bookshop) proposed a travelling exhibition, the exhibits being let into recesses in table-top display cases. His proposal was accepted and an informative catalogue, *Book Collecting for Everyman*, incorporating a list of ABA members, was printed to accompany it. Ninety-three libraries asked to take the exhibition for a minimum of two weeks each.

On two occasions during the 1960s, joint meetings were held with the Rare Books Group of the Library Association. The first took the form of a debate about current price levels for rare books, the librarians arguing that they were too high, whilst the dealers claimed that the sums asked were reasonable and that good copies of desirable books could not be had for less. The second meeting was more constructive. It dealt with security, various aspects of the subject being addressed by speakers with special knowledge.

'I had a diploma, a brand new diploma ...'[4]

Right from Frank Karslake's day, through Lionel Robinson's (President from 1938 to 1942) and that of Mark Cohen (1943), the Committee had constantly sought to provide improved training for assistants and for aspiring master booksellers. In 1924, for example, arrangements were made for senior assistants of member firms to enrol in a dedicated class at the London School of Printing; visits to the Royal Library at Windsor and the Library of Eton College were also planned.

If the master booksellers had their association, so too did their employees. Founded in 1950, the Society of Antiquarian Booksellers' Employees, better known as 'The Bibliomites', soon had more than 150 members. Their names, and the names of their employers, were listed in the society's newsletter in 1952 and included a number of people who went on to play an important part in the work of the ABA itself. Peeping out from the list of names are Frank Doel (Marks & Co.), Bernard Simpson (E. Joseph), Ken Russell (Francis Edwards), Bob Forster, Raymond Kilgarriff (Quaritch, later Howes) and many others. The Bibliomites' activities in 1952 included a dinner dance, a day in Brighton and various lectures – from A.T. Miller (Frank Hollings) on modern first editions, Handasyde Buchanan (Heywood Hill) on coloured botanical books, and Peter Murray Hill on 'The XYZ of Bookselling'. As well as subscriptions from its members, the society received regular grants from the ABA and informal cash subsidies from some master booksellers. It is sometimes said that the Bibliomites was a social club rather more than an academy for young booksellers, but its meetings did provide booksellers' assistants, particularly those living in London or the south-east of England, with the opportunity to chat with fellow members about bibliographical topics. It is a pity that the Bibliomites, which flourished during the 1950s and 1960s, is not active today.[5]

In 1994 the Association made its most ambitious foray into the world of professional training. The Diploma in Antiquarian Bookselling offered by the ABA from 1994 was a noble attempt to provide sound, well-constructed training for would-be entrants to the book trade. It was the late Barry Bloomfield, retired head of collection development at the British Library and bibliographer of W.H. Auden and Philip Larkin, to whom the Association turned when its *ad hoc* Education Committee wanted advice. Barry quickly pointed out that much of the ideal academic training for antiquarian booksellers was already being provided at library schools to those studying to become rare book librarians: half the course for our diploma could be adopted with a little fine tuning; the rest could be provided in a series of lectures given by carefully selected booksellers. The subjects would include fields of specialization, ethics, buying and selling at auction, historical bibliography, and so on.

This was put to Robin Alston, then head of the School of Library, Archive and Information Studies at University College, London, who liked it very much. It came to full flowering under the supervision of Robin's successor, Ia McIlwaine, and her colleagues. In the first year there were a dozen students. They worked hard and produced some good results. There were small problems: for example, the students felt that too much of their time was taken up with the technical side of computerized cataloguing.

A work placement in an ABA member's business, a rare book library or an auction house was considered an important part of the training. One young lady we sent for a placement interview so impressed the owner that he offered her irresistibly attractive terms, resulting in her leaving the educational programme that very day, without attending a single lecture.

The course was offered as either a full- or part-time option, and that sometimes made difficulties in the timetable. But there was another, weightier, problem which we could not solve, and that was the cost. For the course to be self-financing it needed an annual intake of ten students. While it was proving itself, local authorities were not obliged to provide grants to help students to pay their way, and overseas students were required to pay £6,000 for tuition alone. With the high cost of living in London, the bill was more than many could manage and the diploma course foundered. Perhaps it will be resurrected one day, but meanwhile the Rare Book Society, founded by ABA members and endorsed by the Association, is setting out to offer internet-based 'distance learning' courses instead.

The ABA supports a good reference library for its members, specializing in bibliography. The honorary librarian (for many years Raymond Kilgarriff of Howes Bookshop, who was succeeded by Miles Bartley, and now by Roger Treglown of Macclesfield) can often answer bibliographical questions by telephone, but many of the bibliographies can be borrowed by post. ABA members who compile or publish bibliographies tend to have the pleasant habit of giving copies to the ABA library, while an annual purchase grant enables the librarian to fill other gaps on the ABA shelves.

Home and abroad

We have seen that the United Kingdom was the first country to offer a trade association to its rare book dealers, and that it also invited distinguished dealers from other countries to join its ranks. Between 1920 and 1930, recruiting drives aimed at overseas booksellers brought many Americans into the ABA. Things did not stay like this for very long, since dealers from other nations saw the advantages of banding together and began, some sooner and some later, to form their own national associations: the Antiquarian Booksellers' Association of America, for instance, was founded in 1949. There were occasional complications when overseas booksellers who had joined the ABA wished to continue to shelter under the 'International' suffix to the ABA's name. To turn them out would have seemed uncharitable, yet to keep them in – or to recruit more dealers from overseas – would have appeared an unfriendly gesture towards the other associations. In the end an agreement was reached to the effect that no foreign dealer could belong to the ABA unless he or she was also a member in good standing of his or her own national association. For social reasons, and to enjoy the status of belonging to the ABA, a number of foreign dealers opted to retain ABA membership.

Comparatively recently, notably in 1990, a number of British dealers opted for dual membership for a different reason. The excellent reputation of the book fairs run by the German association (the Verband Deutscher Antiquare e.V.) caused those fairs to be oversubscribed. This irritated some members of the ABA and of the Antiquarian Booksellers' Association of America, both of which welcomed overseas exhibitors at their own fairs and in many cases reserved stands to accommodate them. After much burning of the midnight oil, it was accepted that if dealers from other national associations joined the Verband, they would stand a better chance of getting a booth at the German fairs.

The International League of Antiquarian Booksellers

In the years immediately after the Second World War dealers were working hard to revive the international trade in antiquarian books, especially across national frontiers in Europe. Wartime divisions had still to be healed, but dealers at the head of national associations in their own countries were beginning to talk about joining together in a spirit of goodwill to further common interests. At a preliminary conference held in Amsterdam in 1947, it was decided to hold a Congress in Copenhagen the following year. Percy Muir, who was President of the ABA in 1946 and 1947, was invited to take the chair. Twenty-four delegates represented the founding members, who were the national associations of Denmark, France, Great Britain, the Netherlands, Sweden and Switzerland.

The objects of the League were stated to be 'the co-ordination of all efforts and projects having in view the development and growth of the trade of antiquarian bookselling, thereby creating friendly relations between antiquarian booksellers throughout the world'. The rather cumbersome nature of this statement suggests that it may be a translation. It is both a weakness and a strength of the League that it is a bilingual body and that all its proceedings have to be recorded in French as well as English – an expensive and time-consuming business.

By the 1980s the biennial congresses were attracting several hundred delegates. A certain amount of business gets transacted (the subjects cropping up most frequently being standards of collation, the training of new entrants to the trade, and relationships with the auction houses). Its harsher critics say that the League is only a talking-shop – and it is true that the social side of congress life is very pleasant, the national association sponsoring each congress taking great care to mount an interesting programme. Highlights have included a visit by private train to the library at Chatsworth, private concerts in the Fenice Theatre and Les Invalides, a barbecue on the Berkelouws' farm near Sydney, a banquet in a palazzo on the Grand Canal, and the whole of our Japanese experience. Deserving special mention is an exhibition at L'Assemblée nationale in 1988, where the *procès-verbal* from the trial of Joan of Arc was put on display. Rumour had it that the personal intervention of François Mitterrand, President of France, was needed for this treasure to be shown. In the atmosphere fostered by such entertainments friendships are easily forged, which can only be a good thing.

Enforcing the rules

If the ABA and the International League are responsible for the upholding of standards, what powers do they have to enforce their decisions? The answer is that the ABA can expel dealers who offend against its code of good practice, and that the League can rescind the affiliation of a national association when and where appropriate. These are stern sanctions and are very seldom called for. This is because of another factor – one which is not written in the rule book.

The twenty national associations representing 31 countries affiliated to the League have a combined membership of well over 2,000 dealers, including the vast majority of the more important booksellers in their respective countries. Let us assume, for example, that the ABA received a complaint from a collector that an ABA member had supplied a book which did not measure up to the dealer's description, and that the dealer refused to accept the book back and refund the collector's money. If the ABA committee agreed with that complainant, the dealer would be instructed to accept the return and make the refund forthwith. To fail to co-operate with this decision would be a short-sighted policy indeed for anyone wishing to be successful in the trade.

The Provincial Booksellers Fairs Association

Seen by many as a rival and challenger to the ABA, the Provincial Booksellers Fairs Association was founded in 1974 'to provide provincial book dealers with a shop window in London by holding a regular bookfair'. It now has some 750 members and organizes 130 or more fairs each year, including fairs in London every month and others, large and small, all over the country. Most of its members are based in the United Kingdom, but its membership roll includes booksellers from North America, Australia and continental Europe. It is perceived as being less 'stuffy' than the ABA, while still maintaining that all the exhibitors at its fairs are 'experienced bookdealers who are vetted before acceptance'. PBFA members are obliged to act in accordance with 'a strict code of practice'. The books offered at the average PBFA fair begin at much more modest prices than one would be likely to find at an ABA fair.

In the early days there was a considerable rivalry between the two organizations, a state of affairs which continued until the cooler heads on both sides began to see that there was room for both. There were ABA dealers who were glad to be able to put appropriate books into a PBFA fair in the provinces, where the costs were not so heavy as at the ABA fairs in Mayfair or Olympia. There were PBFA members who were shrewd enough to welcome the throng of truly serious dealers and collectors whom the ABA's reputation brought to London every June.

A few bold spirits and book fair enthusiasts from the ABA's ranks put out feelers and, discovering that they would be welcome as PBFA members, became members of both. There were ructions at first, and dark mutterings about 'commercial confidentiality' (which mostly meant dates and venues of fairs and sundry publicity schemes for bringing the fairs to the notice of the book-buying public), but the atmosphere when the two sides meet nowadays is greatly improved.

A man who deserves much credit for this was Hylton Bayntun-Coward, twice President of the ABA, first from 1980 to 1982 and then from 1992 to 1993. He was determined that the two trade bodies should work amicably together, and put much energy into building bridges to that end. He was, for example, instrumental in the arranging of an annual cricket match between the two Associations, using his local connections to hire the village ground at Dunkerton and filling his house with the teams and their supporters in a year when heavy rain set in. One hears of gamblers offering odds that the ABA and the PBFA will be united, though perhaps with two grades of membership, before another ten years have gone by.

In the ABA's first hundred years so many members willingly gave their time to work for it that to list them all would be no mean task in itself. To name some who are still living, while omitting others, would not seem right. Among those who are no longer alive, the most notable include Mark Cohen, of Marks & Co., who fought like a tiger to build up the Benevolent Fund. Lionel Robinson, President from 1938 to 1942, constantly battled against export restrictions and sought to improve the public perception of the ABA, as well as working for better training of assistants. Percy Muir (Elkin Mathews), as well as writing books which blazed new trails for collectors and dealers alike, was largely responsible for getting the International League off to such a good start. Bill Fletcher (H.M. Fletcher) built the shelving for the early book fairs with his own hands; and Ben Weinreb wrote long essays for *The Times*, which were printed before the scheduled opening of the annual book fair.

When we look back at the first hundred years of the ABA, what do we see? I suggest that we see successive generations of booksellers aspiring to make the world – the world of books at least – a better place than they found it, and to a large extent succeeding.

Any Other Business: Topics from the First Hundred Years of the ABA's Minute-Books

ANTHONY ROTA

1912 The ABA petitioned London County Council in respect of the Shops Act, which members resented because it imposed a half-day's closing every week. The LCC asked for the Shops Act petition to be re-submitted, signed by all those London members who sought exemption. Five months later the exemption was granted, save for shops in the narrow confines of the City of London itself.

1913 The Committee discussed how modern fore-edge paintings on old books should be described. Fore-edge paintings (notably some purchased from Joseph Clayton (Kyd) Clark) were judged by the Committee to be modern, but the purchaser could not proceed against Mr Clark since he had not described the paintings as old. Nevertheless, the Secretary was instructed to caution him. One member, Mr Bolleter, confessed that he had employed an artist to put pictures on the fore-edges of old bindings. He proposed to hold an exhibition of them, describing them as modern.

1914 The Association subscribed to the German Trade Protection Society in Leipzig, effectively a debt-collecting agency. The decision might have been a wise one, but it was a pity about the timing.

   The thorny issue of the market-overt, quite literally 'open market', arose, not for the first time. Under legislation and custom dating back to 1313, stolen goods could be sold with a valid title provided that they had been displayed at a market-place or at a fair, where they were plainly visible, and that the buyer was acting in good faith. This was very satisfactory to the purchaser, but bad for the victim of theft. After lengthy discussion, the subject was adjourned in July *sine die*.

April 1914 Members were warned not to trade in pirated editions of Oscar Wilde's works, which were widely available at tempting prices. Lord Alfred Douglas, as copyright holder, was quick to sue when there was a breach of copyright.

   Shortly after the outbreak of the Great War, the President, George Gregory, of Bath, wrote to the Committee apologizing for his absence and reporting that trade was bad. This appears to have been the common experience. A special meeting was called to protest against the proposed abolition of the halfpenny post. The ABA joined with sellers of new books in their opposition and wrote to the Chancellor of the Exchequer, complaining that 'it will cause a dislocation and restraint of trade out of all proportion to any possible national advantage to be gained'.

14 December 1914 Following the death of Bertram Dobell, bookseller, poet and publisher, it was proposed that his son Percy be elected to the Committee. Seconding that motion, Mr Bowes 'referred in terms of high appreciation to the character and acquirements of the late Mr Bertram Dobell'.

July 1916 The meaning of the phrase 'on approval' when applied to the sale of books within the trade was debated and a definition given. Prejudice was shown to those with German names, even if they had left Germany well before the war.

1917 saw a shortage of paper. Booksellers had to apply to the Paper Commission for a licence to produce catalogues. This rule was soon lifted, but not until dealers had asked customers to send in written applications to receive catalogues. The firm of Davis & Orioli was elected to membership. Although booksellers, they also published the first edition of Lawrence's *Lady Chatterley's Lover* and books by Harold Acton and Norman Douglas.

At the November committee meeting, the President proposed that members should not trade with Germans for ten years after peace was declared. No action was taken.

February 1918 A letter from the Board of Overseas Trade suggested a meeting at which members could hear proposals for the benefit of the trade. This was held in March, when Mr W.H. Evans (of the Board) explained at length how the Board could help by circulating information gathered overseas: 'You will want a complete classification of the possible purchasers of your books with an accurate record of their tastes or requirements.' The newspaper report of the speaker's address ran to 63 column inches. The strength of German dealers was said to be in complete sets of periodicals: British dealers were exhorted to do more in this field.

1919 'The injustice of the present *ad valorem* shipping rates to America' was discussed. So too was insurance against the risk of buying books to which the seller proved not to have good title.

20 May 1920 Frank Karslake died. His daughter Maud was appointed Secretary in his stead. The subscription was raised from five shillings to ten shillings and sixpence in order to pay the new Secretary's wages.

1920 A programme of lectures, visits and entertainments was arranged. Three hundred or more members and friends attended a concert at

Stationers' Hall. There were educational and social outings to Bath and Cambridge.

June 1923 It was resolved that 'no German booksellers be at present admitted as members of the Association.' (Before the war a number had been, and by 1925 they were welcomed back.)

1925 The Net Book Agreement was formally approved and members duly advised. In response, 140 members returned their copies duly signed as demonstrating their undertaking to abide by the NBA's terms.

Miss Evelyn Banks became the first woman elected to the Executive Committee.

A nominal list of people who were bad credit risks was compiled and its existence made known to members. 160 members asked for a copy of what became known as 'the confidential list'.

1926 An attempt was made to get the US Post Office to increase from 11 lb the maximum weight of parcels they would accept. The British Post Office regretted it had been unable to get its American counterpart to comply. The British Chamber of Commerce in the USA gave its help and the limit was doubled to 22 lb.

1932 Evelyn Banks became the first woman to be elected President.

1934 saw the publication by Constable of Carter and Pollard's *Enquiry into the Nature of Certain Nineteenth Century Pamphlets*. This brilliant exposé of T.J. Wise as a forger – at the very least – was arguably the most important event of the bookselling year, yet no record exists that it was ever discussed by the Committee.

At Lionel Robinson's urging, thought was given to ways of raising the prestige and status of the Association. There should be more activity. The Association should have a badge. The Rules and Objects should be revised. There should be more publicity and advertising. A newsletter was needed. More stringent checks should be made on candidates for membership.

Many of the brief notes on these pages suggest that the ABA Committee was more concerned with members' profit and convenience than anything else, but this is a misleading impression, as the next entries show.

February 1936 Mr Barber reported that he had been in touch with Mr Blackwell about 'the situation of our Jewish colleagues in Nazi Germany'. The President was to sign a letter of protest. In October, the minutes noted that the effect of booksellers from overseas opening up in the United Kingdom was an increase in trade rather than the reverse. In April 1939, Mr Myers read to the Committee letters concerning German and Austrian dealers whose businesses had been confiscated by the Nazi government and, 'whose condition had therefore become pitiable in the extreme'. In some cases they feared for their lives; at best, others expected to be sent to a concentration camp and they asked the Association to save them from this danger. It was therefore proposed that those dealers whose names had been mentioned should have their expenses for twelve months' stay in Great Britain guaranteed by a fund to which individual members would subscribe. Messrs Myers, Bayntun, Maggs, Sawyer, Haas, Marks & Co., Joseph, and Lionel Robinson guaranteed £50 each, and six others pledged lesser sums.

1938 New rules allowed for a President, Vice President, Honorary Treasurer and the three most recent Past Presidents, a representative of *The Clique* as the official journal, and twelve others who would form the committee. Although the practice had always been that nominees for President should be selected alternately from London and 'the Country', this (14 November 1938) is the first written mention of such a policy. In fact Lionel Robinson was asked to serve for a second term.

Advertising and publishing campaign. Distribution of a list of members was planned, as were broadcast talks and participation in the *Sunday Times* Exhibition at Earls Court. The names and addresses of visitors to the Association's stand at the *Sunday Times* Exhibition would be printed and sent to every member. An exhibition in the Association's name would feature in the forthcoming New York World Fair.

1939 John Carter accepted an invitation to write a series of articles encouraging the collecting of books. These would be printed for wide distribution. (This project was later set aside for reasons of cost.) Mr Joseph reported that he thought he could arrange for a television broadcast on rare books and also for the issue of a series of cigarette cards illustrating and describing books, and suggested he be allowed to take further steps in both matters.

Sotheran's protested that the tariff on the import of books containing silk in their bindings taxed such books on their gross value and not on the value of the silk alone.

A letter from Lionel Robinson suggested fixing a minimum rate of commission for representing a client at auction. Ten per cent was agreed forthwith.

Francis Edwards gave a dinner and dance to celebrate the firm's centenary.

Ifan Kyrle Fletcher, an ABA member, was elected President of the International Federation of Theatre History.

1954 J. Stanley Sawyer was elected President of the ILAB. Of the eighteen Presidents of the League since its foundation in 1947, no fewer than six have been British.

October 1960 Mr Peter Kroger was elected to membership of the ABA. With a residential address in Ruislip, he traded also from a back room behind a tobacconist's at the point where Fleet Street meets the Strand. He and his wife, Helen, quickly entered into the social life of the trade and it caused much surprise when they were arrested and exposed as Soviet spies. With the benefit of hindsight, those who had traded with them – and some who had danced with them at the Association's annual dinners – professed that there had always been 'something odd about them' and that it was hard to see how they could have made a living from their very modest purchases and sales. There was nothing particularly significant about this last remark: booksellers have said this about their colleagues since time immemorial.

March 1965 The Board of Trade had asked for a copy of Rule 16 (forbidding participation in a 'ring'). A copy had been supplied, with an assurance that all members had signed an agreement to abide by it. A further report had been requested and a draft was prepared by Ian Grant: 'It is the opinion of the ABA that the present Act is unworkable. We suggest that any Act designed to stop auction rings should make it the responsibility of the auctioneer to ensure that the goods are properly valued. To the best of our knowledge, since Rule 16 of the Association was passed in 1956, participation in a "ring" is not compatible with membership, and rings in book auctions have practically ceased to exist.' Duly delivered to the Board of Trade.

April 1966 The Secretary reported that he had charted the fluctuations in membership over the previous fifteen years, during which time the total had decreased by 45 (but in 1965 the ABA had gained sixteen new members and had lost only five – one death and four resignations- bringing the total to 332).

1967 The Committee considered engaging a public relations firm (Clark, Nelson) year round. But did we *all* want publicity? If an auctioneer gets a huge sum for a rare pamphlet hidden away, that is good for him and the owner. If a dealer makes a similar discovery he might prefer to keep it to himself.

September 1968 Following the death of Will Clark, who loyally served the ABA for 30 years, Joyce Shannon (née Custard), who had worked for the Robinsons, took over as Secretary, splitting her time between that job and her work at Peter Murray Hill's bookshop.

February 1974 Mr Dring told the Committee that Quaritch had decided to price all its stock in US dollars, first in their catalogues but eventually in the books themselves. 'In general the meeting failed to give support to this [proposed] practice.'

By the early 1980s, the dinner and dance on the eve of each annual general meeting had been abandoned owing to a decline in attendance. The larger firms which used to take entire tables, such as Maggs, Quaritch, Francis Edwards, Marks & Co., and E. Joseph, no longer did so, and the high cost of tickets discouraged the smaller firms. Parties at Christmas, and dinners (without dancing and without long speeches) after the last night of book fairs, filled the gap in the social programme.

1987 Early in her Presidency, Mrs Senga Grant (John Grant, Edinburgh) received a strongly worded letter from the Minister for the Arts, asking the ABA's attitude to the breaking of books for the display of maps from atlases and illustrations from colour-plate books. Mrs Grant swiftly replied that the Association deplored any form of 'vandalisation' of books.

Another topic under discussion was the likelihood or otherwise of the imposition of Value Added Tax on books. Resistance to the notion continues to this day.

Not all the Benevolent Fund entries were routine reports of interest rates on funds on deposit. Generous help was available where it was needed: in one instance, a respectable sum was paid to a member whose own business had suffered badly because of the enormous amount of time he had had to spend on the Association's affairs. In the same year, help was given to a 'runner' or 'scout' (as Americans prefer) who was fatally ill. A further grant was paid to his widow. Benevolent Fund trustees may now use their discretion in allocating funds in proportion to need and in considering applications from all those who have worked in the antiquarian book trade, regardless of whether they are members of the ABA.

APPENDICES

Prices and Exchange Rates

ANGUS O'NEILL

Prices in the UK in the twentieth century: inflation and indexation

THE hardest evidence of changing tastes is changing prices. But how can these be realistically compared over a century which saw vast upheavals in every sphere of human activity? There are any number of different ways of comparing prices, which all give different (sometimes dramatically different) results.

The 'retail price index' measures the cost of the goods and services purchased by a typical household or consumer. It works best with commodities whose use has been stable over a long period: food, drink and so on. It is less suitable for items subject to rapid technological change such as electronics or computers.

'Average earnings' are the mean average, over the entire working population, of wages and other payments, including bonuses, commission and so on. This measure allows for demographic changes in the working population, but it is perhaps not quite right for our purposes as it does not take into account increased accumulated wealth.

Gross domestic product (GDP) is the total output of a national economy. Comparisons made on the basis of GDP can be applied to all types of monetary amounts – commodities, income, wealth, expenditure, and so on – but they are most often made when dealing with larger sums such as government expenditure or large construction projects.

Per-capita GDP reflects average income more efficiently than 'average earnings', because not only wages but also other sources of income (interest, dividends, rents, etc.) are included. It may perhaps be understood as the average share of a person in the total output of the economy. This measure appears most suitable for salaries and other incomes, as well as wealth and assets. It is perhaps not ideal for dealing with the very highest of 'high spots', but since most of the trade is conducted at more humble levels, often with quite valuable books being bought by people of modest means, it seems to be generally adequate.

All these measures give widely different results, unsurprisingly. The retail price index saw the 1902 pound equate to £66.38 in 2002; average earnings over the same period rose by a factor of 342, and gross domestic product by no less than 549. Clearly no single one of these indices is sufficient on its own, but economists suggest that for our purposes (broadly defined here as the comparison over time of prices of valuable, or 'collectable', books, rather than secondhand ones) the most useful of these is 'per capita' GDP, which works out at 388.63 over the period in question.

For the routine buying and selling of ordinary secondhand books, the RPI might be more suitable – indeed, an extraordinarily precise illustration for this exists. David Low, in his memoir '*with all faults*' (Tehran, 1973), describes Thomas Thorp's shop in Cecil Court, *c.*1930, as offering books from his window priced '"All at two shillings", followed by "One shilling", and the final wild "Sixpenny" scramble'. The present writer's shop, also in Cecil Court, offers books outside priced initially at £4, then £2, then, finally, £1: equating exactly to the forty-fold rise in RPI over the period. 'Rare' books, however – first editions, presentation copies and the like – are generally bought by the relatively rich, out of 'spare money' (though not all spouses would agree), and rightly or wrongly are often seen as part of their owner's financial assets: so 'per capita GDP' is the more suitable index to use when trying to assess their prices in real terms. It is far from perfect, but it provides a useful basis for discussion.

Year	RPI	Average earnings	Per capita GDP
1901	1.000	1.000	1.000
1910	1.064	1.068	1.046
1915	1.355	1.339	1.394
1920	2.703	3.181	3.000
1930	1.717	2.240	2.208
1940	1.989	3.098	3.269
1945	2.517	4.251	4.422
1950	3.153	5.683	5.776
1960	4.693	10.857	10.937
1970	6.984	20.610	20.610
1975	12.878	43.769	41.763
1980	25.189	86.791	91.010
1985	35.646	133.770	139.341
1990	47.508	202.395	214.305
1995	56.174	254.586	273.257
2000	64.161	316.959	357.033
2004	70.340	369.886	431.128

Sterling/dollar exchange rate fluctuations

Rates given below are annual averages, or ranges of annual averages: the exception is the year 2005, for which the full range is given in order to illustrate the width of fluctuations. The rate over the century varied from about $1.05 in 1985 (high US interest rates, the miners' strike in the UK) to over $5 in 1934 (following Roosevelt's revaluation of the dollar price of gold).

Year	£1 = US $	Year	£1 = US $	Year	£1 = US $
1900-13	4.86-4.87	1939	4.43	1983	1.52
1914	4.93	1940	3.83	1984-85	1.30-1.34
1915-18	4.76-4.77	1941-48	4.03-4.04	1986	1.47
1919 (a)	4.43	1949 (b)	3.69	1987-92	1.64-1.78
1920	3.66	1950-66	2.79-2.81	1993-96	1.50-1.58
1921	3.85	1967 (c)	2.75	1997-99	1.62-1.66
1922-24	4.42-4.58	1968-73	2.39-2.50	2000-02	1.44-1.52
1925-30	4.83-4.87	1974-75	2.22-2.34	2003	1.63
1931	4.54	1976-79	1.75-2.12	2004	1.83
1932	3.51	1980	2.33	2005	1.70-1.93
1933	4.24	1981	2.02		
1934-38	4.89-5.04	1982	1.75		

Notes: (a) in 1919 Great Britain abandoned the gold standard; (b) in September 1949, sterling was devalued by 30%; (c) in November 1967, sterling was devalued by 14%.

A Note on the Dating of Catalogues

ANGUS O'NEILL AND H.R. WOUDHUYSEN

1902 London telephone exchanges (Central, City, Mayfair, Western, Victoria, etc.) introduced.

1917 London postal districts (W, WC, NW, SW, etc.) acquired number suffixes.

1959 STD dialling codes began to be introduced.

1960 Telex began to be widely used.

1966 All-figure telephone numbers introduced nationally.

1971 Decimal coinage introduced, on 15 February.

1973 VAT introduced at 12.5 per cent; raised to 15 per cent in 1979; to 17.5 per cent in 1991.

1974 Postcodes introduced nationally.

1980s Telex replaced by fax.

1984 Domain names introduced on the internet.

1989 Invention of HTML. Internet became generally available.

1990 01 London telephone numbers replaced by 071 and 081.

1993 World Wide Web introduced; first web browsers released.

1995 All-figure telephone numbers changed nationally from 0 to 01; 071 and 081 London telephone numbers replaced by 0171 and 0181.

2000 0171 and 0181 London telephone numbers replaced by 0207 and 0208.

Founder-Members of the Antiquarian Booksellers' Association, 11 December 1906

JOHN CRITCHLEY

AT the inaugural meeting in the Criterion Restaurant on 11 December 1906, Frank Karslake 'announced a preliminary membership of 112, giving the names and reading extracts from letters by the various well-wishers of the Association.' No record is known to have survived, however, of the names which were then read out.

The list of original members of the ABA in this appendix was reconstructed initially from the names mentioned in the minutes of the inaugural meeting and in subsequent minutes (apart from those recorded as having been elected to membership after the inaugural meeting) and from the Directory of Members contained in the first Annual Report dated 1908.

The list was refined and the subsequent history of the founder-members was then traced in outline by cross-checking against the following sources:

1908 to 1945 Directories of Members (contained in the Annual Reports; copies held at the ABA Office)

Minutes of Committee meetings from the inaugural meeting to December 1956 (all minutes of Committee meetings are held by the ABA but cross-checking has so far only been carried out to December 1956)

1927 *Directory of the Principal Antiquarian Booksellers in the British Isles*

1932 *Directory of the Principal Antiquarian Booksellers in the British Isles*

1948 list of ABA members in Percy Muir's *Book-Collecting: More Letters to Everyman* (1949), pp. 141-52

1949, 56, 72, 74, 78, 81, 83, 85, 88, 89-90, 90-91, 91-92, 92-93, 93-94, 94-95, 96-97, 97-98, 98-99, 99-2000, 2000-01, 01-02, 03-04 and 2006 ABA Directories of Members

The resulting list contains the names of 114 booksellers who could have been founder-members. It has not been possible to identify with certainty the two extraneous names.

It is hoped that the information given below will be useful for establishing the dates at which some of these firms were in business. Of the 114 original members, 33 had left membership by 1916. After 25 years, only 60 original members remained, and this number had fallen to 32 after 50 years. Twelve further members had left the Association by the 75th anniversary, and one more, William Smith, by 1989. Five original members, Deighton Bell, George Gregory, Albert J. (and later Winifred A.) Myers, Thomas Thorp and Wheldon & Wesley, survived into the twenty-first century before ceasing to trade or resigning.

Nine original members remain as members at the 2006 centenary - albeit as eight businesses, some having merged with other businesses and modified their names, and one despite gaps in the continuity of membership. These are:

B.H. Blackwell Ltd; now Blackwell's Rare Books
Thomas Chatto (Trading as Pickering & Chatto); now Pickering & Chatto
H.M. Gilbert (continuity broken between 1922 and 1954)

Alfred Halewood; now Halewood & Sons
Maggs Bros Ltd
Chas P. Porter; now Galloway & Porter
Bernard Quaritch Ltd
Henry N. Stevens; now Henry Stevens, Son & Stiles
R.E. Stiles; now Henry Stevens, Son & Stiles

Founder-Members of the Antiquarian Booksellers' Association

Allsup & Stanley, Preston (not in 1921 Directory)
Baker, E., Birmingham (retired March 1922)
Baldwin, J., London (not in 1921 Directory)
Barnard, P.M., Tunbridge Wells (died 1942)
Baxendine, Edinburgh (Andrew Baxendine & Sons 1932; not in 1938 Directory)
Blackwell, B.H., Ltd, Oxford (Blackwell's Rare Books, 1983)
Bones, W.A., Devizes (not in 1922 Directory)
Braun, L.C., London (not in 1938 Directory)
Brown, C. & E., London (not in 1933 Directory)
Brown, Harold, London (not in 1909 Directory)
Brown, Henry J., B.F. Stevens & Brown, London (died 1948)
Brown, W., Bookseller Ltd, Edinburgh (W. Brown died Dec. 1906; J.H. Brown 1908; William Brown 1927; Trustees of William Brown 1932; William Brown elected June 1943; not in 1978 Directory)
Brown, Wilfred, London (not in 1913 Directory)
Buchanan, John, London (not in 1932 Directory; A.E. Hextall 1932)
Carver, T., Hereford (not in 1913 Directory)
Chatto, Thomas (Trading as Pickering & Chatto), London (Hon. Treasurer, 1906-24; membership under Pickering & Chatto in 1927; died Oct. 1929; of Pall Mall, after taking over Dawson's, from 1983; of St George Street from 1997; of New Bond Street from 2006)
Clegg, J. (Rochdale; James Clegg died March 1917)
Commin, H.G., Exeter (Bournemouth 1908; not in 1912 Directory; re-elected June 1916; J.G. Commin 1930; not in 1948 List; died Oct. 1952?)
Conlon, J., Leeds (not in 1915 Directory)
Crowe, F., Wrexham (not in 1917 Directory; Crowe Bros, Wrexham, April 1939; not in 1972 Directory)
Daniel, Walter V., London (Hon. Member, Feb. 1919; died Nov. 1928)
Day's Library Ltd, London (resigned March 1924)
Daymond, H., London (not in 1922 Directory)
Deighton Bell & Co., Cambridge (& Co., Ltd, 1927; taken over by W. Heffer & Sons Ltd in 1989; resigned and business wound up 2000)
Dickinson, R.D., & Co., London (not in 1938 Directory)
Discount Book Co., Preston (A. Halewood 1927; not in 1925 Directory)
Dobell, Bertram, London (died Jan. 1915; Percy G. Dobell Jan. 1915; Arthur Dobell; resigned Feb. 1956)
Downing, William, Birmingham (died Feb. 1910; C. Downing 1911; W.H. Downing 1912; not in 1931 Directory)
Dunlop, W., Edinburgh (not in 1972 Directory)
Eclectic Book Co., York (not in 1913 Directory)
Edwards, D.W., Hull (L.H. Edwards 1930; not in 1938 Directory)
Edwards, J., London (not in 1926 Directory; died June 1927)
Fagg, W., London (died Dec. 1934)

Forrester, R., Glasgow (not in 1916 Directory)

Gadney, H.G., Oxford (not in 1923 Directory)

George, E.W., London (not in 1916 Directory)

George, W.C., London (not in 1916 Directory)

Gilbert, H.M., Southampton (not in 1922 Directory; H.M. Gilbert & Son elected March 1954; Winchester branch opened 1972 and closed 1999; Southampton shop closed 2002, since when business has operated from Winchester private address)

Gill, F., Weston-super-Mare (not in 1915 Directory)

Glaisher, J., London (removed Feb. 1919 for non-payment of subscriptions)

Goad, F.W., Bath (not a member 1914)

Gray, Henry, Acton (H. Gray & Co. 1927 *Directory of the Principal Antiquarian Booksellers in the British Isles*; George E. Harris 1935; not a member 1938)

Gregory Book Store, George, Bath (died September 1930; Geo. Bayntun & W.J. Crudgington 1927; H.H. Bayntun-Coward 1985; resigned 2000 after death of H.H. Bayntun-Coward)

Halewood, Alfred, Preston (died 1938; Halewood & Sons 1956; Harold R. Halewood December 1926; see Discount Book Co.)

Hamblen, T., Leamington (not in 1912 Directory)

Haxton, David, London (not in 1913 Directory)

Hector, E., Birmingham (not in 1913 Directory)

Heffer, W., & Sons Ltd, Cambridge (E.W. Heffer died 1949; not a member in 1974; see Deighton Bell)

Hill, B.R., Newcastle upon Tyne (not in 1915 Directory)

Hiscoke & Son, London (also Hiscoke's Library, Richmond, in 1927; not in 1935 Directory)

Hitchman, J., Birmingham (not in 1910 Directory)

Hopkins, Hugh D., Glasgow (died Jan. 1947; H. Hopkins 1956; not in 1972 Directory)

Howell, E., Ltd, Liverpool (F.R. Howell 1924; not in 1933 Directory)

Hunt, H.W., Norwich (not a member in 1938)

Jones, T., Hull (not in 1923 Directory)

Joseph, E., London (Jack and Sam Joseph March 1920; not a member in 1996)

Karslake, Frank, London (Hon. Secretary from 1906 until he died in April 1920)

Keener & Co., London (not in 1914 Directory)

Lamley & Co., London (not in 1941 Directory)

Leighton, W.J., London (died Nov. 1917)

Leslie, F., Leeds (not in 1915 Directory)

Loewe, J.R. (Wm. Lesley & Son), London (resigned July 1915)

Long, W.H., Portsmouth (not in 1913 Directory)

Lupton, J.T., & Lupton, W. (Lupton Bros), Burnley (combined under Lupton Bros 1927; not in 1940 Directory)

Mackenzie, J., Glasgow (not in 1910 Directory)

Maggs, B.D., London (died Oct. 1935; C.A. Maggs died June 1922; E.U. Maggs died June 1955; Maggs Bros 1927; Maggs Bros Ltd, 1956)

Marston, R.B. (*The Publishers' Circular*), Dec. 1906 (not in 1920 Directory)

Mason, S.M., Carlisle (died 1937 or 1938)

Massey, E., Dublin (not in 1914 Directory)

Miles, James, Leeds (James Miles (Leeds) Ltd elected March 1950; not in 1972 Directory)

Milligan, J., Leeds (not in 1915 Directory)

Milligan, T., Leeds (not in 1914 Directory)

Mills, T.B., London (not in 1929 Directory)

Murray, Francis E. (The Clique), Derby (London in 1908; D.M. Murray in 1930 Directory; C.S. Davis in 1932 Directory; The Clique continued as a member under its own name from 1933, but was not in the 1978 or subsequent Directories)

Museum Book Store Ltd, London (not in 1972 Directory)

Myers, Albert J., London (Myers & Co. in 1927; died 27 Nov. 1944; succeeded by Winifred A. Myers; Myers & Co. (Booksellers) Ltd, 1956; Ruth Shepherd 1985; retired 2001)

Naunton, F.W., Bury St Edmunds (not in 1913 Directory)

Norton, W. & B., Cheltenham (not in 1918 Directory)

Pitcher, W.N., Manchester (not in 1915 Directory)

Porter, Chas P., Cambridge (became Galloway & Porter in 1927)

Preston, J., & Co., London (not in 1972 Directory)

Quaritch, Bernard, Ltd, London (B.A. Quaritch died Oct. 1913)

Read and Barrett, Ipswich (became E. Barrett in 1907; not in 1929 Directory)

Redway, R.E. (Frank Hollings Ltd), London (died 1946; Frank Redway, Wimbledon, Oct. 1910; succeeded Frank Hollings, Feb. 1919; not in 1948 List)

Richardson, C., Manchester (not in 1936 Directory)

Rider, D.J., London (not in 1917 Directory)

Ridler, William, London (not in 1914 Directory)

Robson, B., London (Robson & Co. 1908; Ltd 1927; not in 1937 Directory)

Sawyer, Chas J., Ltd, London (not in 1972 Directory)

Slatter, A.J., London (not in 1931 Directory)

Smith, W.J., Brighton (died Jan. 1912)

Smith, William, Reading (Wm. Smith & Son 1908; not in 1989 Directory)

South, A., London (not in 1914 Directory)

Stevens, Henry N., London (Founding President 1906; Henry Stevens, Son & Stiles 1912; died May 1930; also New York branch 1948; Farnham 1972; Williamsburg, VA, 1985; Farnham and New York branches now shut)

Stiles, R.E., London (Henry Stevens, Son & Stiles 1912)

Streicher, C.A., York (not in 1913 Directory)

Suckling & Co., London (not a member in 1983)

Sutton, A., Manchester (died Nov. 1922; Albert Sutton in 1927 *Directory of the Principal Antiquarian Booksellers in the British Isles*; not a member in 1956)

Thomas, J., London (not in 1916 Directory)

Thomson, J., Edinburgh (not in 1917 Directory)

Thorp, Thomas, London & Reading (also Guildford 1924; Thomas Thorp died March 1937; succeeded by son Thomas C. Thorp; retired 1983; succeeded by son Jim Thorp; business moved from London to St Albans 1983; Guildford business shut 2002; Jim Thorp resigned membership on retirement Jan. 2006)

Thurgate, R., London (Myers & Co. 1908; not in 1913 Directory)

Thurnam, C., & Sons, Carlisle (not in 1942 Directory)

Tickell, W.H., London (not in 1919 Directory)

Tregaskis, James, London (died Nov. 1926; Hugh Tregaskis Dec. 1920; James Tregaskis & Son 1927; resigned October 1937)

Vincent, H.D. (J. & E. Bumpus), London (not in 1924 Directory)

Voynich, W.M., London (not in 1931 Directory)

Walker, H., (Bookseller) Ltd, Leeds (not in 1938 Directory)

Waters, A.W., Leamington (Simmons & Waters 1930; not in 1940 Directory)

Webb, George, Dublin (not in 1917 Directory)

Webster, D., Leeds (Tunbridge Wells 1927; not in 1936 Directory)

Wesley, E.F., London (Wm. Wesley & Son in 1912; E.F. Wesley resigned July 1915, died April 1929; Wheldon & Wesley 1927; Hitchin 1972; resigned and wound up 2004)

West, G.S., Lancaster (not in 1915 Directory)

Woodhouse, A.D., Birmingham (not in 1916 Directory)

APPENDIX 4

Twentieth-Century Rare and Secondhand Book Trade Archives: A Survey

RICHARD FORD

THE ideal bookseller's archive would be complete. It would comprise: all correspondence, in and out; financial records including records of sales (ledgers and copies of invoices), account books, day-books, and, when applicable, wages books; a record of the stock, usually in the form of a card index until the computer age; a record of books catalogued; a mailing or customer list; publicity material; and a set of catalogues marked with the buyers' names.

A handful of booksellers on the following list have retained comprehensive, nearly complete, archives (Aberdeen Rare Books, Jarndyce, P. & B. Rowan and the manuscript dealer John Wilson). But most surviving archives, however substantial, fall short of this ideal, some woefully. The reasons for this are diverse, and include the fortunes of war – the Blitz destroyed most of Henry Sotheran's archive, and the bombing of Southampton, also in the Second World War, put paid to H.M. Gilbert's archive. There is also the attrition attendant on moves to new premises or the need to make space for something perceived as more valuable. Many booksellers also nurse the conviction that no one would have any use for their records, and hence find them disposable. No reason emerges for the destruction by Lionel and Philip Robinson of their 'archive of correspondence', witnessed by Anthony Hobson, to whom they 'paid no attention when [he] tried to persuade them of its historical importance'.[1] (A few survivors of this destruction recently surfaced at a West London auction and are listed below.)

Some booksellers consider giving information about their archive a breach of confidentiality or an unwelcome addition to their daily grind. Others have been unresponsive to requests for information, broadcast or targeted, for unfathomable reasons. In mitigation, one bookseller who declined an entry here is toying with the idea of donating his archive to the National Library of Ireland.

Richard Hunter of Edinburgh City Archives speculates provocatively that 'the nature of those booksellers inclined to amass their own archives and take steps to ensure their preservation seems likely to present a rather selective and perhaps erroneous impression of the trade'.[2] Perhaps it should be added that many small archives have survived, not by the decision of the bookseller, but by accident. Eric Morten gives this as the reason for the survival of a solitary account book from his acorn days of 1959, which he now keeps for sentimental reasons. He adds the point, supportive of Richard Hunter's view, that many booksellers live from hand to mouth and do not generate the records, catalogues and correspondence which would constitute an archive.[3] The residue of a bookseller's archive, however, may sometimes be found within the archive of a company which has absorbed it – for example, William George's Sons Ltd and other companies in the Blackwell Collection.[8]

Twentieth-century rare and secondhand booksellers' archives have already been exploited in significant works, such as Arthur Freeman and Janet Ing Freeman's *Anatomy of an Auction* (1990) and Donald C. Dickinson, *John Carter* (New Castle, DE, 2004). Scholars who have become interested in why American universities became collectors of rare books see such archives as valuable sources of information.[4] Research is often inhibited by the inadequacy of the cataloguing and the lack, or partial nature, of online access, but this is improving by the day.

The importance of booksellers' archives is now widely recognized, though institutional curators vary in their attitudes towards their donation, purchase or deposit. Arnold Hunt of the British Library says that the Department of Manuscripts would welcome offers of booksellers' archives, but stresses that all offers would have to be considered in terms of their potential research value: 'We would be most interested in marked catalogues, stock-books and other records that might help researchers to trace the provenance of particular items; less so in account-books or routine correspondence relating to the day-to-day running of the business'.[5] Michael Bott, Keeper of Archives and Manuscripts at the University of Reading – the major British repository of publishing archives, but with minimal antiquarian bookselling material – says that in 'principle we'd be interested in acquiring records of booksellers, but space is a problem at the moment, so any new collection will have to be agonised over'.[6] Conversely, B. Breon Mitchell, Director of the Lilly Library, has no obvious space problem and asserts that 'We do like to acquire booksellers' archives if possible',[7] where 'possible' speaks volumes about such factors as availability of funds and a fair price being asked. Dr Iain Brown of the National Library of Scotland would welcome donation or deposit but would be much more selective if payment were required.[8]

The following list of archives is inevitably selective and illustrates various forms of survival ranging from retention by the company (Jarndyce and P. & B. Rowan) to a temporary appearance in another bookseller's stock (W.N. Pettigrew and Andrew Block) – temporary because the usual practice of the bookseller or manuscript dealer would be to cherry-pick a collection for the autograph letters of notable people. But this is the tip of an iceberg since a vast quantity of booksellers' correspondence appears in their retained or surviving correspondence with collectors, research libraries, and fellow booksellers, many of whom are unrepresented or minimally represented here. In many cases such correspondence constitutes a bookseller's only archival hold on immortality. For example, a small quantity of the correspondence of Thomas J. Wise's 'stooge',[9] Herbert Gorfin, survives in the archives of the Rosenbach Foundation, and a bill from him to Wise survives in the Ashley collection (in the British Library). The Rosenbach Foundation, like other archives, is rich in booksellers' correspondence, and here one may find letters from Lionel and Philip Robinson. Some of their correspondence is also to be found in the surviving archive of Peter Murray Hill (see below).

Such correspondence is contained in the general files of the larger American universities, in administrative files kept by curators, and in the archives of American dealers and collectors. Access varies with the institution. The correspondence may be part of the general collections and subject to the 'terms governing such collections [but] if the correspondence is part of the institution's working papers, then expect restriction'.[10]

Among British institutions, the National Library of Scotland keeps 'some correspondence with booksellers if this is in connection with important purchases; but there are no hard and fast rules. ... Sometimes such correspondence is viewed merely as ephemeral and it is weeded from time to time'.[11] The British Library also retains a substantial body of booksellers' correspondence with the Library – 'acquisitions, staff matters, bibliographic enquiries etc'.[12] The National Library of Wales reports that access to such correspondence is now subject to the Freedom of Information Act.[13] For reasons of commercial confidentiality, companies such as Maggs Bros have not deposited their records of the last 25 years at the British Library, and organizations such as the Provincial Booksellers Fairs Association currently restrict access or have a closed archive.

Substantial collections of twentieth-century booksellers' catalogues are held by the Bodleian Library and the British Library. These collections depend upon catalogues which have been sent to the libraries and not every bookseller has thought or thinks it worthwhile to do so. The collections have many incomplete runs, suggesting a patchy policy of retention, or, less likely, booksellers adjusting their mailing lists. The British Library also has an extensive holding of auction catalogues which are described below. Other institutions have large collections of booksellers' catalogues: for example the Grolier Club of New York has a nearly complete run of Francis Edwards catalogues, the firm's own set but unmarked. (A marked set of about 500 of the same company's catalogues is currently held by the Dutch booksellers, Asher & Co. B.V., via Nico Israel and Maggs catalogue 1062 (1985), the latter also the source of the Grolier Club set.) Booksellers (by no means all) keep runs of their own catalogues. Some have accumulated collections of other booksellers' catalogues. Rusty Mott of Howard S. Mott, Inc., for example, could supplement the holdings of the Bodleian and British Library with an incomplete run of Museum Book Store (Leon Kashnor) catalogues. The bookseller William Laywood (Forest Books) owns a substantial collection of auction catalogues from the library of Charles Traylen of Guildford, with annotations revealing Traylen's career in the ring.

I have added information about runs of marked catalogues to this list only if I have listed information about the relevant company's archive – runs of auction-house catalogues, however, are listed whether marked or not.

A major source of information has been Alexis Weedon and Michael Bott's *British Book Trade Archives 1830-1939: A Location Register* (Oxford & Bristol, 1996; hereafter BBTA). Where applicable I have followed Weedon and Bott's custom of referring to the *National Register of Archives* (NRA). Information on archives is also filtering on to the internet via Archives Hub (*www.archiveshub.ac.uk*), A2A (*www.a2a.org.uk*) – both referred to when relevant – and other websites.

I have excluded all booksellers listed in BBTA and elsewhere with no archival material relating to the rare or secondhand book trade, or where none is evident in the information supplied to me by archivists or by printed sources. Trade directories have occasionally provided useful confirmation of a firm's interest in rare and secondhand books. For example, Read and Barrett and William Brown are recorded in the list of original members of the ABA (1906: Appendix 3 above), *The International Directory of Second-hand Booksellers and Bibliophile's Manual*, ed. James Clegg (Rochdale etc., 4th edn., 1894), and the *Directory of the Principal Antiquarian Booksellers in the British Isles* (International Association of Antiquarian Booksellers, 1921).

Information about American antiquarian booksellers' archives appeared in *The ABAA Newsletter* (spring 1997), vol. 8, no. 3.

References to repositories are in brief. Full details of the vast majority may be found in *Aslib Directory of Information Sources in the United Kingdom*, ed. Keith W. Reynard (12th edn., 2002) and, for the American institutions, *American Library Directory, 2004-2005* (2 vols, 57th edn., 2004). The addresses of booksellers currently trading may be found in Sheppard's *Book Dealers in the British Isles* (2005). Further information may also be obtained via the ABA Office, to which supplementary material may be sent for the inevitable revised versions.

ABERDEEN RARE BOOKS, Collieston, Aberdeenshire

'Complete' archive comprising correspondence, financial records, index cards, catalogues 1975-2003.
Aberdeen City Archives. No access until 2014.

J.A. ALLEN & CO. (THE HORSEMAN'S BOOKSHOP) LTD, London

Correspondence, newspaper cuttings and articles, catalogues and personal material about the life of Joseph Allen and his business, some provided by Allen himself.
Private collection. Contact: ABA Office.

JOHN S. ARTHUR, Liverpool

Correspondence, newspaper clippings, photographs *c.*1804-1910 (117 pieces), personal correspondence.
Huntington Library, California.

J. GEOFFREY ASPIN, Little Sutton, Cheshire, and Hay-on-Wye

Correspondence and invoices sent to Professor Vivienne Mylne 1966-85 (*c.*150 items). Aspin specialized in French literature.
Taylor Institution Library, University of Oxford. Archives Hub *GB 486.

H.W. BADLEY, Hawarden, Flintshire

Correspondence files, some literary (one bundle) 1930-9.
Flintshire Record Office. NRA.

JAMES BAIN LTD, London

Correspondence, Memoranda and Articles of Association, minutes, property records, probate records, photographs, catalogues 1842-1979.
City of Westminster Archives Centre. NRA.

GEORGE BAYNTUN, Bath

Correspondence, financial records, sales and stock records, wages books 1922-86.
George Bayntun. Contact: Edward Bayntun-Coward. NRA.

BIRRELL & GARNETT LTD, London

Correspondence 1924-42 (31 box-files), orders from catalogues (4 box-files), administrative documents 1928-33, minute-book of directors' meetings 1927-37, stock (catalogue) cards 1927-38, customer cards, catalogues 1-[45, misnumbered 44] (missing 2-4) (1920-[1934]), marked catalogues 10-44 (missing 1-9, 13, 15, [45], several duplicates) (1925-[1934]), and related material. (Graham Pollard papers: detailed catalogue by Esther Potter available in Room 132, New Bodleian.)
Bodleian Library. NRA.

Cash-book, journal, petty cash-book, sold and stock book, cash sales and bad debts book, accounts for purchases etc., sales, capital loans, rent, etc. 1922-39.
British Library.

BLACKWELL'S RARE BOOKS, Oxford

Archive, mostly concerned with the new books and publishing arms of the company, but also material relating to the Antiquarian Books Department incl. invoices 1925-51, purchases and sales books 1948-51, 1958, 1962-82, correspondence 1968-72, documents concerning the ring 1927-56, marked catalogues *c.*1950-*c.*1985, and other papers. For a more complete description see *A Guide to the Merton Blackwell Collection* (Oxford, 2004). The *Guide* also lists material in this collection from the archives of new and secondhand bookshops mainly in Oxford acquired by B.H. Blackwell, incl. Parker and Son (below), William George's Sons Ltd (below), The Davenant Bookshop (purchases and sales account book), Stone's Bookshop Ltd (annual statements of accounts 1973-77), the Turl Cash Bookshop (annual statements of accounts 1947-63 and 1965-68), and F.A. Wood's Bookshop (financial records 1940-59). See *Guide*, pp. 44-7.
Merton College, Oxford.

ERIC BLIGH, Wallingford

Correspondence, some relating to bookselling, 1904-65, incl. *c.*50 letters to Peter Murray-Hill (below) 1950-7, and customer records (2 vols.); and other material (in the papers of Joan

Feisenberger). Also letters from Eric Bligh to Arnold Muirhead (below) 1929-57.
Bodleian Library. Archives Hub *GB 161.

ANDREW BLOCK, London

Day-book 1954-76, minimal correspondence *c.*1920-81, stock cards, and a small quantity of related material.
Richard M. Ford Ltd. Contact: Richard Ford.

MARTIN BRESLAUER/BERNARD H. BRESLAUER, Berlin, London and New York

Early correspondence, business papers and several catalogues; business papers 1948-78; private documents and correspondence.
Staatsbibliothek zu Berlin.

WILLIAM BROWN, Edinburgh

Records (seven boxes and six ledgers or albums) 1878-1955, a run of catalogues.
National Library of Scotland. NRA.

JOHN & EDWARD BUMPUS, London

Miscellaneous records including correspondence, book orders, bank-books, blocks, etc. 1833-1959. Important literary correspondence (uncatalogued).
City of Westminster Archives Centre. NRA.

CHAUCER HEAD BOOKSHOP (William Downing), Birmingham

Correspondence and miscellaneous records *c.*1870-1940.
Birmingham City Archives. NRA.

DOUGLAS CLEVERDON, Bristol

Correspondence, advertisements, catalogues, lists, invoices, stock sheets, etc., ledgers, scrap-book 1926-41. The Cleverdon papers also include broadcasting and publishing-related material 1926-88.
Indiana University, Bloomington, Lilly Library.

DAWSONS OF PALL MALL, London

See Pickering & Chatto below.

DEIGHTON BELL & CO., Cambridge

Archive, much of which concerns the binding, new books and publishing arms of the company. A comprehensive listing is given by Jonathan R. Topham, 'Two Centuries of Cambridge Publishing and Bookselling: A Brief History

of Deighton Bell and Co., 1778-1998, with a Checklist of the Archive', *Transactions of the Cambridge Bibliographical Society*, vol. xi, part 3 (1998), pp. 350-403, although he discriminates between the new and secondhand only when he lists stock books ('Stock and Sales of Secondhand Books').
Cambridge University Library. NRA.

BERTRAM DOBELL, London

Correspondence, diaries 1868-9, 1881-1914, literary manuscripts and other papers incl. annotated proofs of his first catalogue (1876) and of his *Catalogue of Books printed for Private Circulation* (1906).
Bodleian Library. NRA.

Note: Percy Dobell's diaries 1916-19 survive in a private collection and the correspondence of Percy Dobell with James M. Osborn may be found in the Beinecke Library, Yale University.

DAVID DOUGLAS, Edinburgh

Scrap-books (six volumes) 1847-1903.
National Library of Scotland. NRA.

ELKIN MATHEWS LTD, later Muir & Deval, then Elkin Mathews again, London, Takeley and Blakeney

Correspondence and financial records 1892-1979, stock (catalogue) cards, stock ledger sheets 1894, account books, stock lists, expenses ledgers, customer records, catalogues 1-189 (1922- [1969]), Deval & Muir catalogues 1-25, literary papers of Percy Muir 1933-77.
Indiana University, Bloomington, Lilly Library. Traces of the rare book business of the original Elkin Mathews (Charles Elkin Mathews, died 1921) may be found in his correspondence (Reading University Library, see NRA). Percy Muir, in *Minding My Own Business* (1956), mentions a notebook kept by Mathews (not traced) of 'antiquarian or publishing interest' (p. 11) and suggests that the 'likely contents of his shop are probably reflected in his personal library which was sold at auction by Messrs Hodgson in April 1922' (p. 12).

ELLIS, London

Correspondence, 14 daybooks, 39 letterbooks (total 23 boxes and 38 oversize boxes) 1860-1928.
University of California Los Angeles Library.

Correspondence, George Smith's diary 1890,

newscuttings 1893-1954.
Senate House Library, University of London. NRA.

Marked catalogues 1-259 (1860-1928).
Cambridge University Library.

The correspondence of Frederick Startridge Ellis (1839-1901) may be found in the British Library and elsewhere (see NRA) and a box of his business papers (*c.*1884) in the Grolier Club collections.

C. & I.K. FLETCHER LTD, Newport and London

Correspondence 1953-69, financial records 1963-8, stock (catalogue) cards, marked catalogues 1-232 (1938-69), unnumbered catalogues (1933, 1936), miscellaneous records 1963-8.
London Metropolitan Archives. NRA.

A box of letters (387 items) to Fletcher (1926-69) may be found in the Rare Book and Manuscript Library, Columbia University, New York.

H.M. FLETCHER, London and Much Hadham, Herts.

Correspondence 1955-86, orders 1954-84, invoices and receipts 1960-80, photographs of the book trade (300+ items) *c.*1960-80, catalogues (129, incomplete run from *c.*1920, some marked), ABA Fair Catalogues 1958 to date (missing 1965, 1968), related ephemera and memorabilia.
H.M. Fletcher. Contact: Keith Fletcher.

W. & G. FOYLE LTD (FOYLES), London and Beeleigh Abbey, Essex

Correspondence, early cash-books and financial records, corporate records and accounts, material relating to Literary Luncheons, newspaper cuttings collection and miscellaneous 1903 to date, bound volumes of *Foylibra* 1927-2000, catalogues (Beeleigh Abbey Books), William Foyle's and Christina Foyle's personal 'notebooks' (index cards, a large quantity), Christina Foyle's diaries. Some of this archive relates to the rare and secondhand business.
Private collection.

WILLIAM GEORGE'S SONS LTD, Bristol

Business and other papers 1924-87. (Blackwell Collection, B.H. Blackwell having 'acquired the controlling interest' in George's in 1929.)
A Guide to the Merton Blackwell Collection, p. 46.
Merton College, Oxford.

E.P. GOLDSCHMIDT, London

Financial records 1919-81.
Grolier Club of New York.

Descriptions of books handled ('slips').
Maggs Bros Ltd.

Notes on manuscripts and books examined in Austrian libraries ('Diaries').
Bought at Christie's South Kensington c.1973 by Maggs Bros Ltd. Present whereabouts unknown.

Marked catalogues.
Private collection. Contact: Pickering and Chatto Ltd.

Financial records 1981 to cessation, 'original stock book'.
Jacques Vellekoop. Contact: ABA Office.

JOHN GRANT (BOOKSELLERS) LTD, Edinburgh

Ledgers, cash-books, stock and wages records, agreements, etc. 1886-1960, catalogues 1876- (incomplete run).
National Library of Scotland. NRA.

BERNARD HALLIDAY, Leicester

Invoices 1945-66 (36 items).
Leicestershire Record Office.

HATCHARDS, London

Business records (one box) 1940-7.
City of Westminster Archives Centre.

RICHARD HATCHWELL, Little Somerford and Rodbourne Bottom, Wiltshire

Annual accounts 1953-98, account books 1953-98, indexes of stock *c.*1952-2003, catalogues, some marked, *c.*1954-2003.
Wiltshire and Swindon Record Office.

W. HEFFER AND SONS LTD, Cambridge

Minutes 1905-92, corporate records, accounts, family papers and other papers (various outlets and ventures), some of which relates to their secondhand business incl. a secondhand books trading register 1928-43.
Cambridgeshire Archives Service, County Record Office, Cambridge.

G. HEYWOOD HILL LTD, London

Correspondence, some relating to bookselling, 1930-84.
Indiana University, Bloomington, Lilly Library.

Heywood Hill's letters to Nancy Mitford 1942-73. These letters form the basis of Jonathan Gathorne-Hardy (ed.), *A Bookseller's War. Letters between Heywood and Lady Anne Hill 1942-3* (1997) and of John Saumarez Smith (ed.), *The Bookshop at 10 Curzon Street. Letters between Nancy Mitford and Heywood Hill 1952-73* (2004).
Chatsworth. Private Collection.

Daybook 1939-40 of Michael Williams, bookseller, Curzon Street, London.
Contact: John Saumarez Smith, G. Heywood Hill Ltd.

HOFMANN & FREEMAN, ANTIQUARIAN BOOKSELLERS,
Cambridge, MA, and Shoreham, Kent

Correspondence, financial records, stock (catalogue) cards, marked catalogues 1966-88.
Private collections. Contact: Theodore Hofmann.

WILLIAM JAGGARD, Stratford-upon-Avon

Letter-book November 1907-June 1909, miscellaneous items relating to the Shakespeare Press and the Jaggard family *c.*1900-90.
Shakespeare Birthplace Trust Library.

JANSON & SONS, London

Correspondence, business papers, letter-books and account-books *c.*1873-1929.
Natural History Museum. NRA.

JARNDYCE ANTIQUARIAN BOOKSELLERS, London

Near-complete archive comprising correspondence, stock (catalogue) cards, bank records, marked catalogues 1969 to date.
Jarndyce Antiquarian Booksellers. Restricted access. Contact: Brian Lake or Janet Nassau.

C.C. KOHLER, Dorking

Correspondence, financial records, catalogues of collections (complete set), 'cost cards' (detailed record of purchases for collections) 1963 to date.
C.C. Kohler. Restricted access. Contact: Chris or Michèle Kohler.

E.M. LAWSON & CO., Sutton Coldfield and East Hagbourne

Correspondence, invoices, marked catalogues (nos. 147-315) 1952 to date, catalogue slips, purchase lists and mailing list (cards) 1952 to date. Also the residue of the archive of W.H. (Peter) Lawson, Sutton Coldfield.
E.M. Lawson & Co. Restricted access. Contact: John Lawson.

JOHN & JAMES LEIGHTON LTD,
London

Ledgers, stock books 1886-1918.
British Library. NRA.

H.K. LEWIS & CO. LTD, London

Records 1892-1973 incl. ledgers, letter-books, minute-books, balance sheets and accounts and a quantity of other material, mainly concerning their publishing, printing, new books, and lending library, but incl. information about the secondhand branch established in 1920.
Special Collections Library, University College London. NRA.

TOM LLOYD-ROBERTS, Caerwys, Wales

Correspondence 1968-93, sales journals 1970-88, card indexes of books sold *c.*1970-90, sales ledgers 1970-91, miscellaneous (2 items). Some material under embargo.
National Library of Wales. NRA.

H.K. LOCKYER (BOOKSELLERS),
Abergavenny

Archive boxes, card indexes, accounts collection.
Private collection. No current access.

MAGGS BROS LTD, London

Correspondence and letter-books 1914-78, cash books 1881-1945, ledgers 1933-8, files containing invoices for purchases 1925-61, other financial records 1918-41, miscellaneous records 1914-25, catalogues 1880 to date, over 4,000 volumes. Not fully catalogued.
British Library. Company's permission to consult required.

G. & D.I. MARRIN & SONS, Folkestone

Correspondence 1950-2000, financial (expenditure) records 1965-2000, card index and other records (items relating to Kent history and topography) 1965-90, family records incl. bookselling activities 1945-2000, marked catalogues 1970-2000.
Marrin's Bookshop. Restricted access. Contact: Patrick Marrin.

CHRISTOPHER MILLARD, London

Catalogues (nos. 1-16; all issued) 1919-27 containing relevant press cuttings, cash book with information about customers and their purchases [1919-27].
Stone Trough Books. Restricted access. Contact: George Ramsden.

MORTEN BOOKS, Didsbury and Macclesfield

Miscellaneous papers, account book 1959.
Morten Books. Restricted access. Contact: Eric Morten or Shirley Pryce.

ARNOLD MUIRHEAD, St Albans

Stock (catalogue) cards (*Lime Tree Miscellany*).
Claude Cox Old and Rare Books. Contact: Tony Cox.

PETER MURRAY HILL (RARE BOOKS), London and Stamford, Lincs.

Correspondence (selective) 1949-75 incl. *c.*30 letters from C.B. Tinker of Yale to Lionel and Philip Robinson, day-books 1947-62 & 1965-71 & 1988 to date, stock (catalogue) cards, marked catalogues (nos.1-193, missing 2-8) 1939-2004, marked supplementary lists (nos. 1-75) 1946-73, miscellaneous papers mainly financial *c.*1960 to date, bookselling ephemera.
Peter Murray Hill. Contact: Martin G. Hamlyn.

PARKER AND SON, Oxford

Archive 1794-1987, incl. material relating to secondhand books. (Blackwell Collection, B.H. Blackwell having acquired half the business in 1937.) *A Guide to the Merton Blackwell Collection*, pp. 44-6.
Merton College, Oxford.

W.N. PETTIGREW, Bedford

Correspondence 1951-2, incl. letters from Bertram Rota (*c.*150 items).
Richard M. Ford Ltd. Contact: Richard Ford.

PICKERING & CHATTO, London

Correspondence and financial records 1980 to date, minute-books 1927 to date, sales ledgers *c.*1940-60, client lists 1900-*c.*1955; marked catalogues 1880s to date.
Dawsons of Pall Mall marked catalogues

1951-80, card files (250,000+) 1950-80, purchase ledgers/sales stocklist ledgers 1950-80, client list.
Annotated Christie's and Sotheby's catalogues 1959 to date (some markings indicate ring activity).
Private Collection. Restricted use. Contact: Pickering & Chatto Ltd.

BERNARD QUARITCH LTD, London

Correspondence and papers 1850-99.
Bodleian Library. NRA.

Business archive 1885-1974, incl. day-books 1885-1904, 1943-70, 284 volumes, catalogues 1866 to date. Access restricted to some material relating to the 20th century.
British Library.

Correspondence, stock records, marked auction catalogues and other records (http://www.quaritch.com/resources/archive.asp)
Bernard Quaritch Ltd. Restricted access. Contact: Richard Linenthal.

READ AND BARRETT, Ipswich

Miscellaneous correspondence, book-lists, etc. 19th century-1911.
Suffolk Record Office, Ipswich. NRA.

WILLIAM H. ROBINSON LTD, London

Residue of archive incl. three files of correspondence (Prof. D.B. Quinn 1956-7; Grolier Club visit to London 1959 with related printed material; letters of condolence to Philip Robinson and wife on death of Lionel Robinson 1983), file of book (catalogue) descriptions, printed memorabilia, photographs, photocopy of the corrected typescript of Vernon Bartlett's completed but unpublished account of the Robinson firm, some related material.
Indiana University, Bloomington, Lilly Library.

Agreements for the purchase of the residual Phillipps library, 1945-7.
Private collection.

See also Peter Murray Hill above.

P. & B. ROWAN, Belfast

Near-complete archive 1974 to date, comprising correspondence, stock records (cards to 1984, cards and computer files thereafter), customer records (as stock cards), telephone day-books, commercial records, descriptions of archives and collections handled, valuations, postal receipt

books, marked catalogues, marked Irish auction catalogues, Irish booksellers' catalogues.
P. & B. Rowan. Restricted access. Contact: Peter or Briad Rowan.

CHAS. J. SAWYER, London

Day-books (33 vols.) 1943-80, marked catalogues (total 302 bound in 50 vols.) 1906-79.
Private collection. Contact: Richard Sawyer.

CHARLES SCRIBNER'S SONS, London and New York

Archive 1846-2003, incl. London-New York Office correspondence (John Carter, 1927-53).
Princeton University Library.

Rare Book Department records 1935-68.
Grolier Club of New York.

Carter correspondence and other papers in other locations are listed by Donald C. Dickinson, *John Carter* (2004), in his acknowledgments.

SHERRATT AND HUGHES, Manchester

Two folders containing photographs, newspaper cuttings, manuscript notes and typescript articles [1898]-1996, catalogues (9) 1909-12.
Chetham's Library, Manchester.

RUPERT SIMMS, Newcastle-under-Lyme

Correspondence, some relating to bookselling, 1894-1923.
Bodleian Library. NRA.

G.F. SIMS (RARE BOOKS), Hurst, Reading

Correspondence (5 boxes, part literary) 1942-95, literary papers 1938-97.
Dartmouth College Library, New Hampshire.

Catalogues (most marked) [1]-107 (1948-[1987]).
The family of George Sims. No current access.

KEN SPELMAN, York

Correspondence (five folders and five boxes, unsorted) 1948-86.
York City Archives. A2A.

Marked catalogues 1984 to date.
Ken Spelman. Contact: Peter Miller or Tony Fothergill.

ROBERT D. STEEDMAN, Newcastle-upon-Tyne

Correspondence and invoices (36 items) 1935-47.
Richard M. Ford Ltd. Contact: Richard Ford.

Catalogues 1907-78.
Robert D. Steedman. Restricted access. Contact: Robert D. Steedman.

HENRY STEVENS (HENRY STEVENS, SON, AND STILES), London

Correspondence and papers 1812-1911.
University of Michigan, Ann Arbor, William L. Clements Library.

Henry Stevens died in 1886. Most of his papers 1819-86 are held at the *University of California Los Angeles Library.* Minor locations for his papers (pre-1900) are listed in the NRA.

JAMES THIN, BOOKSELLERS, Edinburgh

Archive 1788-[2004], incl. material relating to their secondhand and antiquarian business. Blackwell's took over James Thin in 2002.
National Library of Scotland. Some closed files, available 2014.

ALAN G. THOMAS, Bournemouth and London

Archive.
British Library. Not yet processed.

WILFRID MICHAEL VOYNICH, London and New York

Business records, incl. account-books, correspondence, and records of books and manuscripts bought and sold 1916-34. Mainly from his New York shop, but incl. correspondence with his London shop.
Grolier Club of New York.

WHELDON & WESLEY LTD, London, Lytton Lodge, nr. Hitchin, and Leighton Buzzard

Marked catalogues 1863-2001, card index of stock books *c.*1940-*c.*2000.
Maggs catalogue 1364, item 505, catalogues, now in a private collection in the USA; Maggs catalogue 1364, item 507, card index, now at Smithsonian Institution, Washington, DC.

JOHN WILSON MANUSCRIPTS LTD (formerly John Wilson Autographs Ltd), London, Eynsham and Cheltenham

Correspondence, financial and business records 1967 to date (computerized from 1981).
John Wilson Manuscripts Ltd. Restricted access. Contact: John Wilson.

AUCTIONEERS

BLOOMSBURY BOOK AUCTIONS,
London

Administrative and finance files 1983-2004, sales and publicity files 1983-2004, complete set of catalogues with prices.
London Metropolitan Archives. NRA.

BONHAMS, London

Near-complete run of catalogues 1962-87; selected catalogues 1988-92.
British Library.

CHRISTIE'S, London

Archive, auctioneer's archival set of catalogues ('auctioneer's books') (marked) 1776 to date.
Christie's. Restricted access.

HODGSON & CO., London

Sale books, bank books, accounts with vendors and with purchasers, cash and day-books, valuations, etc., inventories, valuations etc., 1825-1969.
British Library. NRA.

Correspondence between Sydney Hodgson and John Johnson 1936-55.
Bodleian Library.

Auctioneer's archival set of catalogues 1807-1967. ('Some MS. prices and purchasers' names.')
British Library.

PHILLIPS, London

Auctioneer's archival set of catalogues 1850-1995, selected catalogues 1963-71, selected catalogues 1973-June 1997, near-complete run of catalogues March-December 2001.
British Library.

PUTTICK & SIMPSON, London

Auctioneer's archival set of catalogues 1846-1967, catalogues, 1958-71.
British Library.

SOTHEBY'S, London

Auctioneer's archival set of catalogues 1739-1970, reproduced in microfilm series 'Sotheby Catalogues 1734-1980'. Also Sotheby (UK) catalogues 1930 to date (mixed UK locations arranged by date); Sotheby (Belgravia) catalogues 1971-82; Sotheby (Europe) catalogues 1980 to date (selected catalogues of sales in Europe, Israel and Australia); Sotheby (North America) catalogues 1980 to date (selected); Sotheby (South Africa) catalogues 1986-90 (selected); Sotheby (Hong Kong) catalogues 1982-96 (selected).
British Library.

Working papers, 18th to 20th century, used by Frank Herrmann for his *Sotheby's. Portrait of an Auction House* (1980) donated by the author (41 archive boxes).
Cambridge University Library. Access restricted until 2014.

ASSOCIATIONS AND SOCIETIES

ANTIQUARIAN BOOKSELLERS' ASSOCIATION (ABA)

Minutes 1906 to date, annual reports 1908 to date (missing 1951), *News Letter* (nos [1]-33) 1945-63, *ABA Miscellany* (nos 1-16, missing no. 8) 1967-75, *Newsletter* (nos 1ff.) 1973 to date, miscellaneous records.
ABA Office. Restricted use.

PROVINCIAL BOOKSELLERS FAIRS ASSOCIATION (PBFA)

Minutes, accounts and correspondence 1974 to date, *Newsletter* (later *PBFA News*) c.1975 to date.
PBFA Office, Royston. Closed Archive.

EDINBURGH BOOKSELLERS' SOCIETY LTD, Edinburgh

Archive 1776-[1961], marginal antiquarian book trade interest. Later archives are still with the Society and not available for consultation.
National Library of Scotland. NRA.

Twentieth-Century Rare and Secondhand Book Trade Memoirs: A Checklist of Published Sources

MARC VAULBERT DE CHANTILLY

THIS list is not exhaustive. It includes few items published in periodicals (see separate entries on magazines and newspapers). Items are generally listed by subject rather than author. Place of publication is London unless otherwise stated. Only first publishers and places of publication are given. A section relating to American booksellers follows the main list. British editions are usually cited in cases of works first published abroad. Booksellers' names have not been cross-referenced from the entries for Block's *Short History*, Markham's *Book of Booksellers* or the *Oxford Dictionary of National Biography*.

ALLAN, GORDON – *First and last editions; England's second-hand bookshops* (Brighton: The Alpha Press, 2003)

APPLETON, TONY – *Tony Appleton bookseller; reminiscences of 22 years in the trade 1967-1988* (privately printed, 1997)

[BAIN] Bain, James S[toddart]. – *A bookseller looks back; the story of the Bains* (Macmillan & Co. Ltd, 1940)

—— *see also* Brown and Brett

BAKER, WILLIAM, and WOMACK, KENNETH, eds. – *Twentieth-century British book collectors and bibliographers* (*Dictionary of literary biography*, vol. 201; Detroit: Gale Research, 1999) includes entries by various contributors on John Carter, Norman Colbeck, Percy Muir, Graham Pollard and Bertram Rota

BARKER, NICOLAS – 'Four Booksellers' [James Gordon Akers Campbell, George Valentine Mervyn Heap, Francis Norman, Michael O'Neill Walshe] [reprinted from *The book collector*, autumn 1983, pp. 263-82] in his *Form and meaning in the history of the book; selected essays* (The British Library, 2003)

—— *see also* Wise

BASON, FRED – *Fred Bason's diary; edited and introduced by Nicolas Bentley* (Wingate, 1950)

—— *Fred Bason's 2nd diary; edited and with a preface by L.A.G. Strong* (Wingate, 1952)

—— *Fred Bason's 3rd diary; edited and with an introduction by Michael Sadleir* (Andre Deutsch, 1955)

—— *The last bassoon; from the diaries of Fred Bason; edited and introduced by Noël*

Coward (Max Parrish, 1960)

[BATSFORD] [anon.] – *The house of Batsford; with an account of three centuries of book publishing in Holborn* (privately printed, [1930])

—— Bolitho, Hector – *A Batsford century: the record of a hundred years of publishing and bookselling; 1843-1943* (B.T. Batsford Ltd, 1943)

—— Hanneford-Smith, W[illia]m – *Recollections of a half-century's association with the house of Batsford (1893-1943)* (Printed at The Westminster Press, 'for private circulation', 1943)

BEAUMONT, CYRIL – *Bookseller at the ballet; memoirs 1891 to 1929; incorporating The Diaghilev Ballet in London; a record of bookselling, ballet going, publishing, and writing* (C.W. Beaumont, 1975)

—— Roatcap, Adela Spindler – 'Cyril W. Beaumont The bookseller at 75 Charing Cross Road' in *The Book Club of California quarterly news-letter*, spring 1995, pp. 3-6

—— *see also* Sims (*More of the rare book game*)

BERNARD, PHILIPPA, ed., with BERNARD, LEO, and O'NEILL, ANGUS – *Antiquarian books; a companion for booksellers, librarians and collectors* (Aldershot: Scolar Press, 1994)

['BIBLIO-BOYS'] Introduction by Anthony Rota to Bertram Rota's catalogue 290 (1999), *The biblio-boys; writings about books and bookmen from the library of the late Grenville Cook* [also reprints obituary of Cook by Brian Lake from *Independent*, 24 February 1997]

—— *see* Carter, Muir *and* Pollard

['BIBLIOMITES' (Society of Antiquarian Booksellers' Employees)] *Biblionotes* (privately printed, 1953-?) [The British Library holds numbers 1 (April 1953) to 13 (Spring 1958) from the first series, and numbers 1 ([March] 1960) to 9 (1966) from the second series]

—— [anon.] – *Society of antiquarian booksellers' employees; 'bibliomites'* (eight-page leaflet, privately printed, 1952) [includes report on Peter Murray Hill's lecture 'The XYZ of bookselling']

—— Myers, Robin – 'The bibliomites (1950-)' in *Antiquarian Book Monthly Review*, September 1977, pp. 368-9

[BLACKWELL'S] Norrington, A[rthur]. L[ionel]. P[ugh]. – *Blackwell's 1879-1979; the history of a family firm* (Oxford: Blackwell, 1983)

—— Reid, Julian; Ricketts, Rita; and Walworth, Julia – *A guide to the Merton Blackwell collection* (Oxford: Merton College, 2004)

—— Ricketts, Rita – *Adventurers all; tales of Blackwellians; of books, bookmen, and reading and writing folk* (Oxford: Blackwell's, 2002)

BLOCK, ANDREW – *A short history of the principal London antiquarian booksellers and book-auctioneers* (Denis Archer, 1933) [Edward G. Allen & Son Ltd; James Bain; Thomas Baker (*by himself*); Banks Sisters; B.T. Batsford Ltd; Bickers & Son Ltd; Birrell & Garnett; John & Edward Bumpus Ltd; Davis & Orioli; R.D. Dickinson & Co.; P.J. & A.E. Dobell; Dulau's; Francis Edwards Ltd; Ellis; R. Fletcher Ltd; W. & G. Foyle Ltd; E. P. Goldschmidt & Co. Ltd; Edward Goldston Ltd (*by himself*); Grafton & Company; George Harding; Hatchards; Charles Higham & Son; Hodgsons; Frank Hollings; Ingpen & Co.; Raphael King (*by himself*); J. & J. Leighton Ltd; H.K. Lewis & Co. Ltd; Luzac & Co.; McLeish & Sons; Maggs Brothers; Marks & Co. (*by themselves*); Elkin Mathews Ltd; The Museum Book Store; Myers & Co.; Nattali & Maurice Ltd; Pickering & Chatto Ltd; Arthur Probsthain (*by himself*); Puttick & Simpson; Bernard Quaritch Ltd; Harold Reeves (*by himself*); James Rimell & Son Ltd; William H.

Robinson Ltd; Robson & Co. Ltd; Bertram Rota; Frank T. Sabin; George Salby; Charles J. Sawyer Ltd; Sotheby's; Henry Sotheran Ltd; W.T. Spencer; Spurr & Swift; B.F. Stevens & Brown Ltd; Henry Stevens, Son & Stiles; James Tregaskis & Son; Walford Brothers; Wheldon & Wesley Ltd; A. Zwemmer; *The clique* and the International Association of Antiquarian Booksellers] [previously published, without the entry on H.K. Lewis & Co. Ltd, in Block's *The book collector's vade mecum* (Denis Archer, 1932)]

—— Kidd, Meg – *Four book walls; a memoir of Andrew Block; with forewords by Edward Craig and David Robinson* (Bristol: Brokenborough, 1997)

—— *see also* Brown and Brett

[BLOOMSBURY BOOK AUCTIONS] [anon.] – *Bloomsbury Book Auctions; 10th anniversary; a celebration; 1893-1993* (privately printed, 1993)

—— [anon.] – *Catalogue of brief highlights in the history of Bloomsbury Book Auctions [...] to be given to Frank Herrmann to commemorate his retirement* (privately printed, 2002)

—— [anon.] – *Lord John; an album amicorum* (Steventon: Bennett & Kerr Books, 2002) [Lord John Kerr]

BONDY, LOUIS WOLFGANG, *see* Brown and Brett

[BONNER, ERIC M.] Pollak, Oliver B. – 'Eric M. Bonner, Africana Bookseller' in *African research and documentation* ('journal of the Standing Conference on Library Materials on Africa'), no. 81 (1999), pp. 53-62

BOOTH, RICHARD, with STUART, LUCIA – *My kingdom of books* (Talybont: Y Lolfa, 1999)

—— Cotton, Ian – '2. Book centre of the world' in *Nova* magazine (George Newnes Ltd), May 1968, pp. 28, 32, 35 [feature on Hay-on-Wye including interview with Booth]

—— *see also* Hay-on-Wye

BRASS, DAVID JOSEPH, *see* 'Driffield' (*Not 84 Charing Cross Road*), Joseph *and* Rota, Anthony (*Books in the blood*)

BROOK, G[EORGE]. L[ESLIE]. – *Books and book-collecting* (Andre Deutsch, 1980) [chapter on 'Booksellers']

[BROUGHTON BOOKS] Galinsky, Peter – *Condensed chronicles of the Broughton Bookshop; mcmlxxi-mcmlxxxiii* (Printed by the Dolphin Press, Glenrothes, 1984)

BROWN, RICHARD (photographs), and BRETT, STANLEY (text) – *The London bookshop; being part one of a pictorial record of the antiquarian book trade: portraits and premises; with prefatory reminiscence by Percy Muir* (Pinner: Private Libraries Association, 1971) [James Bain Ltd; Andrew Block; Louis W. Bondy; Stanley Crowe; H.M. Fletcher; Harold Mortlake & Co.; Bernard Quaritch Ltd; Bertram Rota Ltd; Charles J. Sawyer; Stanley Smith; Suckling & Co.]

—— [...] *part two* [...] (Pinner: Private Libraries Association, 1977) [Francis Edwards Ltd; Frank Hollings; E. Joseph; Maggs Brothers Ltd; Marks & Co.; Henry Sotheran Ltd; Harold T. Storey; Thomas Thorp]

CAIRNS, J[OHN]. B. – *Bright and early; a bookseller's memories of Edinburgh and Lasswade* (Edinburgh: Cairns Brothers, 1953)

CAMPBELL, JAMES GORDON AKERS, *see* Barker

[CARTER, JOHN WAYNFLETE] Dickinson, Donald C. – *John Carter; the taste and technique of a bookman; preface by Sebastian Carter* (New Castle: Oak Knoll Press, 2004)

—— *see also* Baker and Womack, 'Biblio-boys', Pollard *and* Wise

[CHARING CROSS ROAD] Suschitzky, Wolf[gang]; and Samuel, Raphael – *Charing Cross*

Road in the thirties (Nishen Photography, [1989])

CLARKE-HALL, JUSTIN, *see* Weinreb

CLEVERDON, DOUGLAS, 'Fifty years' in *The private library*, spring 1977, pp. 51-83
—— *see also* Sims (*The rare book game*)

COLBECK, NORMAN, *see* Baker and Womack *and* Sims (*The rare book game*) *and* Ray (*in American section*)

CORNISH, J.E., *see* Wise

[Cox, CLAUDE] Introduction by 'CWC' [Claude W. Cox] to Claude Cox's catalogue 100 (Ipswich, 1994)
—— [Cox, Tony] 'Wing Commander Claude William Cox, 1920-2006' in Claude Cox's catalogue 171 (Ipswich, 2006)

CROWE, STANLEY, *see* Brown and Brett

D'ARCH SMITH, TIMOTHY, – *The Times deceas'd; the rare book department of The Times Bookshop in the 1960s* (York: Stone Trough Books, 2003)

[DAVID, GUSTAVE] *David of Cambridge; some appreciations* [by T. R. Glover; Sir Arthur Quiller-Couch; W.H.D. Rouse; H.F. Stewart; S.C. Roberts] (Cambridge: At the University Press, 1937)

DAVIS, O[LIVER]. J[OHN]. M[ICHAEL]. – *Second-hand books: a first hand view* (Lewes: The Book Guild Ltd, 2001)

[DAVIS & ORIOLI] Aldington, Richard – *Pinorman; personal recollections of Norman Douglas, Pino Orioli, and Charles Prentice* (William Heinemann Ltd, 1954)
—— Davis, Irving – *A Catalan cookery book; a collection of impossible recipes* (Totnes: Prospect Books, 1999) [contains Davis's fragmentary 'Memories', and reprints Lucien Scheler's obituary of him]
—— Orioli, G[iuseppe]. ['Pino'] – *Adventures of a bookseller* (Chatto & Windus, 1938) [preceded by a signed edition of three hundred copies, 'privately printed for subscribers' by Orioli, Florence, 1937, which, unlike the English edition, has an index by Norman Douglas and, it is said, passages suppressed in the English edition]

[DEIGHTON, BELL & Co.] Topham, Jonathan R. – 'Two centuries of Cambridge publishing and bookselling: a brief history of Deighton, Bell and Co., 1778-1998, with a checklist of the archive' in *Transactions of the Cambridge Bibliographical Society*, 1998, pp. 350-403 (Cambridge: Published for the Cambridge Bibliographical Society)

DENNYS, NICHOLAS ('Nick'), *see* Low, David, and Greene, Graham

DICTIONARY OF NATIONAL BIOGRAPHY, *see* Oxford dictionary of national biography

DOBELL, BERTRAM – 'The battle of the bookstalls' in Bertram Dobell's catalogue 100 ([1902])
—— [anon.] 'The late Bertram Dobell. Some Press Appreciations.' ('Supplement to [Dobell's?] catalogue no. 239', [1915?])
—— Blom, J.M.; and Blom, F.J.M. – 'Bertram Dobell and Samuel Bradbury. The Literary Friendship between a Bookseller and an Industrial Chemist' in *English studies* (Lisse: Swets & Zeitlinger B.V.), September 1998, pp. 447-61
—— Bradbury, S[amuel]. – *Bertram Dobell; bookseller and man of letters* (Bertram Dobell, 1909)
—— [Dobell, Percy J[ohn].] – *In memoriam. Bertram Dobell. 1842-1914.* (privately printed, [1914])

'DRIF', *see* 'Driffield'

'DRIF FIELD', *see* 'Driffield'

'DRIFF' *and* 'DRIFF', *see next*

'Driffield' *or* 'drif' *or* 'Driff' *or* 'driff' *or* 'drif field' [true name unknown] – *d notice* (photocopied and privately distributed 'bulletin' in two series: first series at least fifteen issues between [1989?] and [1990?]; 'new series' at least 47 issues between 1992 and [1994?])

—— *driff's: the antiquarian and second hand book fortnightly* (21 issues between 8 January [without apostrophe in title] and 31 October 1986)

—— [*Driff's Guide*] (six editions: 1st, 1984 (four issues, according to author); 2nd, 1985 ('Driff II.', 'June 85-86'); 3rd, 1986 ('Driff III.', 'September 1986 to September 1987'); 4th, 1991 ('the drif field guide'); 5th, 1992 ('drif's guide II', '1992-93'); 6th, 1995 ('1995-97'))

—— [as 'drif field'] *Not 84 Charing Cross Road; a fiery story* (drif field guides, 1994) [on the legal action concerning E. Joseph Ltd brought by DB Rare Books (David Joseph Brass) against the Antiqbooks Ltd Partnership (Richard Bergman and Jerry Schneider)]

—— Sinclair, Iain – 'Driffield or, The Man Who Thought He Looked Like Raymond Carver' in *Talk of the town* magazine in *The Independent on Sunday*, 17 August 2003

—— Sinclair, Iain – *London orbital* (Granta Books, 2002) ['Driffield', p. 355]

—— Vaulbert de Chantilly, Marc – 'Strange Meeting' in Sinclair, Iain, ed. – *London; city of disappearances; myths and memories retrieved* (Hamish Hamilton, 2006)

—— *see also* Sinclair

DRING, EDMUND MAXWELL, *see* Quaritch

[EDINBURGH] [Gray, W. Forbes; et al.] *A literary centre of a literary capital* (Edinburgh: Robert Grant & Son Ltd, 1946)

EDWARDS, A.S.G., ed. – *The pleasures of bibliophily; fifty years of* The Book Collector*; an anthology* (The British Library, 2003) [reprints Alan G. Thomas's 'Solomon Pottesman' from the winter 1979 issue of the magazine, and Philip Robinson's 'Recollections of Moving a Library, or, How the Phillipps Collection was brought to London' from autumn 1986]

[EDWARDS, FRANCIS] Russell, A.K. – foreword to Francis Edwards' catalogue 1000 (1975)

—— *see also* Brown and Brett

[EDWARDS, H.W.] Powell, Lawrence Clark – *To Newbury to buy an old book* ('Printed for Private Circulation by H.W.E.' [i.e. H.W. Edwards] (Curwen Press, 1954) [reprinted in Powell's *Books in my baggage* and *Bookman's progress*]

[ELKIN MATHEWS LTD] [Ford, Richard M.] – *Bookselling in the 20th century; Elkin Mathews Ltd; an archive; 1928-1979* (Richard M. Ford Ltd, 2002)

—— *see also* Muir

—— Nelson, James G. – *Elkin Mathews; publisher to Yeats, Joyce, Pound* (Madison: The University of Wisconsin Press, 1989)

[ELLIS] [anon.] – 'A short history of the bookselling business carried on continuously at 29 New Bond Street since its establishment by John Brindley in 1728' in *A catalogue of one hundred and fifty choice and valuable books and manuscripts* (Ellis (J.J. Holdsworth and G. Smith), 1913)

—— Smith, George – 'The oldest London bookshop. Ellis, 29 New Bond Street.', in *The library world* (Grafton and Company), March 1932, pp. 195-202

—— Smith, George; and Benger, Frank – *The oldest London bookshop; a history of two hundred years; to which is appended a family correspondence of the eighteenth century* (London: Ellis, 1928)

ETTINGHAUSEN, MAURICE L[ÉON]. – *Rare books and royal collectors; memoirs of an antiquarian bookseller* (New York: Simon and Schuster, 1966)

—— [and King Manuel II of Portugal] *Correspondência de El-Rei D. Manuel II com o Dr. Maurice L. Ettinghausen sobre os 'Livros antigos portugueses'; prefácio do Prof. Dr. M.B. Amzalak* ([Lisbon]: Fundação da Casa de Bragança, 1957) [correspondence, 1925-32, in English and French]

—— *see also* Maggs

FIELD, DRIF, *see* 'Driffield'

FLETCHER, H. M., *see* Brown and Brett

[FLETCHER, IFAN KYRLE] Speaight, George – 'The Bookseller' in *Ifan Kyrle Fletcher; a memorial tribute* (The Society for Theatre Research, 1970)

[FOYLES] [anon.] – *Foyles fifty years; 1904-1954* (W. & G. Foyle Ltd, 'Issued 1954')

—— Fabes, Gilbert H[enry]. – *The romance of a bookshop; 1904-1929* (privately printed, 1929) ['Revised Edition' subtitled '1904-38', 1938]

—— Mountain, Penny; with Foyle, Christopher – *Foyles; a celebration* (Foyles Books, 2003)

—— *see also* Symons, Julian (*under* Symons, A.J.A.)

FRANKLIN, COLIN – 'What Do You Specialize In? A Few Recollections from the Caribbean' in *The gazette of the Grolier Club*, new series no. 55 (2004), pp. 12-28.

FREEMAN, ARTHUR, and FREEMAN, JANET ING – *Anatomy of an auction; rare books at Ruxley Lodge, 1919* (The Book Collector, 1990)

GARNETT, DAVID – *Never be a bookseller; with a postscript by Richard Garnett* (Denby Dale: The Fleece Press, 1995) [previous edition, without postscript, New York: Alfred A. Knopf, 1929]

GEKOSKI, RICK – *Tolkien's gown and other stories of great authors and rare books* (Constable, 2004)

GIBB, TONY – 'Secondhand bookselling in Manchester: a personal backward glance' in *Transactions of the Lancashire and Cheshire Antiquarian Society* (Otley: Smith Settle), vol. 97 for 2001, pp. 153-63

[GODFREY, THOMAS CHARLES] Powell, John S. – *Godfrey of York; a tale of bumps and books* (York: privately printed, 1988)

GOLDMARK, MIKE, *see* Sinclair (*Lights out for the territory*)

[GOLDSCHMIDT, ERNST PHILIP] Dougan, R[obert]. O[rmes]. – 'E. Ph. Goldschmidt, 1887-1954' in *The library* (Oxford: The Oxford University Press), June 1954, pp. 75-84

—— Vellekoop, Jacques – Ernst Philip Goldschmidt 1887-1954 [reprinted from *The book collector*, vol. 3 no. 2, summer 1954, pp. 119-24]

—— Weil, E[rnst]. – 'In Memoriam E. P. Goldschmidt – Bookseller and Scholar' in *Journal of the history of medicine and allied sciences* (New Haven: Yale University), April 1954, pp. 224-32

GORFIN, HERBERT EDWIN, *see* Wise

[HALEWOOD & SONS] [Horace H. Halewood] – *Five generations of booksellers; a unique history; 1867-2000; Halewood & Sons; antiquarian and export booksellers since 1867* (Preston: privately printed, Halewood, 2000)

HAMPDEN, JOHN, ed. – *The book world today; a new survey of the making and distribution of books in Britain; with an introduction by Sir Stanley Unwin* (George Allen & Unwin Ltd, 1957) [Ian R. Grant on 'Antiquarian and Secondhand Bookselling' and John Hampden, 'A Note on the "Book Rings"']

HARDING, GEORGE, *see* Wheeler

HARRIOTT, JOHN F.X. – *Farewell to true bookshops; with an introduction and poem by John Arlott* (Steventon Vicarage, near Abingdon: The Rocket Press, 1984)

—— Karslake, Madge – 'The Late Mr. Frank Karslake; founder and editor of "Book auction records"; ob. 25 March, 1920; a few personal reminiscences' in *Book auction records*, vol.17 (Henry Stevens, Son & Stiles, 1920), pp. xiii-xvii

KERR, LORD JOHN, *see* Bloomsbury Book Auctions

KOHLER, C.C. – *'Not subject to return'; some episodes in the life of a secondhand bookseller* (Dorking: [1974])

KORN, ERIC – *Remainders; from the Times Literary Supplement 1980-1989* (Carcanet, 1989)

KROGER, PETER (Morris Cohen), *see* Low (pp. 105-6) and Snelling (pp. 204-47)

[LAWSON, W.J.] – 'Fifty years of antiquarian bookselling' in E.M. Lawson & Co. catalogue 305 (East Hagbourne, 2002)

[LEIGHTON, J. & J.] Davies, Hugh William – 'Notes on the Firm of J. & J. Leighton and the Old House at Brewer Street' in *The library world* (Grafton and Company), January and February 1932, pp. 149-55, 177-82

[LEWIS, H.K.] [anon.] – *Lewis's 1844-1944; a brief account of a century's work* (H.K. Lewis & Co. Ltd, 1945)

LEWIS, ROY HARLEY – *Antiquarian books: an insider's account* (Newton Abbot: David & Charles, 1978)

—— *The book browser's guide; Britain's secondhand and antiquarian bookshops* (Newton Abbot: David & Charles, 1975)

—— *Book collecting; a new look* (Newton Abbot: David & Charles, 1988)

LINKLATER, CLIVE – *Reflections from a bookshop window* (St Leonards-on-Sea: Hole in the Wall Publishing, 1994)

LOW, DAVID – *'with all faults'; introduction by Graham Greene* (Tehran: The Amate Press, 1973)

—— [and Graham Greene] – *Dear David, Dear Graham, a bibliophilic correspondence* (Oxford: The Alembic Press with The Amate Press, 1989) [Nicholas Dennys]

[MAGAZINES] – *AB bookman's weekly* (American), *Antiquarian Booksellers' Association newsletter* (privately printed), *The antiquarian book monthly review* (renamed *Antiquarian book monthly* in February 1993 and *Antiquarian book review* in February 2002 and *Rare book review* in February 2004), *Biblionotes* [see Bibliomites], *Book auction records* [see Karslake], *Book handbook*, *The bookdealer* [see Markham], *The book collector*, *The clique*, *Desiderata*, *driff's* (q.v.), *The library world* [see Davies, Ellis *and* Voynich], *The private library*, *The publisher and bookseller* [includes articles in 1906 on the 'Famous bookselling houses' of Hatchards; Bumpus; Truslove and Hanson; Jones and Evans; Harrison and Son; B.T. Batsford; Cornish], etc

—— *see also* Newspapers

MAGGS – [anon.] *The house of Maggs; founded 1855* (privately printed, 1939)

—— [anon.] Foreword to Maggs Bros Ltd's centenary catalogue, no. 812 (1953)

—— Barker, Nicolas – introduction to Maggs Bros Ltd's catalogue 1000 (1980)

—— [Maggs, Edward] – *Forgetting to change the filter in the gene pool; a personal look at two episodes in the history of a bookshop* (privately printed, 2003) [Thomas James Wise; the Arthur Cravan forgeries]

—— Maggs, Edward – 'Only the Brave Deserve the Fair: An Inquiry into the Ecology of the Modern Book Fair' in *The gazette of the Grolier Club*, new series no. 54 (2003), pp. 88-96

—— *see also* Brown and Brett *and* Ettinghausen

MARKHAM, SHEILA – *A book of booksellers; conversations with the antiquarian book trade; 1991-2003* (both 'privately printed' and 'Published by Sheila Markham Rare Books', 2004) [Joseph Allen, Stuart Bennett, Leo & Philippa Bernard, Nigel Burwood, John Chancellor, Robin de Beaumont, Peter Eaton, Sally Edgecombe, Nadeem El Issa, Julia Elton, Clive Farahar, Edith Finer, Bill Fletcher, Sam Fogg, Arthur Freeman, Paul Goldman, Simon Gough, Barbara Grigor-Taylor, Michael Hollander, Helen Kahn, Conor Kenny, Raymond Kilgarriff, Eric Korn, Brian Lake, Peter Miller, Eric Moore, Eric Morten, Rusty Mott, Julian Nangle, Anthony Neville, Mitsuo Nitta, Angus O'Neill, John Price, George Ramsden, Hamish Riley-Smith, Albi Rosenthal, Anthony Rota, Rob Rulon-Miller, Charles Russell, John Saumarez Smith, Robert Sawers, Bernard Shapero, Norman Storey, Michael Taylor, John & Juliet Townsend, Charles Traylen, John Walwyn-Jones, Robin Waterfield, Camille Wolff, Laurence Worms] [around half of Markham's interviews from the *Bookdealer*]

[MARKS & CO.] Hanff, Helene – *84, Charing Cross Road* (Andre Deutsch, 1971)

—— Hanff, Helene – *The duchess of Bloomsbury Street* (Andre Deutsch, 1974)

—— Marks, Leo – *Between silk and cyanide; the story of SOE's code war* (HarperCollins Publishers, 1998)

—— *see also* Brown and Brett *and* Snelling (pp. 152-60)

MEYNELL, EVERARD, *see* Sims (*The rare book game*)

[MILLARD, CHRISTOPHER] Burdett, Osbert – *Memory and imagination* (Chapman & Hall Ltd, 1935), pp. 97-108

—— Hyde, H[arford]. Montgomery – *Christopher Sclater Millard (Stuart Mason); bibliographer and antiquarian book dealer* (New York: Global Academic Publishers, 1990)

—— Powell, Anthony – *To keep the ball rolling; the memoirs of Anthony Powell; volume I; infants of the spring* (London: Heinemann, 1976), pp. 90-97

—— Symons, A[lphonse]. J[ames]. A[lbert]. – *The quest for Corvo; an experiment in biography* (Cassell & Co. Ltd, 1934)

—— *see also* Sims (*A life in catalogues and The rare book game*)

MINET, PAUL – *Late booking; my first twenty-five years in the secondhand book trade* (Frant: Frantic Press, 1989)

MOGRIDGE, STEPHEN – *Talking shop* (Lutterworth Press, 1950)

MORTLAKE, HAROLD, & CO., *see* Brown and Brett

MUIR, PERCY (Percival Horace Muir) – *Minding my own business: an autobiography* (Chatto & Windus, 1956) [sometimes cited as *An autobiography; minding my own business*, as the subtitle appears above the title on the title-page] [reprinted, with foreword by Barbara Kaye, as *Minding my own business; an autobiography* (New Castle: Oak Knoll Books, 1991)]

—— unfinished 'Further Reminiscences' in 22 instalments in *The book collector* between autumn 1956 and spring 1964

—— [Deval, Laurie, ed.] – *P · H · M 80* (privately printed, 1974)

—— [Ford, Richard M.] – *Percy Muir; manuscripts, typescripts and correspondence; a catalogue* (Richard Ford, 1996)

—— Kaye, Barbara (Mrs Percy Muir) – *The company we kept* (Werner Shaw Ltd, 1986)

—— Kaye, Barbara (Mrs Percy Muir) – *Second impression; rural life with a rare bookman* (New Castle: Oak Knoll Press, 1995)

—— *see also* Baker and Womack, 'Biblio-boys', Elkin Mathews Ltd *and* Sims (*The rare book game*)

MUNBY, A[LAN]. N[OEL]. L[ATIMER]. – 'Book Collecting in the 1930s' in his *Essays and papers* (Scolar Press, 1978) [reprinted from *TLS*, 11 May 1973]

MYERS, ROBIN – *The British book trade from Caxton to the present day; a bibliographical guide based on the libraries of the National Book League and St Bride Institute* (Andre Deutsch, 1973)

[NEWSPAPERS] – Obituaries, etc., in *Guardian*, *Independent*, *Daily Telegraph*, *The Times*, etc.

—— *see also* Magazines

NORMAN, FRANCIS, *see* Barker

ORIOLI, GIUSEPPE ('Pino'), *see* Davis & Orioli

ORWELL, GEORGE (Eric Arthur Blair) – *Bookshop memories; with a foreword by W.E. Butler* [Baarn, Holland: Arethusa Pers 1987] [reprinted from *Fortnightly*, November 1936, pp. 600-4 and also in *The collected essays, journalism and letters of George Orwell*, ed. Sonia Orwell and Ian Angus (Secker & Warburg, 1968), vol. 1, pp. 242-6]

OWENS, TONY – *Northern soul trader; fifteen years of music books and memorabilia* (Wigan: The Casino Press, 1971)

OXFORD DICTIONARY OF NATIONAL BIOGRAPHY (2004) includes the following twentieth-century dealers in books: Bradley Thomas Batsford; Henry George ('Harry') Batsford; Cyril William Beaumont; Sir Basil Henry Blackwell; Richard Blackwell; Robert Bowes; John Waynflete Carter; Thomas Douglas James Cleverdon; Agnes Joseph Madeline ('Una') Dillon; Bertram Dobell; Peter Eaton; Frederick Startridge Ellis; Frederick Henry Evans; Frederic Sutherland Ferguson; Christina Agnes Lilian Foyle; William Alfred Foyle; Gordon Fraser; Richard Anthony James Wylie ('Tony') Godwin; Reuben George Heffer; Charles Elkin Mathews; Harold Edward Monro; Henry Graham Pollard; Richard Bowdler Sharpe; Leonard Charles Smithers; Edward Stanford; Alphonse James Albert Symons; Alexander Whitelaw Robertson ('Alex') Trocchi; Frederick Warne; Geoffrey Maurice Watkins; John Gideon Wilson; Thomas James Wise

[PEARSON] Navari, Leonora – *The bookseller's art; catalogues issued by the firm of J. Pearson & Co. Ltd* (Maggs Bros Ltd, 1991)

PEARSON, DAVID – *Provenance research in book history; a handbook* (The British Library, 1994) ['Auctioneers' and 'Booksellers' sections]

[POLLARD, GRAHAM] Carter, John – 'Graham Pollard' in Hunt, R.W.; Philip, I.G.; and Roberts, R.J., eds., *Studies in the book trade in honour of Graham Pollard* (Oxford: The Oxford Bibliographical Society, 1975)

—— Potter, Esther – 'Graham Pollard at Work' in *The library* (Oxford: Oxford University Press), December 1989, pp. 307-27

—— *see also* Baker and Womack, Carter *and* Wise

POTTESMAN, SOLOMON, *see* Edwards, A.S.G. *and* Snelling (pp. 98-106)

PRATLEY, HARRY – *A bookseller remembers* (Westerham: Hurtwood Press, 1990)

[PROBSTHAIN, ARTHUR] 'Bookworm' – 'Oriental Literature in London' in *The illustrated country review*, February 1926

—— De Cordova, R. – 'Thumbnail interviews with the great. [...] An Anomalous Bookseller' in *The sphere*, 20 February 1926

—— Sheringham, Lesley – '100th anniversary celebration for Arthur Probsthain bookshop' in *SOAS information* newsletter, week beginning 27 May 2003

—— Wong, David T.K. – 'A London haunt for oriental scholars' in *Wings of gold* ('the inflight magazine of Malaysia Airlines'), July 1993

[QUARITCH] Dring, E[dmund]. M[axwell]. – 'Fifty years at Quaritch' in Linenthal,

Richard, ed., *The Book Collector special number for the 150th anniversary of Bernard Quaritch 1997* (The Book Collector, 1997)

—— *see also* Brown and Brett

[ROBINSON, LIONEL and PHILIP] Hamlyn, Martin – *The Robinson legend* (Stamford: privately printed, 1992) [reprinted from *ABA newsletter*, October 1991, pp. 15-23]

—— Munby, A[lan]. N[oel]. L[atimer]. – *Phillipps studies no. 5; the dispersal of the Phillipps library* (Cambridge: At the University Press, 1960)

—— *see also* Edwards, A.S.G.

ROSENTHAL, ALBI – *Obiter scripta; essays, lectures, articles, interviews and reviews on music, and other subjects; edited for publication by Jacqueline Gray* (Oxford: Offox Press, 2000)

—— Bodin, Thierry, et al. – *In memoriam Albi Rosenthal 5.10.1914–3.8.2004; a catalogue presented as a tribute in gratitude* (Oxford: 2004)

ROTA, ANTHONY – *Books in the blood; memoirs of a fourth generation bookseller* (Pinner: Private Libraries Association, 2002)

—— *The changing face of antiquarian bookselling 1950-2000 A.D.; the 1994 Sol. M. Malkin Lecture in Bibliography* (Charlottesville: Book Arts Press, 1995)

—— *Life in a London bookshop; excerpts from a lecture* (Minneapolis: The Ampersand Club, 1989) [reprinted as prologue to *Books in the blood*]

—— [anon.] – *Anthony Rota* [recollections by various hands for his seventieth birthday] [Printed by St Edmundsbury Press, 2002]

ROTA, [CYRIL] BERTRAM – 'On being 100' in Bertram Rota Ltd's catalogue 100 (spring 1955)

—— *see also* Baker and Womack, Brown and Brett *and* Sims (*The rare book game*)

SADLEIR, MICHAEL – 'A book collector speaks to the trade' in *ABA annual* (Wm. Dawson & Sons Ltd, 1952)

SAWYER, CHARLES J., *see* Brown and Brett

SIMS, GEORGE – *Last of the rare book game* (Philadelphia: Holmes Publishing Co., 1990)

—— *A life in catalogues and other essays* (Philadelphia: Holmes Publishing Co., 1994) [chapter 11, 'Christopher Millard's catalogues']

—— *More of the rare book game* (Philadelphia: Holmes Publishing Co., 1988) [chapter 6, 'Bookseller at the Ballet', on C. W. Beaumont]

—— *The rare book game* (Philadelphia: Holmes Publishing Co., 1985) [chapter 2, 'Three Booksellers and Their Catalogues', on Douglas Cleverdon, Everard Meynell, Christopher Sclater Millard; chapter 5 on Leonard Smithers; chapter 7 on A.J.A. Symons; chapter 11, 'Three Booksellers', on Norman Colbeck, Percy Muir, Bertram Rota]

SINCLAIR, IAIN – 'Drif and Martin Stone' in Atkins, Marc (photographs) and Sinclair, Iain (text) – *Liquid city* (Reaktion Books, 1999) [revised version of '[Heroes & Villains] Martin Stone' in *Independent magazine*, 18 February 1995]

—— *Lights out for the territory; 9 excursions in the secret history of London* (Granta Books, 1997) ['Driffield', Mike Goldmark, George Jeffery, 'Jock the Bookman', Martin Stone]

—— *see also* 'Driffield'

SMITH, STANLEY, *see* Brown and Brett

[SMITHERS, LEONARD] Nelson, James G. – *Publisher to the decadents: Leonard Smithers in the careers of Beardsley, Wilde, and Dowson* (High Wycombe: Rivendale Press, 2000) [first published by Penn State Press]

—— Smithers, Jack – *The early life and vicissitudes of Jack Smithers; an autobiography* (Martin Secker, 1939)

—— *see also* Sims (*The rare book game*)

SNELLING, O[SWALD]. F[REDERICK]. – *Rare books and rarer people; some personal reminiscences of 'the trade'* (Werner Shaw, 1982) [Hodgson & Co.; Peter Kroger; Marks & Co.; Solomon Pottesman]

Society of Antiquarian Booksellers' Employees *see* Bibliomites

[SOTHEBY'S] Herrmann, Frank – *Sotheby's; portrait of an auction house* (Chatto & Windus, 1980)

—— Lacey, Robert – *Sotheby's – bidding for class* (Little, Brown and Company, 1998)

—— *see also* Sowerby

[SOTHERAN'S] S[tonehouse]. J[ohn]. H[arrison]. – Twenty-two chapters of 'Adventures in Bookselling', in the first 22 issues of *Piccadilly notes* (privately printed, 1933-37)

—— *see also* Brown and Brett

SOWERBY, E[MILY]. MILLICENT – *Rare people and rare books* (Constable, 1967) [Voynich; Sotheby's; Rosenbach]

SPENCER, WALTER T[HOMAS]. – *Forty years in my bookshop; edited with an introduction by Thomas Moult* (Constable & Company Ltd, 1923) ['Reprinted 1924. Reissued 1927.']

[STEVENS (B.F.) & BROWN LTD] Powell, Lawrence Clark – '*... and Brown'; a chronicle of B. F. Stevens & Brown, Ltd, library and fine arts agents of London, with emphasis on the years since 1902* (privately printed, 1959)

[STEVENS (HENRY), SON & STILES] Barwick, G.F. – 'The Late Henry N[ewton]. Stevens, M.A.' in *Book auction records*, vol. 27 (Henry Stevens, Son & Stiles, 1930)

STEVENS, HENRY NEWTON, *see last*

[STEVENS-COX, JAMES] [Harding, Robert] – introduction to Maggs Bros Ltd's catalogue 1350 (2003)

[STONE, MARTIN] Baxter, John – *A pound of paper; confessions of a book addict* (Doubleday, 2002)

—— Howard, Peter B. – *Martin Stone, bookscout* (Berkeley: Serendipity Books, 2000) [previously printed in *ABAA Newsletter*, vol. 11, no. 4, summer 2000]

—— *see also* Sinclair

STOREY, HAROLD T., *see* Brown and Brett

SUCKLING & CO., *see* Brown and Brett

SWINNERTON, FRANK – *The bookman's London* (Allan Wingate, 1951) [revised edn., John Baker, 1969]

[SYMONS, ALPHONSE JAMES ALBERT] – Miller, Edmund, 'A.J.A. Symons' in Steven Serafin, ed., *Late nineteenth- and early twentieth-century British literary biographers* (*Dictionary of literary biography*, vol. 149; Detroit: Gale Research Inc., 1995)

—— Symons, Julian – *A.J.A. Symons; his life and speculations* (London: Eyre & Spottiswoode, 1950)

—— *see also* Millard *and* Sims (*The rare book game*)

[THIN'S] *James Thin; 1848-1948* ([Edinburgh: privately printed, 1948])

—— *James Thin; 150 years of bookselling; 1848-1998* (Edinburgh: Mercat Press, 1998)

[THOMAS, ALAN GRADON] de Hamel, Christopher; and Linenthal, Richard, eds. – *Fine books and book collecting; books and manuscripts acquired from Alan G. Thomas and described by his customers on the occasion of his seventieth birthday* (Leamington Spa: James Hall, 1981) [foreword by Lawrence Durrell and introduction by the editors]

[THORNTON'S] Joy, Thomas – *Mostly joy; a bookman's story* (Michael Joseph, 1971)

[THORP, THOMAS] Harris, Walter – 'A backward glance' and 'A second backward glance' in *Biblionotes*, spring 1961, pp. [3]-[10]; and 1964-5, pp. 2-13

—— *see also* Brown and Brett

[VOYNICH, WILFRID MICHAEL] Garland, Herbert – 'Notes on the firm of W.M. Voynich' in *The library world* (Grafton and Company), April 1932, pp. 225-8

—— *see also* Sowerby

WALSHE, MICHAEL O'NEILL, *see* Barker

[WEIL, ERNST] Weil, Hanna – introduction to *Catalogue of books, manuscripts, photographs and scientific instruments fully described and offered for sale by Ernst Weil 1943-1965; original thirty three catalogues bound in two volumes; with a biographical memoir by Hanna Weil* (Storrs-Mansfield: Maurizio Martino Publisher, [1995])

—— *see also* Goldschmidt

[WEINREB, BEN] [Weinreb, Matthew, ed.] – *Ben Weinreb; the history of a bookseller; 1912-1999* ('catalogue 59', 2000) [includes obituaries by Weinreb: 'Justin Clarke-Hall' (reprinted from *ABA newsletter*, May 1983), pp. 92-3; 'The Brothers [Jack and Sam] Joseph' (reprinted from *ABA newsletter*, November 1985), pp. 94-6]

WHEELER, GEORGE A. – 'The random recollections of George A. Wheeler' in *Biblionotes*, October [corrected by hand from April] 1954, pp. 4-6

[WHELDON & WESLEY] 'A brief history of Wheldon & Wesley Ltd' in *Wheldon & Wesley's 150th aniversary catalogue no. 191* (Hitchin: 1990)

—— *Wheldon & Wesley: the company reference library* […] (Maggs Bros Ltd's catalogue 1364, [2004])

WILLIAMSON, R[OBERT]. M[ILNE]. – *Bits from an old book shop* (Simpkin, Marshall, Hamilton, Kent & Co., Ltd, 1904)

[WILSON, JAMES] Wilson, Roger Burdett – *Old and curious; the history of James Wilson's bookshop* (Birmingham: James Wilson, 1960)

[WINZAR, DAVID] Burwood, Nigel – 'Memories of David' in Winzar, David, *Common mallow; poems* (Epsom: Manor Green Press, 1990)

[WISE, THOMAS, JAMES] Barker, Nicolas; and Collins, John – *A sequel to An enquiry into the nature of certain nineteenth century pamphlets by John Carter and Graham Pollard* (Scolar Press, 1983)

—— Carter, John; and Pollard, Graham – *An enquiry into the nature of certain nineteenth century pamphlets* (Constable & Co. Ltd, 1934) [second edn., Scolar Press, 1983, with new material by Nicolas Barker and John Collins]

—— Carter, John; and Pollard, Graham – *Gorfin's stock* (Oxford: Distributed for the authors by B.H. Blackwell Ltd, 1970)

—— Collins, John – *The two forgers; a biography of Harry Buxton Forman and Thomas James Wise* (Aldershot: Scolar Press, 1992)

—— Partington, Wilfred – *Thomas J. Wise in the original cloth; the life and record of the forger of the nineteenth-century pamphlets* (Robert Hale Ltd, 1946) [revised version of book published in America under title *Forging ahead* (New York: G.P. Putnam's Sons, 1939)]

—— Ratchford, Fannie E., ed. – *Letters of Thomas J. Wise to John Henry Wrenn; a further inquiry into the guilt of certain nineteenth-century forgers* (New York: Alfred A Knopf, 1944)

—— Rosenblum, Joseph, 'Thomas James Wise' in William Baker and Kenneth Womack, eds., *Nineteenth-century British book-collectors and bibliographers* (*Dictionary of literary biography*, vol. 184; Detroit, Gale Research, 1997)

—— Todd, William B., ed. – *Thomas J. Wise; centenary studies* (Austin: University of Texas Press, 1959) [includes letters from Wise to the Manchester bookseller J.E. Cornish]

—— *see also* Maggs, Edward (*Forgetting to change the filter*)

[WYLLIE & SON] *A century of bookselling 1814-1914; David Wyllie afterwards David Wyllie & Son; reprinted from 'The Aberdeen book-lover', November, 1914* [Aberdeen: Printed by William Smith & Sons at the Bon-accord Press, 1914]

[ZENO] – *Zeno Booksellers and Publishers; 50th anniversary 1944-1994* (Zeno Booksellers and Publishers, 1994)

[ZWEMMER, ANTON] *Anton Zwemmer; tributes from some of his friends on the occasion of his 70th birthday* (privately printed, 1962)

—— Halliday, Nigel Vaux – *More than a bookshop; Zwemmer's and art in the 20th century* (Philip Wilson Publishers, 1991)

AMERICAN BOOKSELLERS

BASBANES, NICHOLAS A. – *A gentle madness; bibliophiles, bibliomanes, and the eternal passion for books* (New York: Henry Holt and Company, 1995)

—— *Among the gently mad; perspectives and strategies for the book hunter in the twenty-first century* (New York: Henry Holt and Company, 2002)

—— *Patience and fortitude; a roving chronicle of book people, book places, and book culture* (New York: HarperCollins Publishers, 2001)

[BROOKS, EDMUND DeWITT] Grove, Lee Edmonds – *Of Brooks and books* (Minneapolis: The University of Minnesota Press, 1945)

DAWSON, ERNEST, *see* Rosenblum *in this section*

DICKINSON, DONALD C. – *Dictionary of American antiquarian bookdealers* (Westport: Greenwood Press, 1998)

EVERITT, CHARLES P[ERCY]. – *The adventures of a treasure hunter* (Victor Gollancz Ltd, 1951)

GOODSPEED, CHARLES E[LIOT]. – *Yankee bookseller; being the reminiscences of Charles E. Goodspeed* (Boston: Houghton Mifflin Company, 1937)

KOHN, JOHN SICHER VAN EISEN – *see* Rosenblum *in this section*

KRAUS, H[ANS]. P[ETER]. – *A rare book saga; the autobiography of H.P. Kraus* (André Deutsch, 1979)

—— *see also* Rosenblum *in this section*

LEWIS, WILMARTH – *Collector's progress* (Constable & Co. Ltd, 1952)

MAGEE, DAVID – *Infinite riches; the adventures of a rare book dealer; introduction by Lawrence Clark Powell* (New York: Paul S. Eriksson, Inc., 1973)

—— *Chapter II of an unpublished autobiography by David Magee* (keepsake printed by Sherwood Grover for John Borden and Albert Sperisen, San Francisco, 1979)

—— *see also* Rosenblum *in this section*

MANASEK, FRANCIS J. – *Uncommon value; a rare book dealer's world* (Ann Arbor: Arbor Libri Press, 1995)

MONDLIN, MARVIN, AND MEADOR, ROY – *Book Row; an anecdotal and pictorial history of the antiquarian book trade; foreword by Madeleine B. Stern* (New York: Carroll & Graf Publishers, 2004)

NEWTON, A[LFRED]. EDWARD – *The amenities of book-collecting and kindred affections* (John Lane, The Bodley Head, 1920)

—— *A magnificent farce and other diversions of a book-collector* (G.P. Putnam's Sons, [1921])

PAPANTONIO, MICHAEL – *see* Rosenblum *in this section*

POWELL, LAWRENCE CLARK – *Bookman's progress; the selected writings of Lawrence Clark Powell; with an introduction by William Targ* ([Los Angeles]: The Ward Ritchie Press, 1968)

—— *Books in my baggage; adventures in reading and collecting* (Constable, 1960) [section entitled 'Bookman in Britain' includes pieces on C.K. Ogden and H.W. Edwards]

RANDALL, DAVID A[NTON]. – *Dukedom large enough* (New York: Random House, 1969)

—— *see also* Rosenblum *in this section*

RAY, GORDON N[ORTON]. – *Books as a way of life* (New York: The Grolier Club, 1988) [Norman Colbeck, pp. 212-14]

ROSENBACH, A[BRAHAM]. S[IMON]. W[OLF]. – *Books and bidders; the adventures of a bibliophile* (George Allen & Unwin Ltd, 1928)

—— Wolf, Edwin, 2nd; with Fleming, John F. – *Rosenbach; a biography* (Weidenfeld and Nicolson, 1960)

—— *see also* Rosenblum *in this section*

ROSENBLUM, JOSEPH, ed. – *American book-collectors and bibliographers; first series* (*Dictionary of literary biography*, vol. 140; Detroit: Gale Research Inc., 1994) includes entries by various contributors on Ernest Dawson, David Anton Randall, A.S.W. Rosenbach, Leona Rostenberg and Madeleine B. Stern, George D. Smith, Gabriel Wells; *American book collectors and bibliographers; second series* (*Dictionary of literary biography*, vol. 187; Detroit: Gale Research, 1997) includes entries by various contributors on John S. Van E. Kohn and Michael Papantonio, Hans Peter Kraus, David Magee, Otto H.F. Vollbehr

ROSTENBERG, LEONA; AND STERN, MADELEINE B[ETTINA]. – *Between boards; new thoughts on old books* (Montclair: Allanheld & Schram, 1978)

—— *Bookends; two women, one enduring friendship* (New York: Free Press, [2001])

—— *Bookman's quintet; five catalogues about books; bibliography · printing history; booksellers; libraries · presses · collectors; preface by Terry Belanger* (Newark: Oak Knoll Books, 1980)

—— *Books have their fates* (New Castle: Oak Knoll Press, 2001)

—— *Connections: our selves – our books* (Santa Monica: Modoc Press, Inc., 1994)

—— *New worlds in old books* (New Castle: Oak Knoll Press, 1999)

—— *Old and rare; thirty years in the book business* (New York: Abner Schram, 1974) [chapters 6 to 8 by Stern: 'Books After the Blitz', 'The British Succession' and 'English Basements']

—— *Old books in the old world; reminiscences of book buying abroad* (New Castle: Oak Knoll Press, 1996)

—— *Old books, rare friends: two literary sleuths and their shared passion* (New York: Doubleday, 1997)

—— *see also* Rosenblum *in this section*

SMITH, GEORGE DALLAS – Charles F[rederick]. Heartman – *George D. Smith, G.D.S., 1870-1920; a memorial tribute to the greatest bookseller the world has ever known;*

written by a very small one (privately printed from the Book Farm, Beauvoir Community, Mississippi, 1945)

—— *see also* Rosenblum *in this section*

STERN, MADELEINE BETTINA, see Rostenberg *in this section*

STODDARD, ROGER E[LIOT]. – *A library-keeper's business* (New Castle: Oak Knoll Press, 2002) [essay entitled 'Looking at Books, Learning from It, Passing It Along' includes account of visit to England during '1985 European acquisitions trip']

VOLLBEHR, OTTO HEINRICH FRIEDERICH, *see* Rosenblum *in this section and* Ettinghausen

WELLS, GABRIEL – *see* Rosenblum *in this section*

[XIMENES] [Weissman, Stephen; and Tempest, Kathryn] 'Part IV: The Catalogues of Ximenes (1962-1993): An Informal Chronology' in Ximenes's 'Occasional List No. 100' ([1993])

REFERENCES

I. BUYING: HOW THE TRADE ACQUIRED ITS STOCK

FRANK HERRMANN The Role of the Auction Houses

1 *Bibliotheca Osleriana* (Oxford, 1929), pp. xxvii-xxviii, quoted in my *Sotheby's: Portrait of an Auction House* (1980), pp. 92-4.

2 Anthony James West, 'The Market Fortunes of the First Folio', pp. 215-19.

3 The subtitle reads, 'Being a compilation of 2,032 notes from catalogues of book-sales which have taken place in the rooms of Messrs. Sotheby, Wilkinson & Hodge between the years 1885-1909.' To each title listed, Karslake added bibliographical comments, which he thought would help booksellers if and when they included identical books in their own catalogues.

4 H.C. Marillier, *Christie's 1766 to 1925* (1926), mentions only seven library sales between 1900 and 1925, among many hundreds of sales of pictures, jewellery, china, etc., in what was a particularly rich period at Christie's.

5 For the full story see Christopher Mason, *The Art of the Steal: Inside the Sotheby-Christie Auction House Scandal* (New York, 2004). The book was published in the UK only after a long interval as *Lords and Liars: The Secret Story of the Sotheby-Christie Conspiracy* (2005).

6 W.F. Nokes, *The Auctioneers' Manual* (9th edition, 1924), p. 65.

7 C.E. Jerningham and L. Bettany, *The Bargain Book* (1911), chap. xiii: 'The "knock-out" and other customs of the sale-room'.

8 Leonora Navari, 'Bernard Quaritch and John Gennadius: The Development of a Library', *Book Collector* special number for the 150th anniversary of Bernard Quaritch (1997), pp. 76-84.

9 Arthur Freeman and Janet Ing Freeman, *Anatomy of an Auction: Rare Books at Ruxley Lodge, 1919* (*Book Collector* occasional series 1, 1990).

10 Bertram Dobell had achieved minor notoriety in the auction world because of a sale at Sotheby's taken by Tom Hodge at the turn of the century. Dobell had attempted to introduce a note of humour into a rather dreary sale by bidding one shilling for a valuable illuminated manuscript.
'Come, come, Mr Dobell,' said Tom Hodge. 'You ought to know better than that.'
'I'll give a shilling for any lot, Sir,' Dobell responded. And forever afterwards Hodge knocked down to Dobell for one shilling any lot for which there was no bid.

11 E. Millicent Sowerby, *Rare People and Rare Books* (1967), pp. 61-2, 65-6.

12 See also Anthony Rota, *Books in the Blood* (Pinner and New Castle, DE, 2002). In a chapter entitled 'The Ring and the Book', he describes what action he took to quell ringing while he was President of the ABA.

13 It has to be admitted that mischievous anecdotes circulated in the trade which showed Basil Blackwell in a less puritanical light. In particular, Jack Joseph is recorded as having said that

he would no longer do the bidding at rings on Sir Basil's behalf if he did not cease his campaign.

14 This material was published by Muir's widow: Barbara Kaye, *Second Impression* (New Castle, DE, and London, 1995), pp. 328-40. See also above, pp. 313-14, for Anthony Rota's account of the same debate.

15 Sheila Markham, *A Book of Booksellers* (2004), pp. 153, 159, 215-16, 243.

16 Seymour de Ricci, *English Collectors of Books & Manuscripts (1530-1930) and their Marks of Ownership* (Cambridge, 1930), p. 150. These Sandars Lectures still constitute the most concise available account of the most important English book collectors.

17 E.M. Dring, 'Fifty Years at Quaritch', *Book Collector* special number for the 150th anniversary of Bernard Quaritch (1997), p. 35.

18 For a witty and scholarly account of where and for what Yates Thompson acquired his collection, see Christopher de Hamel, 'Was Henry Yates Thompson a Gentleman?', in Robin Myers and Michael Harris (eds.), *Property of a Gentleman* (Winchester, 1991), pp. 77-89.

19 His son, E.M. Dring, known as 'Ted', also became the firm's managing director some years later.

20 The norm at book sales today – though obviously not of the quality of the Yates Thompson sales – is between 120 and 150 lots per hour.

21 Dring had refused to act for Gulbenkian.

22 For example, J.V. Beckett, *The Aristocracy in England, 1600-1914* (Oxford, 1986); F.M.L. Thompson, *English Landed Society in the Nineteenth Century* (1963); Peter Mandler, *The Fall and Rise of the Country House* (New Haven & London, 1997); David Cannadine, *The Decline and Fall of the British Aristocracy* (New Haven & London, 1990).

23 A.N.L. Munby, 'The Library', in Roy Strong, Marcus Binney and John Harris (eds.), *The Destruction of the Country House, 1875-1975* (1974), pp. 106-10.

24 Sales would continue until the end of July and usually began again in mid-November.

25 The stock – which also included a distant warehouse – was bought in its entirety by Ben Weinreb after Crowe's death, and took years to clear.

26 He bought our copy as well!

27 Gordon N. Ray, 'The Changing World of Rare Books', *Papers of the Bibliographical Society of America*, 59 (1965), pp. 103-41; reprinted in his *Books as a Way of Life* (New York, 1988), pp. 47-83.

28 See the present author's *Low Profile: A Life in the World of Books* (Nottingham, 2002), chapter 12, for a full description of the work involved.

RICHARD FORD Private Buying

This chapter has benefited from conversations with Peter Brewer, Tim Warner, Margaret Eaton, Stephen Foster, Patrick Marrin, Eric Morten, Chris Overfield, Chris Saunders, Roger Treglown, Marc Vaulbert de Chantilly, Veronica Watts, Laurence Worms, Graham York. For further details of the booksellers' memoirs cited here, see Appendix 5.

1 (Blackwell's) Rita Ricketts, *Adventurers All*, p. 232; (Robinsons) A.N.L. Munby, *The Dispersal of the Phillipps Library (Phillipps Studies*, 5; Cambridge, 1960), p. 97; Maurice L. Ettinghausen, *Rare Books and Royal Collectors*, p. 47; Robin Waterfield, 'Bookselling as Occupational Therapy' [2000], in Sheila Markham, *A Book of Booksellers*, p. 242; David Low, *'with all faults'*, p. [54]; 'Photo Finish. Jim Thorp in conversation with Sheila Markham' [1995], www.sheila-markham.com; Meg Kidd, *Four Book Walls. A Memoir of*

Andrew Block, p. 66; Paul Minet, *Bookdealing for Profit* (Farnham, 2000), p. 103; Stephen Foster, conversation with writer, 27 May 2005.

2 Information from Rusty Mott, 27 Dec. 2004; Anthony Rota, *Books in the Blood,* p. 72.

3 Percy Muir, *Minding My Own Business,* p. 44; George Sims, *The Rare Book Game,* p. 139; (Block) Kidd, pp. 62-3; (Reeves) Andrew Block, *The Bookseller's Vade-Mecum,* p. 314; E.Ph. Goldschmidt, 'Austrian Monastic Libraries', *The Library,* 4th ser., vol. xxv, nos. 1, 2 (June, September 1944), p. 48; John and Juliet Townsend, 'Country Life', in Markham, p. 99.

4 Charles P. Everitt, *Adventures of a Treasure-Hunter* (1952), p. 150; H.P. Kraus, *A Rare Book Saga* (1979), p. 50.

5 'Unsentimental Journey. Richard Sawyer in conversation with Sheila Markham' [1995], www.sheila-markham.com; Low, pp. 47, 104; Eric Moore, 'The Summing Up' [1995], Markham, p. 145.

6 G. Orioli, *Adventures of a Bookseller,* p. 128; (vet) Rota, p. 163; (Cockerell) E.H. Dring, 'Fifty Years at Quaritch', *Book Collector,* special number for the 150th anniversary of Bernard Quaritch (1997), p. 51; Jamieson, *Echoes and Eccentrics,* pp. 68-71; (Gawsworth) Timothy d'Arch Smith, *The Times Deceas'd,* pp. 103-4; (Hague) Sims, *Rare Book Game,* p. 157.

7 (*Book Auction Records*) Paul Minet, *Late Booking,* p. 77; Roy Harley Lewis, *Antiquarian Books,* p. 129.

8 Muir, *Minding My Own Business,* p. 2; Stephen Mogridge, *Talking Shop* (1950), p. 156; Paul Minet, *Bookdealing for a Profit,* p. 51; d'Arch Smith, p. 54; Rota, p. 274.

9 Lawrence Clark Powell, 'Rendezvous in Cadogan Square', *Books in My Baggage* (1960), p. 132; W.T. Spencer, *Forty Years in My Bookshop* (reissue, 1927), p. 18.

10 (Goldschmidt) Quoted by Gordon Ray, 'The World of Rare Books Re-examined', reprinted in *Books as a Way of Life* (New York, 1988), p. 104; Pratley, *A Bookseller Remembers,* p. 15; Charles Russell, 'Top of the Second Division' [1996], Markham, p. 170.

11 Ian R. Grant, 'Antiquarian and Secondhand Bookselling', in John Hampden (ed.), *The Book World Today* (1957), p. 159; Rota, p. 16; information from John Collins, 2006.

12 Muir, *Minding My Own Business,* pp. 213-14; Clive Linklater, *Reflections from a Bookshop Window* (1994), p. 60.

13 Sims, *Rare Book Game,* p. 1; Orioli, p. 179.

14 Rota, p. 31; D'Arch Smith, p. 102; Pratley, p. 24.

15 The Ballantyne case was chronicled by 'drif field' in his *drif d notices (second series), numbers* 24, 27, 28, 30, 32 (Aug.-Dec. 1993); Ettinghausen, pp. 83-5; (Bunker Hill) Percy Muir, 'Further Reminiscences XIV', *Book Collector* (autumn 1961), pp. 314-16; (Morrell) Muir, *Minding My Own Business,* p. 61.

16 Letter from Dunlop to H.D. MacWilliam, Edinburgh, 1 Oct. 1915, laid down in the latter's home-made bibliography in the present writer's own collection; Muir, *Minding My Own Business,* p. 200; George Sims, *A Life in Catalogues,* p. 2.

17 (Block) Kidd, pp. 68-9; Walter Scott, *The Antiquary* (Everyman reprint, 1977), pp. 34-5; Edwin Wolf with John Fleming, *Rosenbach. A Biography* (1960), p. 386; Kraus, p. 210.

18 Undated, probably in the 1950s, Jamieson, pp. 51-2; ABA minutes, 4 Nov. 1942.

19 Minet, *Late Booking,* pp. 77, 156; Richard Booth, *My Kingdom of Books,* pp. 27-9; Kraus, p. 252.

20 Rota, p. 21; Minet, *Late Booking,* p. 155; letter to Percy Muir, 1969, in the Elkin Mathews archive, Lilly Library, Indiana University, Bloomington.

21 Booth, p. 27; Charles P. Everitt, *Adventures of a Treasure Hunter*, p. 43.

22 Sims, *Rare Book Game*, p. 118; David Magee, *Infinite Riches* (1973), p. 163.

23 Kraus, pp. 238, 240; (Fenwick) A.S.W. Rosenbach, *Books and Bidders* (1928), p. 223; (Swaythling) Wolf and Fleming, p. 295; Ettinghausen, pp. 146-8.

24 (Foyles) Minet, *Late Booking*, p. 188; Booth, pp. 140-9.

25 Booth, p. 112; 'Merchant Adventurer. Kenneth Smith in conversation with Sheila Markham' [1999], *www.sheila-markham.com*

26 (Rowfant) Seymour de Ricci, *English Collectors of Books & Manuscripts (1530-1930)* (Cambridge, 1930), p. 174; (Ogden) Powell, *Books in my Baggage*, pp. 130-36; (Barton) d'Arch Smith, p. 53; Pratley, pp. 13-14; Norman Storey, 'Flights of Imagination' [2001], Markham, p. 260; Townsend, 'Country Life', Markham p. 96.

27 Michael Hollander, 'The A to Zee of Bookselling' [1993], Markham, p. 93; Eric Moore, 'The Summing Up', Markham, p. 147; Sims, *Rare Book Game*, pp. 147, 137 (Bertram Rota); Barbara Kaye, *Second Impression*, p. 283; J.S. Bain, *A Bookseller Looks Back*, p. 209.

28 Wolf and Fleming, pp. 293 (Dufferin), 337 (Marlborough), 221-228 (Holford), 329-37 (York).

29 D'Arch Smith, p. 118; Ettinghausen, p. 71; (HRC) Gordon Ray, 'The World of Rare Books Re-examined', *Books as a Way of Life*, p. 141.

30 Rota, pp. 284-6.

31 (Hamill) Richard M. Ford, *Bookselling in the 20th Century* (2002), Appendix a. The Elkin Mathews archive is now in the collections of the Lilly Library; (Myers) information from Rusty Mott, 17 Dec. 2004; (Woolf) Donald C. Dickinson, *Dictionary of American Antiquarian Bookdealers* (Westport, CT, 1998), p. 92; (food parcels) Kaye, *Second Impression*, p. 223.

32 For example, the purchase of the C.K. Ogden library mentioned above.

33 Kaye, *Second Impression*, p. 5; Low, p. 102; Rota, p. 182.

34 Rota, p. 176; documents relating to the Lillicrap and Rothenstein consignments are described in Ford, *Bookselling*, and are now in the collections of the Lilly Library; (Isaac Foot) information from Martin Hamlyn, 4 May 2005.

35 Nicolas Barker, 'Bernard Quaritch', *Book Collector*, special number (1997), pp. 28-31; Rota, pp. 303-4; Muir, pp. 61-2; Rota, p. 257.

36 *Chicago Daily Tribune*, vol. lxxiv, no. 242C, Saturday, 9 October 1915, part 1, p. 1, see www.geocities.com/voyms/chicago as of 28 June 2005; Sowerby, pp. 133-4.

37 Percy Muir, 'Further Reminiscences', *Book Collector* (winter 1961-spring 1964); (Edwards) obituary in 'News and Comment', *Book Collector* (spring 1980), p. 86; the preface to *The Memoirs of James II* (1962), trans. A. Lytton Sells, gives one account of this coup.

38 (Robinsons) Munby, p. 97; (Vesey) Block, *The Bookseller's Vade-Mecum*, p. 318.

39 Rota, pp. 65-71.

40 Wolf and Fleming, p. 336.

41 Information from Eric Morten, 5 July 2005; Booth, p. 81.

42 Minet, *Late Booking*, p. 167.

43 (Oldbuck) Scott, p. 35; Everitt, p. 125.

44 Booth, p. 27; (Traylen) Roy Harley Lewis, p. 40; Muir, *Minding My Own Business*, p. 203.

45 Ettinghausen, pp. 140-43; Kraus, pp. 314-17; (Goldston) Block, p. 289; (Rosenbach) Wolf and Fleming, pp. 239-42, 548; (Voynich) Orioli, p. 77.

46 Code of Good Practice adopted on 10 Dec. 1997; ABA 'Objects and Rules' (revised 1943).

47 (Rota) Letter to the present writer, 15 Dec. 2004; Rota, pp. 72, 22; Minet, *Late Booking*, p. 155; Spencer, p. 159; information from various dealers.

48 'A Lot on his Pallet. Charlie Unsworth in conversation with Sheila Markham' [1998], www.sheila-markham.com; Booth, p. 28.

49 Spencer, p. 158; Everitt, p. 28.

50 Wolf and Fleming, pp. 386-7; untrue at least in the case of the Holford books for which he did his sums in a hotel room: Wolf and Fleming, p. 222.

51 *Bookdealer*, 12 and 19 Dec. 1996, nos. 1287 & 1288, pp. 3-7 and 3-7; ibid., 12 Dec. 1996, no. 1287, p. 5; ibid., 19 Dec. 1996, no. 1288, p. 7.

52 Jamieson, pp. 49-60; Peter Eaton, 'Straight Talk' [1991], Markham, p. 21.

BARRY SHAW Book Trade Weeklies

1 Andrew Block, *A Short History of the Principal London Antiquarian Booksellers and Book Auctioneers* (1933).

2 Second-hand Booksellers' Association committee meeting, 6 May 1907.

3 ABA committee meeting, 7 March 1932.

4 ABA committee meeting, 12 July 1978: 'The President had received a letter from the Editor of *The Clique* applying to sit in on the Committee. This request was refused.'

5 Originally a talk to the Aberystwyth Bibliographical Group in 1978, reprinted as 'Fifty Years at Quaritch', *Book Collector* special number for the 150th anniversary of Bernard Quaritch (1997), pp. 36-7.

6 In the tradition of book trade weeklies, *Bookdealer* was set in 7pt type and printed as two columns of 14 pica ems (2⅓"), sizes designed to allow most author/title 'Books Wanted' requests to fit on a single line.

7 A selection of 50 interviews were privately printed in 2004 as *A Book of Booksellers: Conversations with the Antiquarian Book Trade*.

II. SELLING: HOW THE TRADE SOLD BOOKS

MICHAEL HARRIS The London Street Trade

1 For Dobell's deliberate challenge to the Westminster City authorities, see Anthony Rota, *Books in the Blood* (Pinner and New Castle, DE, 2002), pp. 34-6; for Quaritch and FitzGerald, see Arthur Freeman, 'Bernard Quaritch and "My Omar"', *Book Collector* special number for the 150th anniversary of Bernard Quaritch (1997), pp. 60-75.

2 W. Roberts, *The Book Hunter in London* (1895), p. 161.

3 Interview by Sheila Markham, *A Book of Booksellers* (2004), p. 19, and at www.sheila-markham.com, 'Peter Eaton'.

4 Roberts, *Book Hunter*, p. 158. London County Council Report (1893), p. 121 (see note 7).

5 Introduction by Donald Thomas in *Memoirs of Dolly Morton* (Paris, 1899; reprinted, 1970), p. 12.

6 Roberts, *Book Hunter*, p. xxi.

7 'Special Report of the Public Control Committee Relating to Existing Markets and Market

Rights and as to the Expediency of Establishing new Markets in or Near the Administrative County of London' [1893]; 'Report of the Chief Officer of the Public Control Department as to the Street Markets in the County of London' (1901). Both reports held at the London Metropolitan Archives, PC/SHO/3/8.

8 George R. Sims (ed.), *Living London* (3 vols., 1901), vol. 1, p. 382.

9 Roberts, *Book Hunter*, p. 152.

10 *Post Office Directory* (1902): 'John Jeffery second hand bookseller, 115a, City Road, EC'. This may refer to George Jeffery I's father's shop; R.M. Healey, 'Return to Bookseller's Row', *Rare Book Review*, vol. xxxii, no. 3 (April 2005), p. 24, suggests (without identifying his source) that George Jeffery I had opened a bookshop in East Road near Old Street in the 1880s and moved to the Farringdon Road in 1909.

11 For the impact of the construction of the road and the railway on existing communities, see Gareth Stedman Jones, *Outcast London* (Oxford, 1971).

12 The complex process by which the eighteenth-century Fleet Market metamorphosed, in part at least, into the Farringdon Road vegetable market can be tracked in the coverage by *The Times* from the 1830s.

13 'A Gossip about Bookstalls', *Temple Bar,* March 1882, p. 423; Roberts, *Book Hunter*, p. 153.

14 References to the specific locations associated with the phrase 'Booksellers' Row' appeared in the *Daily Telegraph*, 17 January 1902, and the *Daily Chronicle*, 8 January 1902. Both were cited in the introduction to Bertram Dobell's *One Hundredth Catalogue* [1902], pp. 6, 8. There is a lively account of the original booksellers' row in W. Heath Robinson, *My Time of Life* (1938), p. 32.

15 For reports of the campaigns organized around the Farringdon Road costers: *The Times*, 3 December 1889; 12, 19 and 20 September 1892.

16 Charles Booth, *Life and Labour of the People in London* (17 vols., 1902-03), 2nd ser., 'Industry', vol. 1, pp. 270-71. The police regulations of 1869 applied for four miles around Charing Cross and defined the size and position of barrows: *The Times*, 13 September 1869.

17 Jerry White, *London in the Twentieth Century* (2002), p. 247; *The Times*, 8 April 1951.

18 Interventions in the Portobello Road and in Tottenham were part of a wider pattern of local authority action involving ex-servicemen. Before the war groups of immigrants, including Jews and Poles, provided an impetus to the expansion of street trading.

19 This was on top of the weekly pitch charge of between 6*d.* and 3*s.* a week for refuse removal. As early as 1887, Whitecross Street costers had met to protest about the 1*s.* a week levy imposed by St Luke's vestry: *The Times*, 5 October 1887.

20 *The New Survey of London Life and Labour* (9 vols., 1932), vol. 3, 'Survey of Social Conditions', p. 298.

21 By 1930 the Clerkenwell Street Traders had five branches and between 800 and 1,000 members, *New Survey*, vol. 3, p. 270.

22 The introduction of designated streets generated some comment in the press: *The Times*, 13 May 1947 and 25 April 1949; *Punch*, vol. 222 (Jan.-June 1952), p. 362.

23 Roberts, *Book Hunter*, pp. 158-9.

24 *New Survey*, vol. 3, p. 306.

25 Such informal arrangements were progressively undermined by legislation on child labour. For a specific proposal to restrict the use of minors in street markets, see *The Times*, 20 October 1952.

26 *Times Literary Supplement*, 4 January 1957. I am grateful to Kim Jeffery for this reference

and for arranging a useful and interesting conversation with Joan Richards.

27 Wolf Mankowitz, *Make Me an Offer* (1952), p. 27. Although a work of fiction, the lively account of the trade in bric-à-brac is realistic in detail.

28 The non-appearance of a bookstall keeper was noted in David Rogers (ed.), *A Victorian Schoolboy in London: The Diary of Ernest Baker 1881-2* (Geffrye Museum, [1989]), p. 21.

29 Roberts, *Book Hunter*, p. 160.

30 J.H. Slater, *Round and About the Bookstalls: A Guide for the Book Hunter* (1891), p. 83; for Dabbs, see Roberts, *Book Hunter*, p. 159.

31 *Victorian Schoolboy*, p. 16.

32 Slater, *Bookstalls*, p. 113.

33 Arthur G. Morrison, 'Whitechapel', *The Palace Journal*, 24 April 1889. I am grateful to Sue Morgan for this and other useful references.

34 Slater, *Bookstalls*, p. 60.

35 Ibid, p. 64.

36 Roberts, *Book Hunter*, p. 159.

37 Ibid, p. xxiii.

38 Ibid, p. 162.

39 O.F. Snelling, *Rare Books and Rarer People* (1982).

40 Mary Benedetta, *The Street Markets of London* (1936), pp. 19-64. She noted the mixing up of books with other materials, including the pram wheels already mentioned. For a later view which also focused on the customers and under-priced books see C.A. Prance, 'The Farringdon Road Bookstalls', *The Private Library*, 25 (January 1963), pp. 86-90.

41 Some biographical information about George Jeffery III appeared in obituaries published early in 1995, including the *Guardian*, 9 January 1995, and *The Times*, 21 January 1995.

42 The best visual record of the Farringdon Road experience is offered by the anonymous 'one who was there'. In a series of photographs linked by a laconic narrative, *Saturday Morning, Farringdon Road* [2005], privately printed for the bookseller Christopher White, provides a clear sense of many of the components of street bookselling and buying at this location.

43 Information from John Collins.

44 One such box, containing a rare series of letters sent to the Western Front during the First World War, was purchased by Nigel Tattersfield.

45 It is tempting to think that the volumes might have formed part of the working experience of Graham Greene during his short and not very successful spell on the paper during the late 1920s. He was a customer at the Farringdon Road and left a short, atmospheric account of the environment in 'George Moore and Others', *Collected Essays* (1969).

46 The Brooklyn Public Library books came through Bloomsbury Book Auctions, who sold on to Jeffery a large group of books which had been deemed unfit for cataloguing. The entire library of the Gibraltar garrison was bought by Martin Orksey and Ben Weinreb, who sold the residue to Jeffery: Snelling, *Rare Books*, p. 179, and information from John Collins.

47 The material cited is from the Mass Observation Archive, in the University of Sussex Library, Special Collections: 'Reading Habits 1939-1947', TC 20, Box 6, 1942, 'Books and Book Buyers'.

48 The quotation from Monkbarns, a collector from Edinburgh, and the subsequent comment appeared in a letter from W. Roberts to *The Times*, 22 December 1901, reprinted in Dobell, *One Hundredth Catalogue*, p. 4.

49 Slater, *Bookstalls*, p. 95; Roberts, *Book Hunter*, p. 160. Both terms seem to have been in general use to describe practitioners of this form of commercial enterprise.

50 Iain Sinclair, *Landor's Tower, or the Imaginary Conversations* (2001).

51 Snelling, *Rare Books*, p. 169.

52 For an account of the changing character of the London street market between the wars, see White, *London*, p. 248.

53 By the 1980s the book fairs were an established alternative to the street trade in books. They were included in Alec Forshaw and Theo Bergstrom, *Markets of London* (1983), p. 28.

PHILIPPA BERNARD The Bookshops of London

1 Richard Brown and Stanley Brett, *The London Bookshop* (2 vols.; Pinner, 1971-7). Cf. Andrew Block, *A Short History of the Principal London Antiquarian Booksellers and Book-Auctioneers* (1933).

2 Percy Muir, *Minding My Own Business* (1956), p. 129.

3 *Views of Some of the Rooms in the House of Maggs Brothers, London & Paris* (Maggs special catalogue 35, 1927) shows the premises at 34-35 Conduit Street and 130 Boulevard Haussmann; *The House of Maggs* (Maggs special catalogue 36, 1939) shows 50 Berkeley Square.

4 *Book Collector*, special number for the 150th anniversary of Bernard Quaritch (1997), edited by Richard Linenthal.

5 Martin Hamlyn, *The Robinson Legend* (Stamford, 1992), pp. 4-5. Cf. A.N.L. Munby, *The Dispersal of the Phillipps Library* (*Phillipps Studies*, 5; Cambridge, 1960), pp. 98-9.

6 Anthony Rota, *Books in the Blood* (Pinner and New Castle, DE, 2002), p. 281.

7 Brown and Brett, *The London Bookshop*, vol. 1, p. 8.

ELIZABETH STRONG
Town and Country Bookshops in Scotland and Northern Ireland

I am extremely grateful to the following, who have helped me with this piece, and I apologize in advance to anyone whom I may have forgotten to mention: James Abbey; Special Libraries and Archives, University of Aberdeen; William F Bauermeister; Tony Drennan; Kulgin Duval; Jack Gamble; Senga Grant; Cooper Hay; Spike Hughes; David Hyslop; Donald MacCormick; Edward Nairn; Trustees of the National Library of Scotland; Professor Roland A. Paxton; Paul Roberts; David Steedman; the late Agnes Steven and Yla Steven; Gillian Stone; Ainslie Thin; Gordon Wheeler (from whose notes I have quoted extensively in the Northern Irish section).

1 'Timolean' [Sir William Y. Darling], *King's Cross to Waverley* (Glasgow, 1944).

2 *James Thin: 150 Years of Bookselling. 1848-1998* (Edinburgh, 1998). For the Edinburgh book trade, see also J.B. Cairns, *Bright and Early. A Bookseller's Memories of Edinburgh and Lasswade.* (Edinburgh, 1953); W. Forbes Gray et al., *A Literary Centre of a Literary Capital* (Edinburgh, 1946); James Thin, *Reminiscences of Booksellers and Bookselling in Edinburgh in the time of William IV: an address delivered to a meeting of booksellers' assistants, in the hall of the Protestant Institute, Edinburgh, October 1904* (Edinburgh, 1905); James Thin, *1848-1948* (Edinburgh, 1948).

3 National Library of Scotland (NLS) Acc. 5024.

4 NLS Acc. 12384/114.

5 NLS Acc. 12384/152.

6 R.M. Williamson, *Bits from an Old Book Shop* (London, Edinburgh & Glasgow, 1904).

7 John Hill Burton, *The Book Hunter* (new edition with a memoir of the author; Edinburgh and London, 1882).

8 Sara Stevenson and Julie Lawson, *Masterpieces of Photography from the Riddell Collection* (Scottish National Portrait Gallery, Edinburgh, 1986).

9 NLS Acc. 5024.

10 Edward Nairn's report of conversations with Robert Aitken.

11 NLS Acc. 5024.

12 D.E. Griffiths, 'The Sarolea papers in Edinburgh University Library', *The Bibliotheck* 3, no. 1 (1961), pp. 24-31; Peter France, 'Charles Louis-Camille Sarolea (1870-1953)', *Oxford Dictionary of National Biography* (Oxford, 2004).

13 NLS Acc. 11018; Olive M. Geddes, 'Shopping in the 1930s', *Folio* (winter 2005), pp. 2-5.

14 Rewritten from my obituary of Mrs McNaughtan, published in part by *The Scotsman*, *The Herald*, and *The Times* and in full by *The Bookdealer* and the *ABA Newsletter*.

15 NLS Acc. 11253.

16 Iain Beavan, 'Notes on the Aberdeen Booksellers' Societies', *The Bibliotheck* 10, no. 6 (1981), pp. 158-69.

17 Aberdeen University Library MS 3205 records some of Wyllie's publishing and remainder bookselling activities between 1848 and 1938.

18 *Scottish International*, no. 13 (February 1971).

H.R. WOUDHUYSEN Catalogues

I would like to acknowledge the great amount of help I have received in writing this chapter from John Collins, Christopher Edwards, Arnold Hunt, Jim McCue, Giles Mandelbrote and Angus O'Neill.

1 Ernest Raymond, *Mr. Olim* (1961), p. 125.

2 Michael Sadleir, *XIX Century Fiction: A Bibliographical Record*, 2 vols (London and Los Angeles, Calif., 1951), I, xx-xxi.

3 'Floreat Bibliomania', in *Essays and Papers*, ed. by Nicolas Barker (1977), pp. 37-41 (pp. 38-9).

4 Clive Hurst, 'Selections from the Accession Diaries of Peter Opie', in *Children and their Books: A Celebration of the Work of Iona and Peter Opie*, ed. by Gillian Avery and Julia Briggs (Oxford, 1989), pp. 19-44 (p. 33).

5 'The World of Rare Books Re-examined', in Gordon N. Ray, *Books as a Way of Life* (New York, 1988), pp. 84-152 (p. 116).

6 David Pearson, *Provenance Research in Book History: A Handbook*, 2nd edn (London and New Castle, DE, 1998), pp. 134-5.

7 See Harold Forster, '"Munby Ltd"', in *The Pleasures of Bibliophily: Fifty Years of* The Book Collector, ed. by A.S.G. Edwards (London and New Castle, DE, 2003), pp. 153-8.

8 'The Accession Diaries of Peter Opie', p. 27.

9 Pearson, *Provenance Research in Book History*, pp. 144-6.

10 For a brief but useful overview of the US, see Eric Holzenberg, 'Book Catalogue Collections in Selected American Libraries', *Papers of the Bibliographical Society of America*, 89 (1995), 465-7.

11 *Catalogus der Bibliotheek van de Vereeniging ter Bevordering van de Belangen des Boekhandels te Amsterdam*, 8 Catalogus 1932-1973 (Amsterdam, 1979), pp. 113-380; see also volume 4 (The Hague, 1934), pp. 65-214.

12 Jeanne Blogie, *Répertoire des Catalogues de Ventes de Livres Imprimés*, 3 *Catalogues Britanniques Appartenant à la Bibliothèque Royale Albert Ier* (Bruxelles, 1988).

13 'The Accession Diaries of Peter Opie', p. 38.

14 Pearson, *Provenance Research in Book History*, p. 143.

15 John Power, *A Handy-Book about Books* (1870), pp. 65-82, 203-4; the figures are: London booksellers 167, 113 issuing catalogues; booksellers outside London 343, 57 issuing catalogues.

16 See especially Andrew Block, *The Book Collector's 'Vade Mecum'* (1932), Appendix B, pp. 270-335, and Pearson, *Provenance Research in Book History*, pp. 154-69, where he describes the major firms founded before 1930 which issued catalogues and where in the UK their catalogues are to be found.

17 See Pearson, *Provenance Research in Book History*, pp. 155, 162, 163, where he mentions: Blackwell's, *Centenary Catalogue of Antiquarian and Rare Modern Books*, A-1 (1979); H.C. Maggs, *A Catalogue of Maggs Catalogues 1918-1968* (1969), covering catalogues 365-914, and for later catalogues Maggs, catalogue 1000 (1980); for Pearson, see L. Navari, *The Bookseller's Art: Catalogues Issued by the Firm of J. Pearson & Co. Ltd.* (1991) and Maggs, catalogue 1118 (1991), describing Pearson catalogues issued after 1900; for Edwards, see John Collins and Penelope Rudd, *A Selection of Reference Books and Bibliographies, from the Reference Library of Francis Edwards Ltd.*, Maggs catalogue 1062 (1985), including 'A preliminary checklist of Francis Edwards Catalogues'. The sort of discursive account of a dealer's catalogues supplied by the American firm Ximenes in occasional list 100 [1993] is unfortunately very rare.

18 Richard Brown and Stanley Brett, *The London Bookshop*, part 2 (Pinner, 1977), p. 26.

19 See John Hart, catalogue 67 [c.2004]), item 124.

20 See *New Review*, vol. 3 no. 29 (August 1976), 35-42, and Peter Parker, 'June Guesdon Braybrooke', in *ODNB*.

21 James Fergusson, 'Catalogues', in *Antiquarian Books: A Companion* ed. by Philippa Bernard with Leo Bernard and Angus O'Neill (Aldershot and Brookfield, VT, 1994), pp. 111-20, provides a valuable account of the various issues to be discussed from the bookseller's point of view.

22 See *The Letters of A.E. Housman*, ed. Henry Maas (1971), p. 393.

23 For other dealers (among them Frank Hollings, Maggs, Quaritch, Sotheran, and Tregaskis) who bought heavily at the Browning sale and then issued catalogues devoted in part to their purchases, see Philip Kelley and Betty A. Coley, *The Browning Collections: A Reconstruction with Other Memorabilia* (Waco, TX, London, Winfield, KS, 1984), pp. xxxv-xxxvii.

24 David Low, *'with all faults'* (Tehran, 1973), p. 32.

25 *Ibid.*, p. 19.

26 See Anthony Rota, *Books in the Blood: Memoirs of a Fourth Generation Bookseller* (Pinner and New Castle, DE, 2002).

27 See Seymour de Ricci, *English Collectors of Books & Manuscripts (1530-1930) and their Marks of Ownership* (Cambridge, 1930), p. 181.

28 Nicolas Barker, 'Bernard Quaritch', *Book Collector* special number (1997), pp. 3-34 (p. 24).

29 Block, *Book Collector's 'Vade Mecum'*, p. 310.

30 For a memoir, see Maggs catalogue 1350 (2003).

31 Percy Muir, *Minding My Own Business: An Autobiography* (1956), pp. 22-3, 26-7, 103.

32 Pearson, *Provenance Research in Book History*, p. 158.

33 'The Accession Diaries of Peter Opie', p. 39.

34 Muir, *Minding My Own Business*, p. 56.

35 Maggs, catalogue 918 (1969), p. 2.

36 'The Accession Diaries of Peter Opie', pp. 31, 38-9.

37 Taken from catalogue 66 (1921).

38 Muir, *Minding My Own Business*, p. 83.

39 See Low, *'with all faults'*, p. 7 and Rota, *Books in the Blood*, p. 44.

40 Muir, *Minding My Own Business*, pp. 49-50.

41 Roger Burdett Wilson, *Old & Curious: The History of James Wilson's Bookshop* (Birmingham, 1960), p. 71; see also *The Times*, 6, 9 March, 21 August 1917. The restrictions were issued by the Paper Commission under the authority of the Board of Trade.

42 See Lawrence Clark Powell, *Books in My Baggage* (1960), p. 121.

43 Block, *Book Collector's 'Vade Mecum'*, p. 320.

44 Michael Sadleir, 'Bookshop and Auction Room', in R.W. Chapman *et al.*, *Book Collecting: Four Broadcast Talks* (Cambridge, 1950), pp. 37-45 (p. 43).

45 Muir, *Minding My Own Business*, p. 83, cf. p. 125.

46 Nicolas Barker, *Stanley Morison* (1972), pp. 245, 279.

47 See Rota, *Books in the Blood*, p. 153.

48 The Edinburgh firm was originally formed by Richard E. Dana and John Price; its title alluded to their lack of hair and glanced at the eighteenth-century booksellers R. and J. Dodsley, as well as at a popular food shop in the city which bore the same pair of initials.

49 Sadleir, 'Bookshop and Auction Room', p. 43.

50 See John Collins's introduction to the Bloomsbury Book Auctions sale, beginning 24 June 1998.

51 For an account of their relations, see Maggs catalogue 918 (1969), pp. 2-3.

52 Cf. Wilson, *Old & Curious*, pp. 32-3.

53 Block, *Book Collector's 'Vade Mecum'*, p. 291.

54 Arnold Hunt, 'E. Gordon Duff', in *ODNB*.

55 Pearson, *Provenance Research in Book History*, p. 160; Low, *'with all faults'*, pp. 33-4.

56 Nicolas Barker, 'Four Booksellers', in *Form and Meaning in the History of the Book: Selected Essays* (2003), pp. 438-47 (p. 443).

57 For Lewis, see Philip Robinson, 'Phillipps 1986: The Chinese Puzzle', *Book Collector* 25 (1976), 171-94 (p. 179); for Wolff, see E.M. Dring, 'Fifty Years at Quaritch', *Book Collector* special number (1997), pp. 35-52 (p. 38).

58 Dring, 'Fifty Years', p. 50.

59 See http://www.sheila-markham.com/sheila_markham.html.

60 Cf. Dring, 'Fifty Years', p. 39.

61 See catalogue 1000 (1975), pp. 8-9.

62 Cf. Jim Thorp to Sheila Markham, 1995.

63 Graham Weiner to Sheila Markham, 1999; Simon Finch to Sheila Markham, 1992.

64 'The World of Rare Books Re-examined', p. 106.

65 Barker, 'Four Booksellers', p. 442.

66 Cf. Low, *'with all faults'*, p. 33.

67 Iain Sinclair, *White Chappell: Scarlet Tracings* (Uppingham, 1987), p. 40.

ANTHONY HOBSON The Phillipps Sales

1 Philip Robinson, 'Recollections of moving a library', *The Book Collector*, 35 (1986), pp. 431-42; reprinted in A.S.G. Edwards (ed.), *The Pleasures of Bibliophily* (London and New Castle, DE., 2003), pp. 160-7.

2 The attribution was contested by Norman K. Farmer, Jr, in *Papers of the Bibliographical Society of America*, 66 (1972), pp. 21-34. This drew a vigorous riposte from P.J. Croft, *ibid.*, pp. 421-6.

3 He died, suddenly and tragically early, in 1975. His successor, recommended by both Dr Richard Hunt and Dr Neil Ker, was Christopher de Hamel, now Fellow and Parker Librarian of Corpus Christi College, Cambridge.

CHRIS KOHLER Making Collections

1 Thanks to Henry Woudhuysen for alerting me to this.

2 Leonora Navari, *The Bookseller's Art: Catalogues issued by the Firm of J. Pearson & Co. Ltd.* (Maggs Bros Ltd, 1991).

3 'Morgan Collections Correspondence' (accession number MA 1310), The Pierpont Morgan Library, New York. Thanks to John Bidwell, Astor Curator of Printed Books and Bindings, and Christine Nelson, Curator of Literary and Historical Manuscripts, both at The Pierpont Morgan Library, for clarifying aspects of the Pearson/Morgan relationship and identifying correspondence.

4 *The Collection of Books used by James Spedding as his Working Library in preparing his Edition of the Works of Sir Francis Bacon* (Bernard Quaritch, [1917]).

5 *Catalogue of a Most Important Collection of Publications of the Aldine Press, 1494-1595* (Bernard Quaritch Ltd, 1929). Thanks to Nicholas Poole-Wilson and his colleagues at Quaritch for sharing this information with me.

6 See above, Henry Woudhuysen, 'Catalogues', p. 155, and Maggs catalogue 918, *A Catalogue of Maggs Catalogues 1918-1968* (1969), pp. 51-4. Thanks to Robert Harding of Maggs Bros for directing me to this material and interpreting it – and for his other help with this chapter.

7 James B. Coover, 'William Reeves, Booksellers/Publishers 1825- ', in David Hunter (ed.), *Music Publishing & Collecting. Essays in Honor of Donald W. Krummel* (Urbana-Champaign, 1994), pp. 58-9.

8 Interview with William Arnold Reeves, 3 October 2005.

9 http://www.iisg.nl/archives/en/files/k/10753810.php

10 John Harrison, *The Library of Isaac Newton* (Cambridge,1978), pp. 51-3. I wish to thank John Sprague and Vic Gray for their help with this part of the chapter.

11 Sotheran date this flyer as 'post-1936'.

12 Letter from Vic Gray, 2 December 2005.

13 Letter from Raymond Kilgarriff, 15 August 2005.

14 I am grateful to Jolyon Hudson for allowing me to see the Dawson marked catalogues at Pickering & Chatto.

15 http://www.nla.gov.au/history/misc-pages/text.html

16 Email from Toshiaki Kaneko, Hitotsubashi University Library, 31 October 2005.

17 http://spencer.lib.ku.edu/sc/18th.shtml#Curll

18 Emails from Lee Pecht, Rice University library, 30 August and 21 November 2005.

19 Information from Nigel Phillips, 14 September 2005.

20 Information from John Boyle, 22 September 2005.

21 Lawrence Clark Powell, *Books in My Baggage: Adventures in Reading and Collecting* (1960), p. 133.

22 *Bookdealer* 770, 6 November 1986.

23 For further details see Theodore G. Grieder, *The Isaac Foot Library: a report to the university* (Santa Barbara, 1964): http://content.cdlib.org/view?docId=tf1z09n8gb& chunk.id=descgrp-1.7.7

24 Information from Richard Hatchwell, 22 November 2005.

25 Interview with John Lawson, 29 August 2005.

26 Email from Hamish Riley-Smith, 20 October 2005.

27 I wish to thank Susumo Kondo, Toshio Obata and Kikuo Sakamoto for answering my various questions about the Japanese trade and collections.

28 Emails from Kikuo Sakamoto, 2 September and 14 November 2005.

29 Emails from Far Eastern, 20 October 2005, Maruzen, 11 November 2005, and Kinokuniya, 24 October 2005.

30 Results of a survey of booksellers conducted by Chris Kohler in late 2005.

31 http://www.indiana.edu/~liblilly/overview/fineprinting.shtml]

32 C.R. Johnson, *Provincial Poetry 1789-1839: British Verse printed in the Provinces: The Romantic Background* (1992).

33 *Bookdealer*, March 2002; Sheila Markham, *A Book of Booksellers* (2004), pp. 292-3.

34 *Bookdealer*, December 1999; *A Book of Booksellers*, p. 227.

35 *Bookdealer*, October 1994.

36 Phone conversation with Jeffrey Stern, 10 December 2005.

MICHÈLE KOHLER The British Trade and Institutional Libraries

1 Andrew Block, *A Short History of the Principal London Antiquarian Booksellers and Book-Auctioneers* (1933), p. 2; Cornell University Archives #13/3/706.

2 Block, *A Short History*, p. 61.

3 James Bain, *A Bookseller Looks Back* (1940), p. 217.

4 Bain, *A Bookseller Looks Backs*, p. 271.

5 Roger Burdett Wilson, *Old & Curious: The History of James Wilson's Bookshop* (Birmingham, 1960), p. 77.

6 Thanks to Jolyon Hudson for finding this resource for me.

7 http://www.princeton.edu/~ferguson/h-ant-b.html

8 Correspondence with Iain Campbell, 23 August 2005; *The Antiquarian Bookseller and His Customer: a member's exhibition arranged by Iain Campbell* (Liverpool Bibliographical Society, 1976).

9 Barbara Kaye, *Second Impression* (New Castle, DE, and London, 1995), pp. 181-228.

10 Anthony Rota, *Books in the Blood* (Pinner and New Castle, DE, 2002), pp. 100-107; *Anthony Rota* (Bertram Rota Ltd, 2002).

11 Interview with John Lawson, 29 August 2005.

12 Thanks to Robert Harding for his readings from the Maggs Bros minute book.

13 C.C. Kohler, *Exhibition Catalogue. American Tour 24th Oct. – 7th Nov. 1968* (Dorking, 1968).

14 Interviews with Nicholas Poole-Wilson of Quaritch, 10 August 2005, and Katherine

Reagan of Cornell University, 16 September 2005, and email from Dan Traister of the University of Pennsylvania, 5 October 2005, all mentioning Edwards and Gaskell as among the most dynamic younger booksellers.

15 Interviews with John Coombes, 1 September 2005, and John Lawson, 29 August 2005.

16 Paul Wilson, 'Out of Print and Secondhand: a View of the Antiquarian Booktrade', in *African Bibliography 2001*, compiled by T.A. Barringer (Edinburgh, [*c*.2002]), pp. vii-xiii.

17 Information from John Titford, 13 July 2005, and interview with John Coombes, 1 September 2005.

18 'Silver Anniversary. The First 25 Years of the Kenneth Spencer Research Library': http://spencer.lib.ku.edu/exhibits/25th/special_collections.html

19 http://www.indiana.edu/~liblilly/guides/smith/smith.html and http://www.indiana.edu/~liblilly/lilly/mss/html/browning.html

20 'RES Gestæ, Libri Manent. An exhibition and symposium celebrating the career of Roger E. Stoddard', *Harvard Library Bulletin*, new series vol. 15, nos. 1-2 (spring-summer 2004), pp. xv-xvii.

21 Ian Rogerson, *Shakespeare Head Press. An exhibition of the books of A.H. Bullen and Bernard Newdigate* (Manchester, 1988). Thanks to Barry McKay for this reference.

22 Interview with Charles Cox, 10 November 2005.

23 Email from Helen Solanum, West European Collection, Hoover Institution, 18 April 1997.

24 Lawrence Clark Powell, *A Passion for Books* (1959) and *Books in My Baggage: Adventures in Reading and Collecting* (1960).

25 Louis B. Wright, *The Folger Library: Two Decades of Growth: An Informal Account* (Charlottesville, 1968), p. 75.

26 Interview with Martin Hamlyn, 23 August 2005; M. Hamlyn, *The Robinson Legend* (Stamford, 1992), p. 5.

27 Wright, *Folger Library*, pp. 91-2.

28 Email from Linda Matthews, Vice Provost and Director of Libraries at Emory, 23 November 2005.

29 Email from Ginger Cain, 14 November 2005.

30 [Emory] Campus Report, 28 September 1980. Thanks to Ginger Cain for this reference and for the following one.

31 Annual Report of the [Emory] General Libraries, 10 August 1981.

32 Email from Brian Lake, 15 November 2005. His reference is to Robert Lee Wolff, *Nineteenth-century Fiction: A Bibliographical Catalogue* (5 vols.; New York, 1981-6).

33 Maggs Bros minute book, 28 July 1960; http://www.sheila-markham.com/Archives/kfletch.htm

34 Email from Ivan Page, 12 July 2005, and Margaret Dent, 2 April 2006.

35 *The Cornell University Library: Some highlights* [Ithaca, 1965] and http://www.infoplease.com/ipa/A0112633.html. I would like to thank Donald Eddy, retired Rare Book Librarian, Elaine Engst, Director and University Archivist, Katherine Reagan, Curator of Rare Books and Manuscripts, David Corson, Curator, History of Science Collections, and their many helpful colleagues in the library for their kindnesses during my visit. Thanks also to David Brumberg, retired History Bibliographer in the library, and Joan Jacobs Brumberg, Stephen H. Weiss Presidential Fellow and Professor of History, Human Development, and Gender Studies at Cornell for their support, hospitality and friendship of many decades.

36 #13/3/705, vol. 78.

37 #13/3/705, vol. 79.

38 #13/3/705, Bills vols. 80-81 and vol. 43.

39 #13/3/1084 Box 1. Felix Reichmann Papers. Report on European Trip and Articles about Trip, January 1956.

40 #13/3/1084 Box 4. 1960 European Acquisitions – England.

41 #13/3/1084 Box 4. Letter to Luzac.

42 #13/3/1084 Box 4.

43 #13/3/1084 Box 1. Howard Adelmann File, 28 May 1958.

44 #13/3/1084 Box 14. Reichmann to Maggs, 2 July 1962; email from Robert Harding, 28 March 2006.

45 #13/3/1084 Box 20. European Acq. England 1968; Box 21. European Acq. England 1969.

46 Interviews, 7-9 September 2005.

DAVID CHAMBERS Dealers and the Specialist Collector

1 John Carter and Graham Pollard, *An Enquiry into the Nature of Certain Nineteenth Century Pamphlets* (2nd edn., ed. by Nicolas Barker and John Collins, 1983); Fannie E. Ratchford (ed.), *Letters of Thomas J. Wise to John Henry Wrenn* (New York, 1944); D.F. Foxon, *Thomas J. Wise and the Pre-Restoration Drama* (Supplement to the Bibliographical Society's Publications, 19; 1959).

2 Percy Muir, 'Ian Fleming: A Personal Memoir', *Book Collector*, 14 (spring 1965), pp. 24-33.

3 Bertram Rota, 'The George Lazarus Library', *Book Collector*, 4 (winter 1955), pp. 278-84; Anthony Rota, *Books in the Blood* (2002), chapter 20.

4 Albert Ehrman, 'The Broxbourne Library', *Book Collector*, 3 (autumn 1954), pp. 190-97; Giles Mandelbrote, 'A New Edition of *the Distribution of Books by Catalogue*: Problems and Prospects', *Papers of the Bibliographical Society of America*, 89 (1995), pp. 399-408.

5 Anthony Hobson, 'John Roland Abbey', *Oxford Dictionary of National Biography*, ed. Colin Matthew and Brian Harrison (Oxford, 2004); A.R.A. Hobson and A.N.L. Munby, 'John Roland Abbey', *Book Collector*, 10 (spring 1961), pp. 40-48.

6 Geoffrey Keynes, *The Gates of Memory* (Oxford, 1981), chapter 25.

7 Simon Nowell-Smith to Percy Muir, 17 and 20 August 1961: Percy Muir papers, Lilly Library, Indiana University, Bloomington, IN. Transcripts of these letters kindly supplied by Arnold Hunt; my thanks to Mrs Judith Adams, Simon Nowell-Smith's widow, and to the Lilly Library for permission to print them.

8 Simon Nowell-Smith, 'The Ewelme Collection', *Book Collector*, 14 (summer 1965), pp. 185-93; *Wordsworth to Robert Graves and Beyond* (Bodleian Library, Oxford, 1982); Bertram Rota catalogue 300: *Poetry: The Simon Nowell-Smith Collection* (2002).

9 H. George Fletcher (ed.), *The Wormsley Library* (London & New York, 1999); Nicolas Barker, 'Sir Paul Getty', *Book Collector*, 53 (summer 2004), pp. 181-212.

III. CREATING FASHIONS AND CHANGING TASTE

DAVID PEARSON Patterns of Collecting and Trading in Antiquarian Books

1 N. Barker, 'The book trade in 1984 – and after?', *Book Collector*, 33 (1984), pp. 417-30 (p. 417).

2 'Some recent phases of book-collecting', *The Times*, 26 December 1906, p. 6.

3 G.L. Brook, *Books and Book-Collecting* (1980), p. 91.

4 'The Amherst of Hackney sale', *The Times*, 27 March 1909, p. 10.

5 A.J. West, 'Sales and prices of Shakespeare First Folios: a history, 1623 to the present (part two)', *Papers of the Bibliographical Society of America*, 93 (1999), pp. 74-142 (pp. 94-5).

6 H. George Fletcher (ed.), *The Wormsley Library: A Personal Selection by Sir Paul Getty* (London & New York, 1999).

7 'News and comment', *Book Collector*, 39 (1990), p. 78.

8 Bernard Quaritch Ltd, *A Catalogue of Books in English History and Literature* (1922), no. 345.

9 *The Library of William Foyle*, part III, 12-13 July 2000.

10 C.J. Sawyer and F.J.H. Darton, *English Books 1475-1900: A Signpost for Collectors* (1927), vol. 2, p. 314.

11 P.B.M. Allan, *The Book-Hunter at Home* (2nd edn., 1922), pp. 202-3.

12 C. Porter (ed.), *Miller's Collecting Books* (1995).

13 S. de Ricci, *The Book Collector's Guide* (Philadelphia and New York, 1921), p. viii.

14 For the growing interest in science, see also E. Weil. 'Milestones of civilization', in P.H. Muir (ed.), *Talks on Book-Collecting* (1952), pp. 75-84.

15 Maggs catalogue 387 (1920); another on the same theme (no. 435) was issued in 1923.

16 [J. Carter (ed.)], *Catalogue of an Exhibition arranged to illustrate New Paths in Book-Collecting* (1934).

17 Obituary in *The Times*, 7 April 1999, p. 21.

18 *Book-Prices Current*, vol. 13 (1899), p. vi.

19 Allan, *The Book-Hunter at Home*, p. 195.

20 F.B. Adams, 'Introduction', in J. Peters (ed.), *Book Collecting: A Modern Guide* (New York, 1977), pp. xi-xix (p. xv).

21 W. Partington, 'The post to paradise: the uses and abuses of second-hand booksellers' catalogues', *The Bookman's Journal*, 3rd ser. 15 (1927), pp. 189-93 (p. 193).

22 A. Wantage, 'Forgotten books – Sandys' Travailes', *The Bookman's Journal*, 1 (1919), p. 14.

23 'Book collecting on a small budget', *The Times*, 28 April 1960, p. 10.

24 Wantage, as note 20.

25 A.N.L. Munby, 'Book-collecting in the 1930s', *Times Literary Supplement*, 11 May 1973, p. 536.

26 G.T. Tanselle, 'The literature of book collecting', in *Book Collecting: A Modern Guide*, pp. 209-71 (p. 209).

27 C. Edwards, 'English literature', in *Miller's Collecting Books* (1995), 32-5 (p. 35).

28 Cf. P.H. Muir, 'The nature and scope of book-collecting', in Muir (ed.), *Talks on Book-Collecting*, pp. 1-23 (pp 20-22).

29 J.H. Slater, *How to Collect Books* (1905), pp. 122-3.

30 For more details of all these developments, including the early history of the Bibliographical Society, see *The Bibliographical Society: Studies in Retrospect* (1945).

31 J. Carter and P.H. Muir (eds.), *Printing and the Mind of Man: The Impact of Print on Five Centuries of Western Civilization* (1967).

32 P. Davison (ed.), *The Book Encompassed* (Cambridge, 1992), pp. 122-9.

33 S. Weissman, 'What use is bibliography? *The Life and Opinions of an Antiquarian Bookseller*', *Papers of the Bibliographical Society of America*, 89 (1995), pp. 133-48 (p. 135).

34 D. McKitterick, 'The young Geoffrey Keynes', *Book Collector* 36 (1987), pp. 491-517 (p. 515).

35 J. Carter, 'The technical approach', in *Book Collecting: Four Broadcast Talks* (Cambridge, 1950), pp. 29-38 (p. 30).

36 Weissman, 'What use is bibliography?', p. 139.

37 G. Uden, *Understanding Book-Collecting* (Woodbridge, 1982), p. 26.

38 Sawyer and Darton, *English Books 1475-1900*, vol. 1, p. 189.

39 J. Carter, *Taste and Technique in Book Collecting* (3rd impression with corrections, 1970), p. 29; Slater, *How to Collect*, p. 10.

40 A.E. Newton, *The Amenities of Book-Collecting* (1920), p. 54.

41 I.O. Williams, *The Elements of Book-Collecting* (1927), p. 42.

42 Carter, 'The technical approach', p. 32.

43 Carter, *Taste and Technique*, pp. 172, 175.

44 B.C. Middleton, *Recollections: A Life in Bookbinding* (New Castle and London, 2000), pp. 40-41.

45 J. Carter, *ABC for Book-Collectors* (1952), pp. 144-5; J. Carter and N. Barker, *ABC for Book Collectors* (8th edn., New Castle and London, 2004), pp. 177-8. Cf. D. Pearson, *Provenance Research in Book History* (1994).

46 F.W. Ratcliffe and D. Patterson, *Preservation Policies and Conservation in British Libraries*, Library and Information Research Report 25 (1984).

47 'The dignity and charm of old books', *The Bookman's Journal*, 1 (1919), p. 120.

48 M. Perkin, *A Directory of the Parochial Libraries of the Church of England* (2004), p. 180 (Coniston).

49 B.M. Rosenthal, *The Rosenthal Collection of Printed Books with Manuscript Annotations* (New Haven, 1997).

50 Bernard Quaritch Ltd, catalogue 1329 (2005), no. 61.

ANTHONY JAMES WEST The Market Fortunes of the First Folio

1 For a detailed treatment of the First Folio in the market place over nearly four centuries, see my volume I in the Oxford University Press *History of the First Folio: An Account of the First Folio Based on its Sales and Prices, 1623-2001* (Oxford, 2001) (SFF I). For details of condition, provenance and bindings of the nearly 230 extant First Folios, see volume II: *A New Worldwide Census of First Folios* (Oxford, 2003) (SFF II). Volume III (SFF III), a *catalogue raisonné* of all copies world-wide, is in preparation. The data in this article are largely drawn from SFF I and II.

2 Sidney Lee, 'The Shakespeare First Folio: Some Notes and a Discovery', *Cornhill Magazine*, n.s. no. 34 (1899), p. 451; and 'A Survey of First Folios' in Israel Gollancz (ed.), *1623–1923: Studies in the First Folio Written for the Shakespeare Association in Celebration of The First Folio Tercentenary* (1924), p. 98.

3 Invaluable as a collective, scholarly resource, these are now in the Folger Library in Washington, DC.

4 See the 'Listing of First Folio Auctioneers and Booksellers' (pp. 360-3) and census entries in SFF II.

5 For a preliminary survey of suffering, see 'Enemies of First Folios', SFF II, pp. 293-6.

6 Arthur and Janet Ing Freeman, *Anatomy of an Auction: Rare Books at Ruxley Lodge* (1990), pp. vii, 61-2, and 94-5.

7 As David Pearson notes in his chapter in this volume, 'Price comparisons over time are always difficult'. I address this issue at some length in SFF I, pp. 55-66, 'First Folio Sales and Price Trends'. For consistency of comparison, all auction prices given here are hammer prices, i.e., without premium or sales tax. Thus the figures since the introduction of premiums (1975) understate the prices buyers were willing to pay.

8 Respectively West 206 and West 175. Price for West 175 calculated at 56 per cent of the total price for copies of the four seventeenth-century Folio editions sold as a single lot.

9 I deal with the meaning of 'price' and price comparisons in SFF I, p. 17. In SFF I, a step towards comparable condition, at least among First Folios, was to use only Lee's Class I copies for one set of comparisons.

10 West 217: the Knight/Clowes copy.

11 West 145.

12 Quoted by Sidney Lee in *Cornhill Magazine* (1899), cited above, p. 452.

13 *Book Prices Current*, II (1889), p. vi.

ANGUS O'NEILL Patterns of Collecting and Trading in 'Modern' Literature

The author wishes to record his gratitude to Iain Campbell, Jolyon Hudson, David Rees, Anthony Rota, Julian Rota and Henry Woudhuysen for their help with this chapter.

1 For Fleming's collection, much of it now in the Lilly Library at Indiana University, see Percy Muir, 'Ian Fleming: A Personal Memoir', *Book Collector*, 14 (spring 1965), pp. 24-33, and Joel Silver's article in *Dictionary of Literary Biography*, vol. 201: *Twentieth-Century British Book Collectors and Bibliographers*, ed. by William Baker and Kenneth Womack (Detroit, Washington DC & London, 1999), pp. 81-8.

2 The only silent rewriting of the NUC known to this writer is the removal from the electronic version of the footnote to the entry under WOLVERIDGE – 'Any one paying good bucks for the crap in this catalog has been royally screwed by us' – which is no great loss to scholarship, but it was probably the only joke in all 754 volumes and as such is lamented; and if a graffito can be removed, so can other things, perhaps with more serious consequences.

3 Allen and Patricia Ahearn, *Collected Books: The Guide to Values* (New York, 2001).

4 P.H. Muir, *Book-Collecting as a Hobby* (London & Chesham, 1944), pp. 11, 52.

5 These prices equate to around £7,500 and £750 respectively in 2006 prices: the Doyles would have to be fine indeed to fetch any more than that today, while the Stevenson would have to be quite rough not to be worth rather more.

6 The reader may prefer Eric Korn's more succinct definition, from *Remainders* (Manchester, 1989): '"completist" is booksellers' euphemism for "monomaniac"'.

7 The source of this quotation has proved elusive, perhaps thereby confirming the remark. Even the *Oxford Dictionary of Quotations* could do no better than ascribe it to *The Mail on Sunday*, in a section entitled 'Quotes of the Week', early in 1997. Wilensky himself has apparently dated it to 1996, while a similar point was made less elegantly by Blair Houghton, discussing USENET, in 1993. The monkeys/typewriters hypothesis itself dates back at least as far as a paper by Émile Borel of 1913! The subject is most fully discussed on, of course, the internet, at http://www.angelfire.com/in/hypnosonic/Parable_of_the_Monkeys.html .

8 Dating of P&C catalogues is difficult, as most were issued (in order to benefit from reduced postal rates) in the form of a continuously paginated periodical. The date of 1892 is obtained from a bound volume of the firm's own marked copies: the other dates given are approximate.

9 The indexation of prices from this period is problematic. The RPI translates 6s. to £21 and £36 to about £2,500; per capita GDP gives figures of around £160 and £19,000 respectively. The first seems too low, the second unrealistically high.

10 It might be supposed that the present (2006) assiduous marketing of new books might act with considerable force on the collectors' market. In fact the impact is surprisingly patchy. Many commercially successful novelists are hardly collected at all. And books with 'television tie-ins' are practically unsaleable even from the shelves outside. For every Harry Potter, there are a hundred titles which may be piled high in Waterstone's, or even Tesco, but this writer's central London shop can do nothing with them.

11 I am grateful to Jolyon Hudson for this interesting suggestion.

12 These four all feature in contemporary auction records, while Eliot, Pound and Woolf do not.

13 Cf. an auction price of £10 in 1923.

14 Two copies sold at auction in 1924 for £3.7s.6d. and £3.10s., without any additional matter. Synge autograph material is rare.

15 Common sense suggests that this small differential merely reflects the fact that, so soon after publication, most dustwrappers had not yet been discarded. However, I believe this to be wrong. Most books in England at that time lost their wrappers soon after purchase and before shelving, for reasons (depending on one's outlook) of snobbery or taste. Once the book was shelved, it was likely to remain as it was – with a few exceptions, such as *Brighton Rock* (1938), whose notoriously scarce crimson wrapper clashed with the scarlet cloth of the book; it was consequently often jettisoned as soon as it began to fray. Another possible reason for the relative scarcity of English dustwrappers from this period is that until around 1942, most English books tended to be decently bound, with flimsy and unappealing dustwrappers; after approximately that date, binding standards declined and wrappers became visually more interesting, so fewer were discarded. A far higher proportion of American books from the twenties and thirties have survived with their original dust-wrappers.

16 As we go to press in 2006, it is still there, and down to £100. The 1931 price was not wayward: a copy had fetched £28 at auction a year earlier, sold to 'Leng'. This was almost certainly Kyrle Leng, who shared a house with Robert Gathorne-Hardy of the firm Elkin Mathews – in which Leng was a shareholder. The two owned a hand-press, and under the imprint of The Mill House Press published very limited editions of Bridges among other authors, all of which suggests that the demand for *Testament of Beauty* was a steady one.

17 Several copies of the Chagall appeared at auction around 1964, with prices varying between £22 and £80.

18 Could this have been the 'Fair copy, inscribed' which fetched £200 at a Christie's sale in 1960?

19 This is the only signed edition known to the present writer to have been published ten years after the author's death: the delay was, of course, caused by the Second World War.

20 I have been unable to identify these precise copies among several in recent auction records, but the ratio is correct.

21 Hemingway did, in fact, take considerable interest in the early English editions of his books, usually to deplore his publisher's tendency to self-censorship: Gekoski records a copy of *In Our Time* (Cape, 1926) inscribed by the author 'This all rewritten by Cape's bitches', and with various autograph changes, such as replacing the words 'a disease' with 'gonorrhea', reinstating Hemingway's preferred version of the text.

22 'Sophistication', *Book Collector*, 55 (Spring, 2006), pp. 11-27.

23 James Fergusson, correspondence in *Bookdealer*, 2005.

PAUL MINET A Short Look at *ABMR*

1   For Nothmann, see *ABMR*, vol. 1, no. 7 (August 1974); for the finances of Dawson's, Francis Edwards, Maggs and Quaritch, see David Buchler, 'The First Division', *ABMR*, vol. 2, issue 2, no. 12 (February 1975), pp. 2-6.

2   For an account of *The Book Collector* and its predecessor *Book Handbook* (1947-52), see *The Pleasures of Bibliophily: Fifty Years of The Book Collector* (2003).

3   *Driff's Fortnightly*, no. 22 (14-28 November 1986).

IV. PERSONALITIES: A TRADE OF INDIVIDUALISTS

ARNOLD HUNT Foreign Dealers in the English Trade

My thanks to all those who have helped in the preparation of this chapter, with particular thanks to Nicholas Poole-Wilson and Katherine Spears for granting me access to the archives of Bernard Quaritch Ltd; to Ed Maggs and Robert Harding for granting me access to the archives of Maggs Bros Ltd; to Christine Nelson and Roger S. Wieck for providing photocopies of Voynich's letters and invoices from the archives of the Pierpont Morgan Library; to Jacques Vellekoop and the Houghton Library, Harvard, for permission to quote from Goldschmidt's unpublished letters to W.A. Jackson; and to Bernard Rosenthal, Jacques Vellekoop and Nicholas Poole-Wilson for their reminiscences.

1   Percy Muir, 'Further Reminiscences V', *Book Collector*, 8 (1959), p. 46.

2   Wilmarth Lewis, *Collector's Progress* (New York, 1951), p. 120.

3   Muir, 'Further Reminiscences VII', *Book Collector*, 8 (1959), pp. 278-9.

4   Arthur and Janet Freeman, *Anatomy of an Auction: Rare Books at Ruxley Lodge, 1919* (1990).

5   Muir, 'Further Reminiscences VII', p. 281.

6   The phrase is John Carter's, in *Taste and Technique in Book Collecting* (2nd edn., 1970), p. 232. For a brief but valuable account of the German and Austrian refugee booksellers, see Ulrich Bach and Bjorn Biester, 'Exil in London: Zur Emigration deutscher und oster-reichischer Antiquate nach Grossbritannien', *Aus dem Antiquariat*, 5/2002, pp. 250-65.

7   Anne Fremantle, 'The Russian Best-seller', *History Today*, 25 (1975), pp. 635-6. This article is chiefly about Ethel Voynich's bestselling novel *The Gadfly*, but also contains some important biographical information on W.M. Voynich, unpublished elsewhere and apparently derived from interviews with Ethel Voynich.

8   The diaries of Richard Garnett's daughter Olive, published as *Tea and Anarchy! The Bloomsbury Diary of Olive Garnett 1890-1893*, ed. Barry C. Johnson (1989), provide a fascinating glimpse of this milieu.

9   Donald J. Senese, *S.M. Stepniak-Krachvinskii, the London Years* (1987), pp. 80-81.

10 'Mr W.M. Voynich', *The Times*, 25 March 1930, p. 21.

11 *A First List of Books Offered for Sale by W.M. Voynich & C.A. Edgell* (1898). Charles Arnold Edgell (1870-1905) was a graduate of King's College, Cambridge, and later 'engaged in private tuition' (Venn).

12 See A.W. Pollard's preface to Robert Proctor, *Bibliographical Essays* (1905), p. xxix.

13 Quaritch trade day-book, 1899-1900: BL Add 64153, p. 4327.

14 *A Second List of Books Offered for Sale ... by W.M. Voynich* (1900).

15 E. Millicent Sowerby, *Rare People and Rare Books* (1967), p. 11.

16 Giuseppe Orioli, *Adventures of a Bookseller* (1938), p. 77.

17 A slip inserted inside his *Sixth List* claims that between three and four thousand copies of previous catalogues were printed.

18 *A Ninth List of Books Offered for Sale ... by W.M. Voynich* (1902), note inside front cover.

19 Minutes, Reports, Letters (1906): British Library archives, DH2/70.

20 The other is Torgrim Hannås, another foreigner in the English trade – and as independent-minded as Voynich – who presented his collection of Scandinavian linguistic books to the BL in 1984.

21 W.R. Newbold, *The Cipher of Roger Bacon* (Philadelphia, 1928).

22 Robert S. Brumbaugh, *The World's Most Mysterious Manuscript* (1977).

23 Leo Levitov, *The Solution to the Voynich Manuscript* (Laguna Hills, California, 1987).

24 Andrew Cook, *Ace of Spies: the True Story of Sidney Reilly* (2004).

25 Gerry Kennedy and Rob Churchill, *The Voynich Manuscript* (2004), pp. 226, 248. Notwithstanding a certain naivete in its portrayal of the rare book trade (e.g. its reference to 'the gentle world of the auction house', p. 8), this book is by far the best account of the Voynich Manuscript currently available.

26 Voynich's application for naturalization, 1904: National Archives HO 144/751/117022. The application is endorsed by a Home Office official: 'The Referees are well known people and enquiry seems superfluous'.

27 H.P. Kraus, *A Rare Book Saga* (1979), p. 222.

28 'Mr W.M. Voynich', *The Times*, 22 March 1930, p. 17.

29 Jessie Conrad, *Joseph Conrad and his Circle* (1924), p. 196. Bruce Harkness, 'Conrad's *The Secret Agent*: Texts and Contexts'. *Journal of the Joseph Conrad Society (U.K.)*, 4: 3 (Feb. 1979), pp. 8-9.

30 Quaritch to Voynich, 21 October 1910: letter in Quaritch archives. Quaritch trade ledger 1913-15: BL Add 64227, p. 389.

31 Olschki's purchases in 1903 are annotated in the Quaritch trade day-book: '1 Pcl [= parcel?] Voynich, 2 Pcl J. & J. Leighton, 1 Pcl Sothebys' (BL Add 64157, pp. 500-1).

32 Voynich to Leighton, 14 Nov. 1916: BL Add 45169, f. 188.

33 Quaritch to Dring, 12 Feb 1909: letter in Quaritch archives.

34 Herbert Garland, 'Notes on the Firm of W.M. Voynich', *The Library World*, 34 (1931-32), p. 227.

35 Voynich to Belle Greene, 6 July 1911: Morgan Library archives.

36 F.S. Ferguson to E.H. Dring, 2 March, 5 March and 19 March 1915: letters in Quaritch archives.

37 Kennedy & Churchill, *The Voynich Manuscript*, p. 226. Garland, 'Notes', p. 228. Invoices in Morgan Library archives.

38 James Westfall Thompson, 'W.M. Voynich', *Progress of Medieval Studies in the United States of America*, Bulletin no. 9 (1931), p. 90.

39 *The Times*, 20 Nov. 1974, p. 19.

40 Maurice Ettinghausen, *Rare Books and Royal Collectors: Memoirs of an Antiquarian Bookseller* (New York, 1966), pp. 8-9.

41 For a nice example of Ettinghausen's sales technique, see Bernard M. Rosenthal, 'Cartel, Clan, or Dynasty? The Olschkis and the Rosenthals 1859-1976', *Harvard Library Bulletin*, 25: 4 (1977), p. 398.

42 Ettinghausen, *Rare Books*, pp. 50-52. J. Davidson Ketchum, *Ruhleben: A Prison Camp Society* (1965), pp. 115-17. Some of the cards sent from Ruhleben by Ettinghausen to his

first wife, showing the synagogue in Barrack 6, are in Southampton University Library.

43 Ettinghausen, *Rare Books*, pp. 58-9.

44 Ettinghausen, *Rare Books*, p. 88.

45 Brooke Crutchley, *To be a printer* (1980), p. 53.

46 Ettinghausen, *Rare Books*, p. 94.

47 'Proposals for enabling the USSR Government to dispose of its surplus objets d'art, antiques, coins, books [etc] to the best advantage' (1931), Maggs archives 2871.

48 Ettinghausen, *Rare Books*, pp. 171-2.

49 The sale price was rumoured to be £30,000: see Edwin Wolf & John Fleming, *Rosenbach: a biography* (1960), p. 361.

50 Ettinghausen, *Rare Books*, pp. 175-83.

51 Wolf and Fleming, *Rosenbach*, pp. 367-8.

52 Geoffrey Quaritch-Wales to J.H. & C.Q. Wrentmore, 20 Dec. 1945: letter in Quaritch archives.

53 P.R. Harris, *A History of the British Museum Library 1753-1973* (1998), p. 511.

54 Carter, *Taste and Technique*, p. 231.

55 The history of the Paris office, which I hope to tell in more detail elsewhere, is very fully documented in the Maggs archives.

56 Maggs archives 2541.

57 Directors' minutes, 2 Sept. 1938, 9 June 1939.

58 Directors' minutes, 6 Dec. 1935.

59 Mlle Kormann to Ernest Maggs, 25 July 1946: Maggs archives 2490.

60 Ernest Maggs wrote a letter supporting Otto Haas's application to establish his business in London, and was later instrumental in securing Albi Rosenthal's release from internment: see the introduction to Otto Haas Catalogue 40 (2003). Maggs Bros also contributed generously to the ABA relief fund for refugee booksellers: see Anthony Rota's chapter in this volume.

61 Ettinghausen, *Rare Books*, p. 185.

62 Ettinghausen, *Rare Books*, p. 188.

63 Directors' minutes, 5 July 1940.

64 Goldschmidt to Jackson, 10 June 1941: Houghton Library archives.

65 Directors' minutes, 13 March 1942.

66 *Ex inf.* Bernard Rosenthal.

67 *Ex inf.* Bernard Rosenthal. Ettinghausen's son Walter (1910-2001) was Director-General of the Israeli Foreign Ministry, and thus a close political colleague of Ben Gurion's.

68 Leona Rostenberg and Madeleine B. Stern, *Old and Rare: Thirty Years in the Book Business* (1974), p. 126.

69 Anton Gerits, *Books, Friends and Bibliophilia: Reminiscences of an Antiquarian Book-seller* (2004), pp. 230-1.

70 *Ex inf.* Nicholas Poole-Wilson.

71 *Ex inf.* Ian Jackson.

72 Clifford Maggs, in *The Book Collector*, 17 (1968), pp. 95-100.

73 John Carter, 'E.P. Goldschmidt: A Personal Note', *Antiquarian Bookman*, 10 April 1954, p. 1076. For Aurispa, see Goldschmidt, 'The Period Before Printing', in P.H. Muir, ed., *Talks on Book-Collecting* (1952), pp. 37-8.

74 E. Weil, 'In Memoriam: E.P. Goldschmidt – Bookseller and Scholar', *Journal of the History of Medicine and Allied Sciences*, 9 (1954), p. 224.

75 Goldschmidt describes his visits to Admont and Melk in 'Austrian Monastic Libraries', *The Library*, 4th ser., 25 (1945), pp. 46-65.

76 For Goldschmidt's offer to buy Quaritch (surely one of the greatest 'what-ifs' in the modern history of the trade), see Jacques Vellekoop's introduction to the sale-catalogue of the Goldschmidt stock and reference library (Christie's, 8-9 July 1993); and for his acquisition of Gilhofer & Ranschburg, see R.O. Dougan, 'E.Ph. Goldschmidt, 1887-1954', *The Library*, 5th ser., IX: 2 (1954), p. 76.

77 Most of the details in this paragraph are taken from Robin Halwas's unpublished paper '45 Old Bond Street', with some details on the geography of the West End trade taken from Carter, *Taste & Technique*, pp. 230-32. I am very grateful to Robin Halwas for generously sharing a copy of his paper with me.

78 For an occasion when he failed to arrive in time, see the note to lot 416 in the Alan Thomas sale catalogue (Sotheby's, 21-22 June 1993), quoting a letter from Munby to J.R. Abbey, 1947.

79 Weil, 'E.P. Goldschmidt', p. 230.

80 *Ex inf.* Bernard Rosenthal.

81 *Times Literary Supplement*, 6 June 1924.

82 Weil, 'E.P. Goldschmidt', p. 225.

83 *Ex inf.* Jacques Vellekoop.

84 Weil, 'E.P. Goldschmidt', p. 224. See also Goldschmidt's Catalogue 100, pp. 66-8.

85 Goldschmidt to John Carter, 1 October 1947: Cambridge University Library, Add 8238.

86 Goldschmidt, 'Notes on Geoffroy Tory and Oronce Finé', unpublished paper of 1937, bound into a volume of pamphlets and offprints from Goldschmidt's reference library, now in my possession.

87 Goldschmidt to Carter, 1 October 1947; see also Carter, *Taste and Technique*, p. 20.

88 Carter, *Taste and Technique*, p. 116.

89 Goldschmidt, 'The Period Before Printing', pp. 26, 28.

90 Many of the sale catalogues in the second part of the Breslauer sale (Christie's, 22-23 March 2005) came from Goldschmidt's own collection.

91 Goldschmidt, 'The Period Before Printing', p. 29.

92 Goldschmidt to Jackson, 15 Sept. 1945: Houghton Library archives.

93 Goldschmidt to Jackson, 30 October 1947: Houghton Library archives.

94 Carter to Stanley Morison, 18 March 1954: Cambridge University Library, Morison papers, I/88.

95 Weil, 'E.P. Goldschmidt', p. 225.

96 Goldschmidt to Jackson, 27 September 1949: Houghton Library archives.

97 Bernard M. Rosenthal, *The Gentle Invasion: Continental Émigré Booksellers of the Thirties and Forties and Their Impact on the Antiquarian Booktrade in the United States* (New York, 1987).

98 Goldschmidt to Jackson, 28 November 1949: Houghton Library archives.

99 Goldschmidt to Jackson, 31 January 1949: Houghton Library archives.

A.S.G. EDWARDS The Antiquarian Book Trade and the World of Scholarship

For assistance of various kinds I am much indebted to Nicolas Barker, John Collins, Jamie Fergusson, Anthony Hobson, Arnold Hunt, Peter Murray Jones, Richard Linenthal and (especially) Giles Mandelbrote.

1 A number of figures mentioned here also appear in Julian Roberts, 'The Bibliographical Society as a Band of Pioneers', in *Pioneers in Bibliography*, ed. Robin Myers and Michael Harris (Winchester, 1988), pp. 86-99.

2 I have tried, wherever possible, to give appropriate biographical documentation, but this has not been done systematically or exhaustively. Where more than one contemporary obituary exists in newspapers of a figure discussed here I have been selective, usually only citing one. Other obituaries or biographies are cited according to my sense of their relevance. The following are cited in abbreviated form: *DLB*, for *Dictionary of Literary Biography*, vol. 201: *Twentieth-Century British Book Collectors and Bibliographers*, First Series, ed. William Baker and Kenneth Womack (Detroit, Washington DC & London, 1999); *ODNB*: *Oxford Dictionary of National Biography*, ed. Colin Matthew and Brian Harrison, 60 vols. (Oxford, 2004).

3 For a memoir of Dobell see Robert John Dobell, *Percy J. Dobell, Enlightened Bookseller* (Tunbridge Wells, 1956).

4 His only substantial publication was *Two Augustan booksellers: John Dunton and Edmund Curll* (Lawrence, KA, 1958).

5 In for example, his article on 'Constance Holme', *Book Collector*, 5 (1956), 250-55 or on 'Lawrence of Arabia and the Seven Pillars of Wisdom', *Texas Quarterly*, 5 (1962), 46-53. On Rota (1903-66) see Anthony Rota in *DLB* pp. 282-8, and Simon Nowell-Smith, *Book Collector*, 16 (1967), 76-9.

6 For details of his writings see *Frederick H. Evans: selected texts and bibliography*, ed. Anne Hammond (Oxford, 1992); see also Beaumont's memoir, *Bookseller at the Ballet* (1975).

7 For example, in *The British Court: its tradition and ceremonial* (1963), and in his contribution to *Famed for the Dance: Essays on the theory and practice of theatrical dancing in England, 1660-1740* (New York, 1970).

8 For example, 'The literature of splendid occasions in English history', *The Library*, 5th series, 1 (1946/7), 184-96 and *Edward Gordon Craig: A bibliography* (1967). For a memoir and partial bibliography see *Ifan Kyrle Fletcher: A memorial tribute*, [ed. George Speaight] (1970).

9 There is an obituary in *The Book Collector*, 24 (1975), 276.

10 For an obituary see *The Times*, 11 November 2004.

11 There is a bibliography of Munby's writings (with a number of omissions) by Nicolas Barker in his edition of Munby's *Essays and Papers* (1977), pp. 235-41.

12 There are obituaries in *The Times*, 31 August 1984, *The Book Collector*, 33 (1984), 495-7, and the *Annual Report of King's College*, 1985, pp. 24-7.

13 Dr Beal is now preparing a revised electronic edition of this index.

14 There is a bibliography of his writings in a Festschrift in his honour, *Bookbindings & Other Bibliophily*, ed. Dennis E. Rhodes (Verona, [1994]), pp. 351-64; this reprints (pp. 13-20), a biographical sketch by Nicolas Barker that first appeared in another Festschrift for him, in *The Book Collector*, 40 (1991), 299-314.

15 For some astute comments on Hobson's contributions to bookbinding history, see David McKitterick, 'Customer, Reader and Bookbinder: Buying a Bible in the 1630s', *Book Collector*, 40 (1991), 382-406.

16 Norma Hodgson and Cyprian Blagden, *The Notebook of Thomas Bennet and Henry*

Clements (Oxford Bibliographical Society Publications, new series vi (for 1953); Oxford, 1956).

17 There is an obituary in *The Independent*, 12 January 1998.

18 There is a biographical sketch and bibliography of Pollard's writings in *Studies in the Book Trade in Honour of Graham Pollard*, ed. R.W. Hunt, I.G. Philip and R.J. Roberts (Oxford, 1975), pp. 3–9, 379–86; see also Esther Potter, 'Graham Pollard at Work', *The Library*, 6th series, 11 (1989), 307–27; and *ODNB*.

19 It was reprinted in an edition of 500 copies by the bibliography specialist Tony Appleton: *Catalogue of … Typefounders' Specimens … offered for sale* (Brighton, 1972).

20 *The Library*, 4th series, 18 (1937/8), 235–60.

21 'Book Production and Distribution 1500–1600' (I, 345–64), 'Book Production and Distribution 1660–1800' (II, 81–107), 'Book Production and Distribution 1800–1900' (III, 70–106).

22 Published in summary form after his death as 'The English Market for Printed Books', *Publishing History*, 4 (1978), 7–46.

23 For a detailed assessment of this book see Giles Mandelbrote, 'A New Edition of *The Distribution of Books by Catalogue*: Problems and Prospects', *Papers of the Bibliographical Society of America*, 89 (1995), 399–408.

24 'Changes in the Style of Bookbinding, 1530–1830', *The Library*, 5th series, 11 (1956), 71–94; 'The Construction of English Twelfth-century Bindings', *The Library*, 5th series, 17 (1962), 1–12; 'The Names of Some English Fifteenth-Century Binders', *The Library*, 5th series, 25 (1970), 193–218; Some Anglo-Saxon Bookbindings', *Book Collector*, 24 (1975), 130–59; 'Describing Medieval Bookbindings', in *Medieval Learning and Literature: Essays Presented to Richard William Hunt*, ed. J.J.G. Alexander and Margaret T. Gibson (Oxford, 1975), pp. 50–65.

25 *The Times*, 16 November 1976.

26 There is a one-volume reprint with introduction by Timothy D'Arch Smith (1967).

27 There is a biography of Millard by H. Montgomery Hyde, *Christopher Sclater Millard (Stuart Mason) Bibliographer & Antiquarian Book Dealer* (New York, 1989).

28 The story is recounted in George Sims, 'Who Wrote *For Love of a King*? Oscar Wilde or Mrs Chan Toon?', *Book Collector*, 6 (1958), 269–77.

29 Reprinted in Hyde, pp. 157–74; see also Anthony Powell's recollections of Millard in *Infants of the Spring* (1976), pp. 91–7.

30 On Dobell see *ODNB*; there is a partial bibliography in S. Bradbury, *Bertram Dobell: Bookseller and Man of Letters* (1909).

31 In addition to *An Outline of the History of Printing* (1917) and *Printing: A Short History* (1927), Peddie compiled the bibliography to Sidney and Beatrice Webb, *The History of Trade Unionism* (1894), following this with *Engineering and Metallurgical Books* (1912), *Railway Literature, 1556–1830* (1931) and *Subject index of books published up to and including 1880*, 4 vols. (1933–48). There is a brief portrait in Munby's *Essay and Papers* (1977), p. 220.

32 I draw in part on the obituary by Nicolas Barker in *The Book Collector*, 29 (1980), 85–8 and Muir's absorbing autobiography, *Minding My Own Business* (1956), supplemented by a series of 'Further Reminiscences' that appeared in *The Book Collector* between 1956 and 1964.

33 For a list of his writings see Barbara Muir, *P. H. Muir: A Checklist of his published work* (Blakeney, 1983).

34 (Cambridge, 1948; reprinted, with an epilogue, London, 1970)

35 There is no full record of Carter's writings but one is in preparation by Dr G.T. Tanselle; see also the biography by Donald C. Dickinson, *John Carter: The Taste and Technique of a Bookman* (New Castle, Delaware, 2004) and *ODNB*.

36 The original edition had appeared in 1963.

37 There were a number of publications by Carter and Pollard which they saw as necessary preliminaries to a second edition: *The Firm of Charles Ottley, Landon & Co., a Footnote to an Enquiry* (1948), and the series of 'Working Papers for a Second Edition of 'An Enquiry into the Nature of Certain Nineteenth-Century Pamphlets': *Précis of Paden or the Sources of The New Timon* (Oxford, 1967); *The Forgeries of Tennyson's Plays* (Oxford, 1967); *The Mystery of The Death of Balder* (Oxford, 1969); *Gorfin's Stock* (Oxford, 1970). They also made contributions to *Thomas J. Wise Centenary Studies*, ed. W.B. Todd (Austin, TX, 1959). There are also various occasional articles by Carter, including 'Thomas J. Wise and his Forgeries', and 'Thomas J. Wise and H. Buxton Forman'. Both are reprinted in his *Books and Book Collectors* (1956), pp. 129-49, 150-6.

38 The interconnecting circles as they existed in the 1930s are set out diagrammatically by Dickinson, *John Carter*, p. 280.

39 *A Bibliography of the Writings of Edward Gibbon* (Oxford, 1940). Her edition of Gibbon's letters appeared in 1956. For a brief memoir see *The Book Collector*, 12 (1963), 18.

40 For a sensitive portrait of Worthington, a man who oscillated between the worlds of bookselling and business, see Muir, *Minding My Own Business*, especially pp. 70-3, 111-18.

41 There is a brief memoir of Gathorne-Hardy by John Carter, *Book Collector*, 22 (1973), 229-30.

42 *A Bibliography of William Somerset Maugham* (1931).

43 On Block see Meg Kidd, *Four Book Walls:A Memoir of Andrew Block* (Bristol, 1997).

44 *The Book Collector's Vade Mecum* (1932; revised edn., 1938): one of the appendices to this work was reprinted separately as *A Short History of the Principal London Antiquarian Booksellers and Book-Auctioneers* (1933); *Sir J. M. Barrie: His First Editions: points and values* (1931); *The English Novel, 1740-1850* (1939).

45 These include his various series of *Modern First Editions: Points and Values* (1929, 1931); *John Galsworthy: his first editions* (1932); *D. H. Lawrence: his first editions: points and values* (1933), *The First Editions of A. E. Coppard, A. P. Herbert and Charles Morgan* (1933); and *The First Editions of Ralph Hale Mottram* (1934).

46 As he observed in an article on 'Books on Bookbinding', *Book-Collector's Quarterly*, vii (July-September 1932) '... it is quite useless for anyone to take up the study of bindings who cannot read French and German at least. Dutch, Swedish, Italian, and Spanish will also be found useful' (p. 70).

47 His *Studies in the History of Bookbinding* (1988) collects most of his periodical essays.

48 For his biography see *ODNB* and the obituary by A.N.L. Munby, 'The Bookbinder's Historian', *Times Literary Supplement*, 22 January 1949, p. 62.

49 John Carter, *Taste and Technique in Book Collecting*, 2nd edn., p. 221.

50 Goldschmidt, in the preface to *Gothic & Renaissance Bookbindings*, traces its beginnings to 'my undergraduate days, when I was permitted by the Librarian of my College to make a catalogue of the bindings in the library of Trinity College, Cambridge'.

51 For a sketch of his early years see the memoir by his partner, Jacques Vellekoop, 'Ernst Philip Goldschmidt 1887-1954: The Evolution of a Great Bookseller', *Book Collector*, 3 (1954), 119-24. For more extensive assessments of his career see: R.O. Dougan, 'E. Ph. Goldschmidt, 1887-1954', *The Library*, 5th series, 9 (1954), 75-84; Ernst Weil, 'E. P.

Goldschmidt, bookseller and scholar', *Journal of the History of Medicine and Allied Sciences*, 9 (1954), 224-32; the introduction by Jacques Vellekoop to the sale catalogue of the firm's stock at Christie's, 8-9 July 1993; and the chapter by Arnold Hunt in this volume, pp. 261-6.

52 A.W. Pollard in his review in *The Library*, 4th series, 9 (1928-9), 102-5 (105); Pollard also reviewed it for the *Times Literary Supplement*, 1 March 1928, p. 146.

53 In *The Bibliographical Society: Studies in Retrospect*, ed. F.C. Francis (1945), p. 175.

54 For a brief memoir of Ferguson by one who worked with him, see E.M. Dring, *Book Collector*, 16 (1967), 371-2; see also *ODNB*.

55 'Additions to *Title Page Borders 1485-1640*', *The Library*, 4th series, 17 (1936/7), 264-311; 'A bibliography of the works of Sir George Mackenzie, Lord Advocate, founder of the Advocates' Library', *Transactions of the Edinburgh Bibliographical Society*, 1 (1935-38), 1-60; 'John Siberch of Cambridge: an unrecorded book from his press, new light on his material', *Transactions of the Cambridge Bibliographical Society*, 1 (1949-53), 41-5.

56 'Book-selling he rather disliked and, since the slump had deprived us of most of our customers, he was apt to spend four days a week at the British Museum working on the revision of the Short-Title Catalogue', A.N.L. Munby, 'Book Collecting in the 1930s', reprinted in his *Essays and Papers*, p. 219.

57 For an appreciation of Breslauer see *The Book Collector*, 47 (1998), 470-507. There are obituaries in *The Times*, 27 August 2004 and *The Book Collector*, 53 (2004), 606-9.

58 The bibliographical part of his collection, *Bibliotheca Bibliographica Breslaueriana*, was dispersed at three sales at Christie's, New York, in 2005: parts I and II (21 March and 22-3 March) and Part III (28 June). From his collection also comes the *Collection of Historic and Artistic Bookbinding from the Bibliotheca Bibliographica Breslaueriana*, with a catalogue by Breslauer and an introduction by J. Toulet (Brussels, 1986).

59 There are obituaries in *The Times*, 25 August 2004 and *The Book Collector*, 53 (2004), 603-6.

60 *Albert Einstein: A bibliography of his scientific papers* (1960). There is an obituary of Weil by S.H. Steinberg in *The Book Collector*, 14 (1965), 160-4.

61 *Sale Catalogues of Libraries of Eminent Persons*, vol. 11: *Scientists* (1975).

62 *Notes and Records of the Royal Society*, 21 (1965), 42-55.

63 *Love in Earnest* (1970); *A Bibliography of the Works of Montague Summers* (1964), published in revised form as *Montague Summers: A Bibliography* (Wellingborough, 1964); *R. A. Caton and the Fortune Press* (1983); *The Times Deceas'd* (York, 2003).

64 There is an obituary by Anthony Rota in *The Independent*, 9 November 1999.

65 *A Bibliography of Norman Douglas* (1955); *A Bibliography of Frederick Rolfe, baron Corvo* (1957; revised 1972).

66 *Great Books and Book Collectors* (1975; reprinted 1988); this is an expansion of his earlier *Fine Books* (1967).

67 See, for example, his 'Recollections of a Durrell Collector', *Book Collector*, 9 (1960), 56-63 (with L.C. Powell) and *Lawrence Durrell: an illustrated checklist* (Carbondale, Ill., 1983).

68 'An introduction to the bibliography of William Cobbett', *The Library*, 4th series, 20 (1939/40), 1-40; 'A Jeremy Bentham Collection', *The Library*, 5th series, 1 (1946/47), 6-27.

69 There is an obituary in *The Book Collector*, 48 (1999), 450.

70 *Bruce Chatwin, Martin Amis, Julian Barnes: A bibliography of their first editions* (1992); *Muriel Spark, William Trevor, Ian McEwan: A bibliography of their first editions* (1992).

71 *Provincial Poetry, 1789-1839: British verse printed in the provinces: the Romantic background* (1992).

72 *William Golding: A Bibliography 1934-1993* (1994).

73 *John Payne Collier: Scholarship and Forgery in the Nineteenth Century*, 2 vols. (New Haven, CT, 2004).

74 *Beyond Decoration: The Illustrations of John Everett Millais* (2005).

75 Edited by Philippa Bernard, with Leo Bernard and Angus O'Neill (Aldershot, 1994).

76 *The Two Forgers* (1992).

77 Quoted in Nicholas Basbanes, *Patience and Fortitude* (New York, 2001), p. 280.

78 On Colbeck see W. Fredeman in *DLB*, 57-63, and George Sims, *The Rare Book Game* (Philadelphia, 1985), pp. 127-34.

MARC VAULBERT DE CHANTILLY
Booksellers' Memoirs: The Truth about the Trade?

The reader is referred to the checklist (Appendix 5) for full references.

1 Spencer, p. 277.

2 Snelling, pp. 12-13.

3 Peter Murray Hill, 'The first antiquarian bookseller's directory', *ABA Annual* (1952), p. 41.

4 Snelling, p. 14.

5 Bason, *3rd Diary*, p. 87.

6 Minet, p. 68.

7 A. and J.I. Freeman, *Anatomy of an Auction*; Jonathan Tootell interviewed by Markham, *Bookdealer*, 11 November 1999; Edward Goldston in Block, *Short History*, pp. 20-21; Eric Morten in Markham, p. 213; Cynthia Morris in *ABMR*, February 1977, pp. 56, 58.

8 'Fortean Times – Iain Sinclair interview' at <http://www.forteantimes.com/articles/147_iainsinclair.shtml> on 1 March 2006.

9 Nigel Burwood, 'Memories of David', in David Winzar, *Common Mallow*.

10 List, by John Howkins, pp. 73-4.

11 Jason Tomes on Christina Foyle, *Oxford DNB*.

12 Snelling, p. 12.

13 Fabes, 1929 edn., p. 10.

14 Fabes, 1929 edn., pp. 18, 38.

15 Norrington, p. 58.

16 Bain, p. 266; *The Publisher and Bookseller*, 19 August 1905, p. 458; John Symonds, *The Great Beast* (1951), p. 268.

17 Fabes, 1929 edn., p. 32.

18 Fabes, 1938 edn., p. 32.

19 Fabes, 1929 edn., p. 32.

20 *Ibid.*, p. 40.

21 Low, p. 19.

22 Revised by G.R. Davies.

23 *The Oldie*, 1 April 1994, p. 58.

24 Julian Symons, *A. J. A. Symons*, chapters 4 to 6.

25 Rota, *Books in the Blood*, p. 166.

26 d'Arch Smith, p. 15.

27 Low, p. 4.

28 *Manchester Guardian* review, quoted in advertisement in *The Times*, 12 October 1923.

29 Low, p. 4.

30 Spencer, p. xxiii.

31 *Ibid.*, pp. xxiii, 89.

32 *Ibid.*, p. 6.

33 *Ibid.*, p. 91.

34 *Ibid.*, p. 33.

35 *Ibid.*, pp. 25, 165, 247, 277-9.

36 *Ibid.*, pp. 78, 96.

37 Low, p. 4.

38 Snelling, p. 13.

39 Newton, *Amenities*, p. 27.

40 Collins, *The Two Forgers*, p. 161.

41 d'Arch Smith, pp. 42-4.

42 Lewis, p. 41.

43 Spencer, p. 273.

44 d'Arch Smith, p. 11.

45 Spencer, pp. 273, 274.

46 Ratchford, p. 532; Partington, pp. 235-6; Ettinghausen, p. 72.

47 *84, Charing Cross Road*, p. 94.

48 Marc Connelly in Hanff, *The Duchess*, p. 75.

49 Snelling, p. 155.

50 *driff's*, no. 11 (29 May 1986), p. 377.

51 *Bookdealer*, 19 March 1992.

52 Block, *Short History*, p. 38.

53 *Infinite Riches*, p. 72.

54 In 'A Brief History – Page 2' [by Steve Maggs] at <http://www.84charingcrossroad.co.uk/hist2.html> on 1 March 2006.

55 Low, pp. 12-13.

56 Snelling, pp. 153-5.

57 Rota, *Books in the Blood*, p. 254.

58 Markham, p. 263.

59 Rota, *Books in the Blood*, pp. 171, 229.

60 *Biblionotes*, March 1960, p. 1.

61 At <http://www.84charingcrossroad.co.uk/> on 1 March 2006.

62 Hanff, *The Duchess*, p. 114.

63 *Ibid.*, p. 62.

64 Marks, *Between Silk and Cyanide*, p. 1.

65 *Ibid.*, p. 155.

66 *Ibid.*, p. 444.

67 *Ibid.*, p. 157.

68 *Ibid.*, p. 154.

69 *Ibid.*, pp. 110-11, 153.

70 Minet, p. 13.

71 *Daily Telegraph* obituary, 23 January 2001.

72 Marks, *Between Silk and Cyanide*, p. 154.

73 *84, Charing Cross Road*, p. 25.

74 Obituary, 8 November 2002.

75 Markham, p. 73.

76 In auction catalogues now owned by Richard Ford.

77 Pratley, p. 7.

78 Low, *'with all faults'*, p. 42.

79 *The Times*, 15 and 20 December 1966.

80 Rota, *Books in the Blood*, p. 215.

81 Pratley, p. 12.

82 Markham, p. 71; Block, *Short History*, p. 42.

83 *Biblionotes*, spring 1961, p. [4].

84 Bradbury, p. 7.

85 'The battle of the bookstalls', pp. 1-2.

86 'Mr. Gatti' in *The Times*, 17 January 1902.

87 Rota, *Books in the Blood*, p. 36.

88 *Ibid.*, p. 260.

89 *Ibid.*, p. 87.

90 *Ibid.*, pp. 3, 199, 235.

91 *Ibid.*, pp. 15, 31, 168, 190.

92 *Ibid.*, p. 253.

93 *Ibid.*, pp. 167, 170, 172.

94 *Ibid.*, p. 160.

95 *Ibid.*, pp. 251, 262.

96 *Ibid.*, pp. 139-40, 289.

97 *Ibid.*, p. 44.

98 Sims (*A Life in Catalogues*, p. 55) says 1959; Rota (*Books in the Blood*, p. 65), 1961.

99 Sims, *Rare Book Game*, p. 128.

100 *Ibid.*, p. 129.

101 Sims, *A Life in Catalogues*, p. 2.

102 *Ibid.*, p. 28.

103 *Ibid.*, p. 14.

104 Ray, *Books as a Way of Life*, pp. 212-14.

105 Colbeck in Sims, *Rare Book Game*, p. 144.

106 Julian Symons, *A. J. A. Symons*, p. 61.

107 Rota, *Books in the Blood*, p. 81.

108 d'Arch Smith, p. 19.

109 *Ibid.*, p. 17.

110 Sims, *Rare Book Game*, p. 49.

111 p. 29.

112 Orioli, p. 49; Mark Holloway, *Norman Douglas* (1976), p. 409.

113 Orioli, pp. 58-9.

114 Sowerby, pp. 7, 17, 27.

115 Herrmann, *Sotheby's*, p. 215.

116 Booth, p. 80.

117 Sowerby, pp. 39, 66.

118 Sowerby, p. 32.

119 Orioli, p. 76.

120 Orioli, pp. 143, 174.

121 *Book Collector*, autumn 1967, pp. 370-1.

122 Brown and Brett, pt. 1, p. 10.

123 *The Times*, 18 June 1985.

124 *Driff's Guide*, 1985 edn., p. 37.

125 *The Times*, 18 June 1985.

126 Bason, *1st Diary*, pp. 91, 157; *2nd Diary*, p. 16; *3rd Diary*, p. 8.

127 *Book Collector*, summer 1959, p. 163.

128 *Biblionotes*, 1964-5, pp. 8-9.

129 Hanneford-Smith, p. 29.

130 Obituary of Clifford Maggs, *The Times*, 13 December 1985.

131 Low, p. 46.

132 Davis, *Second-Hand Books*, p. 75; Coombes interview in *Bookdealer*, 27 June 1996.

133 *Biblionotes*, spring 1961, p. [6].

134 *Ibid.*, p. [9].

135 *Ibid.*, January 1954, p. 7.

136 *Ibid.*, p. 6.

137 *Book Collector*, summer 1993, p. 256.

138 *Biblionotes*, January 1954, pp. 8-9.

139 *Ibid.*, p. 8. Needless to say the book does not exist.

140 Muir, p. 78.

141 *Second Impression*, pp. 135-6, 243, 245.

142 Muir, p. 104.

143 *Book Collector*, spring 1968, pp. 96, 99.

144 *Ibid.*, spring 1962, p. 57.

145 Snelling, p. 153.

146 Quaritch, p. 49.

147 Booth, p. 30.

148 Booth, pp. 84, 87, 135, 316; Minet, p. 119; *Nova*, May 1968, p. 32.

149 17 December 1998, pp. 5-6.

150 Minet, pp. 6, 10, 144, 190, 191, 192.

151 Barry Shaw in Markham, p. 11.

152 Markham, p. 15.

153 In a communication to Richard Ford.

154 *A Book of Booksellers*, p. 7.

155 *Bookdealer*, 4 August 1994.

156 *d-notice*, [New Series] no. 27 (20 September 1993), p. 4.

157 1985 *Guide*, p. 39; 1984 *Guide*, entry 1.

158 1985 *Guide*, p. 83.

159 Rota, *Books in the Blood*, p. 116.

160 Interview with Martin Cropper, *The Times*, 14 October 1992.

161 1995 *Guide*, p. 16.

162 'Strange Meeting', in Iain Sinclair (ed.), *London: City of Disappearances*.

163 *Books in the Blood*, p. 117.

164 *driff's*, no. 21 (31 October 1986), pp. 717-18; 1992 *Guide*, pp. 180-6.

ANTHONY ROTA Defending and Regulating the Trade

I should like to express my gratitude to Martin Hamlyn, whose nine-page history of the first 50 years of the ABA was distributed at the London Congress of the League in 1956. My thanks for information and help go also to Keith Fletcher, and to John Critchley and his staff at the ABA office.

1 See Appendix 3.

2 *Catalogue of an Exhibition of Books, Broadsides, Proclamations, Portraits, Autographs, etc., Illustrative of the History & Progress of Printing and Bookselling in England, 1477-1800* (1912).

3 For a very good account of the history of the ring, see Arthur Freeman and Janet Ing Freeman, *Anatomy of an Auction* (1990).

4 This phrase comes from *When We Were Rather Older* (1926), Fairfax Downey's witty parody of A.A. Milne's *When We Were Very Young*.

5 For the Bibliomites, see *Biblionotes* (1953-66) and Robin Myers, 'The Bibliomites (1950-)', *ABMR*, September 1977, pp. 368-9.

APPENDICES

RICHARD FORD

Twentieth-Century Rare and Secondhand Book Trade Archives: A Survey

I have received valuable comments and suggestions from those mentioned within this appendix, as well as Maureen Bell, Robin Halwas, Anthony Hobson, Michèle Kohler, David McKitterick, Paul Minet, Esther Potter and Marc Vaulbert de Chantilly. Numerous archivists, librarians and booksellers have been generous with time and information.

1 A.R.A. Hobson, letter to compiler, 3 October 2005.

2 Email to compiler, 27 April 2005.

3 Conversation with the compiler, 5 July 2005.

4 Stephen Ferguson, Princeton University, email to compiler, 16 January 2005.

5 Email to compiler, 8 September 2005.

6 Email to compiler, 25 November 2004.

7 Email to compiler, 12 December 2004.

8 Email to compiler 29 November 2004.

9 The word used by Nicolas Barker and John Collins, *A Sequel to An Enquiry* (1983), p. 57.

10 I am indebted to Stephen Ferguson for this analysis: email to compiler, 16 January 2005.

11 Dr Iain Brown, email to compiler, 29 November 2004.

12 John Hopson, British Library Archivist, Corporate Information Management Unit, email to compiler, 15 June 2005.

13 Huw Ceiriog Jones, Senior Assistant Librarian, National Library of Wales, email to compiler, 4 January 2005.

GENERAL INDEX

INDEX OF BOOKS

INDEX OF BOOKSELLERS

This book could not have been completed without generous donations from the following members and friends of the Antiquarian Booksellers' Association

Gutenberg Donors

Maggs Bros Ltd
Piccadilly Rare Books
Jonathan Potter Ltd
Bernard Quaritch Ltd
Henry Sotheran Ltd
Frank R. Thorold (Pty) Ltd

Caxton Donors

Peter Eaton (Booksellers) Ltd
Raymond Kilgarriff
Bernard J. Shapero Rare Books

Kelmscott Donors

Centro Antiquário do Alecrim, LDA.
Alex Alec-Smith Books
Altea Gallery
Any Amount of Books
Ash Rare Books
H. Baron
Steve Baxter
George Bayntun
Robin de Beaumont Antiquarian Books
Librería Para Bibliófilos
Blackwell's Rare Books
J. & S.L. Bonham
Bow Windows Book Shop
John Boyle & Co.
Boz Books
David Brass Rare Books, Inc.
Broadhurst's of Southport Ltd
Bromlea Rare Books
Ms Andrea Brown
Tim Bryars Ltd
Clive A. Burden Ltd
Pablo Butcher
Fiona Campbell
Cathach Books
Cavendish Rare Books Ltd
The Chaucer Bookshop
Chelsea Rare Books

Clarke's Africana and Rare Books
Collectable Books
A.J. Coombes – Bookseller
Charles Cox Rare Books
Claude Cox Old & Rare Books
Kay Craddock Antiquarian Bookseller
  Pty. Ltd
Mr & Mrs John Critchley
A. & Y. Cumming Ltd
James Cummins Bookseller
G. David
Wilfrid M. de Freitas – Bookseller
Demetzy Books
John Drury Rare Books
William Duck
Christopher Edwards
Elton Engineering Books
Emerald Isle Books Ltd
Exeter Rare Books
Fishburn Books
H.M. Fletcher
Sam Fogg Ltd
Paul Foster
Stephen Foster
Alex Fotheringham
Robert Frew Ltd
Galloway & Porter Ltd
Elizabeth Gant
Michael Garbett Antiquarian Books
Garwood & Voigt
R.A. Gekoski Booksellers
Gibb's Bookshop Ltd
H.M. Gilbert & Son
Nancy Sheiry Glaister · Fine and Rare
  Books
Nicholas Goodyer
Major Iain Grahame
Michael Graves-Johnston
Grosvenor Prints
Otto Haas
Halewood & Sons
Amanda Hall Rare Books

Anthony C. Hall
Robin Halwas Ltd
Rebecca Hardie Rare Books
Adrian Harrington Rare Books
Peter Harrington Antiquarian Books
John Hart
John and Judith Head
Jean Hedger
Heritage Book Shop, Inc.
G. Heywood Hill Ltd
Kenneth Hince Old & Fine Books
Ian Hodgkins & Co. Ltd
Judith Hodgson
Holybourne Rare Books
Andrew Hunter – Rare Books
Inch's Books
Jonkers Rare Books
C.C. Kohler
M.E. Korn Books
E.M. Lawson & Co.
John Lewcock (Maritime Bookseller)
Steve Liddle
Lucius Books Ltd
McLaren Books Ltd
McNaughtan's Bookshop
Carol Manheim
Barrie Marks Ltd
Marine & Cannon Books
Marrin's Bookshop
John Marrin Rare Books
Bruce Marshall Rare Books
Howard S. Mott Inc.
Anthony Neville Bookseller
Nicolas Antiquarian Ltd
The Old Hall Bookshop
Omega Bookshop
Laurence Oxley Limited
P & P Books
Hugh Pagan Limited
Colin Page Antiquarian Books
Paolo Pampaloni
Antiquariaat Papyrus
Diana Parikian
The Petersfield Bookshop

Nigel Phillips
Pickering & Chatto
M. Pollak Antiquariat
Patrick Pollak Rare Books
John Price Antiquarian Books
Quadrille
Richard C. Ramer, Old & Rare Books
John Randall (Books of Asia)
Paul Rassam
Rees & O'Neill Rare Books
M. & D. Reeve
Reg & Philip Remington
John Roberts Wine Books
John Robertshaw
Rogers Turner Books
Rothwell & Dunworth
Susanne Schulz-Falster Rare Books
The Schuster Gallery
Michael Silverman
Sokol Books Ltd
Ken Spelman Booksellers
Robert D. Steedman
Henry Stevens Son & Stiles
G. & R. Stone
A. Tavares De Carvalho
Thomas Thorp
Thulins Antikvariat AB
Tiger Books
Tooley Adams & Co.
Travis & Emery Music Bookshop
Roger J. Treglown
Tusculum Rare Books Ltd
Unsworth's Booksellers
John Updike Rare Books
Ventnor Rare Books
Waterfield's
R.E. & G.B. Way
Richard Way, Bookseller
Graham Weiner
Nigel Williams Rare Books
John Wilson Manuscripts Ltd
J. Howard Woolmer – Rare Books
Ximenes Rare Books, Inc.

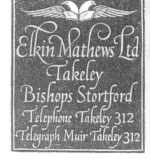